sight and mind

sight and mind

an introduction to visual perception

LLOYD KAUFMAN
New York University

New York
OXFORD UNIVERSITY PRESS
London   Toronto   1974

This book is dedicated to
Hans Wallach
for revealing the beauty
of visual perception to so many of us
and for the important work
he is still doing

preface

In writing *Sight and Mind* I have tried to produce a well-balanced and self-sufficient introduction for an undergraduate course in visual perception. Since a textbook, if it is to be helpful, should treat the topics of perception in accordance with both their historical and current importance, and also develop the fundamental concepts needed to understand these topics, the materials considered in this work range from the study of the visual system's sensitivity to light and color and flicker and contour, to the perception of size and space and movement and form. The mechanisms that are believed to underlie perceptual processes are described, together with the methods being used to gain insight into them. But the emphasis here is not on mere findings; the findings are presented in the context of the theories to which they relate.

This strong emphasis on theory serves two purposes. First, theories provide a framework within which to display facts, and thus serve a useful didactic purpose. They orient the student and enable him to see why some facts are more important than others. Second, since in my view theories are the engines of science inasmuch as they serve to motivate experiments, in this book I hope to make such motivation clear.

Visual perception is a living science, not a catalogue of dry facts the mastery of which will give one a command of the field. With every passing day new insights are being pursued by scientists from many disciplines. These insights are consistent with trends or styles of theorizing that I have been at pains to discern and describe for the reader. That such trends are always evolving and also reappearing in various forms is one of the facts of scientific life. I have here tried to give the flavor of this aspect of science.

In keeping with the importance I ascribe to theory, I have consciously avoided compiling an encyclopedic survey of the facts of perception. It was simply not possible to include everything that is known about perception in a volume of this scope. Many of the findings not discussed here can, however, be understood within the framework of the issues I have described. In view of the fact that I could not cover the entire literature, I have provided a sampling in the Bibliography, so that an interested reader can refer to the articles and books cited here and open to himself virtually the entire literature on any of the topics.

Some of the findings I have left out are traditionally covered in books on perception. The reader will look in vain for a discussion of the transactional approach to perception, for example. My decision concerning any given topic was predicated in part on my opinion as to the possibility of integrating that topic with the main directions of contemporary research in perception. My own point of view with regard to these directions is made explicit in Chapter 1. Other items were omitted despite the fact that they are consistent with the directions of contemporary research. In such cases I was guided merely by limitations of space and my own discretion in the belief that what was included sufficed to make the main issues clear.

In spite of these self-imposed limitations, the instructor who plans to use this book may still find more material than can be covered in an elementary course. In that event I might suggest that the chapters on flicker (Chapter 4), binocular stereopsis (Chapter 8), and pattern analysis (Chapter 13) could be omitted as required reading for a one-semester course. If the class is enthusiastic and relatively well-prepared, these chapters would make excellent supplementary reading. The topics considered in these three chapters would of course be essential ingredients in a more advanced course.

It is my singular good fortune to have had as teachers, friends, and colleagues some of the most important workers in the field of visual perception. Hans Wallach was my first teacher. Without his inspiration I would probably not be working in this field and therefore could not have written a book on visual perception at all. Also, while still a graduate student, I had the privilege of working under the supervision of my friend Irvin Rock. By his example I learned to recognize boldness, creativity, and independence in scientific thought. I hope that the lessons I learned from him and am still learning are reflected to some degree in these pages.

I must also thank Theodore Gold, who gave me my first opportunity to work professionally in the field of visual perception. Moreover, he taught me much about the art of experimentation and of the values of inventiveness and careful analytical thinking. I hope that this too is reflected in the book.

My friends Leon Festinger, Julian Hochberg, and George Sperling deserve a special note of thanks. I have learned much in my contacts with these men over the years.

George Sperling deserves an additional accolade, since he was kind enough to read several large portions of the manuscript and to save me from making some grievous errors. Also, my very brilliant colleague Jean Claude Falmagne must be thanked for insisting that I rework certain pages again and again until I was sure that I had them right.

Many other of my friends have read and commented on various parts of the book. Murray Glanzer, who read one chapter very carefully, helped me to do a much better job on it than I could have done without his help. As my chief at New York University he was supportive in other ways as well. Help was also generously provided by Carl Zuckerman, Gay Snodgrass, and Doris Aaronson. My student Joshua Bacon read much of the manuscript, and his professional and perceptive comments were extremely valuable to me. I owe a very special debt to my friends Walter Heimer and Whitman Richards, both of whom analyzed the entire manuscript and commented on it in considerable detail. Any errors of fact and style are due to my own obstinacy and not to their oversight.

All these dear friends and colleagues enabled me to learn at first hand how some of the foremost scholars in visual perception go about their business of developing our science. They have encouraged me continually during the writing of this book. Whatever its virtues, they are due in large part to the influence these people have had upon me.

Andrea Rubin and Mary Peters were responsible for expert, intelligent, and uncomplaining typing and retyping of the various versions of the manuscript. Their help was invaluable.

Finally, I must thank my wife and children, who spent so many evenings and weekends without me.

Roslyn Heights, New York   L.K.

acknowledgments

The author is grateful to the following publishers and authors for permission to reproduce and modify copyrighted illustrations.

Acta Physiologia Scandinavia, for my Figure 6–21 from Svaetichin, G., *Act. Physiol. Scand.*, 1956, 39, V Suppl. 134, 17–46.

American Association for the Advancement of Science, for my Figure 6–18 from Wald, G., *Science*, 1964, 145, 1007–17, and Figure 13–10 from Blakemore, C., and Sutton, P., *Science*, 1969, 166, 245–47.

American Psychological Association, for my Figure 9–17 from M. Fineman, *J. Exp. Psychol.*, 1971, 90, 215–21; my Figure 11–12 from Harris, C. S., *Psychol. Rev.*, 1965, 72, 419–44; my Figures 12–14 and 12–18 from Coren, S., *Psychol. Rev.*, 1972, 79, 359–67; and my Figure 12–22 from Attneave, F., *Psychol. Rev.*, 1954, 61, 183–93.

Associated Book Publishers, London, for my Figure 3–14 from Pirenne, M. H., *Vision and the Eye*, 2nd ed., 1967.

W. H. Freeman and Co., for my Figures 6–15, 6–16, 6–17 from Rushton, W. A. H., *Scientific American*, 1962, 205, 120–32.

Giunti-Barbèra Universitaria for my Figure 12–14 from Kanizsa, G., *Rivista di Psicologia*, 1955, 49, 7–30.

Institute of Electrical and Electronics Engineers, for my Figure 12–4 from Julesz, B., *IRE Trans. on Inf. Theory*, 1962, It-8:8492.

Journal of the Optical Society of America, for my Figure 4–20 from de Lange, H., *J. Opt. Soc. Amer.*, 1958, 48, 777–84; Figure 4–22 from Kelly, D. H., *J. Opt. Soc. Amer.*, 1961, 51, 422–29; and Figure 5–9 from Ratliff, F., Hartline, H. K., and Miller, W. H., *J. Opt. Soc. Amer.*, 1963, 53, 110–220.

North Holland Publishing Co., for my Figure 14–1 from Sperling, G., *Act. Psychol.*, 1967, 27, 285–92.

Pergamon Press, for my Figures 3–11 and 3–12 from Barlow, H. B., Levick, W. R., and Yoon, M., *Vis. Res.*, 1971, 11, Suppl. 3, 87–101; Figures 6–23 and 6–24 from Festinger, L., Allyn, M. R., and White, C. W., *Vis. Res.*, 1971, 11, 591–612; Figure 6–14 from Tomita, T., Murakami, M., and Pautler, E. G., *Vis. Res.*, 1967, 7, 519–31; and Figure 12–15 from Lawson, R., and Gulick, W. L., *Vis. Res.*, 1967, 7, 271–97.

Rockefeller University Press, for my Figure 5–8 from Ratliff, F., and Hartline, H. K., *J. Gen. Physiol.*, 1959, 42, 1241–55.

Scala Fine Arts Publishers, Inc., and the Uffizi Gallery, for my Figures 7–1, 7–2, 7–3, and 7–4.

The University of Chicago Press, for Figures 2–6, 2–8, and 2–10 from Polyak, S., *The Vertebrate Visual System*, 1957, and Figure 8–14 from Julesz, B., *The Foundations of Cyclopean Perception*, 1971.

The University of Illinois Press, for Figures 8–29, 8–30, and 8–31 from Kaufman, L., and Pitblado, C., *Amer. J. Psychol.*, 1965, 78, 379–91; for Figure 12–9 from Beck, J., *Amer. J. Psychol.*, 1972, 85, 1–20; Figure 9–3 from Holway, A. H., and Boring, E. G., *Amer. J. Psychol.*, 1941, 54, 21–37; Figure 9–6 from Gilinsky, A., *Amer. J. Psychol.*, 1955, 68, 173–92; Figure 9–5 from Gogel, W. C., Wist, E., and Harker, J. S., *Amer. J. Psychol.*, 1963, 76, 537–53; and for Figure 14–2, Neisser, U., *Amer. J. Psychol.*, 1963, 76, 376–85.

contents

1

introduction to perception

1

on the nature of perceiving

What is perception? Despite many books and countless papers dealing with this fascinating subject, there exists no widely accepted definition of perception. Psychologists and physiologists have been theorizing about it for a long time; yet they have been no more successful in this task of definition than have the philosophers who have been concerned with the same problem for many centuries.

Although we cannot agree on its definition, we may try to describe the kinds of phenomena with which perception deals. We know, for one thing, that perception concerns phenomena resulting from excitation of sense organs. We also know that these sense organs are stimulated in ways that vary widely from one moment to the next. Yet we perceive a stable world containing objects of consistent shape, color, and texture. These facts, and many others as well, form the traditional subject matter of visual perception. When confronted with these same facts, a number of different theories have been proposed by thoughtful men to explain how the brain enables us to perceive. We shall examine the facts of perception together with the more important of the explanations that have been offered to us.

In addition to describing facts and theories from within the domain of visual perception, we shall present the subject from a special point of view that may be characterized as consistent with a form of behaviorism. Perceiving is not viewed here as the forming of an image of an object on some inner screen. Instead, it is seen as an active process in which the observer is keeping track of what he had been doing. Awareness, experience, and cognition are seen as after-the-fact constructions formed partly by the need to communicate events to others. This point of view will affect our interpretation of the facts and theories of perception. Nevertheless, every attempt is made to relate as fully and fairly as possible the classic concepts from within the field of perception as well as from related areas. To make a start in elaborating our approach to the subject, let us turn to philosophy, where concern for sense perception first arose.

SOME PHILOSOPHICAL BACKGROUND

Among the philosophers who concerned themselves with sense perception were the famous British Empiricists. John Locke, a member of that school, came to the view that knowledge of material objects arises only from our sense organs. Events originating in the sense organs produce "ideas," and these are then perceived by the observer. Since ideas themselves are not part of the objects that gave rise to them, we cannot know the objects directly but can know or apprehend only the ideas. Similarly, there are ideas arising also from a process Locke labeled "reflection"--i.e., an immediate awareness of our own mental states, our knowing, believing, thinking, willing, and doubting. Hence we may define perception in terms of awareness of ideas or mental events arising either through sensation or through reflection. A science of perception on that basis would be concerned solely with the study of how ideas or mental events become organized to yield the impressions of objects and of states of the observer.

John Locke's approach is perhaps closer than we realize to what some psychologists actually assume. Locke, a psychophysical dualist, held to the position that there really are objects "out there" that reveal themselves through perception. It is not uncommon today for psychologists to view perception as being concerned with relations between physical objects and experience. We may know, for example, that two lines are of the same length; and yet the observer reports that under certain conditions one line is longer than the other. The problem for the psychologist is to find out why the physical reality differs from the perception.

Of course, if we press Locke's position too far we find ourselves agreeing with Bishop Berkeley, who found no good reason for believing that physical objects reveal themselves in perception. Berkeley argued that all qualities of an object may change with the state of the observer, and that as each attribute of the object is examined, its dependency upon the observer becomes apparent. Since for Berkeley the only real objects are those that we perceive, he denied the existence of a material substance and held that all events are mental. Mental events, for him, occur in a mental substance.

David Hume went even farther than Berkeley. In his *Treatise on Human Nature,* Hume asserted that physical substance is unknowable, and that moreover, we can know no substance of any kind. He did allow for mental events that can be known immediately, but held that the notion of substance arises from the repeated contiguity of impressions or ideas. Ultimately, for Hume, these contiguous ideas come to be associated with each other, and we reach the conclusion that they arise from a common substance. Beyond the feeling of likeness arising from the repeated association of ideas, there is no basis for believing in substance. While we may relate and compare mental events, says Hume, there is an inevitable limit to the knowledge that man can obtain about his universe. No possible basis exists for asserting that there are either material or mental substances. There are mental events that may or may not be representations of objects that may or may not exist.

When confronted with such arguments, the psychologist, in his bewilderment, recognizes that they have little to do with his study of perception. If he took them too seriously, he might be led to a crippling solipsism and be unable to justify his own work. He prefers to go along with Hume, who held in the latter part of his Treatise that though we may doubt the existence of objects, it might be more prudent to assume that they really do exist after all. Thus most workers in this field believe that objects exist, that they emit or reflect light, that this light causes neural activity, and that the brain then synthesizes some representation of the original object. This is Locke's position. While the psychologist is not necessarily an ontological dualist (one who believes in two substances, mental and physical), most psychologists may be described as uncritical epistemological dualists. The most prevalent tacit belief is that there are objects and that there are data furnished by the senses ("ideas") representing both the objects and relations among them. The sense data or brain events are not themselves part of the object from which they arise. Sensory experience may reflect physical reality or it may not.

On this account of the matter, the business of the psychologist is to discover how perceptions of objects correspond to physical reality as defined by physics, and also to account for discrepancies between the domain of physics and that of experience. This epistemological dualism, however, can lead to a picture-in-the-head psychology—one that postulates the presence in the brain of a full representation of the visual world. It is probably safer to assume that a complete representation of the visual world is never present in the brain at any one time. Just as a computer solving a problem must have within it representations of parameters of the problem, so must the brain contain events representing aspects of a scene. Nevertheless, not all aspects of a scene need be represented at any one time, and in fact the representation of some aspects could be contingent upon prior representation of others. Thus, a picture of what is going on in the brain at any instant of time would probably never correspond to what the owner of the brain said that he was seeing. In the act of describing what he was seeing, he may well construct a representation of the world his listener could never identify as represented in his nervous system. Moreover, the experience an observer describes to himself may, for the same reasons, be unrepresented in the momentary pattern of activity of his nervous system. For this reason I believe that the picture-in-the-head psychology has had an unduly limiting effect upon research in perception. Nevertheless, the picture-in-the-head psychology is one of the major assumptions underlying research in the field of perception.

THE ASSUMPTION OF PSYCHOPHYSICAL ISOMORPHISM

While there is no consensus of assumptions underlying perception research, the literature of the field does reveal a set of loosely connected assumptions that are rather widely held. An explicit statement of these assumptions is important inasmuch as the assumptions held by a scientist dictate the kind of research he does. Kuhn (1970), in his very revealing book, *The Structure of Scientific Revolutions*, makes the point that normal science is a kind of mopping-up operation. When a particular paradigm or achievement is widely recognized as being important and has been found to be successful, most scientists in that field proceed toward testing the limits of the *paradigm*. Thus, Ptolemy's computations of the laws of planetary motion were applied for centuries by many astronomers in their studies of the heavens. Copernicus' alternative paradigm was resisted in part because of the success already experienced with Ptolemy's methods.

In psychology today we can detect several paradigms that are proving successful. One is the discovery that there are microscopic neural events that are analogues of reports of sensory experience. One such analogue is the experienced Mach bands (see Chapter 5), whose properties are predictable from the physiological facts of lateral inhibition. There is, moreover, the fact that neurons in the brain respond to features of visual patterns. These neurons are referred to in many theories designed to explain psychological phenomena. As a result of such success, many psychologists and physiologists are designing experiments to show perceptual occurrences predicted from consideration of how the neurons might be working.

In 1967 Sir Peter Medewar made the insightful comment that science is a matter of confronting the world of facts with a view of how nature might be configured. Thus, while the preconceptions we have about nature are tested by the facts, the facts we choose to look at are determined by the need to test our hypotheses. This approaches much more closely the true nature of science as it is practiced than does the notion of science as a mindless collecting of facts. So while it is perfectly natural and desirable that the study of perception should proceed as an exploitation of paradigms such as the single-cell analogue alluded to above, it is equally important that we be aware of the further implication of paradigms and of other less clearly formulated assumptions influencing the nature of perception research. We shall clarify some of these throughout this chapter.

As already indicated, one basic assumption held by many psychologists and physiologists is that perceptions can be "explained" if it is shown that there are brain events related in a one-to-one fashion with what is perceived. This is the picture-in-the-head assumption. Thus, as we shall see in Chapter 8, it is widely held that binocular depth perception may be explained by the finding that objects are represented in three dimensions in a volume of brain cells. This need not be a literal representation such that an actual recognizable picture of objects may be found in the brain if we know how to look for it. The assumption we are discussing does, however, seem to require that brain events (which are chemical in nature) must be related in a one-to-one fashion to the perception so that, no matter how distorted the picture, it is uniquely related to the experience or perception. It is only on this basis that one may justify a conclusion that a particular set of electrophysiological findings "explains" a class of perceptions.

The assumption we are discussing works two ways. If it is true that brain events are uniquely related to experiential events, then we should be able to say something about the brain even though we study only the subject's experience. Drawing inferences about the brain from perception is a common practice today.

Readers already familiar with perception will recognize that we are considering the doctrine of *Psychophysical Isomorphism*, which was put forth by Köhler (1929) as a justification for the study of experience. He was the first to assert that there is a one-to-one topological correspondence between what goes on in experience and what goes on in the brain. This is like saying that there is a picture in the head which is in topological correspondence with the picture in the mind—a parallelistic position. The beauty of this position is that it makes it possible to determine what is going on in the brain on the basis of what is going on in experience. Thus, if a bright patch becomes apparently dimmer after it is surrounded by a still brighter background, one might justifiably infer that the patch of excitation in the brain produced by the original patch also becomes less intense.

Though psychophysical isomorphism is still tacitly accepted by many workers in the field of perception, it is used in connection with a more sophisticated understanding of how the brain works. For example, when the patch mentioned above becomes dimmer it is now possible to say with a wise nod that this is an instance of lateral inhibition. Though the theory behind the latter statement differs considerably from the field theory Köhler had linked to isomorphism, the attribution of an apparent change in brightness to lateral inhibition is an argument from analogy which is possible only if isomorphism is accepted. For isomorphism is the rule essential to make argument by analogy an acceptable scientific device. If, on the other hand, the assumption of isomorphism is based upon tenuous evidence, then the attribution of a phenomenon to a known physiological mechanism is mere argument by analogy; and though this form of reasoning is good for political speeches, it should for that reason be suspect. Analogies in science are useful only in providing motivation for experimentation. They are not a proof; and psychophysical isomorphism is not supported by any substantive evidence.

Though brain events must underlie events that are reported, brain events relevant to behavior are far more numerous than those associated with what can be reported. There is a many-one relation that makes it extraordinarily difficult to see how a unique configuration of brain activity can be arrived at from a particular set of experiences. The experiences are themselves more complicated than any report or experiment can reveal. The brain activity underlying the totality of behavior, including that which is reportable, is even more complicated. It is therefore unwise to say that because a particular tissue preparation gives an electrophysiological result that formally resembles the properties of a perceptual response, this particular physiological mechanism must therefore underlie or explain the perception. A more convincing indication of a causal relation existing between physiology and psychology may be obtained when events in both domains are manipulated simultaneously in an experiment. Though such causal relation is not proven in experiments, we shall give somewhat more weight to experiments in which psychological and physiological variables are manipulated together than to separate physiological experiments giving results that merely resemble psychological processes. Nevertheless, it should be kept in mind that the most direct evidence about the nature of perception comes from psychological experiments. Physiological experiments are most useful in suggesting and verifying the existence of underlying mechanisms.

PERCEIVING AND THE ELEMENTS OF CONSCIOUSNESS

One universally accepted idea is that neural signals set up by images on the retina are processed in the retina and then transmitted to the brain for further processing. As we shall see in Chapter 2, however, the complexity of the neural pathways involved in the visual process precludes identifying a single place in the brain where pictures of perceptions may be formed. Isomorphism, at least in its simpler form as described here, is simply not viable. Nevertheless, the relation of neural function to perception is still one of the most important scientific and philosophical problems of our age.

To gain any insight at all into this relation we must be clear as to what we mean when we talk about perception and experience. One of the reasons for the rise of the picture-in-the-head psychology is that there may be a tacit acceptance of the idea that perceptions are themselves like pictures. Since the perception of an object is not the object itself, the perception must be like a picture of the object. This leads quite naturally to the idea that all we have to do is find a representation of that picture in the head and we may then explain the perception. While this view is not entirely wrong, it can be misleading.

The epistemological dualism described earlier in this chapter has been a major influence on the history of psychology. As already intimated, one need not be a vitalist—a believer in a vital force distinguishing living from non-living matter—to be a dualist. All one need accept is the notion that physical things are not our perceptions of them. In the early days of scientific psychology, this dualism was accepted by the *structuralists*, who started with flying birds, smiling people, and sparkling colors, but assumed that perception of such complex events was made up of analyzable elements called sensations. Sensations (which are very much like Locke's simple "ideas") were conceived of as building blocks for perceptions; and perceptions, taken all together, comprise the structure of the conscious mind or consciousness.

We have introduced a new term here—"consciousness." There was at one time a stormy argument about the proper business of psychology. A fine discussion of this problem is given by Boring (1933) in his fascinating study of the sensations, their attributes, and consciousness. For our purposes it is sufficient to point out that just as it was widely accepted that physics is engaged in investigating the fundamental nature of the physical universe, so should psychologists investigate the fundamental nature of the mind. The goal was to use the scientific method (construed as analysis) in achieving the ultimate periodic table of the constituents of the mind. For if perceptions are comprised of sensations, and if they are parts of conscious experience, then the discernment of the constituent sensations should be the way to an understanding of consciousness. Identification of the elements of consciousness was the goal of the structuralists. This is why the structuralists have been described as "elementarists."

The structuralist view was assailed by many authors. Among the more important criticisms of their elementarism was the view of the Gestalt psychologists that we cannot analyze perception into invariant underlying sensations. Sense data entering through the eye and ear are irretrievably transformed by their contexts. In other words, a patch of light on the retina is a different patch of light when its background or context changes: perceptually it might be a gray patch in a bright background, and white in a dark background. No single sensation corresponds uniquely to the original patch of excitation. Thus, the Gestalt psychologists denied the *constancy hypothesis*—that a given excitatory event leads to an invariant sensory response regardless of surrounding conditions. This hypothetical one-to-one relation between stimulation and sensory response implies that sensations are additive—i.e., that different sensations can be mixed together and not influence each other. According to the Gestalt psychologists, who denied that sensations are additive, if the combination of two sensations produced an effect that is not the sum of the two sensations taken separately, then the structuralist program is impossible to implement.

While there is no doubt that the Gestalt psychologists were quite right in this criticism, and thus contributed to modern thought, they chose to take the wrong path in much of their subsequent work. For one thing, they focused upon the fact that spatially separated retinal events show signs of interacting with each other in experience (Koffka, 1935). This looked very much like action-at-a-distance and hence led to the unfortunate Gestalt field theory. Thus, since things act upon each other through a distance, there must be some medium in which the action takes place; and following the lead of their cousins in physics, the Gestaltists assumed that the medium must be some kind of field. We know now that the rich complexity of neural interconnections make it unnecessary to postulate such a field. Moreover, the physical field is a poor analogy of how the brain really works.

Despite their rejection of the idea that psychology should be concerned with the discovery of the elements of consciousness, the Gestaltists conceded that its proper concern is direct experience. In accordance with their principle of psychophysical isomorphism, they thought of experience as a means for obtaining direct access to the brain. In its emphasis on experience, their psychology is like the phenomenology of Edmund Husserl (1962), which is concerned with the phenomena of experience independent of any a priori notions one may have of these phenomena. The idea is to get to the thing in itself and ignore all the expectations and superfluous meanings that past experience has taught us to associate with the phenomenon. Though Gestalt psychology was not so rigorous in its application of the phenomenological method (the so-called method of phenomenological reduction) as Husserl would have liked, it did gaze inward, so to speak, to identify the laws of organization of consciousness. It looked not to static elements of consciousness but toward the dynamic, self-organizing properties of the mind. Although the conscious mind was still the domain of psychology, elementarism was abandoned by the Gestalt psychologists.

The notion of additive sensations is not entirely dead, however. Because of the survival of the notion James Gibson (1966) recently criticized the idea that sensations are constitutents of perceptions. He was reacting to the idea that sense data—the physiological counterparts of experienced sensations—are processed by the organism to produce perceptions. Gibson proposed instead that if sensations exist at all they are mere byproducts of perceptions and arise only in special circumstances, such as in experiments where observers are constrained to respond to only limited parts of the complex array of impinging stimuli.

Gibson's point of view is illustrated by his experiment in which subjects had to discriminate between objects by touch alone. Ten different fingers could touch the objects in any number of combinations to obtain a bewildering variety of cutaneous pressure "sensations." Under the conditions of the experiment these sensations alone could never be related uniquely to an object. In spite of the diversity of information pick-up from the skin and joints of the fingers, objects could be recognized. Gibson thus conceived of perception as being detection of invariant properties of objects and environments revealed over time. There is no room in this concept for the combining of independent sensations.

But old ideas die hard. Julesz (1971) notes that though sensations may not be the elements of perception, they have been supplanted with new higher-order "molecules" of perception. These molecules are somewhat more complex than elementary sensations, and yet they are still building blocks. The molecules, according to Julesz, are representations in the brain of visual stimulus properties such as corners, straightness, velocity, position, and orientation. There is some ambiguity about this new interpretation of perception, however. That is, while sensations were thought of as available to consciousness, there is no widely accepted notion that the new molecules are similarly available. We shall set this idea aside for the present with the observation that the stimulus features extracted by the brain are considered implicitly by some to be the elements of which pictures may be constructed in the head.

THE INCLUSIVENESS OF CONSCIOUSNESS

Thus it is not just any psychological activity that comes under the traditional subject matter of perception. The perception psychologist is not necessarily interested in how things get stored in memory (although he might be), nor is he necessarily interested in repression, problem solving, and concept formation. He is traditionally concerned with how we come to see or hear or feel; and he might be interested in hallucinations, since these events are similar to perceiving objects. Nevertheless, the hallmark of the discipline of perception has been investigation of the properties and determinants of what people are aware of—however "awareness" is defined. Figural aftereffects, space perception, color perception, perceived orientation in space, movement perception—all these traditional topics center on the idea that there are *experienced* events that demand explanation. As we shall see, the explanations of such events may themselves employ concepts originating in the experiential domain (e.g., Rock, 1966), or in the neurophysiological domain (e.g., Ratliff, 1965). But the fundamental problem concerns the bases of immediate conscious experience. I propose to raise some questions about this point of view.

My first question concerns the inclusiveness of consciousness. Classical academic psychology chose as its domain the analysis of consciousness. With one important exception, it left out the aspects of mental life that might be classed as unconscious. Freudian psychology, originating in a clinical setting, sought to explore this latter realm instead. These two schools of thought—the academic and the Freudian—are so divergent that they have virtually no language in common. Here and there in academic psychology we find reference to unconscious events underlying perception. Most important in this connection is Helmholtz's doctrine of unconscious inference. Also, there has more recently been a spurt of interest in so-called subliminal perception. This, however, has led to the almost derisive objection that if a thing is subliminal, then by definition it cannot be perceived. The way out of the logical quandary produced by such a term is to assert that the subject's criterion of judgment may alter in a given experimental situation so that the input is not subliminal after all. Despite such exceptions to the rule, academic psychologists have traditionally limited their concerns to phenomena existing in awareness. Conscious experience, then, is the traditional subject matter of the psychology of perception.

Clearly, the number of things I can report as having seen at any time far exceed the number of things I actually report. I say that the apple is red, and its stem green; that the wall is yellow and the table top gleams. Is that an exhaustive account of what was available in the visual field when I looked at the apple on the table? If pressed, I might add that while the apple was red it had some green spots. And—oh yes—the experimenter was present also. What else was going on? Well, I had forgotten. Or perhaps I didn't notice.

As Sperling proved in his important work on short-term memory (1960), a great deal of information is potentially available to me right after looking at any scene. I could have reported on many different aspects of the scene if only I had the intention of doing so when I first glanced at it, or were asked about some aspect of the scene immediately after glancing at it. It is obvious that very little of the potential information entered my awareness at the time I looked at the apple.

Just look around you and then record what you noticed. Look again later and see what you didn't notice the first time. Many of the things at first unnoticed could have influenced your perception of the object of attention, and yet these things might never have entered your awareness. So we must conclude that the number of reportable events that are in awareness are very few as compared with the number of events entering into a sensory process. Consciousness, whether it is defined as the domain of reportable events or as the domain of a more comprehensive immediate awareness, utilizes only a small fraction of what might be registered by the sensory apparatus.

THE IMMEDIACY OF EXPERIENCE

The second question about experience concerns its immediacy or directness. Though no one any longer holds to this view, it might be proposed that experience is temporally isomorphic to stimulation. Common-sense observation seems to suggest that a temporal series of experienced events is in a one-to-one relation to the sequence of stimulating events. Thus, if A occurs before B in experience, then A must occur before B in the stimulus. We know this to be false, since (as will be discussed later), A may occur at the same time as B and still be perceived as occurring later if it is, for example, dimmer. But such phenomena, which are fairly common, have little profound significance in the way in which they are usually treated. For example, the dimmer stimulus appears to occur later than the actually simultaneous brighter stimulus, since it takes longer for its neural representation to be propagated down the optic nerve. The stimuli to the brain actually arrive at different times. Hence, by recourse to peripheral mechanisms we might still preserve the isomorphism between experienced sequences and temporal physiological sequences. Though such mechanisms do exist and are extremely important in different contexts, they do not illustrate the point I want to make.

The question we are considering may best be illustrated with the example of apparent movement. In Figure 1–1 there are two points, A and B. Suppose that a light is made to flash at point A. After the termination of that flash and a brief blank interval, another light is made to flash at point B. If the timing of these events is just right, you will see a single light move from position A to position B. This is known as optimum apparent movement or *beta* movement. You actually see the light move through space from A to B, even though two physically separate lights are used to produce the illusion.

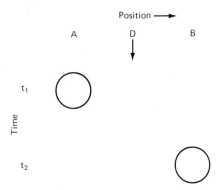

Figure 1–1. At time **t₁** a light (open circle) is made to flash on at position A. The light is then turned off and, at time **t₂**, another light is made to flash on at position B. Assuming that a light is perceived as traveling from A to B, when is it perceived as passing through position D?

Suppose now that I ask you to tell me when you saw the light at position D, a point in Figure 1–1 halfway between A and B. You will tell me that the light was at position D before it got to position B, even though it was never at position D physically. Now suppose that I place my hand in front of position B so that you cannot see the flash when it occurs in that place. Under this condition you could see only the light flash on and off at A. You would never say that it moved through D to get to B. This proves that in order for you to see the light move through D to B it must first be flashed at B. *Thus, the flash at B must occur before you can see the light pass through D.*

This is the paradox. How can you see the light at D—an event occurring in perception before the flash at B—if it must first be flashed at B? The obvious answer is that the entire sequence of movement from A to B must be constructed after the events that are basic to the occurrence of apparent movement. As John Dewey (1929) put it, "We are aware only of stimuli to other responses than those we are now making" (p. 334). If this is generally true, it can have important implications for the theory of perception. We shall trace some of these implications, for they might well allow us to define consciousness and attention.

PERCEPTION AND MONITORING

Observations such as these suggest that the perception of an event may be constructed after the occurrence of a set of constituent events. But immediacy has also been used with a somewhat different meaning in the history of psychology. Sensory experience was once held to be "immediate experience" or direct, as distinct from deduction or inference. Though such immediate experience was the subject matter of Wundt's (1896) psychology, the subject matter of psychology was construed by Kulpe (1904) to be essentially mediate or inferential.

According to Kulpe, there is no formal difference between the kind of inference made about physical reality in physics and the kind made about psychological reality in psychology. Boring's (1933) restatement of this position did not deny that immediate experience exists; it simply held that immediate experience does not enter directly into scientific psychology but is learned about through inferences from psychological experiments. Hence, there is no essential disagreement among many thinkers concerning the existence of immediate experience. The disagreement arises only about whether it is a direct datum of psychology. The constructive character of perception would tend to blur the distinction between immediate and mediate experience. The position taken here is that there is no such thing as immediate experience either of objects and events or of the observer's own inner states. All the events that might be termed instances of immediate experience are themselves constructions occurring over time and after the fact. Hence any program designed to account for immediate experience is doomed to failure.

If perception does not reflect immediate experience, we are still left with the question of its nature. Though there is no entirely convincing answer to this question, we may begin with the idea that perception as-reported-by-an-observer is constructed as reported. But there is also another—and not inconsistent—way in which to view perception.

Perception may be thought of as a way in which the organism keeps track of what it is doing. This monitoring process is evident in speech. When a person makes a statement, he does not first think or have in consciousness every word he is going to say just before he pronounces it (Ryle, 1949). The words come out in good grammatical order and convey his meaning more or less well without any conscious effort. Even meanings remote from each other in time form during a spontaneous monologue a coherent complex argument that can be outlined clearly after the fact. It is possible that the only thing the speaker can report being conscious of is what he had just said. He can construct or generate his basic theme on request, even though he does not have this at the forefront of his mind while speaking. He will not remember his precise words in the more distant past, and he would find it impossible to state precisely the words he will use in the not-too-distant future. Hence, his "awareness" is like a pencil beam of light illuminating only what had just gone by.

Even here there are some restrictions. The speaker is rarely aware of the minor fluctuations in his voice level or of the changes in the timbre of his voice unless these are large and disturbing. Rapidly occurring events do not enter awareness—only events with a time course that is within some channel capacity of the person. While this capacity has yet to be defined, clearly perception of one's own performance in any task is limited in terms of the self-produced events. Very long-term and very short-term events simply do not enter awareness during a performance. Thus, in driving a car, rapid minor adjustments of the steering wheel are made automatically, and the driver need not recite over and over to his conscious self that he is going to Aunt Minnie's house. The new driver may well attend to shorter-term events, thereby making it more difficult for him to pay proper attention to the larger aspects of driving like avoiding collisions or turning at the proper intersection.

Returning to speech: this focused awareness or perception plays a role in permitting the speaker to guide himself. His observation of his own performance may act like negative feedback, since it permits him to detect and correct his errors. It permits error correction on the simplest level and may allow for integration, differentiation, or other more complex operations. But even here the feedback need not be an awareness of events as they occur. There is always some phase lag between the performance and the feedback, and this may be due in part to a processing or encoding of information obtained through the sense organs.

The particular awareness or monitoring of past activity is reportable. As it is reported, however, it may undergo transformation, and this makes it virtually impossible to describe completely by verbal means alone what was going on in a performance. On the other hand, it may be possible that a reasonably accurate representation of the state of the subject during part of a performance could be revealed by careful experiments, as will be recounted in subsequent chapters. In any event, the report is not of immediate experience.

Since the "awareness" we are discussing is part of a feedback loop, that which the subject does report being aware of is bound to be modified by his own activity. As his eyes move or as they change their state of accommodation, the feedback is altered and so too may the subject's report of this state be altered. More important, however, is the way in which the sensory input used for feedback is processed. There are theories (e.g., Sokolov, 1963; Mackay, 1966) that perception entails comparison of the input with a model in the nervous system. Mismatches produce orientation responses, and these in turn alter perception. Similarly, there are theories (e.g., Von Holst and Mittelstaadt, 1950) that a comparison goes on between the orders sent out to the sense organs by the brain and the input to the brain from the sense organ. Such theories hold that when there is a mismatch between these two sets of data, the brain makes inferences about the environment that are quite different from those made when the input and output are in agreement. We shall discuss this "corrolary efferent discharge" theory at greater length later but it serves now to point up the fact that perception is not simply witnessing events played on some inner screen by passive sense organs.

An even more extreme illustration of this dynamical approach to perception is the efferent readiness theory of Taylor (1962) and of Festinger *et al.* (1967) who hold that perception is determined by the signal to the muscles driving the sense organ even if the signal does not actually get sent to the sense organ. This makes perception a monitoring of potential outflow, and this, in turn, is determined by the input and the past experience of the observer.

All these approaches are, I believe, closer to the truth than is the approach of classical sensationism or of the picture-in-the-head Gestalt school. I believe also, however, that such approaches are too specific in the sense that they arise from a consideration of too limited a domain of phenomena. Thus, the corollary discharge theory stems from the riddle of how the world is seen as stationary when I move, and as moving when *it* moves. The Sokolov approach originates in the study of the orientation reflex, a study that has nothing to say about most of the problems of perception as classically considered. Since the efferent readiness approach takes its departure from perceptual adaptation phenomena, it is hard to see how it can accommodate the experience of color, for example.

The idea underlying all these approaches, and others as well, is that perception involves more than the reception of information: it involves an active contribution on the part of the organism. Though this is not the place to elaborate the points of view mentioned thus far, it is necessary to point out that none of the theories see acts of perceiving as playing a role in behavior. The corollary discharge theory asserts that a neural representation of the input is compared with the output so that the perception may be determined. The perception is a consequence of some kind of comparison; it is not effective itself in modifying behavior. The orientation reflex elicited by mismatch between the model and the input increases sensitivity, thereby making perception a consequence of behavior and not a contributor to behavior. Finally, the efferent readiness theory permits perceiving to be modified—indeed, determined—by outflow, but the sensory input *per se* does not elicit perception. As we shall see later, perception may be thought of as a means utilized by the perceiver to govern his behavior directly and then be modified by that behavior.

This role for perception as a controlling factor in behavior does not exclude the logical possibility that sensory input need not be perceived (in the sense that it be reportable) but may still be necessary in governing behavior. The degree to which the organism is dependent upon the "pencil of light" mentioned above is an empirical question that cannot be decided here. The mere fact that this question can be raised, however, places awareness—even the derivative awareness we are discussing—in a distinctly less important place than it occupied in the earlier psychology. Nevertheless, perception as a monitoring operation in which the organism keeps in touch with what it is doing in the interest of governing its activities is still an important topic for research. We shall return to this in a later chapter.

ATTENTION AND PERCEPTION

One of the most fascinating anomalies in human thought is the prevalent notion that somehow perception and attention are distinct psychological processes. Hochberg (1970) is one of the few who suggests that they may well be aspects of the same process. No matter how the present writer tries, he cannot isolate the two processes. Whenever one attends to something, he is, by definition, perceiving it. Similarly, when one perceives something, then he must have paid some attention to it. A sleeping person cannot perceive physical objects—though he might dream about them; and he cannot attend to them either—though he might be attentive to his dream objects. If perceiving is thought of as a form of feedback through which the performer may govern certain kinds of behavior, then the objects involved in this perceiving are also attended to. There is no attention apart from perceiving. Deutsch and Deutsch (1963), among others, suggested that attention is a filter placed between a response and an input already analyzed for meaning. This is very close to the present notion that perception is itself a construction after the fact. By this logic, then, if one is to study attention, he must also study perception. One does not pay attention to a perception. By perceiving an object he attends to it.

You are not at this moment likely to be aware of the pressure of your clothing against your skin. Now that I have drawn your attention to it you may notice the greater sense of pressure against your armpits or perhaps around your waist. If you seek further you may become aware of subtler pressures. This noticing is perceiving and attending—the terms are synonymous. It is not as though all possible perceptions are laid out around you for selection and that this selecting from perception is attending. Though it seems true that some anticipatory behavior may be involved in attention (Hochberg, 1970), attending is not a selection from among reportable events.

Some perceptions, such as itches, tickles, loud sounds, or very rapid changes in light level, force themselves upon the observer. Irresistible tickles have perceptual priority, probably because such stimuli trigger reflexive responses on the part of the subject regardless of his intentions. This reflexive behavior is what is noticed and what overrides anything else the subject may be doing. Similarly, reflexive defensive postures may well occur with loud sounds, brilliant lights, or the sudden extinguishing of lights. The postural changes or orienting reflexes may be the prerequisities for establishment of perceptual priority. When such demanding stimuli are not present as distractions, the perception is likely to be of things associated with what the subject is doing. In this sense the perception may be thought of as an encoding of sensory input for action. When the subject is doing nothing in particular, he is likely to report that his attention is wandering. This simply means that he does little unconnected things and, all the while, is keeping track of what he is doing.

PAST EXPERIENCE AND PERCEPTION

Early behaviorism insisted that sensory psychology had no right to exist. This was a crass distortion of positivistic philosophy, and has fortunately been dismissed by the objectively oriented psychologist of our time in favor of a more tolerant point of view. For reasons we shall outline shortly, however, objectivism became tied to the idea that all perceptual behavior is learned, that past experience plays a paramount role in perception. Before turning to the problem of past experience, however, we must consider the implications for the study of perception of what we have termed "objectivism."

The positivist philosophers demanded that we take an approach entailing the testing of our assertions in the public domain. Subjectivism—introspectionism—is suspect for the reason that it employs as data events occurring in the private minds of observers. Since an observer's introspections are not available for public scrutiny, his testimony about them is not suitable scientific data.

It should be pointed out that no science requires that all of its entities be directly observable. If this were so, physics would have to delete all reference to electrons from its text books. Effects of hypothetically present electrons in the form of tracks in cloud chambers (the track is not an electron) or of attractions between different substances serve to anchor the concept of the electron in a matrix of public observations. Similar arguments may be raised about the intervening variable of learning theorists. The same may well be true of perception or experience. God made a secretive universe, but there are ways in which to explore its hidden recesses.

To ameliorate this problem there is the idea attributable to Ryle (1949) that an observer does not have privileged access to his own states. He must judge them just as you and I judge his states. This means that most of what I say about another is quite as good as that which he might be able to say about himself. In some cases he may be in a better position to make the judgment because he may have more information available—but this is a trivial difference. Objectivity is still preserved. Though Ryle's position has some clear affinities for a kind of behaviorism, it does not limit perception to mere verbal responses. Clearly, any experience is more complicated than the report of the experience. The report is merely a sign of some experience, and it is the experimenter's problem to find out more.

It should be clear from what has been said thus far that there is no necessary connection between an empiricistic theory—one that relies upon past experience to account for perception—and an objectivist approach to perception. Yet this is what happened historically. Behavioristically inclined psychologists have universally theorized that past experience is the essential ingredient of perception. As a matter of fact, the dialogue between the behaviorists and the Gestalt psychologists seems to have centered upon the relative importance of past experience and innate organizing properties of the brain (cf. Koffka, 1935). The empiricistic point of view found its most convincing exponent in Donald Hebb (1949). The nativism-past experience argument is still with us (Hochberg, 1962; Zuckerman and Rock, 1957).

The position taken in the present book is that there is no question that past experience plays a role in perception, but this is not incompatible with the idea that there is built-in wiring in the nervous system. If evolution can shape a body it may also configure its brain. The real question concerns the way past experience influences perception. Gibson's (1966) notion is very appealing—that past experience plays a selective role in determining the *aspect* of a situation to which one tends to respond. Still, the question of this role is an empirical one that must be considered in the context of specific functions of the organism—as we shall so consider it.

THE POSSIBILITY OF A STRICTLY COGNITIVE PSYCHOLOGY

A phrase in common usage today is "cognitive psychology." There are institutes devoted to psychology of this kind, and books written about it (as e.g., Neisser, 1967). There are also the closely connected "information processing" approaches to perception (see Haber, 1969). Both the cognitive psychologists and the information processors quote the same body of literature, which covers topics like short-term memory, brief-exposure experiments involving backward masking and meta-contrast, and also visual scanning experiments. The theme underlying all this appears to be merely a roughly circumscribed range of topics. There is no coherent theory to cover it all, but rather a commonality of interests that make the topics discussed in writings from the cognitive psychology school relatively predictable.

Among the predominant interests is computer modeling. In this approach the general-purpose digital computer is used as a rough model of how the mind works. Thus we find reference to buffer storage as a description of short-term memory, and here and there the use of words like "access" and "address." It is my feeling that this is all to the good, in the sense that psychological experiments are being used very cleverly to probe the different layers of processing of sensory data by the nervous system. More importantly, it views perception as involving serial and parallel processing of data over time. I do not feel, however, that an approach to problems constitutes a theory or a unique school of psychology. In this instance, we can only applaud the diligent workers in the area and hope that they will truly illuminate our understanding of perception. Meanwhile, work in this "cognitive style" cannot really be distinguished from experiments dealing with perception before the word "cognitive" became fashionable.

The term "cognitive psychology" can have a much more profound meaning than that given to it today. It can mean a psychology that does not and should not invoke non-psychological processes as explanatory mechanisms. In this psychology there is no basis for explanation except whatever is already within the psychological domain. Although it is a caricature of approaches taken by some psychologists, and does not do full justice to their understanding of these problems, this is a possible approach and must be confronted.

The belief that explanations of psychological events must be sought on the psychological level is associated with the belief that perceptions cause perceptions. We shall term this latter the idea of "psychological determinism." As an example there is the attempt by Rock and Ebenholtz (1962) to explain apparent movement in terms of a change in position in phenomenal space. Here we have one perception effectively causing another perception. Since we shall have more to say about this problem, it is sufficient here to express the belief that such explanations will ultimately be physiological in nature. It may well be necessary as an intermediate stage to erect some formal model of the mechanisms underlying some psychological occurrence.

A more satisfying explanation would require that the model be given physiological form. The resulting theory could then be evaluated in terms of its applicability to the phenomenon it pretends to explain as well as its capacity to explain and predict still other phenomena. It is because of this preference that I have included so much in the way of physiological methodology and results in this book. It should be pointed out, however, that physiology is just not up to the task of explaining very much in perception. In explaining phenomena it is therefore necessary for pragmatic reasons to invoke also non-physiological models at various levels of formal sophistication. Basically, then, we want to know how the system works. We shall use whatever concepts we can to construct some heuristic theories as to how it does its business.

BIOELECTRIC INDICATORS

The physiological events that accompany living, reception, and perception are chemical in nature. These chemical events have electrical consequences establishing that some tissue is more or less active. The measurement of such activity is accomplished at two levels. First, there is single-cell recording in which cells chatter at a neurophysiologist whenever they change state because of metabolic fluctuations or some incoming signal. As indicated, this method allows one to study the nervous system one cell at a time, and during the past few years it has yielded extraordinarily exciting data that will figure prominently in our discussion of the mechanisms underlying perception. The point of view outlined in the discussion of isomorphism will of course constrain the freedom of interpretations based on this data.

The second class of data derives from measurements made with large electrodes. Such measurements may be made in acute preparations and also remotely—at the scalp in human subjects, for example. This method has been informative about the behavior of large populations of cells. Although there is need for a technology capable of covering relations among smaller populations of cells, data obtained with this crude large-electrode method will be considered because it permits simultaneous behavioral and electrophysiological experiments with human subjects.

It should be obvious by now that physiological and structural factors will figure largely in this account of visual perception. This does not entail commitment to a picture-in-the-head psychology or to the principle of psychophysical isomorphism. It does, however, reflect a preference for explanation at a level below that which is being explained. It is possible, for example, to assume as did Freud, that there is an unconscious mind operating in a way reminiscent of the operations of the conscious mind. Unconscious inference would be an example of such a process.

Moreover, the operations of this unconscious mind could be thought of as accounting for the things of which we are aware—hence perception. But if one views perceiving as an active process of monitoring one's own behavior, the whole notion of an unconscious mind becomes less tenable. To be more specific, if we are not sure of what awareness is really like, it just may not be appropriate to explain the phenomena being studied in terms of mental conduct. The operations underlying perceiving are performed by the brain. It is more likely that meaningful theories will arise if they are formulated in terms of the functions of the brain. We can only aim at this now and here. Perhaps within the next few decades it will be possible to go farther.

2

light and the visual pathways

This chapter introduces some basic information concerning the stimulus to vision, as well as the anatomy and physiology of the visual pathways. The reader already familiar with such topics could skim this chapter, since their treatment here is for the most part at an elementary level. As the need arises, we shall later reconsider these topics in greater detail. The purpose of the present chapter is simply to lay the foundation for this more detailed discussion of the stimulus to vision and of the physiological substrate of perception.

THE STIMULUS TO VISION

In the nineteenth century light was viewed as a wave of electromagnetism that fluctuated transversely in a luminescent medium called *ether*. What made visible light different from other forms of electromagnetism was its frequency. If the waves moved past a point in space with the proper frequency, they could excite visual sensations. At other frequencies, both lower and higher, the electromagnetic waves could not produce visual effects. These latter were the radio waves, the cosmic waves, X-rays, infra-red rays, and others. The entire electromagnetic spectrum includes oscillations ranging in frequency from 10^2 to about 10^{27} oscillations per second. Since the term "oscillations per second" is unwieldy, the symbol "Hz" (pronounced "Hertz" in honor of the discoverer of radio waves) is customarily used to denote frequency. Thus, light is

Table 2–1. The electromagnetic spectrum.

Type of radiation	Approximate frequency (Hz)	Approximate wavelength (nm)
Cosmic rays	10^{26}	3×10^{-9}
Gamma rays	10^{23}	3×10^{-8}
X rays	10^{18}	3×10^{-1}
Visible light	$5 \times 10^{14} - 10^{15}$	$6 \times 10^{2} - 3 \times 10^{2}$
Infrared rays	10^{12}	3×10^{5}
Radar	10^{10}	3×10^{7}
FM-TV	10^{8}	3×10^{9}
Radio waves	10^{6}	3×10^{11}
Electrical disturbances	10^{2}	3×10^{15}

the band of electromagnetic waves having a frequency of between 5×10^{14} and 5×10^{15} Hz.

The various kinds of electromagnetic energy and their frequencies are listed in Table 2–1. Still another useful measure is the wavelength of electromagnetic energy—the distance between the peaks of the waves of the electromagnetic phenomena when they are in a vacuum. Since waves of light are slowed down when they pass from air into glass, the distance between two successive peaks is also reduced. Hence, the wavelengths associated with the frequencies of the diverse electromagnetic phenomena listed in Table 2–1 are correct only when the energy is propagated in a vacuum. It will be seen in the table that radio waves are very long, and light waves quite short. The velocity of light in vacuum is 2.99776×10^{10} cm/sec. The product of wavelength and frequency is equal to the velocity of light.

The different kinds of electromagnetic phenomena behave somewhat differently. Light exhibits some interesting properties, and these were what originally suggested that it was wave-like in nature. One such property is that light waves may interfere with each other, as occurs when two waves are simultaneously present. When their peaks are in alignment (as shown in Fig. 2–1) they tend to reinforce each other, but when the peaks and troughs are in alignment, they tend to cancel each other. Diffraction (see Fig. 2–1) is also a product of the wave-like nature of light. It was evidence like this that led to rejection of Newton's earlier idea that light was made up of discrete corpuscles emitted by a luminous source.

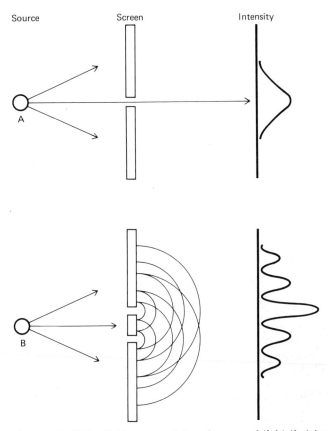

Figure 2–1. If the light source at A emits rays of light that travel in straight lines, then a small aperture in the screen should pass a very small bundle of rays. The measured intensity of light on the right side of the screen, however, shows that the light passed by the aperture is not limited to a small area but is actually spread out. This spreading of light is known as diffraction. The screen at B contains two apertures. The distribution of light intensity on the right side of the screen is not simply the sum of two spread functions such as the one shown at A, but looks like a series of alternating light and dark rings. This may be explained if the light passed by each aperture is wavelike and if the two sets of waves interfere with each other. Hypothetical waves are shown on the right side of the screen. Wavelike behavior of light can explain both the interference phenomenon depicted at B and the diffraction phenomenon illustrated at A.

Experiments by many physicists began to reveal certain anomalies that did not fit into the wave picture. Small particles, for example, can display diffraction, they can act like waves. The study of these phenomena (which lies beyond the scope of this book) led the modern physicist to the conclusion that electromagnetic waves may also be described as particles—the *quanta* of modern physics. Moreover, in the physics prior to the rise of quantum mechanics, it was believed that energy is continuous. According to the modern view, however, energy comes in discrete packets. This is as true for light energy as it is for any other form of energy. The packets of light energy are quanta known as *photons*. The photon is the smallest conceivable unit of light energy. It cannot be subdivided.

If a large electric current is passed through a coil of thin wire, the wire will become hot. If the wire grows hot enough, it will glow. At lower temperatures the wire will glow red. If the temperature is high enough, the wire will become "white hot." If the wire were in air, it would oxidize quickly. That is why the thin tungsten wires of incandescent lamps are enclosed in a glass envelope filled with an inert gas.

The heating of metal in this way agitates its molecules. At room temperature, in fact, the molecules of all substances are always vibrating to some extent. The atoms comprising these substances are always taking on or absorbing energy, and this energy is stored for a very short time and then emitted as photons. By reason of complicated interaction effects associated with the bonding of atoms to each other as molecules, the emitted photons have many different frequencies or energy levels. In essence there is a statistical distribution of the photon frequencies. At room temperatures these frequencies are most common in the infra-red region and are therefore invisible to the eye. Nevertheless, infra-red sensitive film can record images of these infra-red radiating objects.

If the objects are very cold, they will emit relatively little infra-red light. As they are heated up, they will emit more infra-red light and also more of the higher frequency photons. A great deal of heating will cause the object to emit sufficient light at the red end of the visible spectrum, so that it will appear to glow red. Still more heating will cause it to glow yellow and, if the heating effect is sufficient, even white. Hence, the temperature of a wire will determine a whole continuous spectrum of wavelengths emitted by the wire (Fig. 2–2).

Incandescent lamps with tungsten wire filaments are not the only light sources of use in visual perception. Some lamps are filled with gases such as neon, mercury, or xenon. When a voltage is applied across such a gas-filled tube, electrons pass at high velocities from a cathode at one end of the tube to an anode at the other, and displace some of the electrons in the outer orbits of the atoms of the gas. The atoms that lose electrons are ionized and therefore repel each other. They collide with the

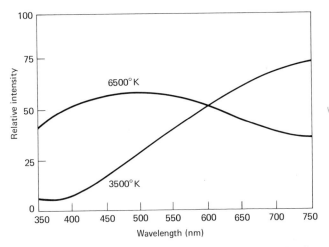

Figure 2–2. Relative energy of light emitted by a tungsten lamp as a function of its wavelength. At the lower temperature of 3500 degrees Kelvin there is relatively more energy at the red end of the spectrum. At the higher filament temperature of 6500 degrees Kelvin, the lamp emits more light from the blue end of the spectrum.

atoms that had not lost electrons and thereby impart energy to them. This energy is stored in potential form, since one of the electrons jumps to a higher level or orbit.

Electrons do not wander about in just any orbit of an atom, nor change their distances from nuclei by continuous amounts: they jump discretely from one orbit to another. Thus, the orbits are said to be quantized. Further, orbits of lower energy are occupied before those of higher energy. When energy is added to the atom, its electrons can climb to higher levels; but they remain in this state for only a short time, quickly jumping back to lower levels or orbits. In the process they liberate the stored energy in the form of photons. These photons are the light emitted by the gas-filled tube.

The atoms of gas such as a mercury vapor have only a small number of discrete orbits, and hence only a particular set of photons of particular energies or wavelengths can be emitted. Hence, too, in such a gas discharge tube, where the atoms are widely separated so that interaction effects are slight, only a discrete number of wavelengths is represented in its light output. This may be contrasted with an incandescent lamp whose output contains all different wavelengths in different amounts. In a neon lamp, the long wavelengths are most strongly represented. A mer-

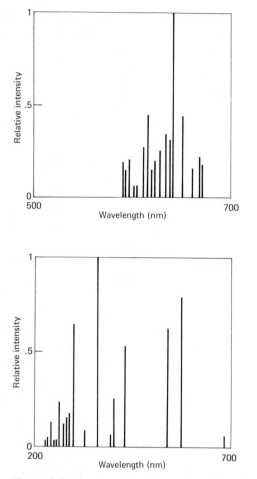

Figure 2–3. Line spectra of neon lamp (upper graph) and of mercury lamp (lower graph). Most of the energy emitted by the neon lamp is in the red and orange portion of the visible spectrum; most of the energy emitted by the mercury vapor lamp is from the blue portion.

cury lamp emits most of its energy at short wavelengths, although there are spectral lines at other wavelengths. This is what gives the neon lamp its reddish glow and the mercury lamp its bluish glow (Fig. 2–3).

Certain substances called phosphors react in a similar way when they are bombarded by a stream of electrons. Some phosphors used to coat black and white television screens are compounded of many different elements and therefore emit photons of many different energies or

wavelengths. Other phosphors composed of special elements emitting photons of limited numbers of wavelengths are used in combination to produce the colors in color television sets. Still other substances emit light
at some wavelengths when they are bombarded by photons of other
wavelengths. This is known as fluorescence.

The laser is a device that amplifies light of a particular wavelength
when excited. Thus, it emits but one kind of photon, depending upon the
materials comprising the laser. A graph illustrating the energy emitted by
a laser as a function of its wavelength would therefore be a single line.
This is known as a line spectrum.

As we shall see later, the eye is not equally sensitive to all wavelengths of light. A red light with a wavelength of 620 nm may not be so
visible as a yellow light (580 nm) of equal intensity. Similarly, a blue
light (400 nm) is not so capable of producing a visual response as a green
light whose wavelength is 510 nm. This means that a simple measure of
electromagnetic energy is not an appropriate index of the effectiveness
of a light in evoking visual sensations.

The energy of a photon is the product of its frequency and a constant. Thus, according to Einstein,

$$E = hv$$

where E is the energy of the photon, h is Planck's constant (which is
equal to 6.624×10^{-27}), and v is the frequency of the photon.

In dealing with large objects capable of emitting light—an incandescent lamp, for example—it is possible to measure the amount of energy
emitted by that object. This energy could be expressed in terms of the
sum of the energies of the photons emitted by the lamp over a period of
time. Thus, the radiant energy in *ergs*/sec of a source is simply the sum
of the energies of the emitted photons in one second—but, it is more convenient to express the energy emitted by the source in other terms.

RADIOMETRY AND PHOTOMETRY

There are substances whose resistance to an electric current will vary
with their temperature. Fine wires of such a substance are used in a device called a *bolometer*. If the wire is embedded in a blackened material,
its temperature will increase with the amount of radiant energy incident
upon it, for the reason that blackened substances reflect very little of the
light falling upon them and thus most of the incident light is absorbed

by the substance. This increase of the energy of the bolometer causes it to grow warmer, and the resulting change in resistance can then be measured. This measurement is proportionate to the amount of radiant energy falling on the bolometer.

Since the bolometer is "blind" to the wavelengths of the incident quanta, both visible and invisible electromagnetic energy can cause it to respond. Therefore, the radiometric measurements obtained with such a device do not specifically reflect the effective intensities of visible energy. To make use of such a device in measuring visible light energy—i.e. to use it as a *photometer*—it is necessary to place filters between the light source and the bolometer. These filters mimic the light sensitivity of the human eye.

Filters are of several types. One type is simply a piece of gel or glass in which a dye is embedded to give the glass a color. This means that some wavelengths are transmitted through the glass and others are absorbed by the dye. Though such filters are rarely precise enough to measure very narrow spectra of light, others known as interference filters do have very sharp filtering properties.

If the proportion of incident light of a particular wavelength transmitted by the filter is known—and this may be determined from the specifications published by its manufacturer—then it is possible to use a device like a bolometer or one of the newer solid-state devices to discover how much light is emitted by a source one wavelength at a time. The sum of the weighted energies of visible light at all different wavelengths emitted by a source and picked up by the photosensitive device can be related to the so-called *photometric intensity* of the source. This is necessary because, as noted above, the eye is not equally sensitive to all wavelengths. Thus, if a moderate amount of very long wavelength light from the infrared region of the spectrum were to fall on the bolometer, it could indicate the presence of that moderate amount of energy in the output of the source. Since these wavelengths are invisible, however, there is little point in measuring them to determine the magnitude of a stimulus to vision. This energy would have to be excluded by the filter placed before the bolometer. Moreover, the eye is less sensitive to red light in the region of 620 nm than it is to light at, say, 540 nm, so that equal amounts of energy at these wavelengths could not be given equal weight in determining the effectiveness of a stimulus. The light at 540 nm would have to be given more weight in computing the total photometric energy than light at 620 nm.

Table 2–2. Photopic (V_λ) and scotopic (V'_λ) luminosity factors tabulated at 10-nm intervals.

Wavelength (nm)	V_λ	V'_λ
390	0.0001	0.00221
400	0.0004	0.00929
410	0.0012	0.03484
420	0.0040	0.0966
430	0.0116	0.1998
440	0.023	0.3281
450	0.038	0.455
460	0.060	0.567
470	0.091	0.676
480	0.139	0.793
490	0.208	0.904
500	0.323	0.982
510	0.503	0.997
520	0.710	0.935
530	0.862	0.811
540	0.954	0.650
550	0.995	0.481
555	1.000	0.402
560	0.995	0.3288
570	0.952	0.2076
580	0.870	0.1212
590	0.757	0.0655
600	0.631	0.0315
610	0.503	0.01593
620	0.381	0.00737
630	0.265	0.003335
640	0.175	0.001497
650	0.107	0.000677
660	0.061	0.000313
670	0.032	0.000148
680	0.017	0.000071
690	0.0082	0.000035
700	0.0041	0.000018

The efficiency of the eye in detecting light at different wavelengths has been determined in careful parametric experiments whose results have been tabulated to give the so-called V_λ values of the different wavelengths of light. These values are shown in Table 2–2. The luminosity coefficients of V_λ can be multiplied by the measured energy emitted by a source at each wavelength to determine the effective photometric energy of the source.

Two complications must be borne in mind. First, the sensitivity of the eye to different wavelengths depends upon the state of adaptation of the eye. The values of V_λ given in the table are valid in the central fovea when the eye had been exposed to normal daylight levels of illumination prior to and during an experiment. If the eye had been kept in the dark for about 40 minutes before the experiment, a different set of luminosity coefficients must be used, those tabulated as V'_λ in Table 2–2. The latter coefficients are referred to as the *scotopic* luminosity coefficients; V_λ is referred to as the *photopic* luminosity coefficient. The theoretical basis for this difference will be discussed in Chapter 3.

The second complication associated with the use of the data in Table 2 is that the listed coefficients represent the spectral efficiency of a standard or ideal eye. In point of fact, there is considerable variability from one person's eye to another person's eye, so that the given values are only approximately correct and their use must be judiciously applied, depending upon the accuracy needed in a given experiment.

Filters approximating the spectral sensitivity of the standard eye are available. These filters will pass light of the visible wavelengths in different amounts, depending upon their luminosity coefficients. Thus, less red light than yellow light will be passed. By placing such a filter in front of a bolometer or a similar device, one may measure directly the photometric energy emitted by a source. If one should place a photosensitive device already calibrated for the spectral sensitivity of the eye near a point light source, the reading obtained would depend upon the distance of the device from the source. Indeed, the magnitude of the reading would vary with the square of the distance from the source. The size of the light-absorbing surface of the photometer would also influence the reading. If the surface were to be increased in size, it would absorb more energy; and thus it is important to take into account the size of the absorbing surface of the photometer in measuring the amount of incident light.

A small source emits light in all directions. Since the amount of light emitted in one direction does not always equal the amount emitted in other directions, the position of the light-measuring instrument must also be taken into account in measuring the light emitted by a source.

The intensity of a source is generally scaled in terms of a standard source. Hidden in the recesses of a vault in one of the capitals of the world resides an object emitting a given amount of light. At one time this object may have been a wax candle of particular size and material composition, and arbitrarily said to emit one candlepower of light. Nowadays, the candle has been replaced by a bar of pure platinum heated to a very high and precisely controlled temperature. The new standard is called the *candela*. If the standard is kept 1 meter away from a surface, we say that 1 *lux* of light is illuminating the surface. The lux is the unit of *illuminance*. In the older, now obsolete system of light measurement, the standard was kept one foot from the surface and it was said that one *foot-candle* defined the unit of illuminance.

If the surface on which the light is incident is a perfect reflector (though such a substance does not actually exist, a good approximation to it is a block of magnesium carbonate which diffusely reflects about 98 per cent of the incident light) we say that the surface has a *luminance* of lux $\times$ $1/\pi$ or 1 nit. The *nit*, a new term, is equivalent to the older though still widely used term *candela per square meter* (cd/m^2) or *meter-candle*. Multiplying the nit by the factor 0.292 gives the luminance in *foot-lamberts*, another widely used measure of luminance.

For our purposes it is important to recognize that a source of light may be compared to the standard light, or candela, to determine its intensity. Of course this intensity measure stands for the emission of a particular number of photons per unit time. Since these photons are given different weights, depending upon their effectiveness in producing sensations of light, a light source may have to emit more or fewer photons, depending on their wavelength, if it is to be as intense as a standard candela. Any particular source may be compared to the candela by holding a properly calibrated instrument at a particular distance from the source and comparing the resultant reading with the reading obtained when holding the instrument the same distance away from a secondary standard that is matched to the original standard. By placing this now-calibrated light source at some distance from a surface, it is possible to compute the illuminance of that surface simply by dividing the number of candelas emitted by the source by the square of the distance to the surface. This is sufficiently accurate for most purposes if the surface being illuminated is small. For larger flat surfaces, the edges of the surface are more distant from the source than is its center. Methods are available for taking this into account (see Le Grand, 1968).

If we know both the illuminance of a surface in lux and also its reflectance, it is possible to compute its *luminance*, which is proportional to the product of its reflectance and its illuminance. A piece of white paper may reflect as much as 90 per cent of the light incident upon its surface. A dark fabric, on the other hand, may reflect only 3 per cent of the incident light. Hence, even though both the paper and the fabric have equal illuminances, their luminances will be quite different. In the case of the fabric, if the illuminance should be one lux, then its luminance will be $1/\pi \times 0.03$ nits, or cd/m^2.

The reflecting surfaces we have been considering may be thought of as comprised of an infinite number of point sources with each point source emitting light in all directions. When such a surface is viewed by the eye, an image of it is formed on the retina at the back of the eye. The intensity of the light comprising that image is a function of the diameter of the pupil of the eye. If the pupil contracts, then less light can enter the eye than when the pupil was larger. Consequently, the product of the luminance of an object in cd/m^2 and the area in mm^2 of the entrance pupil of the eye defines the unit of retinal image intensity called the *troland*. It is customary in many vision experiments to place a small aperture called an artificial pupil in front of the eye. Since the diameter of the artificial pupil is known, the number of trolands may be computed simply by multiplying the luminance of the object by the area of the artificial pupil, thereby avoiding the vagaries of measurement due to changes in the diameter of the natural pupil of the eye.

The luminance of a surface has been defined as its "photometric brightness." In one sense it is true that the apparent brightness of a surface is correlated with its luminance: e.g., a grey surface illuminated by a high-intensity lamp may look brighter than an equally grey surface illuminated by a low-intensity lamp. As we shall see in Chapter 5, however, the "greyness" of the surface may be relatively unaffected by the differences in luminance. If we consider the whiteness, greyness, or blackness of a surface as representing different degrees of *lightness*, then over some range this lightness is relatively independent of the luminance of the object.

The luminance of an extended surface is independent of the distance between the eye and the surface, except when the distance is very large, in which case the particles in the air attenuate the contrast between the image and its background. Over distances where the effects of the atmosphere are negligible, however, the luminance of an object is a representative measure of its photometric brightness.

The reason may be simply stated. As one moves away from an object, the image it forms in the eye becomes smaller and smaller in area. Thus, though the light intensity emitted by every point on the object falls off with the square of the viewing distance, the density of the images of the

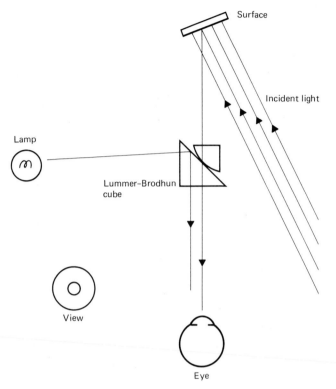

Figure 2–4. Principle of MacBeth Illuminometer. Light reflected by a surface passes through the center of the prism to the eye. This special prism is known as the Lummer-Brodhun cube. Light from the lamp is reflected by the cube to form an annulus surrounding the light from the surface being measured. The amount of light reaching the eye from the lamp can be varied by changing the distance between the lamp and the cube. When the boundary between the disc and annulus disappears, the luminance of the surface is equal to the known luminance of the annulus.

points on the retina increases. This increased density offsets exactly the loss of light intensity. Now since the intensity of the total radiant flux within the image is constant, regardless of the viewing distance, the retinal illuminance, measured in trolands, is independent of the distance from which an object is viewed.

Because the sensitivity of the eye to light depends upon the wavelength of the light, it is sometimes easier to use the eye itself as the light-measuring instrument. A convenient method employs the MacBeth Illuminometer illustrated in Figure 2–4. In this instrument a patch of known luminance is compared with a stimulus and in this way luminance is measured directly by matching the photometric brightness of the standard to the luminance of the stimulus. In most commercially available instruments this measure is given in terms of foot-lamberts. If the value in foot-lamberts is divided by the constant 0.292, the value of luminance in cd/m^2 may be obtained. The advantage of this visual-matching photometry is that one need not take the V_λ function into account, since the eye itself is the measuring instrument; but care and practice are needed to get reliable results.

This brief introduction to the visual stimulus should help the reader to distinguish between the concept of illuminance and that of luminance. The illuminance of a surface is a measure of the amount of light falling upon it; the luminance is a measure of the amount of light reflected by the surface, which is independent of the distance to the object reflecting the light. Illuminance, on the other hand, is not independent of the distance between the source of light and the object it is illuminating. The term "intensity" refers to the amount of light energy emitted by a self-luminous source. This measure of light energy will provide an illuminance that depends upon the distance between the source and the object illuminated by it.

Visible light acts upon the nervous system because it has effects upon the receptors in the eye. As we shall see in Chapter 3, photons are absorbed by pigments in the receptors. These pigments are changed by the absorbed photons to produce biochemical events in the receptors, and these events lead ultimately to nerve impulses that are propagated in the central nervous system. We shall now consider the pathways in which these nervous events take place.

THE EYE AND THE VISUAL PATHWAYS

That the eye is an organ of sight is obvious to anyone who closes his eyes. The way in which the eye functions, however, was for centuries an elusive problem. Aristotle knew that the eye was filled with fluid, and believed that this fluid was a photoreceptive substance—that it was sensitive to light. The Pythagoreans proposed that the eye emitted rays illuminating objects in the world and played upon objects like a spotlight as the eye moved about. A better analogy, perhaps, would be that of the fingers reaching out to touch and palpate objects in the world. This emanation theory bedeviled scientific thought until the seventeenth century, when

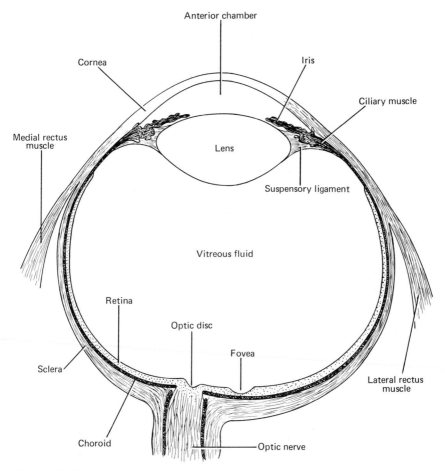

Figure 2–5. The human eye.

Kepler correctly proposed that the eye is an optical instrument capable of forming an image of a scene on its own retina.

The eye is a globe about 1 inch in diameter. As is obvious from Figure 2–5 (which shows only some of its parts) the eye is a complicated structure. Several muscles are attached to the eyeball by means of ligaments. These six muscles (two are shown in Fig. 2–5) serve to pull the eye in a rotary fashion, i.e., to allow the eye to roll up and down, left and right, and, in a limited way, to corkscrew (roll out or in). These movements will be discussed in greater detail in Chapter 7.

The cornea, a transparent covering in front of the eye, admits light through the pupil, which is the aperture within the ring-like iris. After entering the pupil, the light is brought to a focus on the retina by the lens. As we shall see later, both the cornea and the lens bend the light rays so that an image of the world may be formed in the back of the eye. This image formed on the retina is optically similar to the image formed on a screen by a slide projector, and thus is known as a *real image*. One of the amazing things about the eye is that it is capable of bending light from very distant objects so that this light becomes focused to form an image on the retina, which is itself extremely close to the lens. As we shall see, this means that the eye is an extraordinarily powerful optical instrument.

The anterior and vitreal chambers of the eye are filled with fluids, and these also have optical properties that affect the bending of the light rays.

The lens is held in place by the suspensory ligament. This ligament is stretched by the ciliary body, a muscle surrounding the lens. By the action of this muscle the ligament is made to exert different amounts of force on the lens, and this affects its curvature. In Chapter 7 we shall see how this changing of the curvature of the lens may alter the focussing power of the eye—a process known as *accommodation*.

The retina. The retina is a membrane covering the interior surface of the eye. It is an extraordinarily complicated nervous structure that is actually an outgrowth of the brain itself. It contains many nerve cells (neurons) and glial cells. Among the neurons are cells specialized to respond to incident light and known as *rods* and *cones*. When the rods and cones are stimulated by light, they cause signals to be sent through other cells in the retina to the optic nerve, which then transmits signals to the central nervous system. Perception entails the processing of these neural signals.

The retina contains two distinctive regions, identified in Figure 2–5 as the fovea and the optic disc. In Figure 2–6, reproducing a photograph of the interior of a living human eye, the fovea and optic disc (or *papilla*) are easily seen as specialized features of the retinal surface. The optic disc represents the exit point from the retina of the nerve fibers that make up the optic nerve. It is a collection point for all of the messages to be sent to the brain from the photoreceptors. The disc is itself free of photoreceptors, and hence is effectively blind. For this reason the optic disc is sometimes referred to as the *blind spot*. It is possible for an observer to "see" his own blind spot, as is illustrated in Figure 2–7.

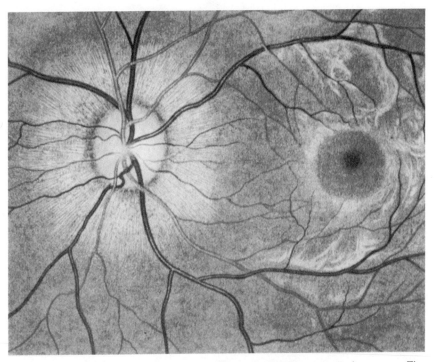

Figure 2–6. Interior of the left eye of a girl as seen with an opthalmoscope. The optic disc is on the left and the circular fovea on the right. The fovea is centered within a yellow spot known as the macula. (After S. Polyak, 1957)

The fovea, richly endowed with photoreceptors, is the shallow pit centered within the yellow spot (or *macula*) shown in Figure 2–6. This yellow spot contains many cones, and they increase in number toward the center of the spot. The fovea itself contains only cones, and it is free of rods. This is the region of maximum visual acuity. When a person wants to look at a thing, read a word, or follow a moving object, he will gener-

Figure 2–7. The blind spot. The reader must stare at the X with his left eye, with his right eye closed. The page should be held at a comfortable reading distance— about 12 inches from the eye. Moving the page slowly toward and away from the open eye will enable the reader to get it into a position where the black disc disappears. When the disc disappears, its image is within the blind spot.

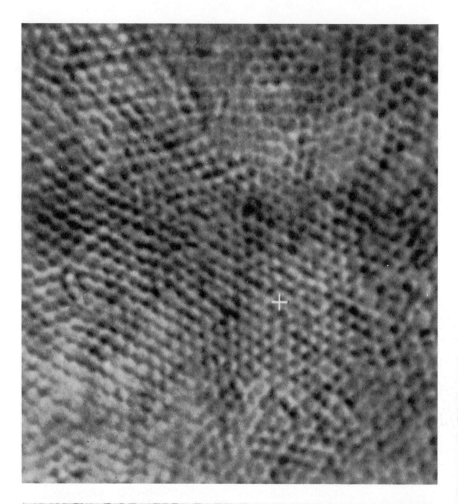

ally turn his eye so that the image of the object of interest falls within the fovea. The cones are also specialized for the seeing of color. As we shall see, color perception depends upon cone stimulation, whereas rods do not permit discrimination based upon color alone.

As we proceed out from the fovea, the cones become less numerous, and the rods more numerous. The fall-off in cone density happens to be exponential, and there is a similar accelerating rise in the density of rods as we proceed into the peripheral retina. Since the rods are specially adapted for responding to stimuli at very low light levels, they have been alluded to as structures used for night vision. Nocturnal animals have rod-filled retinas and lack cones; others, like the tree squirrel, have only cones. As befits the human habit of going forth by day and by night, we have what is known as a *duplex retina*. In Figure 2–8 containing photomicrographs of the human and monkey retinas, one shows a section taken through the human fovea. The "paving stones" making up this section are cones. The other photomicrograph is taken from a more peripheral portion of the similar retina of a monkey. The small dark spots are rods interspersed among the cones.

In the retinal structure (shown in greater detail in Figure 2–9) we see both rods and cones and their connections with the bipolar cells. The bipolars synapse with ganglion cells. The axons of the ganglion cells travel across the retinal surface to form a bundle at the optic disc. The figure shows, too, the horizontal cells and amacrine cells also abounding in the retina. The complexities of this lateral interconnection will be taken up later. As shown in Figure 2–9, there are several retinal layers between incoming light and the photoreceptors themselves. The incoming light must pass through these layers before it can affect the rods and cones.

The tissue layer between the retina and the external sheathing of the eyeball is the *choroid* membrane. In humans this membrane is dark in color, apparently so as to allow the membrane to absorb the light that is not taken up or absorbed by the pigments in the rods and cones. If the choroid membrane were light in color it would reflect incident light back

Figure 2–8. The photomicrograph above is from a section through the central rod-free fovea of the human retina, magnification 3,718. The foveal center is ·partly out of focus with cones slightly disarrayed. The photomicrograph below is from the edge of the fovea of a Rhesus Macaque monkey. This region is not rod-free and is quite similar to that of the human retina. Magnification is 1,053 times. Note the small clusters of rods among the cones in this section. (From S. Polyak, 1957)

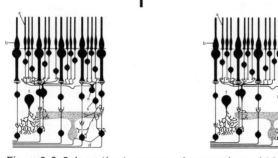

Figure 2–9. Schematic stereogram of connections within the retina. Light enters from the bottom of the drawing and must pass through the various retinal layers before it is absorbed in rods and cones. Activity in rods (a) and cones (b) affects bipolar cells of various types (c). Activity of these units then affects the ganglion cells (d). The outputs of rods and cones affect also horizontal cells (e), and the outputs of bipolars affect amacrine cells (f). Horizontal and amacrine cells provide extensive lateral interconnections that are undoubtedly involved when stimulation at one retinal place affects the response to stimulation at another retinal place. The axons of the ganglion cells leave the eye at the optic disc and are formed into a bundle known as the optic nerve.

into the retina, thereby reducing the sharpness of vision. In animals adapted for nocturnal life the homologous membrane was evolved to reflect light back into the retina. In the cat, for example, the *tapetum* coating the back surface of the retina reflects a substantial amount of incident light back out through the retina. The reason the cat's eyes seem to shine at night is that the light reflected by the tapetum emerges through the pupil. This gives the receptors a "second chance" to pick up incident light—i.e., when the light is reflected back through the retina, the first chance being when the light passes inward through the retina. The use of this reflected light must be at the expense of some sharpness of vision, however.

Figure 2–9 shows some of the major interconnections within the retina. The rods connect to bipolar cells—usually many rods connecting to a single bipolar cell in the retina. The cones, too, connect to bipolar cells, but it is much more common for each cone to connect with several different bipolars—although single cone-to-single bipolar connections are not uncommon, and sometimes several cones connect to single bipolars.

The cones also excite horizontal cells, and these in turn are believed to affect the outputs of other cones as well as of rods. Still other interconnections exist. The bipolars converge onto the large ganglion cells. As indicated, the axons of these cells make up the optic nerve. There are about 7,000,000 cones and about 120,000,000 rods. Yet in the optic nerve there are only about 1,000,000 fibers. This means that information collected in many different photoreceptors is encoded in such a way that it can be carried over many fewer fibers toward the brain.

The pathways. The fibers comprising the optic nerve may be thought of as divided into two intermixed bundles. One bundle contains fibers originating from cells on the temporal side of the eye, and the other bundle contains fibers originating at the nasal side of the eye. The fibers originating temporally go back to the *ipsilateral* hemisphere—the hemisphere of the brain on the same side of the head as the eye in which the fibers origi-

Figure 2–10. Some of the major pathways from the eyes into the central nervous system. Fibers of the optic nerve from the temporal hemiretina remain on the same side of the head, going to the ipsilateral hemisphere of the brain. Fibers originating at the nasal hemiretina cross at the optic chiasma and then go to the contralateral cerebral hemisphere. (After Polyak, 1957)

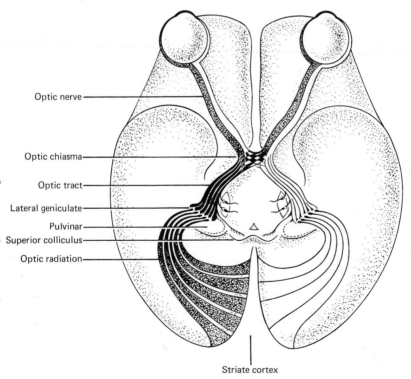

Optic nerve

Optic chiasma

Optic tract

Lateral geniculate

Pulvinar

Superior colliculus

Optic radiation

Striate cortex

nate. The nasal fibers cross over and go to the opposite, or *contralateral,* cerebral hemisphere (see Fig. 2–10).

Simple lenses produce images that are upside down, and the eye does the same. Thus, if a human figure were viewed by either an eye or by a simple lens his image would be inverted so that the head would be down and the feet up. Moreover, his left side would be on the right side of the image, and his right side on the left side of the image. Thus, the inversion is actually a rotation of 180 degrees. This means that the image of the left side of a scene is formed toward the right side of the retina. In the case of the right eye, for example, points in the scene which lie to the *right* of the direction of gaze would be imaged on the *left* side of the retina—i.e., nasally. These nasal images would lead to neural signals that are transmitted across the optic chiasma toward the contralateral (or left) cerebral hemisphere. Similarly, points to the *left* of the direction of gaze would be imaged in the *right* hemi-retina and signals produced by these points would be transmitted toward the right cerebral hemisphere. This leads to a simple mnemonic. Points imaged on the left side of either retina produce signals that are transmitted toward the left cerebral hemisphere, and points imaged in either right hemi-retina affect the right cerebral hemisphere. We shall see later that the crossing of signals to contralateral hemispheres plays an important role in binocular depth perception. Approximately 70 per cent of the total number of fibers originating in one eye cross over at the optic chiasma while 30 per cent remain uncrossed and go to the ipsilateral cerebral hemisphere.

As shown in Figure 2–10, most of the fibers in the optic tracts go to the *lateral geniculate nucleus.* It is here at the lateral geniculate that we find the first synapse after the retina. Each fiber arising in the retina synapses upon several cells in the geniculate. Fibers arising in the ipsilateral eye terminate in layers 2, 3, and 5 (see Fig. 2–11). There appears to be no significant blending of the inputs from the two eyes in the lateral geniculate. The fibers remain separated in their separate layers.

Before getting to the lateral geniculates, some fibers in the optic tracts change their paths and go instead to the *superior colliculus.* This structure in the midbrain receives strong innervation from the crossed fibers, and a weaker innervation from uncrossed fibers after they have left the chiasma. There appears to be a coarse mapping of the entire retinal surface at the colliculus. Moreover, there is some chance that the fibers from the two eyes synapse onto common cells in the nucleus.

There are other accessory fiber tracts going to parts of the midbrain

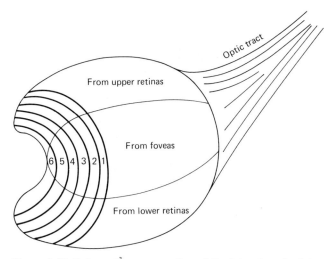

Figure 2–11. Schematic cross-section of the lateral geniculate nucleus.

from the optic tract. Little is known about the functions of these portions of the nervous system (see Marg, 1964).

Returning to the classical visual pathway, the optic radiation contains roughly six times as many fibers as does the optic tract. These fibers proceed from the lateral geniculate bodies to the occipital portion of the brain. Extending from the inner surfaces of the posterior portions of the hemispheres back to the occipital pole is a region known as the *striate cortex* or area 17 of Brodmann. Most of the striate cortex is in the calcarine fissure. The striate area gets its name from the fact that in a fresh human brain it has a striped appearance. This striation is due to a fiber layer that lies between two layers of largely fine granular cortical cells. These two layers are called layers *4a* and *4c;* the fiber layer is called layer *4b.* Another name for layer *4b* is the stripe of Gennari.

Fibers in the optic radiation receiving input from the photoreceptors in the macula, synapse upon cells from just inside the calcarine fissure and outward into the occipital pole. The macula is connected to a truly vast number of cortical cells in this region. Marshall and Talbot (1942) claimed that a small region of excitation in the macula will cause cells within a region 10,000 times the size of the original area of retinal excitation to respond. This means that there is an extensive branching of input from the central fovea in the striate cortex. In fact, the small fovea is represented over a cortical area that is proportionately many times larger

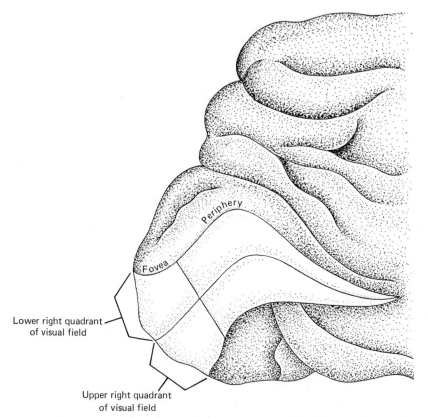

Lower right quadrant
of visual field

Upper right quadrant
of visual field

Figure 2–12. View of the left hemisphere's occipital region from inside the calcarine fissure. The fovea is represented inside the lip of the fissure and around it onto the occipital pole. The peripheral retina is represented deep within the fissure. Note that the amount of cortical tissue representing the fovea is quite large, and that representing the much larger periphery is relatively small.

than the cortical representation of the rest of the retina (see Fig. 2–12).

Two other areas in the occipital portions of the brain, known as the *peristriate area* (area 19 of Brodmann) and the *parastriate area* (area 18), are involved also in the visual process. In man these two areas, taken together, are almost three times as large as area 17. The boundaries of the two areas are poorly defined but, roughly, area 18 surrounds the occipital pole and area 19 surrounds area 18. It should be noted also that many other portions of the brain must be involved in visual perception. A portion of the frontal cortex, the so-called *frontal eye fields*, for example, are clearly involved in eye movements. Visual stimuli have also been found to affect cells in the temporal lobes of the brain. Also, Penfield and Jasper (1954) were able to produce visual sensations in humans by electrical stimulation of points in both the temporal and parietal lobes of the brain. The parietal cortex is probably involved in space perception.

The two hemispheres are interconnected by bands of fibers known as the *cerebral commisures*. The *corpus callosum* is the more important of these by virtue of its being the larger of the commisures and also, for our purposes, because it is the tract that co-ordinates visual functions in the two hemispheres. Thus, when an object is imaged in the left visual field, information about that object is conveyed directly to the right cerebral hemisphere along the classical visual pathways and then conveyed by the intercerebral commisures to the left cerebral hemisphere. Figure 2–13 is a block diagram illustrating some of the many interconnecting portions of the visual system.

Figure 2–13. Block diagram showing the interconnections among some of the more important portions of the visual system. LE = left eye; RE = right eye; LGN = lateral geniculate nucleus; Sup. Col. = superior colliculus; P = pulvinar, a body lying adjacent to the thalamus.

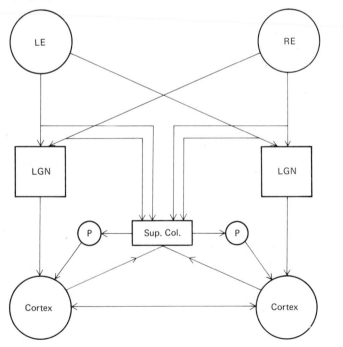

ON THE FUNCTIONAL ARCHITECTURE
OF THE VISUAL SYSTEM

If there is one truth about the visual system it is that there is no simple point-to-point correspondence between positions on the retina and places in the brain. It has been found, for example, that the retina, when stimulated, is capable of eliciting responses in the striate cortex, in the parastriate and peristriate cortexes, the inferotemporal cortex, in the superior colliculi, the lateral geniculate nuclei, the pontine nucleus, and even the cerebellum. Of course, some of these regions of the nervous system serve as relay stations between certain other regions. Nevertheless, stimulation of the retina can be represented independently at several different places at once.

There are two traditional ways in which to explore the nervous system to discover the conditions under which a region may be made active by retinal stimulation. The first method employs a technique in which a rather large electrode is placed in or near the area of interest. The potential difference between that electrode and a remote place on the body then may be measured. By means of special signal-processing methods it is possible to determine whether an intermittent stimulus is producing an in-step intermittent change in electrical potential between the area of interest and some other "electrically indifferent" point on the body. By manipulating the characteristics of the stimulus and also the state of the observer it is possible to find some covariation in the potential measurement and the stimulus. This can be done using intact human subjects.

A much more finely grained method than the one mentioned above has come into extensive use in the last decade. While this method is similar to the first in that a potential difference is measured between two electrodes, the active electrode is of an extremely small size, commensurate with the diameter of a single cell. When this microelectrode is placed near an active cell it is possible to record the impulses or spike potentials produced by that cell in response to sensory stimulation. As of this writing several thousand cells have been studied in several different species of animals. This work has had an enormous impact on the study of visual perception, since it has led to the discovery of previously unsuspected characteristics of the nervous system. In this chapter we shall simply outline some of these characteristics.

One very important concept is that of the *receptive field*. If a small spot of light should be used to explore the retina while a microelectrode is recording the activity of a nerve cell, it may be possible to find a region on the retina which, when stimulated by the spot, will affect the behavior of the cell. Thus, in some positions the spot may reduce the spontaneous activity of the cell, and in other positions, it may increase its activity. The cell itself may be a ganglion cell in the retina or a neuron at any other place in the nervous system. Nevertheless, the region on the retina which when stimulated affects the behavior of the cell is known as the receptive field of that cell.

When the receptive fields of retinal ganglion cells are mapped by means of a small spot of light, it is typically found that the receptive fields are approximately circular in shape. Moreover, even within such a circular receptive field the spot of light may have different effects, depending upon its location. Thus, as Kuffler (1953) has shown, some receptive fields in the cat's retina are organized concentrically. A circular central area may be surrounded by a ring-shaped area. The effect of stimulation of the central area on the ganglion cell may be opposed by the simultaneous stimulation of the outer ring. Thus, a spot of light in the central area may lead to an increase in the activity of the cell while a spot of light in the outer area could lead to a decrease. Again, if a light stimulus were to be removed from the outer area, the activity of the cell might increase, whether or not there is stimulation of the inner area. Such a concentric receptive field has been labeled an "on" center–"off" surround field. Figure 2–14 illustrates the behavior of cells having concentric receptive fields.

Some of the concentric fields are opposite to the "on" center–"off" surround reception fields. Thus, when a light imaged in the center is turned off, the ganglion cell will respond. Introduction of the light in the center will inhibit the activity of the cell; introduction of the light into the outer zone will cause the unit to respond. This is called an "off" center-type of receptive field. Similarly organized receptive fields have also been found in the lateral geniculate nuclei (Hubel and Weisel, 1961).

As we advance to higher levels in the nervous system, the retinal receptive fields of cells become more complicated. The work of Hubel and Wiesel (1962, 1965) has revealed that cortical cells have a wide variety of receptive fields. As shown in Figure 2–15, some of the simpler of these fields are elongated so that the optimum stimuli for activating the cells are small lines of particular orientations. Still other cells can be activated only if their receptive fields are stimulated by lines moving through them in particular directions. Many investigators have attributed movement

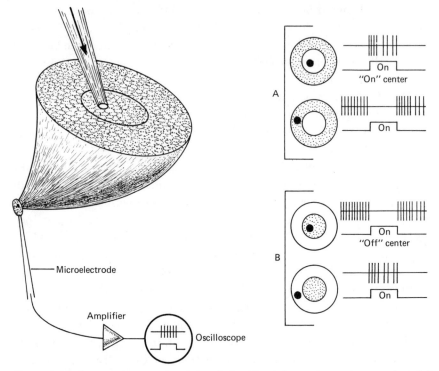

Figure 2–14. Concentric receptive fields. Left side of figure shows the experimental arrangement. The electrical activity of a ganglion cell is picked up by a micro-electrode, amplified and displayed on an oscilloscope (upper trace). The lower trace on the oscilloscope indicates when a small exploring spot of light is turned on (up-ward deflection) and off (downward deflection). In the illustration the cell responds with a spiking discharge when the spot of light is turned on. On the upper right side of the figure, at A, a small spot causes a cell to respond when it is turned on in the central region of the cell's receptive field. The cell will respond also when the light is turned off in the surrounding. Stimulation of the center of the receptive field in B will cause the cell to cease firing. Stimulation of the surround by the spot of light will cause the cell to commence firing.

perception to the activity of these cells. Since the receptive fields we have been discussing appear to be adapted for stimulation by different features of objects, e.g., movement, bars or edges, the cells belonging to them have been called feature detectors.

This sketchy outline of findings in the field of electrophysiology should serve two purposes. First, some of the terms used in this very exciting area have been introduced for later use. Second, it should be clear now how exceedingly naïve it is to think that anything resembling a "picture" of the visual world is formed in the brain. Any representation of the world may be thought of as a pattern of cell firings in many different places and at many different times. This pattern is probably related to features of the world in a highly abstract way. Even though we are still a long way from cracking the code of neural activity in the visual system, some richly suggestive discoveries have been made and these must figure importantly in the study of visual perception.

Figure 2–15. On the left side a luminous bar is rotated within the receptive field of a cortical cell. When the bar is at right angles to the elongated "on" portion of the receptive field (indicated by the outline bar), turning the stimulus bar on or off does not produce a response in the cell. When the stimulus is nearly in alignment with the "on" portion of the receptive field, turning the light on will produce some response in the cell. With the luminous bar squarely centered in the "on" portion, a strong response is produced. The black bar on the right side of the figure represents a moving black bar on an illuminated background. If the bar is moved downward and to the right, it causes a cortical cell to respond vigorously. Movement upward and to the left produces little if any response. When the same bar is rotated through 180 degrees and then moved up and down through the same receptive field, it produces little if any response. Other more complicated kinds of receptive fields have also been discovered. (Hubel and Wiesel, 1962)

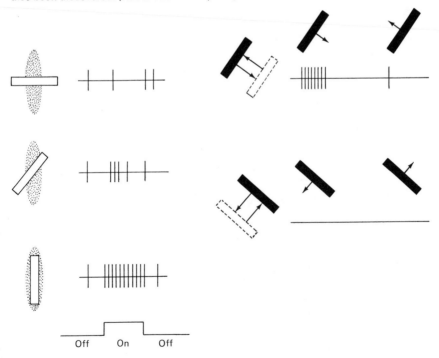

Off   On   Off

II
light and color

3

sensitivity to light

Suppose that an observer is sitting in a darkened room and staring at a small spot of red light. Some place near that light a spot of white light will be presented for a brief moment. The probability that the observer will detect the spot of white light is a function of many different variables. One is the amount of time that he was in the darkened room before the first flash of the white light; another, the luminance of the spot of light will also affect its detectability, as will the size of the pupil of the observer's eye. As we saw in Chapter 2, pupil size will affect the luminance of the retinal image of the spot. Also, the duration of the period of the flash may be important. So will the size of the spot of light. Finally, the distance of the spot from the place of fixation will have a profound effect on its detectability.

All the factors described above have been studied in psychophysical experiments. Our purpose here is to obtain some insight into the mechanisms influencing the detection of light. In order to do this we must first address ourselves to some methodological questions.

THE ABSOLUTE THRESHOLD AND THE PROBLEM OF SIGNAL DETECTION

In the early days of sensory psychology it was believed that one could meaningfully determine the minimum amount of light energy needed to detect a target. It was reasoned that there exists a hypothetical amount of

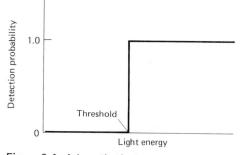

Figure 3–1. A hypothetical step function showing that when light energy is below some threshold value the light cannot be detected. If the light energy should exceed this threshold value, the light will always be detected.

energy enabling the observer to see the target. If the target is seen, we can say that the target energy is above its threshold level. Moreover, if the target should emit a lesser amount of light energy, it would not produce a positive response. Therefore, a hypothetical step function, like the one illustrated in Figure 3–1, was believed to demonstrate the relation between the detectability of a spot of light in the dark and the amount of electromagnetic energy emitted by the spot. The step in the function defines the absolute threshold under the conditions of the experiment.

We could imagine an experiment designed to demonstrate this absolute threshold. Suppose that an observer were seated in a darkened room and told to maintain fixation on a small continuously visible point of light. He could have been kept in the dark for a predetermined period of time prior to the experiment. Further, he might be looking at the fixation target through a 2-mm diameter artificial pupil so that the total light flux entering his eye would be independent of fluctuations in the pupillary diameter. The target spot of light that the observer must detect could be maintained at a uniform size of, say, 3 minutes of arc, and it might be presented consistently 10 degrees off to one side of the fixation point. Moreover, the target may be flashed for a duration of 100 msec. Prior to each flash of the target, the observer might be warned by means of a tone that the target was about to appear. His task would simply be to report whether he had seen the target.

The parameters of period of time in the dark, pupillary diameter, target size, position, and duration are all maintained at a constant value in this experiment. The only independent variable is the luminance of the target. From trial to trial the target's luminance may be changed so that it has one of several different predetermined luminances. The purpose of the experiment is to find the luminance threshold for the target.

Let us suppose that 7 different levels of target luminance are employed in this experiment. These 7 levels range from extremely low to a level so high that the observer has no difficulty in seeing the target. Thus, we are covering a range of luminance that includes the threshold level. In the experiment the different luminance levels are presented in a random order. Each level is presented 50 times so that we can get a good representation of the proportion of trials at each luminance level on which the observer is likely to say that he sees the target. We could then make a graph showing the proportion of trials on which the observer reports seeing the target *vs.* the luminance of the target.

A typical result of such an experiment is represented by the *psychometric* curve in Figure 3–2. The curve does not resemble the step function of Figure 3–1, but is a smooth S-shaped curve known as an ogive. It shows that there is merely an increase in the probability that a target will be detected as its luminance is increased. There is no well defined threshold.

Despite the smooth shape of the empirical psychometric function relating detection probability to target luminance, some workers continued to believe that the underlying threshold is a discrete step from non-detection to detection. The smooth functions obtained in actual experiments were attributed to noise or uncontrolled variability in the experiment.

Figure 3–2. A psychometric function indicating how the probability of detecting a target varies with the energy it emits or reflects.

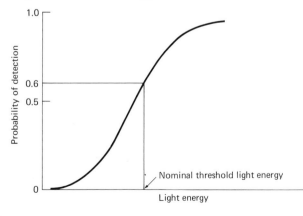

Thus, though the observer is instructed to maintain constant fixation, his eye may wander inadvertently. Since the retina is not uniformly sensitive to light, this wandering of fixation could have caused variability in detection at each light level. But even if it were possible to control all of the parameters in such an experiment, it is impossible to remove all the noise.

Before we can go farther with this discussion of the sensitivity of the visual system to light, it is necessary to describe some of the properties of *noise*. Experimental noise is analogous to audible noise. A pleasing musical tone is not "noisy," but an aperiodic sound containing many different audible frequencies is usually judged to be "noisy." A more formal description would hold that the sound pressure level at any particular time cannot be predicted with precision from previous sound pressure levels, which is to say that what characterizes noise is its *randomicity*.

There are many types of noise. By analogy with white light—light that contains energy at all visible frequencies—a white noise is a sound containing all audible frequencies in equal amounts. The wind rustling in trees produces a good example of white noise. Other noises do not contain all different frequencies in equal amounts, but are biased to include certain frequencies in greater amounts than others. In any case, the thing that characterizes these kinds of noise is their essential randomicity or unpredictability.

Noisy or random processes are not limited to the auditory domain. A speck of pollen floating on the surface of water moves about in a "noisy" or random manner. This is known as Brownian movement. The magnitudes of its excursions from one place to another will be affected by the temperature of the water, since the water molecules bounce about more vigorously at higher temperatures than they do at lower temperatures. Despite this, the future position of the particle is not predictable from its present position.

By now it is commonplace to describe any type of data as noisy if it has a random component. Moreover, such data are inevitably encountered when one uses an extremely sensitive measuring instrument or when one is working in the domain of the very small and the very weak. Thus, a sensitive amplifier that makes an extremely weak signal very large, will generate a hum or noise of its own accord—since thermal and other disturbances in its components are also amplified. In addition to this hum the instrument will make an electrical signal larger. But if the signal should be weak relative to the noise even after it is amplified, it may be difficult to discriminate the presence of the signal in the noise. The same is true of the eye when it is used to detect weak lights.

Light itself is quantal in nature, and the number of quanta emitted by a light source will vary from instant to instant. There is an average number of quanta emitted per second by a source, but there is variability about that average. When the energy emitted by the source is high to begin with, then the variability in the number of quanta emitted per unit time is small relative to the total output. When dealing with a very weak light source, however—one that emits relatively few quanta per second—its variability constitutes a significant portion of its output.

In addition to the inherent and inevitable variability of a source of light, there is also some variability in the visual system's sensitivity to the light. When we consider how weak a visually detectable signal can be, it will become apparent that metabolic fluctuations alone can contribute significant variability to the response of an observer. Since the flash of near-threshold light is weak to begin with, the background metabolic noise can be relatively large, and thus the observer has the task of detecting the flash while it is embedded in other random activity in the visual system. This is not unlike trying to detect a weak radio signal amid the hum of the amplifier and the chatter of atmospheric disturbances: the observer might confuse random activity of his own nervous system with the signal. As we shall see below, the degree of confusion will vary somewhat with the care that the observer uses in making his judgments.

So we see that there are many sources of noise influencing the measurement of the absolute threshold; and yet, since this noise is appreciable when we are dealing with fine-discrimination tasks, it is a physical impossibility for a step-function threshold to exist. As in atomic physics, the deterministic laws of the very large dissolve into statistical laws of the very small. There is always a degree of uncertainty in all measurement, both physical and psychological. This is why all psychometric functions are smooth ogives and can never even theoretically be step functions.

Since the kinds of measurements we are describing are inevitably statistical in nature, we are still left with the problem of defining the amount of energy that just allows an observer to detect a spot of light. We could solve this problem by saying arbitrarily that threshold energy is the amount of energy that allows correct detection on 60 per cent of the trials. Accordingly, as shown in Figure 3–2, the energy level allowing detection with a probability of 0.60 is the nominal absolute threshold (it must be understood, however, that on occasion genuine detection of the target occurs at lower energy levels). It could therefore make equally good sense to select the stimulus magnitude that leads to 50 per cent detectability as the threshold. For practical purposes it may in fact be desirable to designate 90 per cent detectability as a threshold since we may want to be reasonably sure that a target will be detected. Thus, there is no magic about the 60 per cent threshold value: it is only reasonable to expect that if a person can discriminate a target on 60 per cent of its presentations, then that target must be having some effect on his nervous system.

The noise accompanying any detection process may be thought of as going on even when there is no target to detect. Thus, in any given interval of time a target may or may not be presented. It may be assumed that during the intervals in which the target is present the observer is affected by both the target and the noise, and that conversely, when the target is absent the observer is affected by noise alone. So it is that on some trials where there is no target the observer may say that one is present solely because of the spontaneous activity of his own nervous system.

One way to study the effects of this kind of noise is to include catch trials in experiments such as the one we have been discussing. In these trials there is no stimulus, and the observer is required to state whether the stimulus is present. Now, if the stimulus itself is so weak that it may actually be confused with noise, then the observer may more likely say that the stimulus is present on the catch trials. If on the other hand the stimulus is very strong to begin with so that it is easily detected, then the observer is very unlikely to say that the target is present on a catch trial. Clearly, then, the expectancy of the observer concerning the strength of the signal vis-à-vis the noise level plays a role in setting his criterion as to the presence of a signal.

Actually, we could select a single target luminance from those employed in our psychophysical experiment and show that the criterion employed by the observer can affect its detectability. Suppose, for example, that one of the luminance levels was associated with a detection probability of 0.80—i.e., the target was detected on 80 per cent of the trials on which it was presented. Now this target could be presented on some trials, and no target at all on other trials. If the observer were told that the target was to be presented on very few of the trails, and that on most occasions no target would be presented after the tone, the likelihood of the target's being detected on its presentation will be adversely affected.

It has been found, for example, that an observer will be less likely to detect a given target when it is presented relatively infrequently than he would if it were presented more frequently—i.e., when there are fewer catch trials (Green and Swets, 1966). The different likelihoods of target presentation which are known in advance by the observer appear to affect the level of visual activity he is willing to accept as representing the presence of a target. If the target is to be presented relatively infrequently he is less likely to interpret the ongoing low level of noise present on all trials as caused by the target. If the target is presented on most trials, however, he may set his criterion at a lower point so that even low-level noise will be interpreted as representing the effect of the target.

SIGNAL DETECTION THEORY

All of this has been given formal treatment in a theory known as *Signal Detection Theory* (SDT), which provides a useful method for separating the effect of the observer's criterion from his sensitivity. According to SDT the noise level is changing randomly. As we have seen, some random activity is always going on even when a sense organ is unstimulated. While this noise may have a greater or lesser effect on the observer from instant to instant, it does have an average effect on the visual system. It is generally assumed that the effect over time is normally distributed. Thus, a hypothetical observer always has some visual sensations, even in the dark. Such sensations have an average magnitude and fluctuate in magnitude in a random manner about that average. It is assumed also that presentation of a signal or target does nothing more than shift this distribution of noise activity upward on a scale of sensation magnitude, as is illustrated in Figure 3–3. Thus, the addition of one noisy process to another produces a similar noisy process. If a relatively weak signal were to be added to the noise, it would produce a small shift upward on the "sensation magnitude" scale. A strong target signal, of course, would produce a large shift in the distribution. The measure of the magnitude of the shift is an index of an observer's sensitivity to the target.

By accepting the assumption that the effects of noise and of signal plus noise are distributed normally, signal detection theory makes it possible for us to obtain a measure of the observer's sensitivity.

A normal distribution is characterized by two statistics, the *mean* and the *standard deviation* (SD) (see any textbook on elementary statistics for an explanation of these terms). The assumption of SDT is that adding a signal to noise simply shifts the distribution, thereby changing

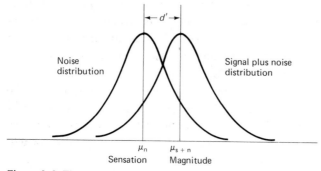

Figure 3–3. The two hypothetical normal distributions of signal detection theory.

the mean but keeping the SD (standard deviation) constant. So, if u_n is the mean of the noise distribution and u_{s+n} is the mean of the signal plus noise distribution, then the difference between these two means is a measure of the observer's sensitivity to the signal. This measure or index of sensitivity is called d′ (see Fig. 3–3). The difference between the means of the distributions can be expressed in terms of standard deviation units. Thus,

$$\frac{u_{s+n} - u_n}{SD} = d'.$$

It is possible to derive an estimate of d′ from one set of trials where some are catch trials, and others where a target is actually present.

In the discussion to follow we shall need two new terms: *false alarm,* which refers to a report that a target is present on a trial where there was no target; and *Hit,* the correct identification of a target.

The curve shown in Figure 3–4 is known as the *Receiver Operating Characteristic* (ROC) curve. It shows how Hit probability may vary with the probability of a false alarm in a signal detection experiment. A typical experiment may have involved three different sessions. In the first, the target would have been presented on relatively few trials while most of the trials contained no target at all. In the second, 50 per cent of the trials may have contained the target while the remaining 50 per cent were catch trials. In the third, most of the trials contained the target while relatively few were catch trials. Prior to each session the observer was informed of the proportion of trials that were to be catch trials, as this is presumed to affect his criterion of judgment. Point 1 on the curve in Figure 3-4 represents the probability of correct detection *vs.* that of a false alarm in the first session. The results of the second session are shown at point 2, and results of the third at point 3. It is obvious that the smoothed ROC curve changes slope as the criterion shifts from rigorous at one end of the curve to very loose at the other.

A criterion line may also be drawn through the overlapping normal distributions of noise and signal plus noise in Figure 3–5. If the observer sets the criterion so low that he is likely to say that a target is present on most trials, he will also report many false alarms. If he sets his criterion high, however, he will exclude many false alarms but pay the price of missing genuine occurrences of the target. If we were to plot the probability of a false alarm against the Hit probability as we slide the criterion line in Figure 3–5 along the *x*-axis, the result would be the ROC curve shown in Figure 3–4. Thus, given the assumptions of SDT, it is possible to obtain an objective index of the observer's criterion as well as of his sensitivity to the signal.

Figure 3–4. Receiver operating characteristic (ROC curve) obtained with a single stimulus magnitude.

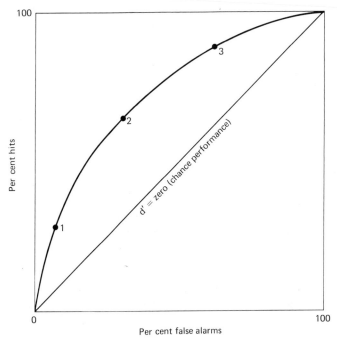

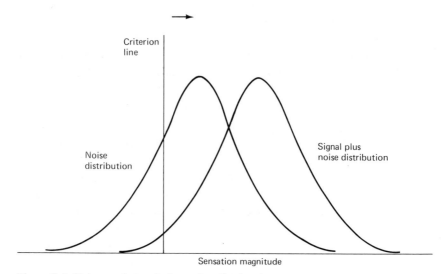

Figure 3–5. Noise, and signal plus noise distributions, with criterion line.

As the observer's criterion is changed in the course of an experiment, the criterion line sweeps across both of the hypothetical underlying distributions. At any position of the criterion line the observer will generate a particular proportion or rate of Hits and of false alarms. The Hit rate is a measure of the area in the signal-plus-noise distribution lying to the right of the criterion line. The false alarm rate is a measure of the area in the noise distribution lying to the right of the criterion line. Given a single pair of Hit and false alarm rates, it is possible to compute d′ and the location of the criterion line. With several different criteria, yielding several pairs of Hit and false alarm rates, it is possible to generate the entire ROC curve. A simple explanation of how to do this is given by Snodgrass (1972).

It is not necessary to assume that the variances of the noise and signal-plus-noise distributions of SDT are alike. This merely introduces some complexity in the calculations involved. Moreover, there are many ways of manipulating the criterion employed by the observer. He may, for example, merely rate a given trial as to the degree of confidence he has in his judgment upon the presence of a signal. The important thing to note here is that we may now approach the problem of sensitivity measurement by explicitly and rationally taking effects of criterion into account. This method should prove very useful in studies of size and distance perception in which instructions are known to affect judgment. In the present context, however, the thresholds measured in a given experiment cannot be thought of as fixed values. The psychometric functions such as shown in Figure 3–2 will slide somewhat along the x axis together with variations in criteria.

One of the problems with SDT is the assumption that the signal and noise are essentially independent and additive; thus, the ongoing noise is presumed to be unaffected by the presence of the signal. Still, as we know from electrophysiological studies, the inherent hum of the visual pathways is modified when light is presented or removed (see Arduini and Pinneo, 1963). When a light is turned on, this hum may decrease in level. Presumably the interaction between a stimulus and ongoing activity will increase with the intensity of the stimulus. Thus, at very low levels, at which one is studying sensitivity to minimum energy levels, the signal may produce an unnoticeable effect on the noise. On the other hand, it is possible that deployment of SDT to situations of high stimulus intensity levels could be invalid.

THE DIFFERENCE THRESHOLD

Perception involves the detection of differences in amount of light energy. Though stimuli may be well above the absolute threshold, differences in their magnitudes need to be discriminated. This kind of discrimination is also accomplished with greater or lesser sensitivity. At times great differences in light energy may be just barely discriminable, while at other times small differences may be discriminable. The study of sensitivity to differences in light energy is a cornerstone of the science of visual psychophysics.

Suppose that you are looking at a dim red fixation point. Two patches are presented shortly after a warning tone, one on each side of the fixation point. One of the two patches—say, the one on the left of the fixation point—is always of some fixed or standard luminance, and is known as the *standard stimulus.* The other patch may have one of several possible luminances, and so is known as the *variable stimulus.* Your task as an observer is to determine whether the patch on the right appears to be "brighter" or "dimmer" than the standard patch on the left.

When the variable patch is very much dimmer than the patch on the left, you will have no trouble at all in saying that it is dimmer than the standard. Also, if the luminance of the variable is several times greater

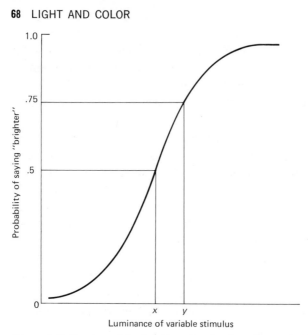

Figure 3–6. Psychometric function showing how the probability of saying "brighter" may vary with the luminance of the variable stimulus. When the luminance of the variable is **x** it is equal to the luminance of the standard. Point **y** on the abcissa corresponds to the 0.75 probability difference threshold.

than that of the standard, you will have no difficulty in judging it to be brighter. If, however, the luminance of the variable is nearly the same as that of the standard patch, then you may have some difficulty in making your judgment. At times you may feel that it is brighter and at other times you may feel that it is not brighter. This leads to essentially statistical results, as in the case of determining the absolute threshold.

In this experiment you are forced to guess that the variable patch is either brighter or dimmer than the standard, but are never allowed to say that they are equal. If we exclude bias effects, on half the trials when the luminances are equal you will probably say that the variable is brighter; on the other half you will say that it is dimmer. We could plot a psychometric function such as the one in Figure 3–6, which shows how the probability of saying "brighter" varies with the difference in luminance of the two patches. When the two are exactly alike, the luminance of the standard patch may be x. It can be seen in the figure that when the luminance of the variable is set to x, the probability of saying "brighter" is 0.5. Now, when the luminance of the variable patch is set to some greater value, say y, the probability of saying "brighter" increases.

In the older psychophysics it was believed that one could find some value y of the variable stimulus to exceed a threshold for the detection of differences. This was known as the *difference threshold*. Since thresholds are statistical quantities, we now say that some value of the luminance of the variable stimulus is associated with a given probability of discrimination of a difference. If this probability exceeds some arbitrary value, then we can say that the difference in luminance has exceeded a threshold. This difference may be one that is detected on 75 per cent of the trials or even one that is detected correctly on 87.5 per cent of its exposures, for example.

Figure 3–7 shows two hypothetical psychometric functions: that on the left obtained with a very dim standard luminance; that on the right obtained when the standard stimulus had a much higher luminance. Let us call the luminance of the standard used in obtaining the left hand ogive x and the higher luminance of the other standard x'. In both cases when the variable was equally often called "brighter" and "dimmer" it was set to have luminances x and x'. This is indicated by the line connecting both ogives with the 0.5 probability of saying "brighter." A second horizontal line is also present in this graph. This line connects both ogives with the probability 0.75. Luminance differences which lead to a probability of

Figure 3–7. The psychometric functions obtained with the standard at two different luminances, **x** and **x'**.

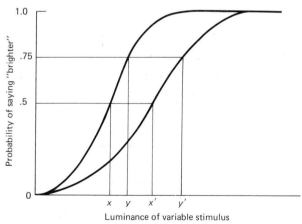

Luminance of variable stimulus

saying "brighter" of 0.75 are our arbitrarily designated difference thresholds. In the case of the two psychometric functions shown in Figure 3–7 these luminance differences are $x - y$ and $x' - y'$. It will be observed that the difference in luminance between x and y is much smaller than the difference in luminance between x' and y'. Thus, the magnitude of the difference threshold increases with the luminance of the standard stimulus.

Let us see how this might work in a more concrete situation. If the luminance of the standard stimulus is set at 1 cd/m², the variable stimulus might have a luminance of 1.02 cd/m² if it is to be discriminated as "brighter" on 75 per cent of its exposures. If, however, the standard stimulus were set to have a luminance of 10 cd/m², then the variable might have to have a luminance of 10.2 cd/m² to achieve the same probability of being adjudged to be "brighter."

For any given standard stimulus x, we can think of the threshold variable stimulus y as being equal to x plus some small increment $\triangle$. The increment associated with a particular threshold probability can be indexed with a subscript. Thus, in our experiment, where the threshold probability was 0.75 the increment in luminance needed to achieve that probability is called $\triangle_{.75}$.

As the nineteenth-century psychologist E. Weber observed, for a wide range of standard stimulus values the increment $\triangle_{.75}$ is a constant percentage of the magnitude of the standard stimulus. Thus, in our concrete example the magnitude of $\triangle_{.75}$ when the standard $x = 1$ cd/m² was equal to 0.02 cd/m². Also, when the standard $x = 10$ cd/m², then the increment $\triangle_{.75}$ was 0.2 cd/m². The ratio of the increment to its standard is 0.02 in both cases. In general, Weber proposed that

$$\triangle_{.75} / x = C$$

where C is a constant. This relation has been known as *Weber's law*. The Weber fraction is independent of the absolute magnitude of the standard stimulus. Thus, if the Weber fraction is known, one can define the difference threshold for any value of the standard stimulus.

If it is assumed that Weber's law is valid, it is possible to predict exactly how much energy must be added to any stimulus to produce a difference that may be discriminated with a particular probability from a standard stimulus. Thus, it is 75 per cent probable that adding 2 per cent of its luminance to any stimulus will make it appear to be brighter than the stimulus to which the increment had been added. Therefore, if we plot increments of equal discrimination probability *vs.* stimulus magni-

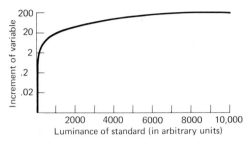

Figure 3–8. Graph showing how the increment in luminance needed to elicit a particular threshold judgment that the variable is "brighter" than the standard grows in magnitude with the luminance of the standard.

tude we will end up with a graph such as that shown in Figure 3–8. As this graph indicates, in order to achieve a 75 per cent probable discrimination of an increase in luminance, a 2 per cent increment must be added to any level of luminance. Thus, .02 nits must be added to a 1-cd/m² stimulus when it is being compared with a 1-cd/m² stimulus; 0.2 cd/m² must be added to a 10-cd/m² stimulus; 2 cd/m² to a 100-cd/m² stimulus, and 2000 cd/m² to a 100,000-cd/m² stimulus.

To place what we have done thus far in a historical perspective . . . The ordinate of the graph in Figure 3–8 usually has a different label. At one time it was believed that the Weber fraction enabled one to determine precisely how much energy has to be added to a stimulus to produce a discrete *just noticeable difference* (JND). The JND was thought to represent an increment in the magnitude of a sensation produced by a stimulus, and noticeable increments in sensation had to have equal psychological sizes, even though the physical stimulus increments needed to produce them might be very different—after all, equal increments in sensation produce equal discriminability. If a dim light has a small increment added to it to produce an increment in discriminability, and an intense light has a large energy increment to arrive at the same incremental discrimination, then these two very different energy increments must be producing the same psychological effect. Since, however, it is really not necessary to speak in terms of sensations and sensation increments, we shall speak solely in terms of probabilities of making discriminations as a function of changes in stimulation.

If the curve shown in Figure 3–8 were to be replotted in a graph where the abscissa is the logarithm of stimulus luminance, the function relating the increments of equal discrimination probability to luminance

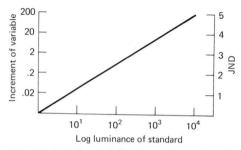

Figure 3–9. Increment needed to elicit the judgment that the variable is "brighter" than the standard, **vs.** the logarithm of the luminance of the standard.

becomes a straight line, as is shown in Figure 3–9. Logarithmic scales compress the high values of a parameter and expand the low values. Thus, by expressing the values of luminance in powers of ten, e.g., $10^0 = 1$ cd/m², $10^2 = 100$ cd/m², and $10^3 = 1000$ cd/m², and using these powers of ten as equally spaced intervals on the x-axis of the graph, we can produce the desired compression.

The fact that there is a proportional relation between the Weber fractions associated with a fixed probability of discriminating an increase in luminance and the logarithm of the stimulus luminance is known as *Fechner's law*. This law has the form

$$\triangle_{.75} / x = k \log x + A$$

where $\triangle_{.75} / x$ is the Weber fraction needed to produce a 0.75 probability of detecting an increment in luminance, x is the luminance of the comparison stimulus, A is the absolute threshold for luminance, and k is a constant of proportionality.

In the older psychophysics Fechner's law was taken as showing that the magnitude of a sensation grows with the logarithm of the magnitude of the stimulus. Many of the criticisms of this law are still of interest. One objection is that the difference threshold is not always a constant proportion of the luminance to which the increment is added. Another is that the difference threshold obtained when one adds a bit of energy to a baseline stimulus is not the same as the threshold obtained when a bit of energy is subtracted from the baseline stimulus. For these and other reasons Fechner's law has been disputed. Moreover, since Weber's law is not always valid, and Fechner's law is based upon Weber's, it too is open to criticism. As it turns out, these criticisms are not fatal. A more general form of the two laws may be stated to take account of them. To see how this is accomplished, let us turn once again to Figure 3–7.

It will be recalled that the difference in luminance between the stimulus values x and y is less than the difference between x' and y'. Despite this difference, the probability that y will be judged as brighter than x is the same as the probability that y' will be judged to be brighter than x'. Now, is it possible to transform the abscissa (scale of luminance) in Figure 3–7 so that the distance between x and y and the distance between x' and y' will be equal? In other words, can we transform the abscissa so that the psychometric functions in the graph will be parallel to each other?

The problem of finding such a transform, which has been called Fechner's problem (Luce and Galanter, 1963; Falmagne, 1974), states in the most general terms what it was that Fechner must have had on his mind when he developed his law. The problem has a solution if certain requirements are satisfied.

Suppose that the probability of discriminating the difference between x and y is equal to the probability of discriminating the difference between x' and y'. Then Fechner's problem has a solution if—and only if—there is a function u such that

$$u(x) - u(y) = u(x') - u(y').$$

If the original Weber's law is correct, then the function of x that would satisfy this requirement is $\log x$. Even if Weber's law does not apply well enough, there may be another function u of the physical stimulus which would do so.

It is possible to perform a test to discover whether the transform u can really make the psychometric functions parallel to each other. We can begin by assuming that the probability of discriminating correctly between x and y is the same as that of discriminating between x' and y'. It may also be assumed that

$$u(x) - u(y) = u(x') - u(y').$$

Now, suppose that we pick some other values on the abscissa of Figure 3-7, namely z and z'. Also, let $z > y$ and $z' > y'$. Moreover, applying the transform u, the values of z and z' should be such that

$$u(y) - u(z) = u(y') - u(z').$$

Taking the algebraic sum of the foregoing two equalities yields

$$u(x) - u(z) = u(x') - u(z').$$

This new equality implies that the probability of discriminating the difference between x and z should be the same as the probability of discriminating the difference between x' and z'. This conclusion can be tested empirically for any function u. Such an experiment would test for additivity of the functions of the stimuli and can therefore determine whether psychometric functions such as those illustrated in Figure 3-7 can be made parallel. A transform having this property is a generalized version of Weber's law (Falmagne, 1974).

In the relatively recent past Fechner's law was subject to rather strenuous criticism (Stevens, 1957). To understand the basis for this criticism, consider the case in which an increment in light energy is added to a low level of light energy. Suppose also that this increment produces a just noticeable increment in its brightness when it is compared with another light of the original low energy level. In this case the JND is defined as the increment needed to produce a response that the light is "brighter" on 75 per cent of its exposures. Thus, we might with some justice use the expression JND$_{.75}$ as compared with the traditional use of JND without an index.

Now suppose that we start with a much higher level of light energy. To produce the same JND$_{.75}$ we would have to add much more energy to this light than we did to the first one. Again, in the traditional psychophysics we could have assumed that these two JNDs are identical in the sense that they produce the same increments in discriminability. Thus, they can be described as producing equal increments in sensation-magnitude. There is no direct evidence that equal JNDs do in fact produce equal sensations.

One alternative to Fechner's approach to the measurement of sensations is to replace discrimination data with judgment data, so that one could ask an observer to estimate the size of his sensations directly. As an example, one might show an observer a patch of light and tell him that "this is 10 units bright." Upon seeing other patches of different luminance, the observer could then judge each of these patches relative to the brightness of the modulus or standard patch. If, e.g., one of the test patches should appear to him to be half as bright as the standard, he could then say that it is five units bright. This method of magnitude estimation was favored by Stevens (1957). A curve showing the relation between estimated stimulus magnitude and the actual stimulus luminance is shown in Figure 3–10. This curve may be described by the function

$$M = kL^n$$

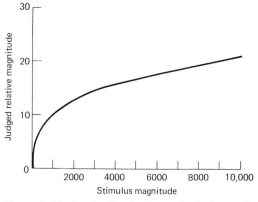

Figure 3–10. Graph showing how the judged relative brightness ("sensory magnitude") of a light may grow with its luminance.

where M is the magnitude of the sensation produced by the patch of light, L the luminance of the patch, and k a constant of proportionality. The exponent n is the power to which the luminance L must be raised to get a straight-line relation between estimated magnitude and stimulus luminance. In the case of a 5-degree visual angle patch seen by the dark adapted eye, the exponent $n = 0.33$. When the target is a point source the exponent $n = 0.5$. Thus, different stimulus characteristics yield *power functions* with different exponents. The "sensations" do not grow at the same rates in the power law as they do in Fechner's law. Which, then, is better—Fechner's law or Steven's power law? Most writers on perception are content to let the two laws stand as competing alternatives. Unfortunately, there is at present no sound reason for preferring judgmental data to discrimination data such as is collected in the traditional psychophysical experiment.

As we have already seen, it may in fact be possible to find a transform of the stimulus dimension—a new Weber's law—which would give a better fit to data than is now possible, and yet we could still be left with the problem of deciding which is the better to use. Fortunately, we need not be left in this quandary forever.

A useful analogy to the difference between judgmental data and discrimination data is that of two different methods that may be used for weighing objects.* In one method we may suspend an object from a

---

* The author is indebted to J. C. Falmagne for suggesting this analogy (in a personal communication).

spring. The length to which the spring is stretched by the object is some function of the weight of the object. This operation is conceptually similar to Stevens' method of directly observing magnitudes of "sensation." Alternatively, we could place known objects on one pan of a two-pan balance. An unknown object could be placed on the other pan. A sufficient number of known objects can be placed on the first pan to null the tilting of the balance. This corresponds to a discrimination method. In this case the weight is given by the number of known objects, while in the case of a spring scale the weight is given by the length of the spring. The two methods thus give different numerical results. A unifying theory would allow us to predict the amount of spring-stretching produced by an object if it needed a particular number of known objects to be balanced on the two-pan balance scale. The same situation applies to psychophysics.

One way to accomplish this goal in the case of weighing objects is to find some transform of spring-length that would then give the weight of an object in terms of number of counterbalancing weights. In the case of the generalized version of Weber's law, a transform u can be found. Now if a linear function of this transform also predicts judgment data, then a similar unifying theory would be available to psychophysics. There is considerable promise that this type of program will be successful (Falmagne, 1974), though as of the present writing, insufficient work has been done in the domain of visual psychophysics to help us with the problem of choosing the appropriate method.

RESULTS OF SOME SENSITIVITY EXPERIMENTS

In a now-classic study by Hecht, Schlaer, and Pirenne (1942), a 510-nm light was formed into a spot about 10 minutes of arc in diameter and was imaged about 20 degrees to one side of the fovea. The light was presented as a brief flash of .001-second duration. The observer was kept in the dark for 30 minutes prior to each experimental session. The task of each of the seven observers used in this experiment was to report whether or not he had seen the flash on each of its exposures.

The absolute threshold reported by Hecht *et al.* was a light energy of about 3.9×10^{-10} erg. This is a measure of the amount of radiant energy reaching the cornea of the observer's eye. Since one quantum of light at 510 nm has an energy of 3.89×10^{-12} erg, approximately 100 quanta reached the eye of the observer during the 0.001-second interval of target presentation. Thus, on 60 per cent of those trials in which 100 quanta reached his cornea, he was likely to say that he had seen a target.

Some quanta are reflected by the cornea; others enter the eye. Of the remaining quanta a large number is absorbed by the media in the eyeball, and only a few remaining quanta actually reach the photosensitive receptors in the retina. It has been estimated that only about seven quanta actually reach the receptors in producing this threshold response.

The image of the ten-minute target used in this experiment is somewhat spread out on the retina because of diffraction. When the effect of diffraction is taken into account, the spot of light covered a region containing an estimated 500 rods. Since only seven or so quanta are likely to fall within this spot, and since they will have a random distribution within the spot, it was concluded that it is extremely unlikely that more than one quantum would ever impinge on a single rod. It was concluded from this that a single quantum is sufficient to activate a rod receptor in the retina.

Although it is quite reasonable from these data to suppose that one quantum is sufficient to activate a rod, it must also be true that the activation of one rod is not sufficient to produce a sensation of light. The inherent noise in the nervous system is always producing changes in the states of rods. This is a random process however, and hence it is unlikely that a number of rods lying close to each other will change state simultaneously. But when 7 quanta impinge on rods near to each other, this will produce a simultaneous change in their state. According to this view, the detection of a target is a matter of discriminating a signal from the spontaneous fluctuations of the receptors. In this case it must depend upon the collection of activity from several receptors at some common center and, perhaps, comparing the output of this center with the output occurring at other times.

Barlow (1956) made the point that spontaneous changes in the states of rods are indistinguishable from the effects of absorption of quanta by the rod pigments. Spontaneous noise such as this may be called *dark light* since it can be confused with the ultimate effects of quantum absorption at the ganglion cells of the retina.

In a very interesting experiment, Barlow, Levick, and Yoon (1971) attempted to measure the number of quanta that must be absorbed by a single rod to produce impulses in single ganglion cells in the cat's retina. A microelectrode was placed near a ganglion cell in a cat's retina. The cell

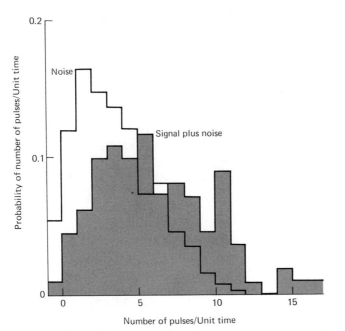

Figure 3–11. Distributions of probability of occurrence of ganglion cell spike potentials in the dark ("noise" distribution) and with a 5-quantum/sec stimulus at the cornea ("signal plus noise" distribution). (After Barlow, Levick, and Yoon, 1971)

emitted spike potentials when a very small 10-msec flash of light was focused at the appropriate point on the retina. The light was then made very dim, and the spikes emitted by the cell were counted over a period of time following each flash. Taking extraordinary care to calibrate their light source, Barlow, Levick, and Yoon were able to determine the average number of quanta reaching the cornea of the cat's eye during the 10-msec flash. They were then in a position to determine the average number of quanta needed at the cornea to produce a significant increase in the number of spikes emitted by a single ganglion cell. By making a number of reasonable assumptions about the absorption of light by the extra-retinal substances within the eye and the distribution of the quanta on the retina, they came to the conclusion that one quantum absorbed by a rod could produce several spikes at the level of the ganglion cell.

The ganglion cells in this study tended to produce spike potentials even when no stimulus was applied to the eye. This was presumed to represent the effect of the dark light or receptor noise mentioned above. By plotting the probability of occurrence of a given number of spikes within a 200-msec. period, Barlow, Levick, and Yoon obtained an approximately normal distribution of spontaneous activity. This is a direct measure of the distribution of the effect of noise on the ganglion cells. Thus, for a given ganglion cell, a mean number of spikes is likely to occur within a 200-msec. interval. Moreover, the variability about this mean value gives the probable occurrence of different numbers of spikes within any 200-msec. interval. Such measurements were then repeated with a very weak stimulus. The addition of the stimulus caused a shift upward in the mean number of spikes produced by the ganglion cell. Typical distributions are shown in Figure 3–11. Since they had the distribution of the effect of noise alone, and also the distribution of the effect of noise plus signal, Barlow, Levick, and Yoon were able to specify the detection capability of the ganglion cell.

One may measure the areas under the two curves in Figure 3–11 to the right of any point on its abscissa. One area represents the probability

Figure 3–12. Receiver operating characteristic of ganglion cell based upon Figure 3–11. (After Barlow, Levick, and Yoon, 1971)

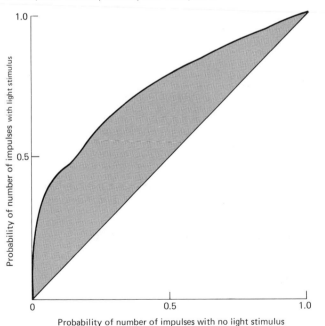

Probability of number of impulses with light stimulus

Probability of number of impulses with no light stimulus

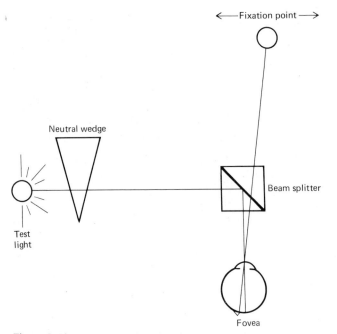

Figure 3–13. Neutral wedge is used to control the amount of light reaching the eye from a test lamp. The position of a fixation point may be changed, so as to shift the position of the image of the test lamp on the retina.

of recording a particular number of spikes without a stimulus, and the other that of recording a particular number of spikes when a stimulus is added to the ongoing noise. These two probabilities give the co-ordinates of a point on the ROC (Receiver Operating Characteristic) curve shown in Figure 3–12. This same procedure may be repeated at some higher point on the x-axis of the graph containing the two distributions, thereby providing another point on the ROC curve. By doing this at various points along the x-axis of Figure 3–11, it is possible to describe the entire ROC curve. It should be noted that this procedure amounts to the same thing as shifting a criterion line along the x-axis of Figure 3–11. Thus, when a point is picked at the far left of the x-axis, the experimenter is saying in effect that he is setting his criterion so low that he is willing to accept any number of spikes as representing the effect of a stimulus. This yields a point in the upper right-hand corner of the ROC graph indicating that a "signal" is detected with a high probability and also that there is a high probability of recording a signal even when there is no stimulus.

If the stimulus had no effect on the distribution of spikes emitted by the ganglion cell, then the straight-line function shown in the ROC graph would have been the result. Since the ganglion cell was responsive to the flash of light, however, the empirical ROC curve bows upward, thereby indicating that the effect of the stimulus was added to the noise.

For one quantum to cause several spikes, there must be some effective amplification of the output of a rod before it reaches the ganglion cell. The experimenters proposed that this might be accomplished by having the output of the rod fed to several bipolars simultaneously. The outputs of the bipolars may then converge onto a common ganglion cell. The joint effect of the bipolars is the production of several spike potentials. Presumably the central nervous system compares the output of the ganglion cell within a given time interval with its output at other time intervals. When there is a sufficient discrepancy between the average spontaneous activity and activity at any particular time, then the conditions are satisfied for the decision that a light is present in the visual field.

Rod and cone thresholds. The great care that went into the classical experiment of Hecht, Schlaer, and Pierenne is typical of the many fine experiments designed to study visual sensitivity. To review all of these experiments, one after the other, would of course be a tiresome task for the non-specialist reader. To spare the reader, as well as because of the detailed complexity of this literature, we shall describe hypothetical experiments summarizing the salient findings of numerous studies of visual sensitivity. If the reader seeks more details he is referred to the books by Pirenne (1967) and Davson (1962); and Cornsweet's (1970) excellent discussion of the visual process.

Figure 3–14. Relative sensitivity to a small spot of white light as a function of the position of the image of the spot on the horizontal meridian of the right eye's retina. (After Pirenne, 1967)

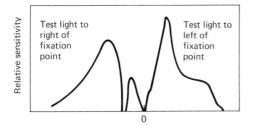

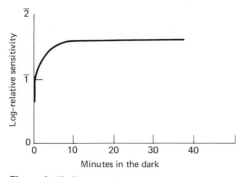

Figure 3–15. Change in sensitivity of the central fovea to target luminance as a function of time in the dark.

One of the purposes of experimentation in the field of visual psychophysics is to define the different functions of the rods and cones. In one hypothetical experiment we shall use a white light as a stimulus. A neutral density filter will be employed to control the amount of light reaching the eye of the observer. This filter may be thought of as a wedge with variable thickness so that less light will pass through its thicker end than through its thinner end (Fig. 3–13). We shall employ also a fixation point. This very dim point of red light may be moved about in the visual field so that for any angle of fixation we can define the retinal region in which the white target light will fall.

Our observers will be volunteers, and they will maintain fixation on the fixation point through an artificial pupil—ensuring that the pupillary diameter of the observer's eye is constant. Further, they will be willing to sit with their eyes covered to keep them in darkness for controlled periods of time prior to any experimental session. Prior to certain sessions the observers will look into a bright uniformly illuminated surface. The observers are all presumed to be highly motivated, they will utilize a consistent criterion throughout the experimental sessions. Our observers must have infinite patience and time, since they will have many thousands of trials under many different stimulus conditions. These many trials will allow us to plot our results as smooth functions representing performance averaged over the many trials.

To begin with, we might consider how the eye's sensitivity varies with the position of the incident light when the eye had been in the dark for about 40 minutes prior to the experimental sessions. As a result of many measurements, it is found that the sensitivity of the eye is greater in the periphery than it is in the center. The results indicating that the sensitivity to the light varies as a function of its position on the retina are summarized in Figure 3–14. To read this figure correctly one must be aware that if a region in the eye is very sensitive to light, then less light is required to produce a *Yes* response than is required at some region with lesser sensitivity. Thus, an increase in sensitivity in the graph means that less light is required to produce a threshold response.

According to Figure 3–14, more light is needed in the fovea if the light is to be detected. About 20 degrees away from the fovea nasally, where the target is imaged in the blind spot, the observer never detects it. Moreover, the eye is most sensitive to the light about ten degrees away from the fovea on the horizontal retinal meridian.

Now, supposing that the previous experiment is repeated several times, on each repetition the observer would spend less time in the dark before his session begins. Moreover, we might modify our procedure somewhat by having the observer slowly increase the amount of light energy reaching his eye until he reports just detecting the target. This will insure that a bright target on a particular trial would not affect the adaptation of his eye on subsequent trials.

Figure 3–15 shows what happens when the target is imaged in the center of the fovea. The sensitivity to the target luminance increases by a factor of ten if the eye is kept in the dark at least 10 minutes before the exposure to the stimulus. A more conventional plot of this change in

Figure 3–16. Change in target luminance needed to produce a threshold response of the rod and cone systems as a function of time in the dark. Upper curve is for cone vision, lower for rod vision; the dotted curve is a composite of both functions.

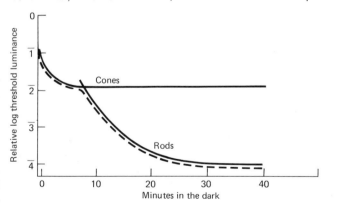

sensitivity is shown in Figure 3–16, which represents the change in target luminance needed to obtain a threshold response as a function of time in the dark. This figure contains a curve for cone vision and another for rod vision. The rod vision curve represents the change in sensitivity as a function of time in the dark when the target is imaged well off to one side of the fovea. The sum of these two curves, indicated by the dotted line, is what may be found if a spot of light is located on the retina so as to excite both rods and cones.

It will be observed from Figure 3–16 that rod sensitivity increases by a factor of about 1000 with time in the dark. It takes about 40 minutes in the dark for the rods to become maximally sensitive to light. Moreover, when the eyes were in the light just prior to the testing conditions, the rods became far less sensitive to light than the cones. If the stimulus in this experiment had been a red light rather than a white light, the resulting data could have looked just like the cone function, and the rod function might have been absent. Moreover, in patients who have lost foveal vision due to a pathological condition, a white light would have revealed a rod curve, and no cone segment would have been observed.

It is obvious from the results of our experiments that the threshold varies with retinal position and also with time in the dark.

THE SENSITIVITY FUNCTIONS

Now let us suppose that instead of using a white light as a target we use colored lights subtending an angle of about 5 degrees. Moreover, rather than expose the observer to several different periods in the dark, we shall use but two periods, and one of them will be very short. The observer will start to detect targets of different color directly after exposure for several minutes to a brightly illuminated surface. Alternatively, he will begin his detecting task after 30 minutes in the dark.

From our previous experiment we may assume that the observer with the light-adapted eye—the one exposed to white light just prior to the experiment—will use his cones to detect the targets. But since cones become relatively less sensitive than rods after some time in the dark, the dark-adapted observer's data will reflect largely the sensitivity of his rods to the colored lights.

Figure 3–17 shows how sensitivity varies as a function of wavelength when the eye is light-adapted and when it is dark-adapted. In general it is true that the eye is not equally sensitive to all wavelengths of light: it is

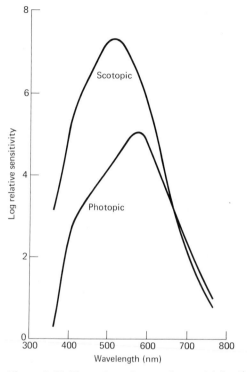

Figure 3–17. Photopic and scotopic sensitivity functions.

less sensitive to the blues and reds than it is to the greens and yellows— less light energy is needed to elicit a response to yellow light than to red light. Thus, if one were to look at a spectrum of colors ranging from red at one end to blue at the other, and if all of the wavelengths were of equal energy, then the yellows and greens would appear to be brighter than the reds and blues. Moreover, the light-adapted eye is maximally sensitive to light of about 555 nm; the dark-adapted eye, to light of about 505 nm. The curve obtained when the eye is light-adapted is known as the *photopic sensitivity function,* and the curve obtained with the dark-adapted eye is the *scotopic sensitivity function.* The fact that the rods are more sensitive after some time in the dark, while the cones become relatively insensitive, is indicated by the different amplitudes of the two functions.

An interesting feature of the photopic and scotopic sensitivity functions is the fact that their maxima are at different wavelengths. This is evident to the observer when he looks at a spectrum of colors first with a dark-adapted eye and then with an eye that had been exposed to a bright light so that it becomes light-adapted. The green (505 nm) region of the spectrum appears to be brighter when it is viewed with the dark-adapted eye, while the yellow (555 nm) portion appears to be brighter when the same spectrum is viewed by the light-adapted eye. This phenomenon, known as the *Purkinje shift,* is attributed to the fact that the pigments in the rods and cones differ in their selective absorption of wavelengths of light.

PIGMENTS AND SENSITIVITY

It is agreed that the differences in the two sensitivity functions are due to differences in the light-absorbing substances residing in rods and cones. A pigment is a substance that absorbs certain wavelengths more than it does others. Those not absorbed by the pigment are reflected by it, and this gives the pigment a colored appearance. The absorbed quanta change the states of the absorbing molecules in the pigment (Wald, Brown, and Gibbons, 1963). Although the intermediary steps are unknown, a change in the state of a pigment molecule can produce activity in a rod, and this is ultimately transmitted as a signal along the optic nerve.

The pigment in the rods is known as *rhodopsin.* Because of its purple color when isolated and kept in the dark, it is known also as *visual purple.* After removal of the pigment from the rods of an eye, it is possible to pass a beam of light through the sample of rhodopsin and watch it change in transparency. After some time in strong light the pigment becomes pale yellow, and considerable light can pass through it. The pigment's purple color derives from the fact that it absorbs light from the middle of the spectrum more than it does light from the red and blue ends of the spectrum.

The selective absorption characteristics of the pigment can be measured. When rhodopsin is isolated from a retina and then mixed in a transparent container with another fluid, light of different wavelengths may be passed through it. The ratio of amount of light entering the container to the amount passing through it is a measure of the absorption of light at that wavelength by the rhodopsin, the container, and the medium in which the rhodopsin is dissolved. The absorption characteristics of the container and the solvent alone can also be measured and subtracted from the total absorption of the container with rhodopsin, thereby giving the absorption characteristics of rhodopsin alone. After correcting for density

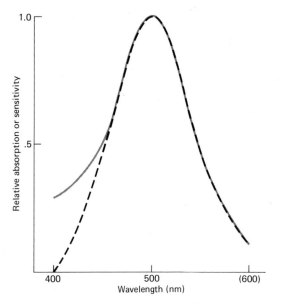

Figure 3–18. Relative absorption of light by rhodopsin in solution as a function of wavelength (solid curve). Dashed curve represents the psychophysically determined relative sensitivity of the dark-adapted peripheral retina as a function of the wavelength of the stimulating light. The discrepancy between the two curves is due to the selective absorption of short-wavelength light by the lens and other intraocular media.

differences, absorption can be plotted as a function of wavelength to give a *density spectrum* for rhodopsin (Dartnall, 1957).

Figure 3–18 shows the per cent absorption of light by rhodopsin in solution as a function of its wavelength. This density spectrum is matched closely by the dashed curve which reflects the sensitivity of the dark-adapted eye to light of different wavelengths. There can be no doubt that it is the absorption characteristics of rhodopsin that account for the spectral sensitivity of the rods.

Rushton and Campbell (1954) succeeded in measuring the changes in the absorption of light by rhodopsin as a function of light adaptation in the living human eye, and did so with an apparatus similar to that shown in Figure 3–19. Light entering the eye is reflected back out by the dark, choroid sheath behind the retina. The light reflected by the choroid passes through the retina twice. If any of the light is absorbed by pigments in the retina, it will be absent from the reflected light measured by the experimenter.

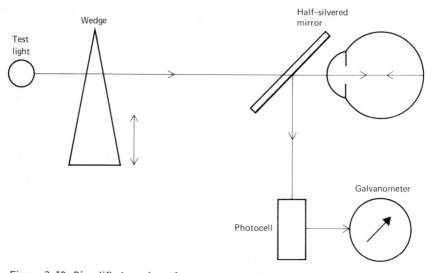

Figure 3–19. Simplified version of apparatus used by Campbell and Rushton (1955). Some of the light emitted by the test lamp enters the eye and is reflected by the choroid sheath behind the retina. This reflected light leaves the eye and is reflected by a half-silvered mirror onto a sensitive photocell. The galvanometer provided a measure of the amount of light reflected from the eye when the eye was dark-adapted, and then after the eye's exposure to a high-energy-adapting light. The bleaching effect of the adapting light causes more of the test light to be reflected by the choroid sheath, since there is less rhodopsin available to absorb the test light. The wedge is then moved to reduce the amount of test light reaching the eye so that the galvanometer reading matches that obtained prior to light adaptation. The difference in test light energy needed to obtain the match is an index of the proportion of the rhodopsin bleached by the adapting light.

Using a blue-green light, Campbell and Rushton (1955) were able to show that more light is reflected from the back of the eye after exposure to a bright light than is reflected prior to exposure. This implies that the bright light bleached the rhodopsin in the retina, thereby making it more transparent—i.e., less likely to absorb light quanta. The same effect did not occur when an orange-red light was used, since very little of the light at this wavelength is absorbed by rhodopsin.

With this method of retinal densitometry, Campbell and Rushton found that there was very little effect of adaptation when the blue-green light was reflected from the central fovea which is rod-free. Similarly, there was no effect when the light was reflected from the blind spot. The effect of the bleaching light varied with rod density across the retina.

In one experiment the amount of light absorbed before reflection was measured at different times after exposure to a very strong bleaching light. This white light bleached nearly all the rhodopsin in the region of its image. Immediately after exposure, and then at different times after this exposure, an increase was found in the capacity of the eye to absorb light from the small test flash. This is reflected by the monotonically increasing curve in Figure 3–20, which indicates that rhodopsin regenerates in the dark, and complete recovery takes about 30 minutes.

The scalloped curve in Figure 3–20 illustrates the fact that during continuous exposure to a bleaching light the rhodopsin bleaches less and less rapidly over time until it reaches a steady state level. When the bleaching light is weak, as in the curve segment labelled '1' in the figure, the steady state level is reached rather quickly. With bleaching lights of stronger intensity (segments labelled '5' and '100'), the time required to reach a steady state takes longer. The steady state level is consistent with the idea that rhodopsin molecules regenerate even while other molecules are being affected by incident quanta. At some point the regeneration rate

Figure 3–20. Relative amount of light absorbed by rhodopsin during bleaching by a weak adapting light (segment '1') and by adapting lights 5 and 100 times more intense. The smooth curve is a record of the relative amount of light absorbed by rhodopsin in the living human eye as a function of time after exposure to a bright adapting light.

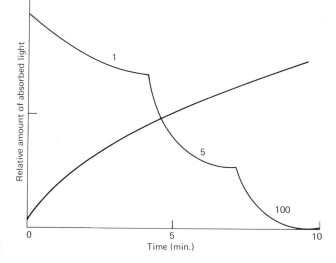

equals the bleaching rate so that the two processes cancel out each other. This balance may be disturbed by either increasing or decreasing the adaptation light level.

Rushton, Campbell, Hagins, and Brindley (1955) observed that an observer's sensitivity to light cannot be determined exclusively by the capacity of rhodopsin for capturing light quanta. Thus, 7 minutes after exposure to a strong bleaching light (see the smooth curve in Figure 3–20) half the available rhodopsin has regenerated. One might assume from this result that the threshold light level for detection would also be lowered by half, thereby making the eye twice as sensitive to light. On the contrary, 7 minutes after exposure to such a bright light, the threshold level is very much higher. Instead, the logarithm of the sensitivity to light (which is the reciprocal of the threshold light level) is approximately proportional to the concentration of rhodopsin or unbleached pigment (Dowling and Wald, 1960).

Using a more sensitive technique (though still similar to that employed in studying rhodopsin in the human eye), Rushton (1958) studied cone pigments also—with results we shall treat in the chapter on color perception. For the present it is sufficient to point out that cone pigments are also bleached by light, and that the amount of light reflected from the area just behind the central fovea will accordingly vary with the intensity of an adapting field.

The difference in amplitude at their highest points between the photopic and scotopic sensitivity functions shown in Figure 3–17 is about 2 log units. This means that sensitivity to light at 505 nm in the dark-adapted eye is about 100 times the sensitivity to light at 555 nm in the light-adapted eye. This difference in sensitivity may be attributed in part to differences in sensitivity of individual rods and cones. Thus, while rods can be excited if they absorb but one quantum, it might be concluded that more quanta need to be absorbed by cones if they are to be excited.

Brindley (1960) calculated the number of quanta which must be absorbed by cones if a sensation of light is to be experienced with a probability of 0.5 or greater. Using data reported by Stiles (1939) and a number of reasonable assumptions about cone density and quanta absorption by the intervening media, he came to the conclusion that a cone may be excited if it absorbs about five light quanta. A recent report by Fain and Dowling (1973) indicates that in the mud puppy individual rods are 25 times more sensitive than cones, and the authors suggest that this may be true for other vertebrates as well. The remaining differences in apparent sensitivity of rods and cones may be due to the fact that the cones are directional sensitive receptors.

The Stiles-Crawford Effect. The directional sensitivity of the cones is illustrated by a phenomenon known as the Stiles-Crawford effect. Figure 3–21 depicts one kind of apparatus for demonstrating the Stiles-Crawford effect. Light from the pinhole or artificial pupil in the figure enters in the center of the pupil of the observer's eye. If the pinhole is moved so that light from it enters near the edge of the natural pupil, a small light source viewed through the pinhole will appear dimmer.

Stiles and Crawford (1933) found that when light enters the pupil near its edge, it must be made much brighter than another light entering the eye from near the center of the pupil if the two lights are to appear equal. As a matter of fact, light entering through the center of the pupil needs to be only 1/10th the level of light entering near its edge if both lights are to appear to be equally bright.

Figure 3–21. The Stiles-Crawford effect. A light source viewed through an artificial pupil placed in line with the center of the natural pupil of the eye (upper part of figure) appears to be brighter than it does when the artificial pupil is displaced away from the center of the natural pupil of the eye (lower drawing).

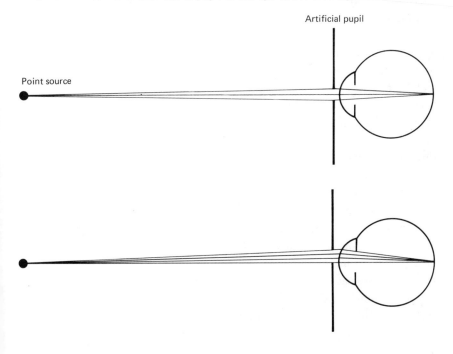

Artificial pupil

Point source

It is now known that the Stiles-Crawford effect is linked to the cones of the eye and does not appear in the dark-adapted eye. The probable reason for the Stiles-Crawford effect is that light impinging on cones at an angle is less likely to affect their pigments than light intercepting the cones head-on. This view led O'Brien (1946) to construct model cones of foam to test for funneling of microwave signals whose wavelengths were in the same proportion to the sizes of the artificial cones as the wavelength of light is to real cones. O'Brien found that the angle of incidence of the waves on the artificial cones had a strong effect on the intensities of the waves measured at their opposite ends.

The Stiles-Crawford effect suggests that the troland, which depends upon pupil size as well as upon target luminance (see Chapter 2), is a bit imprecise as a measure of retinal illuminance. It does not take into account the fact that the rays entering the pupil from near its edge are visually less effective than are rays entering near its center. In any event, the fact that cones are less affected by light entering from the edge of the pupil is another reason that cones appear to be less sensitive than rods. The effective intensity of a sheaf of rays spread over the entire corneal surface is less when the eye is light-adapted than when it is dark-adapted. The magnitude of this effect is small but, together with the actual differences in rod and cone sensitivity, the difference between photopic and scotopic sensitivity can be accounted for.

Spatial Summation. Suppose that a tiny spot of light were to be formed on the retina 10 degrees off to one side of the fovea. The threshold detectability of this spot could be expressed in terms of the light energy it contains or in terms of the number of quanta that impinge per unit time in the area defined by the spot. Once the threshold energy is determined in an experiment, the spot could then be enlarged and the absolute threshold energy determined once again. It has been found in such experiments that just so long as the spot is smaller than about 10 minutes of arc in diameter, the energy needed to elicit a threshold response is constant. Just so long as the total energy of the spot is constant, it will be equally detectable no matter how the energy is distributed in an area about 10 minutes in diameter. The spot could be very tiny so that the energy is concentrated in a single point, or it could be spread out on the retina. In both cases the spot will be equally detectable.

It is believed that this phenomenon occurs because the outputs of the rods within a 10-minute region are brought together at common neurons. This funneling of energy (known as *spatial summation*) is characteristic of the rod system. The region over which spatial summation occurs is not sharply defined. In fact, some summation occurs over areas much wider than 10 minutes of arc, although the funneling effect becomes much weaker as area grows larger. Spatial summation, characteristic of the rod system, is most pronounced outside the fovea in the dark-adapted eye. Attempts to measure spatial summation in the fovea of the light-adapted eye show little if any summation (Brindley, 1960).

The finding that spatial summation occurs depended upon the use of very small and dim spots of light. The psychophysical method of threshold measurement made it possible to discover the process, and thereby revealed interesting differences between the rod and cone systems. These differences are consistent with anatomical findings that show that many more rods converge onto common bipolar cells than do cones. More, spatial summation may contribute to the differences between photopic and scotopic sensitivity. The visual system is, however, far more complicated than is indicated here. We shall now turn to some of these complexities.

4

the perception of flicker

The perceived world is constructed from many glimpses of objects in space. The eye is ever on the move, flitting from one thing to another. At each of its positions the eye may pick up an entirely different distribution of light energy. It is obvious that the response of the visual system to time-varying stimulation is of central importance to perception. To ultimately understand the processes underlying perception, we must explore the response of the visual system to rather elementary time-varying stimulation. The present chapter deals with some effects of such elementary stimulation and discusses the powerful concepts being used to explain them.

TEMPORAL SUMMATION

The visual system collects energy distributed over time just as it collects light energy distributed in space on the retina. This follows from the fact that the detectability of a target may be enhanced by presenting it for a longer period of time—a phenomenon known as *temporal summation*.

Suppose that a flash were detected by an observer on only 40 per cent of its exposures. As we already know, the probability of seeing this target may be enhanced by increasing its luminance. But the probability of seeing the small flash could be improved also by increasing its duration. More formally,

$$C = t \times L$$

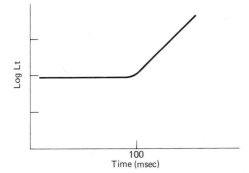

Figure 4–1. Time-course of temporal summation. The ordinate represents the logarithm of the product of luminance and target exposure time needed to achieve detection of the target with a particular probability. As exposure time is increased, less target luminance is needed for detection. When duration of exposure exceeds about 100 msec, the detectability of the target is proportional to the logarithm of the product of luminance and exposure time—i.e., the luminance must remain constant as duration increases if the target is to remain detectable.

where C is a constant effect of a stimulus on the observer, t is the duration of the flash, and L is its luminance. This relation, known as *Bloch's law*, says in effect that if we add energy over time then this energy can have a cumulative effect that enhances the detectability of the flash.

Temporal summation does not go on indefinitely. In fact, there is interchangeability of luminance and time for about 100 msec. Thus, the constant effect of the product of time and luminance is to be expected over rather short periods of time. With increases in duration beyond about 100 msec. the probability of seeing the flash becomes dependent almost exclusively upon its luminance and hardly at all upon its increased duration. The curve describing the way in which time and luminance interact to produce these effects is shown in Figure 4–1.

As we have already seen, spatial summation is more pronounced in the periphery than it is in the fovea. Temporal summation, has nearly the same time course in both areas—according to Bartlett (1965), who compared data obtained by other investigators in the fovea and in the periphery. One reason to doubt Bartlett's interpretation is that temporal summation does vary with the state of adaptation of the eye (Herrick, 1956; Barlow, 1958). In general, as the background luminance to a target is increased (thereby increasing the degree of light adaptation of the eye), the less pronounced is the effect of target duration on its detectability. Or, to state it in another way: with increasing light adaptation the detection threshold comes to depend more exclusively on the luminance of the target and is less subject to variation with the duration of its exposure. This suggests that cones and rods have different temporal integration properties, since the relative sensitivities of these elements will also vary with the state of adaptation of the eye.

There may be an even finer difference between different classes of photoreceptors than a mere change in the course of temporal integration with light adaptation. More recent data by Mollon and Krauskopf (1973) and by Krauskopf and Mollon (1971) indicate that the temporal integration of the effect of light energy on cones depends upon the wavelength of the incident light. This is consistent with the idea that there are several different types of cone receptor, each with its own pigment and with its own temporal response properties (see Chapter 6). Basically, Krauskopf and Mollon found that when a spot of colored light is presented against an adapting background of colored light, the period over which temporal summation occurs depends strongly upon the difference in the wavelengths of the target and of the background. If these are widely separated in wavelength, the luminance of the background has no effect on the period of temporal summation. If they are close together in wavelength, there is an effect of background luminance on the period over which summation occurs. This result is consistent with the idea that the sensitivity of one type of cone may not be affected when light that normally excites a different type of cone is used to adapt the eye (Stiles, 1949).

Moreover, each of these cone-types have their own time constants, and these will influence the period over which summation occurs strongly. Krauskopf and Mollon suggest also that the differences in period of temporal summation is probably due largely to photochemical properties of the pigments in the cones rather than to the neural structures succeeding them in the retina. It is important to recognize, however, that even though different receptors may have different temporal summation characteristics, the neural circuits beyond the receptors themselves undoubtedly play a major role in producing temporal summation.

One bit of evidence for this latter conclusion is the fact that there is an interaction between temporal and spatial factors. Barlow (1958), for example, found that temporal summation occurs over a longer period of time when the stimulus is small than it does when the stimulus is large. Thus, there appears to be an inverse relation between temporal and spatial summation. Indeed, spatial summation occurs over wider retinal regions during short-duration exposures than it does during long-duration exposures. This interaction between the temporal and the spatial collections of effects of energy is a strong argument for a neural basis of both processes. They could hardly interact if temporal summation is a purely photochemical process while the other depends upon the funneling of neural data from different receptors to a common neuron.

Temporal summation implies that the detection of a spot should be independent of how energy is distributed in time during a summation interval. A spot flashed twice during an interval of a few milliseconds should be just as detectable as a single flash with double the energy. Obviously, if two flashes are separated widely in time, they will be distinguishable from each other, and if they are at or near threshold level the detection of one would be quite independent of the presence of the other. As the time interval between them grows smaller, however, a residual effect left by the first flash will ultimately combine with the effect produced by the second flash, thereby enhancing its detectability. The process by which an effect of one event is stored so that it adds to the effect of a subsequent event is basic to many perceptual phenomena, including the perception of flicker. Before turning to the topic of flicker perception, however, we must review some basic ideas that have led to a unification of this field.

LINEAR SYSTEMS ANALYSIS

A system is any assemblage of parts to form a complex whole. Thus, e.g., the lens, camera body, range finder, and film are elements of a photographic system. The assembly of neurons, receptors, end plates, and glial cells comprise the entity we call the nervous system.

None of the systems we normally encounter is truly independent and self-sufficient. The nervous system, for example, cannot survive in isolation from the rest of the organism. *System* is moreover a rather arbitrary designation: the nervous system, for example, may with equal justice be considered as a subsystem of the system known as the organism. When we use the term *system* we actually mean any complex device or collection of devices with some identifiable function or functions. There is the steering system of an automobile, the navigation system of a ship, and the visual system of an organism. In general terms, a system may be thought of as a device that produces an effect as a result of some input. A mass suspended on a spring, for example, is an oscillating system that will

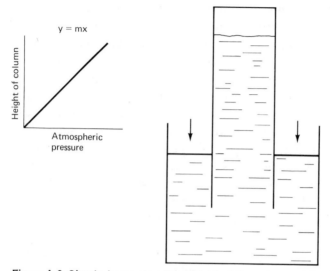

Figure 4–2. Simple barometer. The height of the column of liquid is proportional to atmospheric pressure.

bounce up and down for some time after the mass is elevated and dropped while the other end of the spring is anchored in place.

One important distinction is the one we make between *linear systems* and *nonlinear systems*. A linear system is one whose behavior can be described by means of linear equations—i.e., the output of the system is always proportional to its input. Consider the case of a simple device designed to reflect barometric pressure. A long tube similar to the one shown in Figure 4–2, containing a column of water and placed in a vessel full of water, is such a device. Since the empty upper portion of the tube contains a vacuum, the pressure of the air in the atmosphere is sufficient to maintain a column of water in the tube. This occurs because the air presses down with a particular force on the surface of the water in the vessel. Now, if the barometric pressure should grow smaller, the height of the column of water in the tube would also grow smaller.

A graph showing how the height of the column of water varies with atmospheric pressure is shown in Figure 4–2. It will be observed that the graph is a straight line and can be expressed mathematically with a linear algebraic equation, as shown in the figure. Now, if the water were to be replaced with mercury, the height of the column of mercury will be much smaller than the corresponding height of the column of water. This follows from the fact that mercury is much heavier than water, so that more pressure is required to elevate it by the same amount. Nevertheless, variations in the height of the column of mercury will still follow a straight-line function.

The behavior of a linear system is entirely predictable. In the case of the barometer, so long as we know the air pressure and the constant of proportionality in the equation describing its behavior, we can always predict the output of the system.

The linear system we have been describing is very simple: air pressure normally varies very slowly over time, and we can take our time about measuring the height of the column of mercury. It is possible, however, to have linear systems whose inputs vary relatively rapidly—as in the case in which a brief impulse is the input. If the system is capable of mirroring the input precisely, then no problems arise; but there are linear systems whose components do not respond instantaneously to an input and, moreover, do not stop responding after the input has ceased. A capacitor together with a resistance form such a component.

Two metal plates separated by a gap of air comprise a capacitor. When a battery is connected to the two plates, as in Figure 4–3, positive charges accumulate on one plate and negative charges on the other. If a resistance were to be placed between the positive pole of the battery and the capacitor, it might require a substantial period of time before the capacitor is fully charged after the switch is closed. The *time constant* of this circuit is the amount of time in seconds before the voltage across

Figure 4–3. When switch is closed, one plate of the capacitor takes on a positive charge, and the other plate a negative charge.

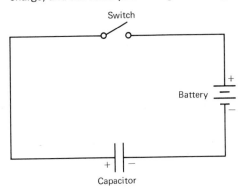

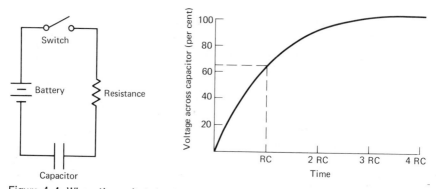

Figure 4–4. When the switch is closed the resistance impedes the charging of the capacitor. The time constant of the circuit is depicted in the graph, which shows how the rate of charging of the capacitor varies with time after the closing of the switch. RC is the amount of time in seconds before the voltage across the capacitor reaches 63 per cent of the applied voltage after closing the switch.

the capacitor reaches 63 per cent of its maximum value. It turns out that the time constant T is simply the product of the resistance R in Ohms and the capacitance C in Farads. The time course of the growth of potential across the capacitor is illustrated in Figure 4–4.

An RC circuit such as that shown in Figure 4–5 requires time to discharge the potential stored by the capacitor. The input signal is turned off by opening the first switch. The capacitor will then maintain its charge, which may leak off very slowly. If the second switch in the figure

Figure 4–5. Capacitor is charged by closing switch S_1 with switch S_2 open. After opening switch S_1, the capacitor will discharge through the resistance R_2 when switch S_2 is closed. The discharge is an exponential function of time, as shown in the graph.

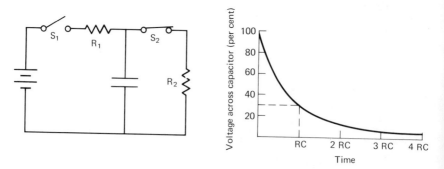

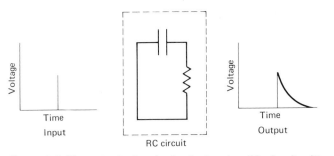

Figure 4–6. The output of a slowly discharging RC circuit with an impulse applied as an input.

is closed, though, the charge across the capacitor will be fed into the second resister R_2. The speed with which this charge is dissipated depends upon the product of C and R_2. The time course of this discharge is exponential—i.e., the rate of discharge at any point in time depends upon the level of remaining charge. Thus, the discharge rate becomes slower and slower as the amount of remaining charge grows smaller. Here too, the time constant is the time required for the level of voltage across the capacitor to reach 63 per cent of its maximum value.

If an impulse voltage were to be applied directly across a capacitor without going through a resistance, then the capacitor would achieve its maximum charge instantaneously. Since R is zero, the value of RC is zero also, and the time constant is therefore infinitely fast. Let us now suppose (as shown in Figure 4–5) that the resulting charge of the capacitor is discharged through a resistance. This means that there will be a gradual fall-off of the voltage, since the resistance impedes current flow. If this

Figure 4–7. Typical distortion of a square-wave input by an RC circuit.

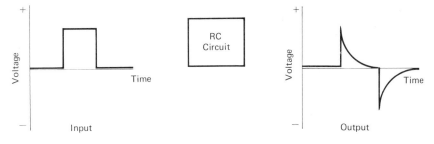

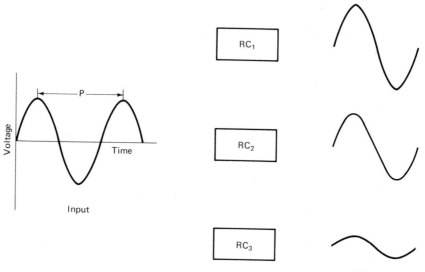

Figure 4–8. Effect of three different time constants on the amplitude of a sine wave input signal. The time constant RC_1 is less than the period P of the input. RC_2 is slightly longer than P, and RC_3 is much longer than P. The effect of these circuits on the phase of the input signal is ignored.

instantaneous charging and slow discharging is considered to be the response of the system, it will be seen from Figure 4–6 that the output does not resemble the input impulse. This distortion of the input by the capacitor and resistor makes it difficult to predict the output from the input to this system.

Consider the same RC circuit when a square wave input is applied to it (see Figure 4–7). The output (also shown in Figure 4–7) appears to be quite distorted. Again, how can we predict output of this kind from the input?

There is only one kind of signal that will not be distorted by a simple RC circuit: the simple sine wave. All that an RC circuit can do to a sine wave is change its amplitude and phase. If the time constant of an RC circuit is very short relative to the period of a sine wave input, then (as shown in Fig. 4–8) a sine wave will appear at the output with little or no attenuation of its amplitude. If, however, the time constant of the circuit is commensurate with the period of the input sine wave, then the output sine wave will be attenuated in amplitude. Nevertheless, the shape of the input is preserved at the output. Of course, if the time constant is very long relative to the input period, then the output will be vanishingly small. This simply means that the circuit is not capable of passing the input.

Sine waves are passed in varying amounts without distortion by all linear circuits. The beauty of this fact is that it enables us to predict with precision the behavior of a linear system in response to virtually any kind of input, even impulses and square waves. This stems from a very basic mathematical discovery—namely, a periodic function can be represented as a sum of many sine waves of different amplitude and phase. This discovery of the French mathematician J. B. Fourier is the cornerstone of some recent and exciting work in visual perception.

A periodic event is something that repeats itself over and over in time. One such periodic sequence is illustrated in Figure 4–9. It will be seen in the figure that this complex wave may be thought of as the sum of two simpler sine waves, where one of them is at twice the frequency of the other. We could make a graph indicating the amount of energy in the complex wave as a function of the frequencies of its components. This

Figure 4–9. The complex wave can be synthesized by adding the simple harmonic oscillations **f** and **2f**.

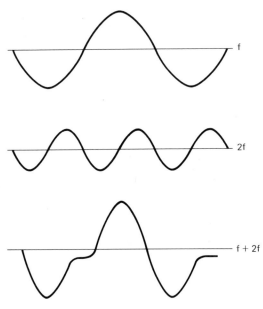

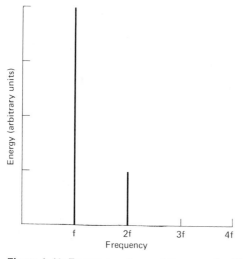

Figure 4–10. Energy spectrum of the wave **f** + **2f**.

graph, known as an *energy spectrum* (see Fig. 4–10), indicates that there is four times as much energy in the low-frequency wave as there is in the high-frequency wave.

The low-frequency component in the complex wave of Figure 4–9 is known as the *fundamental* or *first harmonic* oscillation of the complex wave, as there is no lower-frequency component of the wave. The higher frequency component is known as the *second harmonic* of the complex function. The energy of each of these components is proportional to the squares of their amplitudes. The total energy in a complex wave is proportional to the sum of the squares of the peak amplitudes of its components.

Fourier analysis makes it possible to identify the various harmonic components of a complex wave, as well as their amplitudes. While the various harmonic components of a square wave are actually infinite in number, the wave may be approximated by summing a finite number of its components, such as are shown in Figure 4–11. Fourier analysis teaches us that there are an infinite number of odd harmonics in a square wave and that their amplitudes vary as a function of their order. Thus, in addition to a fundamental component whose frequency is the same as the repetition frequency of the original square wave, there is another component at 3 times the frequency of the fundamental and one-third of its

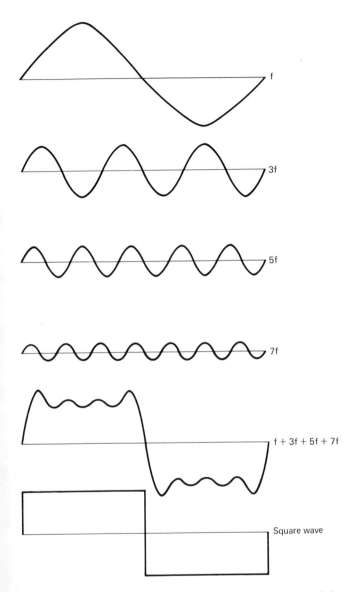

Figure 4–11. Approximating a square wave by summing a finite number of simple sinusoids.

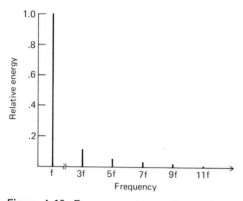

Figure 4–12. Energy spectrum of a periodic square wave. Individual higher harmonics contribute an extremely small amount of energy to the total energy of the wave.

amplitude. There is another component of 5 times the frequency of the fundamental and one-fifth of its amplitude, and so on. The energy spectrum of a periodic square wave is shown in Figure 4–12; that of an infinitely sharp periodic impulse, in Figure 4–13.

Now consider a single non-periodic impulse. If we imagine that this impulse does really recur at some indefinite time in the future—say, in

Figure 4–13. The energy spectrum of a periodic and infinitely sharp impulse. The spectrum contains an infinite number of Fourier components, all of equal energy and all multiples of the basic impulse frequency.

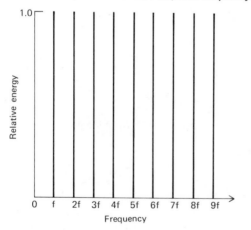

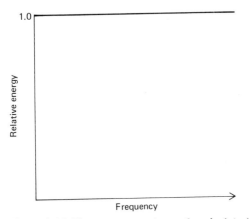

Figure 4–14. The energy spectrum of an isolated impulse. All frequencies are represented with equal energy.

one year—then we can still draw an energy spectrum for the impulse. Since there are 31,536,000 seconds in one year, the basic repetition frequency of the impulse is 1/31,536,000 times per second. This means that the spectral lines in the spectrum of this impulse are separated by the tiniest fraction of a second. If we were to assume that the impulse repeats itself at even greater intervals, then the spectral lines would approach being infinitely close together, thereby producing a continuous energy spectrum for a single impulse. In this way even a single apparently isolated event can be thought of as the sum of an infinite number of sine waves. This spectrum is shown in Figure 4–14.

Now let us return to the system comprised of a capacitor discharging across a resistance. The output of this system in response to an impulse input may also be described in terms of Fourier analysis. If the time constant of the circuit is very short, then the exponential fall-off will take less time than if the time constant is longer. Therefore, the system with a short time constant will pass more of the higher frequencies in the input than will the system with a longer time constant. Figure 4–15 shows how the spectra of outputs of such circuits may vary with increases in their time constants. Thus, though some circuits pass higher frequency components of the inputs than do other circuits, they are all still linear circuits.

One way in which to describe linear systems is in terms of how well they pass different input frequencies. A plot of amplitude of the output

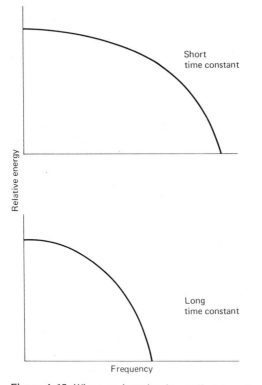

Figure 4–15. When an impulse is applied to a linear circuit with a short time constant, it passes more of the higher frequencies than does a circuit with a longer time constant.

relative to the input as a function of frequency is an *amplitude spectrum* known as the *transfer function* of a system. The transfer function indicates how well any system will pass an input as a function of its frequency. One reason impulse functions are used to test systems is that such functions contain all frequencies in equal amounts, so that by measuring the amplitudes of the various frequency components of the output of a system to which one had applied an impulse as an input, it is possible to define its transfer function.

Our account of the characteristics of linear systems is still incomplete. Consider what happens when two independent sources of light energy are turned on separately and then together. When they are turned on separately and aimed at a photocell, the photocell could be employed to measure the strength of the received energy from each source separately. Now, when the two sources are turned on together, the amount of light energy will obviously equal the sum of the light energies delivered by the two sources separately. When this happens we say that the *superposition principle* is applicable since the effects of the two lights are superimposable. If the amount of light emitted by one source should be lowered when the other source is turned on—perhaps because the activation of the second source depletes the power available for the first source, then the total energy emitted by both sources might be less than the sum of the energies emitted by the two sources separately. In this case the two sources cannot be treated as independent of each other. The superposition principle does not apply, since the two sources interact with each other.

If two inputs should be applied to a linear system, the superposition principle may be used to describe the result, for it is only in a system in which the output is proportional to the input that the superposition principle is applicable. Thus, if one input should be applied, the output may be determined by the linear equation describing the system. Similarly, if the second input should be applied, the response to that input should be equally determinable from the known characteristics of the system. Now, if both inputs were to be applied simultaneously, then the output should be the simple sum of the outputs obtained when the inputs were applied separately. If it turns out, though, that the output in response to the combined input signal is not equal to the sum of the two independently measured outputs, then the system is nonlinear.

Let us now return to the problem of how the visual system responds to flashes of light. Each flash may be thought of as an impulse initiating a train of events in the nervous system. The outcome of all of this may be the response "I see a flash." If many such flashes should be presented, then it is possible for the observer to report that he sees a flickering light. If the flashes are presented close to each other in time, then the observer may report that he does not see a flickering light but that he sees a steady light. This, after all, is the result of looking at an ordinary incandescent lamp. In this case the lamp is flickering with its first fundamental frequency at 120 Hz, in step with twice the frequency of the power-line voltage. At some frequency less than 50 Hz, however, the observer may report a barely perceptible flicker. The point at which he reports this flicker represents the maximum flicker that he may see reliably. The flash frequency at which a flickering square-wave light appears to be a steady light is known as the *Critical Flicker Frequency* (CFF). The CFF is clearly influenced by the temporal summation properties of the visual system, and up to a point its study lends itself nicely to the methods of linear systems analysis.

FLICKER PERCEPTION

Flicker phenomena have been studied for many years. At one time it was common for experimenters to employ trains of brief square waves of light in an attempt to show how diverse parameters might affect the CFF. Thus, the effect of placing the proximal stimulus at different locations was studied by Abney (1897). When Hecht and Verrijp (1933) studied the effect of both retinal location and square-wave peak luminance on the CFF, they found that when the peak retinal illuminance produced by the light was increased, the eye became more sensitive to higher-stimulus frequencies. This effect was most pronounced in the fovea and became much smaller 15 degrees out into the periphery. Effects of background luminance, stimulus area and color were also studied. Nowadays, however, the tendency is to use sine-wave modulated light in the study of flicker perception.

Although Ives (1922) was the first investigator to utilize sinusoidal stimuli in the study of flicker perception, his work was largely ignored until de Lange (1952, 1958) published his important papers. De Lange used a modulated light, which may be described as a steady light level made to increase and decrease in amplitude as a sinusoidal function of time. (This kind of stimulus is illustrated in Figure 4–16.) Two param-

Figure 4–16. Sinusoidal modulation of a light.

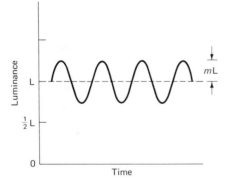

eters are needed to describe this stimulus—one, the average light level L; the other, the depth of modulation m. The peak amplitude of modulation mL is a fraction, m of L.

An expression that describes the foregoing stimulus X_{in} is

$$X_{in} = L + mL \sin wt$$

where w is the frequency of the stimulus, L is the average level of the stimulus, and mL is the peak amplitude of the modulation. One trick employed by de Lange was to use a relatively small per cent modulation of L in his experiments. He reasoned that the visual system would be more likely to respond in a linear manner to a relatively small modulation than it would to a large depth of modulation of the light. To understand this we must now consider some of the consequences of non-linearity when dealing with periodic stimuli.

As indicated in the preceding section of this chapter, the output of a linear system is proportional to the magnitude of its input. If the input of a linear system is a pure sine wave, then the output will also be a pure sine wave of the same frequency as the input. Moreover, if two sine waves of different frequency should be used to stimulate the same system at the same time, then the output would simply contain these same two frequencies. This follows from the superposition principle. To be sure, the amplitudes of the two output sine waves may not be in the same ratio as the corresponding input amplitudes, but only those two input frequencies will be present in the output. The actual amplitudes of the output sine waves will be determined by the transfer function of the system.

To express this mathematically, if $A \sin w_1 t$ and $B \sin w_2 t$ are the inputs, then the relation between the output and the input can be expressed as

$$X_{out} = k \, (A \sin w_1 t + B \sin w_2 t).$$

In this case we assume that one of the periodic functions is not attenuated more than the other by the system.

In the case of a non-linear system the output is not proportional to the input, and consequently a pure sine wave stimulus will be distorted by the system. This is known as *harmonic distortion*. The distorted output wave is itself a complicated wave, and can be described as the sum of simple sinusoids. In most cases the output wave will contain a sine wave at the frequency of the input sine wave, and another wave at twice its frequency. Higher harmonics may also be present.

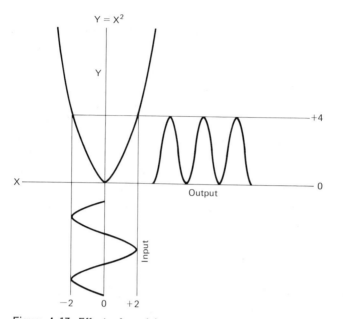

Figure 4–17. Effect of applying a sine wave with a mean amplitude of zero to a square-law device so that for every value X of the input, the output Y = X². The output is at twice the input frequency.

Let us consider a simple example of how a non-linear device may distort a sine wave. Suppose that for every instantaneous value of a signal going into the device, its output will be the simple square of the input. This is diagrammed in Figure 4–17. The function describing the relation between the input and the output is known as a square-law function. The output is always the square of the input. For a sine wave input A sin wt the output

$$X_{out} = A \sin^2 wt.$$

From elementary trigonometry

$$A \sin^2 wt = A/2 - A/2 \cos 2wt.$$

This means that for every input frequency the output is at twice the input frequency. Therefore, a pure square-law device will generate an output that is always at twice the frequency of the input. Moreover, the amplitude of the output cosine wave is one-half the amplitude of the input wave. In addition, there is a steady or zero frequency output which is also at one-half the amplitude of the input wave.

Most of the non-linear devices we encounter in daily life do not produce so extreme a distortion as a doubling of the frequency of an input wave. Thus, a high-fidelity amplifier that distorts an input slightly will still produce the original input frequency, but in addition will also emit an output at the second harmonic of the input frequency. This occurs typically when the input to the amplifier is so high that the amplifier cannot follow it. The peaks are attenuated so that the output wave is somewhat flattened.

As we saw in Chapter 3 the sensation of brightness may grow linearly with the logarithm of the luminance of the stimulus. This follows from Fechner's law. Thus, if a light is made ten times more intense, the observer may say that it has grown by a factor of only two in brightness.

Figure 4–18. A system whose output is proportional to the logarithm of the input will distort a sinusoidal signal. The distortion is obvious when the average level of the input is low (solid curve) and less pronounced when the average level is high (dashed curve).

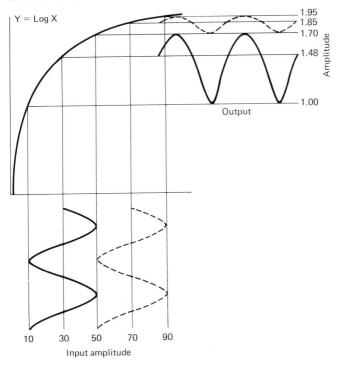

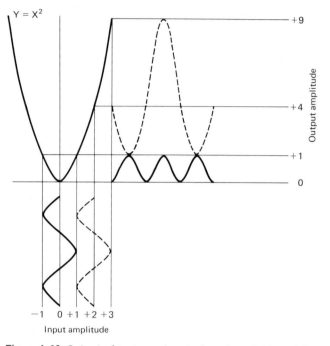

Figure 4–19. Output of a square-law device when the input sine wave is symmetrical about zero (solid curve), and when it is offset from zero (dashed curve). Note that the solid output curve has twice as many peaks as does the dashed output curve.

Assuming this to be true, when luminance is made to change in a sinusoidal fashion, as in the case of de Lange's stimulus, then the corresponding change in the sensation of brightness will not follow exactly the physical change in luminance.

It is possible to show theoretically what happens to a sine wave after it is passed through a device that responds in proportion to the logarithm of the input. A typical example appears in Figure 4–18, where it is seen that the peaks of the wave are flattened and the troughs are made sharper. A Fourier analysis of this wave shows that it contains substantial second harmonic content. Now, the interesting thing is that if the average level L of the wave were to be increased, the relative size of the second harmonic in the resulting wave is reduced substantially. With further increases in the average steady component of the wave, there is further reduction in the higher harmonics produced by simply taking the logarithm of the total input function.

An even more dramatic example occurs when one looks at the result of adding a steady component to a sine wave before applying it to a square-law device. As we saw earlier, the square-law device doubles the frequency of an input wave. As shown in Figure 4–19, the addition to the input of a steady component, whose amplitude is at least as great as the peak amplitude of the original sine wave, will prevent the doubling altogether. The output wave is now basically at the frequency of the input wave! Thus, with a sufficiently large steady component, it is possible to get a non-linear device to behave like a linear device—at least in certain respects.

Still another reason for using small modulation depths in flicker experiments is that one does not run the risk of overdriving the visual system. Large swings in stimulus amplitude can cause a saturation of the visual system or a reduction in its ability to respond. This saturation effect produces distortion of the input signal by the system. If one assumes that the visual system will respond in a linear manner to small depths of modulation, it is possible to define its transfer function. De Lange did this by measuring the CFF as a function of the modulation depth of the stimulus. The graph shown in Figure 4–20 illustrates some of de Lange's results. It is customary to plot the logarithm of stimulus frequency on the x-axis and, on the y-axis, the reciprocal of the logarithm of the per cent modulation needed to just detect flicker. This serves to compress the scales so that results obtained with low frequencies and at small modulation depths can be illustrated in detail, though the results at high frequencies are illustrated in less detail. The reason for this is clear: there is much less responsiveness when stimuli are at high frequencies than when they are at low frequencies. The curve shown in Figure 4–20 is known as a *de Lange curve*.

It is obvious from Figure 4–20 that far less modulation depth is needed to just perceive flicker at low frequencies than it is at high. At very high frequencies—more than 50 Hz—modulations of 100 per cent do not produce the sensation of flicker, though at 10 Hz about 1 per cent modulation may produce the sensation of flicker. Therefore, the eye is more sensitive to low flicker frequencies than to very high flicker frequencies.

De Lange (1952, 1958) showed that as average luminance grows higher, observers are more likely to report flicker in viewing high-frequency flicker. Thus, sensitivity to flicker increases with the average luminance of the stimulus field. This result is in general agreement with

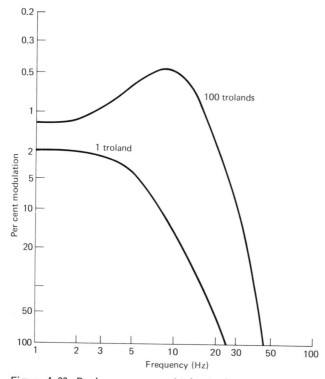

Figure 4–20. De Lange curves obtained with a 2-degree foveal stimulus of white light at two different average retinal illuminances (1 troland and 100 trolands). (After de Lange, 1958)

the results of older studies that did not employ sinusoidal stimuli. The general shapes of de Lange curves lead quite naturally to the observation that the visual system has some of the characteristics of a *low-pass filter,* a device that passes frequencies ranging from zero (*dc*) to some low value. Higher frequencies are attenuated, and very high frequencies are not passed by the filter at all. A low-pass filter model was proposed by Levinson (1968) in a very readable article on the subject of flicker perception.

In a tutorial article on flicker, Sperling (1964) described a low-pass filter model that accounts approximately for the general outlines of the de Lange curve. Figure 4–21, a reproduction of the figure used by Sperling in describing the model, demonstrates that when an impulse function (one that contains all frequencies in equal amounts) is applied to ten successive RC stages, the Fourier content of the output does resemble the high-frequency side of the de Lange curves. Sperling also pointed out, however, that this model cannot account for all the important features of the curves. For one thing, the decision as to whether flicker is present must itself be a non-linear operation. A complete model of flicker perception would include a detector capable of giving an output of "yes, it is flickering" or "no, it is not flickering" when the input to the detector is above or below some threshold or criterion value. These binary outputs are not linear functions of continuous inputs. Second, an RC analogy does not account for the fact that there is lesser sensitivity in the de Lange curves for very low frequencies than there is for intermediate frequencies; when, e.g., the average luminance is high there is a pro-

Figure 4–21. Comparison of systems containing 1, 3, 5, and 10 identical RC stages. The input, an impulse, is identical for each system. The outputs are illustrated in the center. As the number of RC stages is increased, more of the higher frequencies are attenuated, as indicated by the curves on the right. These curves, called "attenuation characteristics," show how the ratio of the amplitude of each sine wave component f of the output e_o, and the corresponding component of the input e_i, varies with the number of RC stages. The logarithm of the ratio e_o/e_i becomes smaller as e_o becomes smaller than e_i. (After Sperling, 1964)

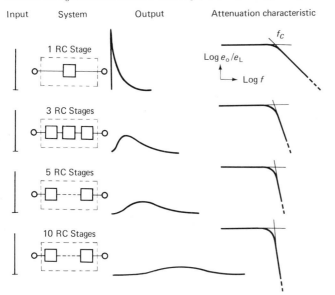

nounced enhancement of sensitivity to flicker at 10 Hz relative to sensitivity at 1 Hz.

In de Lange's experiments the flickering light was embedded in a steady field of light whose luminance was equal to the average luminance of the flickering light. Kelly (1959) suspected that the sharpness of the resulting contour between the surrounding field and the flickering spot could serve as a clue to the presence of flicker. This, he suggested, might make it appear as though the eye is more sensitive to flicker than it really is. Accordingly he created a stimulus in which there was no sharp dividing contour between the flickering center spot and its surrounding field. He used a large test field with a uniform luminance in its center, and the luminance tapered off around the edge of the spot to become zero far in the periphery of the retina.

Kelly found that the eye is far less sensitive to the lower flicker frequencies with the large stimulus field than it is with the small spot in a uniform background (see Fig. 4–22). It is obvious that the low-pass filter is a very poor model of flicker perception when Kelly's stimulus is used. A better analogy is the band-pass filter, which is sensitive to a particular range of frequencies and attenuates frequencies that are below and above that range.

WEBER'S LAW AND FLICKER PERCEPTION

Kelly (1961) obtained data showing how sensitivity to different flicker frequencies varies as a function of the average level of the stimulus. Using his large stimulus with the blurred border, Kelly obtained the results portrayed in Figure 4–22. The average retinal illuminance produced by the stimuli is given in trolands. Absolute sensitivity to flicker is defined in the graph as the reciprocal of the modulation amplitude mL needed to just perceive flicker. It will be seen that at high-average retinal illuminances there is far less sensitivity to the lower flicker frequencies than there is when the average retinal illuminance is low. This means that the depth of modulation can be far less at low average retinal illuminance levels than at high to produce the sensation of flicker. It turned out that these differences in amplitude of modulation are all nearly constant percentages of their respective average retinal illuminance levels. This reflects the operation of something like Weber's law.

It has been suggested that Weber's law does not apply to the higher flicker frequencies, since at higher frequencies the de Lange curves

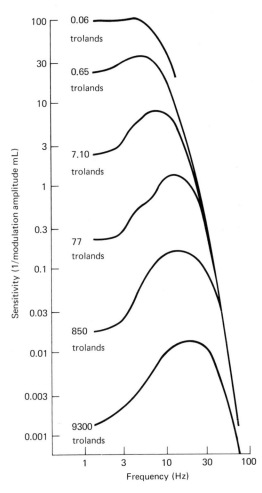

Figure 4–22. Variation of sensitivity to flicker as a function of stimulus frequency when the stimulus has several different average levels of retinal illuminance. (After Kelly, 1961)

shown in Figure 4–22 appear to fall onto a common downward sloping curve. Kelly concluded from this that the sensitivity to flicker above 20 Hz becomes dependent upon the absolute modulation amplitude and is independent of the average retinal illuminance produced by the stimulus. From inspection of the curves shown in Figure 4–26 this effect is most pronounced above 40 Hz.

The idea that two mechanisms are involved in flicker—one mechanism reflecting the operation of Weber's law at low frequencies, the other reflecting sensitivity to absolute amplitude of modulation at high frequencies—appears to be unwarranted by the data. Figure 4–22 shows that the amount of modulation needed to produce the perception of flicker at 50 Hz is about 100 trolands, which corresponds to a sensitivity of 0.01 on the y-axis of the graph. In the case of an average retinal illuminance of 77 trolands or less, it is a physical impossibility to produce this degree of modulation: in order to do it the experimenter would have to produce "negative light." Now, since the 850-troland and 9300-troland curves do not in fact fall on a common descending slope at 50 Hz, there is no evidence for the assertion that absolute amount of modulation determines sensitivity to flicker at the higher flicker frequencies. As a matter of fact, Weber's law is an approximately accurate description of the data at 10 Hz, where sensitivity to flicker is most pronounced in all the de Lange curves. At the higher frequencies of 20 and 30 Hz the ratios of the amplitudes of modulation needed to produce flicker perception and the average retinal illuminances of the stimuli are not constant. As we shall see below, the results obtained by Kelly are not incompatible with Weber's law.

It is likely that many mechanisms interact to produce flicker phenomena. The difference between the lower and higher frequencies may well be due to the fact that some of these mechanisms have time constants differing from the time constants of the other mechanisms. At the present time it is probably unsafe to say that flicker is basically a two-mechanism affair. The nonlinearities deducible from the flicker data prevent us from making models with precise predictive value. Sperling and Sondhi (1968) described a nonlinear model that does predict some of the coarse features of the de Lange characteristics, including the effects of different adaptation levels of flicker perception. Sperling's (1964) simple RC model could not do this. Thus, the primary advantage of this new model is that it shows how flicker perception may be influenced by the average luminance of the stimulus.

The basic idea underlying the Sperling-Sondhi model is that the output of a filter can be made to vary with the strength of the input. One part of their model consists of a filter that reduces the amplitudes of the higher frequencies of stimulation as in the simple RC circuits described earlier. The major difference between the new model and the older linear model is that the resistance R is made to vary as a function of the intensity of the input stimulus. This is done by feeding back a portion of the output of the filter to change the values of the resistor. As the input grows stronger, the time constant of this portion of the model becomes shorter, with the result of a decrease in the filter's sensitivity. Thus, as the signal increases in strength, the output becomes more greatly compressed. This behavior is typical of the visual system, which grows progressively less sensitive to light as the light energy increases.

The output of the feedback filter just described is then applied to another filter capable of comparing an input at one time with the time-average of inputs provided earlier. This filter is sensitive to the ratio of a change in stimulation relative to the average of stimulation provided over some previous period of stimulation. Thus, it is capable of simulating the effect of Weber's law since its output in response to some change in stimulation is governed not by the absolute amount of change but by the ratio of that change to baseline activity. The output of this second filter is then applied in the model to a low-pass filter with six stages. Finally, the signal goes to a detector to decide if a signal has exceeded a fixed threshold.

By estimating several parameters, Sperling and Sondhi were able to predict the results of actual experiments in which an observer must detect an increment or decrement in luminance of variable duration—i.e., in these experiments a brief stimulus was superimposed on a background of many different luminances. The model was then applied to predict the response of the visual system to sinusoidally modulated light. They found that the model predicts de Lange's actual data for flicker frequencies higher than 10 Hz. It is interesting to note that the model, which predicts a Weber ratio in increment detection experiments and an approximate Weber ratio for flicker detection at high frequencies, fits the data well at the higher frequencies. This is another reason for the assertion that the ratio of modulation depth to the average luminance of the stimulus plays a role in detection of high-frequency flicker, although the model does not predict the attenuated sensitivity to low-frequency flicker. On the other hand, it is at low frequencies that data from different experiments differ most widely, for reasons that are not yet understood.

It has been suggested that eye movements play a role in flicker detection (Cornsweet, 1970). Thus, if the eyes move so that the edges of a flickering spot on the retina move back and forth across receptors, then the eye may be more sensitive to flicker than if the image of the spot does not move across the retina. In Kelly's experiments the blurred edge of a large spot will not permit so much of the on-off activity associated with eye movements as occurs when viewing a small well-defined spot. This relatively smaller effect of eye movements could therefore be invoked as the basis for the attenuation of sensitivity at the lower flicker frequencies in Kelly's experiment.

Kelly (1964) has described some unpublished data of Keesey and Lindsley (1962), who stabilized the image of a small spot on the observer's retina. While this procedure prevented the image of the spot from moving across the retinal surface, there was no increased loss in sensitivity to the low-frequency flicker predicted by the eye movement theory. This result bears further study, for if eye movements do not produce the attenuation of sensitivity to low-frequency flicker, then other mechanisms must be sought. Neural and photochemical processes must act jointly to produce the effect of a band-pass filter.

It should be observed that, although Weber's law may predict differences in sensitivity to flicker at a single flicker frequency, it does not predict differential sensitivity to different flicker frequencies. Simple psychophysical laws do not of themselves have very much predictive power. Once some baseline of responsiveness is established, it may be possible to determine how the responsiveness will change with a change in the stimulus level. Other mechanisms, however, must be invoked to explain the baseline responsiveness with which we began. It will become increasingly clear in subsequent chapters that perception cannot be explained in purely psychophysical terms. The system is far too complicated to be described adequately by the simple relations derivable from psychophysical laws.

FLICKER-EVOKED POTENTIALS

As we have already seen, in some cases it may be possible to utilize small amplitudes of modulation of light and a constant adaptation level to linearize the behavior of a system. Merely doing this, however, does not insure that a system will actually behave in a linear manner. Some systems are characterized as essentially nonlinear. In such cases tricks like these might fail, and it would be very difficult to apply the methods of linear analysis to the study of the system. As Sperling (1964, p. 9) has so aptly put it, if a system is essentially non-linear, "The experimenter then knows he must rely on his ingenuity more than on his training."

The problem of characterizing the non-linearity of the visual system has been approached in electrophysiological studies. Electrophysiological recordings from single photoreceptors and at the horizontal cells in gold-fish and carp, for example, indicate that at this early stage the system is linear (Tomita *et al.*, 1967; Spekreijse and Norton, 1970), although non-linearities arise immediately after these early stages.

Experiments employing the method of the *average evoked potential* have clearly demonstrated these non-linearities. It is well known that a fluctuating electrical potential exists between two electrodes placed on the human scalp. This fluctuating voltage, known as the *electroencephalo-gram* (EEG), describes the spontaneous electrical activity of the brain. Although all frequencies between dc and about 40–60 Hz are present, the predominant frequency of these voltage changes is in the vicinity of 10 Hz. The famous *alpha* wave has a periodicity of about 10 peaks per second; but, since it is not a pure sine wave, it contains many frequencies with 10 Hz as the major component. The *alpha* wave occurs more readily when the subject is in a relaxed state and it tends to disappear when he becomes attentive or when he opens his eyes to look at an illuminated room. At such times it is replaced with a lower-voltage and higher-fre-quency wave of approximately 20 peaks per second.

When a light is flashed into the eye of an observer, it is possible to pick up an electrical response to the light from the occipital region of the skull. The effect of this flash is hidden in the ongoing EEG activity and can be discerned only rarely in the raw EEG record. The effect of the light has a complex origin since it results from a blending of many kinds of potential change within the brain. In general, it is not believed that spike potentials contribute to the evoked potential, though summed dendritic potentials and both excitatory and inhibitory post-synaptic po-tentials have been mentioned as contributors. In any case the evoked potential is a consequence of stimulation and can serve as a very coarse index of how the brain is affected by the stimulus.

Because of the fact that evoked potentials are masked by the ongoing EEG, it is necessary to utilize special methods to reveal their nature, such as that involving the technique of signal-averaging. A periodic stimulus, such as the kind used in flicker experiments, is well suited to this method. In the case of a periodic stimulus the experimenter knows precisely when a cycle of stimulation begins and ends. If he keeps an electrical record of all brain activity immediately after the start of each cycle of stimula-tion, it is possible to amplify the effect of the stimulus relative to the un-related ongoing brain activity.

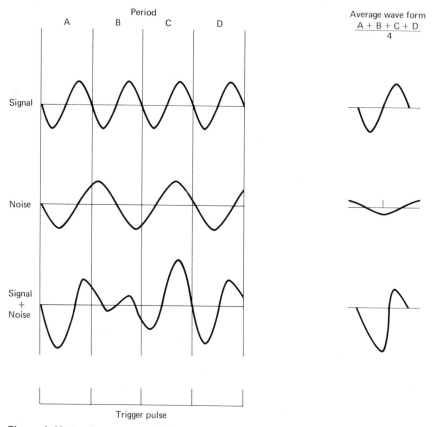

Figure 4–23. An "evoked potential," labeled **signal,** can be averaged by adding the waves in the periods following each **trigger pulse.** The resulting average of four periods is shown on the right. An irrelevant wave, labeled **noise,** produces a much smaller average waveform, since it changes phase from one averaging period to the next. The sum of signal and noise waves illustrates how an evoked potential may be masked by irrelevant ongoing activity. As shown on the bottom right, however, the average of this complex wave resembles the pure signal, even though only four periods are averaged together. In a real experiment several hundred such cycles may enter into an average, thereby obtaining a much better approximation to the underlying evoked potential.

Figure 4–23 shows how electrical records of brain activity may be used to recover stimulus-related activity while unrelated brain activity becomes relatively attenuated. The record obtained during each cycle of stimulation is simply added to those obtained during all other cycles of stimulation. If a signal is present and phase-locked to the stimulus, it will grow in size during the cumulation of the EEG records. The growth of the stimulus-related signal during cumulation is a linear function of the number of cycles of activity added together.

Other unrelated activity, however, does not fare so well during this process. As indicated in the figure, unrelated activity changes phase from one cycle of recording to the next. These extraneous signals tend to be self-canceling. Thus, stimulus-related activity grows arithmetically with the number of cycles being cumulated while unrelated activity grows at a much slower rate. If enough cycles are added together in this way, it is possible to recover a signal that is actually much weaker than the on-going background activity. Once this cumulative record is obtained, it is necessary only to divide each point on the record by the number of cycles added together to obtain the average wave. The resulting waveform is known as the *average evoked potential* (AEP).

The AEP is a complex wave containing several different frequencies. It is important to recognize that the only meaningful components of this average wave are integer multiples of the fundamental stimulus frequency. Activity at other frequencies would necessarily change phase from one record to the other and therefore become attenuated during the averaging process. If, however, the ongoing EEG should contain a spontaneous frequency component that happened to be very close to the frequency of the stimulus, then it too would be reflected in the AEP. Such unwanted signals are referred to as *coherent noise*. There is little that the experimenter can do to eliminate these contaminants of his record. Since the EEG does change over time, however, repeated experiments would indicate the presence of coherent noise. It should be noted also that if a stimulus should affect activity not at the frequency of the stimulus or of one of its harmonics, this influence of the stimulus could not be observed after simply averaging the EEG.

With this background in mind, we may now consider a few of the pertinent results obtained in this field.

When van der Tweel and Verduyn Lunel (1965) utilized sinusoidally modulated light at several different frequencies as a stimulus while measuring AEPs, they found that in general the AEPs at several frequencies contained strong second harmonic components even though these components were not present in the stimulus. This was particularly true when the stimuli were at 5 Hz and at 25 Hz. Thus, very often the response to a 5-Hz stimulus was almost exclusively at 10 Hz, the response to a 10-Hz stimulus was often, but not always, at 20 Hz.

There are two possible explanations for this. First, it is possible that the naturally occurring or spontaneous activity of the brain can be driven by the stimulus. This driving may be likened to the resonance phenomena of acoustics. A tuning fork, for example, has a natural resonant frequency. Stimulating it with an impulse or any other strong sound will cause it to vibrate at this natural frequency. If the 5-Hz stimulus in van der Tweel and Verduyn Lunel's experiment happened to get in step with a spontaneous cycle of brain activity, it could have caused the brain to continue to oscillate at its own natural frequency but more or less in step with the stimulus.

This entrainment explanation is probably incorrect, and for the reason that measurements of electrical energy at all frequencies of the spectrum of brain activity show that in most instances such driving does not take place (van Leeuwen, 1964). When a 5-Hz stimulus is used, the spectrum of brain activity measured during stimulation shows that the ongoing activity at 10 Hz is unchanged as compared to its level when other stimulus frequencies were used. Thus, *alpha* activity is relatively unchanged when stimuli of different frequency are employed.

The second explanation of this doubling phenomenon is simply that the tissues involved are non-linear. As we saw earlier in this chapter, if the input signal is strongly distorted by a non-linear resistance, strong second harmonics of the input frequency will be generated.

Spekreijse and van der Tweel (1972) have shown that it is possible to linearize the system that produces the AEP. Their method is similar to that of de Lange, though instead of using a steady background light they used a light that was flickering either at some high frequency or at some random function of time. The frequency of this background light was not an integer multiple of their sinusoidally modulated stimulus light. Although the background light was flickering, it had the effect of producing in the visual pathway an average steady-state background for the stimulus. Thus, when the flickering background light was employed, a stimulus that otherwise led to a response at twice its own frequency now produced a sinusoidal response at its own frequency.

The non-linearities observed by van der Tweel and Verduyn Lunel occur early in the visual system. Spekreijse and van der Tweel (1972) applied a sinusoidally modulated light to one eye and a randomly flickering background light either to the same eye or to the other eye. When the randomly flickering light was in the same eye as the stimulus, the linearization effect occurred; but when the background light was applied to the other eye, the response to the sinusoidally modulated light was at twice its frequency. This implies that the nonlinearity producing the double-frequency effect occurs prior to the mixing of signals from the two eyes at the cortex. Since other nonlinearities are undoubtedly present at the cortical level (Kaufman and Locker, 1970), it is probable that the theories we now have about flicker phenomena are too simple.

A number of problems should be clarified before the evoked-potential technique can be fully utilized in the study of flicker perception. Among these is the fact that although a 5-Hz stimulus produces an AEP at 10 Hz, the stimulus does appear to flicker more slowly than does a 10-Hz stimulus. Further, AEP amplitude does not always vary with the stimulus frequency in the same way that sensitivity to flicker varies with stimulus frequency (Spekreijse and van der Tweel, 1972). However, when the stimulus is not a simple sinusoidally modulated light but is a complicated pattern of bars, then there is a greater resemblance between the electrophysiological data and the psychophysical data (Sternheim and Cavonius, 1972). Perhaps when viewing such a complicated pattern uncontrolled eye movements add noise to the visual system as the eye scans the pattern. This noise could linearize the response to the basic modulation frequency of the stimulus as in the experiment by Spekreijse and van der Tweel. Clearly, one task for researchers in this field is the clarification of the reasons such conflicting results.

5

contrast and contour

The preceding chapters emphasized the processes underlying the detection of light and introduced the measurement of sensitivity to differences in light. Despite the apparent complexity of these processes, the detection of light is a rather primitive feature of the visual system. After all, it is conceivable that an eye with a single photoreceptor would be capable of detecting a change in light level. The actual retina, however, has a multitude of photoreceptors spread out over two dimensions. The retinal sheet is suited for the sensing of spatial information as given by spatial inhomogeneities of light. In this chapter we shall introduce some of the phenomena studied by visual scientists in an effort to understand the processes underlying the sensing of spatially distributed information. These processes are basic to form and space perception.

LIGHTNESS CONSTANCY

By now the reader should be aware that the visual system does not respond in a simple way to changes in light energy. The way in which a patch of light is perceived will vary depending upon many different circumstances. One dramatic phenomenon illustrating this point is that of *lightness constancy*.

The lightness of a surface is defined in this book at its whiteness, greyness, or blackness. A white shirt is lighter than a grey dress; a lump of coal has less lightness than a piece of white paper. Moreover, the lightness of an object is largely independent of its illumination. Thus, far less light may fall upon a white paper in a dimly illuminated room than upon a piece of coal in bright sunlight, and yet the paper appears to be white and the coal is perceived as black. This would be true even if an observer were to look at the paper in the room and then immediately shift his gaze to a window so that he could then view the piece of coal out-of-doors. The paper reflects less light to the eye of the observer than does the coal, but the paper is still perceived as lighter.

Although the lightness of a surface does not depend upon its luminance, the value of lightness is correlated with the relative reflectance of the surface. The piece of paper in our example may reflect as much as 90 per cent of the incident light to the eye of an observer. The coal, on the other hand, may reflect as little as 5 per cent of the incident light. Thus, the greater lightness of the paper relative to the coal is correlated with its greater reflectance. If an observer could perceive the reflectance of a surface, he could also exhibit lightness constancy. Unfortunately, reflectance is a physical property of an object and is not directly available to perception.

A substance will absorb more or less incident light, depending upon its pigmentation and texture. The light that it does not absorb is reflected. The edge of a one-inch high stack of razor blades reflects very little light to the eye, since most of the incident light is absorbed by the stacked sharp edges. This very black surface resembles the theoretical "blackbody" of physics, which absorbs all of the incident radiation. Yet when the observer is far away from the stack of razor blades he could not perceive the sharp edges in the stack. It still appears to be very black. Hence, the texture of the surface which determines its reflectance is not available to perception.

Since reflectance *per se* is not used by the observer, it has been suggested that it is inferred by him from other stimuli. Thus, according to Helmholtz (1924) an observer can determine the reflectance of an object if he simply compares the illumination falling on the object with the amount reflected by it. Thus, if the observer knows that a particular amount of light is incident upon our stack of razor blades, and that a very small amount is reflected by it, he can infer its reflectance. In reality, the reflectance of an object is the ratio of the illuminance of the object and its luminance, and may be determined by dividing the amount of light reflected from an object by the amount of light falling upon it. Thus, one might hold to the idea that lightness is determined by an unconscious

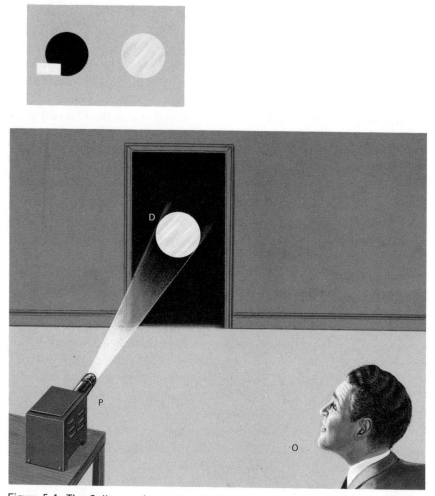

Figure 5–1. The Gelb experiment. A spinning black paper disc D is illuminated by a projector P. Stray light enters the room behind the disc so that it cannot be seen by the observer O. The disc appears luminous except when a small piece of white paper is placed in the path of the projector light.

computation of reflectance in which the observer takes the ratio of luminance and illuminance.

Another way of stating the theory is that lightness constancy occurs because the observer takes the illumination into account. This is parallel to size constancy in which the observer takes account of the distance to an object in computing its linear or distal size (see Chapter 9).

If an observer does have knowledge of the illumination of an object and the amount of light the object is reflecting he could in principle compute its reflectance. Thus, though the amount of light falling on a white paper may be small, it might still be perceived as white if one also knew that it reflected a large proportion of the light falling upon it. This theory, however, assumes that one can "know" illumination. This is not possible.

The only light that affects the nervous system is that entering the eye. When one looks at a scene, the only light entering the eye is that reflected by objects; the amount of light falling upon the object does not reach the eye. How, then, is it possible for an observer to sense the illumination of the objects? Since sensing illumination is a physical impossibility, we must reject the simple form of the *unconscious inference theory* of lightness constancy described above. A better theory has been proposed to account for lightness constancy, but before adverting to it, we must consider another phenomenon.

Figure 5–1 shows an experimental arrangement utilized by Gelb (1929), who illuminated a spinning black paper disc in a dimly illuminated room. The disc was spun so that its texture would be blurred. When the disc was illuminated by a hidden projector it did not appear to be black, but had instead a luminous white appearance—not unlike that of the moon when seen in a rather dark sky. And yet as soon as Gelb placed a small piece of white paper in the path of the projected beam of light, the disc appeared to be black and the paper appeared to be white. We may infer from this lovely demonstration that blackness and whiteness depend upon the simultaneous presence in the visual field of objects with different degrees of reflectance. Upon removal of the white paper, Gelb's disc appeared to be white once again.

The results obtained by Gelb suggested to Wallach (1948) that lightness constancy may be attributable to simultaneous contrast. To test this idea Wallach projected a disc of light onto a white screen. When the room was totally dark, the spot appeared to be luminous—as though it were generating its own light; yet, when the disc was surrounded by an annulus of a different luminance, as shown in Figure 5–2, the disc had a definite neutral color or lightness. Thus, when the annulus had a much higher luminance than the disc, the disc appeared to be black. When the luminance of the annulus was reduced slightly, then the same disc appeared to be dark grey in color. With further reductions in the luminance

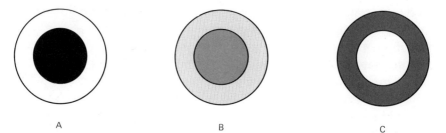

A   B   C

Figure 5–2. The Wallach experiment. The central disc has the same luminance in all three stimuli. Yet it appears to be black in A, where the luminance of the annulus is much greater than that of the disc. The same disc in B appears to be grey when the luminance of the annulus is slightly greater than that of the disc, and white in C, where the luminance of the annulus is much less than that of the disc.

of the annulus, the surrounded disc became progressively lighter in appearance. Finally, when the annulus had a much lower luminance than the disc, the disc was white in color.

In a further experiment, Wallach utilized two discs and two annuli. One disc and its annulus were set to have a particular ratio of luminance —e.g., the disc may have had half the luminance of its annulus. Even though the absolute values of the luminances of the disc and annulus may have been changed from one experimental session to another, the ratio was kept constant. The other disc was also fixed in luminance, but its annulus was free to be varied. The observer's task was to adjust the luminance of this second annulus until its disc had the same degree of lightness as the disc enclosed by the other annulus.

Wallach found that in general the disc surrounded by the variable annulus was matched in neutral color to the other disc when the two sets of stimuli had the same luminance ratio. Thus, when the annulus was set so that it had twice the luminance of its disc, then the disc matched the neutral color of the other disc, which also had half the luminance of its annulus. This was true even though the absolute luminances of the two discs were very different. This tendency to set the two annuli and their enclosed discs to have equal ratios of luminance was found over a wide range of different ratios. Thus, stimuli will have equal lightnesses if their luminance is in the same proportion to their surroundings.

There were many precedents to Wallach's experiment. A similar experiment was conducted in the nineteenth century by Hess and Pretori (1894). Hsai (1943) also investigated how judged lightness was influ-

enced by background luminance. A better known experiment was conducted by Katz (1935), who found that papers of equal reflectance were
judged to be of equal lightness even though they were illuminated by different amounts of light; and yet when the same pieces of paper were
viewed through apertures in a uniformly illuminated screen, they no
longer appeared to be of the same degree of lightness. Katz attributed
this to the fact that when the screen with apertures is not in place, the
observer can take into account the fact that the papers are illuminated
differently. With the aperture screen in place, the observer is deceived
into thinking that the papers have the same illumination. This view is
consistent with the unconscious-inference theory cited above. Now, however, we can see that the aperture screen provided a surround of one luminance for both pieces of paper. Since the pieces of paper seen through the
screen were illuminated differently, the ratios of their luminance to the
screen luminance differed, and this produced the difference in their apparent lightness.

Wallach's experiment is important for two reasons. First, he demonstrated that the neutral color of a surface—its lightness—is relationally determined. In simple situations the relation determining the neutral color
of a surface is the ratio of the luminance of the surface and its surround.
Second, the experiment related lightness constancy to the same ratio principle. A white shirt in a dimly illuminated room reflects a particular proportion of the light incident upon it. This is true also of the background
to the shirt. When the level of illumination is changed, these same proportions are still reflected by the shirt and its background, so that the luminances of the shirt and background are in a constant ratio regardless of
the level of illumination. According to Wallach, since lightness is determined by the ratio, the color of the shirt remains constant.

The ratio theory of lightness constancy is only approximately correct.
It applies in simple situations and only over a range of luminance levels.
Heinemann (1955) conducted a very systematic study that defined some
of the limits of the ratio principle. He presented a disc surrounded by an
annulus off to one side of a fixation point. The disc was set at a luminance
value that varied from session to session over a range of about 10,000
cd/m^2 (about 3,000 milli-lamberts). A single disc of light was also presented off to the opposite side of the fixation point, as shown in Figure
5–3. This disc was adjustable in luminance.

The luminance of the annulus surrounding the disc on the left side of
the fixation point was adjusted by the experimenter. The observer's task

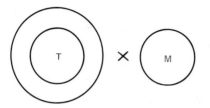

Figure 5–3. Arrangement used in Heinemann's experiment. The observer adjusts the luminance of the matching disc M until its "brightness" appears to match that of the test disc T. The luminances of the test disc and its surrounding annulus are manipulated independently by the experimenter.

was to adjust the luminance of the isolated disc until it appeared to match the "brightness" of the enclosed disc at each setting of its annulus. Thus, in every session the enclosed disc had a constant luminance and, as its surround was varied from one luminance to another, the observer matched the enclosed disc with a luminance setting of the isolated disc.

Even though wide ranges of annulus and disc luminance were used, a single matching luminance was selected just so long as the disc and annulus were in a constant ratio. Thus, when the luminance of the disc was about 80 per cent of the luminance of its surrounding, the matching disc was set to a luminance of about 30 cd/m². This was true even when the absolute luminance of the disc was as high as 10,000 cd/m²! But when the annulus had either a lower or a very much higher luminance than the disc, there were substantial departures from this ratio principle.

When the luminance of the surrounding equalled that of its disc, the observer matched it with a much lower luminance. In fact, the matching luminance was about one-third that of the disc and annulus regardless of the actual value of the latter luminance. Thus, when the disc and annulus matched each other in luminance, the luminance of the matching disc was set to a much lower value. This result appears to be somewhat anomalous, since one would expect the match to be very nearly equal to that of the equal-luminance disc and annulus. After all, in this instance the observer is simply matching one disc to a somewhat larger disc. The larger disc is present because when the annulus has exactly the same luminance as the inner disc, the contour dividing the two should disappear.

When the luminance of the annulus was made smaller than that of the inner disc, the luminance of the matching disc was then made greater than that of the inner disc. In other words, reducing the luminance of the annulus enhances the "brightness" of the disc it surrounds, for when the annulus was not present, the two isolated discs were made about equal in luminance.

As an annulus is made progressively dimmer the inner disc at first grows "brighter" and then grows dimmer once again. Moreover, the increase in "brightness" of the inner disc is not the same when the luminance of the disc is in the same ratio to annuli of differing luminance. Thus, with the annulus dimmer than the disc, a constant ratio of their luminances does not produce a constant lightness enhancement effect. The ratio principle does not apply to a disc-annulus arrangement when the luminance of the disc is greater than that of the annulus. The ratio principle also breaks down when the luminance of the annulus is very much greater than that of the disc.

Both these failures of the ratio principle may be thought of as resulting from *saturation*. That is, when the difference in luminance between a disc and its surround is sufficiently great, the disc can appear either white or black—depending upon the direction in the difference in luminance. Further increases in the difference in luminance cannot make the disc appear either whiter or blacker. The range of possible luminance adjustments exceeds the range of experience of lightness. This situation may be likened to that of a sponge that has absorbed as much water as it can. The now saturated sponge can absorb no more water even though it may be immersed in water for a long period of time.

The term "brightness" used to describe the matches made by Heinemann's observer has been placed in quotation marks because it may be genuinely distinguishable from "lightness," which refers to the whiteness, greyness, or blackness of a surface. As we have already observed, a patch of light seen alone in a totally dark space appears to be luminous. Adjusting its luminance does not change its neutral color or lightness. The patch can never be seen as black. Just so long as it is visible the patch will be dimmer or brighter but never appear as a white, grey, or black surface. The dimness and brightness of a luminous patch is another dimension of the visual appearance of illuminated regions.

In his experiment Heinemann utilized an isolated disc that had no immediately adjacent surrounding. If it were truly isolated, this disc could vary only in brightness or dimness. The enclosed disc, had, however, a surround that gave it a neutral surface color. The isolated matching disc could have been used by the observer as an indirect means for registering the relative values of lightness of the disc. Thus, if the observer had been given a rod of variable length, he could have registered his impression of the disc's change in lightness when the luminance of the annulus was changed by selecting some new rod-length. This method of estimating magnitude could in fact have given qualitatively similar results. The isolated disc was not completely isolated, however: it was near enough to the annulus and its disc to be viewed with constant fixation of the eye, and, consequently, the annulus and disc could have affected the apparent lightness of the matching disc. Though the effect was bound to be weak, its true magnitude is not known. Even a small interaction between the thing being measured—i.e., the lightness of the enclosed disc— and the measuring instrument or matching disc could have biased the outcome of so precise an experiment. Nevertheless, the experiment by Heinemann is the most comprehensive conducted thus far in this field.

In addition to the fact that the ratio principle has only a limited domain of applicability, still other difficulties arise when an object is viewed in a complex field. In both the Wallach and Heinemann experiments a single disc was presented in a uniform surround. In normal life, however, objects are rarely viewed against uniform and isolated backgrounds. The white shirt of our examples is seen against walls, floors, chairs, pictures, and textured wallpapers. Clearly, even if the ratio principle is applicable in simple situations, we are still left with the problem of deciding how lightness constancy works in daily life.

An experiment by Jameson and Hurvich (1961) illustrates this point rather well. They presented simultaneously a number of adjacent rectangular patches of different reflectance. The illuminance of the array of patches was varied over about one log unit. The ratios of the luminances of the patches in the field were preserved even though the absolute luminances of the patches did vary. Each of the five patches in the array was matched by an isolated comparison stimulus at each level of illuminance of the array. If lightness constancy were perfect, the same match would have been made to each patch regardless of the illuminance of the array. Patches of intermediate luminance did in fact display lightness constancy, and yet the lower-luminance patch actually appeared to grow darker when its luminance was increased! Moreover, the lightest of the patches in the array appeared to grow lighter as its luminance increased.

The fact that one of the patches seemed to grow darker when its luminance was increased has a plausible explanation. According to Hering (Hochberg, 1971), when a space is completely dark, nothing can be seen. As the illumination level is increased slightly, one sees objects dimly: they are not well defined. With a further increase in illumination the objects become well defined. This suggests that a low-luminance patch may not have been clearly visible at the lower-illuminance levels of Jameson and Hurvich's display. With an increment of illuminance this patch became well defined. This well-defined object is clearly black and not blended with the over-all grayness of the surroundings as it is in low-illumination surroundings. The increasing lightness of the lighter of the patches cannot be explained in this way, however, since this departure from lightness constancy is in clear violation of the ratio principle. It may well be that complex interactions between relatively distant parts of the display influenced lightness judgments.

The experiments we have been discussing thus far were all conducted under laboratory conditions, and so it is not really possible to claim that they have covered all the factors underlying lightness constancy. Objects in the every-day world are not viewed with constant fixation; they are not matched with a comparison patch of adjustable luminance. We have a limited vocabulary with which to describe lightness. A white object in one circumstance may not really look exactly like another white object, and yet they may both be called white. A white paper with a shadow falling across half of it does not look like a white paper that is not partially shadowed, and yet they are both called "white." We speak of light gray, medium gray, and dark gray, and yet there are many more discriminable shades of gray for which we have no names. Before it is possible to explain lightness constancy with a simple ratio principle it is necessary to discover just how constant lightness really is. That is why it is of importance to recognize that though ratios of luminance have a powerful influence on lightness perception, we may not yet have a satisfactory explanation for the reason that the phenomenon we are trying to explain is itself not well defined. The interested reader should refer to Hochberg (1971) for a description of factors influencing lightness other than those we have considered here.

SIMULTANEOUS CONTRAST

Figure 5–4 shows a gray disc in a black field, and another gray disc in a white field. The two gray discs are identical, even though the one in the white field appears to be darker than the one in the black field. This effect of the surrounding on perceived lightness is considered to be an instance of simultaneous contrast—a phenomenon that is really a weak version of

Figure 5–4. Simultaneous contrast.

Wallach's demonstration of strong interaction between adjacent regions of different luminance.

The contrast effect in Figure 5–4 is weak because the gray stimuli and their backgrounds are not isolated from other backgrounds. If the discs were patches of projected light on a darkened screen, the effect would be much stronger. The gray patch in the white field might appear to be black while an equiluminous patch in a much darker field might appear to be white.

If we restrict ourselves to the simple situation in which the lightness of one patch of light is strongly affected by the luminance of an adjacent patch, it is easy to see how physiological mechanisms may be involved. As it will be recalled from Chapter 2, Kuffler identified concentrically organized receptive fields in the retina. In a typical experiment a microelectrode may be inserted in a retina to pick up the activity of a ganglion cell. A small spot of light may then be used to explore the retina until the ganglion cell responds to it—in the form of an increase in the number of spike potentials recorded from the cell. In general, the spot may be moved to any place within a given region, and the ganglion cell will respond whenever the spot of light is turned on. This region also exhibits properties of spatial summation—i.e., two small spots turned on simultaneously in the same region will cause the ganglion cell to respond more than it would to one spot alone. Now, if the spot is moved outside the region capable of exciting the cell, then turning on the spot does not result in an increase in the firing rate of the cell. On the contrary, turning on the spot can produce a reduction in its firing rate, and the firing rate might increase when the spot of light is turned off. Moreover, there may even be an intermediate region on the retina where turning the spot either on or off produces an increase in the ganglion cell's response.

In general then, turning on a small spot of light in one region may cause a ganglion cell to fire. Turning on the same spot in a region surrounding this first region may suppress or inhibit the activity of this same ganglion cell. These regions—the "on" center and its "off" surrounding—comprise the receptive field of the ganglion cell. Wagner, MacNichol, and Wolbarsht (1960) found precisely this kind of "on" center receptive field in the retina of the goldfish, and found a complementary kind of receptive field as well. In this "off" center receptive field, turning off a spot of light in a circular region on the retina reduced the activity of a ganglion cell. When a spot of light was turned on in an area surrounding this circular region, the activity of the ganglion cell increased.

The point here is that a spot of light in one place can inhibit activity of a ganglion cell, though it may enhance the activity of the same ganglion cell if it is turned on in a nearby place. Moreover, if one spot should fall within an "on" region while another spot is turned on in an "off" region, then the two spots will work against each other. In this way, the activity induced by turning a spot on in the "on" region of a receptive field may be inhibited by simultaneously turning a spot on in an "off" region of the same cell's receptive field.

This organization in the retina of a vertebrate has its antecedents in invertebrate animals. Hartline's (1942) important work on the compound eye of the horseshoe crab (Limulus) first revealed these phenomena. This structure, which is similar to that of the common insect eye, is comprised of many facets called *ommatidia*. Each ommatidium funnels light down to a receptor bipolar cell that is surrounded by eccentric cells. Activity induced in these cells by the action of light builds a mosaic picture of the world for the animal. The activity in one of these ommitidia is not independent of what happens in others. In fact the presence of light on one of these receptors can decrease the response of another nearby receptor to light (Fig. 5–5). Hartline's discovery of this physical *lateral inhibition* has become the basis of many mathematical models of contrast phenomena.

Let us now return to contrast phenomena. Suppose that a patch of light excites one retinal region. This produces a particular impression of brightness in the owner of the excited retina. Now, if an adjacent retinal region should be excited by another patch of light of different luminance, this second patch may well have an inhibitory effect on the first. Such reduction in activity in the cells responding to the first patch could account for the apparent reduction in its lightness.

An experiment by Fry and Bartley (1935) is illustrative of this point.

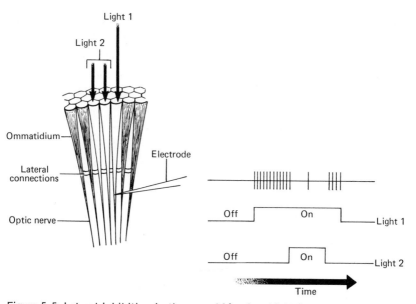

Figure 5–5. Lateral inhibition in the eye of **Limulus.** Light 1 causes a fiber to fire in the optic nerve. The addition of light 2 results in a cessation of firing, and turning light 2 off produces a recovery of firing.

They found that when a line of a particular fixed luminance is moved into the vicinity of another line, the brightness of the line seems to be reduced. In a related experiment of Stecher (1968), observers attempted to discriminate the difference in luminance between two patches of light. The difference threshold was found to vary, depending upon the separation between the patches. The observer was much more sensitive to differences in luminance when the patchs were separated by only 30 seconds of arc—i.e., when they very nearly shared a common boundary. With an increased separation, however, sensitivity to luminance differences decreased monotonically. Stecher concluded that lateral inhibition rendered luminance differences between the fields more perceptible when they were closer together.

The fact that the vertebrate ganglion cells having concentrically organized receptive fields respond when a light is turned on or off is also of considerable interest. As is pointed out in Chapter 7, the eye is in a constant state of motion. This means that the retinal image of a steadily illuminated distal stimulus is always moving from one retinal place to another. This motion of the retinal image excites different regions of the eye from one moment to the next. If the stimulus should be a patch divided by a border into two halves of different luminance, then the brighter half of the stimulus will alternately excite different receptor cells in the eye. The activity evoked by this half of the stimulus may well inhibit the activity evoked by the dimmer half—thereby accentuating or enhancing the difference in activity induced by the two halves if they were stationary. Stabilized retinal images disappear for the reason that lateral inhibition is not so effective without the intermittency of stimulation produced by eye movements.

THE MACH BANDS

In the nineteenth century Ernst Mach (Ratliff, 1965) discovered the visual phenomenon that now bears his name. The "Mach bands" may be

Figure 5–6. Mach Bands. The white and black bands in the figure simulate the Mach bands that can be produced in the laboratory. The luminance varies across a surface, as illustrated in the graph. The simulation of the effect was produced by an artist using an air brush.

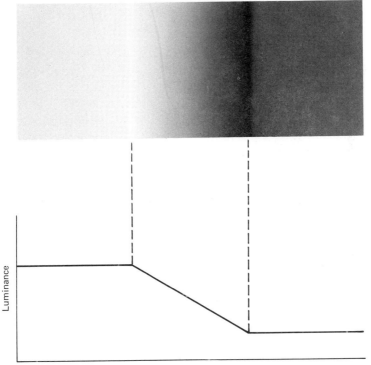

Distance

seen in a luminance distribution such as the one illustrated in Figure 5–6. The upper half of the figure contains three regions: on the left side, a region of uniform high luminance; on the right side, a region also of uniform luminance but of a lower level; and the middle region, of uniformly graded luminance so that it changes from light to dark between the left and right sides. The graph in the lower half of the figure shows how the luminance in the upper half is distributed across the figure from left to right. The reader may see a light band adjacent to the left-hand border of the upper half of the figure, and a dark band alongside the right-hand border. Such bands are not present in an actual distal stimulus. These Mach bands are created by the visual system. Figure 5–7 is a graph indicating how the lightness of the perceived pattern may vary from left to right.

The Mach bands are of considerable interest because their existence suggested the presence of lateral inhibition to Mach even before there was any relevant physiological evidence for it. Moreover, models designed to elucidate the mechanisms underlying the Mach band phenomenon may be deployed to explain other simultaneous contrast phenomena. As we saw in the preceding section of this chapter, Hartline had demonstrated the existence of lateral inhibition in the eye of the Limulus. Ratliff and Hartline (1959) demonstrated the relation between this lateral inhibition and the presence of a phenomenon very much like Mach bands in this same animal.

Figure 5–8 shows three curves. The upper curve (inset) is a luminance distribution similar to the kind typically used to demonstrate the Mach band phenomenon. This luminance distribution was the stimulus for their experiment. Ratliff and Hartline recorded the discharge of impulses from

Figure 5–7. Representation of how perceived lightness varies across a surface in a typical Mach band experiment.

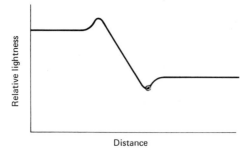

Distance

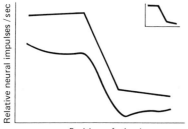

Figure 5–8. Graph showing how neuronal impulse rate from a single receptor in **Limulus** varies with the position of a complex distribution of luminance (**inset**) on the animal's eye. (After Ratliff and Hartline, 1959)

a single receptor unit in the eye of the Limulus. In the first part of their experiment they covered the animal's eye with a mask so that only the ommatidium from which they were recording was exposed. By moving the stimulus across the eye of the animal they exposed this ommatidium successively to each light level in its luminance distribution. It may be seen from the second curve in the graph that the firing rate of this unit varied more or less in proportion to the light level at each position in the luminance distribution.

In the next stage of their experiment the authors removed the mask from the animal's eye. Now ommatidia all around the original unit were also stimulated. They once again moved the stimulus from one side to the other, thereby duplicating the stimulation of the unit from which they were recording. The only difference now is that surrounding units were also being stimulated. The third lower curve in the figure shows how the discharge of impulses varied as a function of the position of the luminance distribution. The "overshoot" phenomena so typical of the Mach bands are evident in this response curve. It is obvious that their occurrence is dependent upon the simultaneous stimulation of ommatidia surrounding the one Ratliff and Hartline were recording from.

Two ways in which receptor cells may be interconnected to produce these phenomena is illustrated in Figure 5–9. The circuit shown in the left side is known as a *recurrent inhibitory system*. Corollary fibers from both neurons cross over to inhibit activity ahead of the site at which impulses are generated. In the circuit on the right, illustrating a *nonrecurrent inhibitory system*, the inhibitory influences occur after impulses are generated by the receptor.

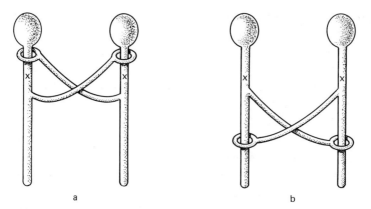

Figure 5–9. Recurrent (a) and nonrecurrent (b) inhibitory systems. (After Ratliff, Hartline, and Miller, 1963)

In the case of recurrent inhibition the magnitude of inhibition of one unit by the other depends upon the number of impulses generated in the inhibiting unit and not upon the magnitude of the stimulus to that unit. The value of this scheme is that other neighboring receptors that inhibit the activity of the inhibiting unit can serve to reduce its inhibitory effect.

Let us suppose that only two units are excited—say, the two units shown on the left side of Figure 5–9—and also that the stimulus applied to the left-hand unit is weaker than the one applied to the right-hand unit. Since the right-hand unit is more active than the left-hand unit, it will tend to depress that one's activity. Moreover, since the activity of the left-hand unit is depressed, it will have a lower capacity to inhibit the activity of the right-hand unit than it would if it were more strongly stimulated. Now suppose that other units also are stimulated and that these units are adjacent to the right-hand unit in the figure. These units will tend to inhibit the right-hand unit, thereby decreasing its capacity to inhibit the activity of the left-hand unit. Thus, the stimulation of a third unit could serve to disinhibit the left-hand unit. This disinhibitory effect has been observed in the eye of Limulus.

The nonrecurrent inhibitory system on the right side of Figure 5–9 does not of itself allow for such disinhibitory phenomena. The amount of inhibition of one unit by the other depends upon the stimulus strength rather than upon the discharging of the unit *per se*. It has been shown, however, that multiple layers of such non-recurrent units can in fact display disinhibition. At the present time there is no way to determine which of these two mechanisms is involved in the human visual system.

Although it is not possible at this time to define the precise neural circuitry underlying lateral inhibition, several abstract models have been proposed to elucidate the phenomena. One such model, designed to provide a quantitative method for describing how Mach bands might arise, was provided by von Békésy (1960).

According to this model a single point of stimulation produces an area of excitation surrounded by an inhibitory area. This inhibitory area will reduce the effectiveness of a second stimulus that might happen to fall within its boundaries. Von Békésy called this latter excitatory area surrounded by an inhibitory area a *neural unit*. Although the neural unit may have a shape similar to the one in the upper half of Figure 5–10, for simplicity we shall follow von Békésy in assuming the rectangular shape shown in the lower half of the figure. The height of the excitatory area is an index of how much excitatory activity is induced by the stimulus; the height of the inhibitory region is an index of how much the stimulus can reduce the sensitivity of the surrounding region—i.e., inhibit the excitation produced by some other nearby stimulus. The magnitudes of the excitatory and inhibitory effects produced by a stimulus depend upon the light energy falling on the retina. Thus, a stimulus with high luminance will produce more excitation and more inhibition than will a stimulus point of lower luminance.

Figure 5–10. Two hypothetical neural units. Unit **a** is one conception of how excitation and inhibition vary about a point stimulus. Unit **b** is an alternative graphical representation of a neural unit, and one that is easier to use for purposes of computation.

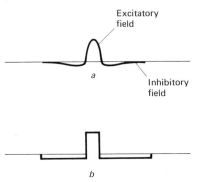

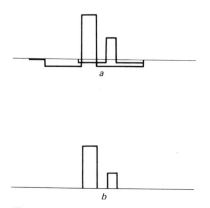

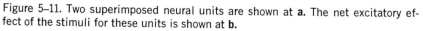

Figure 5–11. Two superimposed neural units are shown at **a**. The net excitatory effect of the stimuli for these units is shown at **b**.

Suppose now that two points are imaged near each other on the retina. If the excitatory region of the neural unit stimulated by one point should fall within the inhibitory region of the neural unit stimulated by the other point, then the inhibitory effect of the latter unit will subtract from the excitatory effect of the first unit. Moreover, as is illustrated in Figure 5–11, if one of the stimuli should be stronger than the other, the reduction in the excitatory effect of the weaker stimulus will be greater.

Now imagine that the luminance distribution shown in Figure 5–12 is actually composed of an infinite number of points. The points in the flanking regions of uniform luminance stimulate overlapping neural units. The higher-luminance points have stronger excitatory and inhibitory effects than do the points of lower luminance. As shown in Figure 5–12, points on the region of graded luminance have neural units of graded size. Since a neural unit just to the right of the right-hand border has a stronger inhibitory effect than does a neural unit just to the left of that border, the excitatory effect of the latter unit will be diminished.

Moreover, this unit on the left of the border has a relatively weak inhibitory effect on the unit just to the right of the border. Therefore, this unit has a greater net excitatory effect than do other units farther to the right of the border. These latter units all inhibit each other and the net effect at some distance from the border is a diminished level of excitation relative to the excitation close to the border. Therefore, a bright band should appear just to the right of the right-hand border. Similar reasoning underlies the prediction that a dark band would appear just to the left of the left-hand border.

This model of von Békésy is a subtractive model. It assumes that activity induced at one point produces effects that may be subtracted from activity at some distant point. Thus, it is a linear model in the sense that the effects produced in overlapping neural units are superimposable. Similar linear models are described in Ratliff's (1965) fascinating book on the Mach bands.

The problem with a linear model of Mach bands is that it cannot easily handle the ratio data obtained by Wallach and Heinemann in simultaneous contrast experiments. If lateral inhibitory processes underly both the Mach bands and contrast phenomena, then a model of one process should elucidate the other. Although the summation of inhibitory and adjacent excitatory effects can account qualitatively for the appearance of Mach bands, this same process cannot account for the fact that the lightness of a surface is, over a large range, defined by the luminance ratio between the surface and its surrounding. Thus, if we assume that a patch of light is inhibited by a surrounding, and that the degree of inhibition is determined by the ratio of the patch and surrounding luminances, then one must assume that the nervous system is responsive to this ratio. It does not respond simply to the absolute magnitude of the difference between the luminance of the spot and of its surrounding area. Thus, one

Figure 5–12. Neural units associated with points along a luminance distribution. The dashed line is a qualitative indication of the shape of the net excitation resulting from the algebraic summation of the inhibitory and excitatory effects of superimposed neural units.

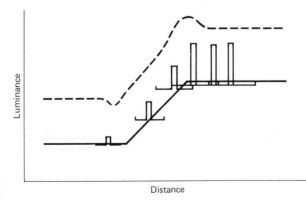

Distance

wants to divide an excitatory effect by an inhibitory effect rather than take their sum in accounting for contrast phenomena.

Let us consider how neurons in the inhibitory and excitatory regions of a cell's receptive field may affect the ganglion cell. Assume that one neuron has an excitatory effect, on a ganglion cell, and another neuron has an inhibitory effect. If light should cause both neurons to fire, the effect of one of them on the ganglion cell will tend to offset the effect of the other, since one effect is excitatory and the other is inhibitory. This is tantamount to subtraction. As Ratliff (1965) has explained, however, the firing rates of the two neurons could be proportional to the logarithm of stimulus intensity. Subtracting logarithmic transformations of a parameter is equivalent to direct division. Therefore, the output of the ganglion cell depends upon the ratio of the stimuli affecting the two input neurons. So we can see that subtractive processes can produce a ratio-sensitive system if receptors and subsequent neurons respond in an exponential manner to incoming stimuli. There is substantial evidence that this is the case. This same scheme may be applied to other kinds of neural circuitry.

THE SHARPNESS OF CONTOUR

The Mach band phenomenon may be thought of as a contour-enhancing process. This property of vision makes a great deal of evolutionary sense. A uniformly illuminated field gives no information to an observer at all. In fact, when the eye is exposed to a completely uniform field of light the observer quickly loses any sense of the brightness or even color of the empty field (Metzger, 1930; Hochberg, Triebel, and Seaman, 1951). The uniformly illuminated surface of the empty field (*Ganzfeld*) quickly disappears, and the observer experiences merely a bulky gray fog, even when the illuminant is colored. Introduction of a contour in this surface, however, quickly restores normal vision. Thus, the empty field or *Ganzfeld* phenomenon is really the prototype for the phenomenon of the disappearance of the stabilized image. The eye needs spatio-temporal changes in light if it is to function normally.

Contours are normally thought of as borders between lighter and darker regions in the visual field. The stimulus conditions that give rise to these borders are usually abrupt changes in luminance between adjacent points on a surface. Thus, if the luminance distribution on a distal surface should approximate a step function, such as the one illustrated in Figure

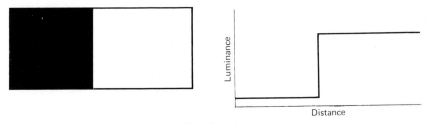

Figure 5–13. Step function distribution of luminance.

5–13, a contour may be seen. The pattern of illuminance on the retina produced by such a stimulus, however, is never a step function. Imperfections of the cornea, lens, and other optical media in the eye actually blur the image of the step function.

Westheimer and Campbell (1962) and Krauskopf (1962) formed the image of a fine luminous line on the retina. A reflection of this image could be picked up by an opthalmoscopic device, and then be reflected by the device to a light-measuring device. Thus, the image of the line at the light-measuring device was comprised of light that had passed twice through the media within the eyeball. The light-measuring device scanned this image to determine the shape of the distribution of the illuminance produced on the retina by the original line. These data were corrected for the fact that the light had passed twice through the same distorting media, and a new luminance function was generated. The results of these two investigations were quite similar. In general, they found that a sharp line forms a blurred image on the retina. The distribution of illuminance on the retina was similar to that shown in Figure 5–14. This distribution

Figure 5–14. Line spread function.

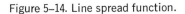

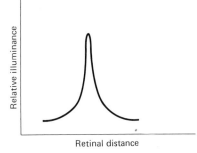

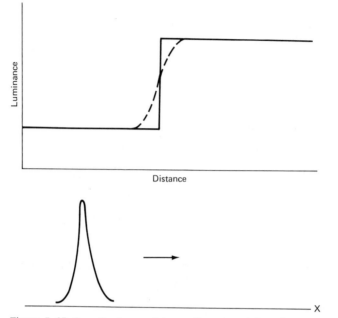

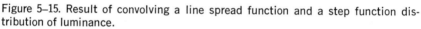

Figure 5–15. Result of convolving a line spread function and a step function distribution of luminance.

describes how the image of a very thin line is blurred on the retina, and hence it is known as a *line spread function*. The width of the distribution becomes greater with a larger pupillary diameter, but its shape is more or less the same. The line spread function, once it is known, can be a very useful thing. Methods exist for determining how any distribution of light will be blurred on the retina once the line spread function is known. This can be accomplished by *convolving* the line spread function and the luminance distribution of the distal stimulus.

In essence, convolving involves sliding the line spread function across the luminance distribution being processed. At each point on the x axis of Figure 5–15, the sliding line spread function is multiplied, point for point, with the luminance distribution above it. The resulting products are stored and added to the new products generated by the multiplication process as the function advances along x. This results in a totally new distribution, and one that is, in fact, a very good representation of the distribution of illuminance resulting on the retina. The illuminance distribution for the step-function stimulus luminance distribution is indicated by the dotted lines in Figure 5–15. It can be seen that there is no sharp step in the retinal stimulus, even though such a step might be present in the distal stimulus.

Although the distribution of retinal illuminance is blurred in the presence of a border, there must still be a relatively sharp change in luminance across a surface if a contour is to be seen. If a sufficiently abrupt change of illuminance is present, lateral inhibition within the retina itself can serve to sharpen the differences in the effects of light on either side of the border. The low-illuminance side of the border will have a lesser effect on the observer than it would if the adjacent higher-illuminance portion were not present. The fact that borders do sharpen apparent lightness differences can be illustrated with an example.

Koffka (1935) described a situation in which a wall was shadowed so that its luminance was graded smoothly between two points. Although observers in general are not sensitive to smooth linearly graded changes in luminance, when a very thin line was drawn on the wall bisecting the area of graded luminance, the observer saw that area as being divided into two regions, apparently of uniform but different lightnesses. The region on the side of the line that was, on the average, the darker of the two, appeared to be uniformly darker. Cornsweet (1970) has made some lovely demonstrations of such phenomena.

THE ADEQUACY OF LATERAL INHIBITION

Thus far we have adopted the now-current view that lateral inhibition within the retina is a powerful tool in explaining phenomena such as simultaneous contrast and lightness constancy. Several words of caution are needed, however. For one thing, cognitive factors may well play a role in these phenomena. Thus, it is known that when a bent card is illuminated so that one part of it is in shadow while the other half is well illuminated, the two halves of the card can appear to be equally light (Hering, 1964). This occurs when the card is viewed binocularly and good cues are available to the bend in the card. When the card is viewed monocularly so that the bent card appears as though it is flat, the half in shadow appears to be darker than the half in good illumination. Similar results have been obtained by Beck (1965) and by Coren (1969) with a different kind of stimulus. In a similar vein, Festinger, Coren, and Rivers (1970) conducted experiments indicating that attention may well influence simultaneous contrast and related phenomena. Hence, even though the effects of cognitive factors are not nearly so strong as simple effects of luminance ratio *per se,* they should be considered.

One more theoretical point is also worth mentioning. A patch of light at one retinal place produces a particular amount of neural activity, and this activity may be depressed by the inhibitory influences of a second nearby patch of greater luminance. Thus, the effect of lateral inhibition is merely to reduce the activity produced by the dimmer patch. This same effect can be produced simply by reducing the luminance of the first patch while the second patch is absent. As we have already observed, a mere change in the luminance of an isolated patch may change its brightness, but it can never make it appear to be white or dark gray, as this requires the presence of other levels of luminance in the distal stimulus. Consequently, the presence of other levels of luminance in a field must do more than merely inhibit the activity produced by a test patch. The reduction of neural activity in a local region cannot of itself produce the impression of a different shade of lightness.

Two possibilities suggest themselves. First, there may be successive stages of inhibitory processes at higher levels in the nervous system, and their activation may be necesary to produce the neutral surface colors. This can occur only when several different levels of luminance are present simultaneously in the visual field.

The second possibility is perhaps a more parsimonius one. The action of lateral inhibition does not simply reduce the activity produced by a patch of light. As we saw in the Mach band phenomenon, the effect of lateral inhibition is stronger near a border than it is far away from the border. This implies that a single patch of non-uniform luminance, with the luminance near its edges lower than the luminance in its center, would simulate the effect of lateral inhibition. It may then be possible to cause the patch to appear gray and even black in a dark field. This idea remains to be tested. Meanwhile, it would be best not to allow ourselves to be seduced into thinking that lateral inhibition is a complete answer to the problems of lightness constancy and simultaneous contrast.

the perception of color

Thus far we have concerned ourselves solely with the problem of the detection of light and of changes in light energy. The human eye is not equally sensitive to light of different wavelengths. As we have seen, the eye is more likely to detect a yellow wavelength light than it is a red wavelength light of equal energy. This difference could exist without the observer's being aware that the two lights have hues with different names. Some color-blind people in fact recognize the difference between red and green traffic signals solely because of the differences in their apparent brightness. If the traffic signals were not in consistent spatial positions and if they had equal effective luminance, the color-blind person could not tell them apart. A normal-sighted person, however, can distinguish between the red and green lights even if they have equal luminance. This ability to discriminate solely on the basis of hue or quality is the subject of the investigation of color perception.

THE COLOR SOLID

Suppose that you were confronted with a large number of colored chips—of red, blue, pink, orange, green, yellow, brown, purple, or whatever—and were asked to order them in terms of their similarity. In the process of creating such an ordering of colors, you will discover that orange is more similar to red than is yellow, and accordingly you will place the reds and oranges next to each other. Similarly, the yellows resemble the oranges more than they do the greens and blues, and thus the yellow would be placed near the oranges. Finally, the greens would be placed between the yellows and blues. The purple chips, however, seem to resemble both the blues and reds. If you are very clever you will realize that the entire array of chips must be arranged in a circle, with the purples between the blues and reds. This provides a satisfactory ordering of colors in terms of their similarity. The resulting *color circle* is illustrated in Figure 6–1, facing p. 206.

The pinks, navy blues, browns, and other shades and tints of colors provide a special problem, for none belong between the pure colors arranged on the color circle. Some are lighter and some darker; others are equally light in appearance but seem to be impure—i.e., the hues on the chips are mixed in various amounts with white. The degree of apparent impurity of a color is its *saturation*. The chips on the circle are very saturated, but those of different shades and tints are relatively unsaturated.

If we agree that all the chips may be ordered in three-dimensional space, then it is possible to get an arrangement in which all chips are placed near other similar chips. Thus, unsaturated chips that are about as bright as those on the circle may be ordered along radii of the circle. A pure red, for example, would be on the rim of the circle, and reds that are less pure will be placed inside the circle. The less saturated the red, the closer it will be to the center of the circle. A grey chip could then be placed at the very center of the circle with the least saturated chips of all colors surrounding it.

By extending the color space upward and downward it is possible also to incorporate the lighter tints and darker shades of the colors. A light pink could be placed above the radius on which are located the reds of different degrees of saturation. The navy-blue chip could be similarly placed below the line of blue chips, and so on. This procedure will finally result in the *color solid* illustrated in Figure 6–2.

The color solid represents the different dimensions of color perception. The white-gray-black axis of the solid stands for the continuum of the experience of lightness. The hues on the rim are examples of the different qualities of light. The dimension of saturation illustrates the fact that colored light may be more or less pure. Finally, the least saturated colors have a wider range of shades and tints than do the more saturated colors. As we progress through this chapter we will come to understand how it is that colors do vary along the dimensions we have been describing.

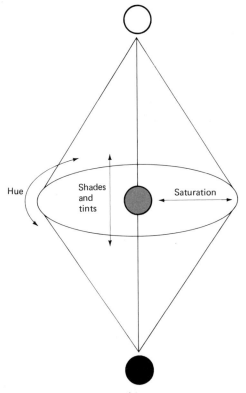

Figure 6–2. The color solid.

NEWTON'S COLOR CIRCLE

If we were to abandon the colored chips and use spectral colors in their place, it is still possible to construct a color circle. Isaac Newton, in his epoch-making experiments in optics, did precisely this, first dispersing sunlight through a prism and then separating various portions of the resulting spectrum by means of small holes in an opaque screen. The colored lights coming from each of these holes were then mixed by superimposing them on a screen with lenses. Newton found that for one color—say, a red light—he could also find another color, blue-green in this case, which when mixed with the red light produced the impression of a neutral or grey light. This was to him a rather amazing event, since he had previously shown that mixing the entire spectrum of colors also produces

Figure 6–3. Newton's color circle. The line connecting Y-G and R represents a mixture of yellow-green light and red light in proportions indicated by the position of the dot on the line. The arrow passing through the dot from the center indicates the resulting color of the mixture.

a white light. The fact that he obtained a similar effect with only two colors was unexpected.

If the holes in Newton's screen were spaced at various distances from each other, the mixture of two colors led to different effects. For example, a mixture of red and yellow made orange, said Newton, and a mixture of orange and yellowish-green made green. Newton also reported that a mixture of yellow and blue light made a green light, but he was mistaken about this, for mixed yellow and blue lights yield only desaturated blues or yellows. As we shall see later, green can be compounded of yellow and blue pigments but not of yellow and blue lights.

In essence, Newton discovered that if the spectral lights are close to each other in the spectrum, their mixture produces the same color as the color of a light that is intermediate between the mixed lights on the spectrum. If the mixed colors were far enough apart, however, they mixed to form a neutral light. If the colors were very far apart—say, a violet and deep red—their mixture produced a color that was not in the spectrum: purple. It was for this reason that Newton imagined a color circle of the type shown in Figure 6–3. The colors that mix to form a neutral color—the complementary colors—were placed at the ends of diameters of the circle. These diameters all pass through the center of the circle, which represents the "color" white. Newton described white as the "middling" color.

Ever since the time of Newton, one of the primary concerns of researchers in color vision has been the problem of color mixture. How is it possible that the mixture of two spectral colors can produce the impression of a third spectral color? As we shall see, the fact that color mixture does occur is the basis for the most important theories of color vision.

Suppose that we mix two colors on the rim of Newton's color circle—say, the colors yellow-green and red as indicated by the line connecting Y-G and R on the circle in Figure 6–3. If we include more yellow-green light than red light in the mixture, the resulting color will be greener than if the two colors were mixed in equal amounts. If red light is the preponderant element in the mixture, the resulting color will be "yellower" in appearance. Mixing the two colors in equal proportions produces an intermediate yellow. The point on the chord connecting Y-G and R represents the amounts of these colors entering into the mixture. If we were to

Figure 6–4. Young's color triangle. White is at the center of the triangle. A mixture of spectral red (R) and spectral yellow-green (Y-G) produces a saturated yellow color.

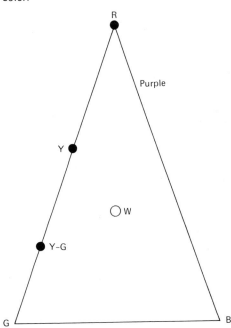

draw a line or radius through the white center of the circle and the point on the chord connecting Y-G and R, we can identify the color produced by the mixture. This is the point on the circle intercepted by the radius. Moreover, the saturation (purity) of the produced color may be represented by the distance of the point on the chord from the center of the circle.

In general, a color produced by mixing two spectral colors does not appear to be as saturated as a spectral color. As Linksz (1952) pointed out, however, the colors produced by mixture do not appear to be as desaturated as Newton's diagram might lead one to believe. Thus, the indicated mixture of red and yellow-green in Figure 6–3 should appear to be a very desaturated yellow. Though the resulting yellow is not highly saturated in appearance, neither does it appear to be as desaturated as the diagram suggests. According to Linksz, this led Thomas Young to suggest that a circle might not be the best way in which to represent the organization of colors.

THE COLOR TRIANGLE AND YOUNG'S THEORY

Let us suppose that the colors are not organized on a circle. After all, the only reason colors were organized in a circle was that we needed a closed boundary to handle the color purple. In the early days there were no good psychophysical methods to allow us to measure the saturation of a mixture of spectral colors. All that we really knew was that purple lies between blue and red, and that a mixture of purple (blue or violet plus red) and green produces white, as indicated by Newton's diagram. This leads quite naturally to the conclusion that the color-space is enclosed by a boundary of pure colors. But the boundary need not be circular in shape. In view of the poor saturation predicted by the color circle, Young suggested that a triangle would prove a better shape for the color-space.

Suppose we place the colors red, green, and blue at the apexes of a triangle, as shown in Figure 6–4. We might also place white at the center of the triangle. Now, if we were to mix red (R) and yellow-green (Y-G), the line connecting these two spectral colors will lie on the boundary of the triangle. The resultant mixed color will be as saturated as the pure color to which it corresponds. Moreover, since the triangle is a closed boundary, it also predicts purple; and drawing lines through complementary colors also produces the impression of "white." Though Young's diagram is not an accurate representation of color perception either, it seems to move things in the right direction. It predicts fully saturated mixtures. This is not correct, since mixed colors are not quite so saturated as pure spectral colors; and yet, it is a closer approximation to what actually happens than is the color circle.

That red, green, and blue are at the apexes of Young's triangle is an interesting fact. Although this view was not given its full and clear formulation until Müller (Boring, 1942) stated the *doctrine of specific nerve energies* it was already suspected that different sensory qualities are mediated by different mechanisms in the nervous system. According to this doctrine the experience of light depends upon excitation of the optic nerve, that of sound by excitation of the auditory nerve, and that of smell by excitation of the olfactory nerve. It doesn't matter how the excitation arises, since merely pressing upon the eyeball can produce sensations of light. If we extend Müller's doctrine we must conclude that the perception of different colors requires the excitation of different parts of the nervous system. When one considers, however, that a normal person is able to distinguish between thousands of different hues, this idea becomes ludicrous. It is just not reasonable to believe that each of these thousands of different kinds of sensory quality has its own receiving mechanism in the eye. One solution is to propose that all color sensations are mediated by activation of a few mechanisms in different amounts. The apexes of Young's triangle suggest that there may in fact be three mechanisms that are sufficient, when activated in different amounts, to account for all of the perceived colors.

THE YOUNG-HELMHOLTZ THEORY

Young's theory was publicized by Helmholtz (1924) in the nineteenth century, and is called today the Young-Helmholtz theory of color vision. Following Young's lead, Helmholtz suggested that there are three kinds of "fibre" in the eye and that they produce three kinds of color sensation whenever stimulated. One fibre produces the sensation of "blue" when it is excited; another the sensation of "red"; and the third, the sensation of "green." The "red" fibres are most easily excited by red wavelength light; the "blue" fibres, by blue wavelength; and the "green" fibres, by green wavelength light. The fibres are excitable to some degree by lights that do not bear their names. Thus, the "green" fibres can be excited in a certain amount by red light—but not nearly so much as by green light.

Nowadays we know that the fibres Helmholtz was describing are the

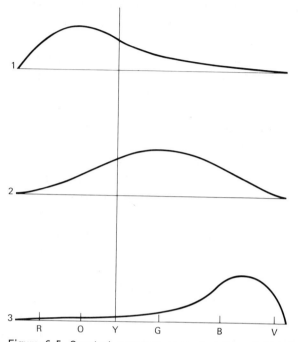

Figure 6–5. Spectral response characteristics of Helmholtz's hypothetical color-sensitive fibers. Curve 1 represents the magnitude of the response of a fiber affected most strongly by light from the red end of the spectrum. Curve 2 represents the spectral response of a fiber affected most strongly by light from the middle (green) portion of the spectrum. Curve 3 represents the spectral response of the fiber most sensitive to short (blue) wavelength light.

cones, since at twilight, when the rods are most active, things appear to be colorless. Red flowers appear to be black, and yellow flowers white. At photopic levels of illumination, however, objects take on their characteristic hues. Thus, it is agreed that cones are the receiving mechanism that transmit color information to the brain.

Light affects photoreceptors in the eye because it is absorbed by pigments carried within the cones. The Young-Helmholtz theory implies that there are three basic types of pigment borne in different cones. The blue cone contains a pigment that absorbs blue light most readily; the green cone absorbs light of the green wavelengths most readily; and the red cones absorb red light. Helmholtz' speculative diagram showing how the different wavelengths of light affect the three basic fibres is reproduced in Figure 6–5.

Suppose now that a pure yellow light were to enter the eye. According to the Young-Helmholtz theory this light will activate both the red and green receptors. In fact, as Figure 6–5 shows, the yellow light will affect the red and green "fibres" in nearly equal amounts: the sensation of yellow simply means that there is nearly equal excitation of red and of green "fibres." Consequently, if red and green light of appropriate wavelengths and luminances were to be mixed at the retina, these two lights would produce the same effect as the yellow light. This example shows how a few basic receptors can serve, in combination, to produce a wide range of qualitatively different experiences.

The basic theme laid down in the Young-Helmholtz theory is pervasive in theories of sensory functioning. One theory, for example, holds that there are about seven different basic odor mechanisms, and that their joint activation in different amounts can account for the entire range of different smell qualities. The idea that three channels mediate the perception of all colors is called the *trichromaticity hypothesis*. We shall now see how this hypothesis is used in predicting the appearance of colors produced by mixing lights of different wavelengths.

THE PRINCIPLES OF COLOR MIXTURE

Figure 6–6 shows a disc divided into two halves. One half of this disc may be illuminated by a colored light, and this is to be matched by a mixture

Figure 6–6. A split field that may be used to match one color, in this case white (W), by a mixture of other lights. A null match is achieved when the observer cannot distinguish the line dividing the two halves of the field.

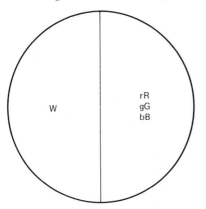

of other lights in the other half. If a perfect match is achieved, the line dividing the two halves will disappear. This nulling method is used commonly in the study of color mixture.

Suppose that the left half of the disc is filled with a white light generated by a tungsten filament. To obtain a good match to this light it is necessary to use differents amounts of three primary colors—say red, green, and blue. This matching can be described by the basic color equation

$$W \equiv rR + gG + bB$$

where W is the white light and r, g, and b the energies of the red, green, and blue primaries needed to match the white light. The equivalence sign between the two sides of the equation means that one cannot perceive a difference between the white light and the mixture of primaries. The plus signs stand for the mixing of the three primaries. Thus, as all authors take pains to point out, the basic color equation is not an algebraic equation but merely describes a set of operations performed in matching two colors. Nevertheless, experiments have shown that by applying the rules of algebra to this color equation one may predict a wide variety of color matching results. The rules of algebra that have been found to be applicable to the color equation are known as Grassman's laws (Marriott, 1962).

A *metameric match* is defined as an exact psychological match of two stimuli that differ from each other physically. The equivalence sign in the basic color equation means that a metameric match has been established.

Colors other than white may also be matched by an appropriate mixture of three primaries. Thus, a yellow light may be matched by a mixture of red and green primaries, with the amount of blue light in the mixture reduced to zero. Thus,

$$Y \equiv rR + gG.$$

Now suppose that we double the amount of light in the yellow sample. To obtain a match to this new sample of yellow light we must also double the amounts of red and green lights in the mixture of primaries. This is an instance of the distributive law of algebra, which is applicable to color matching experiments.

If a white light should have a small amount of blue light added to it, it would appear to have a bluish tinge. To achieve a match to this new sample it would be necessary to increase the amount of the blue primary in the mixture of primaries. Thus, as in algebra, the amount of blue added to the white sample may be offset by adding an equal amount of the same blue to the primaries.

Suppose that a red and green mixture looks exactly like a mixture of pure yellow and a small amount of white light. Now, if these identical-appearing colors are mixed with some other colored light, both will produce the same color. The red and green mixture can replace the yellow plus white—to which it is a metameric match—in any other mixture of colors.

In a very careful study, Wright (1929) chose three spectral colors as primaries and had each of ten normal observers mix these colors in different amounts to match many other colors of the spectrum. The primaries were a red at 650 nm, a green at 530 nm, and a blue at 460 nm. The averaged and smoothed results of this study are shown in Figure 6–7.

Figure 6–7. Equal energy-matching functions based on Wright's (1929) data. The curves labeled $\bar{r}$, $\bar{g}$, and $\bar{b}$ represent the relative amounts of red light at 650 nm, green light at 530 nm, and blue light at 460 nm respectively needed to match all other wavelengths of light. All the wavelengths matched by mixtures of these primaries have equal energy. Equal energy-matching functions of somewhat different appearance have been generated with red, green, and blue primaries whose wavelengths differ from those described here.

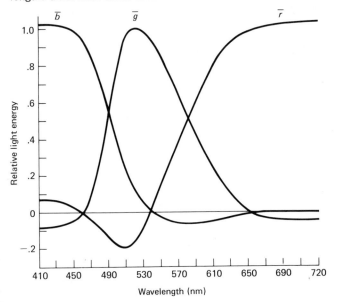

The proportions of the red, green, and blue needed to match each of the wavelengths on the x-axis can be read off the y-axis of the graph. Curve such as these are called *equal energy matching functions,* since all of the wavelengths matched by the primaries were of equal energy.

One curious thing about these data is that negative amounts of one primary were added to the other primaries to match some wavelengths. Thus, to match a blue-green at 500 nm, Wright's observers had to use a negative amount of red light together with equal amounts of blue and green light. The use of negative amounts of light is not so absurd as it may seem. The use of negative amounts of light follows directly from the fact that algebraic operations are permissible in describing color matching experiments. What really happened in Wright's experiment was that no mixture of the blue and green primaries ever looked exactly like the blue-green sample. And yet, by mixing a very small amount of red with the original blue-green sample the match became possible. This addition of red to the sample is algebraically equivalent to subtracting it from the mixture of the blue and green primaries. Thus,

$$X + rR \equiv gG + bB$$

is equivalent to

$$X \equiv gG + bB - rR$$

where X is the sample being matched.

In general, if we are given four colors, where three of the colors are suitably selected primaries, some combination of the three primaries can be used to match the fourth color. At times, however, one of the three primaries may have to be added to the fourth color to obtain apparent equality of the two mixtures.

SOME PRACTICAL IMPLICATIONS OF COLOR MIXTURE

The fact that a limited number of colors may be mixed together to duplicate the appearance of all possible colors is extremely useful. Suppose, for example, that a manufacturer wants to produce a plastic item having the same orange color as that painted on a piece of paper. He could attempt to duplicate the spectral reflectance of the paper but it would be extremely difficult to get a smooth piece of plastic to reflect all wavelengths of light in the same proportions as a rough piece of paper. Since all colors, however, can be duplicated by an appropriate mixture of primary colors, the color of the paper could be specified in terms of the amounts of suitably selected primaries needed to match its appearance. If the plastic object could then be manufactured so that its color could also be specified by the same mixture of primaries, then the color of the plastic would be indistinguishable from that of the paper even if the spectral composition of the light reflected by the plastic differed from that of the paper.

It would be very time-consuming to have to match a particular color with a standard set of primaries every time it is necessary to describe it in terms of the primaries. Fortunately we can eliminate this step, since we already have basic data which describe the color matching behavior of an average or "ideal" observer. These data may be used together with physical measurements of any object to specify the color of the object without having to make actual psychophysical measurements.

The spectral composition of the light illuminating an object can affect its apparent color. Since fluorescent light, for example, has a bluish tinge, and tungsten light is somewhat yellow, the appearance of an isolated object in fluorescent light would differ from its appearance in tungsten light.

As we saw in Chapter 2, a graph can show how the relative energy of light from a source varies with its wavelength. Such an energy spectrum from a hypothetical tungsten lamp is shown at A in Figure 6–8. The graph at B in Figure 6–8 shows the proportion of light at each wavelength that would be reflected by a hypothetical surface if it were illu-

Figure 6–8. The spectral distribution of light reflected by a surface depends upon the nature of the illuminant and also upon the selective reflectance of the surface. Graph A shows how the light energy emitted by a hypothetical illuminant varies with the wavelength of the emitted light. Graph B shows the proportion of light that would be reflected by a hypothetical surface at each wavelength if the surface were illuminated by an equal-energy white light. Multiplying graph A by graph B yields graph C, which shows the spectral distribution of the light that would be reflected by the surface if it were illuminated by the source described in graph A.

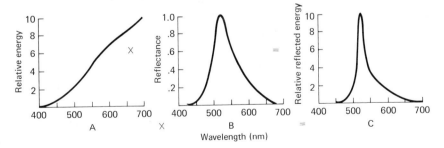

minated by lights of all wavelengths and of equal energy. The surface would reflect but a very small proportion of the red light falling upon it, and it would reflect a much larger proportion of incident yellow light.

These two graphs allow us to determine the spectral composition of the light reflected by the hypothetical surface to the eye of an observer when it is illuminated by the hypothetical tungsten lamp described in Figure 6–8. As we saw in Chapter 2, the amount of light reflected by a surface is the product of the energy of the incident light and the reflectance of the surface. Since we are interested in color, we must now consider the amount of light reflected by a surface as a function of the wavelength of the incident light. This may be determined by multiplying the incident light energy at each wavelength by the capacity of the surface to reflect light at that wavelength. Multiplying graph A by graph B would therefore give the spectral distribution of light energy reaching the eye of an observer viewing the hypothetical surface of our example. This spectral distribution of light energy is portrayed by the graph at C in Figure 6–8.

Now that we have learned to describe the stimulus, we are left with the problem of determining the color that an observer would see. To do this we must use basic psychophysical data such as those obtained by Wright.

The matching functions shown in Figure 6–7 are labeled $\bar{r}$, $\bar{g}$, and $\bar{b}$. A particular value of $\bar{r}$ represents the proportion of the red primary in the mixture of the three primaries needed to match a light of a particular wavelength. Similarly, particular values of $\bar{g}$ and $\bar{b}$ represent the proportions of the green and blue primaries needed to match a particular wavelength. The relative amounts of the primaries have been listed in a table as coefficients to be used in specifying any color. To determine the relative amounts of each of the three needed to match the color of any wavelength of light reflected from a surface, one merely multiplies the amount of reflected energy at that wavelength by the tabulated coefficients of $\bar{r}$, $\bar{g}$, and $\bar{b}$ associated with that wavelength of light.

As indicated in the previous section of this chapter, any color X may be matched by some combination of three suitably chosen primaries as indicated by the equation

$$X \equiv rR + gG + bB.$$

Any other color, say X′, may be matched by different amounts of the same primaries. Thus,

$$X' \equiv r'R + g'G + b'B.$$

It follows from Grassman's laws that

$$X + X' \equiv (rR + gG + bB) + (r'R + g'G + b'B).$$

This is equivalent to

$$(rR + r'R) + (gG + g'G) + (bB + b'B)$$
$$\equiv (r + r')R + (g + g')G + (b + b')B.$$

It follows from these equations that a light consisting of many different wavelengths may be specified also in terms of just three numbers. One of these three numbers is the sum of the amounts of the red primary needed in order to describe each wavelength of the reflected spectrum of light energy; another is the sum of the amounts of the blue primary; and the third is the sum of the amounts of the green primary. For example, if a surface reflects light at just three wavelengths, then multiplying the amount of energy at each of these wavelengths by tabulated $\bar{r}$, $\bar{g}$, and $\bar{b}$ coefficients will define the amounts of the red, green, and blue primaries needed to match each wavelength. The amounts of red needed to match each wavelength may then be added together. This is also done for the amounts of blue and the amounts of green. The resulting three numbers, called R, G, and B, represent the mixture of primaries needed to match the color of the object.

Table 6–1. Standard color matching functions tabulated at 10-nm intervals.

Wavelength (nm)	$\bar{x}$	$\bar{y}$	$\bar{z}$	Wavelength (nm)	$\bar{x}$	$\bar{y}$	$\bar{z}$
390	0.0042	0.0001	0.0201	550	0.4334	0.9950	0.0087
400	0.0143	0.0004	0.0679	560	0.5945	0.9950	0.0039
410	0.0435	0.0012	0.2074	570	0.7621	0.9520	0.0021
420	0.1344	0.0040	0.6456	580	0.9163	0.8700	0.0017
430	0.2839	0.0116	1.3856	590	1.0263	0.7570	0.0011
440	0.3483	0.0230	1.7471	600	1.0622	0.6310	0.0008
450	0.3362	0.0380	1.7721	610	1.0026	0.5030	0.0003
460	0.2908	0.0600	1.6692	620	0.8544	0.3810	0.0002
470	0.1954	0.0910	1.2876	630	0.6424	0.2650	0.0000
480	0.0956	0.1390	0.8130	640	0.4479	0.1750	0.0000
490	0.0320	0.2080	0.4652	650	0.2835	0.1070	0.0000
500	0.0049	0.3230	0.2720	660	0.1649	0.0610	0.0000
510	0.0093	0.5030	0.1582	670	0.0874	0.0320	0.0000
520	0.0633	0.7100	0.0782	680	0.0468	0.0170	0.0000
530	0.1655	0.8620	0.0422	690	0.0227	0.0082	0.0000
540	0.2904	0.9540	0.0203	700	0.0114	0.0041	0.0000
				710	0.0058	0.0021	0.0000

In practice the method described above is more complicated. Surfaces usually reflect a continuous spectrum of wavelengths. The energies of these wavelengths cannot be measured one wavelength at a time, although it is possible to measure relative energy in bands about 5 or 10 nm wide, and this allows us to approximate the continuous spectrum of reflected light.

As already mentioned, negative amounts of light may have to be employed in specifying a color. To avoid this—and other problems not discussed here—an international commission (the *Commission Internationale de l'Eclairage*) recommended the use of three different primaries, usually referred to as the XYZ standard primaries. These primaries are not real colors but are mathematical abstractions from the RGB system of primaries. If one tried to match a mixture of the red, green, and blue primaries to any of the X, Y, and Z primaries, one or more of the red, green,

Figure 6–9. Equal energy-matching functions of the standard XYZ system. The curves $\bar{x}$, $\bar{y}$, and $\bar{z}$ show the relative amounts of the X, Y, and Z primaries needed to match the color of any wavelength of light.

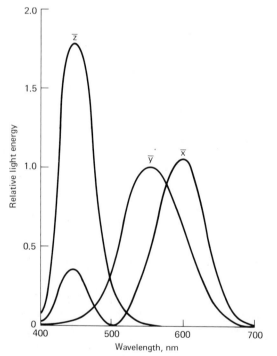

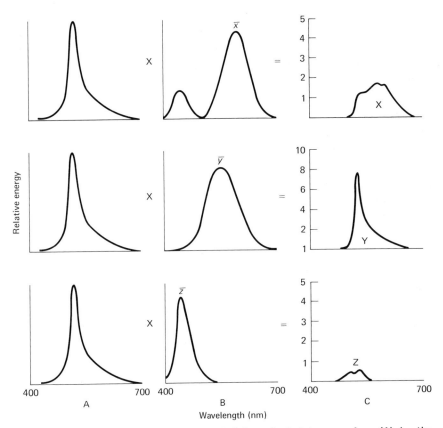

Figure 6–10. Multiplying the spectrum of light reflected by a surface (A) by the standard equal-energy matching functions, $\overline{x}$, $\overline{y}$, and $\overline{z}$ (B), yields the three curves in column C. The areas under these curves correspond to the values of X, Y, and Z needed to describe the color of the surface.

and blue primaries would have to be represented in negative amounts. Consequently, the X, Y, and Z primaries have no real physical existence even though they are very real in the mathematical sense.

The matching functions of the XYZ system, called x, y, and z, were derived from the matching functions of the RGB system. These new matching functions, shown in Figure 6–9, have been tabulated to produce a table of coefficients (Table 6–3) which may be used in the same manner as the coefficients of the $\overline{r}$, $\overline{g}$, and $\overline{b}$ matching functions described above. Thus, any wavelength of light can be represented by three numbers obtained by multiplying the energy at that wavelength by the coefficients listed in Table 6–1. When this is done for several wavelengths, then summing the products of wavelength energy and the $\bar{x}$, $\bar{y}$, and $\bar{z}$ coefficients separately give the values of X, Y, and Z. These three numbers specify the color of the object. Figure 6–10 illustrates the steps needed to obtain the X, Y, and Z values describing the color of an object viewed in a particular illumination. In no case need an actual color match be made by an observer.

At this point the reader must be wondering what he is to do with the values of X, Y, and Z when obtained in the manner described here. How can he determine color and purity from three numbers? One way to solve this problem is by use of the *standard chromaticity diagram*.

THE STANDARD CHROMATICITY DIAGRAM

In discussing the perception of color it is important to keep in mind the distinction between color and brightness. The color of an object in a room does not change significantly if more lamps are turned on. The object may appear to be brighter, but it will still have the same color, provided that the illumination level is made neither extremely low nor radically high. Therefore, to be entirely general in their usefulness, the three numbers needed to specify a color should be independent of the absolute energy reflected by an object. However, the absolute values of X, Y, and Z do change when light energy is changed. Consequently, it is desirable to express the three numbers used to describe a color in terms of proportions or relative amounts. The way in which this is done is by means of the formula

$$\frac{X}{X+Y+Z} + \frac{Y}{X+Y+Z} + \frac{Z}{X+Y+Z} = 1.$$

The XYZ primaries were so chosen that a white light comprised of all wavelengths of equal energy could be matched by equal values of X, Y, and Z. Thus, if a particular level of white light energy should reach the eye, then the stimulus could be matched by an equal mixture of the X, Y, and Z primaries. However, even though they were equal, the absolute values of X, Y, and Z would vary with the energy of the sample being matched. The preceding formula makes it possible to say that X, Y, and Z each contribute one-third of the energy of a mixture that would duplicate the apparent white color of the object, even though the amount of light reflected or transmitted by the object were to vary from one situation to another.

If we let

$$\frac{X}{X+Y+Z} = x$$

and

$$\frac{Y}{X+Y+Z} = y$$

and

$$\frac{Z}{X+Y+Z} = z,$$

then

$$x+y+z = 1.$$

It follows from this that if we know the values of x and y, then we automatically know the value of z because

$$1-x+y = z.$$

These relations make it possible to plot the effects of mixing the standard X, Y, and Z primaries in all possible combinations in a single two-dimensional graph. This strange-looking graph is known as the *chromaticity diagram* shown in Figure 6–11, facing p. 206.

The curved line in Figure 6–11 is called the *locus of spectral colors.* The points on this locus represent the values of x, y, and z needed to produce their colors. The point representing 400 nm, for example, could be matched by a mixture in which the relative value of x is about 0.173 and that of y is about 0.005. Since $x+y+z = 1$, the value of z is about 0.822. By reading x and y from the graph we can determine the value of z even though the graph does not provide a z-axis. Just so long as a surface can be described by the X, Y, and Z primaries in these proportions, it will match the appearance of a spectral light at 400 nm.

We shall now answer the question with which we started: How can we determine the color and purity of a light that is described by three numbers? As we have already indicated, an equal-energy spectrum white light is a metameric match to equal amounts of x, y, and z. Consequently, the location of this white in the chromaticity diagram is at the intersection of lines drawn from the 0.33 point on the x-axis and 0.33 on the y-axis. The z-value is therefore fixed at 0.33 also. Thus, the equal-energy white is located at the center of gravity of the standard chromaticity diagram.

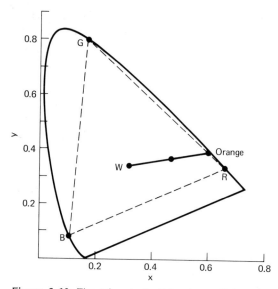

Figure 6–12. The triangle in this chromaticity diagram contains all of the colors that may be matched by a positive mixture of red, green, and blue primaries. The dot on the arrow is the location within the chromaticity diagram of a pale orange color.

As we might expect from the earlier discussion of Newton's color circle, desaturated colors lie inside the locus of the spectral colors. Consider a pale orange, for example. If this color could be matched by a mixture in which the proportions of x is 0.45 and the proportion of y 0.35, as shown in Figure 6–12, the proportion of z is 0.20. The intersection of these values of x and y places the point representing the pale orange inside the locus of spectral colors. The value of the color is determined by a line that may be drawn from the center of gravity of the graph—the position of white— through the point representing the color. The point at which this line intersects the locus of spectral colors determines the value of the hue. The ratio of the length of the line segment between the position of the point of intersection of x and y and white to the total length of the line shown in Figure 6–12 is an index of the purity (saturation) of the color. Thus, the chromaticity diagram may be used in the way that we wanted to use Newton's color circle.

Other primaries also may be used to produce a chromaticity diagram. The only requirement is that the primaries selected be such that no mixture of two of the primaries can match the other primary. The triangle contained within the locus of spectral colors of Figure 6–12 encloses all the colors we can make from positive mixtures of Wright's three primaries. To get the spectral colors lying outside the triangle we must add a quantity of one of the primaries to the spectral color being matched. This would be true of any set of physically realizable primaries.

One might ask why it is that the spectral colors we do see cannot be reproduced by a positive mixture of all three of Wright's real primaries. The answer stems from the fact that a spectral color—say, a blue-green— is absorbed readily by the blue and green light-absorbing pigments and hardly at all by the red light-absorbing pigment. A monochromatic green, however, which has a much longer wavelength than the blue-green spectral color being matched, is absorbed to a much greater degree by the red light-absorbing pigment. Thus, though a mixture of a monochromatic green and a monochromatic blue can produce the same impression as an intermediate monochromatic blue-green, the red light-absorbing cones are excited more by the green in the mixture than they are by the original blue green sample. Accordingly, to get the mixture of blue and green to match the blue-green sample, a bit of red light must be added to the sample to get it to appear the same as the blue and green mixture. In short, then, a blue-green spectral light excites blue and green cones. A green light excites both green and red cones, but the blue light excites only blue cones. This effect on the red cones can be offset by adding red to the original sample. In this light, Grassman's laws are not as arbitrary as they may seem to be. By accepting the simple algebraic laws that they imply, it is possible to account for all perceived colors in terms of a mixture of three spectral primaries.

ADDITIVE AND SUBTRACTIVE COLOR MIXTURE

In the preceding discussion we have assumed that color mixtures are achieved by superimposing lights of different wavelengths—a process known as *additive color mixture*. The results achieved by adding lights to each other differ from the results achieved by mixing paints. Thus, the addition of blue and yellow lights can produce a neutral or white light, but the mixing of blue and yellow paints leads to production of a green paint. Obviously, then, the artist, does not make the same predictions about the outcome of paint mixtures as a visual scientist would make about the addition of lights.

Let us consider what happens to white light when it is incident upon a paint containing a blue pigment. Some of the light is absorbed by the pigment in the paint and some of it is reflected by the paint. The reason the pigment gives the paint its blue color is that the pigment absorbs light of the yellow wavelengths selectively. The dominant wavelengths in the remaining light (which is reflected back to the eye of an observer), are from the blue portion of the spectrum. Of course, the reflected light has a very wide spectrum, and may include green and even some red wavelengths. Thus, an ultramarine blue pigment may have a greenish cast, and a cobalt blue has a different apparent color composition. In the reflected light these differences are mediated by the different weightings given to wavelengths other than blue.

The same is true of a yellow pigment. It looks yellow because blue wavelength light is absorbed by the pigment, and the predominant wavelength in the reflected light is from the yellow portion of the spectrum. Nevertheless, other wavelengths are represented in the reflected light.

Let us now consider what happens when blue and yellow paints are mixed. When white light falls upon this mixture the blue wavelengths are absorbed by the yellow pigment, and, the yellow wavelengths are absorbed by the blue pigment. The light left over is neither predominantly blue nor predominantly yellow, but in fact is usually predominantly green. Thus, the mixture of blue and yellow paints results in green because the blue and yellow wavelengths are both substracted from the white light so that the light remaining for reflection is greenish in color. That is why the mixture of pigments is called *subtractive mixture of colors.*

The pointillist painter did not use subtractive methods to achieve his color effects, but painted each color as a separate dot on the canvas. When dots of blue paint and dots of yellow paint were intermingled, the blue dots still reflected blue light to the eye, and the yellow dots still reflected yellow light. If the observer is far away from the picture, the blue and yellow light reflected by it will mix additively at his eye, with result in the perception of a grey color and not of a green color.

THE OPPONENT PROCESS THEORY

Ewald Hering (1964) proposed an alternative to the Young-Helmholtz theory of color mixture. Hering's theory was based in part on the following observations. Many colors appear to be mixtures of other colors. Thus, orange can be identified even by a naïve observer as a mixture of red and yellow, and purple is apparently a mixture of red and blue. The color yellow, however, is not an obvious mixture of red and green, but appears rather to be a "pure" color in its own right. This observation led him to suggest that there may be four primaries and not the usual three: red, green, blue, and yellow.

A second basis for Hering's theory is that no one has ever seen a greenish red or a yellowish blue. There are yellowish reds—namely, the oranges—and greenish blues, but no colors that are mixtures of red and green and of yellow and blue. This suggests that red and green receptors and yellow and blue receptors may work as opposed pairs. Thus, yellow stimulation may cancel out the effects of blue stimulation, and green stimulation may cancel the effects of red stimulation.

These considerations, and others to be described later, led Hering to the notion that color mixture phenomena may be more aptly explained by invoking the concept of opposed pairs of processes set up by the different colors. Yellow and blue comprise one pair, red and green another pair, and black and white a third pair. In order to understand how these mechanisms might produce the effects of color mixture let us consider a few examples.

According to Hering's theory, any light can affect the black-white mechanism, which conveys information as to lightness, regardless of color. Now, if a mixture of equal amounts of yellow and blue light were to be presented, the black-white mechanism would be activated. But since yellow and blue lights have opposed or self-cancelling effects on the yellow-blue mechanism, the result would be the perception of a light of neutral color. A similar result would be obtained if red and green lights were mixed in equal amounts. Their effects would be counterbalanced and the resulting perception would be of a neutrally colored light.

Now suppose that a mixture of yellow and blue is presented, but that the yellow light has a much higher luminance than the blue. This would lead to perception of a desaturated yellow, since the two lights would have a combined effect on the black-white mechanism, and the blue light would incompletely offset the effect of the yellow light on the blue-yellow mechanism.

If a yellow and red light were presented to the eye, these two lights would affect both the red-green mechanism and the blue-yellow mechanism, and this results in the perception of a mixture of red and yellow or orange.

One of the questions generally raised by Hering's original theory concerns the generation of yellow by the mixture of red and green lights. If red and green lights affect the red-green mechanism, thereby canceling the impression of color, how can a yellow light be experienced? The reason given is that the red and green lights that do mix to yield a yellow are not exact complements of each other, and usually it is a somewhat yellowish green that is mixed with the red, or an orange-red mixed with a green. In both cases one of the lights affects both the red-green mechanism and the yellow-blue mechanism. If the mixture of red and green lights affects the red-green mechanism properly, neither red nor green can be perceived. The residual effect produced on the yellow-blue mechanism is the impression of yellow. A much better explanation of how mixtures of red and green produce yellow will be considered later.

There is considerable evidence that an opponent process mechanism similar to the one envisioned by Hering is actually involved in color vision. At the same time there is strong evidence that only three pigments are involved in color perception. As we shall see later, the opponent mechanisms are basically neural in nature, and the signals supplied to these mechanisms arise in three pigments, as envisioned by Helmholtz.

COLOR DEFICIENCIES

Some of the best evidence for the existence of three pigments comes from the study of different kinds of color deficiency.

There are several different kinds of color deficiency. In very rare cases, people have only rods in their eyes, and hence cannot distinguish between lights of different wavelengths when such lights are adjusted to have equal scotopic luminosities. As we already know, rhodopsin is relatively insensitive to red light, though it absorbs yellow light readily; and thus, for a person having only rods, red objects normally look darker than yellow objects. If a red light were to be made bright enough, however, it could be confused with a dim yellow light. Moreover, a *monochromat*—the person we are describing—will match any light with a mixture of any other lights just so long as their luminances are equal: he is genuinely color blind.

The most common kind of color-deficient person is called a *dichromat*, for the reason that such individuals can match any color with a mixture of two other wavelengths of light, as contrasted with the normal individual, who needs three lights to match all other lights. Further, any match made by a *trichromat* (normal individual) will be accepted by a dichromat.

One way to explain the facts of *dichromacy* is to assume that one of the three normally present cone pigments is missing. Let us suppose, for example, that a subject has red and blue light-absorbing pigments in his cones but is lacking the pigment that normally absorbs green light. Now, if a green light were to be presented to this subject it could not be absorbed by the green light-absorbing pigment. Some of the green light will be absorbed by the blue pigment, however, and a different amount absorbed by the red pigment—as follows from the fact that all pigments absorb all wavelengths of light but in different amounts. Now, the green light can be matched by some combination of blue and red light. This can be done by adjusting the amounts of blue and red light until the red and blue pigments absorb the same amounts of light as they do when the green light is present.

One who lacks the green light-absorbing pigment is known as a *deuteranope*. The term *deuteros* is Greek for "second," and the color green is, by convention, the second primary. The deuteranope may be identified by the difficulty he has in distinguishing between red mixed with a little blue and green. He is, however, sensitive to green light even though he cannot discriminate green from certain combinations of red and blue on the basis of hue alone.

Deuteranopia is the most common form of dichromacy. A less common form of dichromacy, known as *protanopia*, is described in terms of a lack of red light-absorbing pigment (the Greek prefix *protos* indicates "first," and red light is conventionally considered to be the first primary). A protanope is insensitive to long wavelength red light. If a red light is made very much brighter than a green light, these colors could be confused by a protanope. Whereas a normal observer looking at these same lights would perceive that the red light is brighter than the green and also of a different color, the protanope would not detect the difference in brightness between the confused red and green lights. Although the protanope and the deuteranope both confuse red and green lights, the deuteranope is sensitive to the brightness of green light and as sensitive to the brightness of red light as is a normal person. The protanope, on the other hand, is highly insensitive to deep red light. Although these differences in sensitivity are not fully understood, they are consistent with the notion that a protanope lacks the red pigment and the deuteranope lacks the green pigment.

Let us consider Helmholtz's speculative diagram in Figure 6–5. As we recall, this diagram may be thought of as reflecting the different absorption spectra of the three basic pigments in the eye. Now, if the green pigment were missing, the first and third spectral response curves in the figure indicate that the remaining pigments would still be able to absorb substantial amounts of the green light. If the first or red pigment were missing, however, the remaining pigments would be unable to absorb very much of the deep red light. The deep red light could be seen, however, if it were made so intense that it bleached the green and blue pigments. As we shall see later, in the eye the actual absorption spectra of the pigments are qualitatively consistent with this interpretation of the data from color deficiencies. However, not enough green light can be absorbed by the red and blue pigments to account fully for the sensitivity to green in the deuteranope.

If the data on color blindness are to support the idea that there are three distinct types of photopigment in the cones, one would expect to find a third type of dichromacy. There is in fact a very rare condition known as *tritanopia,* which is consistent with the lack of a blue light-absorbing pigment.

In addition to dichromacy there are other kinds of color abnormality. These conditions are usually subsumed under the classification of *anomalous trichromacy,* since subjects with these abnormalities can match any given color by some mixture of three other colors (hence, *trichromats*)— although the mixtures differ from those employed by normal observers. These conditions are usually attributed to relative insensitivity to lights of particular wavelengths rather than to total lack of one pigment or another. Thus, in one kind of anomalous trichromacy, known as *protanomolous* color deficiency, the subject might need more red than does a normal in a red-green mixture that is being matched to a yellow. There is also a condition known as *deuteranomalous* deficiency, in which there appears to be a relative lack of green photopigment.

CHARACTERISTICS OF THE PHOTOPIGMENTS

The study of color deficiencies lends considerable credence to the idea that there are three distinct photopigments involved in color perception. This conclusion, however, cannot be accepted solely on the basis of the fact that color-deficient observers behave as though they are missing one of three pigments. It is also possible that three neural channels are each being fed by many different pigments. In this view—which Brindley (1960) has labeled the *three-channel hypothesis*—several different pigments with overlapping absorption spectra produce activity in a common neural channel. Activity in this channel could signify one color, and activity in other channels could signify other colors. Some color deficiencies could then be attributed not to lack of pigments but to some defect in one or another of the three neural channels.

More direct evidence is available to support the three-pigment hypothesis. First, there is evidence from the recording of the electrical activity of single cone receptors in the eye in response to stimulation by colored lights. Second, there have been efforts to measure the absorption spectra of pigments in cones directly. Third, the methods of retinal densitometry provide evidence also on the characteristics of cone pigments. Finally, the characteristics of the photopigment have been studied psychophysically.

The carp and the goldfish are capable of making discriminations based upon color. Because of their availability and the ease with which they may be studied, these animals are favorites of visual physiologists. In a brilliant experiment, Tomita (1965) succeeded in impaling a single cone on a microelectrode. This was done by vibrating the retina of the carp until one jolt caused one of its cones to be penetrated by a stationary electrode. Once this was accomplished it was possible to illuminate the cone in question and study its electrical behavior. Using this technique, Tomita, Kaneko, Murakami, and Pautler (1967) illuminated an impaled cone with lights of different wavelengths. The lights were produced with a monochromator and calibrated so that they had equal energy. Typical results of their experiments are shown in Figure 6–13, which contains recordings from three different cones. Each of the complicated waves is actually the result of stimulating a cone during successive 1-second intervals with a 0.3-second flash of a different wavelength. Each flash had the effect of hyperpolarizing the cone to a greater or lesser extent.

There is a potential difference between the inside and the outside of any nerve cell, and it is produced by concentration of ions with one charge outside the cell membrane and of ions of the opposite charge inside the cell. In most neurons this polarization may tend to break down as a result of stimulation. If this breakdown or hypopolarization of the potential difference goes far enough, the cell becomes depolarized, and a spike potential results. In the retinal receptors of vertebrates, however, this does not occur, since they do not generate spike potentials. Instead, the cone receptors become hyperpolarized, and the difference in electric potential between the inside and outside of the receptor actually increases. This

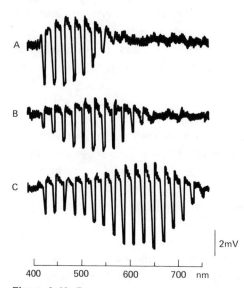

Figure 6–13. Responses of three types of cone to light of various wavelengths. The blue-sensitive cone's response characteristics are described at A, that of the green-sensitive cone at B, and of the red-sensitive cone at C. (From Tomita, Kaneko, Murakami, and Pautler, 1967)

increase in potential is a continuous process as compared with the rapid all-or-none spike potential. Moreover, if hyperpolarization occurs, there will be consequent changes in the polarization of subsequent cells in the retina, resulting finally in the transmission of spike potentials along the axons comprising the optic nerve.

It will be observed in Figure 6–13 that the magnitude of hyperpolarization of a cone depends upon the wavelength of the incident light. Trace A in the figure demonstrates that wavelengths longer than about 550 nm do not cause the cone to become hyperpolarized. There is, however, an increasing tendency for the cone to become hyperpolarized as the stimulating wavelength approaches 455 nm, and this cone appears to be maximally sensitive to wavelengths of about 455 nm. Cone B, on the other hand, is maximally sensitive to green light with a wavelength of about 530 nm, and cone C is maximally sensitive to red light at 625 nm. Thus, Tomita *et al.* (1967) found three types of cone, and these cones do in fact respond maximally to blue, green, and red primaries. It should be borne in mind, however, that the precision of these data probably does not allow us to distinguish among cones with slightly different spectral sensitivities.

Numerous experiments have been performed to measure directly the absorption characteristics of pigments within single cones (Marks, Dobelle, and MacNichol, 1964; Wald, 1964; Wald and Brown, 1965). The general procedure is to focus two tiny spots of light through a microscope on cone cells collected on a microscope cover slip. One spot of light is formed within the outer segment of a cone, the other spot, outside the cone. The amount of light passing through the cone is measured by means of a very sensitive photodetector placed beneath the cover slip. This measurement is compared with the light passing through the cover slip but not through the cone. The difference between these two readings is the amount of light absorbed by the cone itself. This procedure is known as *microspectrophotometry*.

Three classes of human cones have been identified thus far by means of these measurements. The absorption spectra for these cones, shown in Figure 6–14, peak respectively at 445 nm, 535 nm, and 570 nm. Thus, at least three different kinds of cone are present in the human eye.

Using his technique of retinal densitometry, Rushton (1958) has succeeded in measuring the absorption spectra of two cone pigments in the living human eye.

To begin with, it is known that blue light-absorbing cones are relatively sparse in the central fovea. Thus, blue lights imaged precisely in the central fovea are confused with greens, white, and yellows (Willmer, 1946). Moreover, according to Stiles (1949) among people with normal color vision there is a very definite loss of sensitivity to blue light in the

Figure 6–14. These curves show how the relative absorption of light varies as a function of its wavelength in three types of cone from the human retina. (From Wald and Brown, 1965)

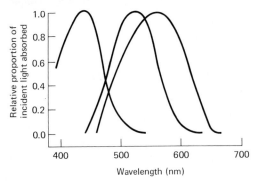

center of the fovea. Relying on these facts, Rushton obtained the services of two kinds of dichromat—a deuteranope, who lacks green-absorbing pigment, and a protanope, who lacks red-absorbing pigment. Though both dichromats may be presumed to have blue light-absorbing pigment, the small amounts in the central fovea might not affect the measurements of the absorption spectrum of the red light-absorbing pigment in the deuteranope and of the green light-absorbing pigment in the protanope.

The first step in Rushton's experiment was to measure the amount of light reflected back from the central fovea in the dark-adapted eye when the wavelength of the incident light was varied. This was done with an apparatus similar in principle to the one employed by Campbell and Rushton to measure the rod pigments (see p. 87). In the case of the protanope the results obtained with the dark-adapted eye were compared with results obtained after the eye was adapted to a bright red light. It can be assumed that the green light-absorbing pigment in the protanope will be bleached to some extent by the red light if the red light is intense enough. As a consequence of this bleaching the light reflected back from the eye when the measurements were taken could increase in quantity, since there is less light-absorbing pigment left after the period of adaptation than there was before it. This difference in pigment density, however, should vary with the wavelength of the light used in obtaining the measurements.

If the green light-absorbing pigment does not absorb light with a wavelength of, say, 640 nm, then, whether or not the pigment is bleached by an adapting red light of 600 nm, there would be no change in the amount of reflected 640 nm light, since it is not absorbed by the pigment in the first place. Now, a light of 540 nm is absorbed strongly by the pigment; and this means that the amount of light reflected at this wavelength would be strongly affected by the degree to which the pigment had been bleached by the adapting light. It is obvious, therefore, that the efficiency with which the pigment absorbs quanta of different wavelengths will determine the degree to which the densitometric readings will be affected by adaptation. A plot of the difference between the absorption of lights of different wavelengths in the dark-adapted eye and the absorption of lights in the light-adapted eye will therefore reflect the degree to which the pigment in the eye is capable of absorbing the lights of different wavelengths. Such a plot, known as a *difference spectrum*, appears in Figure 6–15. The small dots show how the red-adapting light affects the absorption of lights of different wavelengths.

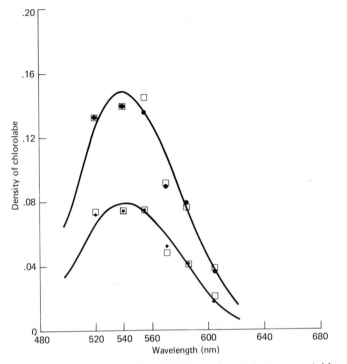

Figure 6–15. Change in the relative density of the green-catching pigment (chloro-labe) in the human eye when it is measured with light of various wavelengths after exposure to either a bright-red-adapting light or a blue-green-adapting light (lower curve), and after exposure to a white-adapting light (upper curve). (After Rushton, 1962)

This procedure was repeated in the protanope, with a blue-green adapting light, and the results are shown by the small squares in Figure 6–15. It will be observed that there is no significant difference in these two sets of data. The blue-green light has the same effect on the eye of the protanope as does the red-adapting light. This means that the difference spectrum is of only one pigment.

To understand the basis for the conclusion that only one visual pigment is present if two different adapting lights have the same effect on the measured absorption characteristics of the eye, consider a hypothetical case. Suppose that two pigments are present, that one of them absorbs red light most readily, and the other absorbs green light most readily. Now, when a red-adapting light is used, the green pigment will not be bleached so much as the red light-absorbing pigment. Consequently, on subsequent test using lights of different wavelengths, less red wavelength light will be absorbed after adaptation than will green wavelength light. If a blue-green adapting light were used, however, the difference spectrum would not be the same as the difference spectrum obtained after using the red-adapting light. This follows from the fact that green light absorption will be more affected by the blue-green-adapting light than it would by the red-adapting light. Since Rushton's protanope did not show this change in the difference spectrum when different adapting lights were used, it is likely that only one pigment was affected by both lights.

When Rushton used a white-adapting light it had the effect of shifting the whole curve shown in Figure 6–15 upward, since the white light had a stronger bleaching effect on the pigment than did either the red- or blue-green-adapting lights. Nevertheless, the shape of the curve is the same as that produced by colored adapting lights, and is similar also to the shape of a psychophysically determined curve showing how the protanope's sensitivity to light varies as a function of its wavelength.

The pigment identified in the eye of the protanope was labeled *chlorolabe*. (Rushton took this term from the Greek because it translates to mean "green-catching") A "red-catching" pigment, called *erythrolabe*, was identified also. As will be recalled, evidence from the study of color deficiencies indicates that the deuteranope has a red light-absorbing pigment but lacks the green-catching pigment. Using the same procedures as with the protanope, Rushton found also that the difference spectrum was no different when the eye was adapted to a red light than when it was adapted to a blue-green light. This suggests that only one pigment was bleached. And yet the difference spectrum obtained in the deuteranope differed from the difference spectrum found in the protanope: the amount of reflected deep-red light was not affected by the adapting light in the protanope, but was affected by the adapting light in the deuteranope. This means that the deuteranope is much more sensitive to wavelengths above 600 nm than is the protanope.

The difference spectrum measured from the eye of the deuteranope is illustrated in Figure 6–16. It will be noticed that the peak of the spectrum is located further toward the red end of the visible electromagnetic spectrum and that the entire spectrum is wider than that measured in the eye of the protanope. The difference spectrum of erythrolabe also shown in Figure 6–16 does not match the curve obtained by taking psychophysical sensitivity measurements from a deuteranopic observer. As suggested by

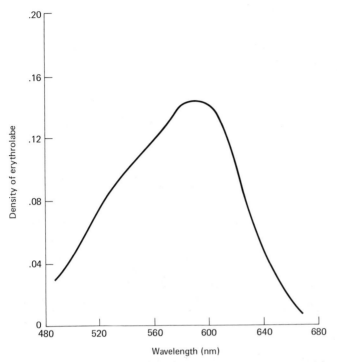

Figure 6–16. Change in the relative density of the red-catching pigment (erythro-labe) in the human eye after exposure to either a blue-green- or a red-adapting light. Both adapting lights produce the same difference spectrum. (After Rushton, 1962).

Rushton, one possible explanation for this is that when erythrolabe is bleached by a light, it produces colored byproducts which reduce reflectivity more at certain wavelengths than at others. This still needs investigation.

Figure 6–17 shows two difference spectra in the normal human eye, one obtained after bleaching with red light, and the other, after bleaching with blue-green light. These two spectra match those of erythrolabe and of chlorolabe, respectively.

There is probably a blue-catching pigment—Rushton calls it *cyano-labe*—whose difference spectrum has not yet been measured. Serious technical difficulties bar the way, prominent among them being that various substances in the eye absorb a great deal of blue light. These include the lens and the macula—the spot containing the fovea—which has a yellowish

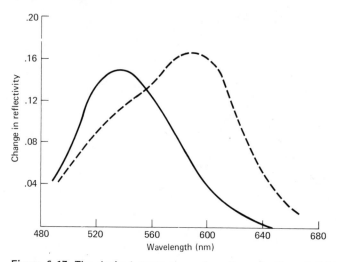

Figure 6–17. The dashed curve shows how the reflection of lights of various wavelength by the normal human retina changes after a red bleaching light is used. Bleaching the same retina with a blue-green light yields the difference spectrum described by the solid curve. The difference between these two spectra indicates the presence of two different pigments. (After Rushton, 1962)

color. Moreover, since the amount of cyanolabe in the eye is probably small relative to that of erythrolabe and of chlorolabe, the differences in reflectivity produced by a bleaching light would be so small that to discern the "signal" from "noise" when taking measurements would be very difficult.

All the evidence discussed thus far suggests that there are at least three pigments in the fovea. Wald (1964) has published three curves (reproduced in Figure 6–18) that are estimates of the absorption spectra of the three pigments. The blue-catching pigment (curve C in the figure) absorbs relatively fewer incident quanta at any wavelength than do the red- or green-catching pigments. The green-catching pigment (curve B in the figure) absorbs as much as 100 times more the number of incident quanta than does the blue-catching pigment. The red light-absorbing pigment is slightly less efficient than is the green-catching pigment. These curves are based upon psychophysical measurements. Other psychophysical techniques have been applied to the study of photopigments. It has been known for a long time, for example, that a brief flash of monochromatic light of very low energy does not have the same apparent color from one flash to the next (see Hartridge, 1950). Krauskopf and Sebro (1965) reconfirmed this finding when they presented a monochromatic light of 580 nm at a near-threshold intensity for a very brief period of time. It was assumed that from flash to flash the photons impinging on the retina would have a random distribution within a circumscribed area, and that consequently the photons would sometimes be absorbed by one receptor only. If this occurred, the color name given the perceived flash should vary from trial to trial.

The observers were given a monochromatic steady field whose wavelength could be adjusted to match the remembered color of the test flash.

Figure 6–18. Psychophysically determined estimates of the absorption spectra of three pigments in the human eye. (After Wald, 1964)

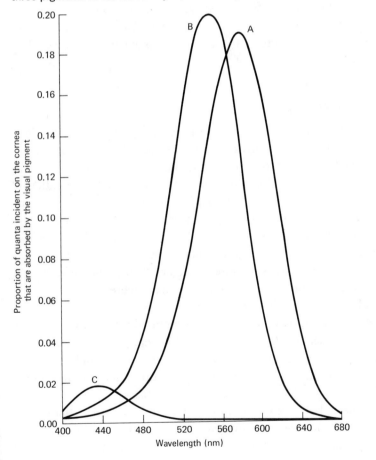

When this matching was done, it was found that the test flashes were always matched to wavelengths described as "orange-red," "red," or "blue-green." On occasion the flashes could not be matched by any wavelength, since they appeared to be "white." This suggests that more than one receptor was excited. The observers never matched the test flash with a yellow light or with a deep-blue light. Plotting the frequencies with which different matching wavelengths were selected against their wavelengths showed a clear bimodal distribution with pronounced peaks in the green and red regions of the spectrum.

By making a number of assumptions, Krauskopf and Sebro were able to generate spectral sensitivity curves for two color mechanisms by means of this method. The curves are not unlike those found by Rushton. The fact that these two authors could not distinguish between the sensitivities to lights named "blue" and those named "green" is consistent with the idea that sensitivity to blue is so much smaller than sensitivity to green that the blue pigment cannot be affected unless other pigments are affected as well. In any case, no independent yellow-sensitive mechanism was found in these studies.

OPPONENT MECHANISMS

As we recall, four basic chromatic mechanisms were postulated by Hering's original theory. These mechanisms worked as opposed pairs so that the effect of red offsets the effect of green while the effect of yellow offsets the effect of blue. In a very informative introduction to their translation of Hering's (1964) *Outlines of a Theory of the Light Sense,* Hurvich and Jameson observe that the opponent process theory was disregarded for a long time because of a mistaken idea widely believed—to the effect that the theory proposed the existence of photochemical substances possibly affected in two different ways by opposed colors. Thus, a pigment may be bleached by the light of one wavelength and made more dense by the opposed wavelength. Thus, the direction of a chemical process induced by the absorption of light quanta may be determined by the wavelengths of the quanta. Chemically, this is not a feasible scheme. As Hurvich and Jameson note, Hering never tied his theory to such a photopigment, and many criticisms of his position are really based upon faulty translation of his writings. Hering held instead that there is a basis for opponent processes in the neural tissues of the retina. This approach is actually well founded on neurophysiological evidence and, when it was proposed, it was far in advance of its time.

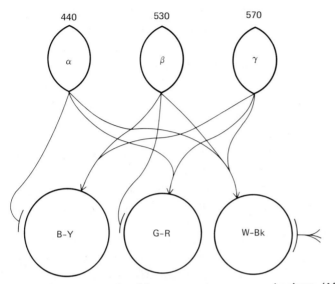

Figure 6–19. Schematic of the opponent process mechanisms. (After Hurvich, 1973)

The general modern form of the theory is suggested by the schematic diagram shown in Figure 6–19. The schematic shows linkages between units containing different photopigments. These pigments, labeled α, β and γ, have absorption spectra peaking at 440, 530, and 570 nm, respectively. They correspond closely to the blue-, green-, and red-sensitive pigments identified by the methods of microspectrophotometry. That is to say, the classical three pigments underlie color sensitivity even in the opponent process theory.

The novel aspect of the theory is the way the photopigments are linked together. In the schematic it will be seen that all three receptors converge further upstream in the retina onto a common unit labelled B-Y. The sum of the β and γ units has an excitatory effect on unit B-Y, while the α unit has an inhibitory effect. Thus, unit B-Y can be depolarized by either green or red light, and it can be hyperpolarized by blue light. The joint effect of green and red light produces an increase in the firing rates of neurons influenced by B-Y; the blue light could reduce the spontaneous firing rates of the same neurons. Since a mixture of red and green may produce the impression of yellow, an increase in the output of B-Y may signify "yellow" to the brain while a decrease in its output could signify "blue." The sum of the β and γ outputs excites yellow activity of the B-Y unit. This is a better account of how red and green lights produce yellow than is the version given by Hering above. Thus, unit B-Y is the blue-yellow opponent mechanism cited in our earlier discussion of this theory.

Unit G–R also receives input from the three cones, though in this case unit β, the green-sensitive receptor, inhibits unit G–R, and both blue and red lights can excite the unit. Red light alone will produce the impression of redness as a result of an increase in the firing rate of G–R; green light will be signified by a decrease in the unit's firing rate. Blue light will produce an increase in the output of G–R concurrently with a decrease in the output of B-Y—a small effect, relative to the effect of red light. This pathway is necessary for the reason that a deep monochromatic blue light produces the impression of a blue color with a tinge of red.

The unit labeled W-Bk, sometimes referred to as a luminosity unit, responds when any light affects any of the three receptors. Moreover, its response will increase with an increase in the number of receptors excited, regardless of their absorption characteristics. Whenever there is an increase in the output of W-Bk there is an impression of an increase in the luminosity of the perceived stimulus.

The luminosity unit is unique in two respects. First, it has a greater sensitivity than either of the other two units in the schematic. These chromatic units need significantly more in the way of input before they will respond than does the luminosity unit. This feature of the luminosity unit was postulated to account for the fact that when a spectrum of colors has a very low luminance it is first perceived as colorless and divided into bands of different degrees of darkness. Thus, the hypothetical W-Bk units have some of the features of the rod system. The W–Bk unit does not transmit color information but it does serve to produce impressions of relative darkness and lightness.

The second way in which the luminosity unit differs from chromatic units is that it is not inhibited selectively by certain colors and excited by other colors. It is inhibited instead by other W-Bk units that can be excited by any one or all three of the primaries. Thus, some cones have ultimate excitatory effect on the unit and other cones of the same type will have an inhibitory effect on the unit.

This latter feature of the W-Bk unit is necessary to account for contrast phenomena. The lightness of a surface, if it is to appear to be white, grey, or black, can be determined by the luminance of an adjacent surface. If the adjacent surface has a very high luminance, then a fixated surface may appear to be black. If the adjacent surface has a very low luminance, the same fixated surface may appear to be a very light grey. These contrast phenomena depend upon the inhibition of the activity of some cells in the retina by the activity of other relatively distant cells. This feature has been incorporated in the opponent process theory as developed by Hurvich and Jameson (1957).

One other feature of this theory is not shown in Figure 6–19. According to Hurvich and Jameson (1957), red light at one place in the retina elicits red activity in R-G units. Moreover, this same red activity in one place inhibits red activity elsewhere in the retina, so that the excitatory and inhibitory connections in the retina are actually more complicated than those suggested by Figure 6–19, and are responsible for *induced color* phenomena produced by simultaneous color contrast. A grey patch surrounded by a red annulus tends to look greenish. The chromatic appearance of a neutral patch when surrounded by a region of some definite hue is induced by the surround. Therefore, the appearance of hue in the neutral patch is termed an *induced color*.

Induced colors presumably are complements of the inducing colors. This can occur only if a response produced by a given color at one point in the retina inhibits activity of the same type in other portions of the retina—and for the same reason the color of a light comprised of many wavelengths has the hue of the dominant wavelength.

A narrow band of red wavelengths may be removed from a white light, leaving all the other wavelengths to stimulate the eye. Although by themselves these wavelengths can produce the impressions of yellow, blue, green, and other colors, the total collection of these wavelengths appears greenish, for the reason that the effect of the green light is no longer offset by the absent red light. Since blue and yellow lights complement each other, their chromatic effects tend to be self-canceling, and thus, the light looks like a desaturated green even though many wavelengths other than the green are present.

As we have seen, a grey patch when surrounded by a red field appears greenish. The grey patch when alone appears to be neutral in color because it reflects all wavelengths back to the eye, and yet when surrounded by a red field it appears greenish—even though it still reflects all wavelengths back to the eye. Hence we conclude that the spectrum of white light reflected to the eye by the grey patch must have a different effect on the retina when surrounded by a red field than it does when in a neutral or dark background. The effect, similar to that of removing red wavelength light from the reflected light before it reaches the eye, can be produced by a lessening of the normal red-responsiveness of the portion of the retina in which the grey patch is imaged. This lessened responsiveness could come about only if red activity in one place selectively inhibits red activity in another place. The opponent process theory is not inconsistent with such mechanisms.

One word of caution, however. From consideration of the so-called *complementary after-image* there is room for the suspicion that an induced color is actually not complementary to the inducing color. After looking at a colored patch of light on a neutral grey background, it is sometimes possible to see the after-image of the patch on a uniform grey field. This after-image is often of a different color—e.g., though the patch may have been red, the after-image is usually green. Brown (1965) has reviewed a substantial body of literature pointing to the conclusion that the color of the complementary after-image is not an exact complement to the color of the patch that produced the after-image. Thus, the after-images of yellow, orange, blue, and blue-green patches are all somewhat redder than the true (additive) complements.

If the after-images were in fact true complements of the real images, they could be explained rather easily in terms of selective fatiguing of opponent mechanisms. Thus, viewing a blue patch would result in a yellow after-image for the same reason that a blue-inducing field ostensibly produces a yellow color by contrast. However, the after-image produced by a blue patch is more orange than it would be if it were a true complement. It may also be true that induced colors are not exact complements of inducing colors. We do not know yet whether this is the case. An experiment which would help us to discover if the induced colors are additive complements of the inducing colors might make use of a small amount of light of the same wavelength as the light of the inducing field. This light could be added to the surrounded patch in a sufficient amount to make it appear a neutral grey. If this added light can cancel the color of the enclosed neutral patch, then the induced color is truly complementary to the induced color; but if some other wavelength masks the induced color more readily, then it is not a true complement. Such experiments remain to be conducted.

There is considerable physiological evidence for the existence of opponent mechanisms in color vision. Wagner, MacNichol, and Wolbarsht (1960) inserted a microelectrode in a ganglion cell in the retina of a goldfish, and then explored the retina with a small spot of light with a wavelength of 600 nm. The spot was moved from place to place and at each place was flashed on for about 500 msec. When turned on in some places it caused the activity of the ganglion cell to increase—the typical "on" response. At other places it caused the cell's activity to diminish. Also, at these same places turning it off produced an increase in the firing rate of the cell—the "off" response. At still other places the ganglion cell responded when the test spot was either turned on or turned off. This is obviously the "on-off" response.

The retinal places at which an "off" response could be elicited tended to cluster together in a region bounded by a region in which "on-off" responses could be elicited. This latter region was surrounded by locations in which only an "on" response could be elicited. A map showing the location of these responses obtained for one ganglion cell is shown in Figure 6–20. It might be inferred that if a light were placed in the "off" region, it would tend to inhibit the effect of another light in the "on" region. This would be an instance of lateral inhibition. The concentrically organized receptive field of the ganglion cell shown in Figure 6–20 is similar to the typical "off" center receptive fields discovered by Kuffler and discussed in Chapter 2.

Wagner, MacNichol, and Wolbarsht (1960) also found "on" center receptive fields in the retina of the goldfish, as well as cells with receptive fields whose organization depended upon the wavelength of the spot of light used to map them. Thus, a portion of the receptive field may elicit an "on" response when the spot of light is at 560 nm, although the same region yielded "off" responses after the termination of a spot with a wavelength of 570 nm. Thus, two wavelengths separated by as little as 10 nm can induce opposed effects in the receptive field of a ganglion cell.

In still other receptive fields of ganglion cells these investigators found more complicated effects of varying the wavelength of the stimulating light. Thus, though a 600 nm stimulus revealed the concentrically organized receptive field shown in Figure 6–20, a longer wavelength stimulus could evoke only one of the responses, either "on" or "off," no matter where the spot was placed in the receptive field. Shorter wavelength stimuli—say, less than 500 nm—produced the opposite response. Thus, short and long wavelength stimuli produced opposed effects no matter where they were localized within the receptive field of the ganglion cell. Other complexities were revealed as well when the wavelength of the stimulating light was varied.

Daw (1968) was able to show that the receptive fields of the Wagner

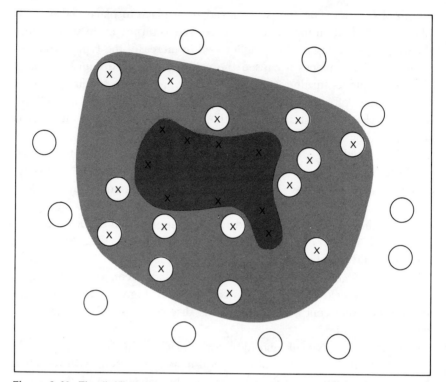

Figure 6–20. The "off"-center receptive field of a color-coded ganglion cell. The open circles represent the positions in which a spot of light produces an "on" response. The Xs indicate the positions where a spot of light produces a response only when it is turned off. Both "on" and "off" responses occur where the circles contain **Xs.** (Wagner, MacNichol and Wolbarsht, 1963)

team are larger when stimulated by colored spots of larger size. Also, "on" responses were obtained when their centers were stimulated by red light, and "off" responses when stimulated by green light. In the annular region surrounding this central portion of the receptive field the "on" response was produced by green light, and the "off" response by red light. It is obvious that these spatially distributed opponent effects could play an important role in theories of the induced color phenomena.

The responses of ganglion cells show that the outputs of a limited number of different cones interact in the intervening retinal layers. Svaetichin (1956) inserted microelectrodes into these intervening layers and detected slow-wave phenomena of several different types. He found a slow wave that varied in amplitude with the wavelength of incident light. With the microelectrode in some cells the slow wave was at a maximum at about 575 nm and had a lower amplitude when the stimulus was at either longer or shorter wavelengths. (These slow-wave or L-potentials are illustrated in Figure 6–21.) These cells respond to the luminance of the stimulus.

With the microelectrode in other cells, different types of response were observed. In one case the potential reached a maximum at about 510 nm (green) and then reached another maximum, but of opposite polarity, at about 640 nm (red). Presumably this switch in polarity of response reflects the operation of an R-G opponent mechanism. Similarly, in still another cell the slow wave reached a maximum of one polarity in the yellow portion of the spectrum and a maximum of opposite polarity when the stimulus was in the blue region of the spectrum. This represents a B-Y opponent process. The potentials reflecting opponent effects of different

Figure 6–21. Typical S-potentials. L-potentials are shown at A, a red-green C-potential at B, and a blue-yellow C-potential at C. (After Svaetichin, 1956)

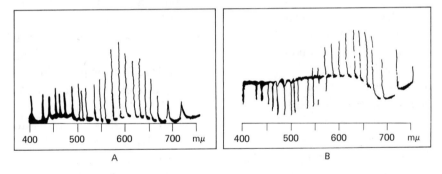

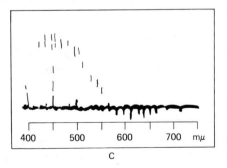

wavelengths of light are called C-*potentials*. All of these graded potentials are called S-*potentials*—for their discoverer.

There is considerable confusion in the literature as to the cells within which these S-potentials originate. Early data (such as that of MacNichol, Macpherson, and Svaetichin, 1957) suggested that L-potentials originate in the horizontal cells, and the C-potentials (chromatic responses) in bipolar cells. On the other hand, Kaneko (1971) concluded in a summary of these data that in the goldfish both the luminosity and chromatic S-potentials originate in horizontal cells at different levels within the retina.

Horizontal cells have very large receptive fields, larger in fact than the areas filled by their dendrites. Kaneko suggested that a direct electrical influence is exerted on one such cell by neighboring horizontal cells. It is not clear how the graded potentials of horizontal cells affect the spike outputs of the ganglion cells. Comparable data are not available from primates, and the fish retina may not resemble the mechanism underlying human color vision.

As we go farther upstream in the nervous system to the lateral geniculate nucleus, it is still possible to see signs of opponent process. DeValois and his coworkers (DeValois, 1960; DeValois, Abramov, and Jacobs, 1966; DeValois and Jacobs, 1968) investigated the response characteristics of cells in the lateral geniculate nucleus (LGN) of the macaque monkey. Behavioral studies had revealed that the color sensitivity of the macaque is not unlike that of the human. For this reason the physiological recordings of DeValois and his associates are particularly relevant to our present topic.

About 75 per cent of the cells in the macaque's LGN are sensitive to color. These color-sensitive cells are generally divided into two classes. The spontaneous firing rates of cells in one class may either increase or decrease when the retina of the animal is stimulated with lights of different wavelength. Thus, a red light applied to the retina may result in an increase in the firing rate of a cell, and a green light would reduce the firing rate of the same cell. Such cells are called "opponent" cells.

The stimulus wavelength capable of evoking a change in the firing rate of a unit differed from unit to unit. Although there were no very sharp divisions between different types of opponent cells, by averaging across many cells it was discovered that there is a statistical separation of cells into four groups. In one of such group a light ranging in wavelength from about 600 nm to 680 nm ("red") caused an increase in the spontaneous rate of firing of an average cell, and a light whose wavelength was shorter than about 590 nm would inhibit the spontaneous firing of this same unit. Although a very broad spectrum of wavelengths could produce a substantial inhibitory effect, the phenomenon appears to be strongest when the stimulus is at about 540 nm ("green"). A second group of cells operated in a complementary manner—i.e., instead of being excited, such units were inhibited by "red" light, yet these same units were excited by "green" light. A third group of cells was inhibited by light from the blue end of the spectrum, though these same units were excited by light ranging in wavelength from about 520 nm to 670 nm. Thus, both green and red lights had an excitatory effect on these units. As before, the fourth group of cells was affected oppositely by these same wavelengths.

It would appear from these results that there are opponent mechanisms in the primate visual system. Still, the traditional opponent process theory does not require the degree of diversity found by DeValois. This variability from one "opponent" cell to another may have significance for future theories of color vision.

The second class of cells discovered in the LGN by DeValois and his coworkers included so-called "non-opponent" cells. About half these cells experienced an increase in firing rate when stimulated by any wavelength of light, and half was inhibited by such stimulation. These non-opponent units are very broadly tuned—i.e., light from a very broad band of wavelengths can affect them. This suggests that the non-opponent units are being excited by more than one type of cone. Thus, the non-opponent units may correspond to the luminosity detectors of Hurvich and Jameson's opponent-process theory.

EFFECTS OF LUMINANCE AND CONTRAST

The picture that has emerged thus far indicates that there are three cone pigments in addition to the rod pigment in the human eye. The outputs of the cones combine to produce both luminosity and opponent responses in the retina and in the LGN. All this suggests that the luminosity mechanism is relatively independent of the chromaticity mechanism. The relation between these mechanisms must now be considered.

As the luminance of a colored stimulus is increased, its apparent hue may undergo a change. With increasing luminance monochromatic reds and yellow-greens become yellower in appearance. Blue-greens, on the other hand, become bluer in appearance. These hue shifts are instances of the *Bezold-Brücke effect*. The numerous theories proposed to explain the Bezold-Brücke phenomenon have been reviewed in a paper by Coren and Keith (1970). As the authors conclude, the phenomenon originates in the neural structures of the visual system and not in the pigments of the cones.

One neural theory of the Bezold-Brücke effect stems from the opponent-process theory (Hurvich and Jameson, 1955), according to which the red-green system has a lower threshold than does the blue-yellow system. Thus, at very low light levels an observer is more likely to discriminate correctly between red and green than he is between blue and yellow. As the luminance of the stimulus is increased, however, the yellow-blue system's responsiveness increases at a faster rate than that of the red-green system. Thus, at very high luminance levels the yellow-blue system is responding more to the same amount of light than is the red-green system. As a result, a green light, which affects both the red-green and the yellow-blue systems, is exciting the yellow-blue system more than it is the red-green system, and as such appears more yellow than it does at lower luminance levels.

As luminance is raised still higher, all colors become less pure in appearance. This whitening process may be attributed to the saturation of all systems, since even when a monochromatic light is used, if it is intense enough it will bleach all pigments and excite all chromaticity mechanisms. This produces the same effect on the system as does white light, which also excites all the mechanisms, so that even a deep blue light can be made to appear white. These effects of luminance on the appearance of a color indicate that there are bound to be departures from Grassman's laws when luminance is high enough. As already indicated, however, colors preserve their appearances over a fairly wide range of luminance levels.

The appearance of a color can be affected by contrast phenomena as well as by luminance. We have already seen that a grey patch may appear to be colored when surrounded by a chromatic background. A different effect may occur when a patch of one color is surrounded by a field of white light. If the surrounded patch is of constant luminance, its appearance may be changed dramatically merely by altering the luminance of the white surround.

If an orange test spot is surrounded by a white field, the orange spot may change in two different ways, depending upon the change in luminance of the surround. With a very high luminance in the surround and a relative low luminance of the test spot, the orange spot may appear to be brown in color. Also, if the surround were now made low in luminance, the spot could appear to be a pastel shade of orange. Thus, the shades and tints of the colors are produced by the interaction of the patch of color with its surrounding field. It is believed that lateral inhibition produces this effect.

If a white surrounding field has more light energy than the surrounded field, predictably it will serve to inhibit the responsiveness of the neurons excited by the patch, and this in turn will reduce the effect of the patch on the central nervous system—thereby changing the lightness of the patch. This suggests that the luminosity mechanism could inhibit chromatic mechanisms.

The second effect of the surrounding field on the patch is to cause its color to change. As Coren and Keith (1970) demonstrated, shifts similar to those encountered in the Bezold-Brücke effect can be produced by changing the luminance surrounding a test patch instead of changing the luminance of the test patch itself. Thus, a green patch surrounded by a field of white light will be matched to a stimulus that is slightly bluer than when it is not surrounded by an induction field at all. Since the magnitude of this color shift is less when the surrounding field has a low luminance, Coren and Keith concluded that the Bezold-Brücke effect has a neural locus.

One word of caution: When a patch of light is imaged on the retina, some light is reflected by the retina and scatters about inside the eyeball, so that the effect of a light stimulus is not limited to the place on which an image is formed. This scattered light is known as *intraocular stray light*. In the Coren and Keith experiment the intraocular stray light from the surround could serve to desaturate the monochromatic stimulus. It may well be that this desaturation is necessary to the production of shades and tints by contrast, as we shall understand when we reconsider the color solid.

The color solid depicted in Figure 6–2 shows that the range of possible shades and tints is larger with desaturated colors than it is with fully saturated colors. According to the color solid, while a pure spectral blue can never appear to be navy blue or as a baby-blue tint, a desaturated blue can have any of a wide range of such shades and tints. Of course the color solid is not a precise model of how colors are perceived, and yet it does suggest that pure colors do not show the same range of contrast-induced phenomena as do impure or desaturated colors.

To be more explicit: as we saw in Chapter 5, a constant white light surrounded by another white light of a variable luminance can be made to appear white, grey, or black, depending upon the luminance of its surround. Thus, if the surround has a very high luminance relative to the constant enclosed patch, the patch may look black. If the luminance difference between the surround and the enclosed patch is reversed, so that now the patch is brighter than the surround, then the patch may appear to be white, and intermediate greys may also be produced. This means that points on the black-white axis of the color solid are determined by simultaneous brightness contrast.

It is reasonable to assume that the shades and tints of colors are also produced by contrast. Now, if a pure spectral color does not show the same range of shades and tints, it may be assumed also that contrast of luminance between a spectral color and its background will not have so pronounced an effect as it does between a relatively desaturated color and its background. Thus, lateral inhibition of one monochromatic patch by its surround may differ in an important way from lateral inhibition of a less pure patch and its surround. This is a subject that needs further investigation.

A border will appear between two adjacent patches of light if the patches differ sufficiently in luminance. If the adjacent patches are of equal luminance, but different color, one might ask whether borders will still appear. Now, it has been known for some time (Koffka, 1935) that the appearance of a border between two adjacent monochromatic patches matched for brightness depends upon the difference in the stimuli's wavelength. Thus, a yellow patch and a yellow-green patch will not have a perceptible border dividing them when they are equated for brightness; but a red patch and a green patch will always have a perceptible, if somewhat ill-defined, border. Thus, one might want to argue that insofar as borders are determined by lateral inhibition, there must be such an inhibitory process between patches of the same luminance but of different color.

There are two reasons for questioning this conclusion. For one thing, the sensitivity of the eye to different colors is not uniform; e.g., a red patch in one place may appear to be brighter than the same red patch elsewhere. Therefore, when a red patch and a green patch are equated for brightness, the equation may be good in the center of the eye but not quite accurate somewhat off to one side of the central fovea. Small eye movements would reveal these differences in brightness, and thereby reveal also a luminance-dependent border.

The second reason for disputing the idea that pure chromatic borders exist flows from the fact that different spectral lights may affect partially independent sets of cones. Thus, a red light may largely affect red-sensitive cones, a green light, green-sensitive cones. Since these two systems are partially independent, the inherent noise in each system will fluctuate independently. This noise adds to the levels of excitation produced by the stimuli. Since noise is, by definition, a random process, the level of activity in the red-sensitive system will fluctuate independently of the level of activity in the green-sensitive system, and these fluctuations could make it physically impossible to attain full equality between the brightnesses of the red and the green stimuli. So it is that borders between colors may be an inevitable consequence of random fluctuations of independent color-sensitive systems, and we have still other reasons to doubt that lateral inhibition among colored lights is of the same nature as lateral inhibition among desaturated or white lights. Of course, very intense monochromatic sources simulate the effects of white light, and we may well expect the achromatic system to predominate. From these considerations, as well as those to be taken up in the next section of this chapter, it is apparent that substantial research is needed to clarify the nature of the effects of lateral interaction among colored stimuli.

LAND'S RETINEX THEORY

Contrast phenomena occur only when there is more than one luminance or color in the visual field. In view of the complexity of lateral connections in the visual system, it is well worth the effort to explore the effects of stimulus complexity on the perception of color.

If a single small patch of light were made up by superimposing green and red light, the amounts of these two lights would determine the color of the patch. If the green and red lights were properly balanced, their joint effect would be that of a neutral light, but if the red light predominated, then the joint effect would be that of a desaturated pinkish light. It is from experiments with such simple stimuli that the laws of color mixture were formulated. Do these same laws apply in the complex scenes of daily life? As we move about in the world, the scenes we see are randomly related to each other. At one instant of time we may view a bowl of fruit containing oranges, red apples, and yellow bananas. At another instant we may look at a television screen and see a blue stream in green woodland. Edwin Land (1959) has suggested that such random-icity and complexity have a strong effect on color perception.

Land took black and white photographs of a scene. One photograph was taken through a red filter, and the resulting picture contained an array of black, white, and grey objects. If an object in the scene reflected large amounts of red light, it appeared white in the photograph; but if it reflected very little red light, then it might appear black in the photo-graph. The other picture, taken through a blue-green filter, produced a black and white photograph as well, but the whiteness or blackness of an object in the photograph was not necessarily the same as that in the first photograph. Thus, an object reflecting red light might appear as black in this second picture, and a green object might appear as white. A white object would appear to be white in both photographs.

Land's next step was to project both black and white photographs so that they were in registration on a projection screen. A red filter was placed in front of the projector containing the slide made through a red filter, and a green filter was placed in front of the second projector. The resulting image contained a wide range of colors—which was not terribly surprising. A mixture of two colors in different amounts can lead to the perception of many other intermediate wavelength colors. The composite picture in this case contained blue colors as well, however. This is surpris-ing since a mixture of red and green does not normally produce the im-pression of blue.

Other results even more surprising were obtained. Using the same two black and white pictures, Land simply removed the green filter from one of the projectors, leaving the red filter in place. This too led to the perception of a wide gamut of colors.

Finally, one projector—the one containing the picture taken through a red filter—was covered by a yellow filter, and the other projector, by a filter that also passed yellow light but at a somewhat shorter wavelength. These two yellow-appearing records when superimposed on a screen led also to the perception of a wide range of colors, among them unsaturated reds, greys, yellows, oranges, greens, blues, blacks, and others. This result cannot be explained solely in terms of the classical rules of color mixture.

The results reported by Land were analyzed by several authors. Both Walls (1960) and Judd (1960) came to the conclusion that many of the colors in Land's displays can be accounted for in terms of mechanisms of color contrast together with the classical rules of color mixture. A direct experimental evaluation of these positions appears to be lacking, and Land (1964) disagrees with their conclusion. His own theory, designed to account for these phenomena, may deserve more attention than it has received. He postulates the existence of three separate systems, called *retinexes*. Each retinex contains a representation of all objects in the visual field: one is predominantly responsive to long wavelength light, another to wavelengths from the middle of the spectrum, and the third to short wavelength light. Thus there are built up in the central nervous system three independent representations of the scene, and they are analogous to black and white pictures taken through three different filters. In the long-wavelength retinex, red objects in the scene produce more activity than either blue or green objects. In the middle-wavelength retinex green objects produce more activity, and blue objects produce more activity in the short-wavelength retinex. According to Land, color perception depends upon the comparison of the "lightnesses" of corresponding regions in the three retinexes.

If a scene containing many objects of different color is bathed in red light, the objects in this scene will have lightnesses determined by many complex factors. Thus, e.g., a red apple in the scene would be very light relative to a green surround, since it reflects more of the red light than does the surrounding, although another even more highly reflective red object placed near the apple could cause the apple to appear less light. Hence we see that contrast as well as reflectance can determine the lightness of any region in the scene. As Land in fact reports, if the light bathing the scene were graded so that at one edge relatively little light reached the scene while much more light reached the other edge of the scene, the relative lightnesses of the objects would be unaffected, since the contrast relations within local regions of the scene would be preserved. Thus, the absolute amount of red light reflected by any point on the scene does not determine the place of that same region on the scale of lightnesses of the entire scene. It is the place on the scale of lightnesses that defines the value of an object within its retinex.

If the same scene is bathed in green light, objects that had a high lightness value in the red illumination may now have a low lightness value; that is to say, objects imaged in the green or middle retinex would have rank orders of lightness differing from the rank orders in the red retinex. The same would be true of the blue or short-wavelength retinex. According to Land, it is the lightness values or rank orders as determined within each retinex that define the color of an object. Thus, rather than considering only the traditional tristimulus values or luminance as determinants of the result of color mixture, Land would employ context-determined lightness values. If these values are the same in all retinexes, the object will have a neutral color. An imbalance in the contributions from the retinexes would produce chromatic colors, as in the traditional color-mixing process. Thus, rather than regard light merely as energy, Land would utilize lightness, which is determined by complex lateral interactions within each retinex, as a determinant of color.

The retinex theory is similar in many ways to the Young-Helmholtz theory and it is really not incompatible with the opponent-process theory. When dealing with mixtures in isolated patches of colored lights, the retinex theory would make the same predictions. It departs from the more traditional approach in that it substitutes lightness for stimulus energy. Moreover, since the lightness of a patch can differ in the different retinexes, the theory would preclude strong lateral inhibition of a patch of one color, which excites one of the retinexes strongly, and an adjacent patch of another very different color. In this the theory would be consistent with our observation that there are no shades and tints of pure colors, whereas desaturated colors do have a wide range of shades and tints. Desaturated colors affect all the retinexes in Land's theory.

Land's two-color demonstrations can be explained by the retinex theory. A black and white picture bathed in red light affects the red retinex, and a particularly bright object in this picture will have a high rank order within the red retinex. A similar picture, one originally taken through a green filter, will excite the red, green, and blue retinexes. The sum of the activity produced by this picture and the activity produced by the red picture in the red retinex produces a pattern of lightnesses differing from the pattern of lightnesses in both the blue and the green retinexes. Objects in the red retinex will have rank orders differing from the rank orders they have in the middle and short wave retinexes. It is these differences that determine the colors. The details of the process of computing the colors—an operation analogous to the multiplication of corresponding regions in the retinexes—have never been spelled out: Land refers simply to a correlation or comparing of the retinexes. The fact is, blue-greens will appear when a region in the short- and middle-wave retinexes has a high rank order of lightness and when the corresponding region in the red retinex has a low rank order. If the region in the red or long-wave retinex has a high rank order, while the corresponding region in the other two retinexes has a low rank order, then it will appear reddish in color.

When the same two pictures are projected through sharp yellow filters, the picture bathed in longer wavelength yellow light will have a stronger effect on the long-wave retinex than on the middle- or short-wave retinexes. Similarly, the picture bathed in shorter wavelength yellow light will have a stronger effect on the middle-wave retinex than it does on the long- or short-wave retinexes. Thus, high rank-order regions in this retinex may appear to be of a desaturated blue color if the corresponding region in the longer wavelength picture has a low rank order.

There is an obvious need for research to test some of these ideas in a precise quantitative manner. While it may well be that induction phenomena can explain these effects, direct tests have yet to be conducted. The idea that lightness plays a role in color mixture in complex scenes is suggestive of many experiments and of interesting neurophysiological mechanisms.

THE NEURAL CODE FOR COLOR

In a very real sense there are no theories of color vision. All the theories and partial theories we have considered are truly theories of color mixture. No one is explicit about the reasons a particular type of excitation leads to the perception of a particular color. The world of the neurophysiologist is devoid of sensations of color, warmth, and pleasure, and simply describes neural correlates of colors and of other experiences. I could, for example, place an electrode in your brain while exposing your eye to red light, and conceivably I could pick up some neural activity differing from the neural activity produced by, say, green light. Nevertheless, the electrical activity that I, as an experimenter, can experience, is not the redness or greenness that you as a subject can experience.

In the older psychology of the nineteenth century the colors were sensations—mental events existing in a mental domain, they were simply parallel to neural events; and for that reason many thinkers were explicitly psychophysical parallelists. Today we are still parallelists, although we rarely admit it. Rather than attempting to solve this great philosophical problem, most contemporary psychologists are satisfied with the identification of neural events that are uniquely related to reported experiences. Thus, the bleaching of different pigments in different amounts is uniquely related to color experiences under laboratory conditions; yet, no one is willing to say that the experience of a color depends solely upon the bleaching of pigments. The tendency is to seek neural events at ever higher centers of the nervous system, so that it is assumed that information about color is preserved at all levels of the nervous system. We are just beginning to consider how this information finally becomes linked to other events, such as information about form or shape. Although apples are both round and red, we are reluctant to consider how these dimensions of experience become integrated. Is there a final common path in which all neural events interact with each other? This question poses many profound problems, and we shall discuss them later. For the present, let us simply consider how information about color is transmitted to the brain.

There are only about one million fibers going from the retina to the LGN, and they must carry information about position, shape, size, texture, brightness, and color. Clearly, this limited channel can carry the information only if it is encoded. It is only by means of unique codes that these dimensions of perception can be separated from each other after traversing a common path. There is no conclusive or even fully convincing theory as to the nature of these codes. In the area of color perception only two theories have been seriously entertained. In one theory, different colors excite different groups of fibers, and so colors are identified by the pathways in which activity is evoked. This, of course, is a version of the doctrine of specific nerve energies, and the code is purely anatomical: there are "red" fibers, "green" fibers, and so on. The problem with this view, however, is that we do not even know whether it is feasible.

It is possible that information about color is carried in fibers that carry information about brightness and shape as well; and there is in fact very good evidence that contour information and color information are closely interlinked in the nervous system (see Chapter 13). Moreover, when one considers the diversity of information that must get to the brain, and the fact that so much information has to get through the bottleneck of the optic nerve, a strict "place theory" of color-coding is probably unacceptable. Nevertheless, the channel capacities of the various pathways involved in perception must be compared with the information actually received by the brain. This has not yet been studied.

The second theory, first proposed by Troland (1921), holds that different colors produce different temporal patterns of nervous activity, but we know very little about how neural events may be encoded over time. One of the phenomena leading to the proposition that colors are

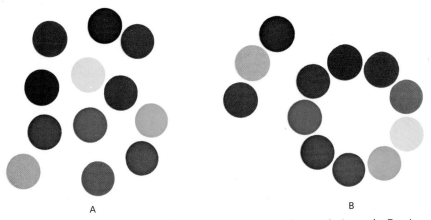

A   B

Figure 6–1. A set of colored chips (A) would be arranged as a circle, as in B, when they are ordered in terms of their similarity. Pink, navy blue, and brown do not fit into the circle.

Figure 6–11. The standard chromaticity diagram.

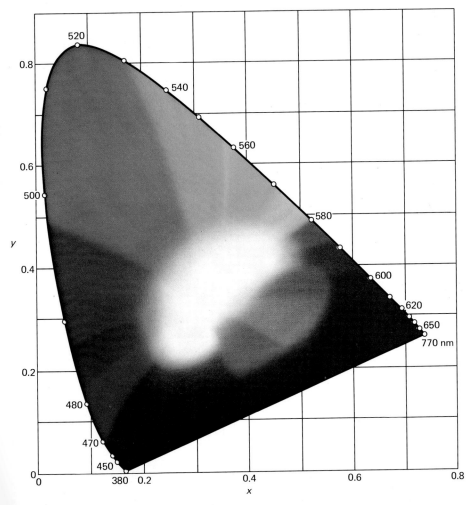

Figure 7–4. Holy Family (15th C.) by Michelangelo Buonarroti
(with permission of the Uffizi Gallery).

Figure 8–4. A typical anaglyph. Stereopsis may be obtained when a red filter is
placed over one eye and a green filter over the other eye. Colored acetate or cello-
phane may be used as filters.

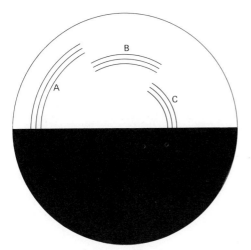

Figure 6–22. Benham's disc.

encoded as temporally varying neural patterns is that of the subjective colors—colors produced by temporally varying patterns of white light, possibly by means of the famous Benham's disc (one version of it is shown in Figure 6–22). When this disc is rotated in a clockwise direction at a rate of from 5 to 10 rps, the lines labeled A will appear bluish, the lines labeled B greenish, and the lines labeled C reddish. With counterclockwise rotation the order of the colors is reversed. The colors appear even though the disc is comprised of black lines on a white and black surface. There have been reports of these colors even when the disc is illuminated with monochromatic light (Cohen and Gordon, 1949). The phenomenon is clearly not due to the bleaching of color pigments in different amounts, as in normal color perception. It has been suggested that the complex flickering patterns set up by the different patterns of light and dark produce time-varying activity in the optic nerve and that this is similar to the activity set up by the photoreceptors when stimulated by colored lights (Fry, 1945).

Festinger, Allyn, and White (1971) investigated the possibility of producing subjective colors with stationary flickering lights. In one of their experiments they utilized a light that could have one of several temporal wave shapes, as illustrated in Figure 6–23. The wave shapes employed were produced by varying the amount of light energy emitted as a function of time by a source known as a glow-modulator tube. The

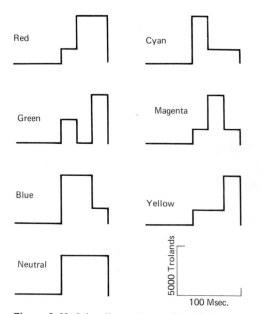

Figure 6–23. Stimuli used in an attempt to produce subjective colors with flickering stationary lights. Retinal illuminance was varied with respect to time in imitation of similar changes in luminance at a point on Benham's disc. The waveshapes on the left correspond to the changes in luminance that occur over time and produce the colors on Benham's disc. The waveshapes on the right are the result of adding waveshapes on the left and then adjusting their amplitudes to produce color "mixtures." (After Festinger, Allyn, and White, 1971)

shapes on the left side of the figure were selected by analyzing the way in which the amount of light reflected from the vicinity of one of the lines on Benham's disc varied over time. Since these time-variations in light are associated with particular colors, it was assumed that similar variations of light emitted by the glow modulator tube would produce the same colors. The wave shapes on the right side of Figure 6–23 are normalized composites of the wave shapes on the left. These composite wave shapes were designed to produce effects of color mixtures. Thus, the wave shape labeled "yellow" is a normalized composite of the "green" and the "red" wave shapes.

While these simple stimuli were not sufficient to produce reliable color impressions, colors were perceived when the stimuli were presented in a background flickering on and off in a square-wave fashion, and in step with the central stimulus. Moreover, these colors could be matched by a true monochromatic source when the source was desaturated with white light. The wave shapes designed to produce a red color were matched consistently with a somewhat reddish matching stimulus. The green and the blue wave shapes also tended to be matched with corresponding colors. The cyan signal, however, did not produce a response differing significantly from neutral light; and the magenta signal led to considerable intersubject variability. In any case, colors could be produced by different time-varying patterns of light stimulation.

The role of the square-wave background in producing these colors has also been explored. Festinger *et al.* reasoned that the square-wave background could, by lateral inhibition, alter the effective intensity of their experimental wave shapes at different points in time, depending upon the relative energies of the background and test stimulus at each point in time. From this they deduced the effective stimulus energy at different temporal points on the wave shapes. This enabled them to design new wave shapes which, they thought, would enable them to get colors without a flickering background (see Figure 6–24). The blue, green, and red signals did produce good reliable colors. Yellow was not

Figure 6–24. Modified waveshapes used to produce flicker colors. (From Festinger, Allyn, and White, 1971)

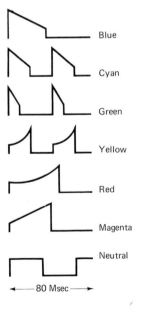

Blue

Cyan

Green

Yellow

Red

Magenta

Neutral

◄──── 80 Msec ────►

consistently different from neutral, however; and although color matches were obtained to the remaining signals, there was considerable variability in their results. These experimenters concluded that although they cannot yet specify a stimulus that would generate neural activity identical to that generated by monochromatic colors, it may be possible to define and utilize the hypothetical temporal code.

An alternative explanation has been offered for the occurrence of subjective colors—that of Pieron (1923), who suggested that the different photo pigments have a different time constant. Thus, a sharply rising flash of light might activate the red system first, and the green and the blue systems later. Festinger *et al.* have argued convincingly that the time constants suggested by Pieron cannot account for color perception in the Benham disc when one considers the temporal flicker parameters that actually produce the colors.

If colors are encoded by means of time-varying neural activity, we may have in hand an explanation for one very puzzling fact. It has already been noted that 75 per cent of the LGN cells are color-responsive. In the cerebral cortex of the macaque monkey, however, there seem to be few if any cells that are also selectively color-responsive. Most cortical cells respond to both luminance and color, so that color identity may be lost. A recent paper by Hepler (1973) raised the question, "Where have all the colors gone?" This is indeed a problem for a straightforward anatomical or place theory of color-coding. For if representations of colors are preserved in anatomically distinct channels, it should be possible to find many color-specific cells in the visual cortex of the primate brain. Of course, it is quite possible that future research will reveal many such cells, since there are vast numbers of cells in the cortex and relatively few have been investigated. It is still possible, however, that there is a temporal encoding of color. Temporal encoding would allow the same pathways to carry information about color as well as luminance. It is important that patterns of activity of neurons over time be studied when the visual pathways are stimulated by lights of different wavelength and energy.

III

space perception

7

the cues to depth

Depth perception is one of the classic problems of psychology. The first writers on perception were concerned with the way the perceiver comes to experience depth even though the retinal image is flat. There is no single solution to this problem. An understanding of how we perceive objects as solid and as arranged in depth requires us to consider the kinds of information we use. Some—but not all—of this information is contained within the stationary retinal image. This chapter describes the information or *cues* utilized by an observer in perceiving depth. It also discusses some of the theories designed to explain how the information is utilized in generating depth perception.

PICTORIAL CUES

The artists of the Western world strove for many centuries to create pictures conveying the impression of depth. In normal life we see things projected in three dimensions, and yet, as we all know, the untrained artist is usually unsuccessful in conveying the same impression with his pencil. As Leonardo da Vinci noted, it is not possible to get the view as seen by two eyes down on paper in a single picture (Boring, 1942). Yet even when we close one eye, the world still has a strong depthful quality. It was only in the fifteenth century that painters learned the techniques basic to representing such "monocular" depth on canvas—the result of the slow realization that certain attributes of scenes convey the impression that some objects are nearer the observer than others.

Figure 7–1. **Rucellai Madonna** (13th C.) by Duccio di Buoninsegna (with permission of the Uffizi Gallery, Florence)

The thirteenth-century Madonnas of Cimabue and Duccio, for example, show little concern for the three-dimensional arrangement of people and objects. The Byzantine style of such paintings conveys the impression of flatness, in which all objects are essentially in the same plane (Fig. 7–1). The decorative angels are usually smaller than the Madonna, but this is more a matter of relative importance than it is of relative closeness or nearness. A few years later, however, Giotto in his *Madonna Enthroned* managed to convey the impression that some of the figures were clearly behind other figures. This he did by letting some figures obscure portions of the others—a use of the so-called cue of interposition. The sizes of the figures, however, were determined more by religious rank rather than by geometrical considerations.

It was not until the mid-fifteenth century that a conscious attempt to represent depth in paintings was discernible. This accompanied the accelerating secularization of art: paintings were made more for decoration and embellishment as such than as religious expression. The rise of the merchant princes, who supported the arts by purchasing paintings and sculpture for the glorious palaces of the Italian Renaissance, was instrumental in this development. According to Bernard Berenson (1957), patrons sought their own immortality by building grand structures and commissioning paintings of themselves to display therein. I suggest that one factor in the development of three-dimensional space in painting was the need for a more adequate and lifelike representation of those who paid for the paintings. In addition to complex factors such as the rise of empirical science and the growing awareness of nature, painters had to create lifelike images of their patrons.

Be that as it may, even in the fifteenth century Paolo Uccello could not create perfectly satisfactory depth in his pictures, as we see in Figure 7–2, a reproduction of his *Battle of San Romano,* in the Uffizi Gallery in Florence. The sense of compressed space conveyed by this picture is produced in part by the awkwardness of Uccello's methods for simulating distance information. The hares running in the background are much too large, as are the soldiers in the field, who because of their size seem so close to a raging battle and yet remain untouched by it, when it was probably the artist's intention to represent them as far removed from combat. But in this same century we find many artists utilizing the background of portraits to present sweeping vistas that recede toward a distant horizon. Piero della Francesca (see his portrait of Federico de Montefeltro, Figure 7–3), Sandro Botticelli, and, a little later, even Leonardo

Figure 7–2. **Battle of San Romano** (15th C.) by Paolo Uccello (with permission of the Uffizi Gallery)

Figure 7–3. **Federico de Montefeltro** (15th C.) by Piero della Francesca (with permission of the Uffizi Gallery)

himself favored this fashionable method of filling space. It was these expanding backgrounds that gave the first compelling impression of depth in paintings.

In the later fifteenth and early sixteenth century we see an extremely rapid increase of sophistication in representing space. The relatively primitive use of space in Piero's portrait was improved upon by many painters, some of them contemporaries of Piero. Michelangelo, who was a young man when Piero died in 1492, painted a Holy Family (Fig. 7–4, facing p. 207) which I consider one of the finest examples of space representation in the history of painting. When we view the picture with one eye, the left arm of the Virgin reaches out of the frame. The Child is a marvelously solid figure. The colors in the foreground are rich, and the contours sharp. The colors in the background fade and verge toward the blue end of the spectrum. The contours of objects become blurred. Light and shade, texture, interposition, perspective, and relative size are all manipulated with sensitivity and knowledge. Though there are more formal pictures exhibiting all these same properties in views of walls, streets, and landscapes, I chose this one because of its extraordinary naturalness. As any art student can tell us, it is a great accomplishment to achieve the true depthful appearance of human figures. It is possible only with awareness of what is involved in creating the impression of depth.

The point is that the sources of information about depth in a static scene are not evident to the casual observer, and yet without an accurate representation of these sources the picture will either go flat or appear distorted, as in the *Battle of San Romano*. These sources of information about depth are called the pictorial cues. They were discovered, not seen; their discovery required several centuries, and, as we have hinted, they must be rediscovered by every art student.

Nearly all the so-called pictorial cues to depth were discovered by the artists. The only contribution of psychologists was to formalize the notion that there are distinctive sources of information about depth; and, as we shall see, they did not do this very well. It is only in recent years, particularly in the important work of James Gibson (1950), that any real progress has been made in developing what the Renaissance gave us with regard to pictorial cues.

What are these pictorial cues? The most important of them appears to be what the artist has labeled perspective. I suspect that it is the most important because it lends itself to formalization and reduction to some very basic and teachable concepts.

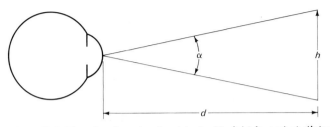

Figure 7–5. The visual angle. An object of height **h,** and at distance **d** from the eye, subtends an angle α.

Perspective. A proper understanding of perspective first requires mastery of the concept of the visual angle—a measure of the size of an object's image on the retina. As shown in Figure 7–5, if an object is at a particular distance from the eye, we may imagine two lines emanating from the eye and diverging so that they just meet the top and bottom of the object. The angle formed between two such lines is the visual angle of the object, and may be expressed either in degrees of arc or in radians. As the object draws closer (Fig. 7–6), the angle subtended by these lines becomes larger. We can have the object subtend the same angle at the eye at the closer distance if, and only if, we shrink the object or cause it to become smaller (Fig. 7–7). So, if we take a constant object—one of invariant linear size—its angular size will be inversely proportional to its distance from the eye. This is known as Euclid's law and it is basic to understanding perspective.

Figure 7–6. If the object of height **h** is moved closer to the eye, it subtends a larger angle, α_1' at the eye

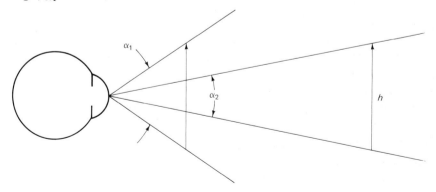

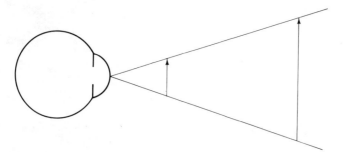

Figure 7–7. An object can subtend the same angle at the eye at different distances if its height is changed in proportion to its distance.

As we move the object in Figure 7–6 farther and farther from the eye, its visual angle will become infinitesimally smaller; but we must move it literally to infinity in order for its visual angle to be reduced to

Figure 7–8. Linear perspective. Parallel rails converge in the distance because the visual angle separating any pair of points grows smaller with their distance from the eye. The dotted lines show how the contours of other surfaces, if extended, also converge at the vanishing point on the horizon.

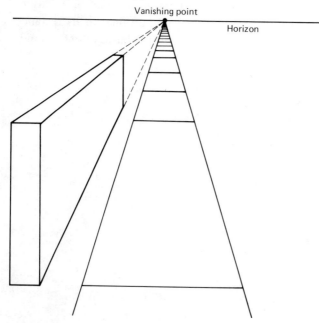

zero. Now, if one imagines the world to be a flat and endless Euclidean space, the plane of the earth's surface reaches infinity at the horizon. This is the place where the world ends—at infinity. Objects on this infinitely distant horizon vanish, to become infinitesimal points subtending a visual angle of zero. Thus, if two straight rails lying parallel to each other extend from the eye to infinity, the visual angle separating points on the two rails will gradually grow smaller, and the rails will meet at the horizon. This abstract principle underlies the convergence of parallel lines in representations of perspective. The vanishing point is at the horizon. As shown in Figure 7–8, this is the way in which two-dimensional planes are represented in perspective.

The foregoing description is of course based on the fictitious assumption that we dwell on an infinite, flat plane. For practical purposes, however, pictures drawn on this principle are virtually indistinguishable from real-life scenes, for although the surface of the earth is round, its radius of curvature is so large relative to our own size that it is practically a flat plane. Also, as we shall see when we discuss kinetic cues to depth, the nature of light and the optical apparatus of the eye make it impossible for us to distinguish points on the actual horizon from fictional points on a fictitious infinitely distant horizon.

Detail perspective. The discussion of perspective dealt primarily with what James Gibson termed linear perspective because it considers contours or lines in its treatment. Gibson (1950) made the point that textural details in the visual field obey the same laws. Thus, if we were dwelling on a sandy surface, the texture of the sand would grow finer and finer with distance from the eye: the textural density would obey Euclid's law. Gibson believed that this textural information may be a prime source of information about distance in the world. The point I wish to make is that both kinds of perspective—detail and linear—are treatable in the same mathematical manner. Both cues are abstractions from the way in which two separated points behave as they are moved toward and away from the observer. The extent to which edges give poorer information about depth than do textures is an empirical question that has yet to be studied adequately.

Size and retinal image. The discussion of Euclid's law indicated that the visual angle is a measure of the size of the retinal image of the object of regard. If the object is familiar and is placed at a distance from the observer different from that of another similar object, then its image size will differ proportionately. It was presumed by Ittleson (1951) that this difference in image size produces the impression that the two similar objects are at different distances. This suggests that somehow the observer achieves an awareness of relative image size *per se* as opposed to relative object size. This notion has great importance for the theory of size perception, and, for example, led Gogel, Hartman, and Harker (1957) to make a distinction between absolute distance and relative distance.

Absolute distance refers to the distance between the observer and an object—i.e., the observer is at point zero, and objects are particular linear distances from point zero. Relative distance refers to the distance between objects independent of the distance from the observer to one of the objects. Utilizing this distinction, Gogel *et al.* found that when the image size of a familiar object was made progressively smaller from one judgment to the next, the judged distance to the object varied in the appropriate direction. In effect, as the image became smaller the observer judged its distance to have become relatively greater. It was concluded by the investigators that relative distance may be given by relative image size where the compared sizes were an image in present time and the memory for the image at an earlier time.

This result is consistent with results reported by Epstein and Baratz (1964), who observed that differences in image size yield judgments of differences in distance (relative distance) when the objects being judged were pairs of familiar objects with familiar linear sizes. But when they trained subjects to associate the distances of nonsense figures with different colors, so that a red figure, say, was always more distant than a blue figure, subsequent tests failed to reveal an effect of image size on the judged distances of these figures. This, however, is not a critical proof that image size is an ineffective cue, since the dimensions along which familiarity may operate in such a situation have never been studied.

In one sense all these cues—relative size, detail perspective, and linear perspective—are partially redundant, and reflect the common operating principle of Euclid's law. Static pictures must show objects growing smaller as they recede into the distance, or else the distance impression is less strong. Moreover, these cues may well be only relative distance cues, for they do not of themselves allow one to judge the absolute distance to an object. Absolute distance may be given pictorially only if the observer apprehends directly the angular size of the object and, at the same time, has information about the linear size of the object. He must also have some standard of what the angular size of an object having a specific linear extent would be at various distances. This is an imposing requirement. It is more parsimonious to assume that the Euclidean pictorial cues described above are cues to relative distance.

In addition to the Euclidean cues we must also consider four other cues often employed by artists. These do not fall into the Euclidean category at all and hence are not necessarily redundant sources of information.

Aerial perspective. As objects become more and more distant they tend to lose their coloration and become predominantly bluish in appearance. In addition, atmospheric haze tends to make the object's contours more blurred. This cue was employed by artists and is evident in the painting by Michelangelo reproduced in Figure 7–4. Though this is an obviously useful means for conveying impressions of great distance, it is probably unimportant for most aspects of living.

Relative brightness. As we saw in Chapter 2, the luminance of an object depends upon the intensity of the light falling upon it and also upon its own reflectance. A lump of coal, e.g., has very little reflectance: it absorbs most of the light incident upon its surface and reflects a small percentage of that light back to the eye of an observer. If the light falling upon the lump of coal were very intense, then the coal could have a high luminance. A piece of white paper, on the other hand, reflects a relatively high percentage of the light falling upon it to the observer's eye. Hence, relatively less light need fall upon the paper to yield the same amount of luminance as the piece of coal.

The amount of light falling upon an object is a function of the distance between the object and a source of light. If the source is a luminous point, the light falling upon the object obeys the inverse-square law—i.e., the intensity of the incident light is inversely proportional to the square of the distance between the object and the source. Hence the distance between the object and the source is important in determining the luminance of the object. As was noted in Chapter 2, luminance is independent of the distance between an object and the eye. Yet as the object is moved toward and away from a source of light—say, a light bulb or a flickering candle flame—the amount of light falling upon it is changed. If both the observer and a small source of light remains fixed in space, then the object will come to have less luminance as it draws away from the light

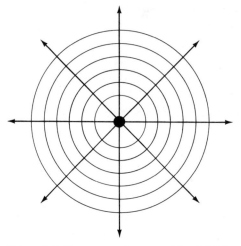

Figure 7–9. The wave and ray models of light.

source. This is a potential source of information about relative distance. An object near the campfire might look bright while a similar object outside the more intense circle of light immediately around the fire would look very dim.

Moving an object toward and away from an observer does not change significantly its distance from the sun. Hence, in bright daylight, unless the object falls into a shadow, its luminance is constant over a wide range of distances. As the distances become very large, however, the particles suspended in the atmosphere act to attenuate the amount of light reaching the eye of the observer. At large distances, moreover, the contrast between the object and its background becomes attenuated and this serves to reduce the visibility of the object. Such effects of large distances are incorporated in the cue of aerial perspective and may by themselves produce relative luminance differences that can be informative about distance.

While testing the idea that brightness differences might serve as cues to depth differences, Ittleson (1960) found that the brighter of two otherwise identical objects viewed in a dark space was reported as nearer than the dimmer object.

Light and shade. Light may be thought of as waves emanating from a luminous source, or, alternatively, as rays traveling in straight lines from their source (see Figure 7–9). These two models—the ray and the wave—are essentially equivalent in certain applications, particularly when tracing the effects of placing lenses in the path of a light beam. To go from one of these models to the other, rays are drawn normal to the tangents to the waves, so that rays emanating from a point source are seen in Figure 7–9 as diverging. If, however, the point source is very far from an illuminated object, the curvature of the wave emanating from the source is virtually planar by the time it reaches the object. The tangent to a plane wavefront is the wavefront itself, and hence all rays normal to the tangent are parallel to each other.

A point on the sun emits light rays that are virtually parallel to each other by the time they reach the earth. If an object is placed in the path of a beam of such parallel rays or collimated light (as in Figure 7–10), then, ignoring effects of diffraction, it will cast a very sharp shadow on the surface on which it stands. Since the sun is an extended source, each point on the sun may be thought of as emitting its own set of parallel rays. These beams of light are at slight angles to each other. Each beam from each point on the sun will strike an object at a slightly different angle and thereby produce its own shadow. This is illustrated in Figure 7–11, which contains representations of three beams arising from three of the infinite number of points on the sun.

Figure 7–10. An object casts a sharply defined shadow in light composed of planar wave fronts originating at an infinitely distant point source. The sharpness of the shadow is actually limited by effects of diffraction.

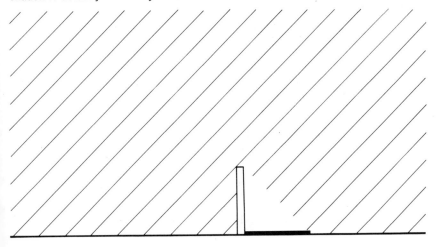

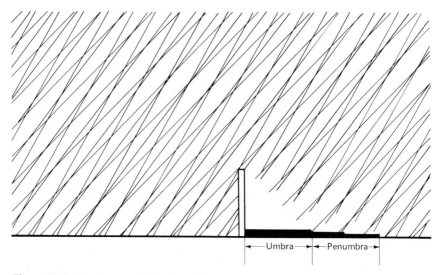

Figure 7–11. Shadows cast by three beams of light originating at three different, infinitely distant point sources.

It will be observed in the figure that the object casts three different shadows, one into each beam of light. Since all three shadows overlap in the shaded region of Figure 7–11 closest to the intruding object, that portion of the shadow is darker than more distant portions of the shadow. This region of maximum darkness is called the shadow proper, or *umbra*. More distant portions are lighter, since light from at least one point on the sun falls within the shadows cast into light from other points on the sun. Hence there is a gradually lightening portion of the shadow, and this is termed the *penumbra*. The presence of a penumbra destroys the sharpness of the shadow. Shadows are sharpest when they are cast into light originating at a point source. The penumbra grows smaller as the source grows smaller. If the penumbra is absent, then the shadow loses its shadow-like quality, and the surface appears darker. The shadow seems to be attached to the surface under those conditions.

A textured surface has small hills and valleys. These hills will cast shadows into the valleys if the incident light strikes them at any angle other than from directly above. These shadows are sufficient to give the world its textured appearance. With very coarse textures it is possible to see more definite shadows of the hills in the valleys. Craters on the moon's surface may well have a depthful appearance because of the modulation of light by shadow.

It is well known that the judicious use of shadow can give substantial relief to paintings and drawings. A picture may look very flat; yet if some shadow is added, it may spring into lively depth, as is evident in Figure 7–12. An array of ellipses becomes an array of craters on a moon-like surface when shadow is added. Shadows will not occur if light comes from all directions at once. Light must come from a limited number of directions if it is to produce shadows. Now the surprising thing is that when a picture such as that shown in Figure 7–12 is turned upside-down, the craters become elevated blisters on the surface. There is no really good explanation for this ancient phenomenon (Boring, 1942).

It has been suggested that the factor determining the direction of depth given by shadow is the direction from which the illumination comes. Thus, by itself shadow produces a depth impression; yet the direction of depth—i.e., which part of the picture is far and which near—is inherently ambiguous unless one knows the direction from which the light is coming. The problem with this is that the direction of depth in a

Figure 7–12. The addition of shadow to ellipses creates the impression of craters. Rotating the page through 180 degrees causes the craters to become elevated "blisters."

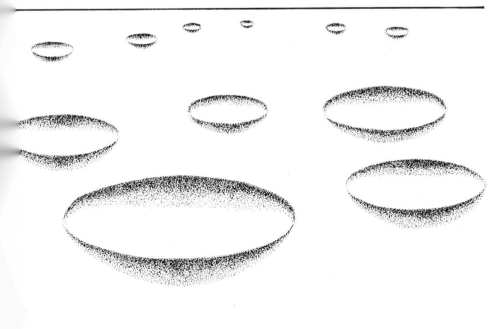

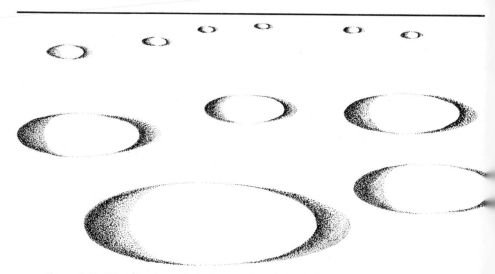

Figure 7–13. The direction of shadow-produced depth is more ambiguous when the shadows are produced by lights coming from above but perspective suggests that one side of the picture is more distant than the other. Figure should be viewed with page rotated 90 degrees.

picture can change when the picture is rotated through 180 degrees. There is no illumination of a raised surface here; there is only a picture of the surface. And thus there must be information allowing the observer to act as though the illumination were coming from one direction rather than another in viewing a picture of a complex scene. As has been suggested (Brewster, 1847), there is a learned predisposition to see a picture as though the light were coming from above it.

The theory is not proved that an assumption of light coming from above influences the perception of relief due to light and shade. There have been no systematic experiments to establish that the only cue present in pictures such as that shown in Figure 7–12 is light and shade. In point of fact, this figure was drawn with a built-in perspective cue: the more distant regions on the surface are closer to the top of the picture than to the bottom. This is generally true of illustrations of this famous effect. Gibson (1950) provides several pictures in which relief may be reversed by rotating the pictures; yet in all of them there is information other than light and shade indicating which part of the surface is more distant from the observer. If a picture like Figure 7–12 is drawn with perspective indicating that the right side of the picture is more distant, but with shadows cast as though light were coming from above, the reversal effect is far more ambiguous. This is illustrated in Figure 7–13. Thus, we come to a problem that will preoccupy us in much of our later discussions —namely, that of the interaction of cues to depth.

The notion that depth reversal produced by rotating a picture such as that shown in Figure 7–12 is due to the assumption that light comes from above can be disputed on the ground that this same phenomenon occurs when there is no shading in a picture. Figure 7–14 shows both the famous Schröder staircase (Boring, 1942) and the Necker cube. There is a general predisposition to see the staircase as a staircase rather than as an inverted staircase projecting from above. As Schröder noted, if the picture is rotated through 180 degrees it will retain its depth until the inversion is nearly complete. It will then reverse its depth so as to appear once again to be a staircase. If the reader does the same experiment with Figure 7–14, he is likely also to notice that the Necker cube has a similar predisposition to keep its lower vertical face as forward. Thus, the Necker cube will also invert in depth as it is rotated.

These figures serve our point that the inversion of depth apparently due to shadow may not be due to shadow at all. The shadow may serve as a depth-producing vehicle in the same sense that the angles in the cube and staircase induce an impression of depth. Since such depth cues are inherently ambiguous as regards their direction, orientational predispositions as well as effects of other cues, such as perspective, may influence the perceived direction of depth. More experimental work is needed to investigate the effects of cues other than light and shade.

Interposition. The Euclidean cues serve as sources of information about relative distance defined in its broadest sense. They tell about the relative

Figure 7–14. The Schröder staircase (A) and the Necker cube (B). Rotating the page through 180 degrees causes depth reversal in these figures as well.

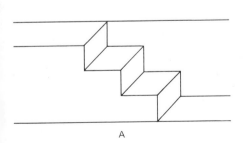

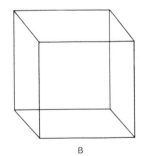

A

B

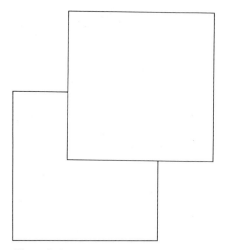

Figure 7–15. The cue of interposition.

distances on a terrain and may also inform to some extent with regard to modeling or relief. Relative brightness seems to be most appropriate to vast distances and sharp differences in illumination. Light and shade serves as a cue to modeling or relief. It also gives the modeling of a terrain and may therefore serve to enhance the effectiveness of the Euclidean cues. Interposition—the cutting off of part of the view of one object by another—is an extraordinarily potent cue to relative distance. The partially occluded object is always seen as behind the nearer object.

On a common-sense level this seems to be a reasonable state of affairs. If the square in Figure 7–15 cuts off a piece of another square, the whole square must be in front of the other. There is a clear and virtually universal tendency to see both enclosed spaces as squares, one in front of the other. But why is the occluded object thought of as a square? If it were an L-shaped object it could be in the same plane as the square.

There are numerous theories as to why depth is seen in such figures as opposed to seeing the figures as co-planar but different. One such theory derives from the Gestalt theory (Koffka, 1935), according to which there is a tendency to see lines as continuous even though portions of them may be occluded. This is attested by the fact that the overlapped irregular figures in Figure 7–16 are perceived as two figures rather than three. The overlapping portions of the shapes enclose a space and may thus be thought of as a third figure. But a "better" figure is made possible by accepting the option of seeing the overlapped portions as belonging to two irregular shapes, since it allows the continuity of their contours to be preserved.

A somewhat more tenable theory is Hochberg's notion that there is a tendency to see things in their simplest terms. The Kopfermann cubes shown in Figure 7–17 may be seen as either tridimensional or flat. The information required to describe one of these "cubes" will vary depending upon whether or not it is assumed to be tridimensional. If it is presumed to be tridimensional it might require a description in terms of a fewer number of different angles than if it is presumed to be flat. Hochberg and Brooks (1960), using many such cubes, found that the judgment of tridimensional *vs.* bidimensional was made in terms of the least amount of information necessary to describe the figure. This same approach may be made to the problem of interposition. An L is a more complicated figure than a square, since it has six angles rather than four. It is therefore simpler to see the L-shaped outline in Figure 7–15 as a square partially hidden by another square.

There is something strained about this kind of reasoning. It is not obvious that seeing an object in depth really makes it simpler. Moreover, the fact of seeing something in depth is not by itself simple—it is an ex-

Figure 7–16. There is a tendency to see two overlapping figures rather than three enclosed areas, all in the same plane.

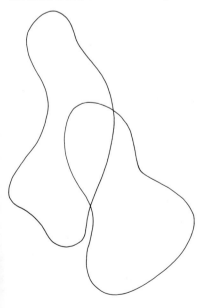

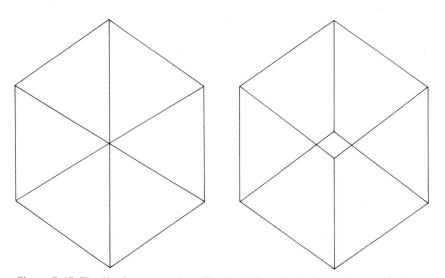

Figure 7–17. The Kopfermann cubes. The "cube" on the left can be perceived as a flat polygon; the one on the right is more likely to be perceived as a tridimensional object.

ceedingly complicated process. The correlation between simplicity and depth noted by Hochberg and McAlister (1953) does not provide a truly satisfying theory, since it does not give us a mechanism by way of which depth makes its appearance. The simplicity may be a result of seeing something in depth, and not a cause.

To return to the Kopfermann cubes: it is possible to explain Hochberg's and Brooks' results in terms of interposition itself. Thus, the cubes seen as tridimensional all have two partially overlapped squares, and thus there is a tendency to see one square as in front of the other. This precondition makes it easier to see them as tridimensional. On the other hand, the cubes not seen as tridimensional have the least overlap of squares; this too is consistent with seeing the cubes as bidimensional. So we see that simplicity may be utilized to "explain" interposition, and interposition may be used to "explain" the depth of the cubes. One explanation seems to be as good as the other.

"Goodness" of form explanations suffer from one major fault, as is illustrated in Figure 7–18. One triangle is seen in front of the other—despite the fact that completion of the "hidden" triangle would involve completing a contour having a change in direction, or discontinuity.

It is obvious from Figure 7–18 that simple good continuation of form cannot be a necessary condition for depth perception caused by interposition. There may well be a host of complex factors operating to produce such depth. It may be, for example, that seeing one triangle whole is a clue to the fact that the partially hidden figure is also a triangle (see Dinnerstein and Wertheimer, 1957). Also, the role of the familiarity of the partially hidden figure may well be a factor in perceiving it as partially hidden. When one human form obscures part of another recognizably human form, the obscured one will be seen as partially hidden rather than as dismembered, regardless of the relative geometrical complexities of the alternatives. We must conclude, therefore, that the cue of interposition does not lend itself to explanation in terms of some simple mechanism.

We have now outlined all the pictorial cues to depth. These are only partially understood by scientists—yet understood well enough to allow their use by the artist. They are not, of course, the only sources of information about depth and distance. Another powerful source flows from the fact that we move about in the world and do not view it always from a stationary position.

KINETIC CUES

As Helmholtz (1925) observed over one hundred years ago, the perception of the layout of things in depth may be derived from transformations of the visual field resulting from the movements of the head. In a classic example of this he described standing in a forest with one eye closed. The stationary opened eye gave the perception of undifferentiated greenery; when he moved his head, however, the branches of the trees and bushes sprang into strong relief, and near things were seen as closer than

Figure 7–18. Failure of good continuation. The trapezoidal shape on the right may be perceived as a hidden triangle.

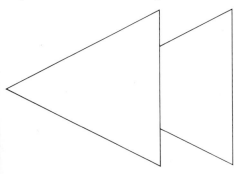

far things. This is the first recorded example of the perfect camouflage created when bodies are disguised with a random texture—the leaves of the trees in this case.

Helmholtz interpreted this phenomenon in terms of the parallax produced by the head movement—though of course, shifting the world relative to the stationary head could produce the same result on the retina. In this general case, whether the head or the world should be moving, we refer to motion parallax.

Motion parallax: Motion parallax can be understood easily if the reader will consider a little analogy—that of a pinhole camera.

Suppose two light sources are at two different distances from the pinhole camera. One of these point sources is, for all practical purposes, infinitely far away—say, at the horizon—and the other source is nearby. The rays of light emanating from the more distant source are all parallel by the time they reach the pinhole. The rays of light emanating from the nearby source are still noticeably divergent when they reach the pinhole shown in Figure 7–19. We shall assume that the pinhole can admit but one ray at a time. This is of course a physical impossibility, but assuming the fiction to be true will help to make things clear.

When the pinhole is in one position it admits one ray from the most distant object. If the pinhole should be moved up or down in the figure, the rays it admits from the more distant object will always intercept it at the same angle, and thus will always fall on the same point on the screen behind the pinhole. This follows from the fact that all these rays are parallel and continue to travel in straight lines after passing through the pinhole. On the other hand, the diverging rays emanating from the nearer object will intercept the pinhole at different angles as the pinhole is displaced up and down in the figure. The position on the screen intercepted by these rays will change with changes in the vertical position of the pinhole in the figure.

The pinhole in the "camera" shown in Figure 7–19 corresponds to the lens in the eye. If a sheaf of rays emanating from a point source enters the lens in the eye, the position of the image formed by the lens on the retina will be determined by the angle at which one ray crosses a point in the lens known as its "node." All other rays are bent by the lens upon entering it, so that they converge on this ray at a focus of the lens, as is indicated in Figure 7–20. Thus, to a first approximation the pinhole acts like a lens.

Since the rays from a very distant source are all parallel, lateral dis-

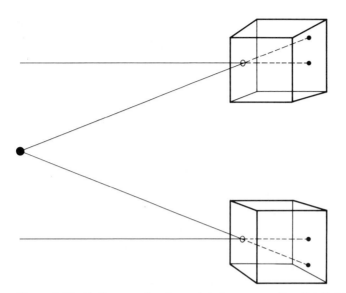

Figure 7–19. Motion parallax in a pinhole camera. Parallel light rays from an infinitely distant source always enter the pinhole from the same angle and intercept the screen in the rear of the camera at the same place, regardless of the vertical position of the camera. If the camera at the bottom of the figure should be moved toward the top, diverging rays from the nearby source of light enter the pinhole from a different angle. These rays intercept the screen at different places as the camera is moved vertically.

Figure 7–20. Rays diverging from a point source on the left side of the lenses are converged on the ray passing through the node of the lens to form an image of the point source on the right.

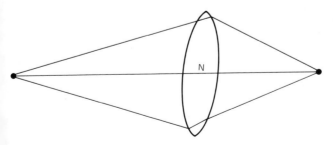

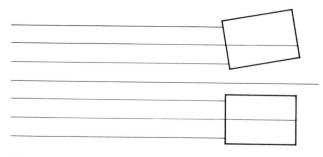

Figure 7–21. Tilting a pinhole camera causes the position of the image of an infinitely distant point to shift on the screen at the back of the camera.

placements of either a pinhole or a lens do not produce any changes in the position of the image of the point on the screen, or on the retina behind the lens. This becomes obvious when one considers the fact that parallel rays correspond to plane wavefronts in the wave model of light. If one displaces a lens parallel to a plane wavefront, the "information" received by the lens does not change, and consequently neither does the position of the image formed by the lens change as the lens is moved. This explains the fact that the moon appears to follow you about as you move your own head, since light coming from each point on the surface of the moon is in the form of parallel rays by the time it reaches the eye. Again, however, the position of the moon or of any other very distant object does change on the retina when the head is rotated rather than displaced laterally. This is explained by Figure 7–21 which shows how rotating a pinhole camera produces a change in the angle at which rays of parallel light intercept the pinhole. This change in angle produces a corresponding shift in the position of the image on the screen behind the pinhole.

As shown in Figure 7–19, when the near point source and the far point source of light are simultaneously present, rays from these two points intercept the pinhole at different angles. Therefore, the ray from the near source impinges on the screen at one place, and the ray from the more distant point, at a different place. When the camera is moved up or down in the figure the rays entering the pinhole from the more distant source keep their position on the screen. Because of the divergence of the rays from the nearer source, however, these rays have different positions on the screen as the camera is displaced. Thus, the image of a near point shifts on the screen relative to the image of a more distant point. The same is true of the eye.

If two objects were presented simultaneously—one at the horizon and the other nearby—lateral head movements would cause the fixated distant object to be imaged at a constant retinal place, and the nearby object's image would move on the retina. Thus, even in the real world, objects or points far away on the terrain would remain stationary on the retina during head movements, and nearby points on the terrain would displace on the retina in the direction of the head movement. In fact a whole gradient of retinal displacements would occur, since points at different distances would have different retinal velocities. The nearer points, whose light waves are curved most when they reach the eye, would move most rapidly across the retina. Points farther away would move less rapidly until, in the case of the farthermost points, if fixated so that the eye does not turn, they would remain relatively stationary on the retina. These differential velocities of points on the retina produce motion parallax during head movements. As it may be inferred, if the eye remains fixed in the head and the head moves laterally with respect to a true three-dimen-

Figure 7–22. Shadows cast onto a screen by discs of equal size will vary in inverse proportion to the distances of the discs from the point source.

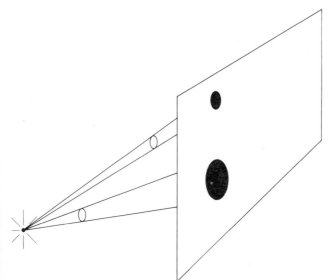

sional scene, then objects relatively far away will move less on the retina than relatively near objects.

There has been some work on the observer's sensitivity to motion parallax, i.e., on the minimum discriminable difference in retinal velocity (Graham, Baker, Hecht, and Lloyd, 1948). Though it turned out that the observer can discriminate very small differences in retinal velocity—a few seconds of arc per second when expressed in terms of visual angle—a far more important question concerns the usefulness of parallax as a depth cue. This was studied by James Gibson and his associates (Gibson, Gibson, Smith, and Flock, 1959).

In what was a fairly clear transposition of Helmholtz's experience of motion parallax from the forest to the laboratory, Gibson and his associates utilized the shadowgraph technique. This method involves placing some object of interest between a small point source of light and a translucent screen. The light emitted by the point source paints on the screen a sharply etched shadow of the object. The smallness of the source minimizes the penumbra. The observer, placed on the side of the screen opposite to that of the point source, can see the shadow on the screen. This device has the advantage that all the shadow images are in the same plane —that of the screen. As is evident in Figure 7–22, points on the object near the point source are imaged as larger on the screen than points farther from the point source but nearer the screen. If all of the points on an object are in a plane and equidistant from the point source, then the shadows of these points will be of the same size. If the shadows are of unfamiliar objects, even if they are in different planes relative to the point source they would be seen in the same plane—i.e., that of the projection screen.

In their experiment Gibson et al. placed two transparent sheets of plastic between the point source and the screen. The two sheets were at different distances from the point source. Paint and powder were splattered on both screens so that a textured shadow of the random arrays of light and dark were imaged on the screen. The shadows arising from both screens were intermixed and, in a static view, the observer saw only a textured visual field where all points were in the plane of the projection screen.

When both splattered sheets were moved at the same velocity and parallel to the projection screen, the shadows of the texture of the sheet nearer the point source moved at a greater velocity across the projection screen than the shadow of the array of points closer to the projection screen. This was equivalent to having the observer move laterally relative to two arrays of random texture one of which was closer to him than the other. These different velocities are instances of motion parallax.

The result of these different velocities was that though the observers noticed that two textures moved with two different velocities, their relative distances were largely indeterminate. The observers could not tell which was nearer and which was farther. Yet when a single sheet of plastic was tilted in the vertical dimension, so that its bottom was nearer the point source than its top, the shadow of its texture was seen as tilted when the plastic sheet was displaced. Movement of the sheet parallel to the projection screen caused those portions of its texture nearer the point source to cast shadows that moved faster than shadows of points more distant from the source of light. This produced a gradient of motion parallax.

Such gradients seemed to Gibson to be necessary to the perception of depth in situations in which motion parallax is the only source of information about depth. Two points alone, of which one is more distant from the observer than the other, cannot be seen in clear depth when the observer moves. Gibson would hold that an array of points providing a gradient of motion parallax is necessary for the perception of depth. Motion parallax *per se* is not sufficient; motion perspective is. Thus, even though pictorial perspective may be absent, points in a tilted array can display a kind of perspective when the observer moves relative to the array. This is a perspective in the sense that the more distant points move with a slower retinal velocity than the nearer points. Unless a whole gradient is present, depth perception is not possible. The same is true of static linear perspective. Two points alone cannot be seen in perspective; an array of points is required before we can discern their convergence toward the horizon.

The kinetic depth effect. Even earlier than James Gibson, Wallach and his associates (Wallach and O'Connell, 1953; Wallach, O'Connell, and Neisser, 1953) utilized the shadowgraph technique to identify the kinds of kinetic information that may be used by an observer in judging depth. Wallach's concern was largely with how congenitally monocular people see things in depth. He reasoned that as we move with respect to objects, their retinal images undergo systematic transformations. Thus, a straight rod tilted away from the vertical may cast a long, slanted image on the retina when viewed from one position, and a shorter vertical image when

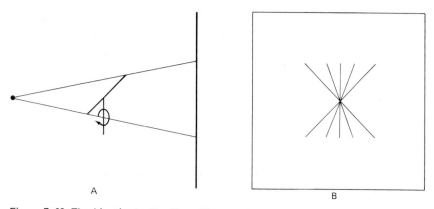

Figure 7–23. The kinetic depth effect. The shadowgraph apparatus at A was used to cast the shadow of a rotating tilted rod on a transluscent screen. The shadows seen on the screen are shown at B, illustrating how the length and direction of the shadow of the rod varied with its rotation.

viewed from another position. This would be true also of a tilted rod placed between a point source and a translucent screen. Its shadow could range from that of a long, tilted line to that of a shorter vertical line as it is rotated (see Figure 7–23).

Wallach and O'Connell (1953) found that a rod rotated in this way is in fact perceived as a rigid object rotating in the third dimension—this despite the fact that from one glimpse to the next the shadow is that of a straight line changing in both slope and length. When the rod, however, is in a horizontal position so that it changes in length but not in slope or direction, depth judgments are very ambiguous. It could not be said that the rod was perceived as a rigid object rotating in the third dimension. They concluded that if the contours of an object change in both length and direction when rotated, it could be seen in depth. This they called the *kinetic depth effect* (KDE).

Wallach went even farther in his collaboration with O'Connell and Neisser and found that when exposure to a rotating stimulus object led to depth perception through the KDE, this depth perception would transfer to the same and other objects presented as stationary. This was termed the memory effect of the KDE, and Wallach *et al.* proposed that it could explain how congenitally monocular people see things in depth.

It should be obvious by now that Gibson's motion perspective and the KDE are really the same cue. As we move with respect to a terrain then the distances between points on the terrain may vary in both direction and extent or length. This is a necessary concomitant of having a textured array stretched out in depth as the stimulus object. Wallach simply connected the points when he studied the contours of objects. If points on contours do not change in *both* direction and length they do not give the perception of depth; so too, the points in Gibson's two sheets of plastic, where only length, but not direction, varied. It is equally obvious that motion parallax, as described by Helmholtz, is not a fully adequate account of the kinetic cues to depth. Not only must the points in the visual field move differentially as the observer moves, they must move differentially in particular ways. This area needs considerable work if we would further elaborate the bases for depth perception in the presence of motion parallax.

PHYSIOLOGICAL CUES

All the cues we have considered thus far have been described solely in terms of the visual field. The information as to depth is available in the world. Perspective, for example, is not in the observer: it is a way of describing a projection of the visual world. Now it is true that if people were built differently they might not respond to the pictorial and kinetic cues we have described. Somehow the wiring of existing nervous systems is adapted to the features of the world as we know them. There is virtually no information at all, however, concerning the physiological processes that respond to these cues. To be sure, these features must be processed physiologically, but for the present we must terminate our discussion of them on the phenomenological level.

There are other cues, however, which involve physiology in a more noticeable manner. If we did not have two eyes in our heads then we could not have the cues of convergence and retinal disparity. If we had no lens capable of changing its curvature in the eye, there would be no accommodation cue. Moreover, we do have information about the central mechanisms underlying accommodation, convergence, and the effects of retinal disparity. It is for this reason that I have made the rather arbitrary and tentative distinction between the pictorial and kinetic cues on the one hand, and the physiological cues on the other.

Accommodation. When attention is shifted from an object at one distance to another object at a different distance from the eye, the curvature of the lens of the eye may change so that the new object will be imaged sharply on the retina. This becomes necessary for the reason that a lens with fixed curvature will focus only those objects at a particular distance in the plane of the retina. Images of objects at other distances would remain blurred. Unlike the case of the camera, the distance between the eye's lens and retina cannot be changed.

The lens of the eye is held in place by the suspensory ligament. This ligament is controlled by the ciliary muscle, which forms a ring around the lens. When the muscle contracts, the suspensory ligament tends to become loose, thereby exerting less tension on the lens. Because of its natural elasticity the lens then tends to bulge or exhibit more curvature. If attention should be shifted to a very distant object, however, the ciliary muscle would tend to relax, with result in an increase in the distance between the muscle and the lens, and this leading to a stretching of the ligament. The ligament would then increase the tension on the lens, and so causing it to draw flat. In this case we say that accommodation is relaxed, since the ciliary muscle is relaxed—and yet in so-called relaxed accommodation the lens is actually under more tension than in viewing nearby objects where accommodation is not relaxed.

Accommodation, particularly for near vision, is under the control of the parasympathetic nervous system. According to Elliot (1963), the pathways for this control have been traced from the pretectal region in the midbrain to the Edinger-Westphal nucleus through the oculomotor nerve to the ciliary ganglion and the short ciliary nerves to the ciliary muscles. While it is widely believed that the visual cortex plays a role in accommodation, the question of pathways from the cortex into the reflex loop governing accommodation is in dispute. Thus it is undecided whether the cortical influence acts in the pretectal region, in the colliculi, or in the Edinger-Westphal nucleus. In any case, even if the cortex does play a role, accommodation is probably not under direct voluntary control.

As we shall see later, stimulation of the parasympathetic oculomotor nerves and nuclei of the midbrain leads to a response of the sphincter (or constrictor) of the pupil as well as the ciliary muscle (Polyak, 1957). There is also some evidence (Adler, 1965) that the sympathetic nervous system is involved in accommodation. This is consistent with the fact that other organs regulated by involuntary muscles have dual innervation: e.g., in the case of the iris the sympathetic system innervates the constrictor or sphincter pupillae. In any case, the sympathetic control

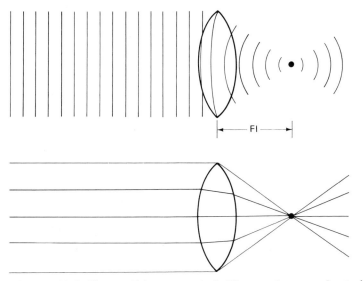

Figure 7–24. Collimated light represented either as plane wavefronts (upper part of figure) or as parallel rays (lower half) is brought to a focus by a lens to form a real image of the original point source. The distance between the real image and the node of the lens is the focal length FL of the lens. Light from an actual source placed at the position of the real image will be collimated by the lens.

leads to a much smaller degree of change in lens curvature than does parasympathetic control.

Relaxed accommodation is necessary if very distant objects are to be imaged clearly on the retina. An increase in lens curvature, on the other hand, becomes necessary as the object of regard draws closer, since in this latter case the refractive power of the lens is greater. This effectively shortens the distance at which an image is formed behind the lens. It is of some importance to understand how an image is formed.

If a plane wavefront intercepts a lens, it will be bent by the lens so that it converges to a point some distance behind the lens. Beyond this point, as shown in Figure 7–24, the wavefront will diverge or be reversed. It is as though a real image of a point had been formed behind the lens, and this real image sent out waves in both directions. The place where this real image is formed is called the focal point of the lens. The ray model, likewise shown in Figure 7–24, is somewhat more explicit. As will be noticed, the parallel rays are bent by the lens so that they cross at the focal point. If a point source were placed at this focal point, the light coming out of the lens in the reverse direction would be parallel, or collimated.

Two factors determine the focus of any lens. The first is the curvature of the lens. Thus, if the lens is very curved, the focus will be short; a relatively flat lens has a relatively long focus. The second factor has to do with the material of which the lens is made. Some materials slow down light more than others. Water retards light more than does air, for example. Some glasses are more refractive than others—i.e., they slow the light more. The reason for this lies beyond the scope of this book but it has to do with an interaction between the electromagnetic light waves and the electric fields of the particles within the substance.

Regardless of how it occurs, if one substance slows light more than some other substance, and if the light intercepts it at some angle, the beam of light will be bent more by the medium that slows it more. Such a substance will have a higher refractive index. If the boundary of the substance is curved, it will bend the light beam differentially along its surface because each ray of light intercepts the surface of the substance at a different angle.

If the refractive index of a substance is known, the angle through which a beam of light is bent when it enters some substance from air can be computed from a rule known as Snell's law.*

If we take two lenses of equal curvature but of different refractive index, and place them in the paths of two parallel beams of light, the light will come to a focus at a shorter distance behind the lens with the higher refractive index. Similarly, two lenses of the same material but of different curvature will in the same circumstances form images at different distances. The lens with the greater curvature will have the shorter focal length. In both cases the lens with the shorter focal length is the more powerful. The power of such lenses is expressed in terms of the *diopter*, which is simply the reciprocal of the focal length. Thus, a lens with a very

---

* This rule holds that the sine of the angle of the incident of light ray is equal to the product of the sine of the angle of the transmitted light and the refractive index of the intercepting medium. More formally,

$$\sin \theta_i = n \sin \theta_r$$

where θ_i is the angle at which the light ray in air intercepts the new medium, θ_r is the angle between the ray and the boundary of the medium it has just entered and n is the refractive index of the medium. Thus, if a ray of light in air (where the refractive index $= 1.0$) intercepts the surface of a body of water (which has a refractive index of 1.33) at an angle of 10 degrees, its angle in water will be 7.5 degrees. This is, of course, the reason a stick partially immersed in water will look bent.

long focal length—of, say 1 meter—is a 1-diopter lens. If several lenses are combined to make an optical system, we may speak of the dioptric power of the entire system. The diopter values of the elements of such systems can be added to give the power of the entire system. In point of fact, the eye is itself a compound optical system.

Since there is a relatively large difference between the refractive indices of the cornea and air, the curved surface of the cornea does most of the refracting of light entering the eye. The aqueous humor lying behind the cornea and in front of the lens also refracts the light, since its refractive index differs from that of the cornea. The next stage is that of the lens, which has a refractive power of between 19 and 33 diopters, depending upon its curvature. The cornea, on the other hand, provides a refractive power of about 43 diopters regardless of the curvature of the lens.

Thus far we have considered only the case in which collimated light impinges upon a lens. If the source of light is close to the lens—say, less than 20 meters away—the light beam entering the pupil is no longer comprised of approximately parallel rays (planar wavefronts). The rays diverge noticeably from the point source. For a given state of accommodation of the eye, the light rays will converge to a focus at a determinate distance behind the lens. This point is not in correspondence with the focal length of the lens as measured with incident collimated light. It is what is known as an image-point, and corresponds to a given object-point which is said to be conjugate to the object-point (distance of the source). Such conjugate points are systematically related. The idea is that the curvature of the lens should be so adjusted that light from relatively nearby sources would be conjugated onto the receptive layer of the retina.

We may now see how an image of an extended object is formed on the retina. Any point on the reflective surface of an object may be thought of as a point source. Light from such a point radiates from it in all directions. A portion, or bundle, of such light rays enters the pupil of the eye, and the optical apparatus of the eye refracts the light so that an image of the point is formed on the retina. Similarly, rays from another point on the object also enter the pupil, but—as shown in Figure 7–25—from another angle. This causes formation of an image of the point at some distance from the first point on the retina. It can be seen from this that all points on the object yield images of themselves so that when taken together they yield an image of an entire object.

We have treated the optical system of the eye as though it were perfect, whereas all lens materials refract light of different wavelengths dif-

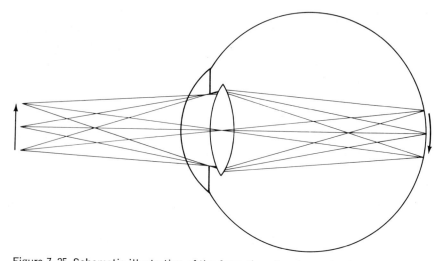

Figure 7–25. Schematic illustration of the formation of an image by the eye.

ferently. A simple glass lens, for example, would bring collimated red light to a different focus than it would collimated blue light. In man-made lenses these chromatic aberrations are corrected by combining different materials to make a lens. In God-made lenses, however, chromatic aberrations are not corrected. Further, not all lenses have good spherical surfaces. Uncorrected lenses produce considerable distortion and blurring in the image. This, too, is true of the eye.

Chromatic and spherical aberrations may be reduced by using only the small central portion of the lens. If the optical system of the eye is not equivalent to a truly spherical lens, rays entering the system at different points on the surface of the cornea will not be bent to converge at a unique point on the retina. This leads to blur even when accommodation is optimum, but this blur may be reduced if the iris cuts the size of the entrance pupil to the eye. In this way, within limits set by diffraction, a smaller bundle of rays enters the eye, and this reduces the size of the blur circles, or zones of confusion, surrounding the image points. In effect the pupil may play the same role as the iris of the camera in controlling the depth–of–field of the eye. The smaller the pupil, the greater the range of sharp vision around the point of fixation. In very bright light, when the pupil is at its smallest, the lens need not change its curvature for small differences in distance between objects of interest. In dim light, when the pupil is relatively large, sharp vision would require that the curvature of the lens be more precisely controlled. It may be seen from this that the pupil is inextricably involved in accommodation. As a matter of fact, when the eye adjusts for near vision there is a reflexive contraction of the pupil coinciding with accommodation of the lens and convergence of the eyes (Lowenstein and Lowenfeld, 1962). This implies that accommodation and pupillary constriction involve the same neural pathways.

All the optical apparatus we have been discussing has as its aim the reduction of the blur circles around image points. Actually it is the blur circles that trigger the occurrence of the accommodation of the lens and pupillary constriction, but these blur circles are effective only if the subject turns his attention to the object producing the blurred image. Thus it is that accommodation involves a voluntary act indirectly and must ultimately be initiated by events in the cerebral cortex. The way in which these cortical events serve to activate the portions of the autonomic nervous system involved in the accommodative reflex is clouded in mystery. At a less profound level, there is also some mystery as to how the relative amounts of blurring of objects at different distances may be used as a cue to depth.

If an image of a point is formed in front of the retina because the eye is accommodated for the distance of some other object, a blob of light (blur circle) will be formed on the retina. A very similar blur circle will be formed also if the image point in question is formed behind the retina. The two blur circles differ in only one respect if the eye is not astigmatic: the lens of the eye has a shorter focal length for blue light than it does for red light. In the case of an image formed in front of the retina, the resulting blur circle would thus have a blue fringe and a red center. With the image point behind the retina, the blur circle would have a red fringe and a blue center. As Fincham (1951) pointed out, such chromatic aberrations could be a source of information about the direction of the difference in distance between an object of regard and some other object. The magnitude of the distance difference, however, could not be derived from the blur circles, since it is also affected by pupillary diameter.

Still another source of information is the effect of astigmatism on the shape of the blur circles. Astigmatism arises from the fact that there is often a barrel-shaped or cylindrical distortion of the surface of the cornea, and because of this the power of the optical apparatus is different for different axes; e.g., in one orientation an incident slit of light would be brought to a different focus than it would at another orientation—as the ray pattern shown in Figure 7–26 will demonstrate.

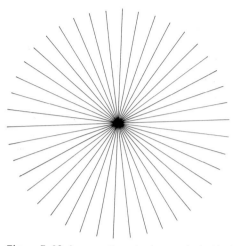

Figure 7–26. A ray pattern to demonstrate the effects of astigmatism.

Most human eyes have a degree of astigmatism. If the reader were to fixate with one eye the center of the ray pattern in Figure 7–26, he would probably notice that some of the lines are dim and others are dark. The dark lines appear to be somewhat sharper than the dim lines, since they are imaged more sharply on the retina. The dimmer lines are brought to a focus either in front of the retina or behind it, because the eye has different optical power in the axis parallel to the dim lines as compared with the axis parallel to the darker lines.

In Figure 7–27, in which a ray diagram shows how this may come about, it will be observed that if a point source of light is placed before the eye, the shape of the circle of confusion will depend upon the retina's position relative to the average focus of the lens. If the minimum-confusion point is in front of the retina, the blur "circle"—or zone of confusion—will be an ellipsoid with a horizontal major axis. On the other hand, if the minimum-confusion point is behind the retina, the ellipsoid on the retina will have its major axis in the vertical dimension.

While it is theoretically possible for such information to be used in determining direction-of-distance differences, we must remember that eyes are not necessarily alike. Even in the same person the astigmatism in one eye may differ from the astigmatism in the other eye in terms of both magnitude and direction. So, if astigmatic errors are sources of information about depth they can be effective only if the organism comes to learn the meaning of its own astigmatism. It might also be pointed out that astigmatism may vary with amplitude of accommodation. This compounds the difficulties associated with learning to use astigmatic errors in discerning depth.

Lest the reader feel that so intricate a task as using astigmatism lies beyond the ability of the human organism, Campbell and Westheimer (1959) found that asymmetry of blurring can be used by an observer in judging depth. In their experiment a monochromatic (green) target eliminated chromatic aberrations as a source of information. Also, spherical aberrations were rendered useless by placing an anular pupil on the eyeball—a pupil that occluded the center of the iris and permitted light to enter by the periphery of the lens only. With a 1-diopter cylinder placed in front of the eye the subject learned quickly to make error-free depth judgments. It might be pointed out also that in monochromatic light alone some subjects lost their ability to make depth judgments with one eye—thus to suggest that they had been using the chromatic aberration information.

Another basis for believing that something like chromatic aberrations or astigmatism may be utilized is provided by the fact that accommodative changes are normally made without an initial error. If the blur circle gave no information about direction of depth differences, the lens should first hunt for the correct direction of change in its curvature. This does not happen very often. On most occasions the lens initially changes its curvature in the correct direction. This could only come about if the nervous

Figure 7–27. An astigmatic lens having greater power horizontally than it has vertically. A point source is brought to a focus as a horizontal line at one point behind the lens, and the same light is brought to a focus as a vertical line at another place. The "zone of minimum confusion" is between these two line-images.

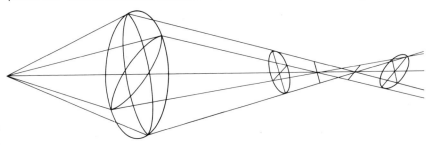

system already knew the direction in which the lens curvature should be changed so that the image would be sharply portrayed on the retina.

In a very real sense, it may well be wrong to say that accommodation is a cue to depth. In point of fact, if there is a cue to depth associated with accommodation it is the information contained in the blur circles. The curvature of the lens is itself irrelevant to depth judgments, since it simply serves to get one object imaged sharply, and the blur circles around more or less distant objects tell us that they are not in the same plane as is the object of regard. This would be consistent with the fact that accommodation is effective over a limited range—e.g., 1 or 2 meters (Graham, 1965a). Under certain conditions, however, the optical apparatus of the eye can distinguish differences in distance far greater than this usable range of accommodation.

The dioptric power of the youthful eyeball has a range of about 12 diopters—i.e., from about 59 diopters for far vision to about 71 diopters for near vision (Helmholtz, 1924). This means that the focal length of the optical system can vary from 17 mm to about 14 mm with the focal length at its shortest when viewing an object at the near point, and longest when viewing an object at the far point. "Near" and "far" are about 20 cm from the eye and optical infinity, respectively. The accommodation no longer relaxes as the object moves farther away than about 10 feet, nor does it increase as the object comes closer than about 8 inches. Nevertheless, objects between the far point and the horizon do affect the optical system differentially. It is quite easy, for example, to pick up the differential velocities arising from head movements when one is viewing the moon and another object more than 100 feet away. Because of its great distance, the nearer object may not be noticeably blurred. This implies that even if an object is farther than 10 feet away, the waves of light coming from that object are still impinging upon the cornea at angles that produce noticeable translation of its image when the head is moved.

Convergence. We have spent considerable time on accommodation because it allowed us to explore the mechanisms of image formation and to explicate some of the very subtle ways in which distance information may be obtained. Accommodation is also a very natural introduction to the more important cue of convergence, since it is inextricably linked to convergence.

Before turning directly to the cue of convergence let us consider what happens when one eye is covered and an object is moved at right angles

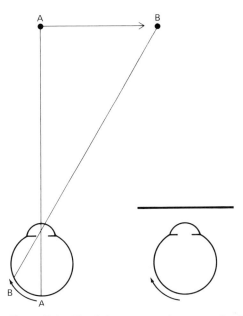

Figure 7–28. The left eye turns from A to B when it follows an object from A to B. The occluded right eye turns in the same direction even though it cannot see the moving object.

to the line of sight of the other eye, as in Figure 7–28. If the left eye in the figure continues to look straight ahead in the direction of A while the object is moved toward the right to B, the image of A moves in the opposite direction, to the left. This is due to the fact that the optics of the eye invert the retinal image. Now suppose that the brain attached to the left eye in the figure decides that it is interested in the moving object. This normally leads to an attempt to keep the image of the object locked into the region of central vision, the fovea. Now, to keep the moving object in the fovea as it goes from A to B the eye would have to rotate to the right. Now the interesting thing about all this is what happens to the other eye—the eye that is occluded. As the object moves from A to B the left eye follows it. The right eye will follow it too, even when it is occluded. The reader can test this for himself. Hold one finger up in front of one eye and keep the other eye closed. Place a finger of the other hand gently against the lid of the closed eye. As the upright fixated finger is moved alternately to the left and right, and if it is followed by the open

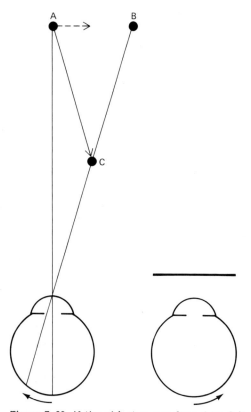

Figure 7–29. If the object moves from A to C it traces the same path on the retina as it would if it moved from A to B. The left eye must also turn through the same angle to keep the image in the fovea. The occluded right eye, however, does not turn in the same direction—it rotates in the opposite direction. This is an example of convergence.

eye, you can feel the corneal bulge under the lid of the closed eye move back and forth in step with the moving finger.

It is obvious from this that the two eyes are yolked together. What one eye does in response to a visual input is done by the other eye too, even if the other eye is unable to see the stimulus. When the two eyes move together in this manner to follow an object translating across the visual field, we speak of conjugate eye movements.

Now let us consider a slightly different case. Figure 7–29 shows what happens on the retina when an object at position A moves to position C, which is closer to the eye. It is rather astonishing that when the object of regard moves from A to C the image point moves in exactly the same way as it did when the object moved from A to B. Displacements toward and away from the observer can be duplicated on the retina by lateral displacements. Moreover, if the observer were to keep the image of the object within the fovea, he would also have to turn his eye to the right. Consequently, the movement of the eye would have to be in the same direction as it was when the image was moved from A to B in Figure 7–28.

But what is happening to the right eye? As before, the right eye is occluded. As the object moves from A to C, the right eye will rotate counterclockwise if it is to keep the image in the fovea. This is opposite to what happened in the case of displacement to B in Figure 7–28. This movement of the eyes in opposite directions is called *convergence*. If the object were to start at C and be displaced to A, the eyes would counter-rotate in the opposite direction in an act of *divergence*.

Convergence and divergence of the eyes are instances of *disjunctive* eye movements, occurring when images move toward and away from an observer. In the case we have been discussing, it is clear that accommodation is involved in reversing the sign of the signal that instructs the non-stimulated eye to move when an image translates across the retina of the exposed eye. For if accommodation were not involved, the stimulus for the exposed eye would be identical to the translation from A to B portrayed in Figure 7–29. In short, if an image were to move from one point on the retina to the other and not change in clarity of focus, the two eyes would move together as the exposed eye tried to keep the image in the fovea. On the other hand, if the image were to move and change only in clarity of focus, then the two eyes would counter-rotate as the exposed eye tried to keep the image in the fovea.

In addition to the fact that correction of blur through accommodation stimulates vergence movements of the eyes, as opposed to conjugate eye movements, there is another factor that might initiate disjunctive eye movements. This factor operates only when both eyes view the stimulus. It is the double images of objects that are not fixated.

Double images arise because the eyes view objects from two different spatial positions. The uninitiated observer is often unaware of the fact that he has double images. In the event that this is true for the reader, I shall suggest a little experiment. Look across the room toward some small object such as a doorknob or light switch. Without being particularly analytical, raise your hand and point to the object. While you keep your hand very still, keep looking at the object, and open and close your

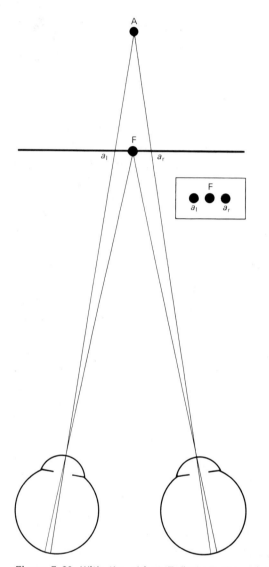

Figure 7–30. With the object F fixated, the object A is seen in the direction $\mathbf{a_l}$ by the left eye, and in the direction $\mathbf{a_r}$ by the right eye. The inset illustrates the left-eye and right-eye views projected onto a plane through F.

eyes alternately. You will notice that one eye's finger is pointing at the object while the other eye's finger is off to one side. Most people point with their right eye's finger. Others—usually left-handed people—point with the left eye. This represents a special kind of eye dominance and also serves to demonstrate that the two eyes do not see all objects as occupying the same visual directions.

Let us try another experiment. Hold your finger upright and look at it carefully. Open and close your eyes alternately. If your fixation is very accurate you will see no movement of the finger from one side to the other. If the finger is held between your eyes and that distant doorknob or light switch, you can try to notice what happens as your eyes are opened and closed. The more distant object, when seen by the left eye, is to the left of where it is seen by the right eye. As a matter of fact, if the finger is exactly in line with the distant object, with the left eye open it is to the left of your finger. This is known as an *uncrossed disparity*, since the left eye's image is to the left of the right eye's image. Now fixate the distant object, keeping your finger in line with it. The relations are reversed, since when the left eye is open, the finger is to the right of the distant object, and with the right eye open it is to the left. This is termed an instance of *crossed disparity*.

Now that you have completed these little experiments you should look at Figure 7–30, which shows schematically what you have experienced. The point F in the figure represents the fixated object. Since it does not change its position as the eyes are opened and closed alternately, we say that it occupies the same visual direction for both eyes: it is seen in the same spatial location regardless of which eye is open. The point A, however, lies in different visual directions for the two eyes. The left eye sees it in the direction of a_l in the figure. The right eye sees it in the direction of a_r, which is to the right of F. If we project the image onto a plane through F, as was done in Figure 3–30, we obtain a diagram that represents the approximate spatial layout seen by the observer with the eyes closed alternately.

Disparate images occupy different visual directions for the two eyes. When an observer is fixating one object and shifts his attention to another object lying at a greater or lesser distance, the disparate images of the new object may trigger what is known as *motor fusion*. There is a tendency to see double images as single (fused) when the object giving rise to them is attended to. To reduce the disparity and achieve motor fusion, the eyes must change their vergence angle. This can happen even when accommodation is not possible.

Convergence due to disparity or double images is different from convergence associated with accommodative changes. Under normal circumstances accommodation and double images supplement each other. As attention turns to an object at some new distance, the state of accommodation changes, the pupil of the eye constricts, and the amount of disparity decreases to provide a sharp and fused image. Convergence behavior is exhibited also by people who cannot accommodate—i.e., when the accommodation is artificially paralyzed (Heinemann, Tulving, and Nachmias, 1959) as well as when the lens is removed surgically. Though centers in the midbrain mediate the vergence responses, people can learn to exercise voluntary control over the extraocular musculature and cross or diverge their eyes at will. It appears that the cortical centers involved in fusional vergence differ from those in accommodative vergence. Moreover, such voluntary changes in vergence may lead to subsequent change in accommodation. It is a common observation that when the eyes are crossed voluntarily there is a period of blurred vision that may subsequently clear up. Hence the two systems of fusional and accommodative vergence are not totally independent of each other.

One of the techniques used to study vergence behavior is to have the subject look at some target for a brief period of time and then suddenly place a prism before one of his eyes. The prism will bend the rays of light entering the eye so that the image of the object formed on the retina is displaced. If the prism is weak, the displacement will be small; and a strong prism produces a large displacement. Such displacements induce a retinal disparity. If the displacement is not too great, the eye will swing through an arc so that both images will once again be imaged in the foveas, and the object seen as single.

Helmholtz (1925) tried this experiment on himself. A prism held with its base toward his nose caused the image to displace in such a way that the eyes had actually to diverge from the parallel in order for him to maintain single vision. He could tolerate as much as 6 or 8 degrees of divergence before the field split into a double image. Helmholtz (1925) gives us some recipes for training the oculomotor system so that it can be controlled voluntarily. From this experience he judges that the lovely coordination of the eyes involved in the maintenance of single vision is acquired.

There is little doubt that convergence operates somehow to inform the observer about the distance to an object or, at least, the distance between two objects. There are really two questions to ask about this: first, what sort of distance information is given by convergence? and second, how is this information developed by the nervous system?

As intimated by the first question, it is possible that of all the cues we have considered thus far, convergence may well be the only one to give absolute distance information. The reader will recall that the Euclidean cues, relative brightness, interposition, the kinetic cues, and even accommodation can inform only about relative distance. Yet to some extent we may certainly judge how far an object is from our own bodies. It is theoretically possible, however, for the convergence angle of the eyes to represent the distance to an object, since it is simple to compute the distance to an object by taking into account the baseline or separation between the two eyes and the angles made by their lines of sight with respect to that baseline. The problem is somewhat more complicated in the case of asymmetric convergence, though it is still soluble trigonometrically (Graham, 1965a).

While it is theoretically possible for the degree of convergence to correspond to a given distance, it may or may not be true that the nervous system utilizes such information. The most important evidence bearing on this question is ambiguous. The so-called wallpaper illusion is a case in point. A visual pattern comprised of a series of vertical stripes may be viewed with different degrees of convergence and still be seen as single. Suppose, for example, that the eyes are converged for the distance of the pattern. In this case all the stripes in the two eyes will fall on corresponding retinal places. Now suppose that the eyes converge too much for the distance of the pattern. If the increased degree of convergence is just right, corresponding retinal regions will still be occupied by similar images of the stripes. There need not be any disparity if the increased vergence angle is an integer multiple of the visual angle separating the stripes. Effectively, then, the binocular view is identical for the two different vergence angles. Now, when this experiment is performed most subjects report that the stripes get thinner. Some report that they also come closer—which would correspond to the increased convergence—while still others report that they become somewhat more distant. Of course, so crude an experiment is inconclusive, since accommodation is free to vary and other cues may well be allowed to operate. A more tightly controlled experiment, such as that of Heinemann, Tulving, and Nachmias (1959), is necessary.

In their experiment these investigators paralyzed the accommodation of their subjects' eyes, and then presented luminous disc stimuli in a totally dark space so that ancillary cues would be minimized. The luminous discs were presented dichoptically—that is, the images to the two eyes were separately manipulable so that their biretinal loci might be varied. With these stimuli it was possible to keep the angular sizes of the discs constant while the degree of convergence needed to see the discs as a single object could be varied. Here too, as in the wallpaper experiment, the disc was seen to grow smaller with increased convergence. Subjects reported also that the disc became more *distant* as convergence was increased. The distance judgment was exactly opposite to what would be expected if convergence were a cue to absolute distance. As we shall see, however, this is not conclusive proof that convergence is not a cue to absolute distance.

An empirical rule known as *Emmert's law* states that the perceived size of an object of constant angular size is inversely proportional to its perceived distance. In the present case the seemingly smaller disc is reported to be more distant—just the opposite from what might be predicted from Emmert's law. Hence it might be concluded that convergence *per se* may affect the apparent size of an object though it does not permit the correct perception of distance. Contrary to this is the theory that convergence alters perceived distance, but this perception of distance is overshadowed by the resulting size difference, which elicits an incorrect judgment (as opposed to perception) of distance. Since this same problem will arise later on, in the context of our discussion of the moon illusion and of the Tausch-Gregory theory of optical illusions, we must leave it now with the tentative judgment that convergence may or may not be a cue to absolute distance.

If convergence is a cue to absolute distance, the problem arises as to how the distance information is produced. One obvious though probably incorrect theory is that stretch receptors in the extraocular muscles send signals back to the brain to provide information as to the positions of the eyes in the head. This is known as the *inflow* theory of Sherrington (1918).

There is no doubt that there are stretch receptors in the extraocular muscles (Daniel, 1946). Further, electrical discharges originating in the afferent nerve endings in the inferior oblique muscle of the goat have been recorded from the oculomotor nerve (Cooper, Daniel, and Whitteridge, 1953). These authors observed a spontaneous discharge from the eye muscle which increased when the muscle relaxed. Despite these physiological and anatomical findings, the psychological evidence suggests that inflow or proprioception is of limited value to the perceptual system.

Helmholtz (1925) observed that the position of an after-image in space does not change when the closed eye is pushed by some external means. More recently Brindley and Merton (1960) grasped the tendon of one eye muscle with a forceps and pulled the eyeball of an observer back and forth. With the surface of the eyeball and the surrounding eyelids anesthetized and with vision occluded, the observer could not tell that his eye was being moved. These results indicate that inflow from the stretch receptors cannot be used by an observer to monitor changes in the positions of his eyes.

Skavenski (1972) and Skavenski and Steinman (1970) have recently raised some questions about these results. As Skavenski argued, pressing on the eyeball with one's finger, as in Helmholtz's after-image experiment, may mask subtle sensations of eye movements. Also, the Brindley and Merton experiment placed the observer under duress, and this could have caused him to overlook proprioceptive information. In the Skavenski experiments a contact lens on the eyeball was attached to a mechanical system which exerted a precisely controlled force in one direction or the other on the eyeball. Two highly practiced observers were able to judge the direction of the mechanically produced turning of their eyeballs in total darkness, even when the surface of the eyeball and the conjunctiva were anaesthetized.

Skavenski and Steinman (1970) also disputed a related finding of Cornsweet (1956) to the effect that if a fixation point is removed from an otherwise empty, dark field and the observer instructed to maintain his direction of gaze, then his eye will wander slowly from the fixation point's position. The eye will jump back to correct the apparently ever-growing deviation relatively infrequently. With the fixation point visible, however, the eye executes many jumps or *saccades*. These corrective saccades occur when the eye has drifted but a few minutes of arc from the fixation position. Nachmias (1959) made similar observations and labeled the jumps in eye position *corrective saccades,* since their direction was opposite to the direction of the slow drifts. For their part, Skavenski-Steinman's two experienced observers were able to maintain their direction of gaze in the dark within 2 degrees of accuracy during a period of more than 2 minutes. In this case corrective saccades were used to maintain the position of the eyeball. Maintenance of eye position in the dark is far less accurate than when a fixation point is available for reference, and yet these results do suggest that there is some inflow available to a trained observer.

Even though the evidence of Skavenski and Steinman suggests that there may be some proprioception, other evidence indicates extreme unlikelihood that proprioception affects visual perception. Matin, Pearce,

Matin, and Kibler (1966) have provided us with some very convincing evidence about the ineffectiveness of proprioception. These researchers recorded the movements of the eye for three seconds after a luminous point stimulus was extinguished. After the three-second period a second luminous stimulus was presented to the subject, and he was required to determine whether the new stimulus was to the right or left of the original point stimulus. If the subject had information about what his own eye was doing in the dark for three seconds, then presumably he would be able to report accurately the true physical relations between the two stimuli. This follows from the fact that if there were proprioception and if the eye wandered from this primary position, the subject would know that his eye had wandered. He would then be able to take into account this shift from the primary position in making his subsequent judgment.

In point of fact, however, subjects make many errors in this kind of experiment (Matin and Kibler, 1966), since very often they will state that the second stimulus appeared to the left, say, of the position previously occupied by the first stimulus, when in actuality the new stimulus is to the right. The beautiful thing about the Matin, Pearce, Matin, and Kibler experiment, however, is that the judged position of the stimulus was usually correct with respect to the retinal location of the previous stimulus. Thus, if the second stimulus was imaged at a place to the left of the retinal place stimulated by the first point, the subject was likely to say that the new stimulus was to the right. This would occur even when the physical location of the second distal stimulus was to the left of the first, and if the eye moved toward the left in the intervening period. These results indicate that if proprioception occurs in the presence of visual information, it is not useful in allowing the observer to compensate for involuntary excursions of his eye.

Naturally enough, the alternative to the inflow theory of Sherrington is called the *outflow theory*. Helmholtz based this theory on the fact that the brain does know when the eyes are turned voluntarily in the dark. How could the brain know that the eyes are turning if there is no inflow? His answer was that in the absence of proprioception the awareness that the eyes are turning could be attributed to the same signals that flow outward from the brain to the extraocular muscles. If these outflowing signals are monitored by the brain, the observer could know that his eyes are turning.

This broadly stated theory is sufficient for the moment to indicate how information about convergence may be used by the observer. If he can monitor the commands to his eye muscles needed to fuse double images, he need not receive a return signal from the muscles themselves to know what they are doing. If proprioception is ineffective, however, the observer would not know what the eyeballs were actually doing if they should not follow the outflowing commands. He could only know that the eye muscles were instructed to rotate the eyeballs.

Skavenski, Haddad, and Steinman (1972) compared this outflow theory to the inflow theory in experiments involving conjugate eye movements. Thus, if the eye is kept pointing straight ahead to look at a target, the muscles must maintain a certain balance. By applying to the eyeball a force tending to turn it toward one side, Skavenski *et al.* caused the signals going to the muscles to be biased so that the eye could maintain its straight-ahead position. The muscles had to be kept in an abnormal state of tension to keep the target fixated. This meant that the outflow to the muscles was biased on one side even though the inflow from the stretch receptors was normal (since the eyes were in fact pointing straight ahead).

Despite the fact that the fixated target was actually straight ahead of the observer, measurements revealed that when the eye was under a load the target was not perceived as being straight ahead. These measurements were obtained by having the observer move a second target until it was perceived as being in the direction of the perceived "straight ahead," though this perceived straight-ahead did not correspond to the direction of the actually straight-ahead target being fixated. This experiment, and others as well, led Skavenski *et al.* to conclude that an observer does not use proprioception when it is in conflict with the outflow to the muscles. Thus, outflow is predominant in visual perception.

One obvious question raised by these results concerns the role of the sensory nerve endings in the extraocular muscles. There is no clear answer as yet. There is still a possibility that these nerve endings are involved in velocity control of the eyes during pursuit movements. Suppose that the eye tries to match the velocity of some moving target. Is the visual input sufficient to permit maintenance of central fixation of a moving target? It may be that such information is supplemented in some way by proprioceptive signals.

Still another possible role lies in the maintenance of muscle tonus. The muscles always exhibit spontaneous contractions and relaxations of a small magnitude when in a resting position. This may represent the typical slight oscillations of a servo system after it had reached some steady state position. Without feedback it might be impossible for the eyes to maintain a steady state even with a visual input. Such information may not be used at all in judging visual direction. This would be consistent with the results of Matin *et al.* (1966) and still provide a role for proprioception.

Another point in this context is that all the results considered so far about proprioception have been obtained in the study of the behavior of one eye as it executes lateral movements. Vergence movements involve different nerve centers than do conjugate movements. It is possible, though unlikely, that the proprioceptive signals go to centers involved in vergence but are irrelevant to conjugate or pursuit eye movements.

Vergence movements are essentially independent of conjugate movements. If, for example, the eyes were to converge in their maximum amount, as when a centrally fixated object is moved to within ten or twelve inches of the nose, and then the object were to be displaced laterally to the right, the angle made by the line of sight from the left eye to the baseline would become still smaller. The left eye would turn still more than it is capable of turning by convergence alone. This indicates that convergence and conjugate movements are additive or superimposable and therefore independent systems (Westheimer and Mitchell, 1956; Rashbass and Westheimer, 1961). Further, the reaction time for convergence is about 160 msec, while that for conjugate pursuit movements is about 125 msec (Yarbus, 1967). Saccades, which are also conjugate, have a reaction time of about 200 msec (Westheimer, 1954). Convergence to a new position may require a period as long as 800 msec, an exceedingly long time as compared to other kinds of eye movements.

Still another source of information about eye movements comes from neurophysiology. Stimulation of area 8—an area of the brain known as the frontal eye fields—will induce saccadic eye movements (Robinson, 1968). Stimulation of areas 18 and 19, in the visual cortex of the brain, excites conjugate eye movements (Wagman, Kreiger, and Bendham, 1958). This suggests that primary control over eye movements derives from the visual input, even though lower brain centers are also in the circuits that drive the eyes. Area 19 is also associated with convergence of the eyes—but so is area 22, which is in the motor cortex (Jampel, 1959). Therefore, overlapping but not identical brain structures may be involved in both the slow conjugate eye movements and in nonconjugate eye movements.

The fact that visual portions of the cerebral cortex are involved in

convergence supports the idea that depth information may be a byprod-
uct of convergence activity controlled by disparity of visual images. If
the eyes have to converge or diverge to see double images as single, the
outflowing signal to accomplish this may be registered at some other place
in the brain to indicate the distance of the object. This outflowing signal
is itself a correlate of distance. Feedback from the muscles is not necessary.

It is important to note that vergence movements may occur when the
disparity is too small to report. Thus, with disparities smaller than 5 or 10
minutes of arc, the observer may not be able to notice his double images
though he may change vergence anyway. Hence conscious awareness of
disparity is not a prerequisite of convergence.

So far we have had very little to say about convergence as a cue to
relative distance. The experiments we have been citing have all considered only the case in which a single object is placed at various distances
and the subject had to report its distance based upon convergence alone
or upon convergence with accommodation. Though judgments of absolute distance based upon convergence alone are not very accurate (Heine-
man, Tulving and Nachmias, 1959), convergence changes do have a large
effect in the sense that apparent absolute distance does change with convergence, albeit in the wrong direction. As we have intimated, the accompanying size changes suggest that convergence information is being used
correctly despite the subject's inability to report distance correctly.

This picture changes considerably in the case of relative distance—
i.e., when two objects at different distances are presented to the subject.
If he has normal binocular vision he can detect exquisitely small difference in the distances between the two objects. Moreover, his judgment
will reflect the correct direction of the difference in distance. There is a
real question, however, as to whether this is really an instance in which
the convergence of the eyes plays a role in making the depth judgment. It
is, rather, like the case in which blur circles are cues to depth instead of
the degree of accommodation of the eyes. In its present instance it is the
relative disparity between the objects that serves as the cue to relative
distance as well as to convergence. As we shall see later, convergence affects the reported amount of depth difference, but disparity alone is sufficient to denote the direction of the depth difference.

Retinal disparity. In the discussion of convergence we considered two
factors involved in initiating vergence changes: accommodation and dis-

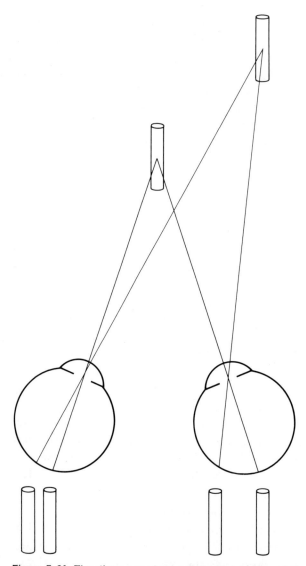

Figure 7–31. The discovery of stereopsis. The images of the two rods in the left eye are closer together than their images in the right eye. If the pictures of these rods are presented to the two eyes in a stereoscope, the observer perceives them in depth.

parity. Disparate images occupy different visual directions for the two eyes. Disparity caused the eyes to change vergence so that the image would be "seen" as single rather than as double. With two objects present and at different distances from the eye, one of the objects might be disparate, though the other, fixated, object might not be imaged on disparate retinal places. With some intermediate fixation, both objects could be imaged on disparate places. As a matter of fact, the total disparity is constant regardless of fixation. With intermediate fixation both objects have some disparity. The sum of the two disparities is equal to the disparity in the images of one object when the other object is perfectly fixated. Hence, the total retinal disparity in a scene is the same even though convergence may be free to vary. This relative disparity is invariant and is mathematically sufficient to denote the depth relations of the two objects. The depth response due to relative disparity, as opposed to convergence *per se*, is known as *binocular stereopsis* or simply *stereopsis*.

Stereopsis was "discovered" by the physicist Wheatstone (1838), when he concluded that the two eyes cannot get the same view of an object in depth. Suppose that two vertical rods were presented at different distances. As will be observed in Figure 7–31, the image of these two rods is different in one eye from their image in the other eye. Specifically, they are more widely separated in the right eye than in the left. Wheatstone wondered what would happen if he drew a picture of the right eye's view of the two rods and one of the left eye's view and placed the two flat pictures so that the right eye could see only its picture and the left eye only its picture. This he accomplished with a system of mirrors we have come to call the Wheatstone Stereoscope. It must have been quite thrilling for Wheatstone to look at these flat pictures in his stereoscope for the first time.

As with all discoveries, Wheatstone's was not without precursors. Leonardo da Vinci (Boring, 1942) had written long before that the two eyes had different views of objects—but he never built a stereoscope. Johannes Kepler could have built a stereoscope because he had a rather good grasp of the principles underlying stereopsis. Still, even though he did not invent the stereoscope or ever experience stereopsis, Kepler gave us the basis for the most widely accepted theory of how retinal disparity leads to stereopsis.

Kepler was walleyed. He was also myopic and suffered on occasion with monocular polyopia (Koestler, 1960). Too myopic to observe the stars (Gillispie, 1959), he relied exclusively on Tycho Brahe's excellent

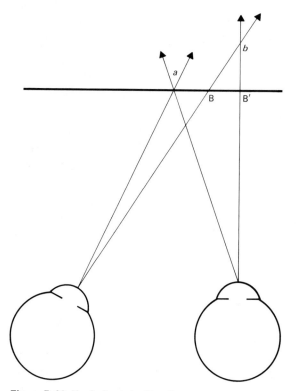

Figure 7–32. Kepler's projection theory.

data in determining the laws of planetary motion. It is interesting to speculate that Kepler's own visual defects may have been important factors in his theories of the visual process. He was the first to realize that the retinal image must be upside down, and probably also the first scientist to publish a theory of stereoscopic depth perception.

Kepler's own double vision may well have caused him to wonder whether other people saw double too. He reasoned that since the two eyes are located at different places when viewing a scene, people should see things double. It was surprising to him that they did not report frequent and striking doubleness of vision, since this was predictable from the geometry of binocular vision. To explain this apparent mystery Kepler proposed a theory labeled the Projection Theory, whose basic structure underlies virtually all the most widely accepted views of stereopsis.

As Koestler (1960) pointed out, Kepler was a strange mixture of modern scientist and Pythagorian mystic. On the one hand he could talk about elliptical orbits of planets and, on the other, seek a mystical geometrical design underlying the dimensions of their orbits. Similarly, he could talk about an inverted retinal image and, at the same time, think in terms of mental rays emanating from the eyes. As Kepler reasoned, if these mental rays emanated in straight lines from the two eyes, people would see the double images as single if they perceived an object point at the place of intersection of the mental rays.

This is illustrated in Figure 7–32, where the arrows represent the mental rays. A ray from one eye would then carry its image of an object and continue its progress through space. A ray from the other eye would also project the image belonging to that eye and ultimately intersect the corresponding ray from the first eye. This place of intersection was presumed by Kepler to be the place at which the object was perceived. As will be noted, the place of intersection at point b in the figure is behind the plane drawn through point a, so that object b must be seen behind object a if it is to be seen as single. The images B and B' are effectively fused at b and then are seen as a single object in depth. So Kepler accounted for the singleness of geometrically disparate images and depth perception at the same time.

As we shall see in the next chapter, Kepler's theory is isomorphic with modern fusional theories of stereopsis. According to these theories, the neural representations of the images in the two eyes must fuse or combine if stereopsis is to occur. It has been known for at least a hundred years that fusion is not really a necessary condition for stereopsis. Stereopsis may occur even when double images can be seen. While this does not disprove fusional theories, it does raise some doubt about adopting a straightforward theory in which phenomenal fusion is always a companion of depth perception. For if fusion is always represented phenomenally as singleness of vision, it cannot be the basis for stereopsis. If fusion can occur at some level other than that of awareness then, as we shall see, stereopsis can occur in the presence of diplopia (double images).

Stereopsis is closely related to convergence. After all, disparity leads to vergence changes, and stereopsis depends also upon disparity. This might recall an old theory maintaining that stereopsis occurs because the depth we see is based upon successive fixations at different vergence angles in the field of view.

Though eye movements have been shown to enhance stereo acuity (see Gettys and Harker, 1967), changes in convergence are not needed for stereopsis. Dove (1841) showed that stereo depth will occur when stimuli are presented by means of a brief electric spark that illuminates the scene for a tiny fraction of a second. This brief exposure time eliminates the possibility of vergence changes while the actual scene is being examined. This proves that active vergence is not essential for the occurrence of stereopsis, and suggests further that disparity may induce a depth effect in its own right and in relative independence of convergence. We shall return to the relation between disparity and convergence in the next chapter.

SUMMARY

In this chapter we have discussed most of the known cues to depth. Beginning with the pictorial cues, we sought to show that information in the static retinal image can be employed in perceiving depth, and discovered that depth perception is not solely dependent upon these static cues, since important information flows also from changes in the retinal image as the observer moves about. In addition to these kinetic cues we encountered cues deriving from the way in which an observer responds to a scene. Thus, we found, the mere act of deciding to look from one object to another may induce changes in both accommodation and convergence, and that, moreover, the blur circles affecting accommodation and convergence, and the double images in the binocular field of view, are important sources of information. This led us to consider some of the complexities underlying the processing of information contained in the binocular field of view.

8

binocular stereopsis

Stereopsis, or binocular disparity, has been studied more extensively than any of the other cues to depth. Because it is the center of much current work in both psychology and neurophysiology and can give us important insights into the functioning of the brain itself, it is, after color vision, the most fully developed area in all visual perception, and consequently it has been possible for workers in this area to formulate some rather elaborate theories to explain it. In this chapter we shall consider many of the facts discovered about binocular vision in order to evaluate these theories, as well as to discover something about the nature of theories in perception.

Before we can turn to the theories of stereopsis, however, we shall set forth some background on the methods used to generate stereoscopic displays. These methods are a natural introduction to the problem of computing depth from disparity, since all theories of stereopsis are concerned with how the brain makes this same computation.

STEREOSCOPIC INSTRUMENTS AND DISPLAYS

Instruments used to display stereograms present one picture to one eye and another picture to the other eye. The ways in which these pictures differ determine whether or not depth will be perceived.

The original stereoscope was designed by Wheatstone (1838) for his early investigations of stereopsis. Although a similar instrument had been built by Helioth four years earlier (Dudley, 1951), Wheatstone's impor-

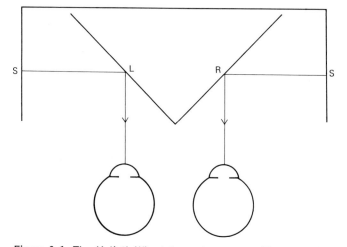

Figure 8–1. The Helioth-Wheatstone stereoscope. The two mirrors L and R are arranged to reflect the images of the stimuli S to the left and the right eye.

tant papers caused his instrument to be remembered. We shall refer to this instrument as the Helioth-Wheatstone stereoscope in belated recognition of Helioth's contribution. As shown in Figure 8–1, the instrument was comprised of two mirrors arranged so that two drawings could be presented separately to the two eyes. When different images are presented separately, one to each eye, the term *dichoptic* will be used (Kolers and Rosner, 1960). If the images presented to the two eyes are the same, the phrase *binoptic stimulation* will be used. If one eye should be closed or occluded while looking at a scene, the term will be *monoptic*.

A version of the Helioth-Wheatstone stereoscope is used today in viewing X-rays. One problem with this type of instrument is that it may create a conflict between convergence and accommodation. The stimulus cards in Figure 8–1 are usually only a few inches from the eyes, so that both eyes must accommodate for a short distance if they are to see the stimuli clearly. If the angles of the mirrors L and R are such that the lines-of-sight of the two eyes must be parallel, as shown in the figure, then the two eyes will be converged for a very distant object. The unpracticed observer may have difficulty in getting the two displays in good binocular registration.

There are two basic approaches to this problem. The first approach entails mounting the mirrors and stimulus cards on arms that can be pivoted around a point between the two mirrors. By adjusting the angle between the two mirrors we increase the convergence angle needed to get the images into good registration. This increased convergence angle is more consistent with the accommodation needed to view the stimuli.

The second approach is to place lenses between the eyes and the stimuli. In the case of a normal youthful eye, it will accommodate for infinity if it views an object at a distance of one meter through a one-diopter lens. This is because an object 1 meter away from a 1-diopter lens is at the

Figure 8–2. The Brewster stereoscope. Each of the stimuli is placed at the focus of its lens so that light from each point on a stimulus is collimated. These parallel rays insure that the image of a stimulus is formed at the same retinal place regardless of variation in the separation of the viewer's eyes and of changes in the lateral position of the eyes.

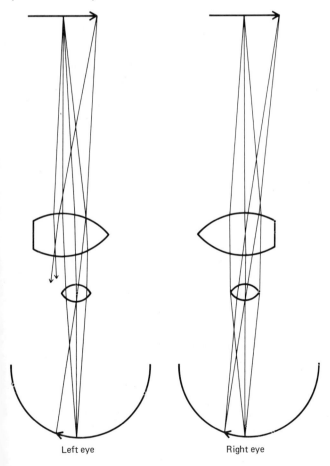

Left eye   Right eye

focus of that lens. As explained in Chapter 7, the light coming from the object through the lens will be refracted by the lens so that it appears to come from infinity. Hence it is that a stimulus seen through the lens is optically at a very great distance from the observer.

The famous Brewster stereoscope makes use of the foregoing facts in eliminating mirrors, as is illustrated in Figure 8–2. The instrument consists of half-lenses serving to collimate light in the same manner as do full positive (biconvex) lenses. If the two half-fields are arranged so that each of them is centered upon the optic axis of its lens, the two eyes will relax accommodation and diverge so that their axes are parallel. This places both half-fields in perfect binocular registration. The lens stereoscope is limited to displays in which the two half-fields have center-to-center separations approximately the same as the interocular separation of the observer—about 2.5 inches. If it is necessary to view large patterns with center-to-center separations greater than the interocular separation, the lens segments may be combined with mirrors or prisms. The common Stereopticon—or parlor stereoscope of Victorian days—was basically a Brewster stereoscope. Oliver Wendell Homes invented a similar stereo-scope for home entertainment.

Another means of viewing stereograms is that of a single mirror. I first saw this method in the laboratory of Dr. S. Papert at the Massachu-setts Institute of Technology. If one half of a stereo display is placed be-fore the left eye, and a mirror-image of the right half of the display placed before the right eye, then a mirror held normal to the surface of the dis-play and between the two half-fields, as in Figure 8–3, will allow normal convergence and accommodation while viewing the display. The eyes will converge and accommodate for the actual distance of the display and pro-vide a view of both half-fields in good binocular registration. This method is commonly used in viewing computer-generated oscilloscope displays.

In addition to the direct optical methods described above for viewing stereograms, there are the common *anaglyph* and *polaroid* methods. The anaglyph (see Fig. 8–4, facing p. 207) is a stereogram in which one half-field is printed with red ink upon the other half-field, which is printed in green ink. When a pair of eyeglasses containing a red filter for one eye and a green filter for the other eye is worn, depth may be seen. The red filter reduces the intensity of the green light so that the eye covered by the filter sees high-contrast black lines in the green portion of the display. Conversely, the green filter cuts down on the red light so that its eye sees the red display as black. This method provides adequate separation of the

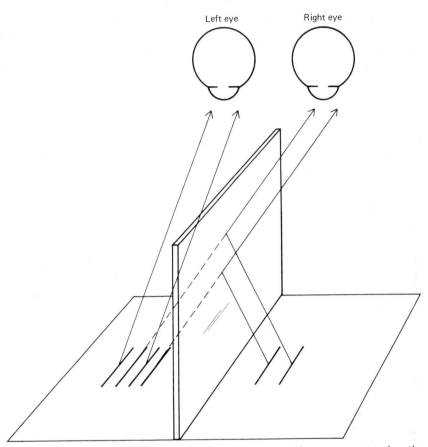

Figure 8–3. This mirror method for viewing stereograms allows one eye to view the virtual image of one half of the stereogram while the other eye views its half of the stereogram directly.

images to the two eyes, and some very convincing depth effects may be obtained. The left eye's image, need not be totally excluded from the right eye, and *vice versa*. As we shall see later, the requisite degree of isolation of the two views from each other may have important consequences for theory.

In the polarization method, which is similar to the anaglyph method, instead of using color as a means for segregating the two images, the angle of polarization of the light coming from the two half-fields is made

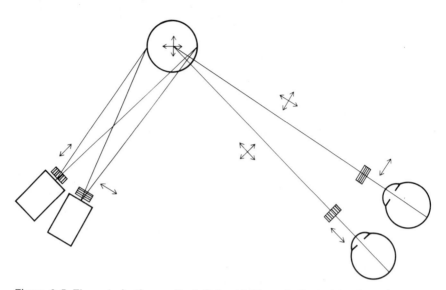

Figure 8–5. The polarization method. Polaroid filters, indicated by the striped rectangles, are placed in front of the projectors and also in front of the eyes. This insures that one eye will see one of the projected images while the other eye sees the other projected image.

different. Then, if polaroid filters are worn, one image may be excluded from one eye and passed into the other eye.

If two projectors were arranged to project the two half-fields of a stereogram onto a screen, the two images could be isolated from each other for stereo viewing if the light beams were polarized. Thus, with polarizing filters oriented at different angles in front of the projectors, the two images may be superimposed on the screen and then sorted out again at the observer's eyes if he is also wearing polarizers. The two polarizers have to be at different angles also—normally 90 degrees out of phase—if they are to do their job. Thus, with a polarizer arranged at an angle over a projector lens so that only vertical electric vibrations are passed onto the screen, a polarizer passing only horizontal vibrations in front of one eye would reject the light from that projector. On the other hand, the image would be seen by the other eye if it were covered by a vertical polarizer (Figure 8–5).

It is important to note, however, that this scheme will not work with just any projection screen. Since light will be depolarized if it is reflected from a diffusing surface, a screen with a metallic coating is necessary to ensure that polarization is maintained after reflection. An aluminized directional screen is commonly used for stereo projection. Just as with the anaglyphs, however, optical "cross-talk" can occur with polarized displays. The interference may arise from inefficient polarizers, which pass considerable unpolarized light. It may also arise at the screen, which tends partially to depolarize light. Despite this, good stereopsis is possible with relatively high levels of cross-talk.

Anaglyph displays may also be projected. Two projectors, one covered by a red filter and the other by a green, can project two differently colored images onto a screen. These images may then be viewed through a pair of filters that sort them out for stereo viewing. Polarized displays are possible with one projector, by means of a special slide known as a Vectograph. This slide combines the two half-fields to give a composite image in which the angle of polarization of the light after passing through the slide depends upon the cross of the disparity. Production of the Vectograph is expensive and requires considerable skill.

THE ESTIMATION OF DEPTH AND DISPARITY MAGNITUDES

Disparity refers to the difference in horizontal angular separation between corresponding elements on the two retinas. Thus, in the classic Wheatstone stereogram the two lines presented to one eye are farther apart than are the two lines presented to the other eye. This stereogram is shown in Figure 8–6 with a somewhat exaggerated disparity. If the left-hand lines in the two halves of the stereogram are bifoveally fixated, they are said to be fused in the sense of motor fusion—that is, the two lines lie along the same visual direction even when the two eyes are alternately occluded. When the left-hand lines are fused by proper convergence of the two eyes, the right-hand lines are unfused or disparate, which means that they lie along different visual directions. When the two eyes are closed and

Figure 8–6. Wheatstone's stereogram.

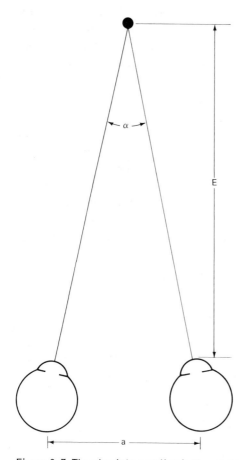

Figure 8–7. The absolute parallax is the angle α.

opened alternately, the line on the right in the monoptic views may be seen as alternately shifting somewhat from left to right.

When viewing such a display, it is possible to shift convergence so that the right-hand lines exhibit motor fusion, and the left-hand lines become disparate. Now, this shift in convergence angle to fixate the right-hand lines has the same angular magnitude as does the retinal disparity. It is in fact possible to define relative disparity in terms of the magnitude of angular convergence change needed to fixate points successively at different distances from an observer.

Considerations such as these led the earlier investigators of binocular vision to define two kinds of disparity. The first kind might be called the *absolute disparity*, or *absolute parallax*, of a point, since the two eyes must view a point from two different positions. It is really identical with the convergence angle needed to get the images of the point centered in the two foveas.

Figure 8–7 shows the two eyes viewing a single isolated point. If we assume that the point is imaged in the centers of the two foveas, the absolute parallax is the angle α. It should be obvious that with the point at a constant distance E, the angle α is dependent upon the interocular separation a. This distance between the centers of the pupils of the eyes is about 2.5 inches (6.4 cm) in the average observer; still, since a varies by as much as 0.5 of an inch from observer to observer, differences between individuals can have a marked effect on the size of α.

The computation of α is quite straightforward when the point is directly in front of the observer and not too far above or below the direction of his gaze. From elementary trigonometry:

$$\tan \alpha/2 = \frac{a}{2E}.$$

For small values of α, α in radians is equal to a/E. Whether α is given in degrees or in radians, it is a measure of how much the eyes must converge to look at a point. If the point is very distant, α becomes very small. At close distances the angle becomes large.

Accurate computation of the absolute parallax becomes somewhat more complicated in the case of asymmetric convergence. This occurs when the point lies off to the observer's side. In cases where the asymmetry is not too large and where α is small, the same equation a/E may be used, since the errors introduced by the asymmetry are very slight (Graham, 1965a). This conclusion was also reached by von Kries (Helmholtz, 1925).

The *relative parallax*, or *relative binocular disparity*, of two points lying at two different distances from an observer is the difference between the angles of convergence which would be required to fixate both images (Fig. 8–8). In this case the relative disparity

$$\rho = \frac{a\,(E_1 - E_2)}{E_1 \cdot E_2}.$$

If the depth interval δ between E_1 and E_2 is small relative to the distance of either point from the eyes, then the following expression may be used:

$$\rho = a\,\delta/E^2,$$

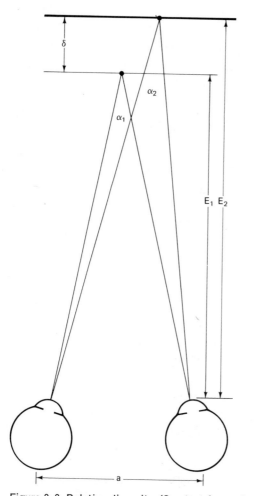

Figure 8–8. Relative disparity. (See text for explanation.)

where E is the average of E_1 and E_2. The binocular disparity as calculated from this formula is inversely proportional to the square of the observer's mean distance from the two points.

THEORIES OF STEREOPSIS

The fusion theory. Most workers in the perception field accept one version or another of the classic fusion theory, whose basic underlying ideas are contained within Kepler's projection theory described briefly in Chapter 7. In Figure 8–9, which depicts the fusion theory, a stereogram is placed before two eyes. The right half-field contains two lines and a large dot, but the separation between the dot and the lines is greater than the corresponding separations in the left half-field. As indicated in this figure, this stereogram causes the perception of the left-hand line to be nearer than the dot, and the right-hand line more distant than the plane of the dot.

The rays connecting the lines and dots with the eyes may be thought to represent Kepler's mental rays. Thus, the rays connecting the central

Figure 8–9. How the projection theory would explain depth resulting from viewing a stereogram.

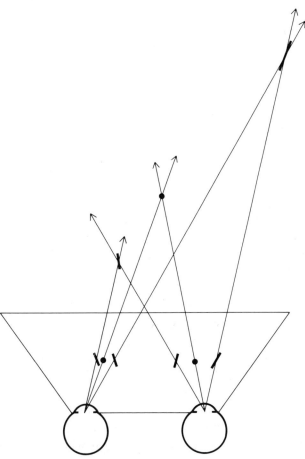

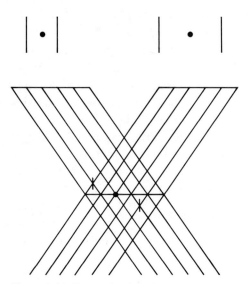

Figure 8–10. The projection field.

dots with the eyes converge behind the stereogram. The rays connecting the eyes with the left-hand vertical lines cross in front of the plane of
the dot. Kepler postulated that the binocularly perceived object would be
seen at the point where such rays cross over. In this case, following the
discussion in Chapter 7, we refer to the *crossed disparity* of the vertical
lines, which become localized forward of the fixation plane. Again, the
rays going to the right-hand vertical lines do not cross either in front of
the plane of fixation or within the plane of fixation. The mental rays must
continue through the plane of fixation until they finally cross behind it.
The right-hand display elements have an *uncrossed disparity,* and so we
see that the depth of an element depends upon where the mental rays
cross or combine in three-dimensional space.

  As suggested above, the modern fusional theories are similar to Kepler's projection theory. In 1933 Boring proposed that there is a nerve net
or projection field in the brain similar to the one shown in Figure 8–10. If
we imagine that there are fixed pathways in the brain that correspond to
specific points on the two retinas, it is easy to see how depth may be computed in such a network. The dots converge, or meet, at the central layer
of the projection field. The left-hand lines combine on one side of this central layer, corresponding to a lesser distance from the eye, while the right-

hand lines combine on the other side of the central layer—to correspond to a greater distance. In essence, this theory states that there is a three-dimensional, or volumetric, model of external physical space in the head.

This internalized version of Kepler's theory was rediscovered several times. In 1951 Lord Charnwood published the same model in his *Essay on Binocular Vision* without mentioning Boring's earlier contribution. Linksz published the same model in 1952—but added something, however. He localized the actual projection field in layer 4 of area 17, with the stripe of Gennari serving the role of the central layer of the projection field; i.e., points in the plane of fixation were presumed to be represented at the stripe of Gennari. This cannot be correct, however, since the stripe of Gennari is a fiber tract. Finally, Dodwell and Engel (1963) also published this model. Their contribution was the addition of a central "recognizer" that serves to detect signals arising from fused image representations in the network.

Discussing this remarkable instance of multiple scientific invention in a personal communication (1964), Boring remarked that certain generally accepted concepts led to this kind of model. It could not have been thought of unless one was ready to accept the notion of projection of the periphery onto the central nervous system. The notion of tridimensional isomorphism is also central to the development. Boring credited Koffka with influencing his thinking in this regard. Thus, if one accepts the concepts of point-to-point projection from the periphery and psychophysical isomorphism, he would be likely to develop the fusional theory of stereopsis.

The basic idea of fusion has appeared in other forms throughout the history of this subject. Von Tschermak-Seysenegg (1952) held that similar elements in the two eyes combine even when they are imaged at disparate places, but did not believe that representations of these elements simply add up to give a more intense combined binocular image. He suggested that with one line imaged in one eye and other line imaged in the other eye, representations of the two images in the nervous system partially inhibit each other, though the remaining level of activity produced by these two lines does add up. In this way he accounted for the fact that in daylight, when one closes one of his eyes, the world doesn't appear to grow dimmer. As we shall see, this is similar to the position taken more recently by Levelt (1964); but von Tschermak-Seysenegg went even farther than this. He proposed also that when two lines are presented to disparate retinal places, as in a dichoptic view, they are attracted toward each other.

234   **234**

567   **567**

Figure 8–11. The displacement phenomenon. When viewed through a stereoscope the numeral 6 appears to lie directly under the numeral 3, even though its half-images are actually placed on either side of the 3 in the separate half-fields.

This attraction he referred to as *assimilation of visual directions,* or *allelotropia.*

Allelotropia is best understood as an apparent shifting of the lateral position of an element when a similar element is presented to a disparate position in the other eye (Figure 8–11). This figure is similar to one in a paper by Werner (1937), an independent discoverer of allelotropia. Werner termed the phenomenon *displacement,* but he was referring to essentially the same facts.

As indicated by Figure 8–11, in displacement, or allelotropia, disparate images may appear to combine in binocular view at an intermediate position. Thus, though the half-images of the numeral 6 in the two sides of the figure are displaced to either side of the central position just under the numeral 3, when the half-fields are combined stereoscopically the fused image is at an intermediate lateral position. Of course, it is also seen in depth.

Many investigators have adverted to the displacement phenomenon. Werner (1937) and von Tschermak-Seysenegg (1952) thought of displacement as an indication that similar disparate images are attracted toward each other to fuse. This is very much like the position of the Gestalt psychologists, who believed that stereoscopic depth may be attributed to an attractive force that tends to cause similar disparate images to fuse in the brain field. The energy involved in the attraction was believed to become translated into an appearance of depth (Koffka, 1935). Charnwood (1951), Linschoten (1956), Sperling (1970a), and Dodwell (1970) also conceived of displacement as representing the fusion or combining of disparate elements. Linschoten accepted a theory reminiscent of the Gestalt notion that fusion occurs in a field. The other authors believed that displacement indicates the occurrence of fusion in a projection field similar to the one described by Boring.

It is important to be clear about the idea that displacement indicates the occurrence of fusion in the projection field. This is tantamount to positing an isomorphic relation between the neurological event of fusion in the projection field and the experience of the unification of disparate images. Von Tschermak-Seysenegg invented the term *sensory fusion* to describe the drawing together and combining of disparate images. He distinguished this from *motor fusion,* which stands for the changing of the vergence of the eyes so that images previously disparate come to fall upon corresponding places in the central retinas.

This latter fusion is a motor response to disparity, and after its occurrence the images of the object are no longer disparate. Sensory fusion, however, is the more interesting concept since it implies that it is possible for the visual direction associated with a given retinal point to change when a somewhat disparate retinal point is stimulated in the other eye. As we shall see later, considerable use has been made of the idea that visual directions associated with given retinal points may be changeable (see Dodwell, 1970), as contrasted with the notion that there is a fixed, built-in relation between points on the retinal surface and directions is visual space (Walls, 1951*a*). In any event, fusion theory entails the idea that visual direction is labile, or changeable, and that such changes may easily be produced by stimulating the two eyes with disparate elements.

Koffka (1935) raised a tantalizing question about the fusion of disparate stimuli. Figure 8–12 portrays a simple stereogram. When the observer converges his eyes so that the lines P and P′ are in good binocular registration, the lines F and F′ are imaged on disparate retinal places—and Koffka wondered why the disparity between F and F′ should determine the occurrence of stereopsis. After all, F is disparate with respect also to other points on the surface on which F′ is drawn. These points all reflect light to the eye. Why, he asked, does F not fuse or interact with the point represented by the dot between P′ and F′? For some reason the points not

Figure 8–12. Koffka's question: Why does F interact with F′ to produce depth, and not fuse with the point represented by the dot near F′?

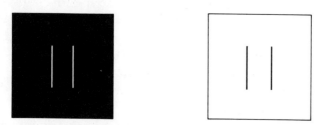

Figure 8–13. An opposite-contrast stereogram.

on F′ do not interact with F. Koffka's answer is that only similar elements will fuse if they are imaged in disparate retinal places. As we shall see in Chapter 12 this is consistent with the Gestalt law that attractive forces exist between similar visual stimuli—and this law of similarity was presumed to be operative in the binocular realm.

Helmholtz (1925) came to a similar conclusion, though he did not propose a mechanism to account for binocular interaction of disparate stimuli. Figure 8–13 shows a stereogram in which the left half-field is a black line-drawing on a white background, while the right half-field is a white line-drawing on a black background. Despite the fact that the two half-fields have opposite contrasts, stereopsis results when this pattern is viewed in a stereoscope. Helmholtz's conclusion was that similar disparate contours interact to produce depth perception. As we shall see, Helmholtz did not accept the idea that similar spatial contours fuse, but this is the inference drawn by many other workers in the field.

Apart from the Gestalt notion of attraction because of similarity, there is another theory of the mechanism underlying fusion of similar spatial contours, this attributable to von Tschermak-Seysenegg (1952). With reference to Figure 8–12, he suggested that line F actively inhibits excitation arising from the uniformly illuminated surface surrounding line F′. This uniform white area is blanked, or inhibited, by line F because the contours presented to one eye are always predominant when a uniform field is simultaneously presented to the other eye. This leaves only line F′ in the vicinity of line F in the binocular field, since line F′ inhibits also the white surface surrounding line F. These remaining contours are therefore free to fuse or combine in the binocular field.

The stereograms invented by Julesz (1964) demonstrate the inadequacy of the foregoing theory. One of these stereograms is reproduced in

Figure 8–14, and the method underlying its construction is shown beneath it. One half-field of this stereogram is comprised of an array of computer-generated random dots. Actually, the two half-fields are identical except that a rectangular inner portion of one of them was shifted slightly toward one side, and the gap introduced by the shift was filled with an independent set of random dots. This shift introduced the disparity. When each half-field is viewed monoptically, the observer sees a uniform texture. When it is viewed in a stereoscope, however, an inner rectangular portion of the array is seen floating above the background texture.

The fact that depth occurs in this stereogram is inconsistent with von Tschermak-Seysenegg's theory. Imagine that the background dots of the two half-fields fall on corresponding retinal places. In that case similar clusters of dots within the inner square will fall on disparate places. Unlike line F' in Figure 8–12, however, for every dot cluster falling in a

Figure 8–14. Julesz' stereogram. The two half-fields are identical random arrays of dots except that the central portion of one of the half-fields is shifted toward one side, as illustrated by the letter matrices. (After Julesz, 1971)

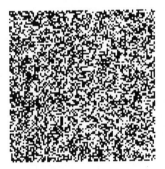
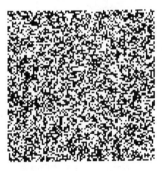

1	0	1	0	1	0	0	1	0	1
1	0	0	1	0	1	0	1	0	0
0	0	1	1	0	1	1	0	1	0
0	1	0	Y	A	A	B	B	0	1
1	1	1	X	B	A	B	A	0	1
0	0	1	X	A	A	B	A	1	0
1	1	1	Y	B	B	A	B	0	1
1	0	0	1	1	0	1	1	0	1
1	1	0	0	1	1	0	1	1	1
0	1	0	0	0	1	1	1	1	0

1	0	1	0	1	0	0	1	0	1
1	0	0	1	0	1	0	1	0	0
0	0	1	1	0	1	1	0	1	0
0	1	0	A	A	B	B	0	0	1
1	1	1	B	A	B	A	0	0	1
0	0	1	A	A	B	A	0	1	0
1	1	1	B	B	A	B	0	0	1
1	0	0	1	1	0	1	1	0	1
1	1	0	0	1	1	0	1	1	1
0	1	0	0	0	1	1	1	1	0

given region on one eye's retina, another dissimilar cluster falls in the corresponding region of the other eye's retina. It is not likely that inhibition could occur here as it might in Figure 8–12.

Fusion theories have been gaining support from recent physiological studies. Hubel and Wiesel (1962) have found that some cells in the cortex will respond when a specific kind of stimulus is presented any place within a circumscribed region on the retina. Thus, a small vertical line will cause a particular cortical unit to fire. If the line is rotated about its center to another orientation, the cell will stop firing, though presumably some other cell will fire in response to the line in its new orientation. In the case of a line of fixed orientation the cell will fire even if the line is moved to different positions on the retina. The region of the retina allowing the cell to respond when a stimulus is placed within it is called the cell's *receptive field.*

As we know, different cells respond to different classes of stimuli, and each of these cells has a receptive field at the retinal surface. The size of the receptive field differs from cell to cell, and cells responding to different features may have overlapping receptive fields. Therefore, though there is a rough correspondence between cortical locations and retinal locations, different units within a cortical region fulfill different functions. Some respond to certain features of the input; others respond to still other features in the same regions. Most feature detectors may be influenced by either eye. Thus, a vertical line presented to one eye may cause a unit to fire, but presenting this same vertical line to the other eye may cause the firing rate of the feature detector to increase. Sometimes a line in one eye will affect a detector, but will not affect it when the line is presented alone to the other eye. The firing rate of the feature detector will be greater when both eyes see the line than when only the first eye sees it.

This phenomenon demonstrates that input to the two eyes may have different effects on different feature detectors. And so we may conclude that regions in the two eyes serve to activate common cortical cells, and that small regions in the two eyes probably activate large assemblies of cortical units.

Barlow, Blakemore, and Pettigrew (1967) found that in area 17 of the cat single feature detectors will respond to stimuli imaged at disparate retinal places. Thus, if a line were presented to one place in one eye, presentation of another line to a different retinal place in the other eye would cause a cortical unit to fire. Some units fired with very small disparities, others fired with wider disparities. As may be concluded, the firing of cortical units in the presence of disparate stimuli represents the fusion of the disparate inputs.

Hubel and Wiesel (1970) performed a similar study on the macaque monkey, whose visual system is much closer to that of the human than is the cat's. While they did not find units responding to specific disparities in area 17 of the monkey, such units were found in area 18, the parastriate cortex—from which we must conclude that Linksz (1952) was in error when he localized the projection field in area 17. Binocular units in area 17 in the macaque fired only when a stimuli fell on corresponding retinal places.

We can see from all this that the built-in wiring of the nervous system does allow for physiological occurrences that are analogous to sensory fusion. If similar spatial contours are imaged at disparate retinal places in the two eyes, then single cortical units will respond. Different units respond when there are different degrees of disparity. Perhaps Koffka's question as to why disparate contours fuse has been answered.

To summarize: According to the fusion theory of stereopsis, disparate similar spatial contours selectively activate common cortical cells. The activation of a common cortical unit is accompanied by a shift in the visual directions of the disparate contours so that they appear to be attracted toward each other. When this shift is complete, we may speak of total sensory fusion of the contours.

Critique of the fusion theory. One of the most serious flaws in the theory is that it is incomplete. The physiological data on which this presentation relies so heavily were obtained in anesthetized animals. These animals could see nothing at all; they were certainly unable to see the depth of an object in the field of view. Unless one accepts the idea that the problem of perception is solved once it is possible to show how some kind of picture of the scene becomes represented in the brain, more work is needed.

Also, from the evidence it is plausible that the disparity detectors actually initiate vergence movements of the eye. Unless it is shown that vergence and stereopsis are mediated by the same mechanisms, then we must reserve judgment as to whether the disparity detectors play a direct role in stereopsis. Nevertheless, it is reasonable to assume that the disparity detectors play some role in binocular vision—indeed, may well constitute an important early stage in the process. But even so, there is still the problem of generalizing from single cortical units to global psychological processes.

Figure 8–15. Another demonstration of the displacement phenomenon. With F and F' fused, **a** may appear to be shifted toward **b**, as indicated by its misalignment with the small line (nonius). This is not a universally perceived effect.

Another problem with the theory is its reliance upon the displacement phenomenon. This became necessary for the reason that stereopsis can occur without complete fusion of disparate half-images (Ogle, 1953). Depth may be perceived in stereograms even though double images are visible. Partial fusion or displacement was therefore considered to be a possible basis for depth perception. Figure 8–15 shows another stereogram designed to demonstrate the displacement phenomenon. This stereogram is similar to a conventional Wheatstone pattern. The lines on the left sides of the two half-fields are labeled with the letters F and F' to indicate that they are to be fixated carefully. The small line in the upper part of the right half-field, placed to the right of F', is known as a *nonius* marker. The distance between the nonius and F' is equal to the distance between F and *a* in the left half-field. The disparity between *a* and *b* is great enough that the two lines may be seen as double images when F and F' are fused. Displacement occurs when the line *a* in the dichoptically viewed stereogram is not perceived as directly under the nonius but is seen instead as shifted toward *b*. This observation led Werner and others to assert that *a* is displaced toward *b* because of an attractive force between the two lines.

The shift of *a* toward *b* can be given another explanation. Suppose, as illustrated in Figure 8–16, that fixation is not exactly on F, but on a point somewhat behind F, so that the half-images F and F' are actually imaged at very slightly disparate places. If this inadvertent fixation disparity should be small enough, the two half-images could not be seen as double. Yet such a disparity of fixation would in fact cause the two lines *a* and *b* to be perceptibly displaced toward each other.

The foregoing explanation, proposed by Ogle (1950), was based upon the fact that many people have a slight *fixation disparity*. Thus, when such people assume that they are fixating on a point, they may actually be fixating slightly in front of the point or slightly behind it. On this basis Ogle proposed that some observers should report displacement in a direction that is actually opposite to that reported by Werner, and that there should be strong individual differences in the displacement phenomenon.

Kaufman (1964a) noted that displacement was observed in a complex stereogram by only two of his nine subjects, but that displacement could be produced and manipulated in all subjects by changing the binocular registration of the fixation elements in the stereogram. Pitblado (1966), in a more systematic study, found that displacement does in fact vary with the individual rather than with either the sign (crossed or uncrossed) or

Figure 8–16. Ogle's theory of the displacement phenomenon. The subject is attempting to fixate the point **a.** In actuality he is fixating on a point in space F, which is behind **a.** The half-images of the point **b** (open circles) projected onto the actual plane of fixation (dashed line) are closer together than the half-images of **b** projected onto the line drawn through **a.** The half-images of **a** on the actual plane of fixation may be so close together that they are perceived as single. This would occur with small fixation disparities, i.e., when F is but a small distance behind **a.** The fixation disparity is exaggerated in this figure.

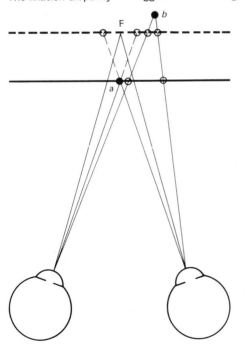

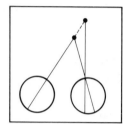

Figure 8–17. Panum's limiting case.

the magnitude of the disparity. He found also that displacement could be affected by the degree of convergence or divergence required to see a fixation point as single. It must therefore be maintained that there is no evidence that displacement represents a shifting of the visual direction of a point when a disparate point is stimulated in the other eye. It is at least equally plausible that displacement is due to unnoticed disparity of fixation as illustrated in Figure 8–16.

Both Werner (1937) and Linschoten (1956) believed that the magnitude of displacement is correlated with the magnitude of perceived depth. For his part, Pitblado (1966) was unable to demonstrate such a relation. Hence it must be concluded that the phenomenon of displacement is not convincing proof of the occurrence of fusion, or of a tendency to sensory fusion.

Still another criticism of fusion theories is that they provide no mechanism to eliminate "ghost" images. To understand this problem we must first describe the so-called *Panum limiting case*, as illustrated in Figure 8–17. The inset shows how objects may be arranged in three-dimensional space to produce the images represented in the stereogram. It will be seen that when two lines are presented to the right eye and one line to the left eye, in the dichoptic view the right-hand line will be perceived as more distant than the left-hand line. This stereogram gets its name from the fact that three lines or points—one for one eye and two for the other— are the minimum conditions for the production of stereopsis.

Fusional theory has no trouble explaining this phenomenon. If the single line in the left eye is superimposed binocularly on the left-hand

Figure 8–18. Multiple fusion.

line in the right eye, it must also fuse simultaneously with uniocular right-hand line. This is illustrated in Figure 8–18, which shows three lines in one half-field and a single line in the other. When the single line is binocularly superimposed on the left-hand line in the other half-field, the remaining two uniocular lines are seen in depth. Moreover, the middle line is closer than the right-hand line—as may also be predicted from the model. The reason this occurs in the model is that the disparity between the fused line and the two right-hand lines in Figure 8–18 is identical to the visual angles separating these two lines from the left-hand line in the same half-field.

Now that we have established the possibility of multiple fusion, we must turn to the diagram in Figure 8–19 depicting the possible fusional

Figure 8–19. "Ghost" images arise in the projection field when F combines with **b** and when F' combines with **a.** There is no provision in the classic fusion theory to prevent these products of multiple fusion.

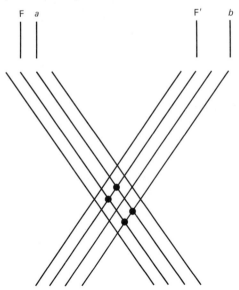

combinations that exist in a Wheatstone stereogram. We see here that the fusion of lines a and b is not the only possibility; the half-image b may also fuse with the line F in the other eye and, similarly, the half-image of a may also fuse with line F'. This means that there are actually four—not two—different fusional possibilities in the projection field. It may be argued from the limiting case that in addition to the fusion of F and F' and of a and b, the fusion possibilities of a with F' and b with F should also be perceived. This does not actually occur in perception. When F and F' are fused, the observer reports seeing only two lines when disparities are small and only three lines when they are large enough to produce double vision (diplopia) of a and b.

There is no mechanism in fusional theory as described here to account for this last fact. Julesz (1971) was one of the first to point out that multiple fusional possibilities or "ghosts" may exist. He was puzzled by the fact that in his random dot stereogram the subject sees two clear planes of depth, and wondered why dots in the disparate regions did not fuse with all of the other nearby disparate dots, thereby producing uncertain depth. In consequence, he proposed a model of stereoscopic depth perception which he believed capable of eliminating ghost images in his stereograms. This model, which he termed the "difference field model," is a modified version of the fusion theory. Unfortunately, the difference field model is unable to eliminate ghosts in ordinary line stereograms.

It can be seen that existing fusional theories have difficulty with several facts. First, complete sensory or perceived fusion is not necessary to the occurrence of stereopsis. Second, partial displacement is not an unequivocal sign of sensory fusion, since there is no proof that displacement may not be caused by fixation disparity. Third, perceived displacement is not correlated with perceived depth. Fourth, fusion theories are haunted by predicted ghost images that are simply not perceptible. Other difficulties will be mentioned later.

On the positive side, fusion theories make use of a simple and direct means for the computation of depth—namely, the projection field network. Also, the data of Hubel and Wiesel and of Barlow, Blakemore, and Pettigrew suggest that such a network may in fact have an embodiment within the nervous system. It may be possible to rationalize some of the difficulties cited above by proposing that the projection field need not be available to perception. Instead, the perceived view is simply that of the superimposed monocular fields, so modified that some of the monocular elements are seen as more or less distant than other monocular elements.

This would certainly get rid of the ghosts and allow for stereopsis in the presence of double images. It is the approach suggested by Helmholtz (1925) and adapted by Sperling (1970*a*).

The theory of local signs. The perceived position of a point in space may vary with the position of its image on the retina. Thus, if an image of a point is formed to the left side of the fovea, an observer is likely to say that the point lies off to the right side of his direction of gaze. If the image were then to be elevated above the horizontal plane, the point might then be perceived as moving downward relative to the direction of gaze. Hence, any point of excitation of the retina could be associated more or less reliably with a given direction in the visual field.

Lotze (Pastore, 1971) held that each point on the retina produces a unique though undefined sensation when it is stimulated. The unique qualities of each such point-stimulation allow the organism to relate them to different spatial directions. This comes about, according to Lotze, because the eye must move through a given angle and in a given direction to get any single image point into the fovea. Thus, if an image of a point were to be located above and to the right of the fovea, the eye would have to move downward and to the left to get the image into the fovea. Since the originally excited point on the retina produced a unique sensation to begin with, in time the organism comes to associate that sensation with the need to move the eye a given amount in a particular direction. Hence, the perceived spatial layout of points distributed on the retina is derived ultimately from the sensations associated with the muscular effort necessary to view objects with central vision. Through experience each point on the retina comes to have a *local sign* to identify the visual direction of an image impinging upon that point.

This empiricistic theory of perceived visual direction could be extended to include depth perception in the following way: Just as a muscular effort is involved in getting a peripheral stimulus into the fovea, so also a muscular effort is involved in changing eye vergence so that disparate images may be seen as single. Experience with vergence changes needed to see things as single leads ultimately to stereopsis. Thus, when half-images are formed in places with different local signs, the disparity produces vergence changes. Vergence changes of different magnitudes come to be associated with different disparities, thereby allowing the ultimate perception of disparate images as being in depth. There is no fusion in this empiricist theory of stereopsis. It simply demands past experience in changing vergence to get disparate images into good binocular registration. It should be pointed out that this theory is not a simple eye-movement theory, such as those we shall consider later in this chapter. It does not demand that the eyes converge actively to perceive depth. As in Hebb's (1949) theory of form perception (see Chapter 12), it simply requires that this must occur in the course of visual development.

Hering (1864) took over Lotze's theory of local signs and modified it considerably. He did not try to show how spatial layout may be derived from some unspecified uniqueness of retinal points, but suggested instead that each retinal point must have a unique spatial significance to begin with. Thus, stimulation of a point to the right of the fovea and slightly above it on the retina signifies innately that the perceived point is to the left of the direction of gaze and somewhat below it. Since learning was not required, Hering was forced to add something to Lotze's theory—namely, that points on the retina are innately identified with points within a three-dimensional coordinate system.

Thus, according to Hering, every point on a retina is identified with three different spatial values. One value is associated with a direction above, below, or vertically in-line with the direction of gaze. A second value, as in Lotze's system, is identified with a direction to the left or right of the direction of gaze. The third value—the one introduced by Hering—is the depth value of a point. In his theory the magnitude of the depth value is proportionate to the horizontal distance of the point from the center of the fovea. Moreover, the direction of depth—i.e., nearer or farther than the point of fixation—is dependent upon the direction of the displacement from the center of the fovea. Nasal displacements are associated with points farther than the plane of fixation; temporal displacements are associated with points nearer than the plane of fixation. Thus, if one point in space should be bifoveally fixated, the introduction of another point to one eye could result only in the perception of depth. A good example of this is the Panum limiting case described above.

Figure 8–18 illustrates how the theory works. Three lines are presented to the right eye, and only one line to the left eye. When the left line in the right eye is fused with the single line in the left eye, the two lines to the right of the left line are perceived as more distant. Moreover, the right-hand line is farther away from the fixation point than is the middle line. The local-signs theory would have it that this is because the right hand line is imaged on retinal points having greater depth values than those associated with points stimulated by the middle line. Moreover, since the right-hand and middle lines are in the nasal hemiretina, the two lines must be seen as more distant than the fixated left-hand line.

To account for stereopsis in the Wheatstone stereogram, Hering proposed cooperation between the images in the two eyes. Reconsider Figure 8–15. When lines F and F′ are fixated, lines *a* and *b* are imaged at disparate retinal places. As described thus far, the theory states simply that these two lines, when considered separately, each have their own local signs. Thus, the line *b* is imaged nasally relative to line F′, and the line *a* is imaged temporally relative to the line F. The direction of depth of this line is forward relative to the plane of fixation. The magnitude of the depth of *a* in the forward direction would have to be less than the magnitude of depth of line *b* in the rearward direction. Now, dual depth is usually not seen on the two half-images *a* and *b*. For small disparities only one line is seen and, when diplopia is present, both lines are generally reported as more distant than the fixation line. To account for such facts, Hering proposed that the local signs of the points associated with the lines *a* and *b* add algebraically. This would give a depth direction that is rearward relative to the fixation line, and a magnitude of depth that is smaller than that associated with line *b* taken alone.

Critique of the local signs theory. Hering's theory of local signs is quite awkward, and on the face of it, appears to offer no advantages over the fusional theory. How would a brain compute the algebraic sum of two local signs? A reasonable approach would in fact posit a projection field which, in effect, performs this same operation. A second disadvantage is that it does not specify the kinds of stimuli needed to produce algebraically combined local signs. The local-signs theory cannot explain how similar clusters of dots in Julesz' random dot stereogram interact to produce depth while adjacent clusters of dots are avoided.

On the positive side are some previously unknown facts about stereopsis. Figure 8–20 shows a stereogram in which three lines are presented to the left eye and two lines to the right eye. The separation between the latter two lines is equal to the separation between the flanking lines for the left eye.

While fusion theory can make no unique prediction about the depth of the central uniocular line when this display is viewed in a stereoscope, the local-signs theory would hold that the direction of depth should be dependent upon the direction of fixation. When the left-hand lines are fixated bifoveally, the uniocular central line is imaged in the temporal

Figure 8–20. Fixation-dependent stereopsis. The central line appears as nearer than the flanking lines when the left-hand lines are fused, and more distant than the flanking lines when the right-hand lines are fused.

hemiretina of the left eye. This means that it has a positive depth value, and should be seen as nearer than the fixated line. Switching fixation to the right-hand line should, according to local-signs theory, result in reversal in the direction of depth. This follows from the fact that with fixation on the right-hand line the central line is imaged in the left eye's nasal hemiretina. This is consistent with observations made by the author, and they may be verified by the reader. Fusion theories cannot explain why the direction of depth should be dependent upon the direction of gaze.

Despite this and similar phenomena, the local-signs theory as expressed by Hering suffers from some severe shortcomings. As it stands it cannot deal with pattern matching such as might occur in the Julesz pattern, nor can it explain the singleness of vision occurring with small disparities.

Suppression theories of stereopsis. The so-called suppression theories of stereopsis attempt to deal with the fact that observers report single vision in the presence of disparate images. One explanation is that the disparate images may fuse; another is that one of the half-images is suppressed, so that the observer actually sees only the remaining half-image.

Suppression theories have a history quite as ancient as that of the fusion theories. Du Tour proposed in the eighteenth century (Helmholtz, 1925) that we actually see out of one eye at a time. In more recent years several attempts have been made to revive suppression theories, among them that of Verhoeff (1935), who asserted that in binocular vision one half-image may replace the other, by virtue of the "attention" values of the two half-images. Thus, if one half-image should be brighter than the other, it would have a greater attention value and therefore be predominant. Such replacement, according to Verhoeff, occurs even when the two half-images are not disparate. Thus, so-called "fusion" of a bifoveally fixated line is really due to the replacement (suppression) of one line by the other. Though this replacement may shift from one line to the other

AB   BC

Figure 8–21. When the letters B are binocularly superimposed, the perceived B is not darker than the uniocular letters A and C.

over time, such shifting is not visible since the two lines are exactly alike, and hence the binocular line appears to be unified. This, of course, is very similar to du Tour's theory.

This approach gains support from everyday experience. If, for example, the reader should close one eye he will notice that the world does not appear to become noticeably dimmer—and yet the total light energy affecting the nervous system is reduced by half when one eye is closed. When both eyes are closed the observer sees a dark field. Presumably when only one eye is closed, that eye is "seeing" the same darkness that it saw when both eyes were closed. Yet the darkness in the closed eye is not seen: it is as though the darkness is suppressed by the presence of an illuminated and textured field in the open eye.

Helmholtz (1925) demonstrated with Figure 8–21 that binocular stimulation need not produce summation of lightness. When the letter B in the figure is fused, the letters A and C are superimposed on the white pages imaged at corresponding places in the other eye. Yet the letters A and C do not appear to be less black than the letter B, and might be made to appear less black only if the superimposed white background in the contralateral eye were to contain some texture, as is illustrated in Figure 8–22. When this figure is viewed as a stereogram the observer will see the fine dots as though they are suppressing small regions of the letter A and C. This too is not lightness summation but rather an instance of *binocular rivalry*.

Figure 8–22. The fused letter B is darker than the uniocular letters A and C.

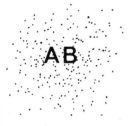 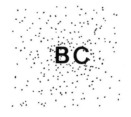

Figure 8–23. When viewing these ray patterns in a stereoscope, moiré fringes are never seen even though convergence may wander. To avoid fusion of the central spots, the page should be tilted when viewing this stereogram.

Binocular rivalry is a phenomenon occurring when the two eyes are presented with different stimuli. The dichoptic view is that of an alternating and shifting pattern in which the two stimuli appear to be competing with each other rather than combining. A dramatic example of binocular rivalry is presented in Figure 8–23. This stereogram may be compared with the picture in Figure 8–24. When the two half-fields in Figure 8–23 are physically superimposed, as in Figure 8–24, the famous moiré fringes are clearly visible. These fringes describe the intersections of the radial lines in the two half-fields, and are analogous to the beats occurring when two periodic tones of different frequency are played simultaneously. The moiré phenomena are even more striking when the two half-fields are moved relative to each other in the monoptic view. In the stereoscopic view of 8–23, however, it is impossible to see the moiré fringes, even when vergence is changing—they are totally invisible. From this it is obvious that, in the vicinity of their intersections, dichoptic contours simply do not combine summatively. Evidence such as this has led to the notion that for both disparate and non-disparate images fusion does not occur, but that instead we see portions of either eye's images.

The most recent experimental data indicate that it is important to distinguish between disparate and non-disparate stimuli. It appears that under certain conditions there may be a degree of combining when the two half-images are formed in exactly corresponding places; and this would conflict with Verhoeff's theory. There is, however, no direct evidence of phenomenal fusion of disparate half-images. If the various theories of stereopsis are to be properly evaluated, the evidence must be reviewed for the tentative conclusions that disparate images may not combine binocularly while non-disparate images may combine.

The perceived lightness of a surface corresponds to its position on the subjective white-grey-black continuum. As we saw in Chapter 5, the fact that a surface may appear to be white or grey or black is not due strictly to its luminance. The specific lightness of a surface is related to the ratio of its luminance and the luminance of its surround. Thus, a small piece of black paper on a white background will continue to appear to be black even though the total level of illumination on the white and black surfaces may be varied over a considerable range. The black paper appears to be black just so long as it reflects a given percentage of the incident illumination and its background continues to reflect a much greater percentage of the same illumination.

As Hering (1964) has argued, if one should mix a solution of 20 per cent alcohol with any amount of the same solution, he could never obtain a solution that is other than 20 per cent alcohol. From this it follows that viewing a surface of different luminances with one eye or with two eyes will not change the ratio of the luminance of the surfaces in the scene; black will continue to look black, white will still be white, and grey will remain grey in both the monocular and the binocular situations. This is probably why the lightness of objects does not appear to diminish when one eye is closed.

Now let us assume that an observer is reading a page of this book with a neutral filter over one eye. The filter serves to reduce by a constant

Figure 8–24. Moiré fringes are clearly visible when the ray patterns of Figure 8–23 are added to each other.

percentage the intensity of the light at every point in the image of the page. If the filter should pass only one-tenth of the incident light, it would effectively reduce by this same factor the luminance of every point on the page; and still the ratio of the luminances of the black print and the white page would be preserved. The page should still appear to be white with black print.

With one eye covered by the filter and the other looking at the page directly, the page does appear to be normal. If the eye covered by the filter should be occluded, however, the whole page appears to grow brighter, and the whites and blacks are more vivid. This observation, first made by Fechner (Hering, 1964), is paradoxical in a way. It is a paradox (and known as *Fechner's paradox*) that though more total light affects the visual system when both eyes are open, the scene appears to be brighter with one eye closed. As Fechner has shown, this paradox cannot be attributed solely to changes in the diameters of the pupils of the eyes (Fry and Bartley, 1933), since the experiment described above will work even when small artificial pupils are placed before the eyes. These pupils keep constant the amount of light entering the eyes, even though the diameters of the natural pupils may change.

Suppose, however, that the visual system responds to the luminance of a stimulus as well as to the ratios of luminance involved in lightness perception. As was pointed out in Chapter 5, there is a degree of sensitivity to brightness *per se*. Thus, a particular lightness—say, a shade of dark grey—can appear as more or less bright under different illuminations, even though it may be identified as the same grey. Under the assumption that this observation represents a general characteristic of the visual system, it is possible to explain Fechner's paradox.

One such explanation is based upon the idea that the visual system responds to the average of the luminances of images in the two eyes. This brightness-averaging idea is inherent in the conclusions drawn by Levelt (1964) from his investigations of binocular brightness summation. As Levelt suggested, if one eye should happen to be more sensitive to light than the other eye, then the more sensitive eye's contribution to the averaged binocular brightness should be given more weight than the contribution of the other eye. Thus, he proposed the formula

$$w_l B_l + w_r B_r = C$$

where B_l is the brightness of the left eye's stimulus, B_r the brightness of the right eye's stimulus, w_l and w_r the weighting coefficients applied to the two eyes, and C the resulting binocularly perceived brightness. If both eyes are equally sensitive and if $B_l = B_r$, then the values of w_l and w_r are equal to 0.5. This makes C the average of B_l and B_r. With unequal values of B_l and B_r, the resulting binocular brightness will be less than that of the brighter of the two half-images.

Levelt (1964) proposed that the actual weight assigned to an eye in his formula depends not only on the sensitivity of that eye to light, but also upon the nature of the stimuli. Thus, if a contour is imaged in one eye, and only a uniform surface in the other eye, the eye seeing the contour will play a much stronger role in determining the binocular brightness. As an example, consider what happens when one eye is closed while the other eye is viewing a scene. The contours in the scene cause the open eye to make a much stronger contribution to the total binocular brightness and in effect suppress the uniform dark field in the closed eye. The dark field of the closed eye makes little or no contribution to the total binocular brightness, since its weighting coefficient goes to zero, whereas that of the brightness of the open eye's stimulus approaches unity.

It is easy to see now how Levelt's formulation may explain Fechner's paradox. The scene viewed by both eyes is contoured, and thus, assuming equal sensitivity of the two eyes, the brightnesses of the two half-images have equal weighting coefficients. The value of C, then, is less than that of the brighter half-image and more than that of the dimmer. Now, if one eye should be occluded the weighting coefficient of the open eye's stimulus will approach unity. This will cause the total binocular brightness to be greater than it was when both eyes viewed the scene.

Levelt's formulation does not provide for a direct averaging of monocular brightnesses to produce the net binocular brightness. The averaging effect observed in Fechner's paradox is achieved by summing weighted values of monocular brightness. When the weightings assigned to the two monocular stimuli are changed because of differences in their contours, averaging may not occur at all. Thus, a contoured image in one eye may completely predominate over a uniform white field, as in von Tschermak-Seysenegg's theory. In this case the net binocular brightness is not the average of the monocular brightnesses.

Levelt's work can explain Sherrington's original experiment (1906) on the binocular perception of a flickering light. As Sherrington reasoned, a flickering light viewed by both eyes simultaneously should appear to become a steady light at a higher flicker frequency than when it is viewed by one eye alone. This follows from the fact that a brighter flickering light will appear to be a steady light at a higher flicker frequency than would a dimmer light. Since he could not find such an effect he concluded that the visual systems of the two eyes are independent. The explanation of this effect is exactly the same as that given above for Fechner's paradox. With one eye open, the weighting coefficient assigned to that eye's stimulus is unity. With both eyes open, the weighting coefficient grows smaller and the other eye contributes the difference between it and unity.

This theory still needs testing. Workers subsequent to Sherrington did find a very small summative effect of binocular viewing on flicker perception (e.g., Baker, 1952). The binocularly viewed light did appear as a steady light at a slightly higher frequency of flicker than when the light was viewed monocularly. This small effect requires that the applicability of Levelt's principles be considered in carefully controlled experiments.

It is important that we keep in mind the distinction between *brightness* and *lightness*. When a field is viewed through a neutral filter its brightness may appear to become smaller. When the filter is placed before the eye, however, black surfaces in the field remain black, and white surfaces remain white. Lightness refers to the neutral color—the whiteness, grayness, or blackness—of a surface. Brightness refers to psychological intensity or brilliance. Thus, brightness and lightness are two different dimensions of perception. It is conceivable that brightness exhibits binocular summation in the manner described by Levelt even though different lightnesses in the two eyes do not.

Suppose that the two monocular images are alike except for the fact that a region enclosed by a boundary in one field is light gray and the corresponding region in the other field is dark gray. Both gray patches are placed in white fields of equal luminance. When such stimuli are viewed in a stereoscope they do not fuse or combine at some intermediate shade of gray. Instead, the observer perceives rivalry between the two shades of gray.

This result was found by Wallach and Adams (1954), who also presented discs of equal luminance within annuli of different luminance. As a result of the contrast between the annuli and the discs, the discs appeared to be of different values of gray and to be moreover in a state of binocular rivalry. For this reason, we cannot conclude that Levelt's results, which were based on experiments using patches of light in a dark background, can be generalized to deal with the binocular interaction of lightness. Clearly, this area is ripe for research to determine the psychological dimensions along which summation may occur and where it may not occur.

Similar considerations apply to colored lights. Thus, for example, Thomas, Dimmick, and Luria (1961) showed that lights of different wavelength may combine binocularly to produce intermediate colors. Yet the farther apart the dichoptic colors grow in wavelength, the more likely it is that binocular rivalry will occur. This, too, is poorly understood. As already indicated, the crucial aspect of suppression theory is that single-ness of vision may be accounted for in terms of suppression just as well as in terms of fusion. Wolf and Zigler (1965) demonstrated that images formed at disparate places do not combine binocularly to enhance de-tectability. More complete data are needed, however. Even if we grant that images formed at corresponding places do combine binocularly and that they inhibit each other when they are on disparate places, it must still be shown that this inhibitory effect can explain singleness of vision during stereopsis.

Singleness of vision is more likely as disparities grow smaller. Diplo-pia is rare if the disparity of half-images is less than about 7 minutes of arc (Ogle, 1950). This number defines the horizontal dimension of an area within which disparate images appear as single—the so-called *fu-sional area* of Panum. Although some authors (see Brecher, 1942) have reported that the size of the fusional area vertically is the same as its hori-zontal size, Ogle (1950) concluded that the area is actually about half the size, thus becoming an ellipsoid in central vision. The fusional areas grow in size as the stimuli are placed farther into the peripheral visual field. Moreover, in brief flash exposures the dimensions of the fusional areas may well be the same vertically and horizontally because of the absence of significant eye movements during the exposure.

Kaufman (1963) presented two lines to one eye and only one line to the other eye, as shown in Figure 8–25. When the two half-fields of this figure are viewed dichoptically, the horizontal single line segment super-

Figure 8–25. The spread of suppression. When in a stereoscope the two vertical lines suppress a segment of the horizontal line.

Figure 8–26. Hochberg's demonstration of suppression of non-overlapping contours. The upper and lower bars tend to suppress each other, even though they do not intersect when viewed in a stereoscope.

imposed on the space between the two vertical lines tends to be suppressed. Moreover, the likelihood of suppression of this line segment is related to the size of the space between the two vertical lines. This probability of suppression was found to be at a maximum value when the space separating the two vertical lines was 14 minutes of arc. Larger spacings produced less suppression; indeed, suppression probability fell off rapidly as the spacing became larger.

If it is assumed that the two vertical lines produce independent and equal zones of suppression (suppressive fields), the magnitude of the suppressive field spreading into the space from each vertical line is 7 minutes of arc when suppression probability is at its maximum. The value is commensurate with Ogle's (1950) estimate of the horizontal size of the fusional areas.

The results obtained with vertical lines causing suppression of a horizontal line were not quite the same as those in which a vertical line is suppressed by two horizontal lines. The vertical spread of suppression occurs less often and across a smaller distance. Suppression of a vertical line segment appears to be maximally likely when the separation between the two horizontal lines is less than 7 minutes of arc. This corresponds to a suppressive field of about 3 minutes of arc. In sum, the vertical zone of suppression of a line is commensurate with the magnitude of Panum's fusional area in the vertical dimension (Ogle, 1950).

Hochberg (1964a) also investigated the possibility that suppression rather than fusion is the basis for singleness of vision. His stereogram is shown in Figure 8–26. With bifoveal fixation of the horizontal bars L and R, the vertically disparate bars *i* and *ii* may be seen in rivalry. This rivalry appeared most pronounced when the disparity was about 15 minutes of arc. Unfortunately, Hochberg did not manipulate disparity in a systematic fashion, and for that reason the function relating rivalry to disparity when bars have the same orientation is not known.

When Crovitz and Lockhead (1967) repeated the Kaufman (1963) experiment using various degrees of contrast rather than simple line stimuli, the results showed that the spread of suppression may be greater if the contrast between the elements of the display is increased. This in turn suggests that the probability of seeing disparate images as single should be studied where the contrasts between the disparate images and their backgrounds are manipulated.

Taken all together, these results indicate how one half-image could be suppressed while viewing a stereogram, as is illustrated in Figure 8–27. This figure shows how a contour may set up both excitatory and inhibitory effects in the binocular receiving areas of the brain. The inhibitory surrounds of the contours are presumed to add together to produce a net inhibitory effect that outweighs the excitatory effect of the enclosed contour in the binocular field. At the same time the excitatory effects combine also when they are produced by half-images that fall on corresponding retinal places. This basic scheme, which is implicit in the work of Hochberg (1964*a*), amounts to a co-ordination or biasing of suppression to produce singleness of vision.

One of the chief criticisms of suppression theory is that it does not account in any way for stereoscopic depth perception—indeed, it has been

Figure 8–27. How contralateral inhibition can explain singleness of vision. The excitatory and inhibitory effects produced by contours combine algebraically in the binocular field, and this results in the suppression of the excitatory effect produced by the right-hand contour on the left side of the stereogram.

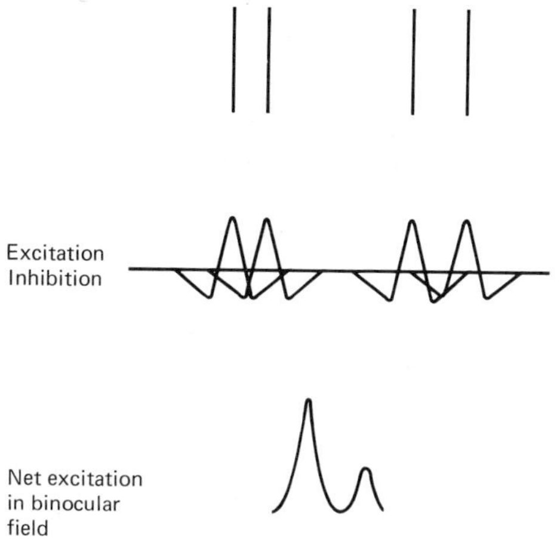

Excitation
Inhibition

Net excitation
in binocular
field

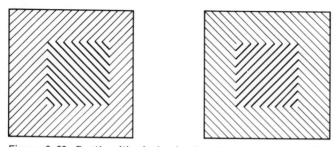

Figure 8–28. Depth with rivalry in the absence of perceptible fusion of similar contours.

suggested that binocular rivalry is incompatible with stereopsis (Julesz, 1971). Moreover, as Helmholtz (1925) pointed out, if something is suppressed it is not available to the nervous system for the computation of depth from disparity. In other words, suppression could actually prevent stereopsis.

This conclusion has been refuted in a number of experiments, such as that of the stereogram shown in Figure 8–28. The lines in the left half-field are all at right angles to the corresponding lines in the right half-field. The inner squares in these half-fields are comprised of lines that are darker than the lines in the backgrounds. Despite the fact that there are no lines for fusion, the inner square may be seen in depth when this display is viewed stereoscopically. Moreover, even when the inner square is seen floating above the background lines in the stereoscope, all the lines are in a constant state of binocular rivalry. There is no singleness of vision here, nor is there any apparent combining of similar spatial contours. We shall see how a modified version of fusion theory might account for depth in stereograms such as this one, since it does make the point that rivalry and suppression are not incompatible with the occurrence of stereopsis. Again, when a dense neutral filter is held before one eye while viewing a stereogram of this kind, the observer may not even be aware of rivalry. He perceives only the brighter half-field and may also experience the depth effect.

To summarize, it appears as though images falling on corresponding places interact in a combinatorial manner at least in part. This combination is reflected by a weak brightness-summation effect. It may be that both inhibition (suppression) and summation contribute to the interaction. Disparate images betray no similar experiential combinatorial tendency, and in fact may inhibit each other if the disparity is small enough. The evidence for this is that vertically disparate images are mutually inhibitory. Moreover, the magnitude of the spread of suppression is commensurate with the so-called fusional areas. Finally, since manifestly rivalrous stimuli can interact to produce stereopsis, there is no reason for insisting that sensory fusion is a necessary condition for the occurrence of stereopsis. And thus, suppression may be sufficient to account for singleness of vision, but it does not account for stereopsis.

Eye Movement theories of stereopsis. According to Helmholtz (1925), Brucke suggested that depth is perceived because our eyes move across the various contours of objects. As they move to various contours at different distances, the eyes must change vergence again and again, and in this way a three-dimensional picture of the object may be built up over time. Since the magnitudes of vergence changes are identical to the relative disparities of the contours, this eye-movement theory has a certain appeal, and yet it must be rejected as it stands, since the eyes need not move at all and objects may still be seen in depth. Despite this criticism, the basic eye-movement theory has been revived from time to time. Then too, it is not at all clear that the mechanisms involved in eye movements are completely separated from the process of disparity detection. Before we turn to these mechanisms we shall weigh the evidence for and against the classic eye-movement theories of stereopsis.

A theory such as Brucke's must be incorrect, and for the reason that stereopsis may be achieved even when a stereogram is exposed by means of a brief electric spark (Dove, 1841). On repeating this experiment, Helmholtz (1925) found that when disparities are small, depth may be seen in the briefly exposed stimuli. With large disparities, however, he reported that double images were seen, and that depth was ambiguous or absent, though these same stereograms may be seen in depth when they are viewed for prolonged periods of time. Observations such as these led Helmholtz to conclude that eye movements may play a role in sharpening the perception of depth. He felt that in some circumstances it might be necessary to shift vergence to get widely disparate images into near correspondence, and that shift could improve the accuracy of depth perception.

Ishak, Radwan, and Ibrahim (1965) and independently Gettys and Harker (1967) performed experiments that support Helmholtz's notion concerning the role of eye movement in sharpening stereoscopic acuity.

In an earlier study of the role of eye movements in stereopsis, Clark (1935) photographed both eyes while the observer viewed an ordinary stereogram. He was able to measure large vergence changes and conjunctive eye movements, but since could find no systematic patterns of movements related to reports of stereoscopic depth perception, he rejected the idea that the system controlling the extraocular musculature is involved in stereopsis. He did point out that stereoscopic vision nonetheless involves the perception of intermittent and continuously changing retinal impressions. This implies that the process of building up a three-dimensional impression depends upon a change over time in the relations among the two retinal images. Such changes can come about from changes in the vergence of the eyes. In any event, no current theorist accepts the idea that eye movements *per se* produce the impression of depth obtained from viewing stereograms.

Image Movement theory of stereopsis. Clark did not ignore the electric spark experiment of Dove when he proposed that changes in the relations among the retinal images may mediate stereopsis. He cited the findings of von Karpinska (1910), who showed that stereopsis rarely occurs during a first brief exposure to a stereogram. According to von Karpinska, several brief exposures may be necessary to perceive depth correctly. Since the eyes may change vergence from one such exposure to the next, relations among the half-fields will differ from exposure to exposure. It might be proposed that these changes from exposure to exposure provide the information needed for stereopsis.

It is now well established that stereopsis may still occur when the images on the two retinas cannot change their relative positions even though vergence may change. Helmholtz (1925) cites several different investigators who reached this conclusion from experiments employing after-images. This same conclusion was reached by Shortress and Krauskopf (1961), who employed an optical technique (see Chapter 10) enabling them to keep half-images on constant retinal places regardless of how the eyes moved. They found that as exposure time was increased, the observers made more accurate discriminations of depth differences due to disparity, even though there was no image-shifting due to eye movements, and inferred thus that time of exposure alone could be involved in building up an accurate impression of the layout of things in depth. This conclusion differs from that of Ishak, Radwan, and Ibrahim (1965) who found better stereo acuity when eye movements were encouraged than when the eyes were kept still during equally long exposures to the stimuli. The dimensions of their stereograms were quite different from those employed by Shortress and Krauskopf, though. The eye movements may have been effective because without them monocular acuity may have been very poor.

Hochberg (1964*b*) suggested that binocular rivalry could provide a substitute for image movements to produce depth in stereograms. A related theory was also proposed by Washburn (1933). According to Hochberg, if one eye is dominant over the other, half-images in the dominant eye will be available for observation for relatively greater periods of time than the half-images in the non-dominant eye. This assumes, of course, that the half-images do not fuse, but that they suppress each other. Now, in the case of a crossed disparity of two half-images, and where the right eye is dominant, the left-hand half-image in the binocular view will be visible for longer periods of time than will the right-hand half-image. On occasion, however, the right-hand half-image will come to predominate over the left-hand half-image, as in binocular rivalry. This would produce an effect similar to stroboscopic movement. As the left-hand half-image disappears, the right-hand half-image becomes visible. This could look like an image moving from left to right.

Just the opposite effect should occur with uncrossed disparity and right eye dominance. Here the left-hand half-image would appear only occasionally and the movement would be from right to left. In this way the relative directions of apparent movement of alternating half-images would indicate the cross of the disparity. The brain associates different disparities with different depth. Hochberg's theory presumes that the central nervous system has no direct information to identify the eye in which a stimulus is imaged. This is consistent with the results of Templeton and Green (1968), who found that with extraneous clues eliminated, observers cannot tell which eye is being stimulated. According to Hochberg, it is image movement, produced by rivalry or by eye movements, that informs the brain as to which eye is being stimulated. Hence, the theory implies that half-images must be available to awareness if stereopsis is to occur.

Critique of the Image Movement theory of stereopsis. The straightforward theory attributing stereopsis to literal movements of the eye has already been shown to be inappropriate as an explanation of stereopsis. More sophisticated theories, such as Hochberg's, can be faulted on still other grounds. First, the theory is completely speculative as to the role of eye dominance. There are several kinds of eye dominance (Walls, 1951*b*). The so-called preferred eye is sometimes determined by giving a subject an aperture to look through. He will tend to choose one eye rather than the other. This does not correlate with other measures. In still another test, the so-called pointing test, the observer points to some fixated object with his finger. It will be discovered upon doing this that only one half-image of his finger is pointing to the object while the other half-image is off to one side. The half-image doing the pointing belongs to only one eye —the so-called dominant eye—even though this eye is not necessarily the one that predominates in a rivalry test of dominance.

A rivalry test of dominance may be performed in the following way. Two pages of different text may be placed in a stereoscope, and a subject is required to read the text. He will tend to read the text in one eye in preference to the text in the other eye. The preferred eye may not be the same as the eye used in pointing. The author, for example, is left-eye dominant in a pointing test and right-eye dominant in a rivalry test. Stimulus characteristics may of course be manipulated to alter the so-called rivalry dominance.

The stereogram shown in Figure 8–29 may be used to illustrate the point in question. Most observers will see rivalrous letters from the two half-fields. But if one half-field should be made less bright than the other —as by looking through a darkened film or glass or by squinting with one eye—the brighter image will predominate. According to Hochberg's theory, if the normally dominant eye is made weaker in this way, then the hypothetical movements of the half-images should be reversed. Nevertheless, the direction of depth does not reverse when the normally weaker

Figure 8–29. A rivalrous letter stereogram. (After Kaufman and Pitblado, 1965)

```
j  yfr   ou  n     f    x    a  gqur gs j p        y  jgh   fd  n     w    t   d  lkjh yt o u
jsy  d  zxc  e  kacs q   yetd x be iuy pq          ytr  u  nbv k  asdf g    bvcx m kj iuy op
s  makc w di  bsg marwq  x  ab  zbf tru yd nh      y  trew s gf nbv lkjhg r  yt piu fds re vc
gsf  z  vb n  hgf u  d rew ghj bv ite n k          qaz   x  sw e dcv f   r  tgb nh y  jm rfv e s
t    shf x qifj  vw ait  asd   mn lkj p   t        l    jhg r wsx  qa tgb  yhn k iu lkj b  t
d  wer uy iu b  fd lkj  e  yt fds    cby  ilgw     c  vbn ml kj  hg fds a qw trey   piu rfbg
q   au sirh d   xirh al sj sie gcy w tr xg         b   mn hgty e redf yn ij kip  mju g re dj
smch    wk aidh    sn q wyd s   d   age t it       plki    fd yhg    fr w qsf t y i   mhr d tv
g   zbd wy d    cnb s xm xbc laut f  tr plm        k   tbf ug x  azx d  sw rsa z cfd h fu mnb
hxb x znb q    rt  fg  ajcg z dbr wt q hv          hgf c wre y   ip bg  mhte d fyt ds t mj
fd cber a st shf ch dit dj c    mnbc tdf           dw piyh v fd hyt dw fsa wq t    ngtr swq
hf ryt s  d    chrt d  lk xj c f eyt d bm          nb dre u  f   grdc k  br fr f d frt k lp
```

eye is made relatively stronger. It may in fact be made so strong that the dimmer image in the normally stronger eye cannot be seen by the observer at all.

The foregoing review of the major theories of stereopsis is not quite complete; there are several possible variants on these theories, as well as approaches incorporating the principal features of a number of them. None of the theories, however, can explain all the important facts of stereopsis. Since theories as such are neither true nor false, the way to evaluate them is to consider the domains of facts that they cover. In this purview, it is evident that the classic fusion theory does cover a wider domain of facts than do any of the other theories, and yet it has some very serious deficiencies. It may well be that these deficiencies could be overcome by modifications and additions to the basic theory. One such modification is that of Sperling (1970*a*), who has added several features of suppression theory to his model and thereby made the basic fusional concept more viable. Later in this chapter we shall attempt to point the way to a still more adequate theory of stereopsis, but before doing so we shall review the nature of the stimulus to stereopsis.

THE STIMULUS TO STEREOPSIS

We have already alluded to the problem of the stimulus to stereopsis. It has been shown, for example, that the notion is incorrect that disparate similar spatial contours are the appropriate stimuli. The contours need not be alike at all, and depth may result. In a series of experiments dealing with this issue, Kaufman (1964*b*, 1965) and Kaufman and Pitblado

Figure 8–30. A letter stereogram with brightness disparity. (After Kaufman and Pitblado, 1965)

(1965) came to the conclusion that disparity of patterns of brightness is a sufficient stimulus to produce stereopsis. Even though these patterns of brightness may be carried by different shapes, stereopsis can still result. An example of this is shown in Figure 8–30. It will be noticed that the stereogram contains letters of two different brightnesses in the two half-fields. The shapes of the letters are identical. If fusion of similar spatial contours is the basis for stereopsis, then depth should not result from viewing this stereogram. The pattern of brightness in the two half-fields contains a disparity, however, and this produces the impression of an inner square floating in depth when the pattern is viewed stereoscopically.

A similar effect may be observed in Figure 8–31, though in this stereogram the letters comprising the pattern are shifted in one direction to produce an element-disparity, while the brightness pattern is shifted in the opposite direction. As a result, two competing disparities are simultaneously present. The reader may observe for himself that in this case the direction of depth is determined by his own desires. If he wants to see the inner square floating above the background, he may see the pattern that way. Alternatively, if he wants to see the inner square behind the background, then he can produce that response too. When he does so he is responding to the brightness disparity. When he sees the inner square above the background he is responding to the crossed disparity of the letters *per se.*

The direction of depth seen in this reversible-depth stereogram is probably determined by the convergence assumed by the observer. Motor fusion of the inner letters seems to produce a response to the letter disparity. Fusing patterns of brightness seems to produce the opposite response.

Figure 8–31. Brightness disparity vs. element disparity. (After Kaufman and Pitblado, 1965)

The purpose of the foregoing example is to show that the single in-variant property of the stimulus leading to depth perception is the corre-lation of brightness levels in the two eyes. A fine-grained analysis of brightness would produce a response to the letter disparity; a coarser-grained analysis would lead to the response associated with the brightness pattern disparity. This conclusion is confirmed by the stereogram illus-trated in Figure 8–28. Depth occurs only when the inner lines are either darker or lighter than their backgrounds. This yields "blobs" of brightness that are imaged on disparate places. The depth effect is independent of the elements comprising such blobs.

It is possible, then, to define the stimulus to stereopsis in terms of geometrical disparity of "blobs" of brightness. If a region in one eye is stimulated by a patch differing in brightness from its background, while a somewhat disparate region in the other eye is also stimulated by a simi-lar patch, then the disparity of the patches or blobs is sufficient to produce a stereoscopic depth effect. Moreover, the contents of the patches need not be alike. Thus, the monocular views could contain discriminably dif-ferent materials that may still interact to produce stereopsis just so long as the average brightness within the region containing the materials differs from that of the background. This geometrical disparity of regions differing from their backgrounds in average brightness may be called *brightness disparity*.

Although brightness disparity is sufficient to produce a stereoscopic depth response, it is not necessary. It has been shown, for example, that when a white disc on a grey background is presented to one eye, and a black disc on the same grey background is presented to a disparate place in the other eye, then stereopsis can occur (Kaufman and Pitblado, 1969). Treisman (1962) had been unable to obtain this result, but her failure to do so may have been due to the fact that in her viewing setup conver-gence and accommodation were inconsistent with each other. She did, however, confirm Helmholtz's result in which opposite-contrast line stere-ograms (Fig. 8–13) gave a depth effect.

The fact that opposite-contrast discs can yield stereopsis allows one to argue in favor of a *contour disparity* mechanism as well as a brightness disparity mechanism. The two mechanisms may be placed in conflict with each other, and this may explain why opposite-contrast Julesz patterns do not seem capable of eliciting a depth response (Julesz, 1971). In these patterns one half-field's black spots are interchanged with the white spots so that the entire half-field is the negative of the other. Disparities of brightness are not preserved in such stereograms while disparity of contour is preserved. Under some circumstances this conflict could inhibit stereopsis. A beginning has been made toward understanding how the patterning of complex stereograms can affect stereopsis (Julesz, 1971), but, as yet we have no general laws which will allow us to make particular predictions.

SPERLING'S THEORY OF BINOCULAR VISION

In view of the inconsistencies between the older theories and the new facts such as those described above, it is important that the stereopsis theories be revised—and several indeed have been proposed in recent years, such as Julesz' spring-loaded dipole model (1971), Dodwell's (1970) modification of fusion theory, and the theory of Lawson and Gulick (1967). Since these theories are accessible to the interested reader, in this section we shall describe only one of the current theories—namely, Sperling's (1970a) theory of binocular vision.

Sperling suggested that the *potential well* model of quantum physics is analogous to the processes involved in binocular vision. In this model a particle (for example, a marble) rolls about inside a bowl filled with a viscous fluid. No matter where the marble may happen to start, it ultimately will roll slowly down the side of the bowl to its bottom. The elevation of the marble represents its potential energy. In rolling to the bottom it uses up its potential energy and becomes entrapped in the bottom of the bowl. The particle can escape from the "energy well" at the bottom of the bowl only when energy is added to the bowl from the outside.

When the eyes are in a state of rest they naturally assume a specific vergence angle. This hypothetical angle of rest corresponds to the bottom of the bowl in the mechanical model described above. Thus, if the eyes are initially divergent, they may drift slowly toward the angle of convergence defining their natural resting position.

Let us now assume that the bowl is made of a rubbery substance capable of being deformed (see Fig. 8–32). When a dimple or indentation is made in the inner surface of this bowl, the rolling marble can fall into the dimple and come to rest. This dimple is produced by the application of the external force, which in Sperling's model results from the presentation of disparate images to the two eyes. When disparate images are presented to the eyes, the eyes assume a convergence angle to minimize the disparity. The only way to get the eyes out of their new positions is to in-

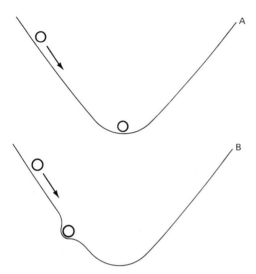

Figure 8–32. A particle rolling about inside an energy well, as in A, will ultimately come to rest at the bottom of the well. If, however, the energy well's surface is deformable, as in B, the particle can become entrapped in a dimple in the surface.

troduce some other disparate stimulus or to turn the direction of gaze so that the eyes will then be free to return to the position of rest.

Several indentations can be made in the bowl at one time, and the rolling particle may then be entrapped in any one of them. Thus, there are several different possible stable states of the particle on the energy surface of the bowl. It would require the application of external energy to enable the particle to climb out of one energy well so that it could then roll into another one. Similarly, in binocular vision the eyes could minimize the disparity of one pair of half-images by assuming one vergence angle while the other half-images remained disparate. A shift of attention or of the direction of gaze could then function analogously to providing a different arrangement of dimples and of their relative sizes in the mechanical model, and thereby cause the eyes to shift vergence to fuse previously disparate half-images.

Thus far the model has described the vergence behavior of the eyes when they are confronted with disparate half-images. This same model may be used to describe fusional depth or stereopsis, though in this case it is applied to small local regions of the retinas rather than to the eyes as a complete system.

Just as the eyes converge or diverge to produce motor fusion, half-images on each retina "displace" toward each other to yield perceptual fusion in a projection field. That is, with small disparities (less than 8 minutes of arc), to achieve a steady state, half-image representations displace and fuse perceptually. In Sperling's model the particle rolls into an energy well that corresponds in this case to perceptual fusion rather than to motor fusion, the case to which the model was applied above.

One important difference between Sperling's projection field and that considered earlier in this chapter is that active neurons at the intersection of the network tend to inhibit or silence the activity of other neurons. This process depends in part upon positive feedback, since a portion of the output of a neuron is fed back to its input. It is known as *regenerative feedback*, since, once excited, such a neuron will tend to maintain its state of excitation even after a stimulus is removed. Hence, the behavior of a neuron in the projection field depends upon prior states of stimulation. This may be likened to the entrapment of a particle in an energy well. New stimulation, which will ultimately silence a previously active neuron, is similar to the addition of energy to the mechanical model described above. This new stimulation can cause the activity of the projection field to assume a new stable state.

The Sperling projection field has an advantage over the classic field in that the number of ghosts arising from multiple fusion (see page 290) is minimized simply because the projection field does not respond to disparities larger than about 8 minutes of arc. Thus, in a Wheatstone stereogram it is only the disparate lines that will fuse if the separations between the lines in each half-field is greater than eight minutes of arc. Further, when the lines in such a stereogram are separated by small visual angles, this model will also produce ghost images.

This new projection field does not compute depth when disparities are large or when the stimuli presented to the two eyes are inherently rivalrous. To accommodate the occurrence of stereopsis in the presence of both large disparities and rivalrous stimuli, Sperling proposed that a second coarse-grained projection field is also part of the depth-computing system. This projection field responds to "blobs" or brightness patches similar to those described in the previous section. Moreover, fusion of these blobs will occur when the disparities are as large as several degrees of arc. Thus, even though line elements may be rivalrous they can still fuse in the coarse, or secondary, projection field. The depth signals generated in this field are added to those generated by the primary or fine projection field. Since the disparities handled by the secondary field are large, the depth signals from the primary field may be thought of as per-turbations on the larger signals from the primary field. Thus we see how this secondary projection field can account for depth in the brightness-disparity stereograms described above.

Since it is the output of the primary projection field that is analyzed for form and texture, it is only this output that leads ultimately to the per-ception of objects. That explains why rivalrous elements may be seen by the observer even though such elements may have relative depths that are determined in the coarse field.

In addition to handling depth with dissimilar and widely disparate stimuli, Sperling's theory attempts to integrate the functions of conver-gence and stereopsis. To accomplish this, depth signals arising from ac-tivity at different levels in the primary and secondary projection fields are weighted according to their retinal locations and then summed. Activity arising from levels on one side of the level corresponding to the plane of fixation have excitatory effects on the centers controlling vergence, and activity arising from levels on the opposite side of the reference level have inhibitory effects. Thus, if a large excitatory signal were present—i.e., one that would indicate a large crossed disparity—and if a small inhibitory signal were present, the sum of the two would have the net effect of caus-ing the eyes to increase convergence. Thus, the weighted sum of the out-puts of the different levels in the projection fields could be utilized to sig-nal changes in the vergence of the eyes. In the case of a bifoveally fixated point, the excitatory and inhibitory effects would cancel each other, and the eyes would tend to maintain their convergence.

Critique of Sperling's theory. In this author's opinion the dual projection field theory of Sperling is a genuine advance over previous theories. It makes it possible to account for depth in the presence of double images as well as depth with rivalrous stimuli, and it shows how disparity can produce both depth and vergence changes.

There are several problems the theory has not resolved, among them the problem of ghosts. Although the problem is minimized in this theory, ghosts are still predicted when the dimensions of a stereogram are small. Thus, if the lines in the half-fields of a Wheatstone stereogram were to be separated by as little as 8 minutes of arc, four lines, not two, should be seen in the stereoscopic view. This author has made such stereograms and cannot see the extra lines.

A second problem is that it relies heavily on displacement as an indicator of fusion in the primary projection field. As we have already seen (page 289), displacement can be explained in terms of fixation disparity. If fixation disparity can produce apparent displacement with large disparities, it must certainly be implicated in displacement of half-images that are only slightly disparate. This follows from the fact that small instabilities and inaccuracies of vergence must be more likely to take place than large.

Despite these criticisms, and others not discussed here, Sperling's theory is clearly superior in many respects to the classical fusion theory. More research should make it possible to test various aspects of this theory, which has been worked out in considerable detail. The fact that it has a dynamic character, as opposed to the static, machine-like nature of its predecessors, makes it particularly attractive.

OVERVIEW AND CONCLUSION

As noted earlier, binocular stereopsis is undoubtedly one of the best developed topics in all visual perception; and yet it is still difficult to assert that this or that theory represents a fully convincing interpretation of all the facts of stereopsis. I for one have serious doubt that a fusional theory of any sort can account for stereopsis. In my opinion suppression mechanisms furnish a better basis for explaining singleness of vision than does a fusional mechanism. And then new experimental findings cast even more doubt on the idea that fusion of the monocular inputs results in an isomorphic representation of three-dimensional space in the brain. We shall describe just a few of these new findings.

In the early pages of this chapter it was noted that stereopsis may occur even when there is considerable "cross-talk" between the two half-fields. Depth may still occur even when both eyes see both half-fields because of imperfect polarization, or, in the case of anaglyphs, poor color filtering. Kaufman, Bacon, and Barroso (1973) investigated this phenomenon systematically.

Figure 8–33 reveals what happens when the two half-fields of an ordinary stereogram are superimposed so that one eye sees both half-fields. Depth still results, since this stereogram satisfies the requirements of Panum's limiting case. If both eyes should see both half-fields, however, there is no geometrical disparity and depth cannot result.

Suppose, now, that one eye sees both half-fields and that these are

Figure 8–33. When the left half of the upper stereogram is superimposed on the right half, as in the lower stereogram, depth still results.

equally bright. The other eye may see both half-fields also, but they could contribute different proportions to the total brightness of the field. At one extreme, one of the half-fields could alone be visible, as in Figure 8–33, and at the other extreme only the other half-field could be visible to that eye. At both extremes depth would result. If both half-fields contributed equal weights then depth could not result, since both eyes receive identical views. But what if the two half-fields contribute unequal weights to the total brightness of one eye's view? Is depth an all-or-none affair in this situation, or does it depend upon the relative brightnesses of the half-fields contributing to the view of that eye?

Kaufman *et al.* (1973) found that stereoscopic depth magnitude is a function of the proportions contributed by the mixed half-fields to one eye's view. Thus, starting with equally bright half-fields in both eyes, when one half-field in one eye was reduced in brightness while the brightness of the other half-field was increased, a depth effect appeared. The magnitude of this effect grew with the difference in the weights given to the two half-fields.

This effect occurs with any type of stereogram: with line stereograms, with stereograms of natural scenes, and with random dot stereograms. One proposal to explain it is that the peaks and troughs of brightness across the superimposed half-fields add in the same way that sine waves of different phase can be added to produce another sine wave of the same frequency but intermediate phase. This would be consistent with Sperling's theory. Yet if this explanation were correct, the depth magnitude when one eye sees both half-fields and other only one half-field should be half the depth magnitude occurring when the stereogram is viewed normally. This is not what was found, since the depth-magnitude in this case was equal to that of the normally viewed stereogram.

The reason this experiment appears to be important is that even though both eyes see the same contours on corresponding places, depth can result. Nothing is known about the disparity detectors of Hubel and Wiesel (1970), or of Barlow, Blakemore, and Pettigrew (1967), to suggest that their detectors respond differently if disparate contours are of different brightness. Moreover, superimposed contours should fuse for the stationary eye even if they differ in brightness. Yet in this experiment disparity of contrast at corresponding places is sufficient to produce stereopsis. There is of course substantial rivalry of contours of different contrast when such contours are imaged on corresponding retinal places. Is it possible that the rivalry makes it possible for the depth effect to occur?

It has been known for a long time that some individuals are stereo blind. This has usually been associated with abnormal vergence of the eyes. Recently, Richards (1970, 1971a) has reported the existence of stereoblind subjects who do not have abnormal convergence and of others who have anomalous stereopsis.

The so-called "stereoanomalous" subjects are of the most interest to us. Some of these people can detect the depth of an object correctly when the disparity of its half-images is crossed but not when the disparity is uncrossed. Others can detect depth when the disparity is uncrossed but not when it is crossed. This observation implies that crossed disparities are processed in one channel while uncrossed disparities are processed in a parallel channel. This view is entirely incompatible with all the theories considered in this chapter and led Richards (1972) to propose his own theory of stereopsis.

Still another, much older problem is that all theories of stereopsis are really inconsistent with the geometry of stereopsis. Referring to page 277 of this chapter, the reader will recall the formula

$$\rho = a\delta/E^2,$$

where ρ is the magnitude of the binocular disparity, a the interocular separation, δ the separation in depth between two points, and E the average distance to the two points. This equation states that the magnitude of disparity is proportional to the product of the distance between the two objects and the interocular separation, and is inversely proportional to the square of the distance between the observer and the objects. If the relative disparity is held constant, it follows that the magnitude of δ will vary in proportion to the square of the average distance E to the two points. Thus,

$$\delta = \frac{\rho E^2}{a}.$$

This proves that if an experimenter were to keep disparity constant while increasing the distance between the observer and the display, the magnitude of perceived depth would increase with the square of the distance. This is a first-order effect that really cannot be ignored by theorists— especially since it has been shown to be approximately valid in an experiment by Wallach and Zuckerman (1963). Despite Foley's (1967) conflicting results, viewing distance has a strong effect on perceived depth. Although Sperling's theory acknowledges a connection between vergence and disparity, it does not account for this striking square-law relation.

Casual observation reveals that there are still other problems to be faced by theorists. It is a common experience that stereopsis may not occur when a complicated stereogram is first viewed. When stereopsis does occur, it does not occur all at once. Depth appears literally to grow over time. Moreover, staring at one point in the stereogram results in the gradual loss of depth—particularly when one is viewing a Julesz pattern. Such observations lead one to the conclusion that at any one time there may not be an isomorphic representation of three-dimensional space in the brain. This representation appears to be constructed over time, perhaps even during a period of time following a brief flash exposure; and scenes may need continual scanning to refresh the impression of objects laid out in depth. These complications, together with the possibility that the direction of depth is dependent upon fixation (page 295), attest that this field is ripe for extensive theoretical development.

the perception of size

Early psychologists considered the perception of depth—of the third dimension—more mysterious than the two-dimensional layout of objects. The reason for this is not hard to understand. Since the retinal surface is two-dimensional, and since an image of an object covers a portion of that surface and has a particular location on it, it may be argued that the amount of retinal surface covered by the object's image determines the size of the object and that the direction of the object is given by the retinal location of its image. Hence, information about size and direction is given directly on the retina.

Depth perception, however, was not so easily related to the peripheral input. As pointed out in Chapter 7, the cues to depth and distance had to be discovered: they were not directly observable. Moreover, not all depth cues are wholly retinal. Convergence, for example, entails activity of the extra-ocular musculature. Since muscular activity could be involved, some were led to believe that depth perception is the result of experience or learning during the formative weeks and months of early infancy. One purpose of this chapter is to explain why the perception of size is really not less a scientific problem than is the perception of depth, but is itself strongly dependent upon the perception of distance. Accordingly, the first section of this chapter deals with the relation between size and distance.

THE RELATION BETWEEN SIZE AND DISTANCE

It is possible to determine the length of an object by observing how many units on a yardstick or a meter stick would be covered by the object. Such operations are utilized by the physicist to define the concept of length. In psychology, however, the concept of length is more difficult to define operationally.

The psychological concept of length can be clarified if we first take up the distinction between the *distal stimulus* and the *proximal stimulus*. All stimuli are physical entities. A simple line drawn on a white card might be the stimulus in an experiment dealing with size perception. The physical length of the line, as measured with a yardstick or a meter stick, would be the physical attribute of the stimulus manipulated in the experiment. The length of the stimulus as well as its other physical attributes are measurable physical quantities, and are, moreover, absolutely independent of the observer. If the observer were to close his eyes or look away from the line, these attributes of the stimulus would remain unaffected. Yet, as we know, we cannot disregard the fact that an observer might not be looking at the stimulus that is at the heart of the experiment. This is why the psychologist makes a distinction between the *distal stimulus* and the *proximal stimulus*.

A distal object or stimulus is situated away from the sense organ. A proximal object or retinal stimulus, on the other hand, is situated at the sense organ—in this case, the retina. While the distal object (stimulus) is independent of the behavior of the observer, the proximal stimulus is very much affected by what the observer does, for if the observer were to look away from the line, its image would shift across the retina and out of the field of view. The proximal object or stimulus also is describable in physical terms. Thus, the retinal image has a size; it may be more or less blurred; it reflects a particular amount of light; it may have a color, and so on.

The physical size of the retinal image is an immediate derivative of the angular size of the object at the observer's eye. As indicated in Figure 9–1, as an object of constant physical size is moved away from an observer, its angular size diminishes; and moreover the image of the object undergoes a commensurate change in its physical or linear size. It is in fact possible to compute the linear size of the retinal image if the angular size of the distal object is known.

Let us assume that the linear size h of the object a in Figure 9–1 is one meter, and that the distance D to object a is 100 meters. The angular size of object a may then be computed from the formula

$$h/D = \tan \alpha. \tag{1}$$

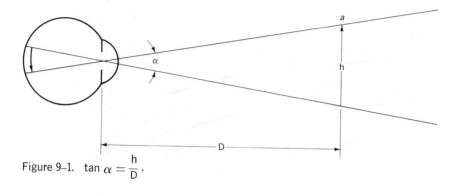

Figure 9–1. $\tan \alpha = \dfrac{h}{D}$.

Consequently,

$1/100 = 0.01.$

It so happens that for small angles—angles smaller than 1-degree—the tangent of the angle is equal to the angle in radians. Since there are approximately 57.3 degrees per radian, we need only multiply 0.01 by 57.3 to discover the angular size of the 1-meter object in degrees. In this case the visual angle of the object is 0.57 degree of arc.

When the eye is accommodated for long distances it focal length is about 17 mm. As we saw in Chapter 7, this is the distance between the node of the eye's compound lens and the retina. Since we know the angular size of the object a, it is possible to determine the linear size of the retinal image from the formula

$$\frac{\text{size of image (mm)}}{\text{focal length of eye}} = \tan \alpha.$$

This formula also provides a way of discovering the angular size of the retinal image of object a at the node of the lens of the eye. This angular size is identical to the angular size of the object a. Since we already know the value of $\tan \alpha$,

size of image (mm) $= 17\,(0.01).$

Therefore, the height of the retinal image of a is 0.17 mm. Thus is proved that the size of the proximal stimulus and the angular size are equivalent measures. It is customary in psychological research simply to cite the angular size of the stimulus employed in an experiment.

Observers of course do not perceive either a proximal stimulus or a distal stimulus. As already emphasized, stimuli are physical entities; they serve to initiate chains of events within the organism. The psychologist attempts to get in touch with these chains of events by asking the observer to describe his experience or to perform a task. The performance of the task is presumed to reflect the perception of the objects by the observer. One such task might simply require the observer to compare the size of two objects. Thus, he may hold a disc in his hand and determine whether one of a set of discs of various sizes on the other side of the room has the same size.

For an illustration of a size-judging task, suppose that the disc held by the observer has a diameter of 5 inches, and that it is held approximately 20 inches from his eye. In this case, the angle subtended by the disc is about fourteen degrees of arc. We shall assume also that the set of comparison discs is located 10 feet away from the observer, and that moreover these discs will range from 1 inch in diameter to 30 inches in diameter. A 5-inch diameter disc placed among these comparison discs would subtend a visual angle of about 2 degrees 20 minutes of arc. Hence, the visual angles of two discs of equal linear diameters would be very different under the circumstances of our hypothetical experiment. And yet, as the reader can determine for himself, the 30-inch diameter comparison disc does have the same angular size as the 5-inch standard disc that the observer is holding in his hand.

If the observer should select the 30-inch diameter comparison disc as the best match to the size of the nearby 5-inch diameter standard disc, we might conclude that his judgment of size is correlated with the proximal stimulus. Alternatively, if the 5-inch diameter comparison disc were the best match for the subject, we should conclude that size judgments are correlated with the physical dimensions of the distal stimulus. On the other hand, if subjects select comparison discs smaller than the 30-inch diameter disc but larger than the 5-inch diameter disc, it is difficult to decide whether subject judgments are based upon the lineal dimensions of the distal object or upon the angular dimensions of the object, or upon some compromise between these two aspects of the stimulus.

The foregoing hypothetical experiment raises a number of interesting questions. Suppose, for example, that judgments of size do correlate with the distal stimulus. This would be a truly remarkable result, since, as we have already pointed out, the distal object is distant from the observer and cannot be sensed directly. On what would such a result be based?

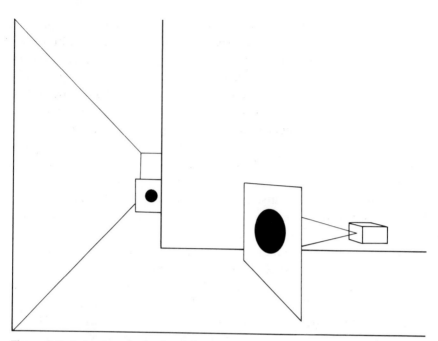

Figure 9–2. Arrangement of stimuli in the L-shaped corridor of the Holway-Boring experiment on size constancy.

How could an observer manage to judge size in such a way that it correlated with the distal object's size? As we shall see later, size judgments can correlate with the physical size of the distal stimulus. Under other circumstances, however, they correlate better with the proximal stimulus, and at still other times they may be intermediate between these two possibilities. Before attempting to interpret such results, we should consider some of the actual experiments performed to discover the characteristics of size perception.

The experimental study of size perception. In their classic experiment on size perception, Holway and Boring (1941) placed two discs in an L-shaped corridor. One disc, which we shall call the variable disc, was located 10 feet away from the observer, and the observer was able to vary its size so that it could be made to match the size of the standard disc placed around the corner in the corridor. The observer had to turn his head through an angle of 90 degrees in order to look from one disc to the other. This arrangement is illustrated in Figure 9–2.

The standard disc was placed at a number of different distances from the observer in its portion of the corridor; these positions ranged from 10 to 120 feet from the observer. Moreover, the size of the standard disc was adjusted at each of its positions so that it always subtended a constant angle of 1 degree at the observer's eye. The task of the observer was to adjust the size of the variable disc, at its constant distance of 10 feet, in order to match the size of the standard disc in the other leg of the corridor.

Let us try to imagine the outcome of this experiment if the observer adjusted the size of the variable disc to match the size of the *distal* standard disc. As indicated, the lineal size of the standard disc was increased with increased distance, so that it would subtend a constant angle at the observer's eye. Thus, the size of the distal stimulus was made proportional to its distance, and, if the judgments of size were correlated with the distal stimulus, the judged size would have to increase in proportion to the distance of the standard stimulus. This would necessarily result in the straight-line function shown in Figure 9–3, as a dashed line labeled "size

Figure 9–3. The results of successive degrees of cue reduction on perceived size. (After Holway and Boring, 1941)

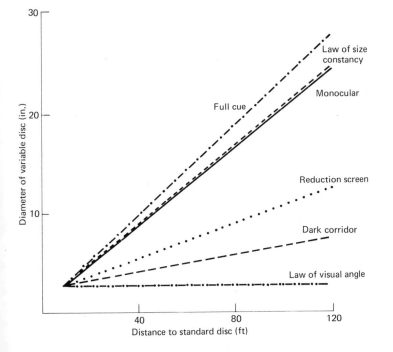

constancy." This line shows how the diameter of the variable disc selected by the observer could increase in proportion to the distance of the standard disc.

Now, if our observer responded in terms of the *proximal* stimulus rather than in terms of the distal stimulus, in this case we would obtain the flat-line function labeled "law of visual angle" in Figure 9–3. The reason is fairly obvious. As the standard disc was moved into the distance, its angular size was maintained at a constant value of 1 degree. To accomplish this it was necessary for the experimenter to increase the lineal size of the distal stimulus. But these changes in the distal stimulus were offset by the increase in its distance, so that the angular size of the disc remained the same. If the observer's judgments reflected the angular size of the disc, and therefore the size of the proximal stimulus, the size of the variable disc would be the same regardless of the distance of the standard disc. This follows from the fact that the variable disc was at a constant distance of 10 feet, and only one particular disc diameter would produce an image with an angular size of 1 degree at that distance.

The term *size constancy* has important implications in the psychology of space perception. It is another way of stating that the *observer responds in terms of the distal stimulus*. If size judgments are correlated with the distal stimulus, then an object, say a man, is perceived as being of a specific size regardless of his distance from the eye of the observer. In this case, a man might be perceived as being 6 feet tall, whether he is standing nearby or some distance away: the perceived size of the man is constant regardless of his distance from the observer. When perceived size is constant, even though the distance of the object observed may change, we refer to the phenomenon of *size constancy*. This phenomenon, however, is merely a special instance of the more general tendency to respond in terms of the distal stimulus.

In the Holway and Boring experiment, to keep the angular size of the disc constant the standard disc was made larger as it was moved away from the observer. If size constancy is present the observer would respond in terms of the distal stimulus—an increase in perceived size would accompany an increase in distance in this experiment. Holway and Boring tested a number of observers to check whether the size constancy function did, in fact, describe their performance. The conditions of their experiment were governed directly by the theoretical consideration of the bases for size constancy.

One of the problems for the theory of space perception is to explain how it is possible that observers perceive size in terms of the distal stimulus. The only information available to the observer is that which is presented to him by his sense organs. In this case, the proximal stimulus, or retinal size, is available at the retina, and yet the subject may respond in terms of distal dimensions. Such a response could come about only if the observer has additional information—information other than that yielded by the retinal size of the proximal stimulus.

The occurrence of size constancy must depend upon the ability of the observer to make use of information given by the cues to distance. If, for example, a man appears to be the same size in the distance as he does when he is nearby, the observer must in some way take the distance to the man into account in making his judgment. If he did not, there would be no way for him to know the size of the man. Another example might make this clear. Suppose that a cardboard disc having the same diameter as a dime were placed on a table. It is conceivable that a person could judge whether the disc were closer in size to a dime than to a penny. Moreover, he could make this judgment whether he were 20 inches or 40 inches from the disc. Such a range of viewing distances would cause the visual angle of the disc to vary remarkably. How could the disc have a stable perceived size under these conditions, unless distance information is utilized by the observer?

It is implicit in our discussion in Chapter 7 that the maximum number of cues to distance is available in a given situation when the environment is fully illuminated and when both eyes are employed in viewing the scene. When the environment is darkened, however, and when it is viewed with one eye only, fewer cues are available on which to base distance judgments. Considerations such as these led to the selection of the different experimental conditions utilized by Holway and Boring. Let us now consider their findings when the corridor they were using was fully illuminated and when the discs were viewed with both eyes.

Under these conditions some of the cues available to the observer were perspective (both linear and texture), convergence, accommodation, binocular disparity, and head-movement parallax. When the sizes of the variable disc selected by the observer are plotted against the distances of the standard disc, we obtain the curve labeled "full cue situation" in Figure 9–3. This curve shows that as the standard disc was moved into the distance, the observer tended to enlarge the variable disc slightly more than necessary to achieve a perfect match to the distal stimulus. We might infer from this that there was a tendency toward a small degree of *over-*

constancy. Over-constancy refers to the fact that the empirical size constancy function, the *full cue situation* curve in Figure 9–3, has a somewhat higher slope than does the ideal or theoretical size constancy function.

In another condition, Holway and Boring had their subjects view the discs monocularly in order to eliminate the cue of binocular disparity. The cues of accommodation and accommodative convergence remained intact, as did the perspective cues and others as well. This simple operation had the effect of depressing the slope of the size-distance function, as shown by the curve labeled "monocular" in Figure 9–3. It follows from this that binocular depth cues play some part in enabling observers to judge lineal size as an object's distance is subjected to change.

In another set of trials, the cues were reduced still more. A *reduction screen* was employed—an opaque screen with a very small aperture. Only one eye could see the stimuli through the aperture, and the lights in the corridor were turned off. Even though some stray light remained to reveal details of the corridor to the observer, cues to distance were less available to him. Moreover, the use of a small aperture for viewing purposes served to reduce the effectiveness of the accommodation cue; and head-movement parallax could not be so effective, since movements of the head would cause the stimulus to go out of view behind the reduction screen. The curve labeled "reduction screen" in Figure 9–3 shows how effective these measures were. The slope of the size-distance function is considerably less than the slopes of the "full cue" and "monocular" curves, and hence the observer was inclined to provide size matches that matched the proximal stimulus more closely than they did the distal standard stimulus.

Finally, having recognized the presence of stray light in their reduction screen condition, Holway and Boring undertook the elimination of this factor in their experiment. To this end they hung draperies in the corridor, with result in the curve labeled "dark corridor" in Figure 9–3. The elimination of stray light, together with the reduction screen, led to a still closer approximation to the law of the visual angle—i.e. proximal stimulus matches—as evidenced by the small slope of the size-distance function.

By way of summary: Holway and Boring demonstrated that size judgments tend to correspond to the distal stimulus when the distance cues are available, but that as distance cues become less available, there is an increasing tendency to judge size in terms of the proximal stimulus. Therefore, they inferred, when distance cues are present, the law of size constancy serves to predict size judgment; when distance cues are reduced, the law of the visual angle may become a better predictor of size judgment.

Equation 1 showed that the angular size of an object is proportional to the ratio of its height and distance. It follows from this that the height h of a distal stimulus may be computed from the product of its angular size in radians (where the angle is small) and its distance D. Thus,

$$h = D \, \alpha \text{ (radians)}. \tag{2}$$

For larger angular sizes, i.e., angles larger than 1 degree,

$$h = D \tan \alpha. \tag{3}$$

It follows from this that if the observer has precise information regarding the physical distance of an object and also "knows" the size of the proximal stimulus, he can compute the linear size of an object, regardless of its distance from his eye.

There is a problem in this approach. As was indicated earlier, one problem of size perception concerns the possibility of perceiving in terms of the distal stimulus, inasmuch as this type of size judgment would have to depend upon the availability of distance information. If the subject registers the physical distance to an object and also its image size, he could, in principle, calculate the size of the distal stimulus. The difficulty with this simplistic geometrical theory is that it requires the observer to register the physical distance to the object—and physical distance is no less a distal attribute than is physical size.

Since it is a question as to how an observer judges distal size, it is equally questionable to assert that an observer can have knowledge of physical distance. Awareness of this problem has prompted psychologists to seek for a better relation than that existing between the distal parameters of physical distance and physical size. One approach toward solving this problem is exemplified by *Emmert's law* (1881), which deals with *after-images*.

An after-image is commonly experienced after looking briefly at a very bright light source or after staring for a minute or two at a high-contrast pattern. The reader may have had the experience of seeing the after-image of the light bulb in his bedside lamp after turning it off before retiring. The after-image of the lamp results from the fact that vision persists for some time after the cessation of stimulation. The proximal stimulus sets up processes in the retina which go on for a considerable period of time after the stimulus is removed. If the eye is kept very still during exposure to the distal stimulus, the ensuing after-image will have a well-defined form, similar to the shape of the original stimulus. In essence the after-image is a proximal stimulus in the absence of a distal stimulus.

Although after-images are painted on the retina, they are localized in space outside the body. This should not be surprising, since all retinal images are located or perceived as being outside the body. Moreover, since after-images have a constant or unchanging retinal size, they resemble the standard stimulus employed by Holway and Boring—i.e., their standard disc was maintained at a constant visual angle although it was moved in distance. Thus, no matter how far away the after-image appears to be, it will always subtend a constant angle at the node of the lens of the observer's eye, and hence have a constant linear size on the observer's retina.

Emmert observed that an after-image will appear to be located on any surface viewed by the observer—i.e., if one has an after-image, he will see it on, or as belonging to, any object of regard. If he looks at a wall across the room, for example, the observer will see the after-image on the wall. Moreover, Emmert noted, the size of the after-image will appear to change depending upon how far away it appears to be, so that if the wall on the other side of the room is ten feet away, the after-image will appear to be larger than it would against a wall only five feet away. Observations such as these led Emmert to formulate his law, which states that the perceived size of an after-image is proportional to its *apparent* distance.

The critical point here is that the effective distance in size perception is not the *physical* distance to the object, but the distance at which it *appears* to be. It is very important to recognize the distinction between physical distance and perceived or apparent distance. If an after-image should be seen against a 10-foot distant wall but the observer were deceived about the actual distance of the wall, then the size of the after-image would not be proportional to the physical distance of the wall. Thus, looking at the wall through a small aperture to reduce the cues to its distance would also reduce the apparent size of the after-image.

Figure 9–4 shows how Emmert's law works. If we assume that the distances to points A and B are apparent distances and not necessarily physical distances, the after-image projected onto a surface at the dis-

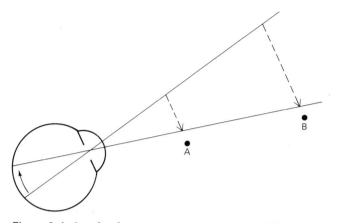

Figure 9–4. An after-image, represented by the solid arrow, is perceived as being twice as large at B as it is at A. This exemplifies Emmert's law.

tance of point B will appear to be twice as large as it would if projected to the distance of point A.

A mere illustration of the effect of apparent distance on perceived size does not of course establish the validity of an empirical law. We need to know whether the law is in actual conformity with empirical data and also whether there are any limitations on its applicability. Thus, though the law may be an appropriate account of size perception under one set of conditions, it may not be adequate under other conditions. In one experiment designed to test for the actual relation between perceived size and apparent distance, Gogel, Wist, and Harker (1963) utilized a novel technique for measurement. Rather than have observers match the size of one object to the size of a similar object, they tried to elicit judgments of the absolute perceived size and absolute perceived distance of an object.

When an observer compares one object's size to that of another, similar object, we can say that he is making a relative size judgment. Thus, if one of the objects is smaller than the other, it may be perceived as such, even though the observer may not know the physical size of either object. Gogel *et al.* suggested that if the observer can see one object and if he gives some indication of its size without literally looking at anything else, then we may say that he is offering us a judgment of the "absolute" size of the object. The term *absolute* in this case is something of a misnomer, for if an observer offers any size judgment at all, that judgment must be made relative to some scale, even though the scale may be different when the observer does not make direct visual comparisons. Therefore, we shall make use of the term, but referring it to comparison with some scale other than a visual scale.

Absolute size judgments were elicited by the Gogel team in the following way: Black rectangular targets were presented at distances of 5, 10, 15 and 20 feet from an observer in an alley 34 feet long and 4 feet wide. The sizes of the rectangles were selected so that their widths would subtend a constant visual angle of nearly 3 degrees regardless of the distance of presentation. The subjects in this experiment were provided with two aluminum rods. One rod was to be grasped with the left hand, and the other, grasped with the right hand, could be moved toward and away from the left hand's rod. Neither rod could be seen by the observer, since they were placed at the level of his knees, and throughout the experiment he had to look through an aperture into the alley. While looking at one of the rectangles in the alley, the observer moved the right-hand rod until the gap between his left and right hands appeared to match the size of the rectangle. The experimenter then read from a scale the distance between the rods. This distance was presumed to reflect the absolute perceived size of the rectangle.

The absolute perceived distance to the rectangle was measured by having the observer throw darts into an alley parallel to the alley in which the rectangles were presented and invisible to the observer. He simply obtained a visual impression of the distance to the rectangle and then threw a dart with sufficient force to reach the target. He never knew how accurately he threw the dart, since he could not see it.

Despite the seeming coarseness of this method, an independent study showed that the length of the dart throw was linearly related to the physical distance in the alley, although the perceived absolute distance as measured by dart throwing did not increase at the same rate as physical distance. That is to say, the distance to which a dart was thrown increased with increasing distance, but the magnitude of the average throw was always less by a constant proportion than the magnitude of the distance of the target. It appeared to Gogel and his associates that the magnitude of the dart-throw was more nearly reflective of the apparent distance to the target than was the magnitude of the physical distance to the target.

In this situation Emmert's law would predict that the judged absolute size of the target would in fact be proportional to the judged absolute

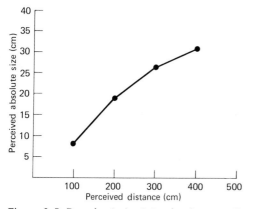

Figure 9–5. Perceived absolute size is not a linear function of perceived distance. (After Gogel, Wist, and Harker, 1963)

distance to the target. When the absolute size judgments are plotted against absolute distance, however, it is apparent that perceived absolute size is not proportional to perceived distance, as indicated by the graph shown in Figure 9–5.

The Gogel team used also a relative-size measure similar to that used by Holway and Boring. Rather than ask the observer to match one object to a similar object, they had him match the separation between two visible rods to the size of their rectangle. When perceived relative size is plotted against physical distance, as in the Holway and Boring experiment, the result is similar. Thus, perceived size is nearly a linear function of physical distance. There is a slight tendency toward over-constancy in the sense that two of their empirical points exhibit perceived size as slightly larger than would be predicted from the law of perfect size constancy.

What are we to conclude from this representative study of size perception? There are at least two alternative interpretations. First, we might conclude, as did the authors of the study cited above, that size is not proportional to apparent distance. The fact that relative perceived size is a function of physical distance raises some questions about this conclusion, however.

The perceived absolute distance to a target, as measured by the dart-throwing technique, is proportional to the physical distance to the target. Hence, we do not obtain much information about apparent distance from this experiment, except that it faithfully reflects physical distance. But the perceived absolute size is not a linear function of distance to the target, though relative size is so related to distance. Why is it necessary to conclude that measured absolute size is a more appropriate measure of perceived size than is the measure of relative size? Gogel and his associates do not provide us with an answer to this question.

Other experiments, too, have proposed that perceived size is not truly proportional to apparent distance. Gruber (1954), in an experiment in which he hoped to measure apparent distance more directly than did Gogel, Wist, and Harker, utilized a technique in which observers bisected a distance to an object. In this procedure the subject had to indicate on a terrain a point that appeared to subdivide that terrain into two equal parts. It was found that observers tended to place the bisecting point closer to themselves than they would have if the ground-plane were actually divided in two. Gruber's inference from this was that the nearer half of the ground-plane is perceived as larger than the more distant half; and this suggests that perceived distance is not proportional to physical distance, since nearer portions of the ground are perceived as larger than physically equal but more distant portions of the terrain. On the other hand, since size judgments indicate that perceived size of an object of constant angular size grows in proportion to physical distance, we must conclude that Emmert's law cannot be a precise expression of the relation between apparent distance and perceived size. This conclusion was supported in similar experiments by Smith and Smith (1966). Jean Piaget (1969) discovered that while perceived size and distance judgments are not related linearly in adults, they do correlate when children make such judgments. This finding has an indirect bearing on the interpretation of Gruber's result.

The bisection method utilized by Gruber may be subject to rather interesting speculation. It may well be that the performance of this experiment requires the observer to adopt an analytical attitude if he is to find a point that bisects a length along the ground-plane. This attitude might prompt the observer to equate two regions on the basis of the angles that they subtend at the eye, rather than in terms of their linear dimensions. This could lead to an apparent overestimation of nearer portions of the terrain relative to equally long but more distant portions. There is some evidence to admit the plausibility of this conjecture.

The effect of attitude on size and distance judgments. Gilinsky (1955) presented a standard triangle at several different large distances—from 100 to 4000 feet—from the observer. The variable triangle was kept at a constant distance of 100 feet from the observer, and it was off toward one side so that he had to turn his head to look from the variable to the standard. The task of the observer was to vary the size of the variable triangle so that it matched the size of the standard when it was at each one of its different distances away.

The matching of size was done by different observers, operating under different sets of instructions. The "objective" instructions required the observer to adjust the variable so that it would equal the size of the standard if they were both measured by a ruler. This, of course, is asking the observer to match the linear sizes of the two triangles—i.e., to match their distal sizes. Under the so-called "retinal" instructions, the observers were asked to imagine that photographs were taken of the two triangles. If a more distant triangle were photographed, it would produce a smaller picture than the nearer variable triangle. The successful accomplishment of this task would, of course, be equivalent to giving matches that varied with variations in the proximal stimulus.

As shown in Figure 9–6, these different instructions did lead to different judgments of size. Under the objective instructions the results reflect a capacity to match the heights of the triangles in terms of their distal dimensions. Actually, there was a tendency toward over-constancy, inasmuch as the variable triangle tended to be made larger than the standard stimulus as distance to the standard was increased. When the retinal instructions were given, however, there was a strong tendency to match the angular sizes of the two stimuli.

Perhaps a word is needed about the graph shown in Figure 9–6. The curves in this graph differ from those in Figure 9–3, for the reason that Gilinsky's standard had the same linear size at all distances, while the standard used by Holway and Boring had a constant angular size at all distances. Therefore, if judgments reflect variations in the distal stimulus, an experiment such as that conducted by Holway and Boring would show that the variable stimulus must be made larger as the distance of the standard increased. Gilinsky's observers, on the other hand, cause the variable to be the same size, since the linear size of the standard was kept constant in her experiment.

Gilinsky's findings have been confirmed by several other experimenters. Epstein (1963), for example, obtained similar results with an improved experimental design. Ono (1966) demonstrated that when many visual cues to distance are available, observers can rapidly learn to

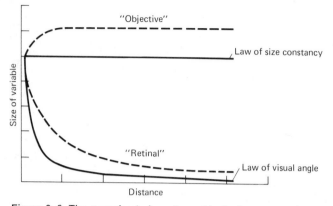

Figure 9–6. The perceived size of an object of constant linear size as a function of its distance under "objective" and "retinal" matching instructions. (After Gilinsky, 1955)

give fairly accurate distal-stimulus matches. When the visual cues to distance are somewhat impoverished, his observers rapidly learned to match on the basis of retinal or projected size. This fits well with Gilinsky's casual observation that the effect of attitude may be easier to discern when stimuli are presented at very large distances from the observer. As is to be expected, distance cues are less efficient when large distances are to be perceived, allowing observers to behave as though they are sensitive to variations in the proximal stimulus.

Returning to the results of Gruber (1954): it may now readily be imagined that when an observer tries to bisect an extent of the ground-plane, he may very well adopt an analytical or "retinal" attitude. Thus, in effect, he could be instructing himself to respond in retinal terms. The same observer, attempting to judge the frontal size of an object, however, could instruct himself to adopt an "objective" mode of behavior, and therefore generate matches closely approximating size constancy. It is clear that careful attention must be paid to the criterion accepted by the observer for the different tasks he may perform in such experiments. This is borne out by Piaget's (1969) experiment, where size and distance judgments are correlated when made by children, but do not correlate when adults try to make them. Perhaps children have less ability than adults to adopt different criteria when asked to do related tasks.

As Rock (1973) has pointed out, perhaps uncontrolled variations in attitude underly much of the variability in the performance of such tasks.

This could explain differences found between different cultures, between adults and children, and also between different persons. Rock's proposition enjoys some support from Leibowitz and Harvey (1967, 1969*a*, 1969*b*), whose subjects exhibited excellent size constancy over a large range of distances for familiar and unfamiliar objects in naturalistic environments. When they varied instructions they were able to change the size constancy functions markedly.

Modes of size perception. The experimental studies of size perception have proven that observers are capable of making judgments in accord with variations in the distal stimulus. The mere fact that this capability exists is far more important than the fact that under some circumstances the law of the visual angle is a better description of size-judging behavior. The problem we must now confront is that of identifying the mechanisms that make size constancy possible. The simple notion that perceived size is proportional to perceived distance does not explain how it is possible for a person to reflect variations in the distal stimulus in his discriminatory behavior. While at the present time no adequate theory exists, it is of considerable value to consider some of the strands from which such a theory may be woven.

Figure 9–7. Many differently shaped objects can produce the same image on the retina.

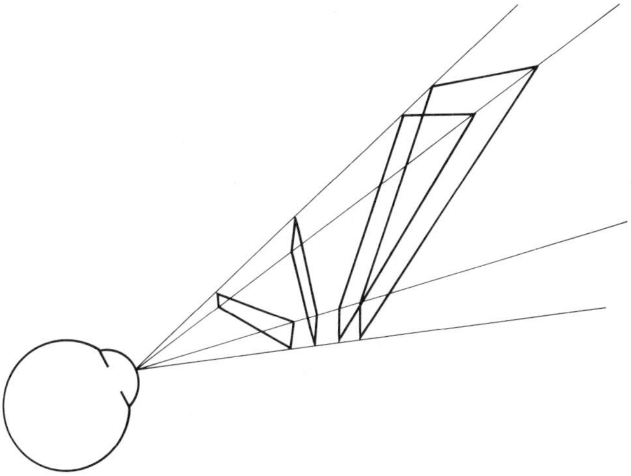

Ittelson (1960) has pointed out that many differently shaped objects may produce the same image on the retina, depending upon the orientation and distance of the distal stimulus (see Figure 9–7). The uncertainty inherent in a situation where an isolated object is presented to an observer will diminish as various cues are presented. The image size alone is an ambiguous indicator of the size of the distal object. Presumably, the size of the distal object becomes available to the observer as the number of cues to its distance is increased. This last point led Wallach and McKenna (1960) to the hypothesis that an object viewed under reduction conditions can have no perceived size. To test this hypothesis they presented a luminous square as the standard in a size-matching experiment. The square was viewed under reduction conditions, and the observers's task was to match its size with one of several white squares of different sizes. The squares of white cardboard were presented one at a time, inside a large, illuminated box that the observer could look into with both eyes. Thus, a non-reduction object was used to match the size of a reduction object.

In general, most of Wallach and McKenna's observers responded inconsistently to the size of the standard luminous square. Since in only a few cases were observers able to match the visual angles of the stimuli, the investigators concluded that viewing the standard object under reduction conditions gives rise only to ambiguous perception of size. It implies also that observers are only feebly aware of the extent of the retinal image of an object—but if so, how then do they match two reduction objects to each other? Gilinsky (1961) suggested that this is done as well as it is because observers assume that the objects are equidistant. The observer need not know precisely how far the objects are from him. Wallach and McKenna accept this explanation for the matching of two reduction objects.

Rock and McDermott (1964) came to opposite conclusions. When their observers matched two reduction objects, they tried to judge their relative distances as well. These judgments were likewise ambiguous. In another experiment they had observers match a reduction object with a binocularly viewed object seen at two different distances. Since the matches differed, depending upon the distances of the non-reduction variable object, Rock and McDermott concluded that the observers were capable of responding in terms of retinal size.

There should really be no doubt at all that observers adopting the appropriate attitude can discriminate differences in angular size. The fact that training enables the artist to create pictures in perspective is eloquent testimony to the existence of this facility. The ambiguous responses encountered by Wallach and McKenna could well have been reduced by training. All this suggests that there are different modes of responding to the sizes of stimuli: some modes incorporate information about distance, others largely make use of the magnitude of the retinal area stimulated by an object. The presence of distance cues could inhibit the latter capability —perhaps in the same way that attitude or instructions tend to favor one kind of response over the other. Before we can consider this possibility, we must turn to some of the factors influencing size judgments.

The equidistance tendency. Gogel (1956, 1965, 1970) has demonstrated that under reduction conditions two objects will be more likely to be judged as being equally distant from the observer as they are brought closer to each other in the frontal plane. This would explain the fact that the observers in Rock and McDermott's experiment gave ambiguous judgments about the relative distance of two reduction objects. The observers had to turn their heads 90 degrees to look from one object to the other. Presumably, they would have judged the objects to be equidistant if they had been adjacent to each other.

A typical experimental arrangement to study the equidistance tendency is illustrated in Figure 9–8. One object is presented so that it may be seen by one eye only; all other objects in the visual field may be seen by both eyes. Gogel assumes that the uniocular object is at an indeterminate distance from the observer, and the other objects are at determinate distances. Now, when the uniocular object is near one of the binocular objects, observers report that it is at the same distance as the nearest edge of the binocular object. Without changing the stimulus arrangement in any way other than shifting the uniocular object's position closer to one of the other binocular objects, its apparent distance may be changed.

The changes in apparent distance of the uniocular object are ascribed by Gogel to the so-called *equidistance tendency.* This is a way of describing the result of placing an object at an indeterminate distance adjacent to an object at a determinate distance; in no way is it an explanation of that fact. Nevertheless, the equidistance tendency that accompanies adjacency can have a powerful effect on size perception. This is markedly evident in an experiment employing an after-image in one eye only.

With an after-image formed in one eye and not in the other, it is possible, by positioning the eye, to place the after-image near the edge of

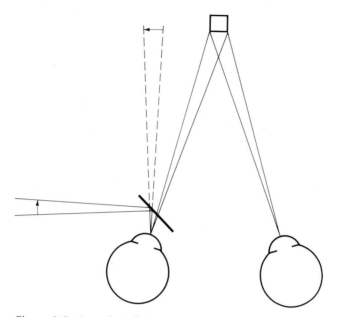

Figure 9–8. A method for demonstrating the equidistance tendency. The virtual image of the arrow is seen by the left eye only. The square is seen by both eyes—directly by the right eye, and through a partially silvered mirror by the left eye.

some other object. The judged size of the after-image will be proportional to the distance of the binocular object—an instance of Emmert's law.

Although the equidistance tendency is easily demonstrated, there is reason to believe that it may simply reflect the influence of the conventional cues to depth. In the experiment using an after-image, the sharpness of the after-image is unaffected by changes in the accommodation of the eye, with the result that both the object and the after-image are seen clearly when the eye is accommodated for the distance of the object. This could yield an equidistance judgment. Similarly, the convergence of the eyes required to see the binocular object as single results also in an apparently single after-image (or any other uniocular image). From this, too, the observer could judge that the uniocular and binocular objects are equidistant.

Despite these reservations, it is entirely possible that as described by Gogel, there is a general equidistance tendency not reducible to the depth cues. Moreover, this equidistance tendency could have a profound effect on perceived size. Distance cues may play a role in producing this tendency. We must now consider how the cues to distance may affect the perception of size.

Size and the cues to distance. In Chapter 7 we reviewed the results of Heinemann, Tulving, and Nachmias (1959), who had studied the effect of convergence on perceived size when the accommodation was paralyzed, and discovered that with increased convergence (which normally occurs as an object approaches) there is an accompanying diminution of the size of a target of constant angular size. This reduction in size is consistent with a reduction in apparent distance, which is a normal correlate of increased convergence. These authors noted, however, that the judged distance of a target that is apparently reduced in size as a result of increased convergence is opposite to what might be expected. The apparently smaller target is judged as distant, and the apparently larger target —because of decreased convergence—is judged as near.

This result is by no means universal. Other studies show that increased convergence leads to an apparent diminution of apparent distance, together with a reduction in perceived size (Gogel, 1961; Richards, 1971*b*; Wallach and Floor, 1971). But not all observers show such effects. Only half of Gogel's (1961) observers exhibited perceived changes in absolute distance with changes in convergence. Richards (1971*b*) found that while about one-third of his observers exhibited a very small change in perceived size with convergence, and a very slight change in perceived distance, two-thirds of his observers evidenced a relatively strong effect of convergence on both size and distance. When convergence is increased from zero (i.e., when the observer is looking at an object at optical infinity) to a near distance of 14 cm, the apparent size of a space separating two pinpoints of light in a dark environment may be reduced by nearly 80 per cent. For these observers there is a proportionate decrease in the apparent distance to the stimulus (see Richards and Miller, 1969). Apparent distance can, however, change by only a factor of four over the entire range of convergence, and this is not sufficient to account for size constancy.

As Gibson (1950) has shown, observers give evidence of perfect size constancy when objects are so far away that they are just visible. Gilinsky (1955), and Leibowitz and Harvey (1967), also demonstrated size constancy over vast distances. Leibowitz, Shiina, and Hennessy (1972) have shown that oculomotor adjustments alone can provide sufficient informa-

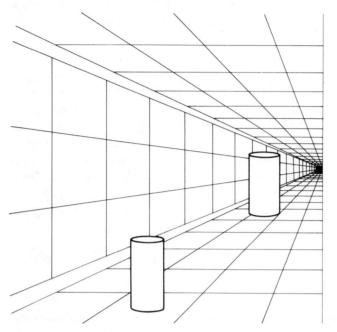

Figure 9–9. The corridor illusion.

tion for complete size constancy over a distance of only 1 meter. At longer distances size constancy must be attributed to pictorial and kinetic cues.

The pictorial cues discussed in Chapter 7 may very well be involved in the constancy of the sizes of objects viewed from large distances. Unfortunately, however, the effect of perspective, interposition, and other pictorial cues on perceived size have barely been studied. We do have optical illusions such as the one shown in Figure 9–9, which demonstrates that the perceived size of an object may be strongly affected by perspective, or perhaps by other features of perspective drawings. The effect of a perspective grid similar to that shown in Figure 9–9 causes the more distant cylinder to appear as much as 12 per cent larger than the nearer cylinder (Richards and Miller, 1971). That the effect of perspective may be stronger than this is suggested by the demonstrations made with Ame's distorted room (Ittelson, 1960).

As shown in Figure 9–10, the actual construction of the room places one corner at a much greater distance from the observer than the other corner. But since the room provides a retinal image identical to the image

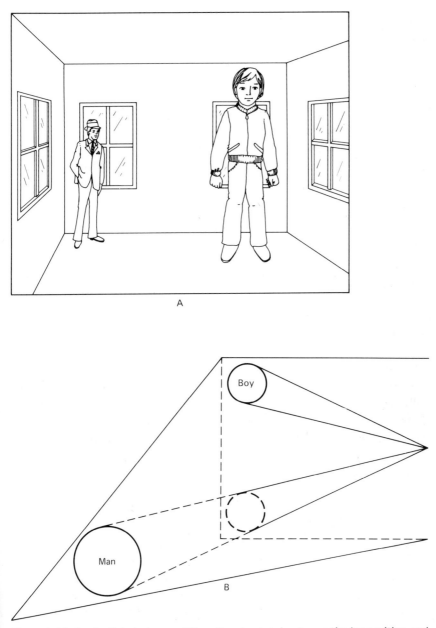

Figure 9–10. Ame's distorted room. When the observer is at a particular position and looks at the room monocularly, as at A, it appears to be a normal room. Since the man is actually farther away than the boy, he subtends a smaller angle at the eye of the observer. Also, the man appears to be smaller because he is perceived as being at the same distance as the boy, as in B.

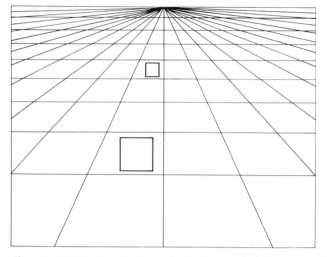

Figure 9–11. The density of terrain texture occluded by an object of constant linear size remains constant with the distance to the object.

produced by an actual rectangular room when it is viewed with one eye from a particular position, the two corners appear to be equidistant. This follows from the fact that a photograph of the room would be identical to a photograph of a rectangular room. Now, if a man is placed in the physically more distant corner, as shown in the figure, and a boy in the nearer corner, the boy will look much larger than the man. So it is that the perspective cues to distance override the effects of such factors as the prior experience we have had with large men and small boys. The magnitude of this effect may be greater than 12 per cent—though systematic data are not available.

One way in which texture perspective might affect the perception of size is yielded by the fact that as an object recedes into the distance, it covers an equal amount of terrain. In other words, the angular size of the object changes together with the angular density of terrain texture. Gibson (1950) suggested that this invariance may well underlie size constancy. Figure 9–11 illustrates this phenomenon. Once again, however, we have little data for determining precisely how perceived size varies as a function of covered terrain texture.

If an object is moved away from an observer in a uniform corridor, the size of the object relative to the surrounding walls of the corridor will remain constant (see Figure 9–12), and this relative size effect can be

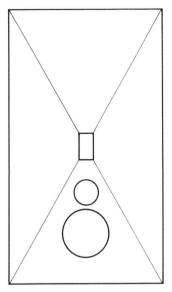

Figure 9–12. An object of constant linear size occupies the same relative space in a uniform corridor regardless of its distance.

separated from perspective. To do so, suppose that an object within a framework is viewed under reduction conditions. While the observer has no information as to the actual distance of the object and its framework, his task is to match the sizes of objects enclosed by frameworks of different sizes. If the sizes of the objects are judged to be equal when they fill equal amounts of their respective frameworks, it may be concluded that the relative size of an object can be determined by the relation between the object and its immediate framework.

This experiment was performed by Rock and Ebenholtz (1959). Their stimuli were two luminous rectangles containing vertical lines, similar to those shown in Figure 9–13. One rectangle was maintained at a constant size; the other was either 2 times, 3 times, 5 times, or 8 times the size of the standard rectangle. The observer's task was to adjust the length of a line in the larger rectangle, so that it appeared to match the length of the line in the smaller standard rectangle. If the surrounding rectangle has an effect on the perceived size of the enclosed line, when the match is made the larger rectangle should contain a longer line than the shorter standard rectangle. If the effect of the relation between the line and its framework completely determines size constancy, then the ad-

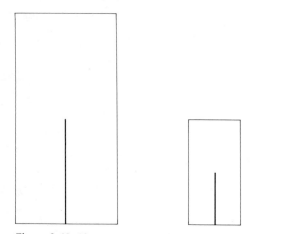

Figure 9–13. Observers tend to judge the central lines in the two rectangles as equal in length when they fill equal proportions of their frames.

justable line should always be in a constant proportion to the height of its framework. Thus, if the standard line is always one-third the height of its rectangle, then the lines in all the larger rectangles should be adjusted so that they, too, are one-third the height of their surrounding rectangles.

The degree to which this is achieved was expressed by the authors in terms of percentage of complete proportionality. Thus, when the variable rectangle was twice the height of the standard rectangle, its inner line was judged to be equal to the line in the standard rectangle when it was 80 per cent of twice the length of the standard line. This is an impressive degree of proportionality of size. As the variable rectangle grew larger, however, the approximation to complete proportionality grew less as well. With the variable rectangle three times the height of the standard, its line was 73 per cent of the length of three times the length of the standard line. The proportionality with the variable rectangle five times the height of the standard was only 45 per cent and, with variable eight times the size, 42.5 per cent.

If we return now to our hypothetical experiment in a corridor, it is evident that when one object is eight times farther away than another similar object, its linear angular size is one-eighth that of the other object. Moreover, the walls surrounding the more distant object provide a framework that is also one-eighth the size of the framework surrounding the closer object. Under these circumstances, as Holway and Boring have shown, size constancy can be complete, and yet the results of Rock and

Ebenholtz suggest that framework alone could account for only a portion of size constancy. This same conclusion might also apply to Gibson's notion that the density of occluded texture can account for size constancy on an open textured terrain.

It should be obvious by now that many factors may operate to produce constancy of apparent size. Depth information clearly plays an important role in size perception; so, too, does the frame of reference surrounding the object whose size is being judged. The mechanisms that make possible these effects of diverse sources of information is as yet unknown. According to Helmholtz' *doctrine of unconscious inference* (1925), which has been invoked to explain size constancy, the observer literally computes the lineal size of an object from neural information representing the size of its retinal image and its apparent distance. This is tantamount to asserting that at some unconscious level the observer computes the product of the distance to the object and the tangent of the angle it subtends at the eye, so that he may arrive at an estimate of its lineal or distal size. This view is accepted by both Gregory (1970) and Rock (1973).

This writer has some reservations about the applicability of the unconscious inference theory to size perception. It will be recalled from Chapter 7 that virtually all cues to depth are relativistic in nature—i.e., indicating that one object is more or less distant from an observer than is another object. None of the relativistic cues can directly inform an observer that an object is at some particular distance from him. Consequently, the distance cues cannot be used in a simple computation of size (as implied by Helmholtz), since they do not indicate absolute distance. It would first be necessary for the relative distance cues to be used in a computation of absolute distance, and we do not know how this might be done.

Convergence, which is the only candidate for the status of cue to absolute distance, might be involved in a Helmholtzian computation of size; and yet we have seen that while this cue is effective over a limited range of distances, at greater distances mechanisms similar to those discussed by Gibson (1950) are more likely involved in size perception. Occlusion of terrain texture, gradients of texture and of retinal velocities, and interposition may all serve to change the scale or frame of reference against which the size of an object is judged. Such cues do not require the observer to compute distance *per se*, but they do imply a somewhat different usage of what we have come to call the cues to distance.

INTERACTION OF THE CUES TO DEPTH

However the cues to depth or distance are used, they are definitely implicated in size perception. Moreover, different cues may have similar effects on the perception of size. When distances become large the oculomotor cues may drop out, and then perceived size becomes dependent upon contextual cues. Also, as in the Holway and Boring experiment, cues in combination may allow for more complete size constancy than do the cues of a less rich environment. All this suggests that cues to distance supplement each other in their influence on size perception. Different cues may have different effects on the appearance of distance and on the perception of size. In combination these cues may well interact with each other in ways not as yet understood. In this section we shall outline some of these ways.

If two cues provide pertinent information about the distance of an object, the probability of judging the distance correctly may be greater when both cues are present than it would if either cue were present alone. Thus, each cue makes it more or less likely that a distance may be judged correctly; together they may make it even more likely. Such cues may be thought of as providing parallel information about a scene. It is as though the two cues are processed in independent channels to which the observer can refer in making his judgments.

Such independence of cues is an instance of the *superposition principle*. If two signals are sent by independent transmitters over independent channels to a single receiver, and if the signals do not interact in the receiver, then the effect of one signal on the receiver will be totally independent of the effect of the other signal. The signals would simply add together in the receiver—i.e., they would be superimposable. It is possible that some cues are similarly superimposable.

A second possibility is that simultaneously present cues produce effects that interact with each other. The effect of one cue alone may be quite different if another cue is simultaneously present. The place and nature of this mutual interaction of cues may also vary. Thus, while two cues are processed in independent channels, they may interact when the observer makes his decision about distance. Alternatively, the cues may be processed in a common channel and interact before decisions can be made.

Finally, some cues to distance may not refer to the same phenomena at all. The cue of interposition, for example, can inform an observer only that one object is closer to him than some other object. Of itself this cue cannot inform him about the distance separating the two objects. This could come from another cue—binocular disparity, for example. It is, however, conceivable that the interposition cue could improve the probability of a correct response in the presence of binocular disparity. In this case we may think in terms not of parallel channels but rather of sequential channels in which the effect of one cue is dependent upon information received over other channels.

The foregoing discussion does not exhaust all the ways in which cues could jointly affect distance and perceived size, but merely points the way toward analyzing the relations among the cues. This systematic approach has not yet been applied to the problem of size and distance perception; instead, most studies have concentrated upon the effects of cue conflict. It is possible to arrange a situation in which different cues provide conflicting information about the depth-relations in a scene. Such experiments have focused on predominance—i.e., on the relative strengths of the cues. Now, while this of itself can never lead to a basic understanding of the processes involved in judging size and distance, it does yield some insights into the nature of the interaction of the cues involved in these experiments.

One example of how cues interact with each other has already been encountered in Chapter 8, where we saw that changes in convergence affect the magnitude of depth produced by a constant binocular disparity. This is not simply a matter in which judgment of a particular depth is made more or less accurate because two cues are present rather than only one. It indicates rather that the effect of one cue—disparity in this case— is altered by the introduction of a variation in the other cue.

A different kind of relation among cues was observed by Harker (1958), who found that when binocular disparity was supplemented with monocular cues to depth, observers had better acuity than when the binocular cues alone were present. Harker suggested that this could be attributed to the fact that monocular and binocular cues provide the observer with independent information about the depth interval between two objects. This, in effect, gives the observer two independent "chances" to identify correctly a small depth interval between two objects—from which Harker implied that the monocular and binocular cues have superimposable effects. This proposal is similar to one reached by Jameson and Hurvich (1959), who conducted a similar experiment. The monocular cues in neither experiment were fully identified. Yet when observers were

Figure 9–14. A stereoscopic Necker cube.

required to judge the magnitude of a small depth interval, the monocular cues produced effects that did combine additively with the effects of the binocular cues. This, however, is not proof that these same cues have superimposable effects on perceived size.

Some monocular cues and binocular disparity may not work in parallel. Figure 9–14 shows two drawings of a wire cube known as a *Necker cube*. In both drawings, depth is based upon monocular cues, but the direction of depth is ambiguous, inasmuch as the viewer cannot tell which face is nearer to him. When this figure is viewed in a stereoscope two interesting facts emerge. The nearer face of the cube is above the more distant face, and the cues do not exhibit the same spontaneous reversals in depth as they do when viewed monocularly. Moreover, the magnitude of the depth between the nearer and more distant faces is apparently greater than in monocular view. So it is that while the available monocular cues provide qualitative information about the existence of depth, its magnitude and direction are given binocularly. It is possible that the monocular cues present complement the binocular cues by giving some crude indication of the object's characteristics and thereby aiding the binocular system in analyzing the scene more precisely.

Analysis of this kind may be carried farther by placing the cues in conflict with each other. In Figure 9–15 the cue of interposition is placed in conflict with the cue of disparity. The interposition cue alone suggests that one square is hiding behind another less distant square; and yet the binocular disparity is arranged so that the occluded square would be seen as closer than the occluding square if disparity alone were operative. If the effects of the two cues were additive, the two cues would tend to cancel each other. However, one has no difficulty in responding to the disparity so that instead of two squares seen one behind the other, the upper shape is seen as nearer than the lower square. The upper shape, in this case, is perceived as a broken outlined square, since the boundary common to the two shapes is perceived as belonging to the lower square.

Figure 9–15. Interposition vs. disparity.

McDonald (1962) studied this relation between interposition and disparity by means of this cue-conflict paradigm. Other scientists who have considered the cues in terms of their relative strengths when placed in conflict include Schreiver (1925), Vernon (1937), Wallach and Norris (1963), Fineman (1971), and even the great Wheatstone (1838), with his pseudoscope.

A pseudoscope is a device permitting the left eye to see the right eye's normal view, and the right eye to see the left eye's normal view—thus reversing the cross or direction of all disparities in the visual field so that if distance judgments are based upon disparity alone, objects physically more distant than other objects will appear to be nearer if viewed through the pseudoscope. While looking through a pseudoscope, Wheatstone observed that regular geometrical objects—such as the wire cube or a crystal—do appear to have reversed depth, whereas more complicated objects, like the human face, are apparently unaffected by reverse disparity. The nose appears to be closer to the observer than do the eyes, even though disparity *per se* indicates that the nose is more distant. In a similar experiment, Schreiver (1925) found that pseudoscopic viewing of perspective scenes produces an impression of depth that is consistent with perspective and not with disparity, and concluded that the monocular cues contained within perspective scenes are stronger than conflicting disparity cues.

These cue-conflict studies have not always been consistent in outcome. The reasons are obvious if one studies stereograms such as that depicted in Figure 9–16, a pseudoscopic view of a perspective scene in which cues other than disparity are also present. At first the global impression is of a normal street scene; after prolonged viewing, however, some parts of the scene do, in fact, appear at depths predictable from disparity. It is by no means obvious that perspective or any other pictorial cue always predominates over disparity. Observation of many pseudoscopic scenes indi-

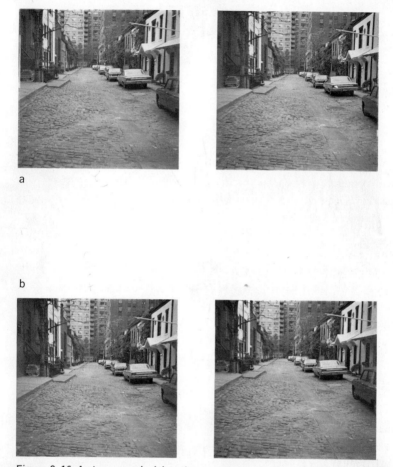

a

b

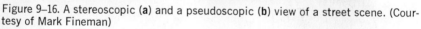

Figure 9–16. A stereoscopic (**a**) and a pseudoscopic (**b**) view of a street scene. (Courtesy of Mark Fineman)

cates that such prolonged periods of viewing together with actively seeking alternative depth relations enable me to "see through" competing pictorial cues and respond to the disparity. This result also supports the contention that at least some of the pictorial cues may be processed independently of the disparity cue. When disparity is in conflict with other cues, the resulting predominance of the pictorial cues in some cases depends largely upon what the observer is trying to do.

Fineman (1971) studied the effect of the relative-size cue on depth due to disparity. The inner sets of letters in his two stereograms (Figure 9–17) differed in size from the letters comprising the backgrounds. In one stereogram the inner letters were larger than the background letters. This size difference alone suggests a depth difference. The smaller inner letters correspond to stimuli more distant than their backgrounds, while the relatively larger inner letters correspond to closer stimuli. The outer letters in both stereograms are alternating V's and O's. The periodic or alternating pattern of background letters provides an ambiguous disparity cue. If the observer fixates the non-periodic central letters in the two half-fields, he may respond to either a crossed disparity or an uncrossed disparity of the background letters. This ambiguity is present by reason of the fact that, with the inner letters fixated, corresponding places in the two eyes are necessarily stimulated by dissimilar shapes—a V in one eye, an O at the corresponding place in the other eye. Over most of the field

Figure 9–17. The large inner letters in stereogram A tend to be perceived as nearer than the smaller background letters, and the small inner letters of stereogram B are experienced as more distant than their background letters. (After Fineman, 1971)

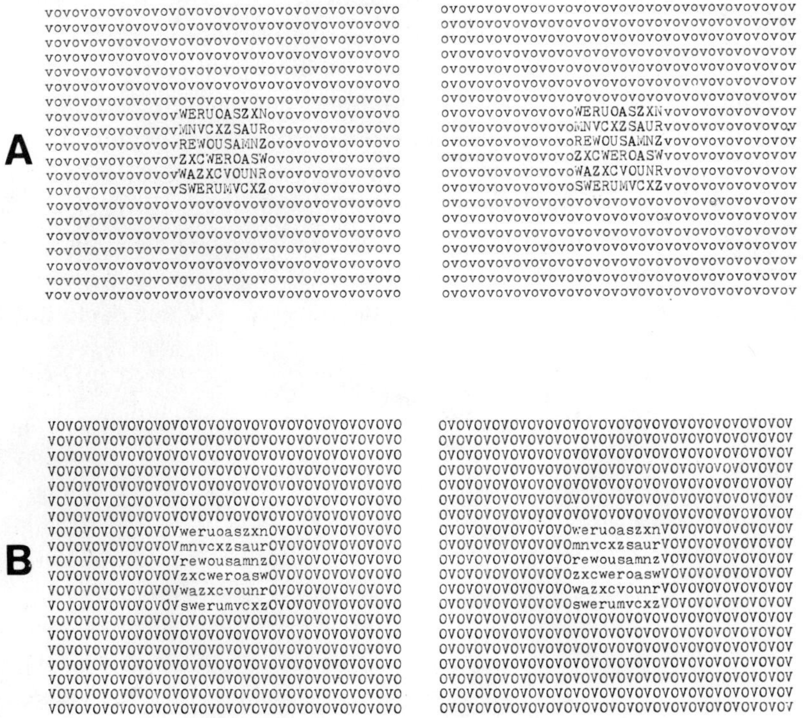

then, a letter in one eye is free to interact with either the similar displaced left or right letter in the other half-field.

Fineman found that when the central letters were larger than their backgrounds, observers tended to react more readily to the uncrossed disparity of the background letters, thereby favoring a stereoscopic response in which the central letters were perceived as nearer than their background. On the other hand, when the central letters were smaller than the background letters the opposite disparity was seen to determine the direction of depth. This finding is consistent with the idea that the relative size cue can serve to facilitate the perception of depth based upon disparity if relative size is consistent with the cross of the disparity. Thus, one distance cue can bias the response to another cue, at least with regard to the perceived order of contours in depth. These cues may be processed sequentially.

As we have seen, then, some cues are at least partially redundant and also independent of each other; and such cues produce additive affects on the probability of judging distance correctly. Moreover, the observer can exercise choice in the use of these cues in conflict situations. Although such cues appear to exist, they have not been clearly identified. Again, other cues are complementary, at least in the performance of certain tasks; and these cues serve to reduce ambiguity or uncertainty about the order of contours in depth. Still other cues appear to interact dynamically with each other in producing the impression of a depth magnitude. Finally, we have little or no knowledge of how cues combine in a constancy task. Those cues that have additive effects on the probability of judging the magnitude of a depth interval may not have the same effect on perceived size. This is an area that is ripe for experimental study, since the problem can be clearly stated and the experiments designed with relatively little effort.

The independent, interactive, and complementary cues to depth are utilized by the observer in making size judgments. Precisely how this is done is not known; it is conceivable, however, that some cues operate automatically, perhaps from birth, in enabling the organism to distinguish between objects of different size. One such cue might be the straightforward difference in retinal size, which serves as the so-called relative size cue. The operation of this cue, however, could hardly produce a tendency toward size constancy. As we shall see in Chapter 11, infants display a remarkable degree of size constancy, and hence, still other cues must be brought into play early in the development of a child. It may well be that a theme—a mode of responding in terms of distal size—is laid down genetically. This tendency toward constancy may exhibit considerable variability, and this in turn is reduced over time with experience in co-ordinating the diversified information about the spatial arrangement of objects offered as the various cues. In Chapter 11 it appears that this co-ordination of cues is subject to modification, even in the adult.

ILLUSIONS OF SIZE DIFFERENCES

Although the two cylinders shown in Figure 9-9 appear to be of different sizes, they are actually of the same size. This illusion is produced by the lines suggesting that the upper cylinder is farther away than the lower cylinder. In other words, the perspective cue to distance is the probable basis for the occurrence of this illusion.

The term "illusion" has a rather unfortunate connotation, suggesting as it does that in some cases the observer is unable to discriminate the actual physical properties of objects. When he is unable to do so correctly and instead gives a report that is not compatible with the physical arrangements of objects in space, we say that he is experiencing an illusion. This distinction strikes me as being somewhat arbitrary—as is illustrated by means of stereoscopic depth perception. Some writers have maintained that when one looks at a stereogram in a stereoscope the depth that he reports seeing is an illusion, since, as they imply, the actual stereogram is a flat picture with lines on it. Since the depth is not present in the physical stimulus, it must be illusory.

It should be clear by now that it serves no useful purpose to describe as illusory the depth perceived in stereograms. The stereogram provides the two eyes with the same proximal stimuli they would receive if they were looking at an actual scene. We can speak of an illusion in this context if, and only if, we maintain also that the observer has some magical means for observing physical things directly. Since the observer knows only what his sense organs tell him, there is no basis whatsoever for describing depth in a stereogram as illusory.

Similar considerations apply to the picture of the cylinders in a corridor. Here there is, however, one important difference. It is true that if two cylinders of equal angular size were presented at different depths in a corridor, the more distant cylinder could be perceived as the larger of the two cylinders. But other cues are present in the picture that would not be present in an actual corridor. The texture of the paper itself indicates that the picture is drawn on a flat sheet. Also, one need not change the accommodation of his eyes to look from the nearer cylinder to the far-

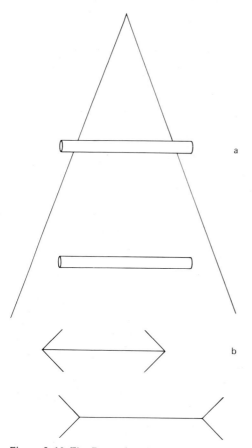

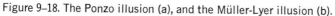

Figure 9–18. The Ponzo illusion (a), and the Müller-Lyer illusion (b).

ther cylinder. These cues are in conflict with the depicted perspective cues. If we assume that these cues to the flatness of the page are some-how more "real" or more important than the depiction of perspective, then it is reasonable to say that the perceived size difference is illusory. On the other hand, if the cues to the flatness of the paper are treated independ-ently from the perspective information portrayed on it, the perceived size differences are not illusory at all.

More generally, there is a class of illusions whose effects are depend-ent upon the presence of cues to depth. The Ponzo illusion (see Fig. 9–18a) is one such phenomenon. As pointed out by Woodworth (1938), Tausch (1954), and Gregory (1963), this illusion may well be due to the fact that the converging lines provide an incipient perspective cue so that the upper horizontal line is perceived as being more distant than the lower horizontal line. Inasmuch as it is both more distant than and of the same angular size as the lower line, the upper line is perceived as larger. Since cues are also present to the flatness of the page on which the picture is drawn, Gregory (1963) considered the apparent enlargement of the upper line to be due to an "inappropriate constancy." Gregory's inappropriate constancy may be regarded as the basis of all illusions involving elements of linear perspective in flat drawings. It is the inappropriateness of the constancy effect that prompts us to describe such size effects as illusory.

Another approach to this same type of illusion is to assert that the cues to flatness operate independently of the effect of the perspective lines. The observer may then simply disregard the flatness cue and respond instead to the portrayal of depth, much as he does to the depth portrayed in an ordinary photograph of a depthful scene. Hence, the appellation "illusion" in such cases may be misleading altogether.

Still another illusion explained by Gregory as being due to inappropriate constancy is the famous Müller-Lyer illusion, which is depicted in Figure 9–18b. The reason one of the horizontal lines in this figure looks larger than the other—even though they are the same size—is presumably due to the fact that the longer line is perceived as though it is the contour of an inside corner of a three-dimensional surface, and the shorter line is perceived as though it is the less distant outside corner, as shown in Figure 9–19. Hence, even the Müller-Lyer illusion may be thought of as an instance of inappropriate constancy.

There are numerous good reasons for disputing the claim that the Müller-Lyer illusion is in the same class as the illusion of the cylinders and the Ponzo Illusion. Day (1965) has reviewed some of them, and an experiment by Pitblado and Kaufman (1967) is consistent with Day's conclusion. In their experiment, Pitblado and Kaufman employed a stereogram similar to that shown in Figure 9–20. In this stereogram the disparity was so arranged that the fins of its upper half were perceived as receding away from the line, and the lines comprising the arrow heads in the lower half were perceived as emerging from the picture plane. This converts the upper half of the pattern into an "outside corner" and the lower half into an "inside corner," just opposite the spatial relations that the inappropriate constancy theory considers basic to the illusion. This stereoscopic manipulation had no effect on the magnitude of the illusion, so that it may be stated that the apparent distance relations among the parts of the

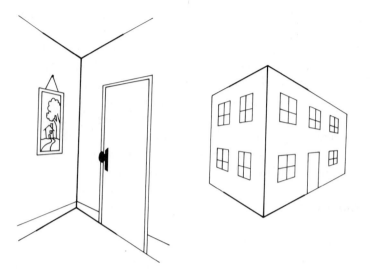

Figure 9–19. Example of the hypothetical apparent distance basis for the Müller-Lyer illusion.

Figure 9–20. A Müller-Lyer stereogram, which reverses the depth relations depicted in Figure 9–19. The illusion is unaffected.

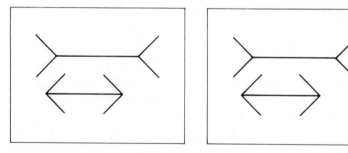

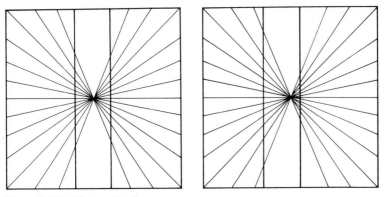

Figure 9–21. A Hering illusion stereogram.

illusion are not central to its cause. Pitblado and Kaufman concluded that the illusion is not a member of the class of distance-dependent illusions.

The Hering and the Ehrenfels illusions depicted in Figures 9–21 and 9–22 respectively, are likewise unaffected by stereoscopic manipulation. The parallel lines in the Hering illusion still look bowed when the figure is viewed stereoscopically, even though the parallel lines are perceived as floating above the plane of the crossed lines. Similarly, the Ehrenfels figure still contains a trapezoid, even though stereoscopic viewing causes the upper horizontal line to be perceived as in the same depth plane as the lower horizontal line. Hence, the perspective cues produced by the converging background lines cannot be the sole basis for this illusion. In Chapter 13 we shall discuss other explanations for some of these illusions;

Figure 9–22. An Ehrenfels illusion stereogram.

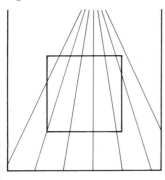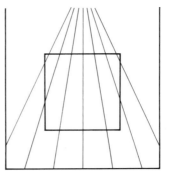

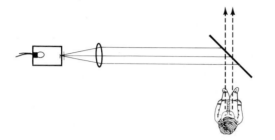

A. Arrangement for viewing horizon moon

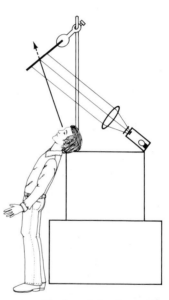

B. Arrangement for viewing Zenith moon

Figure 9–23. Apparatus for studying the moon illusion. A luminous disc of adjustable size is placed at the focus of a lens. The reflected image of the disc is seen through a transparent glass on the sky. The arrangement at A simulates the horizon moon, that at B the zenith moon. The observer can adjust the size of one moon so that it appears to match the size of the other moon.

suffice it here to state that some illusions are distance dependent, others must be explained in other terms.

One of the most ancient illusions known to man is the apparent enlargement of the moon when it is near the horizon. The moon subtends a constant angle at the eye of an observer whether it is seen over the horizon or in the zenith, and yet the horizon moon appears to be much larger than the zenith moon. Holway and Boring (1940) ascribed this illusion to the elevation of the eyes in the head when looking upward toward the zenith, and measured the illusion by having an observer adjust the diameter of a nearby disc until its size appeared to match the size of the moon. When the eyes were held level in the head while viewing the moon, the disc was made larger than it was when the eyes were elevated to view the moon. Although others have found that perceived size does become smaller when one's eyes are elevated, this effect is usually on the order of about 3 per cent (Hermans, 1954; Kaufman and Rock, 1962; Baird, Gulick, and Smith, 1962). The surprising thing about the Holway-Boring result is that with the eyes elevated their observers made the diameter of the comparison disc nearly one-half the match attained when the eyes were level in viewing the moon.

Kaufman and Rock (1962) argued that the nearby disc is incommensurate with the distant moon, as this would be like comparing a reduction object with a non-reduction object, as in the experiment by Wallach and McKenna (1960). It is not known whether eye elevation would produce so great a change in size judgments in the framework of the Wallach and McKenna experiment; but if it should, this phenomenon is not really pertinent to the moon illusion, the moon illusion is experienced when one compares his memory for the size of the moon when it is in one position in the sky with its size when it is in another position. One does not compare the moon to some intermediate object when experiencing the moon illusion.

Kaufman and Rock also argued that when they observed the natural moon, its size did not appear to change very much when their eyes were elevated. They performed an experiment in which artificial moons seen on the sky were compared with each other (see Fig. 9–23). In their first experiments Kaufman and Rock had observers view one moon with eyes level and then adjust its size until it appeared to match the size of the other moon, which was viewed with the eyes elevated. They found a negligible effect of eye elevation. When one moon was placed over the horizon and the other in the zenith, however, the horizon moon was perceived as much larger than the zenith moon, whether or not the eyes were elevated in viewing the zenith moon.

One ancient theory of the moon illusion attributes the phenomenon to the fact that the perceived distance of the horizon sky is greater than the perceived distance to the zenith sky. Since the moon on the horizon

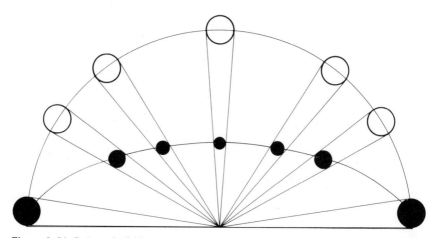

Figure 9–24. Robert Smith's theory of the moon illusion (1767). If the moon is localized on an apparently flattened sky, it will appear to be smaller in the zenith than at the horizon, even though the physical distance of the moon from the observer is approximately constant, regardless of the moon's elevation.

has the same angular size as the moon in the zenith, it should appear larger when it is perceived as being at a greater distance. This *apparent distance theory* of the moon illusion was based upon an observation by Ptolemy (Boring, 1943), who observed that an object seen across a filled space is perceived as more distant than the same object viewed across an equal, though unfilled, space. It is also consistent with the observation that the sky appears as a flattened dome, with the horizon sky apparently farther away than the zenith sky (Minnaert, 1954; Miller, 1943). The apparent distance theory of the moon illusion was accepted in the eleventh century by Alhazen (Reimann, 1902) and also by Smith (1767), whose version of the theory is depicted in Figure 9–24. Miller (1943) observed that the degree to which the sky is perceived as flattened is a function of the amount of cloud coverage and also by the distance to the visible horizon. The sky appears flatter as the cloud coverage increases, less flat as the horizon draws nearer.

In a series of experiments, Kaufman and Rock (1962) and Rock and Kaufman (1962) measured the size of the moon illusion with different degrees of cloud coverage and with the visible horizon at two different distances. They found that the illusion was stronger when the sky was completely overcast—the magnitude of the illusion decreased with decreasing cloud coverage—and also that the illusion was smaller when the horizon moon was seen over the nearer horizon than when the moon was seen over the more distant horizon.

Although these results are consistent with the apparent distance theory, it has been argued that the theory must be rejected on the ground that observers do not report the horizon moon to be more distant than the apparently smaller zenith moon. Kaufman and Rock, on the other hand, suspected that the judged distance to the horizon moon is influenced by the fact that the horizon moon appears larger than the zenith moon. Accordingly, they asked their observers to judge the distance to the horizon sky and compare it to the distance to the zenith sky when the moon was not visible. In all cases, observers reported the horizon sky to be more distant than the zenith sky. Moreover, they projected very large moons to the zenith sky and relatively small moons to the horizon sky. When observers were asked now to judge relative distance to the two moons, they reported that the horizon sky was more distant than the zenith sky. Similarly, with a very large moon at the horizon and a small moon in the zenith, these distance judgments were reversed. In this case, when an observer was asked how he was able to tell that the horizon moon was closer than the zenith moon, he replied that it appeared to be closer because it was larger.

Kaufman and Rock concluded from this that distance judgments when the moons were present do not correlate with the effects of cues to distance because cognitive factors predominated. When an observer is asked to make an explicit judgment, he is likely to respond in terms of the more obvious features of the scene. His judgment, then, would be based upon an apparent size difference—a datum that could have been induced by cues of which the observer was unaware. This is consistent with the idea already expressed in this volume—i.e., the effects of cues are not observable; they must be discovered. Thus it is that naïve observers give judgments of distance based on apparent size and that this in turn is determined by the action of cues to distance.

Restle (1970) has recently argued that the moon illusion is not due to the action of cues to distance. His position is based upon the observation that an object appears to grow smaller as its framework is made relatively larger, and that if the space between the moon and the horizon is made larger, the increase in the expanse of empty space between the horizon and the moon causes the moon to appear to grow smaller. This theory would reduce the moon illusion to an instance of the relational determination of perceived size, as exemplified by the study of Rock and Ebenholtz (1959), discussed on page 347.

A number of objections may be raised to Restle's thesis, the most important flowing from the observation that a screen placed in front of the observer, which simply occludes the terrain from his field of view, causes the size of the horizon moon to become smaller. This screen fills his field of view just as did the terrain, although the cues to distance are such that the observer perceives the screen as a vertical barrier and not as a terrain receding away from him. In any case the amount of empty space between the upper edge of the screen and the moon is the same as that between the horizon and the moon. The relative size hypothesis of Restle would therefore predict that the size of the moon should be unaffected by the presence of the screen. The apparent-distance theory predicts that the moon seen over the screen would be reduced in size. The fact that the screen produces a diminution of the size of the moon indicates that the relative-size hypothesis is not an adequate basis for explaining the moon illusion. This, of course, does not preclude the possibility that factors such as those discussed by Restle are involved in determining the perceived size of the moon. Such factors, however, must operate in addition to the cues to distance clearly involved in producing the phenomenon.

CONCLUSION

Despite all the work undertaken to elucidate the basis for our ability to judge distal size, a completely satisfactory theory is unavailable. Computations of the sort suggested by Helmholtz may be involved, especially over short distances; but this simply states the problem for psychology. We have no knowledge at all as to how the brain makes the computations that must be involved. We also have no idea about how attitude or instructional set would influence these computations. Even if Gibson is right in saying that we scale judgments of size differently at different distances, this too is a complicated process, and requires elucidation.

In this field we are really at the threshold of understanding and must cross that threshold before we have a more nearly adequate theory of the phenomena involved. To be sure, there is some form of "intelligence" underlying size perception. Millions of years of evolution must have produced a brain capable of sophisticated operations, such as those involved in judging size. Some of these operations must involve the co-ordination of diverse kinds of information about the distances of objects. Perhaps further insights will come from considering how this information is processed.

the perception of movement

As the eye moves to scan a scene, the image of the scene glides across the retina. Despite this gliding of the retinal image, the scene is perceived as stationary, and the observer experiences his own eye as moving. This stability of the scene's position can be disturbed when some external device is used to push or pull the eyeball. Pushing the eyeball also causes the image of the scene to change its position on the retina. Yet instead of experiencing his eye as moving, the observer perceives the scene as changing its position.

This early phenomenon has important implications for the theory of perceived movement. As we shall see below, it has been proposed that movement is perceived when an image moves from one point to another on the retina. Though there is little doubt that movement may be perceived when an image changes its retinal position, the constancy of spatial position during voluntary eye movement demonstrates that this need not be the case. As in size perception, a mere account of the proximal stimulus is not an adequate basis for understanding the perception of movement.

It is possible to perceive an object as moving even when its image does not shift on the retina during an eye movement. This phenomenon argues also against an interpretation of perceived movement as being due only to retinal translation. An even more curious fact is that it may be possible to have an experience of movement when the moving object does not change its apparent position. All these phenomena demand a theory of movement perception far more complicated than any theory yet proposed.

Each of the existing theories is more or less capable of handling rather limited domains of facts. While discussing such theories we must be cognizant of the fact that we can discern only the dim outlines of a more comprehensive approach to movement perception.

SOME THEORETICAL BACKGROUND

Nineteenth-century psychologists considered that perceptions were compounded from elements known as sensations. One of their preoccupations was the identification of these elements. Thus, the sensation of redness was thought of as being an element comprising the perception of an apple.

Although this general approach to psychology has fallen into disrepute, recent years have seen its revival in the study of motion perception. Boring (1942) credits several nineteenth-century figures with the idea that movement is a primary sensation in its own right. This idea, which arose in the 1870's, was buttressed by Exner (1875), who presented two spatially separated electric sparks to an observer. The observer had to judge the order in which the sparks were flashed. Exner found that if the sparks were separated in time by less than about 45 msec, the observer could not judge their order correctly. If the sparks were placed adjacent to each other, however, the observer could see one spark move from its position to that occupied by the second spark. The direction of this apparent motion was correctly identified even when the time interval between the sparks was as small as 14 msec—which is smaller than the perceptible time interval of the first experiment. Exner concluded that inasmuch as movement perception is more precise than time-order perception, movement must therefore be a special process—a sensation in its own right—and not a perception compounded from sensations of time and space.

The essentially primitive nature of movement perception was also maintained by Wertheimer (1912). In a classic experiment he presented two separated lines in rapid succession. When the time interval between the lines was just right, the observer reported seeing movement between them—a disembodied movement in which the line did not move from one place to another. Though the observer still saw stationary lines flashing on and off, movement was experienced between them. This is now known as the *phi* phenomenon. Wertheimer, like Exner, concluded that movement has an existence in its own right. The observer need not see the position of an object change over time, provided that the stimulation is sufficient to produce a brain state normally correlated with the experience of movement.

Wertheimer's notions about the brain states underlying perception are no longer accepted. Motion is not simply the correlate of a short circuit between two points of excitation on the visual cortex. All remaining doubt about this was removed by the experiment of Rock and Ebenholtz (1962), discussed on page 400. Still with us, however, is the basic idea that there are physiological functions directly correlated with movement *per se.*

Lettvin, Maturana, McCulloch, and Pitts (1959) found neurons specialized for the detection of movement when a small round object was moved through the frog's visual field. Cells in the tectum responded to the movement but did not respond to the same object when it was stationary. Similarly, cells in the cortex of the cat will respond only when an edge or bar is moved in particular directions across their receptive fields in the retina. This is true also in the rabbit (Barlow and Hill, 1963) and in the monkey (Hubel and Wiesel, 1968). Bishop, Coombs, and Henry (1971) obtained results indicating that the vast majority of motion-sensitive neurons respond to movement in one direction only.

MacKay (1961) proposed that the human visual system contains cells that are sensitive to motion as such. Gregory (1966) took this to mean that one does not have to compute movement at some high level in the nervous system from changes in the position of an object over time. Instead, velocity is directly encoded at an early stage when an image passes across the array of retinal receptors.

A model of a system which would directly encode velocity has been outlined by Schouten (1967). Figure 10–1 shows an array of receptors that are stimulated in sequence by the image of a bar. A movement detector may be excited if the image of the bar passes over two of the receptors within a given period of time. The box labeled t in Figure 10–1 receives signals from receptors R_1 and R_2. When the image of the bar excites receptor R_1 a signal is transmitted to the box t. The activity in t initiated by the signal from R_1 tends to persist. The duration of this persisting activity is determined by the *time constant* of the unit t.

The box or unit t is a coincidence detector. That is, the unit cannot fire or transmit a signal to the movement detector unless it is stimulated at the same time by R_1 and R_2. Since t has a time constant, R_1 need not be active at the time that R_2 is active. It is sufficient that the effect of R_1 on

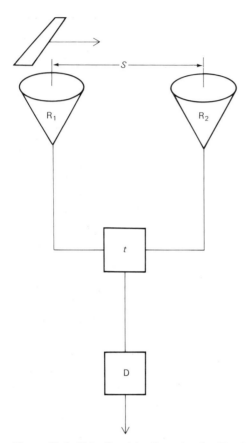

Figure 10–1. Velocity detecting circuit. The bar produces activity in receptor R_1 which is transmitted to and stored at the coincidence detector **t**. If the stored signal from R_1 is present when a signal arrives from receptor R_2, a signal signifying movement is transmitted to the movement detector D.

t persist long enough so that the signal from R_2 will occur while that effect is still going on. Thus, just so long as R_1 and R_2 are both activated within the period of the time constant of t, then a signal will be transmitted to the movement detector.

If it is assumed that the velocity of the image of the bar is constant, then two parameters will determine the firing of a movement detector. These are the separation s between the receptors connected to unit t, and also the time constant of t. If the image should move too slowly, the effect of R_1 will wear off before R_2 is activated by the image. Also, if the space s should be larger, the time between events R_1 and R_2 may also be too long to activate t. Thus, the probability that a particular movement detector will fire will be high only if the velocity of the image is within a range determined by the space s and the time constant of t.

There are two serious difficulties with Schouten's model. First, the movement detecting circuit is not polarized, for it will respond if R_1 is stimulated first and also if R_2 is stimulated first. We now know that physiological movement detectors are sensitive to the direction of movement (Barlow and Hill, 1963). Without this polarization an observer containing Schouten's movement detectors could not discriminate between movement from left to right from movement from right to left. Further, a flash of light stimulating both R_1 and R_2 simultaneously would cause the movement detector to respond. Therefore, several authors have proposed models of directionally sensitive movement detectors (e.g., Barlow, Hill, and Levick, 1964).

Miriam Kaplan (1972) has suggested one model in which R_1 supplies signals to t and R_2 transmits signals directly to the movement detector itself, thus polarizing the circuit. This circuit is shown in Figure 10–2. It will respond to movement if, and only if, the movement is from R_1 to R_2. Presumably there are other circuits in the visual system hooked up in the reverse way—with R_2 supplying signals to t and R_1 to the movement detector. Moreover, if t requires some time before it starts to transmit signals to the movement detector, and also has a delay time, then the simultaneous stimulation of R_1 and R_2 will not cause the movement detector to respond.

When an image is moving at a particular speed across the retina, only a particular set of movement detectors will respond. Presumably the retinal velocity of the target is correlated with the activity of a particular population of the movement detectors. Thus, movement detectors may be tuned to respond to different velocities. Though the Schouten and Kaplan models are suited for the encoding of retinal velocity, they cannot be the sole bases for movement perception. As we pointed out in the introduction to this chapter, images glide across the retina when the eye is voluntarily moved. This would certainly cause movement detectors to become active. Yet the movement perceived is of the eye and not of the objects whose images are moving. Something more must be added to movement detection models to account for this fact.

Still another sign of the incompleteness of the velocity detection proc-

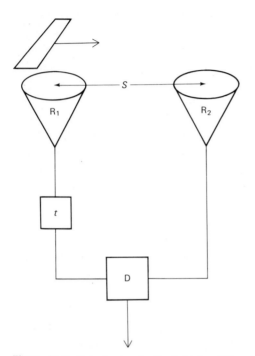

Figure 10–2. Polarized velocity detector. When the bar stimulates receptor R_1 the unit labeled **t** delays the output of R_1 before transmitting it to the movement detector D. If the bar arrives at R_2 concurrently with the arrival of the output of **t** at D, the movement detector will respond to the coincidence of the signal from R_1 and R_2. This movement detector cannot respond when the bar moves from R_2 toward R_1.

ess is that when the eye follows a moving object, the object will appear to move. As we shall see later, the object's image need not move across the retina at all; so long as the eye follows it, the object will move. For this reason Gregory (1966) posited two different systems of movement perception.

The first system we have been discussing: the direct encoding of retinal velocity, which Gregory called the *image-retina system* for movement perception. The second system is called into play when the eye tracks a moving target. The direct detection of retinal velocity need not be involved when this happens. Instead, the nervous system makes use of the fact that the image is stationary on the retina *and* the eye is being signaled to change its position in its socket. The perceived movement of the target must be based upon the fact that there is an attempt on the observer's part to change the position of his eye relative to the position of his head. This, then, is Gregory's second system: the *eye-head system* for the detection of movement.

There is no detailed information on how this eye-head system may work, except that the system does not employ proprioception from the extraocular muscles themselves. As we saw in Chapter 7, there is little evidence for the existence of feedback from the eye muscles which would enable the observer to monitor his eye position. One of the strongest pieces of evidence for this conclusion is the example we provided at the beginning of this chapter. It will be recalled that objects remain stationary when an eye is moved voluntarily, whereas, if the eye is pushed or pulled, the visual scene appears to move. If proprioception were available, the stretching of the eye muscles when the eye is pulled should signal to the observer that his eye is changing its position. The fact that such passive eye movements do not produce the same stability of the scene as that occurring during active or voluntary eye movements suggests that it is the signal to the eye muscles that creates stability. In the absence of this signal the world appears to move.

Careful observation of the behavior of an after-image strengthens this conclusion. If the reader will first look at a bright lamp with fixed gaze for one or two minutes he will continue to see the lamp after looking away from it. If this after-image should fade, it can be restored by blinking the eyes. In any event, a slow turning of the eyes is accompanied by an apparent movement of the after-image, and this will occur even when the eyes are closed. On the other hand, pushing the eye gently with one's finger through the closed lids does not produce this same movement of the after-image. Hence, though the mere shifting of the position of the eye does not produce movement, the active signaling of the eye to move will produce such movement. Richards and Steinbach (1972) have presented some evidence that apparent movement of the after-image may occur before the eyes are actually moved voluntarily. This is consistent with the idea that the programming of the eye movement by the brain is the basis of perceived movement of a stationary image during eye movements.

Additional evidence for this conclusion stems from the fact that when an observer's eye muscles are paralyzed the world appears to be unstable. It has been found (Helmholtz, 1925) that when a person with paralyzed eye muscles attempts to move his eyes, objects in the field of vision appear to jump in the direction of the desired eye movement. This can be understood if it is assumed that there is no effective proprioception from the eye muscles. Insofar as the brain is concerned, the eyes have been instructed to move toward one side. The images on the retina remain stationary because of the paralysis. Hence, the brain must conclude that the objects in the field of view have moved with eyes! So it is that while active contraction of the muscles does not elicit a perception of movement, the act of instructing the muscles does elicit that perception. This is consistent with a theory of von Holst (1954) according to which the signals to the eye muscles are compared with signals arising from the behavior of images on the retina.

We must agree with Gregory, then, that two systems are involved in the perception of movement. One is the eye-head system in which instructions to the extraocular muscles are matched against the behavior of the retinal image. If the image remains stationary on the retina while the eyes are being instructed to move, the image will appear to move. Further, when the image moves across the retina while the eyes are being instructed to move, the image may appear to be stationary.

The second system, the image-retina system, is capable of encoding retinal velocity directly. Even though this system is not adequate to account for perceived movement in all of its forms, if it is postulated that the image-retina system's output is integrated with the output of the eye-head system, a great many facts may be covered. But even here there are phenomena that cannot be fully explained, as we shall encounter later in this chapter when we survey some facts of movement perception.

REAL MOVEMENT

When an object or point is translated across a space, it may be perceived as moving. When perceived movement is associated with such a physically moving distal stimulus it is customary to refer to *real movement*. We should give no more significance to this term than that the distal stimulus to movement perception is a physically moving object.

In perception research it is customary to utilize small dots or points that move with a uniform velocity either horizontally or vertically across the visual field. The field in which the point is displaced may be a dark empty space or it may contain a textured background or framework that remains stationary while the point is in motion.

There are two ways in which a moving point may be viewed. In the one, the observer may fixate some other point in the field while the dot shifts from one position to another. In this case the proximal stimulus contains a moving image of the dot—an image gliding across the retinal surface—and, perhaps, a fixed reference point. Alternatively, the observer may fixate the moving dot so that it remains stationary on his retina. In this case the eye moves with the dot. As we shall see later, these two modes of viewing lead to somewhat different results when sensitivity to motion is studied.

When an observer views the hour hand on his watch he is not able to see it move, since its velocity is below the threshold for perceived movement. Yet if the observer were to look at it again somewhat later, he might discern that it had changed its position. This, however, is not the same thing as perceiving movement: the observer is merely making an inference that movement had occurred from the fact that the hand had changed its position over time.

For experimental purposes we may replace the hour hand with a slowly moving luminous dot. If the dot were displaced at the angular rate of 2 sec/min, it would require 1800 minutes for it to traverse a path subtending 1 degree of visual angle. It is obvious that at such very slow velocities it would be impossible to perceive the dot as moving.

If the dot were to move at a higher physical velocity it might be possible to perceive the dot as moving. Aubert (1886) found that a luminous dot in a dark space may be just perceived as moving if its velocity is between 10 and 20 minutes of arc/sec. Thus, if the dot were 20 inches from the observer's eye, it could be just perceived as moving if it were displaced at a uniform rate through a distance of about 0.1 inch in one second.

With a visible and stationary textured background it is possible to just detect movement when the dot is displaced at a slower rate. Thus, Aubert found that the threshold of movement is as small as 1 or 2 minutes of arc/sec when the dot is moved relative to a stationary background of finely ruled lines. This corresponds to a displacement across a distance as small as 0.01 inch in 1 second at a viewing distance of 20 inches. This is truly an exquisite degree of sensitivity!

This difference in sensitivity to movement may be interpreted in terms of two different levels of movement perception. Thus, when a stable structure is present, the observer has information about the spatial position of the moving target relative to the visible framework as well as the retinal velocity of the target. This information is available even if the position of the eye is unsteady. When the framework is absent the observer may base his judgments upon the retinal velocity of the target only. In this case instability of the eye may become a significant factor. Hence, the presence of the framework, and the positional information it provides, may facilitate the detection of movement.

The results obtained by Leibowitz (1955) are consistent with this interpretation. He presented a moving target for a very short period of time. A typical exposure duration was 0.25 sec. In so short an exposure a slowly moving target cannot change its position by very much relative to a stationary line in the visual field. Thus, if the target were displaced with an angular velocity of 20 min/sec, it could move through an angular distance of only 5 min. of arc in 0.25 sec. Since this excursion might not be discriminated easily in the short exposure time, one might predict that the presence of the stationary line would have little effect on the perception of the displacement of the dot. This is what Leibowitz found. A background line had no effect on movement sensitivity when moving targets were exposed for short periods of time. The threshold for movement was the same as that obtained when the moving targets were exposed for the same short durations in an empty field.

Leibowitz strengthened the argument that both velocity and position information enter into judgments of movement by presenting his targets for long durations also. With a 16-sec exposure he found that the presence of background lines enhances movement sensitivity. This confirmed Aubert's result.

Shaffer and Wallach (1966), using instead of a stationary line a framework surrounding the moving target, did not confirm Leibowitz' result. They found that the framework enhanced motion sensitivity when the stimuli were exposed for very short periods of time. The surrounding framework, however, may also have enhanced sensitivity to position during the brief exposure. That is, the observer may have been able to discern an asymmetric location of the dot within the framework more easily than difference in its position over time relative to the position of a single straight line.

Thus far we have focused on the problem of sensitivity to real movement, but have failed to distinguish between the condition in which the observer fixates a moving point and the one in which he fixates the stationary background while the target is moving. Both Aubert (1886) and Fleischl (Teuber, 1960) observed that a fixated moving target appears to move more slowly than it appears to move when the stationary background is fixated instead. At one time this phenomenon was referred to as the Aubert-Fleischl Paradox, since it was believed that if the eye pursues a target there should be a greater sense of motion than if the eye remains stationary.

This difference in sensitivity observed by Aubert and Fleischl suggests that the sensitivity of the eye-head system to movement is not quite so good as the sensitivity of the image-retina system. An alternative possibility is that information about the position of a target relative to a visible background is less effective while an eye is following a moving target than it is when the eye is stationary and the image of the target slides across the retina.

This alternative gains some plausibility from two facts. First, the eye does not usually track a moving object smoothly. Suppose that a target is moving past an observer. If the observer intends to track the target with his eye he might turn his head to get the image of the target near the center of his retina. Then he could turn his eye in its socket to achieve a more precise fixation on the target. The turning velocity of the eyeball would have to match the angular velocity of the target. This is rarely achieved with complete precision. Sometimes the line of sight lags behind the target, in which situation the eye may make a quick flick or saccade to correct its position, and then the slow tracking might be resumed. Now, during these flicks or saccades visual acuity may be impaired. This phenomenon is known as *saccadic suppression*. The effect of saccadic suppression can be measured by briefly flashing a light at various times before, during, and after a saccade. The intensity needed for the light to be seen is a measure of the magnitude of the suppression. Volkman (1962) found that a light had to be about three times more intense if it is to be seen during a saccade than it was when the eye was stationary. Latour (1962) has shown that the suppression associated with a saccade actually begins about 50 msec before the initiation of the eye movement.*

Since saccadic suppression occurs when a stimulus is presented so rapidly that it has too little time to move a significant distance across the retina, saccadic suppression cannot be attributed solely to the fact that the retinal image is smeared out by the movement of the eye. Still, this smearing effect must contribute to a lessening of acuity for the stationary

---

* Krauskopf, Graf, and Gaarder (1966) could find no significant suppression during small involuntary saccades. Matin *et al.* (1972) succeeded in producing suppression during small voluntary saccades by introducing visual stimuli immediately after a saccade. These introduced background stimuli had the effect of masking a light which was exposed during the saccade. Thus, some saccadic suppression may be produced by parameters in the visual stimulus.

background. Both these effects, then—the inhibition of vision during a saccade and the retinal smearing of the scene during the slow phase of the eye movement—must contribute to a failure in acuity while tracking a moving target. This failure of acuity for the stable background could reduce sensitivity to the position of the target, and this in turn result in an apparently slower target displacement.

We are left, then, with an unresolved problem. The reason a visually tracked target appears to be moving more slowly than a target that is not tracked could be the fact of differences in the sensitivity of the two systems of movement detection. Alternatively it could be attributed to the loss of visibility of the stable background by virtue of saccadic suppression and retinal smearing. The first order of business may well be to see whether the Aubert-Fleischl phenomenon occurs when a moving target is presented in an empty visual field. This would at least determine whether the effect is background dependent.

Thus far we have considered targets that move at slow and moderate velocities. If a target moves at a very high velocity, however, its true shape cannot be differentiated, and it appears as a streak. The picture on a television screen, for example, is written in sequence by a moving dot of light. The spot itself cannot be resolved. For if it could it would be seen fluctuating in brightness and moving from left to right along lines ranging from the top of the screen to the bottom. Instead of seeing the spot the eye constructs a static picture.

This observation proves that there is an upper threshold for movement as well as the lower threshold we discussed earlier. The fusion or streaking of a moving target has been found to occur when a luminous target is displaced across the retinal surface with an angular velocity between 12 and 32 deg/sec (Graham, 1965b). If a target moves repeatedly through an aperture with retinal velocity between 7 and 15 deg/sec, it may still be detected but appear to be blurred, and sometimes more than one target may be visible (Graham, 1965b). The appearance of multiple targets occurs when the target is moving repeatedly through a rectangular aperture. The appearance of the target may persist after it actually leaves the aperture, and remain present when the target reappears in the aperture.

The particular angular velocity at which a target will blur or streak depends upon a number of different parameters. One such parameter is the luminance of the target. Another is the extent to which the eye remains stationary while viewing the target. For if the eye should move while the distal stimulus is being moved, then the velocity of the target's image across the retina will be affected.

In addition to the difference between fixated and non-fixated targets, there is also a variation in sensitivity to motion from one retinal region to another. Thus, though the threshold for movement in the central fovea is between 1 and 2 min/sec, when a stationary background is visible, the corresponding lower threshold 9 degrees of arc to one side of the point of fixation is approximately 18 min/sec (Aubert, 1886). More recent data obtained by McColgin (1960) indicate that sensitivity to movement of a bar decreases montonically as the target is placed farther and farther into the periphery of the retina.

Despite this differential sensitivity to movement depending upon retinal location, it is a well-known fact that movement in the periphery is more *salient* than movement in the center. It is easier to see a moving point in the periphery than it is to see a stationary line (see Walls, 1963). This may be connected with the fact that if an observer fixates a point straight ahead of him and tries to view a stationary line off to one side, the line may disappear. This phenomenon, known as Troxler's effect (Troxler, 1804), is particularly strong at low levels of illumination, but occurs at high levels as well (Aubert, 1865). In the latter case a fog creeps from the far periphery toward the center of the visual field, obscuring objects in the periphery as it progresses toward the center. Objects that have been made to disappear in this manner reappear instantly when they are moved. It is as though peripheral portions of the retina are better designed to detect moving objects than they are stationary objects. This is also true of foveal vision, though the distinction is less marked—possibly because the fovea is more sensitive to movement than is the periphery.

If the last sentence seems paradoxical, still, when properly interpreted it does make sense. To understand this we have only to consider what happens when an image is completely stationary in the fovea.

Ditchburn and Ginsborg (1952) and Riggs, Ratliff, Cornsweet, and Cornsweet (1953) attached a small plane mirror to a contact lens. Reflecting a beam of light off this mirror, as in Figure 10–3, enabled them to measure very fine movements of the eye. Their results were more complete than those of Barlow (1952), who, in a heroic experiment, measured the movements of the eye by reflecting a beam of light off a droplet of mercury in his eye while his head was clamped in a steel apparatus. Barlow could take measurements only during the period between the insertion of the droplet of mercury and his first eye blink. Nevertheless, the

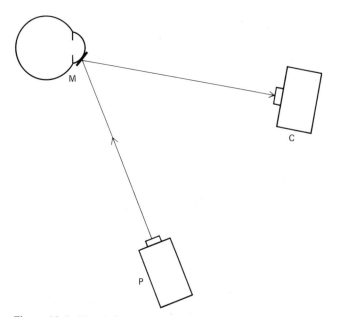

Figure 10–3. Measuring eye movements with an optical lever. Light from the projector at P is reflected by a small mirror M mounted on a tightly fitting contact lens. The reflected light beam leaves a trace on a moving strip of film in a camera at C. The excursion of the spot of light on the film may be large even when the angle of rotation of the eye is small.

results of all of these investigators are consistent. In short, it has been found that the eye engages in a tremor that varies from 10 Hz up to 120 Hz, with an average frequency apparently between 20 and 30 Hz. The amplitude of this tremor is very small—evidently no greater than about 20 seconds of arc.

In addition to the fine tremor or *physiological nystagmus* the eye also drifts slowly even during attempted fixation. When fixating a point the average slow drift is 4 to 6 minutes of arc. After drifting by at least this amount, a small quick movement or saccade occurs. The saccade appears to be corrective inasmuch as it causes the eye to shift so that the image of the fixation point is once again near the center of the fovea. The slow drifting of the eye occurs as often as about 5 times per second. It may occur less often too—e.g., 2 times per second. But even these slow drifts play a vital role in visual perception.

Riggs *et al.* (1953) utilized the contact lens technique (see Fig.

10–4) to discover what role, if any, is played by the various kinds of eye movements in perception. Their results indicate that the fine tremor (nystagmus) does not have any relation to visual acuity. This refutes a theory proposed by Marshall and Talbot (1942) that a fine high-frequency tremor is important in aiding visual acuity. They presumed that a rapid turning on and off of retinal units caused by shifting of the retina relative to images of fine lines, could enhance their perceptibility. Riggs *et al.* found, however, that the slow drifts function to refresh the information received by the nervous system from the retina.

In the modified contact lens method used by Riggs and his associates, an image was reflected off the mirror on the contact lens and onto a screen. The image on the screen was seen by the observer through a sys-

Figure 10–4. The stabilized retinal image. Light from the projector at P is reflected by a mirror attached to the contact lens to form an image of a slide in the projector on the screen. The image on the screen is viewed through a system of mirrors arranged so that the angular movement of the image of the slide on the retina is exactly equal and opposite to the angular rotation of the eyeball. (After Riggs **et al.**, 1953)

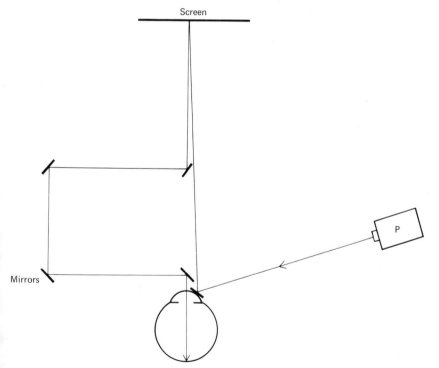

tem of four mirrors that enabled the experimenter to increase or decrease the path length to the image.

When the eye in Figure 10–4 rotates through an angle of 1 degree the image on the screen will move through twice that angle. This 2-degree rotation of the image is due to the fact that the angle of rotation of the eyeball is added both to the angle of incidence of the light beam on the mirror and also to the angle of reflection. By adjusting the spaces between the mirrors it is possible to increase the path traveled by the light reflected from the screen to the pupil of the eye so that it is exactly twice the length of the path between the screen and the mirror on the eye. This compensates precisely for the doubled angular displacement of the image on the screen, thereby causing the image to be fixed on a given retinal place even though the eye is free to move.

The *stabilized retinal image* cannot shift on the retina when the eye's position drifts, and in this circumstance the image disappears soon after it is presented to the observer. It must be concluded, that if an image continues to excite the same receptors, these receptors will cease to transmit information about the presence of the image. If the receptors are excited intermittently, however, as when the image glides across them during eye movements, they become refreshed and information is transmitted. As a matter of fact, a spatially stabilized retinal image will remain visible if it is flashed at a rate of one or two times per second.

Let us now reconsider our statement that movement is more salient in the periphery because the fovea is more sensitive to movement. When an image is stabilized it will disappear in the fovea as it does in the periphery when it is not stabilized. When the image is not stabilized, however, it disappears in the periphery even when the eye wanders slightly during voluntary fixation. This disappearance in the periphery—as in Troxler's effect—may be attributed to the fact that small eye movements are less effective in refreshing information transmitted by the peripheral receptors. Since foveal regions are more sensitive to movement, however, stabilization of the image is required to produce the same disappearance. It follows that, with fixed gaze, objects are not very visible in the periphery, though if the objects or eye should move, these objects become visible. Yet with the same fixed gaze, the foveal images are shifting slightly because of the small slow drifts, and these images never disappear. Therefore, eye movements do not make them more visible than they normally are; and moreover, movement is not more salient in the fovea than it is in the periphery.

RELATIVE AND INDUCED MOTION

Karl Duncker (1929) placed a luminous dot in a dark space. When the dot was moved at a very slow rate, observers could not be sure that it was moving. But when a stationary luminous dot was placed near the first moving dot, all doubt was removed. This is an instance of Aubert's discovery that sensitivity to movement may be enhanced when a moving target is near a stationary object. Now, one of the curious things about this situation is that it is impossible to determine which of the two dots is moving. Even though one of the dots is moving while the other is physically stationary, the observer cannot decide which is moving. We may conclude from this that while relative displacement is capable of producing the perception of movement, it is not sufficient to determine the identity of the moving object.

When Duncker replaced the stationary luminous dot of his experiment with a luminous rectangular framework, as in Figure 10–5, he found that this ambiguity was removed. Observers readily reported that it was the dot, not the framework, that moved.

A most interesting variation occurred when Duncker moved the framework at the same slow rate as the dot in the first experiment and kept the dot stationary (see Figure 10–5). The dot still appeared to move while the frame of reference appeared to be stationary. He referred to this phenomenon as *induced motion,* since the perceived movement of the dot was induced by the displacement of the frame of reference. A common example of induced motion is the perception of the moon sailing across a cloudy sky. It is actually the clouds that are moving; but since they provide a framework for the moon they cause it to appear to be in motion.

Duncker drew two general conclusions from these experiments: first, that *object relative displacement* is necessary to the perception of movement; and second, that the enclosed object appears to move relative to an

Figure 10–5. Induced movement. The stationary dot appears to move toward the left when the frame is moved slowly toward the right.

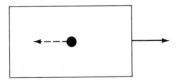

enclosing object. Duncker referred to this second proposition as the *principle of surroundedness.*

The observer may enter into a situation so that in effect he forms the frame of reference for moving objects. This provision was required by the fact that an isolated point may be seen as moving if its angular velocity is great enough. Moreover, under some circumstances the observer may perceive himself as the surrounded object moving within a frame of reference. Thus, rotating a striped shower curtain around an observer can cause him to experience himself as rotating in the opposite direction (Wallach, 1940).

A commonly used example of this phenomenon is the movement experienced by an observer when he is on a stationary train, and another train starts to move on an adjacent track. Though this is undoubtedly an instance of induced motion of the self, it also points to an ambiguity in Duncker's formulation of the principle of surroundedness. In actuality the observer need not be visually surrounded by the moving train to experience himself as moving. The phenomenon occurs when the observer glimpses the moving train with the corner of his eye through a large stationary window. It appears that there are still facts to discover about the conditions under which the observer provides a reference system so that he perceives objects as moving relative to himself, and also when he experiences himself as moving relative to objects. After all, when the eye is pushed by a finger, the observer experiences the world as moving, even though the entire visual surround is being displaced. It must be that other non-visual sources of information influence the perception of movement of the self—a point we shall return to later when we consider the oculogyral illusion.

Brosgole (1968) has observed that all cases of induced motion of an object may depend upon the perceived change in the position of the object relative to the observer. His argument is based on the Roeloffs effect (Roeloffs, 1935), which occurs when a dot is placed off-center in a luminous framework. Even though the dot is straight ahead of the observer, he perceives it as being off to one side of his own perceived direction of gaze. By inference, then, as the framework moves from side-to-side relative to the stationary dot, the dot appears to change position relative to the observer's own perceived direction of gaze. This would reduce all instances of induced motion to a shifting of the position of the dot relative to the observer's perception of the straight-ahead. This approach would involve

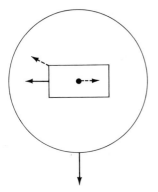

Figure 10–6. Separation of systems. The stationary dot appears to move horizontally toward the right when the rectangular frame is displaced physically toward the left. The rectangular frame appears to move diagonally upward, since the circular frame is moved physically downward. The physical movement of the circular frame has no effect on the direction of movement of the dot.

the observer in induced motion to a much greater degree than was envisioned by Duncker.

Brosgole's approach is consistent with the idea that one perception may be caused by another more elementary perception. In this case the perceived motion is caused by a change in perceived position. This theory, however, may not really clarify the nature of the processes that underlie induced motion, since we are left with the problem of explaining the perception of position and how it is affected by a frame of reference.

We must consider now the principle of the *separation of systems*, exemplified by the experiment illustrated in Figure 10–6. In this figure a dot is surrounded by a rectangular framework, which in turn is surrounded by a circular framework (Wallach, 1959). The rectangular framework is moved to the left, and the circular framework is moved downward. Though the dot is physically stationary, it appears to move.

If both frameworks, the circular and the rectangular, influenced the perception of movement of the dot, we might expect the dot to move along a diagonal path upward and to the right. In point of fact, however, the dot moves along a horizontal path—the same path the dot would take if the outer circular frame of reference were absent. Thus, the system comprising the dot and rectangle is independent of the system comprising the rectangle and the circle. This principle of the separation of systems predicts that the induced movement of an element is influenced solely by its immediate surround.

The phenomenon of induced movement is quite beyond the comprehension of theories stemming from the discovery of the velocity detectors in the visual system. Though there is little doubt that the velocity detectors play an important role in movement perception, it is not possible to deduce the facts of induced motion from their properties. Perceived movement has, or can have, an absolute quality. It is the enclosed object, not its surround, that is seen as moving. Thus, movement may be referred to a stationary object and not to the moving framework. We simply have no models capable of handling this fact.

One might speculate that the moving framework in an induced motion experiment causes the eyes to move and follow it. This could go on without the awareness of the observer. Moreover, the eye movements may themselves be reflexive. Reflexive eye movements are involuntary and affect vision in the same way as does moving the eyeball by some external means. It is well known, for example, that a pattern of vertical stripes moving horizontally is a powerful stimulus to reflexive eye movements. This movement, known as the *optokinetic nystagmus* (OKN), is strictly involuntary. My own observations after being spun around until dizzy indicate that an after-image viewed with eyes closed during the OKN (which persists after being rotated in a structured field) does not appear to move. Now, if a very weak OKN should be present because of the displacement of the frame, the dot's image will glide across the retinal surface. If the eyes are moving involuntarily in one direction, movement will be referred to objects whose images sweep in the opposite direction across the retina.

Unfortunately, there is no evidence in favor of this interpretation. More, the multiple-frame situation used to illustrate the principle of the separation of systems (Figure 10–6) may conflict with it. If the rectangular frame is perceived as moving downward in the circular frame while the dot is simultaneously perceived as moving horizontally, a simple eye-movement explanation would be erroneous. The eyes cannot move in two directions at once. But if the two movements, one sideways and the other downward, are perceived at different times, then an eye-movement explanation might be viable. Clearly, experiments must be performed in which eye movements are measured while perceived movement is reported.

THE PERCEPTION OF SPEED

Thus far the major emphasis in this chapter has been on the sensitivity to movement and to its perceived direction. We have not considered in any detail the perception of the speed of a moving object.

The introduction of a stationary framework may cause a previously subthreshold movement to become perceptible. The introduction of the same framework can cause an object, already perceived as moving, to appear to be moving faster than it was without the framework. J. F. Brown (1931) discovered that a frame of reference can have a very powerful effect on the perceived velocity or speed of a moving object.

Suppose that an object is moving with a uniform velocity across an observer's line of sight in the frontal place. The angular velocity of the object will vary in accord with Euclid's law—i.e., the farther the plane of the object's path, the slower is its angular velocity. Brown was concerned with the possibility that there is a speed constancy analogous to size constancy. As an object moves away from an observer, its perceived size can remain constant even though its angular size varies inversely with its distance. Is it also the case that as a moving object is viewed from a greater distance, its perceived speed will remain constant?

If an observer responds to a moving object in terms of the proximal stimulus, the object would be perceived as moving more slowly than a nearby object moving at the same linear velocity. This could fit the notion that detectors tuned to one retinal velocity will not respond when the same distal stimulus moves at a different retinal velocity. On the other hand, if the observer responds in terms of the distal stimulus, as in size constancy, then the perceived speed of the moving object will be independent of its distance.

To test for the existence of speed constancy, Brown made use of an apparatus similar to a loop of paper placed on two rollers, as shown in Figure 10–7. Black dots were pasted on the loop, and presented within a rectangular aperture. Using two such instruments—one near the observer and the other farther away—he had the observer adjust the physical velocity of one set of dots until its speed appeared to match the speed of the dots in the other display.

Brown found that the perceived speeds of the two sets of dots were equal when their physical velocities were equal. Since this occurred when the displays were at different distances, it appeared that a phenomenon of speed constancy did, in fact, exist. One question did, however, remain:

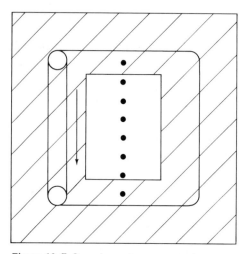

Figure 10–7. Speed constancy apparatus.

Is speed constancy dependent upon cues to distance in the same way that size constancy depends upon these cues?

With Brown's two displays at two different distances, the angular size of the aperture in the more distant display is smaller than the angular size of the aperture in the nearer display. This difference in angular sizes of the rectangular apertures is commensurate with the difference in the angular velocities of the dots moving within them. The rates of change of the positions of the dots within their frameworks are the same, regardless of how far the displays are from the observer. Thus, the amount of time it takes for a dot to go from the top to the bottom of the frame is invariant, even though the distance to the frame may be changed.

Brown reasoned that the speed constancy he found could well be due to the constancy of the rate of figural change rather than to the use of distance cues by the observer. To test his idea he placed his two displays at the same distance from the observer and separated them laterally. The rectangular aperture in one display was made one-half the size of the aperture in the other. Then, the dots in the smaller frame were reduced in size and increased in number so that an equal number of dots could be seen at the same time in both displays. The room was darkened and the loops of paper in the two displays were transilluminated so that the observer saw white rectangular fields containing black dots descending from the tops to the bottoms of the two fields (Figure 10–8).

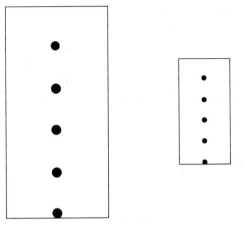

Figure 10–8. The transposition of velocity. The dots in the two displays appear to move downward at the same rate when the physical velocity of the dots in the larger display is twice that of the dots in the smaller display.

As before, the observer adjusted the velocity of one set of dots until its speed appeared to match that of the dots in the other display. When the dots in the two displays appeared to be moving at equal speeds, it was found that they were not moving with equal physical velocities; on the average, the dots in the smaller display were moving at approximately one-half the velocity of those in the larger display. Thus it could be stated that when a display is reduced in size, the perceived speed of its elements is increased in inverse proportion to the change in its size. Accordingly, a change in the size of one of Brown's displays transposes the perceived speed of the moving elements in the display. But this phenomenon, which has been called the *transposition principle,* breaks down when the laboratory is illuminated so that other objects can be seen; hence, the principle of the separation of systems does not apply to speed perception.

As we saw in the preceding chapter, a similar phenomenon is encountered in size perception. Kunnapas (1955) and Rock and Ebenholtz (1959) found that the perceived size of a line may be strongly influenced by the size of its frame of reference. This effect is not strong enough to account for the full magnitude of size constancy, however. In the Brown experiment the effect of the frame of reference is strong enough to account for the full magnitude of speed constancy. Wallach (1939), in an important review of this evidence, concluded that while speed constancy is independent of distance to the moving targets, size constancy entails that distance cues be employed. This leads to the prediction that speed constancy should be absent when a visual frame of reference is absent.

To test this prediction, Rock, Hill, and Fineman (1968) performed an experiment with a display containing a luminous circle on a dark background. The rectangular frame of reference could not be seen by the observer. Nevertheless—and this is the major flaw in their experiment—the circle did have an onset when it entered the invisible aperture, and an offset when it left the aperture. These terminal points could have served as a frame of reference for the observer.

Two viewing conditions were employed. In one condition the two displays were viewed binocularly to allow the observer to make use of the cues of convergence and accommodation. One display was 18 inches from the observer; the other was 72 inches away in another direction. These cues were strong enough to permit accurate judgments of distance, as was proven in an independent experiment by Rock and his associates. In the second condition the two displays were viewed monocularly through artificial pupils. This eliminated the effectiveness of the cues to distance.

When the moving circles were viewed binocularly they were perceived as moving with the same speed when their physical velocities were equal. When viewed through artificial pupils, however, the more distant display had to move twice as fast as the nearer display to achieve a judgment of equal speeds.

These results suggest that there is a tendency to match the retinal velocities of moving objects. Yet, because the terminal points on the path of the moving circle were visible, it is still possible that Brown's transposition principle was at work. If the presence of terminal points was an important factor, it could have contributed to the matching of velocities in the binocular condition. The artificial pupil, on the other hand, could have obscured the terminal points in the nearer display, thereby reducing the effectiveness of this clue to target speed, since an artificial pupil limits the size of the field of view, depending upon how far the pupil is placed from the entrance to the eye. The fact that there was still a tendency toward transposition when the artificial pupils were used supports this contention. For if the artificial pupils were fully effective, the more distant moving circle would have had to move at a velocity four times that of the nearer circle to achieve equal retinal velocities. While this experiment shows that distance cues may influence speed perception, a more conclusive experiment would have utilized a target that moves across the entire visual field so that the end points of its path would not be visible.

Regardless of whether or not cues to distance affect speed perception, it is clear that both the Brown and the Rock, Hill, and Fineman experiments demonstrate a further inadequacy of retinal velocity detection as a basis for movement perception. The detectors alone cannot account for the effects of either the framework or the cues to distance on perceived speed. An alternative explanation of the transposition phenomenon may ameliorate this problem.

Smith and Sherlock (1957) suggested that if an observer simply counts the number of dots appearing in the aperture or disappearing from it in a given period of time, then it would be possible to predict the transposition phenomenon. For if he matches the frequencies of appearances of dots in the frame, the velocities of the two sets of dots will be proportional to the sizes of the frames. This same explanation could be applied also to the experiment by Rock and his associates, even though they had only one circle visible at one time in each frame. In this case the observer could have responded to the period over which a single circle was visible. These periods if matched would have shown speed constancy even though they were totally insensitive to the movements of the circles as such. On this interpretation the experiments were actually dealing not with speed perception but with counting behavior. Still, there are good reasons to believe that a framework can affect perceived speed, one being that when a target moves with a uniform velocity it appears to speed up as it gets nearer to a stationary line. This well-known phenomenon is predictable from the fact that we are more sensitive to movement against a stationary background.

Still another reason for believing that velocity *per se* may be perceived is found in the fact that a person may assess the future position of a moving object. Experiments by Fraisse (1957) and by Bonnet (1964) suggest that an observer may be able to predict accurately the future position of an object that had been seen as moving and then was occluded from his view. The observer's task is to estimate at what time the moving target would reappear from behind a screen after it had moved behind it. If this can be done accurately, it may be assumed that the observer had some impression of the velocity of the target. Since his ability to make this judgment may depend upon how long a time the target was visible before it went behind the screen, it must be that the observer has developed some notion of how long it takes for the object to cover a particular distance. Since velocity is defined in terms of the amount of space traveled per unit time, the observer must have an impression of the velocity of the target if he is to make this judgment accurately. If predictions of future position can be affected by the size of the surround in such experiments, Brown's original interpretation would gain additional support.

Perceived speed must be multi-determined. All the factors of retinal velocity, eye movements, effects of framework, and other stimulus parameters as well, must be incorporated in a comprehensive theory of movement perception. We have not even mentioned the higher derivatives of motion—i.e., acceleration and the third derivative or "jerk"—which have hardly been studied. Is the perception of such kinds of movement affected by the same parameters in the same way as is the perception of velocity? Movement in the third dimension also appears to be a promising field of inquiry. If speed constancy is affected by cues to distance, an object moving in the third dimension should appear to have a uniform velocity in the absence of a visible frame of reference. Also, as in size constancy, the attitude of the observer could affect the perception of real movement. An analytical attitude might serve to vitiate the effect of the framework in the Brown experiment.

APPARENT MOVEMENT

As it will be recalled, real movement was defined as the perception of movement when the stimulus to motion is a physically moving target. In this section we shall be concerned with *apparent movement*—i.e., the occurrence of the perception of movement when the stimulus is not moving physically. In actuality this nomenclature is misleading, for all perceived movement is "apparent." Despite wide recognition of this misleading nature of the terms "apparent" and "real," the usage has persisted. Consequently, we shall follow the convention and use these same words to stand for the two different stimulus conditions of movement perception.

The most intensively studied version of apparent movement is that perceived when two lights are presented at different times and at different places. This is one of the stimulus conditions for producing *stroboscopic motion*. Thus, as shown in Figure 10–9, if a light is flashed at A and a second light flashed somewhat later at B, the observer may report that he sees the light move from A to B.

To contrast apparent movement with real movement, let us consider what happens in both cases when the eye does not move. As per Figure 10–9, in the case of real movement the light literally shifts across the retinal surface, thereby exciting different receptors in order, one after the

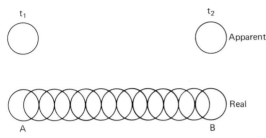

Figure 10–9. Apparent movement may occur when a light is flashed at place A at time t_1 and then at place B at time t_2. Real movement occurs when the light is flashed on at time t_1 and then moved physically to place B during the interval between t_1 and t_2.

other. In the case of apparent movement, however, the light is imaged at but two places and may thus be thought of as a discontinuous stimulus.

One of the most important studies of apparent movement was undertaken by Wertheimer (1912). Wertheimer presented two objects to an observer in an arrangement similar to that shown in the upper part of Figure 10–9. At first, object A was presented at time t_1, and then object B was presented at time t_2. The main variable in this experiment was the difference in time between t_1 and t_2.

When the interval between t_1 and t_2 was large, the observer reported that he saw two objects, A and B, appearing in succession at two different places. When the interval between t_1 and t_2 (hereafter to be called the interstimulus interval or ISI) was about 60 msec in duration, the observer reported that the object at A simply moved across the space to the position B. This was referred to as optimum apparent movement, which was later given the name *beta movement*.

When the ISI in Wertheimer's experiment was made longer than 60 msec, he found that sometimes observers could not see the object move across the space between A and B, but instead reported either partial movement or a disembodied movement (*phi*) across the space. As indicated when this pure motion without a moving object was discussed earlier in this chapter, Wertheimer felt that the *phi* phenomenon reflected the dynamic interactions between spatially separated events in the brain.

When the ISI was zero—that is, when the stimuli were presented simultaneously—Wertheimer's observer reported that the two stimuli were in fact flashing on and off simultaneously. Moreover, as the ISI was increased from zero to some value less than about 30 msec, the observer still reported the stimuli to be flashing on and off at the same time. Movement did not occur unless the interval between the stimuli was greater than about 30 msec. Thus, as Wertheimer found, there was a band or ISI region in which some kind of movement could be seen. This band lay between about 200 msec and 30 msec. Intervals longer than 200 msec led to the impression of succession while intervals shorter than 30 msec led to the impression of simultaneity.

While Wertheimer's results are correct for his experimental situation, the relation between ISI and the occurrence of apparent movement depends upon a number of factors. Thus, as the space between A and B is increased the ISI needed to achieve optimum apparent movement may be greater than it is for small stimulus separations. This is consistent with the findings of Cook and Mott-Smith (1966), who tested for the occurrence of *beta* movement with an oscilloscopic display. With an angular separation between the stimuli of 0.8 degree, for example, the probability of reporting optimum apparent movement was at its maximum with an ISI of about 100 msec. When the angular separation was 3.2 degrees, the ISI for optimum apparent movement was in the vicinity of 120 msec. A 6.4-degree separation was associated with an ISI of about 130 msec for optimum apparent movement. There is however, considerable variability in the data reported by Cook and Mott-Smith.

Factors other than stimulus spacing have also an influence on apparent movement. Among these is stimulus intensity. It has been observed, for example, that optimum apparent movement could be more likely at a particular ISI if the stimulus intensity were increased. More, eye movements may enter into the occurrence of optimum apparent movement. Thus, if one shifts his gaze from A to B during the ISI there is in effect a shortening of the amount of retinal space between the proximal stimuli. Research is needed to determine the effect of eye movements on apparent movement.

The roles of stimulus intensity and stimulus separation in space and time were explored by Korte (1915), who formulated a set of laws that are really statements of qualitative effects of manipulating various stimulus parameters on apparent movement. The parameters are the separation or space between the two stimuli, the duration of the ISI, the period or length of time of presentation of each of the two stimuli, and the intensities or brightnesses of the stimuli.

Korte was the first to discover that if the ISI is lengthened, apparent movement may still be perceived—provided that the space *s* between the two stimuli is made larger. Similarly, if the space *s* were made so large that movement could not be seen, the movement might be restored by making the ISI longer. Also, increasing the intensities of the two stimuli can offset increases in the size of *s* or duration of the ISI. Moreover, increasing the duration of presentation of the two stimuli can offset to some extent an increase in the ISI. Similarly, an increase in stimulus duration may offset an increase in *s*. Korte's findings are not truly precise laws of perception, and they neglect other factors important to our understanding of apparent movement.

The emphasis placed on the effect of stimulus intensity may be misleading, for it is possible to obtain apparent movement when the stimuli do not differ in brightness from their backgrounds. Julesz (1971), for example, showed that the inner square in his random dot stereograms (see page 285) can be seen in apparent movement. This square is produced by a systematic binocular disparity and does not differ in brightness from its background. Yet if it is presented toward one side of its background framework at one time and near the other side at another time, it can be seen in good apparent movement.

Moreover, it is possible to see apparent movement between a white object on a grey background and a black object at another place on the same gray background. The object has perfectly good movement, but it changes color from white to black at some indeterminate point before reaching its second position. It is difficult to see how intensity *per se* is important here. It is more likely that the magnitude of the difference in brightness or the contrast between the object and its background, rather than the absolute intensity *per se*, will influence apparent movement. Needed are definitive studies of the parameters influencing apparent movement, and in such studies, attention should be paid to the role of contrast, as opposed to intensity per se. Further, the fact that movement occurs in the Julesz patterns suggests that movement can be detected after generation of a perceived form. The appearance of the form could be dependent either upon patterns of brightness difference or upon binocular disparity (Julesz, 1971).

THE RELATION BETWEEN REAL AND APPARENT MOVEMENT

One of the earliest questions about apparent movement concerned its relation to real movement—i.e., is apparent movement mediated by the same mechanisms that produce real movement? Until recently the most

common answer to this question was that there is no fundamental difference between the two classes of movement.

There are very good reasons for believing that real and apparent
movement have a common basis. One of these is that apparent movement
resembles real movement. This was noted by Dimmick and Scahill (1925),
DeSilva (1929), and other writers as well. Koffka (1935) made the point
that perceived movement is due to the displacement of an object relative
to the visual field, since as he believed, even a so-called homogeneous field
has a structure yielded by the perceived up-down and left-right directions
of the perceived space. Now, since such structure is naturally not so
strong as that given by a textured field containing other visible objects,
Koffka was not surprised that sensitivity to movement is less in an empty
field than it is in a textured field. Yet he considered displacement relative
to structure to be the basis for movement.

When he pondered apparent movement, Koffka suggested that if an
object is first seen at one point in the visual field and subsequently at
another nearby point, it may have the same effect as it would if it had
been physically displaced. Hence, the basis for apparent movement must
be the same as that for real movement—i.e., in Koffka's thinking, the
stress set up in the activity of the brain by a displacing object.

Gibson (1950) presented a compelling argument for the fundamental
similarity between real and apparent movement in his point that perceptions correspond to physical situations. The stimulus to the perception of
movement need not be a replica of the physical situation—e.g., an image
translating across the retina—but must merely be correlated with a physical
situation. The fact that an object is presented at one point and then later at
another point does correlate with a physical situation in which an object
starts from a standstill and moves to another position where it is stationary one again. This correlation, in Gibson's view, is present in the case of
both real and apparent movement and thus provides sufficient basis for
producing the perception of movement.

Gibson's view is consistent with Schouten's interpretation of apparent
movement (1967). Schouten noted that an object moving across the receptive field of a velocity detecting neuron must cross at least two receptors if movement is to be perceived. In the apparent movement situation
two points illuminated at two different times could produce the same
effect on the velocity detector and thus the image-retina system of velocity detection must mediate both real and apparent movement perception.

Paul Kolers (1963) performed several experiments that prompt us to question this identity of real and apparent movement. In one such experiment he moved a point from one place to another, and a small line was flashed someplace along its path of movement. Kolers found that the detectability of the flashed line was affected by the moving target: it was harder to see the line when the target moved across it than when the target was absent.

Kolers then caused the target merely to appear to move, by first presenting it at one place and then, slightly later in time, at another place. The timing was such that the observer reported that the target was moving from one place to another. As before, the small line was flashed in the path of this movement. It was found that the apparently moving target did not have the same effect on the detectability of the line as did the target that was in real motion. We conclude from this that apparent movement differs in some ways from real movement.

Kaufman *et al.* (1971) studied another aspect of the relation between real and apparent movement—an aspect emerging from the fact that in a typical experiment apparent movement proceeds in rapid jumps. Suppose that two objects, separated by a visual angle of 2 degrees, are presented alternately to an observer. If the ISI is about 100 msec, the observer might see the object jump back and forth between two positions. Now, if an object were actually moving back and forth between two positions separated by the same 2-degree space, and if it were to do this within the same 100-msec interval, the velocity of the object would be 20 degrees of arc/sec. As we saw earlier in the discussion of real movement, an object moving at this velocity would appear to streak: with fixed gaze it could not be perceived accurately as it moves. This observation led to the conclusion that apparent movement may not be directly comparable to real movement, since in real movement objects must have lower velocities to be seen accurately while they are moving.

To compare real and apparent movement Kaufman and his associates used a disc like that shown in Figure 10–10. When the disc was rotated, a short segment of the luminous curve on the disc could be seen—a short luminous line moving back and forth in the slit. Because of the design of the curve on the disc, the observer saw a line segment standing still at one end of the slit, and successively moving across the length of the slit, where it remained stationary once again.

The slit was viewed in three different ways. In the first condition the observer saw the stationary segments as well as the movement of the segment along the slit. In the second condition the moving segment was hid-

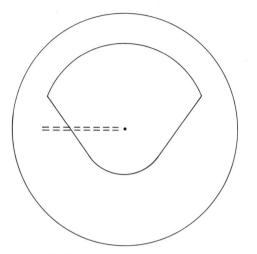

Figure 10–10. Disc used to demonstrate the complementarity of real and apparent movement. Dotted line is a slit, and through it the observer viewed the luminous curve on the rotating disc. (After Kaufman **et al.,** 1971)

den from the observer so that he saw only the alternating stationary end points. Finally, in the third condition the end points were hidden and the observer saw only the moving segment.

When the first condition was employed, the moving line segment appeared to be blurred when its velocity was about 10.6 degrees of arc/sec. A totally fused line that did not exhibit blinking or movement was seen at an angular velocity of 27.9 degrees of arc/sec.

When the moving segment was invisible and only the end points were seen by the observer, the conditions for apparent movement were satisfied, since the observer first saw a luminous line at one point and then another luminous line later at another point. The velocity of the moving invisible segment defines the ISI of this experiment. Apparent movement was just seen by the observers when the ISI corresponded to a velocity of about 8.9 degrees of arc/sec. This 8.9 degrees of arc/sec threshold did not differ significantly from the blur threshold in the first condition. Thus, apparent movement began when an object in real movement started to blur or streak. The upper threshold for apparent movement occurred when the velocity of the moving invisible segment was about 21 degrees of arc/sec. This did not differ significantly from the threshold of total streaking, or fusion in the real-movement condition.

The fusion threshold when the end points were not visible—the third condition of the experiment—was significantly lower than that found when the end points were visible. This suggests that when an object starts from a standstill and then moves across the field, if its velocity is great enough apparent movement will be superimposed on the real movement of the object. This could explain the finding of Smith and Gulick (1957) that an object in motion may be more accurately perceived if it is standing still before it moves.

These data suggest that apparent movement and real movement are complementary rather than parallel processes. If an object is moving slowly, one population of velocity detectors is involved in the detection of the movement. These detectors do not respond when only two points within their receptive fields are stimulated, as in an apparent movement experiment. There could, however, be another set of velocity detectors that respond when two points are stimulated in succession in their receptive fields. These detectors do not discriminate between high-velocity real movement and apparent movement. Indeed, it may be argued that high-velocity real movement is not distinguishable from apparent movement, since the discrimination of such movement depends upon seeing the object as stationary before and after it actually moves.

Thus far our focus has been on the image-retina system. We have concluded that different subsets of velocity detectors must be involved in perception of real and apparent movement. But even with this qualification the notion of velocity detectors is insufficient to explain many instances of perceived movement, as one observation by Ternus (1938) makes clear.

Ternus presented three dots at time t_1 as shown in Figure 10–11. At the later time t_2, he presented a second set of three dots. Two of the dots from the first set of three overlapped the places occupied by two of the dots in the second set. Thus, two of the three dots simply flashed on and off in their same positions. Despite this repeated stimulation of the same retinal places, observers saw the dots moving as a unit from side to side.

○

Figure 10–11. Phenomenal identity. A set of three lights (open circles) is flashed and then replaced by another set of lights (closed circles). The observer perceives the three lights moving as a group from left to right so that the central and right-hand lights preserve their identities.

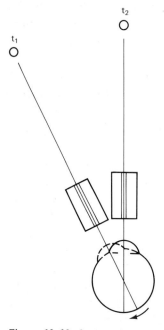

Figure 10–12. Apparent movement without stimulation of disparate retinal places. The eye first fixates a light when it is flashed on at time t_1, and then turns to fixate a second light at time t_2. The observer may see the light moving from one position in space to the other, even though it does not stimulate different retinal places at different times. (After Rock and Ebenholtz, 1962)

The middle dot in the array preserved its identity, so that it appeared to move from side to side even though the same retinal place was stimulated on all presentations of the stimuli. This Ternus referred to as the preservation of *phenomenal identity,* for if the set of dots is perceived to be an organized unit, it will be perceived as moving as a unit even though only the end dots are actually shifted from flash to flash. It is obvious that a simple velocity detector model cannot handle this strong effect.

The important study by Rock and Ebenholtz (1962) creates still other difficulties for theories of apparent movement. As shown in Figure 10–12, these investigators had an observer move his eye from side-to-side to look through very small apertures at two different places, while two lights were flashed alternately. One light could be seen through one aperture, and the other light through the other aperture. If the eye movements were synchronized with the flashing of the two lights, the observer saw a light flashing in one aperture and again in the other aperture. Since the apertures were very small, the two lights were always imaged on approximately the same retinal place, even though the eye occupied two different positions to view them.

In essence, then, the eye moved between two different positions: in one, a light was imaged at one retinal place, and in the other, another light was imaged at the same retinal place. The result was that the observer saw a light moving from one position to another—i.e., apparent movement *without* a change in retinal position.

One way to interpret this result is to conclude that the eye-head system is capable of mediating the perception of apparent movement independently on the image-retina or velocity-detecting system. This would imply that apparent movement may be produced also by the change in an object's position as signaled by the outflow of the eye muscles. Thus, even if an after-image could be made to disappear during a voluntary eye movement, the after-image would appear to move.* The mechanism mediating such apparent movement could be the same as that mediating the perception of the real movement of a target followed by the eye. Note, however, that there is no information that would allow us to judge whether such apparent movement is parallel to real movement or is complementary, as found in the experiment by Kaufman *et al.*

Rock and Ebenholtz subsumed their result under a general proposition that served to explain other kinds of perceived movement as well. As they argued, the flashing light was perceived first in one place and then in another, and this change in perceived position mediated the perception of the movement. This argument is consistent with the general view that the explanation of perception must derive from within the domain of perception as we discussed in Chapter 1. It can be disputed in the present context, however, since one may experience movement without a change in perceived position.

ILLUSION OF MOVEMENT

In the 1860's Helmholtz (1925) discussed the fact that after one has been looking through a train window at a moving landscape the interior of the railroad car appears to move in the opposite direction. This is a special

---

* Daniel Kahneman has suggested that the biological utility of apparent movement is to "fill in" the perception of objects during saccadic suppression (personal communication, 1965).

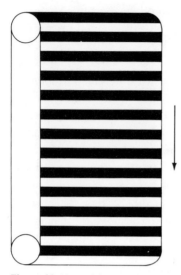

Figure 10–13. A striped pattern for demonstrating the waterfall illusion.

instance of the waterfall illusion produced by viewing a set of moving stripes, as in Figure 10–13. If one should view the stripes for some time while they descend downward in the visual field, and then stop the movement, the stripes will then appear to be moving upward.

One explanation of this phenomenon lies in the fact that the eyes tend to follow the lines as they move downward in the field, and that this sets up an *optokinetic nystagmus* (OKN), in which the eyes follow the stripes slowly and then saccade back to the original straight-ahead position. This is followed again by a slow movement downward, and so on. As indicated earlier in this chapter, the OKN tends to persist after a stimulus is re-moved—i.e., after the stripes have stopped moving, the eyes will continue to move slowly downward, saccade upward, and drift downward again. As we already know, such involuntary movements cause the images of the physically stationary objects in the field—stripes in this case—to move on the retina. Therefore, the physically stationary stripes could appear to move opposite to the direction of the slow eye movements. The diffi-culty with this and with other eye-movement explanations is that they cannot handle the related illusion of the *spiral aftereffect*.

Plateau (1850) painted an Archimedes spiral on a disc (one version is shown in Figure 10–14). The spiral was then rotated. Depending upon the direction of rotation, the spiral appeared either to expand or to contract. After viewing this for some time, observers report seeing opposite movement upon looking at any textured surface—even a human face. It is clear that eye movements could not cause this illusion: the image cannot be made to expand or contract through the action of the eye muscles. Obviously something in the image-retina system is involved in such aftereffects of seen movement.

Interestingly, the spiral aftereffect is not accompanied by any perceived change in the position of the objects experienced as moving. When a page of text is viewed after the spiral has been rotated, the text may move in either an expanding or a contracting direction, even though the letters and words do not seem to change position. This would suggest that the visual system is not detecting a change in position but is encoding velocity directly, contrary to the theory of Rock and Ebenholtz.

When one looks at a rotating spiral with one eye, and another spiral rotating in the opposite direction with the other eye, it is possible to experience two independent spiral aftereffects (Wolgemuth, 1911; also see Anstis and Moulden, 1970). The independence of the aftereffects is most apparent when the observer closes one eye. The open eye sees its aftereffect against a textured background. This argues for the proposition that at least a significant portion of the spiral aftereffect occurs early in the visual system before the views generated by the two eyes converge onto a common

Figure 10–14. Rotating the spiral about its center causes it to appear to expand or contract. After a period of one or two minutes of observing the rotating spiral, any stationary textured surface will exhibit the opposite kind of movement.

population of cells. We cannot conclude, however, that all velocity detection occurs prior to the visual areas of the cortex.

Julesz (1971), using his random dot stereograms, succeeded in demonstrating that there are movement phenomena that could have occurred only after the level of binocular integration. He therefore concluded that movement detection may be possible at many different levels throughout the visual system.

Papert (1964) has shown that the waterfall illusion may be produced with random dot stereograms in which neither eye alone can see a moving pattern of bars, but that when the two eyes view the disparate sets of random dots, a set of bars becomes visible. This set of bars is in continuous movement, as in the conventional waterfall illusion and, after cessation of the movement, an aftereffect occurs. Since this phenomenon is not attributable to retinal displacements of pattern (which are visible only in a stereoscopic view), the aftereffect must be central in origin. This is consistent with Julesz' (1971) view that movement detection can go on at several different levels in the nervous system.

It would appear from these results that velocity detection occurs not only in the image-retina system but also at higher levels in the nervous system, and thus may be quite independent of the perception of position change *per se*. The latter function—detecting position change—can also occur in the image-retina system, and perhaps at higher levels, as indicated by the perceived positions of forms in Julesz patterns. New evidence suggests that the eye-head system provides rather poor information about position (Festinger and Easton, 1974). What we have here is a highly complicated interweaving of many different systems subserving the functions of velocity detection and position detection.

Additional support for the notion that the velocity detection functions are involved in aftereffects of movement is furnished by the work of Sekular and Ganz (1963). These researchers used the contact lens method for stabilizing the image of a rectangular framework on an observer's retina. The stabilized framework contained a striped pattern that could be moved within the framework at any desired velocity, so that the retinal velocities of the stripes were independent of the observer's eye movements. They succeeded in demonstrating that the aftereffect of motion occurs even when the eyes are not free to move relative to the bar pattern, and moreover, that the detectability of moving bars depends upon prior exposure.

Suppose that the bars had been moving in one direction for a long period of time. On subsequent tests the bars were moved in the original direction and in the opposite direction as well. The experimenter increased the luminance of the pattern—very dim in these tests—until the observer reported that he could see the pattern. The luminance required to detect a pattern had to be greater when the pattern was moving in the same direction as in the original prolonged exposure than it did when the bars were moving in the opposed direction during the test. Pantle and Sekular (1968) found that this effect of exposure is orientation-specific. Tilting the bars reduces the effect.

These results are consistent with a conjecture of Sutherland (1959) to the effect that prolonged viewing of movement in one direction fatigues the velocity detectors tuned to that direction of movement. As a result of the fatigue the normal spontaneous firing rates of these detectors becomes attenuated. Meanwhile, other detectors responding to other directions of movement will continue to fire at their normal rates, with the result that the observer sees movement opposite to that which he had seen before.

This theory has an important deficiency: no reason is given for the perceived aftereffect to be *opposite* the direction of movement during the initial exposure. Presumably there are velocity detectors that respond to many different directions of movement. Why then should the after-effect not occur in every direction but that of the exposure stimulus? Why is the movement only in the direction opposed to the one to which the observer was exposed?

This deficiency may be remedied by postulating that velocity detectors come in opposed pairs. That is, there may be detectors whose rate of spontaneous firing decreases in response to one direction of movement and increases in response to the opposite direction of movement (Barlow and Hill, 1963). Excessive exposure to one direction of movement will bias the spontaneous firing rates of these detectors so that the level of the spontaneous firing rate after they are fatigued is interpreted by the brain to mean that there is movement in the opposed direction.

The theory that there are spontaneous events occurring in the image-retina system helps to explain the well-known *autokinetic effect*. This illusion of movement occurs when a single luminous point is viewed in the dark. Even though the point is physically stationary it may appear to be wandering about aimlessly. This wandering is the autokinetic phenomenon, and may well be attributable to spontaneous changes in the firing patterns of otherwise idle movement detectors. This theory appears to be incomplete, since there are reasons to believe that outflow to the extraocular muscles is involved in the autokinetic effect.

It is an old observation (Carr, 1910) that with the eyes turned to view a luminous point in a dark space, the point will seem to move in the direction of the turned gaze—and this uniform movement is not accompanied by an apparent change in the position of the point. Active eye movements could not be detected during the illusion (Guilford and Dallanbach, 1928), although straining of the eye muscles can influence the effect. Gregory (1966) suggested, therefore, that the phenomenon is due to the outflow to the muscles needed to offset instability in the maintenance of fixation. Thus, to maintain fixation off to one side may require more neural activity in one direction than in the other if fixation is to be maintained. This in turn could produce an apparent movement of the point in the direction of gaze, since, so far as the brain is concerned, the eyes are being signaled to move in one direction while the image of the point remains on a constant retinal place.

One result seemingly inconsistent with this interpretation is that obtained by Matin and MacKinnon (1964). These workers used the stabilized image technique to prevent eye movements from influencing the horizontal retinal position of a dot. When the dot was so stabilized, observers reported fewer instances of autokinesis in the horizontal direction than when it was not stabilized. Autokinesis occurred in directions other than the horizontal direction when stabilization was applied. This suggests that involuntary eye movements *per se* could contribute to the phenomenon and that earlier attempts to measure the relation between involuntary eye movements and the autokinetic effect were too limited in sensitivity.

There is one important flaw in both the outflow theory of Gregory and the eye-movement theory of the autokinetic phenomenon: neither view can account for the fact that to produce the phenomenon we must use an isolated point or object in an empty field. If the phenomenon is due to either outflow to the musculature, or the involuntary and unnoticed eye movements themselves during an attempt to maintain fixation, then the entire visual scene should exhibit an autokinetic effect. Let us assume for the moment that the eyes drift involuntarily from their point of fixation. Since there is no proprioception from the muscles, the drifting of the image on the retina causes it to appear to move, as when the eyeball is pushed. This could explain the autokinetic effect—and yet the entire visual field when filled with objects and textures should likewise appear to move under the same circumstances. But the autokinetic dance can be discerned only when the visual field contains isolated points or objects. *Ergo,* it is clear that we have yet to develop a completely satisfactory theory of the phenomenon.

VESTIBULAR EFFECTS

Another illusion that may bear upon the processes underlying the autokinetic effect is the *oculogyral illusion.* This form of apparent movement occurs when the semicircular canals of the inner ear are stimulated.

The inner ear is composed of two major parts: One part, the cochlea, concerned with hearing; the other, consisting of the semicircular canals and the otolith organs, and concerned with body balance. The otolith organs are involved in the sensing of the static position of the head, and the canals are stimulated by accelerative forces. When an observer is rotated, the rotational acceleration is responsible for the stimulation of receptor cells in the canals. Signals arising from these receptors produce a reflexive eye movement known as the *rotational nystagmus.* After cessation of the rotation, the observer's eyes continue to move—a phenomenon known as *post-rotational nystagmus.*

Graybiel and Hupp (1946) found that in a dark room an illuminated object goes through a whole series of movements during and after rotation of an observer. When an observer is rotated to the left the object, which is rotating with him, immediately appears to move with him. After a time the object comes to stand still. Then, when the rotation is stopped, the object appears to rush to the right, and subsequently reverses its direction, once again moving slowly to the left.

To achieve similar effects in a lighted room the observer had to be rotated at a much higher rate than when viewing an isolated object. The reflexive nystagmus induced by the acceleration probably mediates this phenomenon. As we already know, since involuntary eye movements are not sensed by the observer, he interprets the resulting image movement as a movement of the object being viewed. The fact that in a lighted room the acceleration must be stronger to produce this same effect suggests that there is an interaction between the effects of image displacement on the retina during rotation and the effect of the acceleration itself. Thus, in a lighted room the images of features of the room sweep across the retina during rotation. This visual input could produce an optokinetic nystagmus tending to offset the rotational nystagmus and thereby making it more difficult for the full effect of the rotational nystagmus to be experienced. This is purely speculative, since there is no direct evidence bearing upon it. Dichganz and Brandt (1972) have shown, however, that movement of the visual surrounding of a rabbit may produce a modulation of the discharges in its vestibular nucleus. This, and other evidence as well (e.g., Dichganz and Bizzi, 1972), implies that visual stimulation may affect the vestibular apparatus just as the vestibular effects of acceleration affect vision. Such interactions suggest the existence of circuits connecting the movement detection system of the retinal-cortical pathways to the vestibular mechanisms. Such interconnections may well be inborn, for when Tauber and Koffler (1966) placed newborn infants in a rotating striped field they were able to observe an optokinetic nystagmus. This same nystagmus could be observed when the stripes of the field were in apparent motion rather than in real motion.

CONCLUSION

Many sources mediate the appearance of movement, among them the inner ear, eye movements, outflow to the eye muscles, retinal translation, relative displacement of retinal images and of their cortical representations, and perhaps even the attitude of the observer. Undoubtedly many sub-systems are involved. In higher-order systems they include the eye-head system and the image-retina system, which latter is involved in the detection of relative displacement and of induced movement. Both systems appear to mediate the perception of the real and the apparent movement of an isolated object. The complicated interweaving of these systems in the perception of movement in daily life remains to be unraveled by future research.

11
the rearrangement
of perceptual space

Many psychologists believe that perceiving depends upon learning. It is commonly held that the reason the visual world appears to be three-dimensional even though the retinal image is flat is the fact of experience in moving about and touching objects. One type of evidence for this thesis flows from experiments showing that adult sensorimotor co-ordinations are modifiable.

Suppose that a prism were to be placed in front of an observer's eye. As appears in Figure 11-1, the perceived position of the object no longer corresponds to its physical location. Now, when an observer reaches for the object after looking at it and then closing his eyes, he is likely to miss it. In the situation depicted in this figure, he is likely to reach above the object. After repeated trials, however, he will be able to reach accurately for the displaced object with his eyes closed.

The foregoing observation, which was first made by Helmholtz (1925), suggested to some investigators that reaching for the object leads to a change in the perceived position of the object. If the object can be reached for correctly—so this reasoning goes—its perceived position must correspond to its physical position. Although, as we shall see later, there are substantial reasons for giving such phenomena an entirely different interpretation, evidence has been marshaled to support the contention that the perception of the spatial layout of objects is an acquired capability. A review of some of the evidence for and against this thesis leads instead to the conclusion that while perceiving is indeed modifiable, at the same

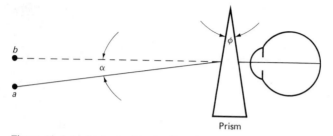

Prism

Figure 11–1. Light from object **a** is refracted by the prism so that it appears to originate at **b**. The shift in direction produced by a prism is always in the direction of the apex of the prism. The angle of deviation α is related to the angle ϕ formed by the sides of the prism and also to the refractive index of the glass. The power of a prism can be expressed in terms of the **prism diopter,** which is 100 times the tangent of the angle of deviation α. Since the tangent of an angle of deviation of 0.57 degrees equals 0.01, a prism producing this angle of deviation has a power of 1 prism diopter.

time such modifications come about within constraints dictated by the innate structure of the organism. The task of psychology is to define these constraints and to explain the nature and range of the modifications that do occur.

THEORETICAL BACKGROUND

The proposition that we learn to perceive has always been an attractive one. Ever since the British Empiricists proposed that all knowledge is based upon experience, many scientists and philosophers have assumed that perceptions arise from associations of sensations (or ideas) which are contingent upon experience. If sensations occur close together in time or space and with some frequency, they may then be perceived and remembered as belonging together. Contiguity (which is really proximity in time) was presumed by David Hume to underlie the perception of causality. Thus, the classical laws of association, which go back to Aristotle, together, perhaps, with the more recently discovered mechanism of reinforcement, are still often considered to be the bases of perceptual learning.

Just as there has always been a strong tendency to believe that perceiving is an acquired capability, so also have there been schools of thought devoted to the opposite thesis. In his *Meno*, Plato described an encounter between Socrates and an uneducated slave. By asking questions Socrates was able to get the young slave to produce a proof of the Pythagorean theorem, and concluded that since the slave had no prior experience of geometry, he must have been born with the knowledge needed to establish the proof. Thus Socrates could argue that all learning is really a matter of remembering what one had come to know in an earlier existence. While no one takes seriously this Socratic reminiscence theory of learning, many thinkers have believed that the organism has innate properties determining the ways in which it will perceive the world and gain insight into its workings.

The Empiricists held that the mind is a blank tablet on which experience writes. Immanuel Kant recognized that this theory implies a number of previously unsuspected assumptions. Thus, in arguing that perceived causation is due to the contiguity of experienced events, Hume neglected to ask how one learns of contiguity itself. In Kant's view it must be that the capacity to perceive the temporal order of events is inborn. Similarly, the perception of spatial ordering must be dependent upon the inherent character of the mind. The "blank tablet" has a prior structure to which experience must conform. Time and space, according to Kant, are organizations imposed by the mind on incoming events. They are the forms of experience.

Hering's notion of local signs was strongly influenced by the Kantian view. So too was Johannes Müller's doctrine of specific nerve energies, according to which each sensory nerve, when excited, leads to a sensation's having a unique quality. Thus, even electrical stimulation of the optic nerve will lead to the sensation of light; the same stimulation of the auditory nerve will lead to the sensation of sound. Such events are innately organized in both space and time.

There are really two levels of experience. On the one hand, there is the experience of the individual. His exposure to diverse circumstances undoubtedly plays a role in moulding his personality and at least sensitizes him to certain events and dulls his awareness of others. On the other hand, there is the experience of the species. As Darwin has taught us, when events exceed the capacity of an individual to cope with them, he may succumb. Those individuals innately capable of dealing with these same events may survive and subsequently reproduce similarly endowed individuals. This "natural selection" is reinforcement on a grand scale. It is only those individuals with a particular genetic constitution who will survive in a particular environment. This, as we all know, leads in time to the remarkable differences among the species. The shape of the horse's eye is a case in point.

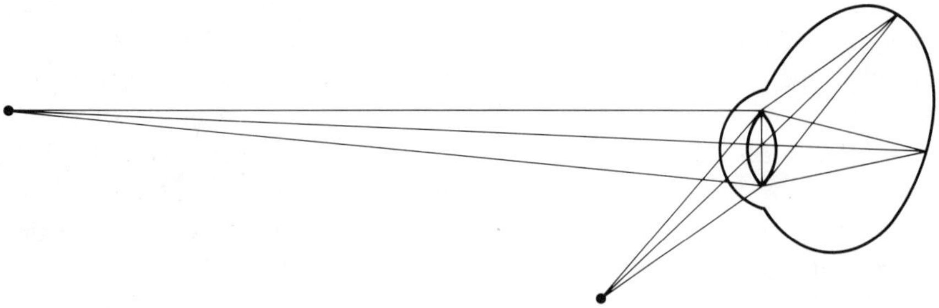

Figure 11–2. A cross-sectional sketch of the eye of a horse. Since the upper portion of the retina is farther from the lens than the lower portion, objects in the distance are brought to a sharp focus on the lower retina, and nearby objects are brought to a sharp focus on the upper retina.

In Figure 11–2, a cross-sectional view of the eye of a horse, it is obvious that objects on the ground and immediately in front of the horse can be imaged sharply on the retina, and that objects in the far distance may also be imaged sharply. Unlike the human, the horse need not take time to change his accommodation to look from far to near.

It is not our purpose to discuss the mechanisms of biological evolution. The eye of the horse is merely a reminder of the fact that the sensory system of an animal may be configured by evolution. If such remarkable structures can evolve, then there is certainly no sense at all in the bland assertion that space perception as such is a learned capability. Much of this so-called learning must take place on the phylogenetic level.

Despite all this, there must be some flexibility in the way the visual apparatus is put to use; as we shall see in Chapter 13, its very structure may even be modifiable in some degree. Helmholtz (1925) had the idea that the ordering of objects in space is innately detectable. Thus, in theory a person with no prior experience is able to recognize the order in which points are imaged on his retina. If three points were imaged on a horizontal retinal meridian, then, according to Helmholtz, an observer with no experience at all should be able to notice that one of the points lies between the other two. It does require prior experience, however, to perceive the magnitude of the separations between the points. This experience may take the form of eye movements to switch fixation from one of the points to another. Thus, if we follow Helmholtz, the calibration of perception is not native, though the experience of relative position is determined by inherent structure.

For the present, we shall assume that perception is not infinitely modifiable. At the very least, a person can never learn to "see" sounds and "hear" lights. Too, it is probably true that there is an inherent spatiality in visual experience, as would follow from the fact that the retina is an extended surface designed by evolution for the detection of spatial information. This does not of itself prove that, if perception is to develop normally, there must be a topological correspondence between the image formed on the retina and the distal object.

It is possible to imagine an experiment in which the retinal image is scrambled, so that points comprising the image need not be in the same order as corresponding points on the object, as shown in Figure 11–3. If the retinal images of a newborn infant were scrambled in this way, one might ask what sort of information the infant could ultimately gain about objects in space. In this imaginary experiment the normal topological correspondence between the proximal stimulus and the distal object is destroyed. An extreme empiricist would maintain that despite this rearrangement of the retinal image, the infant might well develop normally. One of the purposes of this chapter will be to examine evidence concerning this hypothesis.

To anticipate a bit: the weight of evidence does not support the idea

Figure 11–3. Scrambling the image of an L-shaped object.

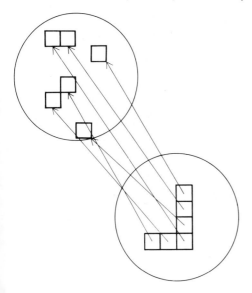

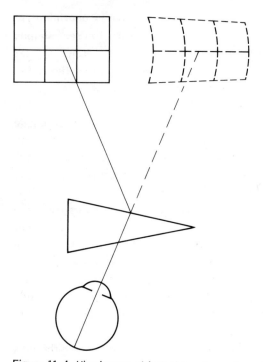

Figure 11–4. Viewing an object through a prism changes its apparent position and also causes its straight vertical contours to be curved. The curvature (exaggerated here) is due to the fact that rays entering the prism at an oblique angle are bent more than rays entering the prism at right angles. Although the dotted figure is a distorted version of the solid figure, topological correspondence is preserved.

that the infant with a scrambled retinal image will develop normal vision, though as Dodwell (1970) has suggested, this infant would probably be able to tolerate and adjust to a range of transformations of the retinal image in which the normal topological correspondence is preserved. According to Dodwell, such rearrangement of the retinal image, which is illustrated in Figure 11–4, approximates a *conformal transformation*. Other examples include minification of the retinal image, magnification of the image and even the rotation of the image through 180 degrees. Rock (1966) also believes that only a limited range of transformations is suitable for adaptation. Except for Dodwell's suggestion, however, no one has conjectured what the limits are.

   The point here is that it may be necessary for the retinal image to have a systematic relation to the physical object producing it if that object is to be perceived veridically. If this is true, it would provide a further constraint on any theory that attributes perceiving to learning, since perceptual learning might not be possible unless certain preconditions are met. These preconditions in turn reflect the native (phylogenetically developed) characteristics of the organism. These ideas have been explored by means of *rearrangement* experiments in which the normal relation between the retinal image and the distal stimulus is altered in some way. Thus, as we have seen, a prism might be placed in front of the eye, thereby causing the positions of objects to change. A number of tests are performed before and after this rearrangement to determine whether exposure to it has produced any sign of perceptual learning. An understanding of the mechanisms underlying such perceptual learning may provide a basis for a theory of perceptual development.

REINVERSION OF THE RETINAL IMAGE

A classic account of the effects of exposure to a rearranged visual stimulus was written by Stratton (1896, 1897). In his remarkable experiments Stratton wore a Galilean telescope of unity power (see Figure 11–5) over one eye, and blindfolded the other. In one experiment he wore the device for three days, and then again for eight days in a repetition of the earlier experiment. The telescope had the effect of reinverting the retinal image. Though the normal retinal image is upside down relative to objects in the world, the reinverted retinal image is right side up.

Stratton performed his experiment to resolve an old controversy. When it was finally proved that the normal retinal image is inverted, many people reasoned that there would have to be some reinversion of the neural representation of the image—otherwise the world would appear to be upside down.. As Rock (1966) has so aptly argued, however, there is

Figure 11–5. The principle of the Galilean telescope. Unlike the normal image, which is upside down, the retinal image of an object viewed through a Galilean telescope is erect.

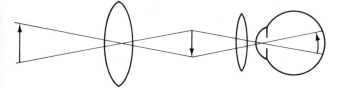

nothing inherent in an upside-down image that would require us to see things as upside down. As did Berkeley before him, Rock reasoned that the terms "up" and "down" are purely relativistic. "Up" is in the direction of the head and the sky, and "down" is in the direction of the feet and the ground. All these relations are preserved when the retinal image is reinverted by a Galilean telescope. When looking through such a device, one can see his hand reaching toward the sky, and his feet in contact with the ground. Since he also accepted these arguments, Stratton tried to demonstrate that the world can appear normal even with a reinverted retinal image.

Of course, when one first looks through a telescope of this type, everything does appear to be upside down. If all the identifying features of verticality are preserved in such transformation, why should the world appear to be inverted? One answer to this question—though by no means the only answer—is that the visual information is in conflict with information from the other senses.

According to Stratton, the conflict comes about because in the course of normal development a particular visual direction or retinal local sign becomes associated with other sensory information. Thus, when a point lies off to the right of the direction of gaze, it is imaged in the temporal hemiretina of the left eye and in the nasal hemiretina of the right eye. When one reaches for this object, his hand extends also out toward the right, so that the sensed position of the hand becomes associated with the stimulation of particular retinal places. Now, when the telescope is worn, the image is rotated through an angle of 180 degrees. This means that the top of the object is imaged on the upper half of the retina, and the bottom is imaged on the lower half. Moreover, the left side of the image is in the left hemiretina, and the right half is in the right hemiretina. Hence, an object off to the right of the direction of gaze will now be imaged in the nasal hemiretina of the left eye and in the temporal hemiretina of the right eye—i.e., just the opposite of what would occur without the telescope. If one were to reach out and grasp the object, though, he would still have to reach out to the right. The proprioception from the arm would therefore be in a novel relation to the retinal position of the image of the object, and this relation might be experienced as a conflict. Thus, e.g., one may see his arm reaching out in one direction and feel it as reaching out in the opposite direction.

Similar points may be made about the other senses: thus, one may hear a tone coming from the right but see its source on the left. Again, the static position of the head relative to the gravitational vertical is sensed by the receptor organs in the inner ear.* This enables one to ascertain even in the dark whether his head is tilted. When one wears Stratton's telescope he may have to tilt his head down to look at an object that is above his head. Once again, this is in conflict with the normal or customary situation in which one tilts the head down to look at an object lying below it.

According to Stratton, when one has had enough time and experience with the telescope he should establish a new set of associations between the different sense modalities. Thus, reaching to the right should ultimately follow naturally from stimulation of points on the right hemiretinas. When a bell sounds on the left, one should naturally turn his head to the right to look at it; one should roll his eyes down to look up at the moon. When such behavior becomes natural, the world should once again appear to be normal to the observer.

What actually did happen to Stratton in the course of his experiment? At first everything appeared to be quite abnormal. If he saw an object off to the right, he would reach for it with his right hand and discover that he should have reached for it with his left hand. He could not feed himself very well, could not tie his shoelaces without considerable difficulty, and found himself to be severely disoriented in general. His image of his own body became severely distorted. At times he felt that his head had sunk down between his shoulders, and when he moved his eyes and head the world would slide dizzyingly around. The normal position constancy of objects was destroyed. Of course, the world appeared to be upside down.

As time went by, Stratton achieved more effective control over his body. He would reach with his left hand when he saw an object on the right. He could accomplish normal tasks like eating and dressing himself. His body image became almost normal, and objects did not appear to move about so much when he changed the positions of his eyes and head. He even began to feel as though his left hand was on the right and his right hand on the left. As long as this new localization of his body was vivid, the world appeared to be right side up. Frequently, however, he

---

* The otoliths in the inner ear are concretions of calcium capable of bending hair cells that send nerve impulses to the brain and thereby indicate deviations of the head from an erect position.

would experience his own body as upside down in a visually right-side-up world. The visual world became the standard within which he localized his body.

At the end of the eighth day Stratton removed his telescope. Although the world had a strange appearance, it now appeared to be right side up. He made incorrect reaching movements, though, and the world once again seemed to move about when he shifted the positions of his eyes and head. From his observations he concluded that if he had only been able to wear the apparatus for a sufficiently long period of time the world would have come to be entirely normal in appearance.

Stratton was not the only person to perform experiments of this kind. Similar apparatus was employed, e.g., by Ewert (1930) and two subjects, who wore a binocular set of telescopes for about 14 days. These experiments took place in the heyday of Watsonian behaviorism, when reports on the appearance of the world would have been "unscientific." Accordingly, Ewert's paper tells us largely about the recovery of sensorimotor co-ordination in the course of the experiment. As we shall see later, the binocular apparatus produces special problems that might well inhibit adaptation effects.

Snyder (Snyder and Pronko, 1952) wore a similar apparatus for 30 days. Here, too, the emphasis was on sensorimotor co-ordination, but Snyder was less reluctant to comment on the appearance of things. Naturally, in 30 days he recovered his ability to get about in the world very nicely, and was able even to drive an automobile. Moreover, toward the end of his experiment, Snyder was not particularly aware that the world appeared to be inverted, though, if he were asked about how things "looked" he became aware of the fact that the world was upside down.

There is still considerable controversy about what actually happened to the perceived orientation of the world during these experiments. According to several authors, Stratton proved that the visual world comes to be right side up after wearing his device for a sufficiently long period of time. Other authors, particularly Walls (1951a) and Harris (1965), have argued forcefully that nothing of the sort happened—on the ground that what actually happened is that the proprioceptive sense, not the orientation of the visual world, changed. Thus, if the left hand in Stratton's experiment came to feel as though it were on the right, this is not to say that the right visual field came to appear to be on the left. Yet either transformation would produce the same effects, according to this theory of adjustment through modification of the felt position of the parts of the

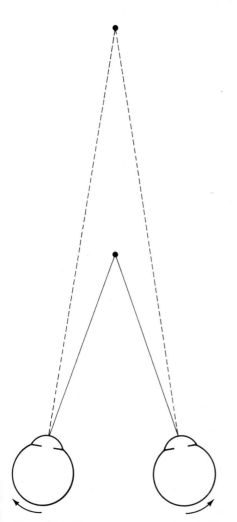

Figure 11–6. The eyes converge when looking from far to near.

body. The theory appears to be quite consistent with reports given by Stratton, by Snyder, and by Ewert, though in direct conflict with Berkeley's idea that touch educates vision. Walls and Harris are asserting quite the opposite of this thesis, suggesting rather that vision is predominant over the touch and kinesthetic senses.

One reason for the attractiveness of this point of view is that there are real anatomical reasons for asserting that there is a fixed inborn rela-

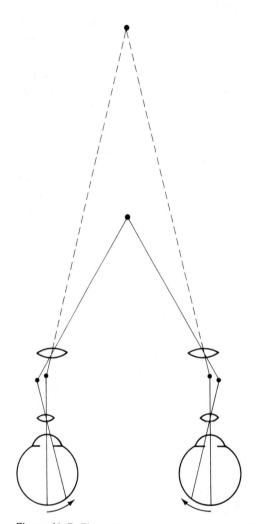

Figure 11–7. The eyes must diverge when looking from far to near while wearing Galilean telescopes.

tion between visual directions and retinal positions. For example, the normally inverted (rotated through 180 degrees relative to the object) retinal images are necessary if vergence of the eyes is to make it possible to maintain singleness of vision. Figure 11–6 shows how the eyes must turn to get disparate half-images into the foveas when these eyes try to fixate a near object after having looked at a very distant object. It is obvious that convergence must increase to get the two temporal half-images to slide toward the foveas. When binocular Galilean telescopes (which reinvert the retinal images) are worn, the half-images of a near object will be in the nasal hemiretinas (as seen in Fig. 11–7) while fixating a very distant object. Under these circumstances the eyes will have to diverge to include the half-images of the near object in the foveas. As Helmholtz (1925) showed a century ago, the eyes cannot diverge more than a very small amount. This appears to be a built-in limitation. Consequently, as Ewert (1930) has verified, it is not possible to eliminate double vision in the near distance while wearing the apparatus. The clinical evidence is very clear that one simply does not adapt to such misalignment of the eyes; rather, a victim of such disorder may suppress vision altogether in one eye—a condition known as *amblyopia ex anopsia*. Moreover, as Wiesel and Hubel (1965) have shown, artificially produced misalignment of the eyes of a kitten can produce destruction of cortical units in the visual areas of the brain.

There are still other reasons for believing that there are fixed inborn relations between visual directions and retinal positions. Schlodtmann (1902) tested three children who had congenital cataracts and who had never once had patterned visual experiences. He pressed against the sclera of their eyeballs with the wooden end of a small penholder, since such mechanical pressure against a normal retina produces the sensation of a small spot of light known as a *pressure phosphene*. (In fact, this procedure may be employed to discover whether a person who is blind because of cataract still has an intact and functioning retina so as to justify a surgical procedure for removal of the cataract.) Now, Schlodtmann's chil-

Figure 11–8. Difference between an image rotated through 180 degrees and one inverted by a mirror.

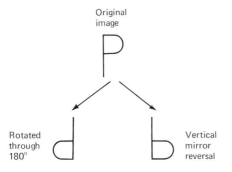

Original image

Rotated through 180°

Vertical mirror reversal

dren all reported seeing a small distinctive spot of light when pressure was applied. Moreover, the spot could be localized by the children relative to parts of their own bodies. Pressure in the upper half of the eyeball moved the children to say that the spot was nearer the chin than the forehead; pressure on the right half of the eyeball they stated to be nearer the left hand than the right hand. Thus, the localizations of the children relative to their own bodies were exactly what one would predict if the normal inverted retinal image were associated with inborn local signs. Even though they had no prior visual experience, different points on their retinas were within a frame of reference provided by the body as a whole.

MIRROR REVERSAL OF THE RETINAL IMAGE

Figure 11–8 shows the difference between a reinverted image rotated through 180 degrees, and a vertical mirror reversal of the same image. In the latter case the top and bottom of the image are interchanged while the left and right sides of the image are in their normal locations. Mirror reversal of the retinal image was studied by Erismann and by Ivo Kohler (Kohler, 1964) with an optical device invented by Erismann and von Kundratitz and illustrated in Figure 11–9. Although Kohler did not men-

Figure 11–9. Mirror-inverting apparatus worn by the subjects of Erismann and Kohler (Kohler, 1964). Since the occluder blocks the direct view of the world, the observer must look over it into the mirror.

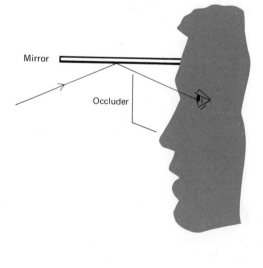

tion the problem of convergence discussed above, this problem is avoided with vertical mirror reversal of the image. Objects on the left of the direction of gaze are still imaged on the right hemiretinas, as in the normal situation; but objects above the direction of gaze are imaged in the upper half of the retinas, and objects below the direction of gaze are imaged in the lower half of the retina. In addition to avoiding the problem of inappropriate vergence, this new device made it possible for the subject to have a wide field of view—about 80 degrees—and a clear view of his own body. The Galilean telescope gave a much narrower field of view, and therefore hid objects not in the vicinity of the direction of gaze.

In 1947 von Kundratitz wore the mirror apparatus for six days. At first he had to be escorted about, since he had considerable difficulty with his sensorimotor co-ordination. On the fourth day, however, he could ride a bicycle and, on the sixth day, went skiing. It would appear that adaptation is much easier with this device than with the telescope. After the device was removed, objects seen in a uniform field without visible boundaries were occasionally reported to be inverted, although they were actually right side up. This would appear to indicate that the retinal position associated with the visual "up" was becoming associated with the visual "down" as a result of the perceptual learning that took place during the experiment.

In another experiment, an observer wore the device for ten days. When this observer reached for and touched an object, it suddenly appeared to be right side up even though it had appeared to be inverted just prior to reaching for it. In this case the observer's hands were the first objects to be seen in an upright position, and the object being reached for followed them. When this same subject read letters they were frequently reversed, as when an *m* was read as a *w*. After two or three days, these reversals did not occur.

Other observations made by Kohler indicated that perceptual adaptation proceeds in a piecemeal manner. Some objects come to be seen as right side up while other objects were still upside down. Finally, however, observers reported completely correct perceptions.

Before the reader hastens to the conclusion that Kohler proved that the adult effectively replaces his customary modes of visual perception with new modes, it must be noted that the evidence is still not clear. We shall consider alternative explanations that depend upon the shaping of proprioception by the exposure condition, but first let us examine one theory consistent with the idea that one learns to perceive visually.

THE EFFERENT READINESS THEORY OF PERCEPTION

J. G. Taylor (1962) hoped to embrace the results obtained by Kohler with a more general empiricist theory of visual perception. According to Taylor, any perception is merely the complex set of simultaneous readinesses to respond behaviorally to objects affecting the sense organs. Thus, perception is not a picture formed on an inner screen by the sense organs. The sensory events produce readinesses to respond—tendencies toward efference—which themselves comprise the perception. That is to say, even though the sensory input were cut off, if the same efferent tendencies were present, the observer would report that he is perceiving.

As Taylor holds, readinesses to respond to features of the environment are parts of conditioned responses. Thus, if the eye is confronted by a straight line, eye movement along a straight path may be needed to keep a segment of the line in the fovea while scanning it, and consequently the perceived straightness of the line may be attributed to the tendency or readiness to respond to such a stimulus by a class of eye movements. Even if the eyes do not move in viewing the line (as in a brief exposure), the line appears to be straight because of the aroused readiness to respond to it with a particular kind of eye movement.

Taylor (1962) tested this idea by wearing contact lenses that effectively bent horizontal lines. The bending was produced by the wedge prisms contained in the lenses, as is explained in Figure 11–4. Although when first viewed through the prisms the line appeared to be bent, after scanning the line by moving the eyes it gradually came to appear to be straight. In one experiment, 20 seconds of scanning was sufficient to produce complete straightening of the line. Essentially the same results were reported by Festinger, Burnham, Ono, and Bamber (1967), who came to the conclusion that efferent signals to the eye muscles determine the perception. A small amount of practice changes their signals and therefore the perception.

Lest the reader think that the repertoire of possible efferent activity is not sufficient to account for the richness of visual experience, he should be aware of the fact that programming of verbal activity is part of that repertoire. The shades and nuances of speech activity are innumerable. Taylor believes that perceptual changes could very well be attributed to a reprogramming of verbal behavior as well as walking, or reaching and maintaining postural control. Moreover, since different responses may be conditioned at different times, the piecemeal adaptation reported by Kohler is to be expected.

If we accept the definition that perception itself is the set of simultaneous readinesses to respond, it is not at all difficult to imagine that visual perception might change in the course of an adaptation experiment. As things stand now, however, there are no grounds for accepting this interpretation and excluding alternative explanations of perceptual change. Indeed, it is not at all clear that certain alternative theories we shall consider are truly incompatible with Taylor's theory. One of the problems with Taylor's theory, however, is that it is difficult to make unique predictions from it about the outcome of rearrangement experiments (Harris, 1965).

REAFFERENCE AND THE EFFERENT COPY

Motor behavior has always figured largely in theories of perceptual learning. In the theories of Taylor and of Festinger it is the programming of motor behavior that determines the perceptions of an observer. In the older theories it was the feedback from the motor behavior itself that determined visual perception. Thus, Lotze's original idea was that the spatial value of a retinal point—its local sign (see page 293)—is determined by how far the eye must rotate to get an image from that point into the center of the fovea. Presumably the sensation of eye movement magnitude becomes associated with the visual sensation arising from stimulation of the original point to give it its local sign. Thus, visual space is constructed by the association of visual sensations with proprioceptive sensations by virtue of their frequent occurrence together.

Nowadays we have more sophisticated ideas of how motor behavior may figure in perceptual learning. First of all, it is strongly doubted that any significant sensations arise from the extraocular muscles (see p. 260). Therefore, it is unlikely that perceptual learning occurs through the association of visual sensations and sensations arising in muscle stretch receptors.

If muscle receptors are not providing the input, then why does the world appear to be stationary during eye movements? One theory designed to explain this phenomenon is that the movement of the image on the retina is compared with a copy of the signal sent out to the eye muscles by the brain. If the movement of the image is predicted by the copy of the efferent signal, then the brain interprets the image movement as being due to the eye movement. If the copy of the efferent signal and the image movement are discordant, however, the brain interprets the displacement of the image as belonging to the distal object.

The foregoing theory was anticipated by many investigators. Nowadays, it is associated with von Holst (1954; see also von Holst and Mittelstaedt, 1950), who gave it its present formulation. Von Holst utilized the term *reafference* to stand for sensory events produced by self-initiated movements of the sense organs. He used the term *exafference* to stand for sensory events produced by the displacements or changes in the stimulus itself. According to von Holst, a copy of the signals sent to the eyes to initiate their movements plays a role similar to that of proprioception in older theories. It is the relation between this *efferent copy* and the *reafferent* signal that may be modified in the course of perceptual learning and development.

Richard Held and his associates have produced an impressive body of literature in their attempt to account for perceptual learning in terms of reafference and the efferent copy. In the course of pursuing this program, Held and Bossom (1961) introduced the term *rearrangement* to stand for the experimental condition in which the normal relation between the distal and proximal stimuli is altered.

One approach used by Held and his associates to measure the effect of rearrangement on perception involved the *negative aftereffect* of the exposure condition. Suppose that a person wears a prism in front of his eye, as shown in Figure 11-1. At first, objects physically straight ahead of him will appear to be off to one side. Now if the visual space becomes reoriented relative to the observer as a result of his continually wearing the prism, these displaced objects will no longer appear to be off to one side. In fact, with complete adjustment to the rearrangement condition, objects physically straight ahead of the subject—i.e., in line with his nose —should appear to be straight ahead of him. Now, with removal of the prism these same objects would be perceived as being off to one side, since the perceived direction to objects has been changed by the adaptation to the rearrangement. Moreover, the direction of this shift in apparent displacement should be opposite the direction of the displacement originally produced by the prism.

In their actual experiment Held and his associates had observers orient themselves to a luminous slit of light in a darkened room so that the slit appeared to be straight ahead. This was done before attaching a set of prisms in front of the eyes and immediately thereafter. Thus, in an ex-

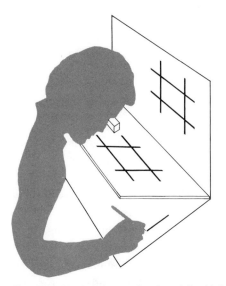

Figure 11–10. Apparatus developed by Held and Gottlieb (1958). The observer can see the virtual image of the square pattern in the mirror but cannot see his hand under it while he is trying to make marks in line with the corners of the square. The effect of having seen his hand moving with the mirror removed can be measured by noting the changes in the positions of the marks when the mirror is restored to its position.

periment by Held and Bossom (1961), observers wore two prisms—one over each eye—for about one hour. Half the observers walked around while viewing the environment; the rest were wheeled about in a wheel chair. At it turned out, the freely moving observers exhibited a significant negative aftereffect: they had apparently adjusted to wearing the prisms to a significant degree since the judged straight-ahead was altered. The wheel chair observers, however, did not exhibit a significant degree of compensation.

In an earlier experiment Held and Hein (1958), using an apparatus designed by Held and Gottleib (1958; see Fig. 11–10), employed a similar methodology to study adaptation to rearrangement under somewhat more constrained conditions. Rather than allow the observer to move his entire body about, they studied the role of active movements of the arm in producing adaptation. The observer saw the reflected image of a square in the mirror shown in Figure 11–10. The mirror served to hide the observer's own hand from his view. His task was to make a mark with the pencil on the paper under the mirror so that the marks would coincide with the seen positions of the corners of the square. Once this was accomplished, the mirror was removed and the observer then looked at his arm through a prism. In this experiment the observers were divided into three groups. Members of one group simply looked at their stationary hands and forearms through the prism. Members of another group moved the hands and forearms from side to side, and these movements were self-initiated. Members of the third group had their forearms tied to a flat board, and the board was swiveled by the experimenter so that the hand and forearm could be seen through the prism moving from side to side; the resulting movements were not self-initiated.

After exposure to these conditions, the observers were tested once again with the mirror in place, by making dots in positions that seemed to correspond to the visual positions of the corners of the square. Let us assume that the prism caused the hand to appear to be shifted to the right of its actual position. If the hand's exposure through the prism resulted in a correction of the perceived position of the hand, then the new position would be shifted to the left, relative to its originally displaced position. Therefore, with the mirror back in place, the marks on the paper beneath the mirror should be shifted to the left of their positions prior to the exposure.

Held and Hein found that the observers able to move their hands freely from side to side exhibited this adaptation effect. The magnitude of the shift was approximately one-third of the original deviation produced by the prism. The other two groups—those whose hands were kept stationary and those whose hands were moved for them—did not exhibit a significant degree of adjustment.

Hein and Held (1962), Held (1965), and Held and Freedman (1963) have furnished summaries of how Held would explain the foregoing results in terms of reafference and its relation to the efferent copy. According to this theory, adaptation to rearrangement must be due to a change in the relation between the efferent copy and reafference. In an adult the efferent copy must have a particular relation to the reafferent signal if the world is to appear normal. Thus, when the eyes are instructed to move to a particular position, the resulting reafferent signal produced by the gliding of the image across the retina will normally have a particular (though unspecified) and invariant relation to the copy of the efferent signal that produced the original eye movement. Thus, the efferent copy and the reafference have a customary correlation as a result of the constant association of the two in the course of development.

In a rearrangement experiment the efferent copy and the reafference are decorrelated. Specific arm movements that previously caused the arm to appear at a particular place in the visual field no longer do so, but rather place the arm at some other visual position. If this new arrangement should persist over time, however, the efferent copy of the instruction to the arm can become associated with the new visual reafference. When this recorrelation is established, the world appears to be normal once again. Moreover, once this new relation is established between the efferent copy and the reafference, removal of the rearranging device—e.g., the prism— results in an abnormal appearance of the world. Hence the negative after-effect.

Since only self-initiated movements of the eyes, limbs, and other parts of the body can produce efferent copies, it is to be expected that adaptation will occur only when the observer voluntarily moves parts of his own body. That is why observers who could initiate their own movements exhibit adaptation. Moreover, Held believes that normal development of the organism requires self-initiated movements accompanied by reafferent feedback. It is the development of correlations between efferent copies and reafferent signals that makes co-ordinated sensorimotor behavior possible.

The kitten carousel experiment of Held and Hein (1963) is consistent with this point of view. In this lovely experiment kittens were reared in the dark except for those periods when they were exposed to the conditions of the experiment. During exposure one kitten was carried in a gondola, and another kitten was free to walk about in the same striped environment as shown in Figure 11–11. Because of the nature of the apparatus shown in this figure, the movements of the locomoting kitten were duplicated by the gondola in which the passively moving kitten rode, which meant that the visual stimulation of the passively moving kitten was essentially the same as that experienced by the locomoting kitten. In von Holst's terms, the passive kitten received only exafference, the locomoting kitten received only reafference.

After several weeks of exposure to these conditions for a period of about three hours per day, the kittens were tested. When normal kittens are moved toward a surface, they tend to anticipate contacting the surface by extending their limbs. This placing response was found to occur readily in the kitten who moved freely while the passively moved kitten did not produce the placing response. More, the passively moved kitten did not blink its eyes when an object was moved rapidly toward it, but

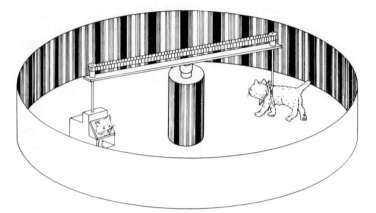

Figure 11–11. Kitten carousel experiment of Held and Hein (1963).

the locomoting kitten did produce this normal response. Finally, when placed on the visual cliff (see p. 456, and Fig. 11–15) the locomoting kitten exhibited behavior indicating that he discriminated between the deep and shallow sides of the cliff while the passive kitten did not. This suggests that depth discrimination may have been affected by the exposure conditions.

One conclusion to be drawn from the experiment is that self-initiated movement accompanied by consistent visual reafference is basic to normal development of sensorimotor co-ordination. And yet one cannot conclude that visual perception is learned, since this theory does not clearly differentiate between sensorimotor co-ordination and visual perception. An equally plausible conclusion is that kinesthesis may be inappropriately related to vision but that either of these modalities can function well independently of each other. After all, the kittens did get along well in the dark. Moreover, people blind from birth develop good motor functions, and people paralyzed from the neck down perceive a visual world.

It would appear that an appropriate interpretation of Held's theory is that one does not necessarily *learn* to see, touch, or hear, but that the relation between sensory and motor activity is modifiable; and moreover, that when motor outflow matches reafference from several simultaneously active sense organs, the motor outflow co-ordinates the diverse sensory inputs. This interpretation differs from that given it by others (e.g., Rock, 1966)—no doubt by reason of the ambiguity in the theory itself.

One problem to be faced concerns the requirement for self-produced movement if adaptation is to occur. Held does not believe that all adaptation requires self-produced movements, but that self-initiated movements still play an important role in development. Thus, one may simply look at a straight line through a prism and ultimately come to perceive the optically distorted line as straight. Moreover, after removal of the prism the straight distal line will look curved in the opposite direction. This, the *Gibson aftereffect,* may occur without noticeable movements of the body or the eyes. It may well be that such phenomena are not important in the development of visual perception but simply reflect other properties of the visual system. In addition to the Gibson aftereffect, however, there are very likely other effects associated with the movement of the body.

Held and Rekosh (1963) placed their prism-wearing observers in a darkened, cylindrical room. The wall of the room was covered with a random array of luminous round spots, so that there were no straight edges in the field of view that could appear to be curved when viewed through the prisms. In this experiment some observers walked about in the cylindrical room; others were wheeled about in a wheel chair. Afterward all observers viewed straight lines through a variable-strength prism, adjusting the strength of the prism until the lines appeared to be straight. On this test the active observers did not perceive the lines as straight unless the prism produced some degree of curvature. The average amount of curvature was the same as that produced by a prism displacing points by about 2 degrees. This corresponds to a prism strength of 3.5 prism diopters (see Figure 11–1). Thus, these observers showed a curvature aftereffect that was not dependent upon exposure to an apparently curved line. The observers who were wheeled about, however, did not show an aftereffect, but perceived straight lines as straight.

The magnitude of the effect found by Held and Rekosh is much greater than that reported by Gibson. Since the Gibson aftereffect is of itself not sufficient to account for such changes they were forced to conclude that active movements causing systematic time-varying changes in a scene are sufficient to produce distortion in subsequent perception of curvature. But the story does not end here. Though active movement on the part of the observer may be sufficient to produce adaptation, it is by no means clear that this is necessary.

Weinstein, Sersen, Fisher, and Weisinger (1964) performed an experiment similar to the one by Held and Bossom (1961), but their wheelchair observers gave the same amount of adaptation as their active observers. The reasons for this inconsistency with the results of Held and

Bossom are obscure, but there were several differences in the experimental procedure.

Wallach, Kravitz, and Lindauer (1963) had observers simply look at their feet through a prism for 10 minutes, but not move about. Nevertheless, on a subsequent test observers could point correctly at targets viewed through the displacing prism. This test confirmed the qualitative observation that when viewed through the prism the observer's torso and legs appeared to be displaced at an angle from the vertical and then, after a few minutes, appeared almost abruptly to be truly vertical.

There is reason to believe that the adaptation found by Wallach, Kravitz, and Lindauer was associated with a tilting of the eyes in the head. McLaughlin and Webster (1967) obtained direct photographic evidence of the fact that the eyes do turn in the head when the observer is asked to look straight ahead after wearing prisms. Still, there is no evidence that maintenance of a constant posture or a constant position of the eyes is associated with the generation of an efferent copy. Presumably this copy is generated only when an order is sent out to an appendage to change its position. Thus, even though a prism adaptation may be associated with maintenance of a new constant postural state, this is not necessarily consistent with Held's theory.

It should be mentioned that even though an experiment does show that adaptation may occur without apparent overt movements of the body, this does not prove that such movements, or other factors related to the movements, do not play an important role in adaptation. Most investigators are agreed that adaptation is usually more rapid when self-initiated movements occur; and this suggests that one cannot simply reject Held's theory.

THE REORGANIZATION OF PROPRIOCEPTIVE SPACE

One of the problems with most experiments dealing with adaptation phenomena is their sheer complexity. Thus, while Held asserts that adaptation comes about through a recorrelation of efferent copy and reafference, others say with apparently equal justice that it comes about through a reorganization of vision. Still others hold to the view that proprioception changes. The reason for this diversity of opinion is that all of these factors —outflow, visual perception, and proprioception—are involved in all of the experiments.

Charles Harris (1965) has made a convincing case for the notion that adaptation occurs through a modification of the felt position of the body or its parts. This is in direct conflict with the theory that touch and motor behavior educate vision—the assumption that looms so large in the thinking of the early empiricists. Before we can deal adequately with Harris' approach to this problem it would be well to review some of the data dealing with the relation between vision and the other senses, particularly proprioception.

Berkeley, one of the first to theorize about the co-ordination of sensory information, believed that one learns to see the third dimension by means of touch—possibly by reason of the general intuition that there is something more "real" about palpated objects than there is about seen objects. That is, the grasped object is contacted directly, while it is merely sensed at a distance by vision. This, of course, is an absurd thesis, since both touching and seeing produce sensory information, and what we make of this information depends upon properties of the nervous system. There is no good theoretical reason for ascribing primacy to the sense of touch —nor, for that matter, is there any good theoretical reason for ascribing primacy to vision. And yet passive touch and sensations arising from active movements of parts of the body have been considered to be primary even though, in point of fact, empirical data suggest instead that vision predominates over these bodily sensations.

In his researches mentioned above, Gibson (1933) reported the experience of his observer Janet Goldschmidt, who wore a pair of prism spectacles for four days without taking them off except to sleep. Now although, as shown in Figure 11–4, it is characteristic of prisms that they cause lines in the visual field to appear to be curved, Goldschmidt reported after wearing the prisms for some time that the curved lines tended to appear as straight; and that, moreover, upon removal of the prisms straight lines appeared to be curved in the opposite direction—a negative aftereffect. This negative aftereffect of exposure to curvature we called the *Gibson aftereffect* above.

Following these initial observations, Gibson performed a more systematic experiment with several observers. It had occurred to him that his curvature aftereffect might be due to a conflict between kinesthesis and vision. Thus, if a meter stick were seen as curved but felt to be straight, and if vision were dominated by kinesthesis, then the kinesthetic sensations might lead to a visually straightened meter stick. Gibson rejected this explanation virtually at the outset of his experiment, on the ground that, when the prisms were first worn, an apparently curved meter stick was experienced as curved when it was touched. So long as the hand was watched while it ran along the length of the meter stick, observers felt the stick to be curved: there was no noticeable conflict in the sensations of touch and vision. When the eyes were turned away, however, the meter stick was experienced as straight. Still as Gibson commented, "This dominance of the visual over the kinesthetic perception was so complete that when subjects were instructed to make a strong effort to dissociate the two, i.e., to 'feel it straight and see it curved,' it was reported either difficult or impossible to do so" (1933, p. 5).

Tastevin (1937) had his observer look at a plaster replica of the observer's own finger. This cast protruded from under a cloth, and his own finger was hidden from view some distance away from it. The plaster finger was made to move in step with the observer's own finger. The observer believed that the plaster finger was his own, attributing his tactual sensations to it. Following Tastevin's nomenclature, Hay, Pick, and Ikeda (1965) labeled this phenomenon *visual capture*, since the visual sense determined the localization of tactual occurrences. Visual capture occurs when the visual sense predominates over other kinds of sensory information in a conflict situation.

In their experiment, Hay and company let observers view their hand through a 14-degree displacing prism. Hidden from view beneath the visible hand they had an array of thirty pushbuttons. With his invisible hand each observer had to select and press the button he believed to be directly underneath the visible hand. For this task the observers used two criteria: first, they pressed the button they believed to be below the location of the visible hand; and second, they pressed the button that appeared to be below the felt position of the visible hand and tried to ignore its visual location. Control measures were also taken with the eyes blindfolded.

The results demonstrated a visual capture effect. There was no significant difference between the judged visual location of the hand and the judged felt location of the visible hand. The displacement of the felt position of the hand was about 8.6 degrees in the direction of the seen displacement produced by the prism. This may be compared with the localization of the hand with eyes covered. The average constant error in this case was only 0.7 degree, and the variability in judgment was about the same as when the hand was visible. The authors concluded that visual capture may be the source of proprioceptive adaptation. The "felt" position of the hand was determined by what the observer saw.

Rock and Victor (1964) showed that vision can be predominant over kinesthesis even when the hand itself cannot be seen. In their demonstration they presented a square object to a subject, and he was to look at it through a special lens capable of making the square smaller in one dimension than the other. That is, the square appeared to be a rectangle with one side twice the length of the other side. The subject in this experiment reached into the box containing the square and was able to touch and grasp it through a black silk cloth, so that his own hand was invisible to him while he was grasping the visible rectangle. In other words, the tactual sensations corresponded to that of a square while the visual impression was that of a rectangle.

The observers in this experiment drew a picture of the object they were touching and seeing. In every case the drawn object was rectangular in shape, and on the average, one side of the drawn rectangle was twice the size of the other side. This corresponded to the ratios in the distorted image of the square and suggested to Rock and Victor that vision is predominant over touch. Their conclusion was supported by two control experiments. In one, in which the square was viewed but not touched, the results were similar to those obtained when the square was both seen and touched. In the second, the square was touched and not seen. Here the response of the observer indicated that the touched object was a true square.

It would appear from all the foregoing data, and from other data as well (e.g., Hay and Pick, 1966), that vision predominates over touch—contrary to the beliefs of the early thinkers in this field. While this conclusion seems reasonable, one or two reservations had best be kept in mind. For one thing, the relation between touch and vision has been studied under a limited number of circumstances. All the visual stimuli were changed in curvature, position, or size by prisms or lenses; and the proximal stimuli contained the same number of corners as the distal stimuli—i.e., in short were conformal transformations of the distal stimuli. What if the observer were able to see his finger move around a sharp corner while there was no tactual input corresponding to moving around a corner? It is a bit hard to believe that if this kind of sensory discordance were present, touch would still be captured by vision. It may well be that in this kind of experiment, with touch and vision providing conflicting information about the presence of discontinuities, instances would be found in which the sensory information in different modalities could be independently responded to. Moreover, it may even be possible to find differences in stimulation enabling touch to capture vision. This, of course, remains to be tested in future experiments.

A second problem associated with the experiments reported here is that of criteria. It may well be that observers tend to respond in pictorial terms. Thus, in the effort to reproduce stimuli by drawing them, as in the Rock and Victor experiment, the observers may represent their memory for the visual form in the drawing. This does not prove that the tactual experience was not registered at some level within the nervous system. This tactual impression could in fact be no different from what it is when visual experience is excluded. As we saw in Chapter 7, cues may be registered without the observer's awareness and still influence his perception. Even when the observer responded in the Rock and Victor experiment by selecting one object tactually from an array of objects touched in sequence he could have based his judgment on a visual memory. This does not prove that vision captured touch, but means only that the observer responds in terms of a visual impression and does not employ the information obtained through his sense of touch. Rock (1966) refers to this as a "visualization" of the stimulus.

This interpretation is applicable to Gibson's observations of "felt" curvature as well. If a person runs his finger along a physically straight edge which is visually curved by a prism, his task is really to describe the nature of the edge. The observer will note that the edge "feels" curved when he looks at the edge while touching it. This does not prove that his tactual sensations now actually correspond to those that would be present if the edge were physically curved; rather it means that the only way in which he can describe the edge is in terms of the visual memory of it. In the presence of visual stimulation, the tactual information is not available to help him describe the edge. This does not prove that the tactual information was altered in some way by the visual information; it is just that his criterion of judgment was biased by the visual impression.

All this leads to an alternative interpretation of the visual capture data. That is, the judgment of a shape or a size is accomplished more accurately by visual means than by tactual means. The two sense modalities are essentially independent. When information is available from both modalities simultaneously, and when the observer is asked to describe the object, his description is likely to be based upon the information derived from the visual modality. This may happen even if he is asked to ignore his visual impression and respond solely in terms of his tactual impressions. Since vision is more accurate than touch, and since pictorial description is more commonly employed than tactual description, it is not surprising that the observer effectively ignores the instruction. It is conceivable that, by careful training and manipulation of his motivation, the observer would be able to reflect his tactual impressions in his judgment. Thus, all the experiments we have been describing obtained essentially negative results. And since it is not possible to conclude from a negative result that a positive result could not be achieved under other circumstances, instead of "visual capture" the term "visual bias in response" might be more appropriate to describe these experiments.

Despite these reservations, more direct support for the notion that proprioception can be modified by visual experience is furnished by experiments by Harris (1963), Hamilton (1964), and Mikaelian (1963). In essence these investigators found that when one views his moving hand through a wedge prism, as in the experiment by Held and Hein (1958), the adaptation does not transfer to the other unseen hand. In this Held and Hein experiment the hand was hidden from view by a mirror after the exposure period; and yet, despite the fact that the hand could not be seen, the observer tended to move his hand too far toward one side when marking the corners of the visible square. This aftereffect was not found when the other hand was employed. Moreover, if the observer were required also to point in the direction of a sound, his unseen adapted hand would exhibit the same error as when pointing in the direction of a visual stimulus, whereas the unadapted hand would not make this error (Harris, 1963). This data suggested that if anything at all changed in the course of the exposure condition, it was the felt position of the arm.

Harris (1965) reanalyzed the results of Stratton and of Kohler in terms of the modification of proprioception. His interpretation of these phenomena is nicely illustrated with a hypothetical experiment in which the left and right directions are reversed by some optical means. Thus, as shown in Figure 11-12a, a blackboard containing the letters L and R is facing the observer. Due to the optical device, the initial appearance of the blackboard is similar to that shown in Figure 11-12b. Assuming that the observer is right-handed, when he raises his right hand to write on the blackboard he feels the hand on the right side of his body. Prior to adaptation this felt position of the hand is on the same side of the blackboard as the letter R. Immediately after he had donned the rearrangement device, however, the felt position of the right hand is on the same side as the backward L on the blackboard (Figure 11-12b). As adaptation proceeds—say, by having the observer write on the blackboard with

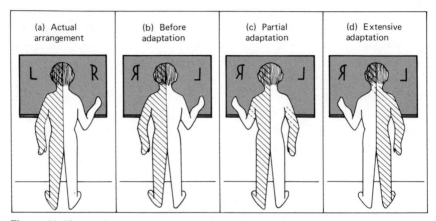

Figure 11–12. Harris' explanation of adaptation to optical rearrangement. (After Harris, 1965)

his right hand—he gradually comes to feel his right hand and arm shift toward the left, since he sees his hand in the vicinity of the backward R on the board. This shift may be due to the visual-capture effect discussed above. When adaptation is complete, as in Figure 11-12*d*, the felt position of the hand corresponds to the seen position of the letter R.

As Harris' subject writes on the blackboard, the portions of his body most involved in the task are his hand and arm, though, other parts are involved also to some degree. He must co-ordinate the behavior of his shoulder; he must maintain an appropriate over-all posture and balance; and he undoubtedly turns his head and eyes to compensate for the prism. Thus, with further adaptation the felt locations of the torso, head, arms, and legs may be altered. Now he can perform other functions that demonstrate co-ordination of the movements of the body with the reversed visual scene.

According to Harris, the visual perception remains unchanged throughout the course of the adaptation; the letters are still reversed. And yet, since the right side of the body is now experienced as being on the left side, and since the backward R is also on the left, the observer is likely to say that the backward R is on the right. After all, it is physically in line with the right hand, and the hand is felt as being in the position of the R—indeed, the observer may even say that the backward R appears to be "normal." This could occur because the mirror image of the R has become familiar and easy to read. In this context, incidentally, printers are accustomed to reading type that is actually the mirror image of the ultimate printed material. This is not very difficult to do, nor are we likely to conclude from exhibitions of this skill that printers perceive mirror images of letters as normal letters.

If Stratton felt that the various parts of his body were in the same places as where he saw them, then he would have responded just as he did. He could have exhibited good sensorimotor co-ordination, and in time he might not have noticed that the world was upside down. Kohler's observers would stop misreading directionally ambiguous letters like *d* and *b*, and would also achieve a high degree of co-ordinated sensorimotor behavior. This is why Harris believes that adaptation to rearrangement of the visual input is due to a change in the sense of the positions of the limbs and of other parts of the body. While he is not explicit about this, an implication of his theory is that in the course of normal development the organization of proprioceptive space—the sensed relative positions of the parts of the body—is determined to some degree by the nature of visual experience. It would be interesting to see how the body "image" of a congenitally blind person differs from that of a person with sight.

Objections have been raised in connection with the proprioceptive adjustment explanation of adaptation to rearrangement. For one thing, critics protest, adaptation is possible even when proprioception is absent. Thus, Taub and his associates (see Taub, 1968, for a review of this important work) have shown that when the afferent nerves from a limb are severed prior to their entry into the spinal cord, a monkey may still exhibit adaptation of reaching behavior while wearing a prism. The deafferentation of a monkey's limb will certainly destroy any proprioception, since the signals from the joints and the deep muscle receptors are blocked before they get to the brain. If proprioception *per se* is absent and adaptation may still occur, in what sense can we maintain that adaptation is due to modification of the felt position of the parts of the body?

Thus far we have adopted the convention that the felt position of a part of the body is attributable to activation of position sensors. Harris, however, was deliberately ambiguous in his use of the term "felt position," and would, in point of fact, be equally at home with the idea that the felt position of a part of the body is due to outflow to the part and not necessarily to sensory data arising from the joints and muscles. Thus, in the case of the eyeball it is commonly believed that there is no useful proprioceptive information transmitted to the brain from the extraocular muscles—or at least, if there is such information, it is not available to the observer so that he can "feel" the position of his eye. The position of the eye, however, is determined by a signal to the extraocular muscles. This outflowing signal also gives the sense of eye position. If this were true to some degree for the limbs and for other body parts as well, then Harris could avoid the criticism inherent in Taub's data by a broader definition of "felt position" so that it transcends the normal understanding we have of proprioception.

It should be noted that adaptation in one experiment with deaf-ferented animals proceeded much more slowly than in animals with intact proprioception from the arm (Taub, 1968). This suggests the possibility that both outflow and inflow are implicated in the development of new co-ordination between motor behavior and vision.

A second criticism of the "felt position" theory falls upon certain results indicating that intermanual transfer may be possible after all. As it will be recalled, Harris, Hamilton, and Mikaelian found that, with an immobilized head, adaptation resulting from viewing one arm through a prism does not transfer to the other unseen arm on subsequent tests. Yet Kalil and Freedman (1966) demonstrated adaptation of the unseen hand in an experiment similar to that of Harris (1963). But in their experiment the observer's head was immobilized, whereas previous studies showing intermanual transfer (see Hamilton, 1964) did so only if the head was free to move. Other experiments (Taub, 1968) used a different display technique and likewise found intermanual transfer. The reasons for this transference are obscure, especially since Harris, Hamilton, and Mikaelian did not obtain the effect.

As with so many controversial issues in this area of research, one is left with the feeling that the complexity of the phenomena has caused a number of variables to be left uncontrolled. Although the head was not free to move in the Kalil and Freedman experiment, there may still have been some slight innervation of the neck muscles; and this produced a tendency toward head movement that was prevented from occurring by the biteboard. Is it possible that such physically prevented movements are implicated in adaptation? It could be that a difference in instruction allowed one experimenter's subjects to try to move their heads, while another experimenter's subjects did not try to move their heads.

In any event, a theory such as this does not stand or fall solely because a few experiments provide seemingly incompatible results. It is always possible that some unsuspected parameter was at work in these experiments and not in the original substantiating experiment. The only terms in which to reject the theory are those of a new theory that embraces a wider range of facts. It is probably true that the "felt position" theory is too simple to account for all of the facts of adaptation. Moreover, the modifiability of felt position has not yet been related to the broader problem of perceptual development. One can accept this theory tentatively, but it should be recognized that it implies that perceptual learning is very limited, and does not allow in any way at all for an influence of prior exposure on vision itself.

Before we turn to theories that postulate experience-induced changes in visual space perception, we should consider the relation between the "felt position" theory and the efferent copy theory. Logically, there are three ways in which the efferent copy and the reafferent signal may become recorrelated: (1) for the representation of the reafference to change its spatial value; (2) for the efferent copy to change its spatial value; and (3) for both to change. In the latter two cases, the Held theory and the Harris theory may become equivalent.

As it will be recalled, Harris does not restrict the felt position of the body or its parts to dependency upon proprioception or inflow from the muscles. He is perfectly happy with the idea that felt position could be at least in part attributed to outflow—i.e., an awareness of the signals flowing out to the muscles. It might well be that the efferent copy of the outflow to a limb becomes recorrelated with a rearranged visual input, and that this may be the basis for the experience of a change in the felt position of the limb. There is nothing in the efferent copy theory requiring this recorrelation to transfer to another limb. The same efferent copy may be generated when one tries to point to an invisible sound. Since the efferent copy now has a different spatial value, the adaptation effect would reveal itself even under these circumstances. Thus, it is not at all certain that the two theories are really mutually exclusive; they diverge only in terms of the importance they ascribe to self-initiated movements.

THE REORGANIZATION OF VISUAL SPACE

The theories presented by Taylor (1962) and by Festinger *et al.* (1967) state that the visual perception of the arrangement of things in space is modifiable. This modification comes about through the reprogramming of motor behavior: it is the program of efferent signals that comprises the perception. The efferent copy theory of Von Holst and of Held also implicates motor behavior in adaptation and perceptual learning, and in this theory it is the relation between the efferent copy and the sensory signals that determines perception. Harris, on the other hand, suggested that the larger portion of the effect of rearrangement is due to a modification of non-visual perceptions—the felt position of the body. Thus, none of these theories propose that adaptation is due strictly to a modification of vision without the mediation of specifically correlated motor behavior. We shall now consider theories that attribute adaptation to a change in visual perception *per se*.

It has long been known that visual processes may be altered simply by exposure. Constant exposure to a bright light, for example, leads to desensitization of the visual apparatus. Thus, a small dim target is less detectable after looking at a bright light than it is after keeping the eyes in darkness. Such visual adaptation phenomena do not have a direct bearing on the development of space perception, but are local effects depending upon the depletion of photosensitive substances in the retina.

Another possible local adaptation effect is the Gibson aftereffect mentioned earlier in this chapter. As we have already noted, Gibson (1933) found that staring at a curved line for a period of time results in the apparent straightening of that line, and that, moreover, when the curved line is replaced by a straight line, the straight line appears to be curved in the opposite direction. This, too, is a local aftereffect, since if the straight line were to be presented at some other retinal location the curvature aftereffect would not be seen.

The aftereffects of looking through a prism while walking about in the world may be affected by local adaptation phenomena such as those described by Gibson. As Held and Rekosh (1963) established, however, they include also non-local adaptation phenomena. Thus, even though an observer may have been looking at a variable scene through the prism, he would display an aftereffect if he stated that a small light off to one side appears to be straight ahead of him. The aftereffect is not dependent upon stimulation of a specific retinal place by a particular proximal stimulus. Are such non-local aftereffects strictly visual in nature?

Irvin Rock (1966) is an explicit proponent of the idea that visual perception can be changed if an observer is subjected to optical distortion. According to Rock, if the subject has adequate visual information on the nature of the distortion, the appearance of the scene will change. One example of such adaptation is illustrated in Figure 11–13, in which a seated person looks at a straight line through a prism. The vertical line appears

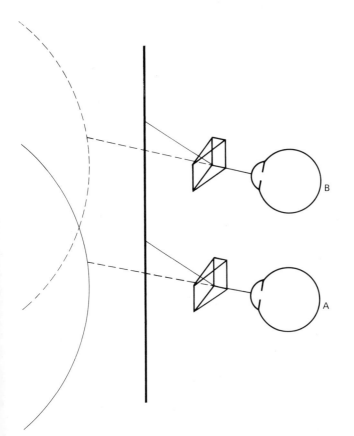

Figure 11–13. Shape of a straight line that is distorted by a prism changes with the position of the observer, as when the eye and prism move from A to B.

to be curved. If the observer stands up, the line is still straight in front of him. Since he is looking at the line through a distorting prism, however, the bend in the line will follow him as he rises to an erect posture. A truly curved distal line would not behave in this way, for if the distal line is actually curved, its maximum point of curvature will remain fixed in its position. This variation in distortion of the proximal line may serve as a cue to the observer that the line is truly straight.

Another way to express this is to invoke a subjective definition of a straight line. A vertical straight line placed directly in front of an observer will remain imaged in his foveas if he moves vertically. This is true even if the line is distorted because viewed through a prism. Hence, the variations in the shape of the line still fit the definition of a straight line. These variations are a source of information about the line. One might argue that this is merely a variation of the Taylor-Festinger observation and might therefore be explicable in their terms. Though this is certainly correct, Rock proposes an alternative explanation for this phenomenon and for other adaptation phenomena as well.

According to Rock, there is no logical reason why the world should appear to be upside down if one wears Stratton's device (as was discussed early in this chapter). Rock's argument is that all the relations between the images of objects are preserved in the reinverted retinal image. Thus, the first postulate of his theory is that any optical transformation that alters the entire retinal image in a systematic manner should not *of itself* result in a change in perception.

In point of fact, however, things do look different when such a systematic transformation is created. To take care of this fact, Rock proposed a very bold hypothesis—namely, that traces of the experiences one normally has are left in the brain, and that these memory traces are of attributes of the proximal stimuli themselves: they are traces of the retinal nature of the stimuli. Hence, the distortions evident to perception when one first dons a prism or an apparatus like Stratton's are due to a conflict between these memory traces of prior images and the new attributes of the rearranged proximal stimuli. This, then, is Rock's second postulate: Conflict between memory traces of visual stimuli and the new perceptual processes set up by current proximal stimuli produce apparent distortion.

Rock discounts theories that base the perceived distortion on conflict among the senses, and is thus in fundamental disagreement with Stratton. The reason for his rejection of the thesis that conflict among the senses leads to perceptual distortion can be explained with the help of a reconsideration of Taylor's experiment. If one looks at a straight horizontal line through wedge prisms attached to contact lenses, the line appears to be curved. As time goes by, it ultimately appears to be straight—possibly because the scanning eye movements that keep the line in the central foveas are themselves horizontal straight-line movements. We saw that Harris might interpret this result as being due to the fact that the felt positions of the eyes change as they traverse the line. This would bring the experienced eye movements into agreement with the perception of a curved line—thereby destroying the ostensive conflict between the felt positions of the eyes and the curvature of the line.

Rock does not see why this should lead to a straightening of the line.

He holds instead that the felt position of the eyes, whether it is due to outflow or to inflow, is governed by the visual-capture effect. Thus, though the eyes may be moving in a straight path, they are felt to be moving in a curved path to match the visual curvature of the line. If this is so, then the line should continue to appear to be curved. Such a resolution of the conflict could hardly be the basis for the ultimate straightening of the line. Thus, on logical grounds, Rock feels that resolution of conflict among the senses is not the basis of adaptation if that adaptation involves a change in visual perception.

According to Rock, adaptation *per se* comes about because the rearranged stimuli produce their own memory traces, and these traces in time come to supplant the traces left by prerearrangement experiences. As this replacement of the old traces by the new ones progresses, the adaptation becomes more nearly complete. This presumably accounts for the partial degree of adaptation encountered in the data of most experimenters. Thus, we might say that the theory has a third postulate—the postulate of the replacement of memory traces. Rock gives us no more than a very sketchy outline of how this may actually occur. He suggests that similarity between a memory trace and an incoming stimulus may cause the memory trace to be recalled. Presumably, the observer is capable of discriminating the difference, if any, between the absolute properties of the current perceptual process and the aroused memory trace.

Thus, if one should look through a lens that reduces everything, the smaller-than-customary retinal images of objects will arouse memory traces associated with prior exposure to those objects. The discrepancy between the stored representation of the memory trace of the retinal size of the original object does not match the representation of the retinal size of the minified object, and as a result, the observer judges that the newly seen object is smaller than it had been before he donned the lens. However, with time new traces corresponding to the smaller size of the proximal stimuli are laid down. These traces ultimately supplant the older ones, and the objects now appear to be normal.

Finally, Rock does allow a role for both efference and proprioception in his system. He asserts that where visual information is ambiguous, proprioception and efference indicating how the body is positioned and moving in space may be factors in adaptation.

The chief criticism of Rock's theory is that it is too general to permit specific quantitative predictions about the course of perceptual adaptation. In other words, though it points to the role of memory processes in what appears to be a cumulative or growing phenomenon, it cannot tell us when and to what degree adaptation is likely to occur. Consider Stratton's experiment, for example. There is considerable room to doubt that adaptation in the form of a genuine reorientation of the visually perceived world ever did occur, since Stratton interpreted his results in terms of a growing agreement between the senses. Intersensory adjustments as we have seen, can be explained in terms of a reorganization of proprioceptive space. Rock could actually accept this interpretation—but on the grounds that the rearrangement of 180-degree rotation of the retinal image is too radical a change for an adult observer to adapt to visually (Mack and Rock, 1968). On the other hand, he would agree that less radical rearrangements, such as those produced by a modest prism displacement of the visual field, do lead to perceptual change. This, it would appear, is not an entirely fair position, based as it is upon *post hoc* hypotheses about the tolerable degree of distortion or rearrangement. Without these the theory predicts full and complete adaptation to rotation.

The startling idea that absolute properties of the proximal stimulus are stored in memory does appear to be required by the internal logic of the theory. Without such storage, observers could not notice that the sizes of objects appear to be smaller when they are viewed through minifying lenses. There are numerous assumptions underlying this new idea, however. For one, even though an observer may be aware only of the distal size of an object, and thus be unaware of its retinal size, some representation of the retinal size is stored. This implies that there is storage of an attribute without awareness of the attribute—a kind of latent perceptual learning. There is no direct evidence for this idea. It would appear to be easy enough to conduct an experiment in which memory for relational properties among images of objects is compared with memory for absolute properties of the images themselves.

It seems that Rock would have to accept the idea that visual events are mapped into an inherent spatial co-ordinate system. For without such a system, memory traces of the sizes, shapes, and distances between images of objects would be impossible. Size can have a meaning only within the framework of some co-ordinate system. Again, although Rock is not explicit about the inherent nature of a spatial co-ordinate system, he does suggest that a representation of a stimulus can have a specific orientation in the "neural substrate." Thus, the neural substrate must itself be a co-ordinate system within which size, orientation, and shape are given a native meaning.

The foregoing interpretation may be inconsistent with some of Rock's other assertions. Although it is somewhat unclear, he seems to believe that the co-ordinate system is modifiable by virtue of a rearrangement procedure. Thus, looking at a vertical line through a device making it appear to be tilted can ultimately lead to a shift in the orientation of the co-ordinate system itself. These ideas do not appear to be fully worked out as yet. Nevertheless, Rock does believe that visual perception can, within undefined limits, be modified by experience. Learning influences the appearance of things, though precisely how this works out in the course of the individual's development remains to be discovered.

While it is intuitively obvious that a conflict between different sense modalities can provide a motivation for adjustment, it is not equally obvious that a conflict between a current perception and memories of attributes of other similar experiences should also motivate adaptation. It is true, as Rock asserts, that the resolution of intersensory conflict need not result in a change in visual perception. Merely achieving concordance between the senses by having vision predominate over proprioception would lead to adequate behavior, and yet still allow physically straight lines to appear to be curved. But much the same criticism can be leveled at Rock's theory. Why should perception change? The same end would be served if the memory of old events became modified to match the new perception. There is no evidence at all for this conjecture, but it should illustrate the point that the mechanisms for ostensive change in visual perception are still poorly understood.

The question as to why discordant sensory information may lead to modification of some sort is barely recognized. It may be that such discordance is inherently aversive (Taub, 1968). Thus, conflict between vision and vestibular cues may lead to seasickness: the organism adjusts in an attempt to avoid such conflicts. Taub and Taylor (1962) both try to embrace adaptation phenomena within the framework of learning theories. Taylor is an avowed Hullian who perceives adaptation in terms of setting up new conditioned responses. Taub attempts to treat adaptation phenomena in the framework of operant behaviorism. Both theorists note that when an observer is allowed to view his hand through a prism, his behavior will be positively reinforced when he sees his hand contact a reached-for target. If he should miss the target, he is negatively reinforced. These events lead to the increased probability of certain responses and the diminished probability of other responses. But why should adaptation occur in experiments in which the observer makes no overt responses and still shows signs of adaptation? A possible answer may emerge from the suggestion about the inherently noxious effect of sensory conflict. At the moment, however, this is like the assertion that nature abhors a vacuum.

Despite the fact that the motivation for at least some kinds of adaptation to sensory conflict is not well understood, there is no doubt that such adaptation does occur.

THE CUE ASSIMILATION HYPOTHESIS

The proposal that adaptation comes about because proprioception or felt position of the body is modified may be a specific instance of a more general process. Wallach, in a series of papers dealing with various kinds of adaptation phenomena, came to the conclusion that there is a general tendency for discordance of perceptual cues to become reduced, to become more nearly alike in their effects. This tendency has been termed the *cue assimilation hypothesis* (Wallach and Frey, 1972). The apparent reduction in conflict between the cues of proprioception and vision may be seen as a result of this general tendency. Moreover, Wallach and Frey believe that this tendency may work in the opposite direction—i.e., it is logically possible that visual cues may have their significance altered vis-à-vis proprioceptive cues. Wallach and his associates performed experiments to show that one can find modification of one, the other, or both of a pair of cues placed in conflict by the rearrangement procedure.

As we saw in Chapter 7, the cues of accommodation and convergence serve to inform the observer about changes in the distance to an object. If the object should move from far to near, the power of the eye's lens increases together with the angle of convergence. These cues involve the interaction of both visual and motor processes. A tendency to minimize blur circles, as well as the magnitude of disparity, serves to produce the muscular changes of accommodation and convergence. More, as an object moves closer to an observer, its angular size will increase. Such changes in retinal size serve also as a cue to the change in distance to the object. Thus we see that changes in retinal size and of accommodation and convergence may all be cues to changes in the distance to an object.

Wallach and Frey (1972) placed the cue of size change in conflict with the cues of accommodation and convergence. They caused a luminous diamond-shaped object to move toward and away from an observer. The actual length of the path of the excursion of the moving diamond was

55 cm. The nearer point on the path was 25 cm from the observer and the most distant point was 80 cm. Though the path length was only 55 cm, the size of the diamond was varied as a linear function of its position on its path. These changes corresponded to what would be seen if the diamond moved along a path about 367 cm long. Thus, at its most distant point the diamond was very small and, as it progressed toward the nearer point, it became larger at a faster rate than it would have done if its linear size had remained constant. This provided a change in retinal size which simulated movement along a path much longer than the actual path, even though the cues of accommodation and convergence were in agreement with the actual shorter path.

As we recall from Chapter 9, the perceived size of an object is proportional to its registered distance. Thus, if the cues to distance indicate that one object is more distant than another object of equal angular size, then the more distant object will appear to be larger. Moreover, as shown in Chapter 8 the amount of depth perceived between two objects is a function of the distance to the objects and of the relative binocular disparity. For a constant relative disparity the amount of perceived depth between the objects varies with the square of the average distance to them. As suggested in Chapter 8, the cue of convergence could well be involved in detecting the distance to an object. Hence, changes in this cue alone would alter the amount of depth between two objects whose images have a constant relative binocular disparity. Thus, if exposure to the conflict between retinal size and accommodation and convergence could produce a change in the scaling of the latter cues to bring them into better accord with the size cue, one would expect that effects of these distance cues on perceived size and perceived depth would be changed.

In testing for this hypothetical effect, Wallach and Frey had the observer estimate the size of the base of a luminous wire pyramid facing him. They then asked him to estimate the magnitude of depth between the base of the pyramid and its apex, which was farther away than the base. This was done with the pyramid at one distance from the observer, and then again with another pyramid at a greater distance from him. This second pyramid was changed in objective size so that its base would subtend the same visual angle at the observer's eye as did the nearer pyramid, and so that the relative disparity of the base and apex of the more distant pyramid would equal that of the nearer pyramid. In this way they were able to measure the perceived size of the base and perceived depth between the base and the apex at two different viewing distances.

The observers were then required simply to sit and look at the moving diamond. While the diamond oscillated between the near and the far point, the observer tracked it with his eyes for twenty minutes. Following this exposure period, the observer repeated his size and depth judgments, using the pyramids.

In the post-exposure tests the size and depth judgments of the observers were substantially changed. The procedure used by Wallach and Frey was to have observers adjust—*by touch alone*—the length of a brass rod until it was of the same size as the diagonal of the base of the pyramid. Following this the observer then adjusted the length of a brass rod until it was apparently equal to the depth between the base and apex of the pyramid. These lengths were all made larger than they were before exposure to the moving diamond. The base of the near pyramid, which was about 33 cm from the observer, was judged to be about 10 per cent larger than it was before exposure. The diagonal of the far pyramid was judged to be about 16 per cent larger. The depth of the near pyramid was about 19 per cent larger than it was before adaptation while the judged depth of the far (67 cm) pyramid increased by about 28 per cent.

The fact that the increase in the magnitude of judged depth was greater for the more distant pyramid than for the nearer pyramid indicates that registered distances to the pyramids was altered by the exposure condition. Since the binocular disparity was the same in both pyramids, the 28 per cent increase in depth of the more distant pyramid suggests that it is perceived as farther away than it was prior to the exposure condition. The increase in the judged length of the diagonal of the base of the more distant pyramid was also to be expected if registered distance was recalibrated by the exposure condition. This increase, however, could not be so great as the increase in depth, since perceived frontal size varies only as the first power of registered distance.

This very strong effect of observing a changing size is consistent with the hypothesis that the distance information given by convergence and accommodation was altered. This occurred despite the fact that the accommodation and convergence cues during exposure were not interfered with at all. By themselves they simply reflected an actual change in distance. As these cues were consistent with the physical situation, the change in their calibration is a departure from veridicality. In this sense the change in accommodation is counter-adaptive. That is why Wallach and Frey used the term *counter-adaptation* to describe their phenomenon. If a cue should shift so that the resulting perception were in greater conformity to the distal situation, the change would then be referred to as *adaptation*. The change in the apparent straight-ahead after wearing a prism, for example, would be an instance of adaptation, since distal points that are actually straight ahead come to appear to be straight ahead after some period of exposure. The shift is adaptive since it produces a more veridical perception.

In another experiment, Wallach and Smith (1972) demonstrated that proprioception may be modified by rearranging the cues of accommodation and convergence. For this procedure their observers wore special spectacles so that convergence for a given distance had to be either stronger or weaker than normal when fixating objects at various distances. The spectacles were also fitted with lenses to produce concomitant departures from normalcy in accommodation. While wearing these spectacles, observers pushed and pulled a large screen containing only a single contour toward and away from themselves. Subsequent tests revealed a shift in the judged position of the hand and the arm but not in perceived depth and size.

In still another experiment Wallach and Karsh (1963) placed the kinetic depth effect (or KDE; see p. 239) and binocular disparity in conflict with each other. This was done with a telestereoscope (Fig. 11–14), which has the effect of increasing or decreasing the normal separation between the eyes. Increasing the interocular separation exaggerates binocular disparity; decreasing the interocular separation decreases the relative disparity.

In their experiment, Wallach and Karsh had observers look at wire objects, such as a wire pyramid, through the telestereoscope. The observers judged the amount of depth between the near and far surfaces of the object. After eliciting these judgments, by having the observer adjust the length of a rod until it seemed to match the seen depth, the wire object was rotated for several minutes. The observer simply sat and watched the rotating object through the telestereoscope. The wire object as seen by one eye would produce the same time-varying configuration as it would if the observer were not looking through the telestereoscope, and consequently, the depth given to each eye by the kinetic depth effect (KDE) is in conflict with the exaggerated or minified depth produced by the telestereoscope.

If the depth effect produced by the KDE were to be altered by an exaggerated disparity, tests after the exposure period should indicate an increase in perceived depth. But if depth given by disparity was altered

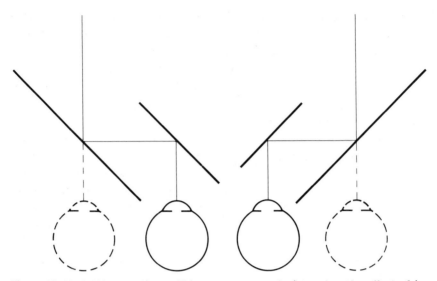

Figure 11–14. A telestereoscope. This arrangement of mirrors has the effect of increasing the distance between the observer's eyes.

by the KDE, then post-exposure tests would indicate a decrease in perceived depth. The latter result was actually obtained, and this led Wallach and Karsh to conclude that stereoscopic depth could be rapidly modified by a conflicting KDE.

So far we have seen that conflict between oculomotor cues and retinal size leads to a modification of oculomotor cues, and that conflict between proprioception and oculomotor cues leads to a modification of proprioception. Since binocular stereopsis is closely related to convergence, these results of Wallach and Karsh suggest also that kinetic cues produce a modification of depth that is dependent upon oculomotor cues. Of course, it is not possible here to determine whether this is restricted to an influence on convergence, or whether the effect of disparity *per se* was modified.

Of itself the assimilation hypothesis of Wallach does not allow us to predict which cue will be modified when two cues are in conflict. The results of their experiments indicate, however, that there is a general tendency for oculomotor cues to be readily modified by strictly visual cues, and that, moreover, there is no direct evidence that the effects of strictly visual cues—e.g., the KDE and retinal size—can actually be modified by such conflicts. Possibly any function involving overt motor behavior is modifiable, whereas purely visual functions are not modifiable. This interpretation is not necessarily in conflict with Held's theory, since he postulates that a change in the relation between efference and afference underlies adaptation. It is also consistent with Harris' theory, in which, as he intended, the concept of "felt position" is broadly defined.

At first glance it would appear that assimilation of cues occurs more readily in some cases than in others. Thus, proprioception can be modified both by conflicting visual cues and by oculomotor cues. And, oculomotor cues can be modified by purely visual cues. It may well be that effects of oculomotor cues cannot be modified by conflicting proprioceptive cues, and it is probably true that visual cues are not changeable as a result of conflict with the other cues. Of course, purely visual adaptation phenomena do occur, but these, like adaptation to curvature, are probably not based upon conflict with other modalities. All this suggests a hierarchical ordering of tendencies toward assimilation; yet, the results obtained by Hay and Pick (1966) suggest that the relations among the cues are far more complicated.

Hay and Pick had their observers wear 11 degrees displacing prisms for 6 weeks, and subjected them to a number of tests before they wore the prisms, immediately upon donning the prisms, and then at intervals while wearing them. The observers were also tested immediately after removal of the prisms.

In one test, observers were required to point in the dark toward a sound. The purpose of this test was to measure the change in the felt position of the arm after prisms had been worn. Another test used by Hay and Pick was similar to that of Held and Hein (1958), in which an unseen hand was pointed toward a visual target. If adaptation to prisms entails a shift in the felt position of the arm, then wearing prisms should result in a gradually increasing error in pointing toward a sound in the dark and a gradually decreasing error in pointing toward a target viewed through prisms.

Hay and Pick did not obtain so clear-cut a result. Just before donning the prisms there was no error in pointing toward either the sound or the visual target. Immediately after donning the prisms there was no error in pointing toward the sound and there was considerable error in pointing toward the visual target. This latter error resulted from the fact that the prisms caused the direction to the visual target to change, and there had been no time to adapt to the change. Since the prisms cannot displace a sound, there should have been no error in pointing toward it in the dark. After one day of walking about with the prisms, however, the direction of pointing toward the sound was in error by about 6 degrees. This is consistent with Harris' observation that the felt position of the arm is altered by wearing prisms. On the second day of wearing prisms, on the other hand, this error actually became smaller: the observer was able to point accurately toward the sound.

In contrast with this reduction in error of pointing toward a sound, pointing toward a visual target improved from an initial error on the first day of about 7 degrees to virtually no error at all on the second day. This visual adaptation remained stable throughout the remaining period of the experiment, while there was a gradual increase in the error of pointing toward the sound for 18 days after the second day of wearing the prisms. Hay and Pick concluded that adaptation to the prisms could not be attributed solely to a modification of the felt position of the arm, since such modification would lead to a consistent relation between the error in pointing toward a sound in the dark and toward a visual target with an unseen hand.

Quite likely, adaptation to prisms involves more than a modification of the felt position of the arm. It could entail also changes in the oculomotor system. The eye may actually come to be oriented obliquely in the head when an observer believes he is looking straight ahead. Modifications in the oculomotor system and the felt positions of the limbs of the body need not be perfectly correlated. This interpretation was accepted by Hay and Pick. Their results may not be explained in terms of a truly visual change coupled with a change in the felt position of the arm, since oculomotor changes were not ruled out in the experiment. Moreover, the results of the experiment imply that the oculomotor system may be modified quite independently of the sense of the positions of the limbs of the body. The hypothesis of cue assimilation cannot predict such results. Clearly, the degree to which various sensorimotor functions are independent of each other is a suitable topic for future research.

ON THE INNATENESS OF SIZE AND DISTANCE PERCEPTION

Much of the work dealing with adjustment to rearrangement was motivated by a desire to cast light on the development of perception. Thus, Taylor's theory implies that all perceiving is the product of the acquisition of multiple states of readiness to respond. Held's theory maintains that relations between efference and reafference are acquired through experience. Wallach's assimilation hypothesis implies that there is a general tendency for diverse cues to come to represent the same perceptual parameters. But virtually all the evidence for these points of view stems from research using adult volunteers as subjects. We turn now to the rather sparse literature on the perceptual capabilities of very young humans.

Obviously it is not possible to enlist the co-operation of an infant in a perception experiment. Since the infant is preverbal and has only a limited repertoire of overt behavior, we know very little of what it can perceive. Yet, to some extent we may infer that the newborn infant exhibits behavior suggesting that there is an innate spatial co-ordination of body movements with sensory stimuli.

Wertheimer (1961) delivered clicks next to the right and the left ears of a newly delivered baby girl. Although the infant was but three minutes old, she moved her head in the direction of the sound source. Now while this result suggests an innate capability for discriminating direction, it is conceivable that the behavioral discrimination was not based upon perception. That is, there may be a purely reflexive tendency to turn the head toward auditory stimuli even if the organism could not perceive the sounds. But even if Wertheimer's infant was exhibiting reflexive behavior, its response does suggest that there is a built-in wiring that relates head movements to the direction of an auditory input.

Similar results have been obtained in the visual domain with somewhat older infants. As we have already seen (in Chapter 10), Tauber and Koffler (1966) demonstrated optokinetic nystagmus when infants were exposed to stroboscopically moving stimuli. Salapatek and Kessen (1966) showed that the patterns of eye fixations exhibited by an infant will vary with the geometrical form of a visual stimulus. Unless the infant were capable of differentiating spatial locations of parts of the form, his eye movements would not be different for different stimuli. Similar results were obtained by Fantz (1961), Hershenson (1964), and Hershenson, Munsinger, and Kessen (1965). The results cited above, together with the impressive study by Schlodtmann (1902), support the conclusion that there is an innate basis for the perception of visual direction. Moreover, most of the theories of perceptual adaptation discussed above allow for an innate discriminability of relative spatial position. It is largely the sensorimotor and intersensory relations that appear to be modifiable by virtue of a rearrangement procedure.

While all this is valid for the perception of relative visual direction,

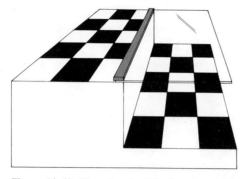

Figure 11–15. The visual cliff. The deep side of the cliff is covered by glass. The subject could be placed on the board between the deep and shallow sides and then move off the board toward one side or the other.

it need not be valid for the perception of size and depth. For example, consider the experiments of Walk, Gibson and Tighe (1957), who introduced the visual cliff as a means for studying the development of depth perception. At first this method was employed with light- and dark-reared rats as subjects, and subsequently with other species, including humans (Walk and Gibson, 1961). Walk (1966) has carried out extensive studies of many species of animals to determine their ability to discriminate depth as a function of age and experience.

In the case of human subjects, babies ranging in age from six to fourteen months were placed on the center platform of the visual cliff (see Figure 11–15). The baby's mother was placed alternately at the deep end and the shallow end of the cliff, and called the baby to come to her. Twenty-four out of twenty-seven babies crawled to the mother when she was on the shallow side, but refused to go when she was at the deep side. This was true even when the baby reached out and touched the glass cover over the deep side. Thus, the baby had tactual information that there was a platform to support him on the deep side but his response was determined by the visual stimulus.

While we cannot conclude from this evidence that newborn infants are innately endowed with a capacity to perceive depth, the presence of this capacity at so early an age is still impressive.

The work with animals is also suggestive. Newly hatched chicks will never hop off the platform onto the deep side but only onto the shallow side. A one-day-old goat will not walk onto the deep side; but if it is placed onto the deep side it will extend its forelimbs as a defensive posture, and then, when it sees the shallow side, leap onto it. Thus we know that at least some species of animals are capable of discriminating depth differences at quite an early age.

The discrimination between far and near involves the use of diverse visual cues. At an early age this may be a rather coarse kind of discrimination, but one that could become sharper with experience. Thus, while a baby might be able to tell whether an object is far or near, he might not be able to respond accurately to the distal size of an object. The retinal size of the object will be more likely to determine the infant's response at an early age than at a later age. Walk (1966) varied the sizes of the checks in the visual cliff so that the retinal sizes on the deep side approximated the retinal sizes on the shallow side. The infants still preferred the shallow side. This result suggests that retinal size *per se*, or the density of optical texture, does not strongly determine the behavior of the infant. The infant must be employing cues to the distance of the textured surface as well as to retinal size.

T. G. R. Bower (1964, 1965) tested very young infants to determine whether they respond to the distal size of an object as opposed to its retinal size. The assumption here is that if the infant can respond to distal size, he must be making use of cues to distance. It has been demonstrated by Haynes, White, and Held (1965) that the focusing ability of the eye of a newborn infant is quite poor. Can slightly older infants who are still incapable of locomoting make use of cues to distance? Bower's infants were from seventy to eighty days old in one experiment (1964) and between six and eight weeks old in another (1965). He utilized an operant technique to get the infants to make a small head movement to a 12-inch cube. This was done by playing peekaboo with the infant when he made the head movement in the presence of the cube. Thus, if in the presence of the cube the infant were to turn his head a slight distance to one side or another, thereby actuating a small switch, the experimenter would pop into view and say "peekaboo." By altering the schedule of this reinforcement, it was possible to get the baby to respond frequently to the cube.

After shaping the behavior of the infant, Bower placed other cubes in the baby's field of view at various distances from him. These cubes were selected to produce the same or different retinal image sizes. Thus, when a cube three times larger than the original cube was placed 3 times farther away, it subtended the same angle at the baby's eye. The infant did not respond to this cube nearly so often as he did to the 12-inch cube at its original distance, or even when placed three times farther away than it was originally. This result is consistent with the hypothesis that the infant can use cues to distance to enable it to recognize the distal size of an object. Even though we do not know precisely which cues were used by Bower's infants, it is clear now that the capacity to utilize distance cues occurs prior to an ability to move about in the world, so that cues to distance do not depend for their development on walking and crawling. Still, movement in the world may serve to sharpen and calibrate distance perception.

One reason for deducing that experience leads to a sharpening of the effectiveness of cues to distance is that size constancy usually improves with age. Zeigler and Leibowitz (1957), for example, showed that 7- to 9-year-olds have less size constancy than adults. Wohwill (1960) has reviewed a substantial literature that supports this conclusion. Yet none of the results are conclusive, since we cannot separate differences in the criteria employed by the subjects in these experiments from the potential effectiveness of the cues. This problem of the effects of different criteria is quite important, particularly in view of recent evidence. As Leibowitz, Graham, and Parrish (1972) demonstrated, hypnotic suggestion to college students that they are 9 and 5 years of age produced a lowering of size constancy similar to that found in actual children. Moreover, nonhypnotized groups instructed to imagine they are 9 or 5 also show evidence of less size constancy. It is as though the mere instruction to imagine oneself as younger produces a tendency toward matching of retinal size rather than distal size. This is clearly a matter of self-instruction to use a different criterion.

The general conclusion to which we must come with regard to size and depth perception is that the organism has a built-in ability to utilize cues to depth, and that, moreover, these cues to depth have an effect on perceived size. Since, however, the effects of these cues are inherently variable, by applying different criteria one can bias size and distance judgments. Greater flexibility in the use of different criteria probably develops as a function of age. Moreover, exposure conditions can probably lead to a degree of recalibration of cues to size and distance. This may be partly attributed to a change in criteria. Clearly, more must be learned about the development of size and distance perception.

ADAPTATION TO IMAGE MOVEMENT

The efferent copy theory discussed early in this chapter is based upon the phenomenon of an apparently stationary world when the eye is moved voluntarily. When one moves his head and eyes the images of objects change position on the retinas. Despite this image movement, the objects themselves seem to maintain a constant spatial position. This phenomenon has been labeled *position constancy*.

There have been several studies of the effects of rearrangement on position constancy. When Stratton's observations were discussed, we skimmed lightly over the first such study. As will be recalled, when Stratton first put on his telescope, the world appeared to move about when he moved his head and eyes. In other words, the normal position constancy was disturbed by the telescope. This disturbance was due in part to the fact that when Stratton rolled his eye to the left, the image of a stationary object shifted to the right on the retina. This is the opposite to what normally occurs, so that the reafference was inconsistent with the efferent signal to the eyes.

As time went by, Stratton noticed less of this movement of the world. Position constancy was restored. But then, after the removal of his telescope the world appeared to be unstable. Something new was learned while wearing the telescope, and this new something supplanted the old customary relation between the reafference and the efferent signal.

This phenomenon was studied by Posin (1966) and by Wallach and his associates. Working at about the same time, Posin and Wallach and Kravitz (1965a) investigated the effect of a change in the normal rate of image displacement on position constancy. In the Wallach-Kravitz experiment the observers wore a minifying lens that effectively slowed by a factor of 3 the normal rate of retinal displacement of an image. After wearing the lens for several hours, the observer was tested. In this test the observer wore a helmet on which was mounted a mirror. A beam of light was reflected from the mirror on to a screen. As the observer turned his head, the beam of light displaced on the screen. A variable transmission was used, so that the angle of rotation of the mirror could be varied relative to the angle of rotation of the head. Thus, the angular displacement of the spot of light on the screen could equal, be slower than, or be faster than, the rate of rotation of the head.

Wallach and Kravitz found that the spot was perceived as being stationary during the test, when it was actually moving at a rate of one-sixth of the head rotation. This represents a 50 per cent adaptation effect. Posin, using a very similar arrangement, obtained qualitatively similar results. (Posin's study is described in detail by Rock, 1966). Posin used also a "passive" movement condition that likewise produced adaptation. This result was confirmed by Wallach and Kravitz (1965b) in another study.

The foregoing studies manipulated the relation between head rotation and distal stimulus displacement. They did not control in any way for rotation of the eye relative to the head. Thus, as the head rotated horizontally, the eyes could have made compensatory movements so that they continued to point at the displacing visual target. Such compensatory rotation is commonly encountered when the head is tilted to the left or right or when it is nodded up and down. If such compensatory movements occur normally, then while a minifying lens is worn, the eye movements will at first be executed at the wrong rate—i.e., they will be too fast. After some time, however, the rate of eye rotation could change, and objects of interest would be more accurately tracked by the eyes. This could conceivably underlie the adaptation effect (see Hochberg, 1971, p. 545).

This conjecture is not inconsistent with another finding of Wallach and Kravitz (1968)—that there was no transfer to an auditory target as a result of adaptation to a magnifying lens that increased the rate of retinal displacement of images. Thus, though the observer perceived a moving visual object as stationary after wearing the lens, an auditory target had to be physically stationary if it were to be judged as stationary while the head was moving. Such transfer will not be expected if the eyes do not turn to track the position of an audible but unseen target.

In the normal situation, when an observer moves about in the world, he perceives the world as stationary and refers the movement to his own body. In the experiments discussed above, the abnormal movements of images produced by the movement of one's own body come to be associated with changes in body position so that these movements are also referred to the body and not to the visual world. The fact that adaptation occurs even though the observer is moved by an external agency does not vitiate this argument. The rotation of the body is a powerful source of information about body movement, since the vestibular apparatus is very sensitive to rotational acceleration. Moreover, there is a strong link between the vestibular apparatus and the oculomotor system. Position constancy is not simply a matter of discounting eye and head movements, but is rather a matter of referring image movements to the body. That this can be learned is another instance of the flexibility of sensorimotor and intersensory relations.

IV

form and information processing

12

the perception
of pattern and form

How do we perceive pattern and form? One explanation that comes to mind is that forms are perceived because they are clearly defined regions of color or lightness. A gray disc is perceived because a region of grayness is bounded with a circular border. This, after all, is a description of the retinal image.

This simple explanation of form perception cannot be correct. The gray disc might be so large, for example, that the observer has to move his eye about in order to see the entire contour clearly. After a period of visual exploration he will be able to say that there is a large disc before him. Yet at no point in time during the period of exploration was there ever a well defined image of a disc on his retina. The perception of form may be constructed over time (e.g., Rock and Halper, 1969). It may be argued that a similar constructive process occurs even when a shape can be resolved by the eye in a single glimpse.

Perceiving and recognizing forms and patterns are complicated processes, and numerous theories have dealt with one or another of their aspects. In this chapter we shall review some of these theories and try to show how current workers in the field are approaching the problem of understanding form and pattern perception.

ORGANIZATION, GESTALTEN, AND SOME ALTERNATIVES

The term "Gestalt" can be translated to mean *form* or *configuration*. Gestalt psychology started with the idea that forms or patterns transcend the stimuli used to create them.

Figure 12–1. The four dots form the vertices of a square.

Consider the four dots in Figure 12–1. These dots are perceived as the vertices of a square. Open circles or even short line segments could have been used in place of the dots. In each case the property of squareness would have emerged. This phenomenon is not unlike that of a melody that may be played in different keys and yet is still recognizable. It is for reasons like these that the Gestalt psychologists concluded that a pattern or form is not the simple sum of the elements of which it is composed. The program they set for themselves was to discover why patterns emerge.

Perceptual organization. The dots in Figure 12–2 are apparently organized into pairs. Why should we not see the dots organized into triads? What principles underlie the organization that does emerge when we look at such patterns?

According to the Gestalt psychologists, elements like dots and line segments do not produce independent effects in the nervous system. They postulated rather the existence of attractive forces among these elements. Because of such forces two elements near each other will tend to be perceived as a segregated unit or group, although, if the space between the elements is large, the attractive force will be relatively weak. The pattern in Figure 12–2 is organized into pairs because the differential spacing among the dots is associated with a differential distribution of forces within the brain. The organization is determined by the stronger attractive forces.

Figure 12–2. Grouping of dots into pairs (the Gestalt law of proximity).

The foregoing theory was designed to explain perceptual organization of patterns. Actually, several different features of patterns may produce organization phenomena. The *field forces* postulated by the Gestalt psychologists were deployed to explain all these occurrences of organization (Koffka, 1935). Since diverse features of arrays of elements can cause them to be organized, several different empirical laws of organization have been proposed (Wertheimer, 1923). These laws must, however, be separated from the field theory designed to explain them. An empirical law simply describes a general relation between events. It may be predicted by a particular theory, but it may also be explained by some other theory. For the present we shall review some of the laws of organization in the context of the Gestalt theory—but we shall also consider them in the light of subsequent theoretical developments.

The first law of organization proposed by Wertheimer is the *law of proximity*. According to this law, stimulus elements that are close together will tend to be perceived as a group. The row of dots in Figure 12–2 exemplifies this law.

A second law proposed by Wertheimer is the *law of similarity* (illustrated by Figure 12–3). The open circles in this figure are perceived as the

Figure 12–3. Grouping by similarity.

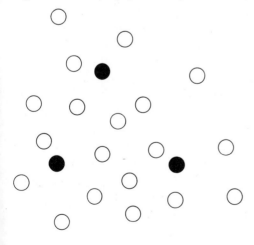

```
CERTAIN QUICKLY PUNCHED METHODS SCIENCE COLUMNS NIATREC YLKCIUQ DEHCNUP SDOHTEM ECNEICS SNMULOC
SCIENCE SPECIFY PRECISE SUBJECT MERCURY GOVERNS ECNEICS YFICEPS ESICERP TCEJBUS YRUCREM SNREVOG
METHODS RECORDS OXIDIZE COLUMNS CERTAIN QUICKLY SDOHTEM SDROCER EZIDIXO SNMULOC NIATREC YLKCIUQ
DEPICTS ENGLISH CERTAIN RECORDS EXAMPLE SCIENCE STCIPED HSILGNE NIATREC SDROCER ELPMAXE ECNEICS
SUBJECT PUNCHED GOVERNS MERCURY SPECIFY PRECISE TCEJBUS DEHCNUP SNREVOG YRUCREM YFICEPS ESICERP
EXAMPLE QUICKLY SPECIFY METHODS COLUMNS MERCURY ELPMAXE YLKCIUQ YFICEPS SDOHTEM SNMULOC YRUCREM
SCIENCE PRECISE EXAMPLE CERTAIN DEPICTS ENGLISH ECNEICS ESICERP ELPMAXE NIATREC STCIPED HSILGNE
SPECIFY MERCURY PUNCHED QUICKLY METHODS EXAMPLE YFICEPS YRUCREM DEHCNUP YLKCIUQ SDOHTEM ELPMAXE
EXAMPLE GOVERNS OXIDIZE ENGLISH SUBJECT RECORDS ELPMAXE SNREVOG EZIDIXO HSILGNE TCEJBUS SDROCER
COLUMNS SUBJECT PRECISE MERCURY PUNCHED CERTAIN SNMULOC TCEJBUS ESICERP YRUCREM DEHCNUP NIATREC
ENGLISH RECORDS EXAMPLE SUBJECT OXIDIZE GOVERNS HSILGNE SDROCER ELPMAXE TCEJBUS EZIDIXO SNREVOG
CERTAIN PRECISE PUNCHED METHODS ENGLISH COLUMNS NIATREC ESICERP DEHCNUP SDOHTEM HSILGNE SNMULOC
OXIDIZE QUICKLY SCIENCE DEPICTS SPECIFY PRECISE EZIDIXO YLKCIUQ ECNEICS STCIPED YFICEPS ESICERP
DEPICTS EXAMPLE ENGLISH CERTAIN RECORDS SCIENCE STCIPED ELPMAXE HSILGNE NIATREC DROCER  ECNEICS
SPECIFY MERCURY GOVERNS PRECISE QUICKLY METHODS YFICEPS YRUCREM SNREVOG ESICERP YLKCIUQ SKOHTEM
```

Figure 12–4. Meaningful items are not segregated readily from meaningless items. (After Julesz, 1962)

vertices of a triangle, even though filled dots neighbor each of the more widely separated circles. The reason given for such organization is that attractive forces exist also among similar stimuli. These forces must, in this case, be stronger than the forces generated by the proximity of dots and circles.

The law of *common fate* is another of Wertheimer's important principles of organization. If a group of dots were moving with a uniform velocity in a field of similar though stationary dots, the moving dots would be perceived as a coherent or unified group. Presumably there are also attractive forces generated by common differential movement of elements.

It is possible to imagine experiments testing for the applicability of these laws to pattern formation as well as for their relative effectiveness (e.g., Hochberg and Silverstein, 1956). Nevertheless, the foregoing laws of organization are really quite imprecisely formulated. What do we really mean by proximity, similarity, and common fate? Can these be defined strictly in retinal terms? It is easy to see how retinal proximity and velocity might be employed as factors in the study of organization, but this is not the case with similarity.

The concept of similarity is difficult to define. Bartley (1969) has suggested that similarity is not a stimulus dimension at all, but rather a human response—in this case the response of the experimenter to the stimuli he decides to use in his experiment. Thus far no really satisfactory methods have been devised to enable us to relate stimulus characteristics to perceived similarity. Similarity is largely context-determined and is probably dependent to a considerable degree upon the prior experience of the observer.

The array of words shown in Figure 12–4 illustrates the fact that prior experience is not the exclusive determinant of organization by similarity. The words in the array have the same apparent texture or granularity, but those on the left side of the array are meaningful, those on the right side nonsensical. Although it is possible to discern the separation between the meaningful and nonsensical words in the array, this discrimination is not spontaneous (Julesz, 1962). One would expect spontaneous organization to occur if similarity were exclusively determined by experiential factors.

The situation is more complicated than this demonstration indicates. In Figure 12–5 the same words are used as in Figure 12–4, but the letters of the words on the right side of the array are mirror images of those in Figure 12–4. Now, the organization of the array into two halves is more pronounced even though the physical granularity of the array is the same over all its portions. Physical differences *per se* cannot explain this organization. People are unaccustomed to seeing mirror images of letters. This differential experience could affect perceived similarity.

Henle (1942) showed that familiar and properly oriented letters are more discriminable in very brief exposures than are mirror images of letters. This result of past experience may so change the response characteristics of an observer when he is confronted with mirror images of letters

Figure 12–5. Grouping can be affected by familiarity, since mirror images of letters are easily segregated from normally oriented letters.

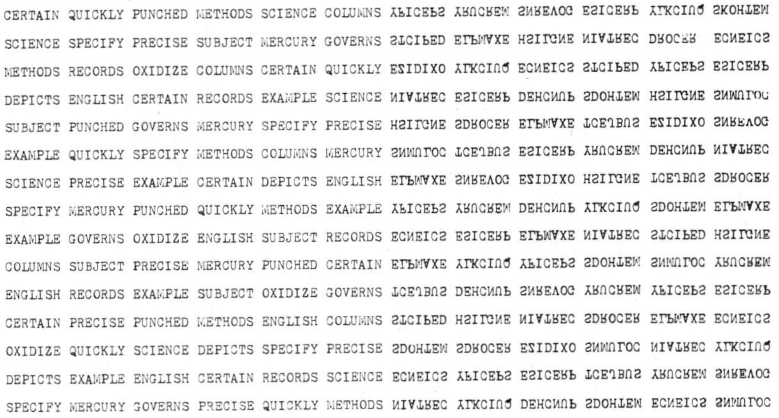

```
CERTAIN QUICKLY PUNCHED METHODS SCIENCE COLUMNS ƛbICEbƨ ƛbПƆ b...
SCIENCE SPECIFY PRECISE SUBJECT MERCURY GOVERNS ...
METHODS RECORDS OXIDIZE COLUMNS CERTAIN QUICKLY ...
DEPICTS ENGLISH CERTAIN RECORDS EXAMPLE SCIENCE ...
SUBJECT PUNCHED GOVERNS MERCURY SPECIFY PRECISE ...
EXAMPLE QUICKLY SPECIFY METHODS COLUMNS MERCURY ...
SCIENCE PRECISE EXAMPLE CERTAIN DEPICTS ENGLISH ...
SPECIFY MERCURY PUNCHED QUICKLY METHODS EXAMPLE ...
EXAMPLE GOVERNS OXIDIZE ENGLISH SUBJECT RECORDS ...
COLUMNS SUBJECT PRECISE MERCURY PUNCHED CERTAIN ...
ENGLISH RECORDS EXAMPLE SUBJECT OXIDIZE GOVERNS ...
CERTAIN PRECISE PUNCHED METHODS ENGLISH COLUMNS ...
OXIDIZE QUICKLY SCIENCE DEPICTS SPECIFY PRECISE ...
DEPICTS EXAMPLE ENGLISH CERTAIN RECORDS SCIENCE ...
SPECIFY MERCURY GOVERNS PRECISE QUICKLY METHODS ...
```

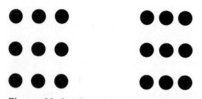

Figure 12–6. When viewed monocularly, the dots appear to be grouped into rows. When combined stereoscopically, however, the dots are organized into columns.

that he does not perceive them as similar to correctly oriented letters. Such data indicate that similarity is not predictable from the physical features of items *per se*. Moreover, it is not possible to make *a priori* predictions about the role of past experience in determining similarity. Clearly, more work is needed here.

We even have difficulty in dealing with the apparently simple concept of proximity. Suppose that one were to view, with one eye only, a pattern of dots, such as the one illustrated in one side of Figure 12–6. The retinal distances separating the dots horizontally is less than the distances separating the dots vertically. When a stereoscope is used to view the pattern, however, the dots will be perceived as slanting into depth from right to left. The lateral separation of the dots in the third- or depth-dimension is greater than their separation in vertical dimension.

Using a stimulus of this type, Rock and Brosgole (1964) discovered that differential retinal separation did not necessarily determine the organization of the array of dots. When the array of dots was viewed with one eye so that the dots appeared to be closer together laterally than they were vertically, they appeared to be organized into a pattern of rows. With both eyes opened, the dots organized as a pattern of columns and not as a pattern of rows. This occurred despite the fact that the lateral separation of dots on both retinas was less than the vertical separation. On the other hand, the disparity cues introduced by both eyes revealed that the lateral separation of the dots in depth exceeded their vertical separations, thereby producing the alternative organization. As a result of this experiment, Rock and Brosgole concluded that organization by proximity results from the relative separations of elements in *perceived* space, and is in consequence a higher-order process than is organization based upon simple retinal separation.

Despite the problems discussed above, there is an undeniable tendency for elements to be perceived as organized patterns. This undoubtedly reflects a natural tendency toward seeking some organization in the world. Organization makes it possible for the perceiver to deal with larger chunks of experience than those given by elements taken in the visual field one at a time. The mere fact that the Gestalt psychologists were so persistent in pointing to the importance of these phenomena is a sufficient contribution to psychology. Despite the importance of these phenomena, there have been relatively few parametric studies designed to reveal the quantitative characteristics of organizational processes.

Gold (1960) reported on one of the few systematic studies of the law of proximity. As one condition of his experiment he placed three dots in the visual field. The position of the middle dot could be shifted from one side to the other of the space between the two flanking dots. When the middle dot was centered in the space, observers reported seeing a triad— a group of three dots. But when the dot was shifted toward one side, observers reported seeing a grouping of two dots on that side.

The amount of displacement of the middle dot from the center needed to just perceive a paired organization was compared with the observer's ability to discriminate a difference between two lengths. Gold found that sensitivity to grouping by proximity does not differ from the ability of the observer to discriminate differences in line length.

If an attractive force exists between two dots, sensitivity to their grouping could be stronger than the mere ability to discriminate differ-

Figure 12–7. Stimuli similar to those used by Gold (1960) in a study of grouping by proximity. The dots are equally spaced in the top row, organized into a group of three in the second row, and organized into two flanking pairs of dots in the third row. These are possible outcomes of shifting the positions of the second and third dots.

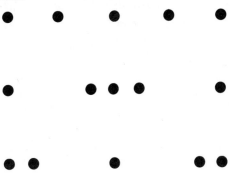

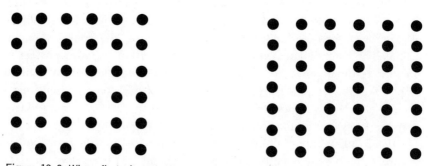

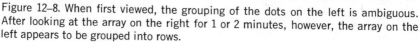

Figure 12–8. When first viewed, the grouping of the dots on the left is ambiguous. After looking at the array on the right for 1 or 2 minutes, however, the array on the left appears to be grouped into rows.

ences in length. Since this was not so, Gold argued that attractive forces were not needed to explain grouping phenomena.

In further support of this idea Gold used a group of five equally spaced dots. The second and fourth dots in the group of five could be moved jointly toward the center dot or away from it, as is illustrated in Figure 12–7. When the second and third dots were nearer the center dot, a group of three dots was perceived. But when they were nearer to the first and fifth dots, they became members of two pairs of dots. In this case discrimination of grouping was actually worse than discrimination of differences in line length. This is exactly the opposite of what an attractive-force theory would predict. Despite the apparent conflict with an attractive-force theory of proximity, this study confirms the fact that grouping by proximity does exist. More work is needed where the observer's criterion as to what constitutes a group is taken into account.

Gold's results are not in conflict with the results obtained by Rock and Brosgole. If Gold had studied grouping in depth he might well have found that sensitivity to such grouping is no better than the ability to discriminate differences of length or distance in the third dimension.

It is becoming increasingly clear that the grouping laws discussed thus far are not elementary processes, and it is further evident from Figure 12–8. On the left side of the figure is a rectangular array of dots, with equal vertical and horizontal distances between the dots. By itself this array has an ambiguous organization. Sometimes it appears as an array of rows of dots, and at other times as an array of columns of dots. The reader may recognize this as an instance of the "bathroom floor phenomenon."

The array of dots on the right side is ordered so that the vertical spacings are smaller than the horizontal. This causes the array to resemble a set of columns. If the reader looks at this pattern for a minute or two and then switches his gaze to the array on the left, the previously ambiguous array is no longer ambiguous, but is organized into rows—just the opposite of the array on the right. By rotating the page while staring at the array on the right, this induced organization can be reversed.

The foregoing experiment demonstrates an aftereffect of exposure influencing grouping by proximity. As we shall encounter other such aftereffects later in this chapter, for the present we need only recognize that even so simple a parameter as proximity cannot be defined in retinal terms or even in terms of the distal stimulus. Prior exposure may also contribute to its definition.

The physical attributes of the stimuli are important. An example of this is provided by the work of Beck (1967, 1972). Using a display similar to those of Figure 12–9, Beck reasoned that if the V-shapes in these displays were dissimilar to their background elements, it should be easier to count them than if they were similar to the backgrounds. He found that counting was faster in Display A than in Displays B and C. On the basis of the kinds of stimuli he employed to obtain such results, Beck inferred that discriminability can depend upon differences in slope. The line-elements comprising the V_s in panel A are oblique relative to the line elements comprising the background stimuli. This, of course, is reminiscent of the work of Hubel and Wiesel.

Beck concluded that grouping depends upon the conspicuity of the elements that are to be grouped. If they are conspicuous relative to background elements, he inferred that they will group together. This conspicu-

Figure 12–9. Discriminability can depend upon the slopes of line elements. (After Beck, 1972)

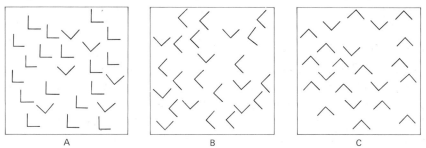

A   B   C

ity is a function of physical differences among stimuli, such as differences in slope, luminance, size, and perhaps color. Thus, the law of similarity probably subsumes many as yet unknown laws of grouping. Theories designed to explain these grouping phenomena have yet to be formulated.

As will be recalled from Chapter 8, stereograms may be constructed from random arrays of dots. These Julesz patterns are particularly interesting because the surfaces seen in depth are not visible in either of the half-fields of the stereogram. In a sense, this too is a grouping phenomenon. The square seen as raised above its background in the Julesz pattern (see Fig. 8–14) is a segregated group of dots. The grouping occurs because the disparity of the dots in one region differs from the disparity present in another region. Since this is not a retinal effect, but depends strictly upon an operation performed by the brain on signals provided by the two retinas, it is clear that cortical processing of information leads to grouping. This is the conclusion of Rock and Brosgole. In the present context, however, it is important to recognize that grouping by disparity is another proof that grouping cannot as yet be subsumed under a few simple rules.

The grouping in depth demonstrated by Julesz is but one of many such kinds of grouping, as described in Julesz' (1971) beautiful book, *The Foundations of Cyclopean Perception.* He describes, for example, a phenomenon that occurs when many tiny needles are rotated at one velocity while many other surrounding identical needles are rotating at another velocity: the enclosed needles appear as a group segregated from its background. Though one might explain this effect in terms of the principle of common fate, this principle could be replaced by a new principle—a principle of depth-segregation—which would cover the same and, perhaps, even a wider domain of facts. The new principle of perceptual organization is derived from a theory presented by Hochberg (1971).

To introduce this idea let us first review the example usually given to illustrate the rule of common fate. A set of dots is moving across a field of stationary dots. The moving dots are therefore seen as a segregated and coherent group. Now consider what would happen if an array of dots were painted on a transparent and invisible plate of glass and placed nearer to the observer than another and larger array of dots. When one eye is closed, movements of the head will cause the images of the nearer dots to move on the retina at a greater velocity than that of the more distant fixated background dots. This, of course, is the motion parallax described in Chapter 7. The result of this "thought experiment" would be

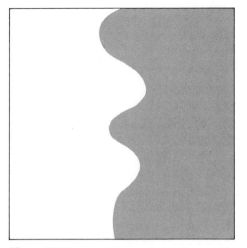

Figure 12–10. An ambiguous figure-ground display.

that the nearer set of dots will also appear to be a coherent organized pattern segregated from its background. Are the differential retinal velocities *per se* responsible for the segregation, or is it the fact that the two arrays of dots are perceived as being in separated planes of depth?

We are left, then, with the proposition that organization does occur—although it may well be a highly derivative process, influenced by many factors ranging from the attributes of stimuli to past experience. There is also considerable ambiguity about some of the rules of organization. Similarity cannot be defined. Effects of common fate may be attributable to segregation in depth, which could occur prior to the organization of a pattern. At the risk of being repetitive, this area, relatively neglected for so long, must be studied again in the light of all the exciting new developments in psychology and physiology.

Figure and ground. Another favorite subject of the Gestalt psychologists is the famous *figure-ground* phenomenon.

Figure 12–10 contains a region of grey and a region of white within a rectangular framework. The contour separating the two regions is perceived as belonging either to the grey region or to the white region. Whichever the region it belongs to—and this is somewhat arbitrary—that region is perceived as a figure, and the other region is perceived as a background to the figure. In fact the Gestalt psychologists maintained that

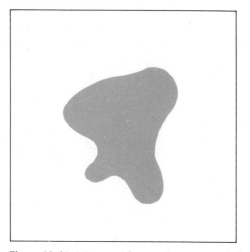

Figure 12–11. A less ambiguous figure-ground display.

one can experience the background portion of the field as extending behind the figure portion (Koffka, 1935). This author does not have that experience despite the fact that it is widely reported. Nevertheless, there is
no doubt that the figure portion of the pattern has a perceptual substan-
tiality that the background does not have.

A less ambiguous version of this figure-ground phenomenon is shown
in Figure 12–11. Though the enclosed grey patch is more often perceived
as figure than is the surrounding background, with a little effort it is possible to perceive the patch as a window through which one is looking at
a background. In both Figures 12–10 and 12–11 the boundary belongs to
the figure and does not belong to the background.

An early Gestalt explanation of this figure-ground phenomenon is
that points comprising the grey region of the pattern are similar to each
other in color, so that, by the rule of similarity, they cohere or group together. Moreover, white points are more like their white neighbors than
like their grey neighbors just across the border. They too group to form a
segregated whole. The border, again, belongs to the figure and not to the
ground.

The one-sidedness of the border may be attributed to organizational
processes too. The small patch in Figure 12–11 is more likely to be seen as
figure than as ground. Presumably forces set up by the contours are
stronger within the contour than without. But where there is no such

biasing effect, as in Figure 12–10, the figure-ground relation is ambiguous. Köhler (1940) suggested that the alternation of figure and ground experienced when looking at this pattern may be attributed to a satiation or fatiguing of the differential cortical processes set up by the border. When this satiation is complete, the cortical processes reverse and the other side of the border becomes the figure.

The satiation theory can also be used to explain the aftereffect shown in Figure 12–8. Köhler (see Köhler and Wallach, 1944) suggested that an electric current flows between two points of cortical excitation produced by two stimuli. After some time this current produces a polarization of the tissues in which it flows and thereby comes to impede its own progress. As the current flow thus diminishes; when one looks at the equal-spaced array on the left side of Figure 12–8 there is now a weaker current flow in one direction than there is in the other, and thereby the perception of the pattern is biased. This theory, we might note, is not unlike the theories of movement aftereffects which attribute such effects to the selective fatiguing of movement detectors (see Chapter 10). Presumably similar processes can account for the figure-ground reversals.

There are alternatives to this Gestalt point of view. In all figure-ground patterns the figure portion of the pattern is perceived as being in front of the background. This perception is not unlike that occurring when one looks at a real object placed in front of some background. Hochberg (1971) has observed that when one looks at such an object and scans it with his eye, accommodation and convergence are set for the distance of the object. The background behind the object is relatively blurred, and points in the background are imaged at disparate retinal places. As the boundary of the object moves into the center of the field of view, it is seen as sharp and well defined, while background points are not. Hochberg suggested that this is why the boundary belongs to the object of regard.

As a result of this experience in the world of three-dimensional objects, the observer comes to expect that points on one side of a boundary will be blurred and insubstantial, and objects inside the boundary sharp and detailed. Thus, when one looks at the enclosed grey form in Figure 12–11, the tendency is to expect points outside its boundaries to be more distant and blurred. This may explain why the enclosed gray region is perceived as figure and the background white region is perceived as background.

We are dealing here with a potentially complicated process. As we shall see later, some theories consider figure-ground formation to be a primitive and perhaps unanalyzable attribute of perception. For these theorists the real problem of perception is that of recognizing forms on subsequent exposures to them. The primitive figure-ground experiences in this view are like pure colors: they are the "given" elements of early experience. In Hochberg's theory, however, the figure-ground organization is derivative, depending upon experience and expectancies built up in the course of acquiring the experience. The expectation that points outside an enclosing boundary will be blurred leads to the perception of the sharply imaged enclosed region and its boundary as a relatively nearby figure.

Hochberg's theory is admittedly unsubstantiated by data, and yet it does point the way toward the kinds of data that may be meaningful. A special instance of such data is the determination of the role of fixation in figure-ground organization. Perhaps the first thing predicted by this theory is that the side of Figure 12–10 that one happened to be fixating should tend to be perceived as figure. My own observation is that this is true, and yet one can get the figure-ground relation to reverse so that the fixated side becomes background and the non-fixated side becomes figure. This, however, does not disprove the theory. As the reader can see for himself, the effort involved in obtaining this reversal of the figure-ground relation is great. It could mean that the observer is somehow altering his expectancies. There are no data on this subject.

There must be some interaction between the effects of fixation on figure-ground segregation and the physical features of the stimulus pattern. Thus, if a field is divided by a contour such as the one shown in Figure 12–12, there may well be a tendency to perceive the left side of the pattern as figure, since the left side of the contour is sharply concave and

Figure 12–12. The left side of this figure-ground display is more likely than the right side to be perceived as figure.

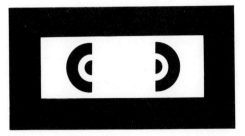

Figure 12–13. Schumann's demonstration of subjective contour.

the right side convex. This sharp convexity is reminiscent of the overlap of the interposition cue to depth. So once again we see that depth cues may be involved in determining figure-ground segregation.

Subjective contour. Contour usually results from some abrupt change of level in the distribution of luminance across a surface, and yet it is possible to perceive contours where there are no such abrupt local changes in luminance. These are called *subjective contours*. Schumann (1904) was the first investigator to recognize these subjective contours. In his demonstration of them in Figure 12–13, a central white square bounded by a complete contour can be perceived. The contour is most pronounced in peripheral vision and also when the figure is small. Kanizsa (1955) constructed a number of patterns displaying these subjective contours. The effects are rather compelling, as may be seen in Figure 12–14. Pattern C, for example, demonstrates that subjective contours may be curved as well as straight.

Subjective contours appear also in Julesz-type stereograms. Shipley (1965) first demonstrated these effects with random dot stereograms, while Lawson and Gulick (1967) found subjective contours in even simpler stereograms, whose basic pattern is illustrated in Figure 12–15. The inner white square at A is seen in depth, but the flanking dots are all flat and in the plane of the page. The contour surrounding the inner square has both vertical and horizontal components—especially when viewed with fixation slightly off to one side of the pattern. According to Lawson and Gulick this "anomalous" contour is generated without disparity. There is, however, a genuine disparity of the white central patch relative to the framework of the entire dotted square (see Kaufman, 1965), and this disparity may give rise to the perception of a white square in depth. Nevertheless, Lawson

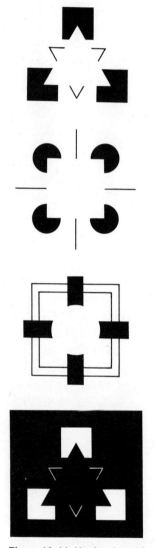

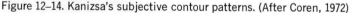

Figure 12–14. Kanizsa's subjective contour patterns. (After Coren, 1972)

and Gulick are correct in pointing out that the resulting contour is anomalous and is probably related to Schumann's subjective contour. On the other hand, if the disparity of the white region is uncrossed in the Lawson and Gulick figure, the observer does not perceive an anomalous contour. This can be proven by interchanging the left and right halves of Figure

12–15*a* to produce Figure 12–15*b*. Viewing this through a stereoscope will reveal that the inner columns of dots go into depth behind the page, as in Panum's limiting case, and the subjective contour is absent. This suggests that subjective contours may appear only when they bound a figure perceived as nearer than its background.

The suggestion made above is consistent with Coren's (1972) explanation of the monocular subjective contours—i.e., that subjective contours are perceived because they are associated with surfaces or planes that are in depth relative to the other portions of the scene. These planes may be created by any depth cue. Lawson and Gulick created a plane by means of the cue of disparity, but other cues as well could produce such effects, as is exemplified in the letter H shown in Figure 12–16. Less than half the boundary of the letter is actually "shadowed" by the black line. Since, as is well-known, such shadowing produces an illusion of depth, there is a pronounced tendency to perceive the completed contour. When this figure

Figure 12–15. Anomalous (subjective) contours appear in **a** but not in **b**. (After Lawson and Gulick, 1967)

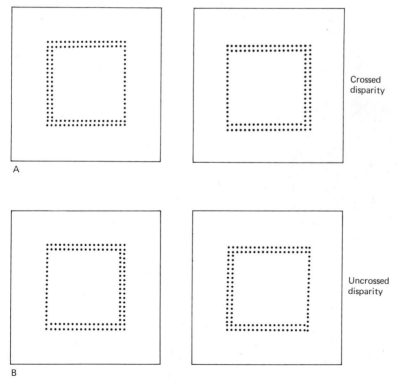

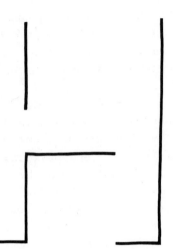

Figure 12–16. When the page is turned upside down, the subjective contour bounding the H is less pronounced.

is inverted by turning the page upside down, the subjective contour becomes far less pronounced. On the basis of what we know from Brewster's study (see Chapter 7) of the effect of light and shade on depth, turning the figure upside down should destroy the illusion of a letter elevated in depth.

Figure 12–17. The ring on the triangle appears to be smaller than the ring outside the triangle. (After Coren, 1972)

Perhaps the most compelling evidence for Coren's theory is the fact that the circular ring in the middle of the subjective contour of Figure 12–17 appears to be smaller than the patch outside the triangle. The patch within the triangle would appear smaller if it were perceived as nearer. Since it is perceived as smaller, Coren argues that the triangular shape is perceived as nearer. A recent paper by Gregory (1972) reports the existence of "cognitive" contours that may be explained in these same terms. Coren's theory of subjective contour is similar in many ways to Hochberg's theory of figure-ground organization. If a region is perceived as figure because of present and, perhaps, expected depth cues, the subjective contours may also be thought of as the boundaries of a figure. Thus, the figure-ground and the subjective contours are related phenomena in which depth cues play an important role.

An alternative to Coren's theory is the Gestalt theory that there is a tendency toward closure or completion of incomplete contours (Pastore, 1971). The small angles formed by the black regions in Figure 12–17 are segments of an actual triangle. This tendency toward closure may cause the observer to perceive a completed triangle. If this theory is correct, a subjective contour should connect the lines forming the small angles in Figure 12–18. Since this does not happen, the closure explanation is probably inapplicable to the subjective contour phenomenon.

Information and organization. One Gestalt law we have not discussed is the *law of good continuation* or "good curve" (Wertheimer, 1923), ex-

Figure 12–18. Subjective contours are absent in this figure, and thus closure is ruled out as an explanation of subjective contour.

Figure 12–19. Good continuation favors seeing two wavy lines.

emplified by Figure 12–19, which shows two wavy lines of dots. The two lines appear to cross each other. One might plausibly predict also that the observer will see angular shapes with their apexes touching each other in the figure. The preferred organization is apparently related to the fact that the wavy lines are continuous, whereas seeing two angular shapes would entail perceiving a discontinuity or abrupt change in the direction of a line of dots.

The preference for good continuation in such patterns may reflect a more profound attribute of the perceptual system. It is possible that the observer will tend to minimize the amount of change or discontinuity in his perceptions. Thus, for example, if a border surrounding a region is symmetrical, the region bounded by that border will tend to be perceived as figure, as illustrated in Figure 12–20 (Bahnson, 1928). The preference for symmetry in figure-ground configurations suggests also that, when confronted with ambiguous stimuli, observers tend to select the simpler of the alternatives. This, of course, is consistent with the results obtained by Hochberg and McAlister (1953) (see p. 231).

Hochberg and McAlister, as well as Hochberg and Brooks (1960), argued that perception is biased in the direction of greater simplicity. If fewer different angles and line lengths are required to describe a figure as three-dimensional, the observer will select that alternative. But if fewer angles and line lengths are required to describe the shape as two-dimensional, observers will tend to make that identification. The good-continuation principle of organization can be subsumed under this general concept as well. Wavy lines are simpler to describe than irregular angles and their discontinuities.

This approach of Hochberg and his associates is related to attempts to apply *information theory* to psychology. To understand this approach to form perception the reader must know something about the abstract nature of *information.*

Information is news (Cherry, 1957). If the news broadcast on the radio were to give us the same old stories from one hour to the next, we would be justified in saying that we are receiving no information. But if the state of the world were to change so that some new and unpredictable event occurs, the content of the newscast would change as well. Then we would be inclined to say that we had received information. Obviously, then, information is related to change.

Information theory is a mathematical theory designed to enable us to measure the information-transmitting capacity of a communications channel. The theory has obvious practical advantages. Such measurement, however, must be independent of the particular messages transmitted over a channel. An engineer seeking to discover how much information a channel can carry is not interested in the state of Aunt Tillie's health or in the latest stockmarket reports. He needs something more abstract by which to ascertain whether information about Aunt Tillie or about anything else can get across to the receiver in a reasonable length of time.

The unchanging sequence of letters AAAAAAA . . . contains no new information after the transmission of the first letter. This sequence of letters is highly redundant, since the same letter A is repeated indefinitely. Obviously, too, there is only a little more information in the sequence AAABBBAAABBBAAA. . . . After the first few letters one can predict what subsequent letters will be; there is no more "news" after a few let-

Figure 12–20. Symmetrically bounded regions tend to be perceived as figure.

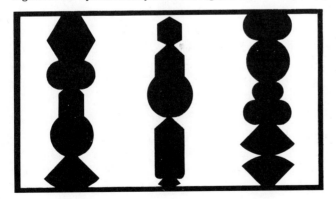

ters. By contrast, the sequence ABAABABBBABBAAABA . . . is loaded with information. A random noise generator (the author) was used to produce this sequence. The reader cannot predict the next letter after being shown all of the preceding letters. The measure of information reflects the amount of this randomicity in a sequence of binary events.

The interested reader is referred to the book by Cherry (1957) for a fine treatment of the formal properties of information theory. For our purposes it is sufficient to point out that the amount of information in any message is related to how predictable one part of the message is on the basis of knowledge about other parts of the message. The degree to which events are predictable is a measure of the *redundancy* of the message. We need to transmit very little information to get a redundant message across a channel. Thus, if most messages are highly redundant we can get along with a limited capacity to carry information. If on the other hand the message is highly random—i.e., if changes are not predictable—we need a channel with a higher information-carrying capacity. Lacking that, a great deal of time is required to get a message with high information content across the limited channel.

In communications channels messages are frequently transmitted in the form of oscillating electromagnetic waves, which means that we can relate the information-carrying capacity of the channel to its ability to transmit and receive waves of a number of different frequencies. This permits us to introduce a useful term—*bandwidth*. By analogy with radio communications, a *wide-bandwidth* system is one capable of carrying a great deal of information per unit time. A *narrow-bandwidth* system carries less information per unit of time. Since the nervous system is rather sluggish by comparison with electronic systems, it is a narrow-bandwidth system.

In actuality, the nervous system is not a single channel with a transmitter of information connected by neurons to a receiver. There are many relay stations and many different pathways. Some of these pathways can carry more information than others. Some pathways are so limited that they form bottlenecks for the flow of information. One such bottleneck is exhibited by the simple fact that the reaction time to an unexpected signal is so very long.

The capacity of an individual to respond to stimuli is quite limited. Reaction time is slower than 100 msec. When an event is unexpected, the reaction time is closer to 300 msec. In this case we cannot respond with an overt action more often than about three times in one second. Speech behavior is somewhat faster, and playing a musical instrument can be still faster (Attneave, 1959). But behavior of this kind, even though very complicated, is programmed in advance by experience and learning. The sequences of action in speech and in making music are not random. Language and music have statistical properties allowing one to prepare his actions well in advance of their execution. The true limit to the information-transmitting capacity of the human is better reflected by these slow reactions to random events.

The sensory systems may well have a greater capacity to transmit information to the brain than do systems involved in executing motor actions. One function of memory is to store sensory information until the motor system gets around to acting upon it.

The fact that the organism selects the simpler of several alternatives may be connected with this sluggishness of the motor system. Continuity, predictability, and order all make the selection of response alternatives easier. Preference for the simpler of several alternatives may well reflect an encoding of information for action. This, however, is all speculative. Not enough attention has been paid to the relation between perceptions and the information-handling capacities of the systems that act upon them.

While the ideas of information theory seemed to have considerable promise when psychologists first became aware of them, this promise has been largely unrealized. Nevertheless, the theory has taught us a way of thinking of perception that will undoubtedly prove very useful in the future.

One of the first scientists to employ information theory in the study of perception was Attneave (1954). In his first studies Attneave pointed out that pictures can be viewed in information-theoretic terms. A bounded

Figure 12–21. Information about form is given by the changes in direction of contour, since observers would place dots at the points of change in curvature in representing the form.

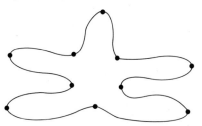

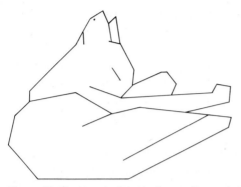

Figure 12–22. Attneave's cat. Connecting points of maximum curvature produces a recognizable picture of a cat. (After Attneave, 1954)

shape can be represented by a few points—a square, e.g., by only four points. A more complex shape, such as is shown in Figure 12–21, contains many changes in direction. Attneave reasoned that the information used by an observer is concentrated at these changes in direction. Thus, given ten dots to arrange to represent such a form, his observers placed them at the places around the form where its contour deviated most from a straight line. The picture of the cat in Figure 12–22 is Attneave's demonstration of the fact that if one simply connects by straight lines the points of maximum curvature of the original picture of the cat, the resulting picture is still recognizable as a cat.

The symmetric forms in Bahnson's figure-ground pattern (Fig. 12–20) may be preferred by the observer because it requires less information to describe them than to describe their assymmetric alternatives. It is difficult to see how one might test this idea in any conclusive way, and yet Attneave (1955) did try to discover whether symmetric forms could be remembered better than assymmetric forms. It is plausible to hypothesize that memory for symmetric forms should be better because less information is needed to represent them. Actually, Attneave found that memory for symmetric forms was somewhat worse than memory for assymmetric forms.

One of the problems with the information-theoretic approach to form perception is that one does not know *a priori* the appropriate unit of information or in what terms to measure it (Garner, 1962). If one effort to systematize data in the framework of information theory should be less than satisfactory, it does not follow that the theory is inapplicable. It may mean that we have yet to identify the appropriate metric or scale by which to measure forms. Many such schemes have been proposed. These are reviewed at length in Zusne's (1970) book, *The Visual Perception of Form*. Rather than duplicate Zusne's excellent review, we shall concentrate on one very general approach that has the virtue of being connected with important developments in physiology.

FEATURE DETECTION AND FORM PERCEPTION

An enormous amount of evidence has been accumulating which relates many of the problems of form perception to the detection of features. As was pointed out previously, Lettvin *et al.* (1959) discovered that neurons in the optic tectum of the frog fire away quite merrily when small shapes are moved across the retina. It is as though there are neuronal circuits configured for the detection of bugs. Hubel and Wiesel (1962) identified units in the visual cortex of the cat whose retinal receptive fields are shaped to optimize their responses to lines of a particular slope or retinal orientation. Other units are responsive to corners of rectangular shapes, and still others are responsive to contours moving in particular directions. All this implies that neurons in the brain are selectively responsive to particular features in the environment.

This physiological evidence has so sensitized psychologists that they are now examining the "features" of the stimuli they use to see whether responses can be predicted from these features. Are features the appropriate units for an analysis of the information assimilated by an organism when it is perceiving? Can the processes underlying feature detection account for the phenomena of perceptual grouping? These are just a few of the questions to be considered here.

Hebb's theory of form perception. The notion of feature detection has been around for some time. Donald Hebb (1949) proposed a theory of form perception which was one of the first to employ the idea that the brain responds differentially to distinctive features of forms. This theory assumes that the visual system can detect a primitive kind of figure-ground segregation, that there is a built-in capacity to detect the segregation of an object from its background. Yet even though this is possible, without experience the perceiver cannot identify or recognize a form. Hebb's theory centers on the mechanisms that make form identification possible.

Suppose that a large triangle is presented to an infant. The triangle is responded to in the sense that it is distinctive from its background; i.e., at first is has no identity. And yet the eye of the infant is attracted to the edge of the triangle. Once the contour of the triangle is imaged in the central fovea, there is a tendency for the eye to move so that the contour remains in the central part of the visual field. Accordingly, the eye moves back and forth along the contour. But, if perchance a corner of the triangle should slip into the center of the visual field, there will be a tendency for the eye to change the direction of its movement and sweep around the corner. These eye movements in the vicinity of corners leads to a pattern of visual stimulation whenever corners are present in the visual field. Repeated exposures to these patterns of stimulation lead in turn to the development of *cell assemblies.*

A cell assembly is a group of cells in the brain which tends to respond whenever a particular feature is present in the visual field. Thus, a line has its own cell assemblies that fire whenever a line is in the visual field. Corners, too, have their own cell assemblies.

Returning to the triangle: with sufficient experience a set of three cell assemblies will be established because of the three corners of the triangle. These assemblies are fired in sequence by the three corners of the triangle. These *phase sequences* of the firings of the cell assemblies come to "mean" that a triangle is present in the visual field. Thus, the cell assemblies may be thought of as feature detectors, and their phase sequences indicate how the responses of the cell assemblies are integrated to indicate the presence of a particular form.

Once cell assemblies and phase sequences are established, the individual need no longer move his eyes about to activate them. While the eye movements are the necessary conditions for establishing the capacity for perception of form, they are not necessary to the perception of form once the capacity has been developed. Mature individuals can recognize forms after a brief exposure. Moreover, they have the capacity to perceive also the similarity among triangles differing in size and shape. The property of triangularity is given because cell assemblies respond in the appropriate phase when any kind of triangle is present. Finally, even when the triangles or other objects are presented in different retinal places, they may still affect similar cell assemblies in the proper phase.

This rather incomplete résumé of Hebb's theory illustrates a number of problems that must be confronted by a theory of form perception. One such problem is the distinction between seeing a form and recognizing it.

It is possible to imagine an observer in the act of seeing a totally new shape unlike anything he has even seen before. It has a unity in the sense that it stands out from its background, and yet it has no name. On subsequent exposures the observer may recognize that he has seen it before. Moreover, if new shapes have been generated by changing the size or orientation of the first shape, the observer may well identify them as belonging in the same class. Again, the shape may be presented at several different retinal places from one exposure to another. A theory could predict that the shape will still be recognized despite the change in its retinal position. Hebb attempted to account for many of these aspects of form perception by employing the concept of feature-detecting circuits built-up through experience. Before turning to more recent theories that also use the feature-detecting concept, let us consider some of the evidence for and against Hebb's theory.

Salapatek and Kessen (1966) photographed the eye of an infant when it was looking at an empty field and then when a large black triangle was introduced at various places in the field. Within the accuracy of their method they showed that fixations wandered far less when the triangle was present and appeared to cluster about one of the apexes of the triangle. Kessen, Salapatek, and Haith (1972) found that infants tend to fixate on vertical contours but horizontal contours do not influence fixation behavior when it is compared with an empty-field situation. In summary, these and other studies by Salapatek and his associates indicate that the human infant does seem to fixate on specific features, contours, and angles, from a very early stage in his development.

Zusne and Michels (1964) found that even in the adult the eye tends to follow the contour of a shape, though such findings are far from conclusive. Yarbus (1967) found that different eye-fixation patterns will appear when an observer looks at a picture under different instructions, since what one looks at is very often a function of what he is looking for. Thus, it is not surprising that Kaufman and Richards (1969) and Richards and Kaufman (1969) obtained results quite different from those of Zusne and Michels. When a large field was divided by a single contour into two regions of different luminance, fixation did tend to concentrate along the lighter side of the contour. If an angle was introduced in the contour, fixation was usually just on the lighter side of the apex of the contour. When small closed forms were used, however, fixation concentrated near the "centers of gravity" of the forms. The contours of the shapes were not scanned.

Concentration of fixations along a single isolated vertical contour could have occurred because there was nothing else to look at. Moreover, in a large field—about 20 degrees across—information about the field could be obtained only by scanning the contour. And with a small 5-degree object in the field of view, the best strategy of an uninstructed observer might be to look at the center of the object. With fixation at the center of gravity he could resolve the whole outline of a small shape at one time. These results, while not a criticism of Hebb's theory, are inconsistent with the idea that results obtained with adults can be used to support the theory. Still, when isolated features are presented observers do tend to fixate in their vicinity.

Hebb relied heavily on research by von Senden (1960) and by Riesen (1947). Von Senden reported on some studies of adults blinded from birth by cataracts. When vision was restored after removal of the cataracts, these patients could not recognize objects visually even though they could identify them easily tactually. Similar effects were observed by Riesen in his dark-reared chimpanzees. Gregory and Wallace (1963) studied a human patient whose sight had been restored after many years of blindness. He, too, was visually handicapped, even though his optical system was intact and functional. Evidence like this can lead to the conclusion that visual experience is necessary for the development of perceptual functions, and yet there is considerable evidence that animals deprived of vision in early life suffer actual destruction of neurons in the central nervous system (see p. 519). Therefore, the results relied upon by Hebb may be attributable to central nervous system damage rather than to a lack of opportunity to build cell assemblies.

The primitive nature of figure-ground can also be questioned. Hochberg's theory, discussed earlier, illustrates the degree of complexity that may be involved in figure segregation.

One class of evidence often cited as favoring Hebb's theory is the observation that stabilized images do not disappear all at once, but rather become fragmented, so that various segments disappear while others remain available for observation (Pritchard, Heron, and Hebb, 1960; Pritchard, 1961). This fragmentation is cyclic: various parts of a figure may disappear and then reappear, and other parts then disappear.

The interesting aspect of these observations is that the parts disappearing or remaining present during fragmentation were identifiable features of the stimuli. Thus, whole corners or angles, as well as lines, tended to disappear as a unit. Moreover, if parallel lines were close together they tended to disappear together. This suggests that the disappearance of stabilized images is due in part to the deactivation of feature-detecting circuits. As we consider other theories of form perception based upon feature detection it will become apparent that these results are not uniquely supportive of Hebb's theory.

Toward analysis by features. The work of Hochberg and McAllister (1953) and of Hochberg and Brooks (1960) is a precursor of feature-detecting theories, for they too focused on lines and angles. There have been recent studies as well, studies directly influenced by the findings of Hubel and Wiesel as well as by the work of Hebb and Hochberg. One such study is that of Vitz and Todd (1971), who attempted to develop a model of how we perceive simple geometrical figures. Actually they addressed themselves to but one aspect of form perception—the judged complexity of a form. They wanted to see whether weighting could be given to specific features of forms so that, when these weightings are taken into account, they could predict the relative judged complexity of the form.

The features singled out by Vitz and Todd were the line segments making up the form, the angles between line segments, and the areas demarcated by the closed boundaries composed of lines and angles in the form. The weightings given these lines, angles, and areas were related to their sizes. Thus, a long line segment had a greater weighting than did a short line segment; a large angle had a greater weighting than a small angle, and a large area a greater weighting than a small.

An analogy may be useful in understanding how Vitz and Todd came to their predictions of form complexity. One of the favorite didactic tools of the statistician is an urn filled with different numbers of black and white marbles. The probability of picking a white marble out of an urn is a function of the relative number of white marbles. The Vitz and Todd model can be understood if we think about three different urns: one filled with lines of various sizes, another with angles, and a third with chips representing different areas. If one of these features, lines, angles, or areas is large it will be represented in large numbers in their urns. In consequence, if an observer were to reach into one of these urns he would be more likely to select a chip representing a large line, angle, or area than he would a small line, angle, or area.

A form composed of lines and angles that enclose areas can be broken up into these individual features. A square, for example, contains four lines of equal size, four angles of equal size, and one area. In terms of Vitz and Todd's model, if an observer reaches into an urn containing the lines of this square, he will always pick a line of the same size. Similarly, the "angle urn" will contain only angles of the same size. Thus, a square is a "simple" shape, since all its angles and lines are equally probable. Also, since there is only one area in a square, the observer can pick only one area from the "area urn."

In the case of a more complicated shape containing lines, angles, and areas of different size, the observer will have to dip into the three urns representing this shape many times to discover what lines, angles, and areas it contains.

The number of samples taken from these hypothetical urns is an index of the complexity of a form. Vitz and Todd found that the total number of trials required to sample the features of a figure was correlated very highly with its complexity as judged by human observers. A correction is needed in their estimate of a form's complexity if the form is symmetric about one or more of its axes. Their results imply that the nervous system may actually undertake a stochastic (random) sampling of the features of a figure in the process of perceiving it.

The model of Vitz and Todd cannot handle curved figures. More, figures that appear to be three-dimensional pose difficulties for their model. Nevertheless, the proposal that figures or forms are analyzed in terms of various features is generally consistent with the idea that the perception of an object consists of analysis of its features.

McFarland (1965) and Julesz (1967) reported on experiments in which different parts of figures were presented at different times. In Julesz' experiment the sides of various regular polygons were presented in clockwise sequence. The rate of presentation of the sides was varied: when the rate was fast, the time of presentation of each side was short; and when the rate was slow, the time of presentation was long. The observer was asked at what point he recognized the form at each of several presentation rates. In this way a threshold of form perception was measured.

The threshold obtained when the sides were presented sequentially was compared with one obtained when the sides were not so presented. Actually, rather than present the sides one at a time, Julesz presented the angles of the figures in a non-systematic order. He found that the angles had to be presented at a much faster rate than the sides if observers were to report seeing a form. This is consistent with McFarland's findings in which the features or elements of the patterns were perceived to join more readily and form a figure when sides were presented in sequence than when angles were presented.

Julesz (1967) interpreted his results as reflecting the fact that form perception in general may well entail the sequential processing of features, one at a time. Since his angles were presented in a non-systematic order, the sequential processing could not be so efficient as when lines were presented in a consistent order. Once again, these data reflect a growing awareness of the importance of feature analysis in form perception.

Piaget (1969) states that a child tends to focus or "centrate" on specific features of a shape at the expense of other features. Thus, there are features which tend to attract the first attention of a child. Presumably, other features are processed subsequently. L. Ghent Braine (1972) has proposed that this sequential processing of shape may well underlie its perceived orientation—i.e., the fact that it has an apparent "top" and "bottom." There does appear to be a general tendency among children to identify a particular feature of some shapes as the "top" regardless of its spatial location. There is, however, no general formula to enable us to determine in advance which feature will identify the "top" of the figure. [*]

One of the major problems with this entire approach to form perception is that it is difficult to state what is and what is not a feature. There are no systematic and universally applicable principles to help us identify the so-called features of all forms and objects. While Chapter 13 describes an approach to the analysis of patterns that might provide us with such principles, in the context of the traditional approaches it is at present impossible to provide a sufficiently general definition of "feature."

Metacontrast. One phenomenon that may ultimately be useful in studying the features involved in form perception is that of *metacontrast.* This phenomenon, discovered by Werner (1935), is the obliteration of the perception of one object when it is followed in time by the presentation of another object. Thus, as shown in Figure 12–23, if a disc is presented at one time and followed some time later by an annulus, the observer may

[*] It is clear that in adults the recognition of a figure may be influenced by its orientation relative to the environment (Rock, 1956; Rock and Heimer, 1957). According to these authors, it is more difficult to recognize a face when it is upside down relative to its environment. Yet, retinal orientation may not affect recognition. An upside-down face is more easily recognizable in an upside-down room than it is in an upright room. Thus, the use of various features in recognition is affected by the circumstances of viewing.

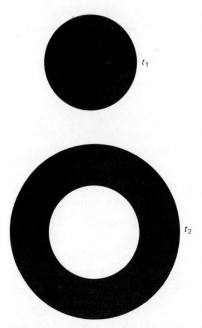

Figure 12–23. Metacontrast. If a disc is presented at time **t₁** and a surrounding annulus in the same place at the later time **t₂**, the disc may not be seen by the
subject.

not be able to see the disc. But if the disc and annulus are displayed
simultaneously, he will have no difficulty in seeing both of them.

There are other phenomena with some similarity to metacontrast,
and the interested reader is referred to Kahneman's (1968) review of this
topic. The metacontrast phenomenon (which is also reviewed by Kahneman) is, however, more pertinent than these others to form perception.

Many parameters have been manipulated in the study of metacontrast. The time between the target and the mask, the duration of presentation of the target, luminances of the stimuli, and the shapes of the
target and mask have all been studied. The fact that metacontrast is not
a purely retinal phenomenon is supported by Koler's and Rosner's (1960)
observation that a mask in one eye can obliterate a target presented earlier in the other eye. Other forms of masking do not occur when the
target and mask are presented separately to the two eyes.

Averbach and Coreill (1961) found that a black ring can mask a
previously presented letter. Mayzner and his associates (see Mayzner,

Tresselt, and Helfer, 1967) used letters to mask another letter presented earlier in an intermediate position. Sperling (1963) employed a random array of small line segments to mask a matrix of letters.

Sperling (1963) suggested that a mask functions to interfere with the processing of visual information by the brain, since, as he reasoned, it requires time for any structured input to be processed. This process may be interfered with by the introduction of other extraneous material during the processing time. If the mask and target stimuli are presented simultaneously, the brain must process a more complicated stimulus. But if the brain is processing the target already when the mask is introduced, interference occurs. Thus, the timing of masking may give us insights into the time required by the brain the respond to forms.

As Haber (1970) has pointed out, the effectiveness of a mask may depend upon the similarity of its contours to the contours of the target. Further research may enable us to determine whether the processing of some features is affected differentially when other similar features are employed as the mask. This could give us some insights into the time-course of processing in the many different channels that may be involved in form perception.

EFFECTS OF PAST EXPERIENCE ON FORM PERCEPTION

Our study is not concerned with the problem of memory for form, for although this is an important topic in psychological research and does involve visual perception, it can be studied in the context of learning theory. Our primary concern here is to discover how memory affects the perception of form, and not the conditions that favor the remembering of form. There is little doubt that prior experience can, under some circumstances, affect the way a thing "looks." Consider the ambiguous form shown in Figure 12–24, which has become known as Boring's (1930) "wife or mother-in-law" figure. It can be seen in two ways. In one of its forms it looks like a young woman; in another, like an old and ugly woman. Those of you who are seeing this figure for the first time see it in one way or the other. If you should be perceiving it as a picture of a young woman it could be very difficult for you to notice its other form. Yet after some time you can finally discern it in either of its forms.

Leeper (1935) provided one group of observers with a version of this picture that was an unambiguous representation of a young woman. Another group was shown an unambiguous version of the old woman. When

Figure 12–24. Boring's (1930) wife or mother-in-law figure.

both groups were shown the ambiguous version illustrated in Figure 12–24, they reported that it looked like what they had seen before. The perception of the ambiguous figure was affected by prior experience with a similar figure.

But does the picture really "look" differently in its two versions? Figure 12–25 depicting Jastrow's (1899) famous duck-rabbit, can be seen as either a duck or a rabbit: the form or outline is the same regardless of how it is seen. An observer required to copy the "duck" could draw the same picture as an observer required to draw the "rabbit." What, then, is the difference when an ambiguous figure is perceived in its two different modes?

We really do not know the answer to this question. In all probability it is the figure's "meaning" that is altered by prior experience and the expectations it induces. Perhaps it is the way in which the form is represented by the set of expectancies induced by the portion of it that is momentarily fixated.

Neisser (1967) discussed the problem of "figural synthesis." According to his view the perception of a form is an active construction on the part of an observer. Hochberg (1968) provided the related theory that the perception of large forms that must be scanned by the eye depends upon the construction of a "schematic map" or *schema* of the form. The schema comes about through the storage of successive glimpses of the parts of the form and their subsequent integration. For the present we point out merely that the identification of a form could be contingent upon the observer's expectancies as to what he should see while scanning, on the hypothesis that the form is this or that object. If these expectancies are fulfilled, the form's identity will be established. There may well be, however, a dual representation of a form to which an observer can respond— i.e., he can respond to the form as an abstract geometrical entity or as an object with an identity.

The work of Posner and Mitchell (1967) is consistent with this idea. They presented observers with two letters in a brief exposure, and asked them to determine whether the letters had the same name. The letters AA are the same and the letters AB are different. In contrast, the letters Aa have the same names, but differ in configuration. Posner and Mitchell found that in general when letters were alike in both configuration and name they were responded to more quickly than when they were alike in name alone. This suggests that there is a capacity to perceive configurational similarity as well as a capacity to assess identity. Both factors may operate in what we call "form perception."

It is becoming increasingly clear that past experience with a form affects its configurational properties under special circumstances. The Gibson aftereffect is such a configurational effect, and we shall see others in the next chapter. These aftereffects require constant exposure for a period of time, and are quite independent of meaning. Apart from such phenomena, the configurational properties of forms are extraordinarily robust in the sense that, at least in adults, they are not affected by past experience.

Figure 12–25. Jastrow's duck-rabbit.

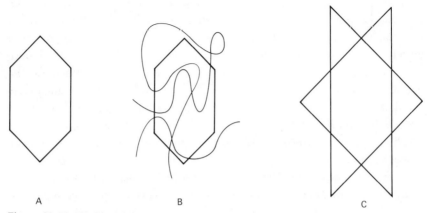

A   B   C

Figure 12–26. The polygon at A is easily detected when it is hidden by curved lines at B. It is much more difficult to discriminate the same polygon at C, since it forms an integral part of the total form.

The literature dealing with this subject is copious, and we shall not attempt to deal with it in detail. Gottschaldt (1926) was one of the first to explore the issue of how prior exposure affects the configurational properties of a form. In his experiment he gave observers considerable experience with a particular outline form, and then embedded the form in another figure. Subsequent testing revealed that the prior exposure did not help observers identify the figure when it was camouflaged by embedding it in the larger form. This work of Gottschaldt led to a fair amount of research which attempted alternately to support or to expose his findings. The upshot is that when the forms are appropriately embedded in genuinely camouflaging patterns, they cannot be detected easily even if they had been seen before. This should not be terribly surprising (see Figure 12–26).

The work of Rubin (1921) is another case in point. He showed figure-ground patterns similar to that illustrated in Figure 12–10 to a number of observers and instructed them to see one part of it as figure. Having seen it once in this way the observers tended to report the same part as figure as they had before, even though the direction of brightness contrast in these patterns was reversed. Rock and Kremen (1957) repeated Rubin's experiment with better control over various biasing factors and could not obtain this same result. Cornwell (1963) attempted another revision of Rubin's experiment, and his results ran counter to those of Rock and Kremen, but supported Rubin's. These results, however, can be challenged.

The basic issue underlying the controversial results obtained by these various researchers concerns the level at which familiarity affects form perception. One formulation is that a perception must become organized before it can be recognized (Wallach, 1949). That is, if the figure is recognized as figure, it must first be perceived; and consequently, the effect of past experience has to be upon an already formed percept.

Recent developments, particular in the fields of information processing and attention (see Chapter 14) indicate that there is in fact a good deal of processing and organizing *before* an observer is actually aware of what he is seeing or hearing. For this reason, it should not be surprising if familiarity can affect the perception of a form. Nevertheless, the level of this effect must be clarified—i.e., is it an effect on identity or on configuration?

13

the analysis of pattern

The foregoing chapter leaves one with the feeling that certain important problems have yet to be clearly discerned. What does it really mean, e.g., to say that the perception of a form may be altered by prior experience with it? As the Jastrow duck-rabbit illustrates so nicely, a picture can look the same and, somehow, still appear to be different from what it was previously. In what way is the perception of the picture changed by seeing it as a rabbit rather than as a duck? Such changes are surely not sensory in nature. This is but one example of how form perception is related to the problem of meaning. We do not know how to ask the right questions about such relations.

Problems exist also at a more primitive level. In the preceding chapter some space was devoted to the proposition that we analyze forms into features, that the visual system may well respond to the lines and angles making up rectilinear forms. Such features have the virtue of being related to the line and corner detectors of Hubel and Wiesel, but since these researchers have not discovered curvature detectors in the cortex, we are left with the problem of defining the features in figures containing curved contours.

A novel approach to the analysis of form and pattern has come to us from the field of electro-optics. This method was developed to permit a more adequate analysis of image-forming mechanisms such as lenses and television systems. While the problem of identifying features has not yet been solved, these new techniques may be very helpful toward that solution. Morover, the new concepts and findings to be described in this chapter are compatible with the findings of the neurophysiologists.

THE CONCEPT OF SPATIAL FREQUENCY

The familiar Snellen chart is one method for measuring visual acuity. If you can discriminate correctly among small printed letters when they are viewed from a large distance, your acuity is better than if you had to come closer to the letters to see them clearly. This method, while suitable for deciding whether you need to wear eyeglasses, is not sufficiently general for describing the resolution of an optical system.

Suppose that you want to select a lens for use in an aereal reconnaissance camera. Your choice of lens may be dictated by several factors, among them the size of the targets you want to photograph, the contrast between the targets and their backgrounds, the altitude of your aircraft, and the density of targets on the ground. If the targets should cluster close together you may not be able to distinguish or resolve the separations between them with a particular lens. One desirable objective is to define a "figure of merit" for a lens in order to predict how well the lens would detect such targets.

A bar grating or pattern of black and white stripes could be used toward this objective. A good lens can resolve the separation between the black and white stripes even when they are very narrow. A poor lens can resolve only widely spaced stripes. Thus, the resolution of a lens can be indexed by the minimum resolvable separation of bars. When applied to human vision this method has shown that a normal observer can resolve angular separations between bars of about 1 minute of arc in a well illuminated environment. This older method for obtaining a "figure of merit" for an optical system has been generalized by the application of Fourier methods (see Chapter 4). These methods have made it possible to describe the quality of an optical system more adequately.

Instead of a grating composed of equally spaced black and white stripes, it is possible to employ a sinusoidal grating, as illustrated in Figure 13–1. The graph shows how luminance varies with horizontal distance across the grating. A sinusoidal variation in luminance across a surface can be described in terms of two parameters: the spatial frequency of the wave, and its contrast.

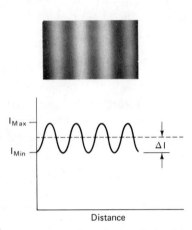

Figure 13–1. Sinusoidal variation in luminance across a surface.

The *spatial frequency* of a grating can be expressed in terms of the number of cycles of change in luminance per unit distance across the display. For our purposes the unit of distance is degree of visual angle. Thus, a high-frequency grating would contain many cycles/deg, and a low-frequency grating might contain but a fraction of a cycle/deg.

The *maximum amplitude* of the luminance of the wave shown in Figure 13–1 is the maximum luminance of the distribution. This amplitude is denoted by the symbol I_{max}. The minimum luminance of the distribution is indicated by I_{min}. The difference between I_{max} and I_{min} is the *peak-to-peak amplitude* of the wave. One-half the *peak-to-peak amplitude* is the *peak amplitude,* which is indicated by $\triangle I$ in the figure.

The peak amplitude or $\triangle I$ is equal to the difference between the mean luminance of the grating and either I_{max} or I_{min}. The mean or average luminance I is $(I_{max} + I_{min})/2$.

The *depth of modulation* of the average luminance of a grating can be expressed as a percentage. Thus,

$$\% \text{ modulation depth} = \triangle I \, / \, I \times 100.$$

This formula is equivalent to one given by Campbell (1968) in which

$$\text{modulation depth} = \frac{(I_{max} - I_{min})}{(I_{max} + I_{min})}.$$

Multiplying the depth of modulation by 100 gives the percentage depth of modulation. Campbell uses the terms *depth of modulation* and *contrast* interchangeably.

A lens may be tested by using it to form an image of a grating. This image could then be scanned by a sensitive photodetector. If the image contains a sinusoidal variation in luminance, then the output of the photodetector will also vary sinusoidally as the image is scanned. But if a very high-frequency grating should be completely blurred by a poor lens, the photodetector may not be able to sense any variation in light energy as it scans the smeared image of the grating, and consequently this grating cannot be resolved by the lens. A lower-frequency grating of the same contrast may not be entirely blurred by the lens. When its image is scanned by the photodetector, the output of the photodetector will reflect some sinusoidal variation in luminance. The amplitude of this sinusoidal variation in light energy may be relatively small, as indicated in Figure 13–2. If, however, the grating is of lower spatial frequency, the sinusoidal output of the photodetector could have a relatively high amplitude. At still lower spatial frequencies, the amplitudes of the sinusoids generated by the scanning photodetector will all be of this same maximum amplitude.

Figure 13–2. The object grating is scanned by a small aperture, and a plot made of the variation in amount of light in the aperture as a function of its position on the grating. The same operation is performed on the image of the grating on the right side of the lens. This new sinusoid has a lower amplitude than does the wave describing the object grating. The ratio of these two amplitudes is an index of the ability of the lens to form an image of the grating.

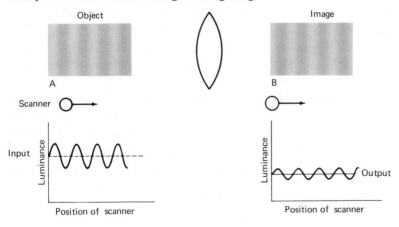

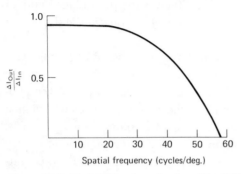

Figure 13–3. Modulation transfer function (MTF) of a hypothetical lens. The graph describes the variation in $\Delta I_{out}/\Delta I_{in}$ as a function of the spatial frequency of the input.

A graph showing how the amplitudes of the sinusoids generated by the scanning photodetector vary as a function of spatial frequency is shown in Figure 13–3. This plot is a transfer function of the lens and is known as the *modulation transfer function* (MTF).

Examination of the MTF in Figure 13–3 reveals that the lens is a *low-pass filter*. That is, it passes lower spatial frequencies but not very high spatial frequencies. A lens with a very wide MTF passes higher spatial frequencies than does a lens with a narrow MTF. The lens with a wide MTF has a greater resolving power than one with a narrow MTF.

As in the case of time-varying sound waves or of flickering lights, an optical scene can be analyzed to reveal its Fourier components. Suppose that we start with a distribution of luminance that varies in a complex manner along one dimension of a surface. As shown in Figure 13–4, this luminance distribution can be broken up into a number of simple sinusoidal components. If the relative phases of these components are preserved, the original scene may be reproduced simply by adding them back together again.

If we know the MTF of a particular lens, it is possible to determine the degree to which a complex image will be degraded by the lens. If only the very highest spatial frequencies are blurred by the lens, then there may be no noticeable degradation of its image. Whereas, if lower frequencies—say, spatial frequencies that can be detected by the human eye—are attenuated significantly by the lens, then the image may be noticeably blurred.

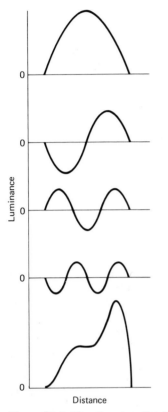

Figure 13–4. The complex distribution of luminance described by the bottom graph is the sum of the sinusoidal distributions above it.

SPATIAL FREQUENCY ANALYZERS

There is little point to building a television system so that it would transmit spatial frequencies that the human eye cannot detect. Hence some practical advantages can accrue from studying the sensitivity of the human observer to different spatial frequencies (Schade, 1964), for once we know the spatial frequencies that observer can detect, we will know what spatial frequencies an optical system would have to transmit if it is to produce an acceptable picture. And hence the importance of discovering the MTF of the visual system itself.

The depth of modulation of luminance is an extremely important parameter when we are dealing with visual processes. It is possible to

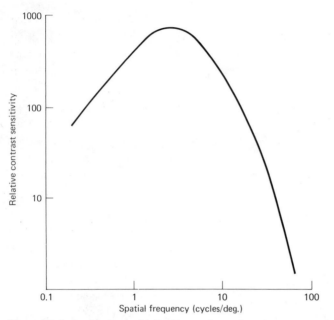

Figure 13–5. Contrast sensitivity (the reciprocal of the amount of contrast needed to just detect the grating) as a function of spatial frequency. It is customary to plot such data in logarithmic coordinates. (After Campbell and Robson, 1968)

keep constant the peak-to-peak amplitude of luminance in a grating while the depth of modulation is varied. Thus, if I_{max} should be 300 cd/m² and I_{min} 298 cd/m², the peak-to-peak amplitude of the grating would be 2 cd/m². Since the depth of modulation is defined as

$$(I_{max} - I_{min}) \, / \, (I_{max} + I_{min}),$$

the average luminance of this grating is modulated to a depth of .0033 or only 0.33 per cent. But if the average luminance of the grating were 5 cd/m² and the peak amplitude 1 cd/m², then the depth of modulation would be 20 per cent. This is a much higher contrast and the grating would be more detectable.

Thus far we have had nothing to say about spatial frequencies and their relation to the concept of "features." We shall now turn to the radical proposition that the visual system analyzes a scene into its Fourier components and processes these components in partially independent channels.

These new approaches to visual processes are reminiscent of the

Helmholtz (Gulick, 1971) theory of audition, in which it was proposed that the ear is a Fourier analyzer—i.e., it detects the Fourier components of complex sound waves and transmits representations of these components independently to the brain. Thus, each place on the basilar membrane in the inner ear resonates in response to a narrow band of audio frequencies. An astute observer can actually hear the different pure tones comprising a complex sound. This was the primary evidence for the so-called *place theory* of audition. Nowadays we know that the auditory system does not work exactly in this way. Nevertheless, some type of harmonic analysis does go on and it does play a role in audition. These more complicated modern views of auditory processes are reviewed in the Gulick book (1971).

If the analogy to the place theory is correct, one would expect the human observer to be differentially sensitive to the Fourier components of a complex visual scene. Campbell and Robson (1968) performed an experiment to test for this possibility. First they measured the sensitivity of the human visual system to sinusoidal gratings as a function of their spatial frequencies. This enabled them to define MTFs for their observers. This was accomplished by presenting a particular spatial frequency at a fixed average luminance and adjusted its modulation depth until the observer reported just seeing the grating. This gave a contrast or modulation depth threshold for the grating. The reciprocal of the contrast threshold is the sensitivity of the observer to the grating. Figure 13–5 shows how contrast sensitivity varies as a function of spatial frequency for one of their observers. The observer was most sensitive to a grating of about 4 cycles/deg and less sensitive to both lower and higher spatial frequencies.

The two experimenters then used a square-wave grating of the same peak amplitude as their sine wave gratings in measuring sensitivity. As will be recalled from Chapter 4, a periodic square wave contains an infinite number of Fourier components, and all the higher components are odd multiples of the fundamental frequency component of the square wave. Thus, if the function has a basic or fundamental periodicity of 26 cycles/deg, it also contains a component at 78 cycles/deg having one-third the amplitude of the fundamental component. From their basic MTF, Campbell and Robson were able to predict that the observer is totally insensitive to a spatial frequency of 78 cycles/deg or any of the still higher Fourier components of the square wave. Consequently, the detectability of a square-wave grating with a basic periodicity of 26

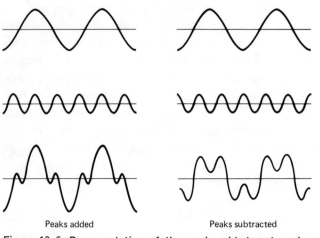

Peaks added   Peaks subtracted

Figure 13–6. Representation of the peaks-added and peaks-subtracted stimuli of Graham and Nachmias (1970).

cycles/deg should be identical to the detectability of a sine wave grating of the same frequency. They found this to be true. But when the square-wave grating has a basic periodicity of, say, 2 cycles/deg, the presence of its third harmonic at 6 cycles/deg could influence the detectability of the grating. The reason for this is that the observer is more sensitive to a simple grating of 6 cycles/deg than he is to a grating of 2 cycles/deg. He could therefore detect the square-wave grating at 2 cycles/deg as soon as its 6 cycles/deg component gets above its threshold.

As further evidence for their thesis, Campbell and Robson adjusted the depths of modulation of sine wave and square-wave patterns until the observer was able to identify them correctly. They found that observers could discriminate a square-wave grating from a sine-wave grating only when the third harmonic of the square wave grating had exceeded its own detection threshold.

Julesz and Stromeyer (1970), working with suprathreshold stimuli, were able to confirm this result. They added visual noise in the form of random bars to a bar grating. The noise was "filtered" so that it contained only low spatial frequencies. The fundamental frequency of the square-wave bar grating was within the spectrum of the noise frequencies. The noise was therefore able to hide or mask the fundamental component of the bar grating. Since, however, the third harmonic of the fundamental frequency of the bar grating had a higher frequency than any of the frequencies in the noise spectrum, Julesz and Stromeyer were able to see a grating that apparently had three times as many bars as did the grating when the noise was not present. This is a rather striking demonstration of the fact that the visual system can indeed respond to different spatial frequencies in a complex waveform.

All of these results support Campbell and Robson's suggestion that the visual system may contain separate channels. They proposed that each channel is most sensitive or tuned to a different spatial frequency.

The trichromaticity theory is a useful analogue to the concept of separate spatial frequency channels. The normal human eye contains three different cone pigments. Each of these pigments is sensitive to a particular band of wavelengths of light. The visual signals arising from just these three pigments interact in various ways to produce the entire range of visible colors. Is it possible that there are spatial channels similar to the

Figure 13–7. A figural aftereffect. After fixating the **x** in the inspection (I) pattern for 1 minute, the squares on the left side of the **x** in the test (T) pattern appear to be farther apart than the squares on the right side.

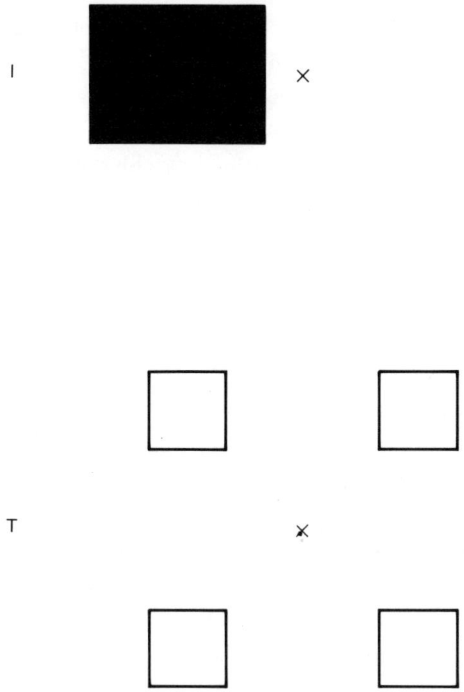

channels involved in color vision? Perhaps at some very late stage in the nervous system, interaction of the outputs of these tuned channels or filters is sufficient to signal the nervous system about the existence of textures and shapes in the visual environment.

In their study of spatial frequency detection Graham and Nachmias (1971) began by distinguishing between what they termed a *single-channel* model and a *multiple-channels* model. The single-channel model implies that a single neural network processes spatial information to transform the optical pattern into neural activity. The organism's perception is determined by this neural activity. A multiple-channels model of the sort envisioned by Campbell and Robson assumes that many channels simultaneously process patterned stimuli by responding differentially to the frequency components comprising the pattern. With this distinction in mind, Graham and Nachmias developed the two spatial gratings shown in Figure 13–6. The graphs of the two gratings show the Fourier components that make them up. Both gratings contain exactly the same frequency components, but have different phase relations. In one phase relation in the grating on the left, the peaks of the two component frequencies add together to give a higher peak amplitude than in the grating on the right. The latter grating is called a peak-subtract grating because the peaks of the two components are always 180° out of phase. In this case the peak-amplitude of the composite grating is the lower of the two.

A single-channel model predicts that the grating on the left, the peaks-added grating, should be more detectable than that on the right. Since the two component frequencies of the two gratings are more than an octave apart in frequency—the higher-frequency component being three times the spatial frequency of the lower-frequency component—the multiple-channels model predicts that both gratings should be equally detectable. This follows from the idea that if two spatial frequencies are sufficiently different, they will be processed in independent channels. If the channels are truly independent, the phases of the component frequencies should not affect their detectability.

The results of the experiment supported the multiple-channels model. The detectability of the grating was not affected by the phase relations of the two components. Graham and Nachmias found that the detection thresholds of both the peaks-added and peaks-subtracted gratings were determined when either of the two components reached the contrast of its own threshold. On the basis of their data involving many different fundamental frequencies in similar experiments, Graham and Nachmias suggest that there may be as many as three channels tuned to respond maximally to three different spatial frequencies. Additional evidence for these separate channels is furnished by the study of adaptation phenomena.

PERCEPTUAL ADAPTATION AND FILTER THEORY

As it will be recalled from the discussion of the Gibson aftereffect in Chapter 7, after an observer looks at curved lines for some period of time, straight lines will appear to be curved in the opposite direction. This is but one of many different aftereffects. Some such aftereffects are consistent with the idea of separate spatial-frequency channels. In the aftereffect studied by Köhler and Wallach (1944), as illustrated in Figure 13–7, a large black rectangle is placed off to one side of a fixation marker in the *inspection pattern* of the figure. After fixating the marker in the inspection pattern for one or two minutes, the observer should shift his gaze to the fixation marker in the *test pattern*. The two small squares on the left side of the fixation marker appear to be farther apart than the two on the right side, and yet the actual vertical separations between the two sets of squares are identical. The increased vertical separation of the squares on the left is thus an aftereffect of viewing the inspection pattern.

When this phenomenon, and others like it, were first studied, it was theorized that electric currents set up in the cortex by the contours of the inspection square polarized the tissues in which they were flowing, and that consequently the currents set up in the same part of the cortex on the left had to find a different path. The displacement of the path of current flow was presumed to be the cortical correlate of the changed perceived positions of the left-hand test squares.

Despite its ability to predict many phenomena, this theory of the *figural aftereffect* is no longer accepted, since if such flows of current actually exist it should be possible to deflect them by implanting mica plates in the visual cortex, and thereby distorting vision. When this was done to monkeys (Sperry and Miner, 1955), their ability to discriminate among different shapes was found to be unaffected.

Among other theories proposed to account for the figural aftereffects is the theory of Osgood and Heyer (1952), which relied on the spontaneous physiological nystagmus of the eyes to explain it. This theory, however, can be discounted, since the aftereffect occurs with stabilized ret-

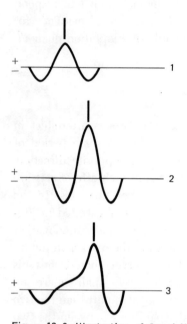

Figure 13–8. Illustration of Ganz' (1966) theory of the figural aftereffects. A contour sets up a region of excitation (+) and one of inhibition (−) that remain for a time after the contour is removed. Such a residual effect is portrayed at 1. A new contour presented at 2 also produces such effects. If the residual effects of the first contour are present at the time of presentation of the second contour, then their excitatory and inhibitory effects combine algebraically. The resultant effect is shown at 3. Note that the apex of the excitatory region of the resultant curve is shifted slightly toward the right.

inal images (Hochberg and Hay, 1956). Still another theory (Ganz, 1966) holds that the aftereffect can be explained in terms of lateral inhibition (see Figure 13–8).

The upper tracing in this figure shows a region of excitation produced by a contour in nervous tissue which is bounded by a region of potential inhibition. The second tracing is the excitation and potential inhibition set up by a contour in another position. When both contours are present simultaneously, the sums of the two patterns of activity they set up results in a displacement of the ridges of excitation. This displacement is the basis for the figural aftereffect.

Ganz' principal point is that a process such as lateral inhibition can account for the figural aftereffect even though the inspection and test figures are shown at different times. The reason is that there is always some effect, like an afterimage, left over after looking at one pattern. This residual effect can function in the same way as would the effect of a simultaneously present contour. Ganz goes on to argue that such phenomena should exist even more strongly when contours are present simultaneously. In point of fact, many of the so-called *geometrical optical illusions* can be explained in these terms. Thus, the Hering Illusion shown in Figure 13–9 contains two parallel bars that look as though they are bowed. Progressive displacements of the vertical bars by the angled bars due to lateral inhibition can account for this illusory bowing.

Several authors have disagreed with Ganz, despite the fact that his theory appears to be consistent with much of the evidence. In any case, the new aftereffects we are about to consider may indicate that this topic should be reviewed once again, since all the theories of aftereffects discussed thus far are single-channel theories.

Pantle and Sekular (1968) and Blakemore and Campbell (1969) have found that adaptation to a high-contrast bar grating of one spatial frequency reduces sensitivity to bar gratings of the same spatial frequency. If you look at a grating of, say, 7 cycles/deg for a few minutes, and then try to detect a grating of the same frequency, it will have to have more contrast to be detected than it did previous to the adaptation period. Sensitivity to bar gratings of less than 3 cycles/deg or more than 14 cycles/deg will hardly be affected at all by exposure to a 7 cycles/deg

Figure 13–9. The Hering illusion. The bowing of the physically parallel lines may be attributed to the processes depicted in Figure 13–8.

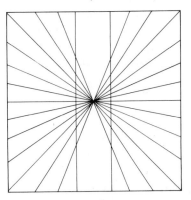

inspection grating. Sensitivity to gratings within a band of from 3 to 14 cycles/deg will be affected, but none so much as one at 7 cycles/deg. This phenomenon occurs even when the eyes are continually scanning the inspection grating, thereby minimizing sharp afterimages of the inspection grating.

The fact that adaptation of contrast sensitivity is frequency-specific is quite consistent with the idea that there are separate channels tuned to different bands of spatial frequencies. But since some aftereffect occurs in bar gratings in a band of frequencies an octave wide, the channels must be rather coarsely tuned. Thus, an aftereffect will occur when the test grating is less than twice the frequency of the inspection grating or more than one-half its frequency. Of course, the effect is strongest when the test and inspection gratings have the same frequency.

Contrast attenuation has been observed also in Köhler and Wallach's figural aftereffect. Ganz attempted to account for this, too, on the basis of lateral inhibition. However, it is difficult to see how lateral inhibition *per se* can account for frequency-specific aftereffects of this type.

Blakemore and Sutton (1969) reported on still another aftereffect that has some of the properties of the displacement phenomenon associated with the figural aftereffect. Their phenomenon is illustrated in Figure 13–10. If the reader will move his eyes back and forth along the small horizontal black bar on the left side of the figure for one or two minutes and then shift his gaze to the dot on the right, he will see this effect. The lower grating on the right will now appear to be more widely spaced than the upper bars.

One explanation for this is that continued looking at the widely spaced bars on the left side selectively fatigues one of the tuned channels. The analogy of color vision may help to explain this effect. Suppose you were to stare at a green light for some time and then look at an orange light. The orange light now appears to be redder than it did before you stared at the green light, since the orange light affects both red and green sensitive channels in the visual system. Staring at the green light alone reduces the sensitivity of the green-sensitive channel so that the activity in the green channel is less while you are looking at the orange light than it was prior to adaptation.

Let us now suppose that there are a limited number of channels transmitting information about spatial frequency. One bar grating may affect two of these channels just as yellow light affects the red and green sensitive pigments in the cones. The relative outputs of these tuned spatial-

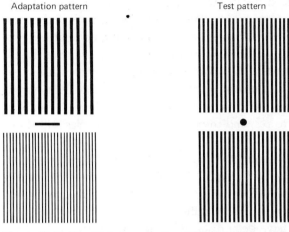

Figure 13–10. The Blakemore-Sutton (1969) aftereffect. After fixating along the small horizontal bar on the left, the upper grating on the right appears to be more narrowly spaced than does the lower grating on the right.

frequency channels represent the spatial frequency of the particular bar grating. But after looking for some time at another grating of a different spatial frequency, one of the two original channels becomes fatigued. Consequently, when the observer looks again at the first grating, the relative outputs of both channels changes. The shift in their relative outputs could signify the presence of a grating of another spatial frequency.

Neither straightforward lateral inhibition nor a field theory such as that envisioned by Köhler and Wallach can account for this aftereffect of Blakemore and Sutton. While we can speculate about the application of these new ideas to the older figural aftereffect, this issue remains to be clarified. The lateral inhibition theory is really consistent with a single-channel theory of spatial pattern perception, whereas the results of Blakemore and Sutton are better explained in terms of a multiple-channel theory. It remains to be seen which approach will be more fruitful in the long run. This author believes that a multiple-channel model will prove the more helpful in stimulating further theoretical developments.

PHYSIOLOGICAL BASIS OF SPATIAL FREQUENCY CHANNELS

Blakemore and Campbell (1969) found that after an observer inspects a grating of a particular spatial frequency for a long time, the average evoked potential produced by an oscillating grating of the same spatial frequency will become attenuated. This result, together with the psychophysical data, suggests that there is a large population of cortical cells tuned to respond to a given spatial frequency. When these cells are fatigued by constant exposure to a particular spatial frequency, they become less responsive to that stimulus. When another spatial frequency is presented, however, the many other cells among the millions of units in the visual cortex tuned to respond to other spatial frequencies will do so vigorously.

Thus far we have not attempted to make any connection between the feature-detecting units found by Hubel and Weisel and the gratings discussed in this chapter. The reader may well ask how it is that numerous cortical units are sensitive to lines of different orientations while the psychological evidence we have been discussing concerns hypothetical channels responsive to spatial frequencies. In point of fact, the hypothetical channels responsive to different spatial frequencies may well include the line and bar detectors of Hubel and Weisel.

Campbell, Cooper, and Enroth-Cugell (1969) recorded from single cells in the visual cortex of the cat while the animal was stimulated by moving gratings that were varied in both spatial frequency and contrast. They found several units whose firing rates were affected differentially by gratings of different spatial frequency. Some units, believed by the authors to be fibers of cells in the lateral geniculate nucleus, were affected by gratings of any orientation. Other units, probably cortical cell bodies, were sensitive only to gratings of a particular orientation. It should be noted, however, that none of the units they studied were responsive to spatial frequencies higher than about 4 cycles/deg, and most units responded best when the spatial frequency was less than 1 cycle/deg. Since humans are sensitive to much higher spatial frequencies, it is difficult to draw clear parallels between the two organisms. Still, it is plain that units in the cortex do respond to grating stimuli as well as to isolated bars or lines.

It is possible to conceive of tuned channels that include line detectors as essential elements. To see how this may work let us consider a hypothetical physical system capable of responding differentially to different spatial frequencies.

Suppose that a bar grating were placed under an opaque plate containing an aperture. The plate may move across the grating so that the aperture scans it. The light passing through the aperture is integrated

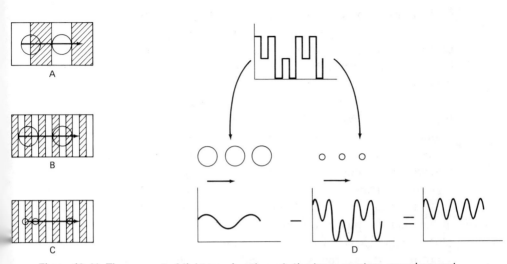

Figure 13–11. The amount of light passing through the large aperture superimposed on grating A will fluctuate with changes in the position of the aperture. Yet, when this same aperture is placed on grating B, the total amount of light collected by the aperture will vary very little as its position changes. Thus, an aperture may act like a low-pass filter, since its output will vary only if the width of one cycle of the grating is larger than the diameter of the aperture. The output of the smaller aperture at C would fluctuate with its position because its diameter is smaller than the width of one cycle of grating C. The smaller aperture has a cut-off at a higher frequency than that of a large aperture. If a large and a small aperture scan the same complex grating, as in D, the large aperture would detect the low-frequency component, and the small aperture both the low- and high-frequency components. The difference between these two outputs is the high-frequency component. Thus, two apertures, one large and the other small, may be used together as a band-pass filter.

and then measured by a photodetector. If the aperture is very large, then even if many fine bars pass under it the integrated light energy detected through the aperture will remain constant during the scanning. If, on the other hand, the bar grating under the aperture is of a very low spatial frequency, then the aperture will pass more light energy when it is sitting on a bright portion of the grating than when sitting on a less bright portion. Thus we can state that the integrated light energy detected through the aperture will vary with the position of the aperture, and moreover, that a large aperture has the characteristics of a low-pass filter responding only when very low spatial frequencies are placed under it. As suggested by Figure 13–11, the width of the aperture should be less than one-half the width of a cycle of the grating if the system is to detect the frequency of the grating optimally. Gratings coarser than this will also be detected. Now, if the aperture were made smaller still, it would be possible for the photodetector to pick up even higher frequencies in the grating. Thus, even a small aperture is a low-pass filter, and yet it passes higher frequencies as well as low frequencies.

It is possible to construct a band-pass filter from two apertures and two photodetectors. If one aperture is small it will pass high and low frequencies; if the other aperture is large it will pass only low frequencies. If we take the difference between the outputs of the two photodetectors, we shall be measuring just the higher frequencies.

The apertures in our system are circular, and hence will tolerate large differences in the orientations of patterns. A very low spatial frequency can be picked up through a rather large aperture even if it is tilted at an angle relative to the scanning path of the aperture. But if the aperture were a narrow slit, it would be very sensitive to the orientation of the grating relative to the scanning path. The output of the photodetector would be markedly reduced if the grating were to be tilted. Several slit apertures at different orientations, however, could be used to scan a grating, and one such aperture would detect the grating—provided that its spatial frequency is low enough for the width of the aperture. Actually, simultaneous recording from two apertures oriented at right angles to each other provides sufficient information to pick up the presence of any grating regardless of its orientation.

Now, we see how line detectors may serve as elements in a spatial filter. It is not necessary that a slit aperture actually scan a grating. If there are many apertures of the same size overlapping each other, differences in the light levels collected by these apertures can indicate the presence of spatial frequencies. Concentric and oriented receptive fields of cortical cells can serve this same purpose. Activity of these cells would indicate the presence of spatial frequencies in the visual field. Moreover, the opposed effects of the centers and surrounds of these receptive fields provide all the requisites of a broadly tuned band-pass filter, similar to the hypothetical channels of Campbell and Robson. Therefore, the units discovered thus far in the cortex could provide raw materials for the construction of spatial frequency filters. These spatial frequency channels must, however, be more narrowly tuned than has thus far been indicated, for otherwise it would be impossible to perceive a scene composed of many different spatial frequencies as being different from a simple sinusoidal variation in light. As in the analogous situation in color vision, spatial frequencies would "mix" to form other apparently simple spatial frequencies.

SENSITIVITY TO ORIENTATION

Gilinsky (1968) found that an observer's ability to resolve a line grating was a function of the orientation and duration of a previously exposed grating of the same spatial frequency. This finding provides further support for the rather widely accepted idea that oriented receptive fields play an important role in spatial-frequency filtering. This, and other evidence (e.g., Gilinsky and Mayo, 1971), suggests that there may be multiple sets of frequency-selective channels designed to detect spatial frequencies of different retinal orientation.

NEONATAL STUDIES

When one is first exposed to this idea of frequency-selective channels, one's reaction is likely to be that this is a rather interesting fantasy. Even though the whole idea seems to lack reality, however, some recent work involving newborn animals should go a long way toward jarring this attitude.

Hirsch and Spinelli (1970) raised kittens wearing special goggles. One eye could see only vertical stripes, and the other eye only horizontal stripes. After some time the cortical units of these kittens were studied. Unlike the normally reared kitten, most of whose cortical cells can be driven from either eye, the Hirsch-Spinelli kittens had cortical units that were largely monocular. Cells driven by the eye that viewed only vertical stripes had receptive fields elongated vertically, and cells driven by the eye that viewed only horizontal stripes had horizontally elongated receptive fields.

Blakemore and Cooper (1970) raised one group of kittens in an environment containing only vertical stripes, and another group in an environment containing only horizontal stripes. All the kittens wore ruffs about their necks so that they could not see their own bodies. After five months they were tested, first, behaviorally, and then electrophysiologically. The animals behaved as though they were blind to contours oriented normally to the contours of their early environment. In the electrophysiological tests, no neurons could be found that responded to contours oriented normally to the ones to which the animal had been exposed.

Although the distribution of receptive field orientations was abnormal in these kittens, the experimenters could find no "silent" areas in their cortexes. This indicated that units had not been destroyed by lack of use, but rather that units that might normally respond to, say, horizontal contours, become tuned to respond to vertical contours if these had comprised the total early visual environment of the animals.

This conclusion is supported by the results of Muir and Mitchell (1973). In behavioral testing of their kittens, these latter authors found a long-term deficit in acuity for contours that were oriented normally to the contours to which the kittens were exposed during their first five months of life. This acuity deficit is not unlike an astigmatism and, despite prolonged living in a normal environment, the kittens never recovered from it. The dramatic behavioral deficits observed by Blakemore and Cooper as well as by Hirsch were temporary in the longer-term Muir and Mitchell study.

Mitchell, Freeman, Millidot, and Haegerstrom (1973) studied humans who suffered with long-standing astigmatism. Astigmatism results in a blurring of contours of one orientation while contours of another orientation are imaged sharply on the retina, and can be corrected by placing appropriate cylindrical lenses before the astigmatic eye. When this is done so that there is little refractory error, persons suffering from long-term astigmatism still have relatively poor acuity for contours oriented in one direction. Moreover, when the refractory errors are corrected, these subjects give smaller evoked potentials when gratings of the appropriate orientation are oscillated before their eyes. Thus, if a person had an astigmatism that blurred vertical contours, after optical correction the same person will exhibit a smaller evoked potential when the stimulus contains vertical gratings than he does when the stimulus contains horizontal gratings. These effects of exposure to blur in one dimension during early childhood are apparently permanent, and suggest that channels tuned to spatial frequencies of a particular orientation will not develop properly unless appropriate stimulation is provided for them at the critical early stage in life.

THE PROBLEMS OF SPATIAL PHASE

While there appears to be great promise in the frequency-selective channels approach to perception of pattern, many problems remain to be solved. For one thing, at suprathreshold levels we are sensitive to the relative phases of superimposed sinusoidal patterns. The peaks-added grating of Graham and Nachmias and the peaks-subtracted grating do look different when they are well above the contrast threshold for their detection. Moreover, even if these spatial filters underlie form perception, if one form is to be distinguished from another when the two contain identical spatial frequencies, this can be done only if phase-differences can be discriminated. Anstis (1973) has shown that prolonged exposure to coarse-grained sandpaper makes print of somewhat larger grain size look larger still. It would appear from this that the frequency content of the sandpaper produces an aftereffect similar to that produced by Blakemore and Sutton and shifts the frequency of content of print in the direction of still lower spatial frequencies. Yet, since we can distinguish between print and sandpaper, the visual system must be sensitive to the phases of different spatial frequencies. More evidence for phase-sensitivity is implicit in a recent study by K. DeValois (1973).

While it is unlikely that there is ever a 1-to-1 representation of a form in an observer's brain at any point in time, the operations performed by the brain must be related uniquely to one aspect or another of the form. Therefore, if tuned channels are involved in the analysis of pattern and form, they must be phase-sensitive if their outputs are to indicate the presence of particular objects. The problem of how information about spatial phase is processed in the nervous system is very far from solution. Without phase-sensitive mechanisms concepts like "local sign" and "visual direction," discussed in earlier chapters, would be meaningless.

Spatial-phase sensitivity is part of the larger problem as to how information about different attributes of objects becomes integrated so that the observer perceives a coherent world. Evidence is now being amassed to indicate that the feature-processing channels of the nervous system serve multiple purposes.

THE CONTINGENT AFTEREFFECTS

One aspect of this problem of integration of different attributes of scenes involves color. How do colors get assigned to representations of objects? Our chapters on color perception and on form perception have for the most part treated these functions as separate processes.

An experiment by Ivo Kohler (1964) illustrates how color perception may be influenced by other perceptual processes. He prepared a pair of spectacles with split lenses, as shown in Figure 13–12; the left half of

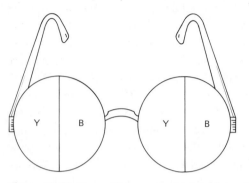

Figure 13–12. The split-lens spectacles of Ivo Kohler (1964). The left half of each lens is tinted yellow, and the right half, blue.

each lens was yellow, and the right half, blue. On rolling the eyes to the left when these spectacles are first worn, the subject sees all objects as tinged with a yellow color. Rolling the eyes to the right causes objects in that direction to appear tinged with a blue color. After a long period the wearer of the spectacles is no longer aware of colors that are contingent upon eye-position, but upon removing the spectacles after this period of adaptation a very strange effect occurs. Rolling the eyes to the left causes objects in that direction to be tinged with a blue color and rolling the eyes to the right causes objects to be tinged with a yellow color.

It is important to recognize that the central foveas of Kohler's observers were exposed to different colors, depending upon the positions of the eyes in their sockets. The effect was not attributed to local retinal adaptation, because the colors seen after wearing the spectacles were contingent upon the direction of gaze—which is why this and related phenomena have been called *contingent aftereffects*. This phenomenon had no clear explanation when it was first reported, and we still have no complete explanation for it. However, a recent study (McCullough, 1965a) suggested that the effect may not be contingent on the direction of gaze *per se* because, though the two foveas were equally stimulated, the right and left edges of the visual field were differentially adapted to blue and yellow light. Nevertheless, other truly contingent aftereffects do exist.

McCollough (1965b) demonstrated still another contingent aftereffect involving color. A grating of vertical lines was projected onto a screen through an orange filter, which caused the grating to appear as a set of orange and black vertical stripes on a screen. This grating was exposed for 5 seconds and was followed by a dark period of 1 second. Immediately after the dark period a second grating of horizontal lines was projected onto the screen through a blue-green filter. McCollough continued to present these gratings alternately for several minutes. Following this period of adaptation the observers were exposed to a vertically oriented black and white bar grating and to a horizontally oriented black and white grating. When looking at the vertical grating the observers reported that it appeared to be blue-green in color. The black and white horizontal grating appeared to be orange in color. When one of these gratings was tilted through 45 degrees of arc the color aftereffect was absent. The orientation contingent color aftereffect persists for several hours although it does grow weaker with time.

The McCollough aftereffect suggests that the feature-detecting channel of the visual system carries information about color as well. Thus, line-detecting neurons in the visual cortex may be tuned also to respond more strongly to edges of one color or another. When edges of one particular color are presented for a long time, the units tuned to that color become fatigued. The remaining color-tuned edge detectors will then respond to a neutral stimulus to produce the impression of an edge tinged with the complement of the adapting color. Harris and Gibson (1968) were able to demonstrate that the McCollough aftereffect could not be explained solely in terms of negative after-images. They proposed also an alternative to the theory that the effect depends upon some units in the cortex that are sensitive to both edge orientation and color.

Hepler (1968) and Stromeyer and Mansfield (1970) have demonstrated movement-contingent color aftereffects. In this experiment a green and black bar grating is continuously moved vertically downward. The alternative stimulus is a red and black bar grating moved vertically upward. After a period of successive exposures to these moving stimuli the observer is permitted to look at a white and black bar grating that is moving either upward or downward. When the neutral grating is moving upward it appears to be tinged with green, and when moving downward it appears to be tinged with red. Stromeyer and Mansfield found that this motion-contingent aftereffect is present as long as six weeks after the adaptation period.

In summary, it may well be that channels within the visual system carry multiple information. Further work in this area will undoubtedly reveal exciting new approaches to the study of the perception of complex scenes.

A RECONSIDERATION OF FORM PERCEPTION

The approach taken in this chapter to the problem of form perception is quite different from the traditional approach. As we saw in the preceding chapter, the early theorists started with topics like the principles of organization and figure-ground segregation, and were ultimately led to the consideration of a rather ambiguous concept of feature analysis. What is to be gained from dissecting an object into representations of its lines and angles, with the task of putting them back together still to be performed? Why shouldn't nature have been satisfied simply with relaying a representation of a form straight to the brain—in other words, with a picture-in-the-head psychology?

If we adopt the point of view set forth by J. J. Gibson (1966), it does make sense to consider feature detection as a basis for form perception. Gibson proposed that there is no picture-in-the-head, that the brain does not construct information from the input of a sensory nerve by any process. For him the information is already there in features of the world; and the brain simply "resonates" to this information. Yet we are still left with the problem of defining the features that constitute the information utilized by the organism. Lines and angles are not adequate; they are not sufficiently general. And still, the spatial frequencies in the two dimensions of the visual field describe not only lines and angles but also any other pattern of luminance. The traditional problems of form perception should be reviewed with this concept in mind.

Patterns organizing by proximity lend themselves very nicely to the Fourier approach. Rows of dots group into couples if their spacing is right. This differential spacing alters the spatial frequency of the distribution of dots, as shown in Figure 13–13. In this figure couples are seen in the upper row, and triads of dots in the lower. In both rows the density of light changes in a periodic manner from left to right. The pattern of light in the upper row has a higher spatial frequency than does the pattern in the lower row. Is organization by proximity merely a matter of responding or resonating to the spatial frequency in the display? While organization by similarity and organization by common fate are not so obviously related to analysis by spatial frequency, it is possible that this approach as well can be applied here.

The information-theoretic approaches to form perception also share some of the attributes of spatial-frequency analysis. A pattern with many different spatial frequencies can appear to be very complicated; but when

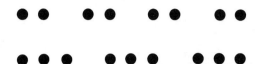

Figure 13–13. Due to differential proximity, the lower row of dots has a lower spatial frequency component than that of the upper row of dots.

a few spatial frequencies define the pattern in two dimensions, it might appear to be relatively simple. In this sense there is more information in the complicated pattern than there is in the simple pattern.

Julesz (1970) has undertaken a program to explore the usefulness of Fourier methods in describing the stimuli to stereopsis. Segregation of form in depth requires that the two half-fields share similar frequency spectra. They can do this and still appear to be very different, as in some of the stereograms discussed in Chapter 8. The effectiveness of a masking stimulus in a metacontrast experiment may also depend in part on its spatial-frequency content, as some recent reports suggest (Weisstein, 1973).

Many problems remain to be resolved, among them that of deciding just how independent the spatial frequency channels are from each other. Interactions among different spatial frequencies are a distinct possibility. Thus, Tolhurst (1972) found that when the fundamental and third harmonic are present simultaneously in a square-wave adapting stimulus, they are far less effective in masking sine-wave gratings of the same frequencies than they are when presented alone. This indicates that the superposition principle does not apply to the visual analyzing systems— which is to say that the system is nonlinear (see p. 109). Consequently, inferences from experiments involving near-threshold stimuli to perception of suprathreshold stimuli may be made only with considerable caution.

14

information processing and attention

In this final chapter we return to some of the topics considered in our first chapter, which dealt with the nature of perception. Perceiving was viewed as a constructive process—not unlike communicating events to others. This dynamic concept was contrasted with the picture-in-the-head theory, which holds that the problem of perception is solved once it is shown how a scene is represented in the brain.

Whichever approach one takes to perception, it is plain that effects of the stimulation of sense organs are processed in the central nervous system. The experiment of Gibson (1966) in which observers handle oddly shaped objects is a useful example of why this must be so. The manifold effects of cutaneous stimulation and of changes in the position in the fingers are infinitely variable. The nervous system must decode this impressive array of information if the observer is to recognize the object.

There are many comparable examples in the visual domain. Thus, Hochberg (1968) showed that an object may be recognized when it is viewed through a small, slowly moving aperture that scans its outlines. Stimulation that varies over time can lead to the construction of a coherent *schema* to represent the object. But the construction of perceptual schemata involves memory. If a person is to extract higher-order information from more elementary events distributed in time and space, at least some of these events must be stored away for future use. Recent work on visual-information processing is relevant because it deals with the problem of the storage of information.

THE VISUAL ICON AND SHORT-TERM MEMORY

Neisser (1967) suggested that psychologists adopt the term *visual icon* to stand for a stored representation of the retinal image which is available for subsequent analysis by the organism. When a subject is shown an array of randomly selected letters for a few milliseconds, it is unlikely that he will be able to remember more than about 4 of the letters a short time after exposure. This fact implies that the "span of apprehension" in visual perception is extremely limited. On the other hand, research by Sperling (1960) revealed that many more than 4 items are left behind by a brief flash.

In one of Sperling's experiments a 4-by-3 matrix of 12 randomly selected letters were displayed for only 50 msec. The matrix was followed by a dark field. One of three tones followed the exposure of the letters. A high-pitched tone signified that the observer had to report the letters he remembered from the top row of the matrix. A tone of intermediate pitch indicated that the observer had to report on the middle row of letters; and a low-pitched tone required him to report on the lowermost row of letters. After each exposure the observer reported the letters in the row indicated.

If the observer could remember only 4 items out of 12, and he did not know in advance to which row he should attend, then on the average he would be unable to recall more than 1 or 2 letters from any one row. Using this *method of partial report*, however, Sperling's observers were able to report 3 or 4 of the 4 letters in any designated row. This meant that 9 or 10 letters out of a matrix of 12 were available for reporting immediately after the exposure. Since the observer was able to name only four of the letters in the matrix if asked to report on its entire contents, it must be that during the time of reporting the stored letters were fading. By the time the observer reported on 4 of the letters, the remaining items in storage were obliterated. If the tone requiring the observer to respond by recalling the letters he had seen was delayed by 1 second, there was a substantial decline in accuracy of reporting (see Fig. 14–1). Using the partial report method described above, Sperling found that observers could correctly recall but 4 of the letters out of the entire matrix of 12 letters after a delay of 1 second—which implies that the stored matrix had decayed beyond recall in a period shorter than 1 second.

These results indicate that for some time after a brief flash the observer may have an actual retinal image of the matrix available to him.

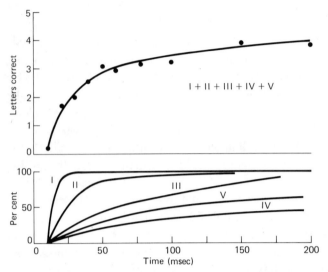

Figure 14–1. The upper graph shows a monotonic increase in the total number of letters reported correctly when an array of five letters is presented in locations I to V on a horizontal line. The lower graph shows the per cent letters reported correctly at each location, I to V. Location I is the left-most letter in the horizontal array.

The action of the retina is not instantaneous: it takes time for electrical potentials to develop and decay in the retina's various layers. The perceived duration of a 1-microsecond flash may not be distinguishable from the duration of a 100-msec flash. Sperling (1960) estimated that visual persistence in his experiment may have been as long as 160 msec. When Haber and Nathanson (1968) used a version of the Parks (1965) effect to measure visual persistence, they discovered that it could be as long as 250 msec.

The Parks effect is the perception of an entire form even though the moving form is viewed through a very narrow slit. If the speed of the form's displacement behind the slit is fast enough, the image appears as a whole with all its parts simultaneously present. It is now believed that the eyes move while the form is being moved behind the slit, thereby causing the form to be "painted" on the retina (Anstis and Atkinson, 1967). A similar painting phenomenon can occur if a stationary form is presented behind a moving slit. As the slit scans the surface, the parts of the form visible in the slit are exposed in succession. Haber and Nathanson found that a form can be seen as a coherent and whole object if the scan period is 250 msec or less.

High-contrast stimuli can be stored on the retina for longer periods than low-contrast stimuli. The state of adaptation of the eye will also affect storage time. In all probability very high spatial frequencies lose their visibility faster than some relatively lower spatial frequencies. In all cases, however, some persistence exists, and the persisting retinal effect may be available for extraction of information. This persisting visual image is known as the *visual icon*. The idea that visual persistence is active in this memory task is supported by Sperling's (1960) finding that a bright post-exposure field reduces the accuracy of recall for the reason that the bright post-exposure field is capable of reducing the visibility of a persisting retinal image.

An observer can verbally report no more than 3 letters in 1 second, and even fewer letters if he has to write them down. Moreover, reporting can occur after some initial delay. Since the iconically stored matrix is seriously degraded before the observer can report on the letters he had seen, there must be some capacity to store the information in the image prior to and during the report. The place of storage is referred to as the *short-term memory buffer*. In effect, the observer scans the visually stored information and reads it into short-term storage. This is not unlike looking up a telephone number and then remembering the number prior to dialing. The fact that the telephone number is typically forgotten after the call is placed suggests a short-term memory capacity.

One question of concern to scientists concerns how information in visual storage gets into the short-term memory. Is the image scanned and read in sequentially, or is it processed in parallel so that some information from the entire array is transferred all at once? Sperling (1967) utilized a post-exposure field of "visual noise" to determine whether the processing of the iconic image occurs sequentially or in parallel. The noise field was composed of bits and pieces of many letters, and effectively obliterated the persistence of five letters presented as test stimuli. By delaying the onset of the noise field by various amounts of time on different trials, the observer had more or less time in which to scan the letters in the image left by their brief exposure.

Sperling found that each additional increment of from 10-to-15 msec allowed the observer to report one additional letter. Moreover, observers tended to report the presence of a letter from the left-most position when the noise field was close in time to the test field. This suggests that letters are scanned sequentially. When the icon is available for a very brief period, the first letter scanned may be the only one stored by the observer. With increasing time before the presentation of the noise field, the observer might start to report letters that were in other positions in the array.

In our culture it is customary to read letters from left to right. As indicated, there was a tendency for observers to report letters beginning with the left-most position after short exposure times. With increasing exposure time, letters toward the right side of the array tended to be recalled more accurately, in spite of individual idiosyncracies in the sequence of reporting letters as exposure time increased.

Sperling observed that even at the briefer exposure times letters at all locations begin to be reported at better-than-chance level. He felt that the apparent serial order of recall with increased exposure time was due to the fact that recall from different locations develops at different rates. Thus, he interpreted his results as providing evidence for an essentially parallel process of letter recognition. Such results, however, may occur also when processing is a mixture of sequential and parallel events. Asymmetry of reporting letters in a row could be the result of a sequential scanning coupled with some degree of parallel processing.

As soon as information is registered in the short-term memory it may well have lost its primarily visual character. Conrad (1964), for example, showed that errors made in recall of visually presented letters tended to resemble acoustic confusions rather than visual confusion. Thus, observers might have responded with a C rather than an E and an S rather than an F. The F and E letters look more alike but the S and F letters sound more alike. Data such as these led Sperling (1967) to the idea that items in visual storage may be rehearsed one at a time and then remembered in auditory storage.

The encoding of visual information into auditory form is likely to occur only when verbal or verbally describable stimuli are employed. Most visual stimuli are not easily described in words: the human face is a good case in point. Moreover, although some complicated scenes may be described verbally, it would take a very long time to do so. The fact that linguistic stimuli such as words, letters, and numbers have been the predominant stimuli in the study of information processing is one of the great limitations in this field.

Classical research in perception is concerned with effects of orientation, spatial position, luminance, contrast, and context on the perception of objects. Studies of information processing, however, have dealt almost exclusively with "items." These are typically letters, words, and numbers. Factors such as contrast, or the presence or absence of a visual framework, are usually not considered. It is as though researchers in this field want to dispense as quickly as possible with the problem of the analysis of the physical attributes of stimuli and deal with them as abstract items being processed in the internal computing machine. Verbal materials are particularly useful for this purpose, since they become units of information or items stored here or there and recalled from this or that portion of the memory. These materials are the classic stimuli used in the study of verbal learning.

Workers in the field of information processing are aware of this problem. Thus, according to Atkinson and Shiffrin (1968), there must be short-term storage of non-linguistic materials but the nature of this storage is not well understood. Despite this limitation, models of memory have been developed to explain a wide variety of phenomena.

The role of rehearsal is quite important in memory. When a person fumbles for coins before dialing a telephone number he has just looked up, he might recite the number over and over again to keep it in memory until it is dialed. Rehearsal of this kind is possible also in a typical verbal learning experiment in which a list of words has to be recalled on subsequent trials. After presentation of one of the words on the list, the subject may repeat it to himself several times in the hope of fixing it more strongly in his memory. Such rehearsal is one means for encoding visually presented material in auditory form (Sperling, 1967, 1970b). Atkinson and Shiffrin (1968) suggested that such phenomena imply the existence of a buffer that holds or stores the items being rehearsed. Items in this buffer may be pushed out by new items when the buffer's capacity has been exceeded. Such items may be lost entirely. On the other hand, items in the buffer are always being transferred to long-term storage—another major component of the memory system.

Items in short-term storage are always being circulated into long-term storage and back again into short-term storage. As a result of this recursive process items become permanently engraved in the long-term memory and remain available for recall into the working short-term memory.

The term "working" was used to indicate that the things one is aware of at any point in time are in the short-term memory. The vast bulk of the things we know are not at the forefronts of our mind. If I were to ask you for your address you would have to retrieve it from your long-term storage, bring it into short term storage and then recite it. Presumably, the representations of complex scenes also are transferred from long-term memory to short-term memory when they are recalled. The nature of this stored information is not known. Most writers in this field believe that when a stimulus is presented it evokes from long-term memory other associated items. Thus, the presentation of a picture of an orange might evoke memories of the word orange, of tastes, textures, odors, and even temperatures. These may all be transferred to short-term memory for subsequent use.

One remarkable thing in all this is that items in memory are treated as though they are independent "particles" that become assembled into constellations by processes such as those described by the laws of association. Until very recently the interaction among items was not dealt with in information-processing theories.

The Leeper experiment described in the preceding chapter showed that an ambiguous figure may be perceived in one way and not in another if the observer has been prepared for it by prior exposure to an unambiguous figure. The resulting appearance of the ambiguous figure could be attributed to the fact that it shares certain features with the previously seen unambiguous figure. These features are associated with particular traces in the long-term memory. The transfer of these traces to the short-term memory may give the ambiguous figure its identity, and thus, information-processing models can lead the way toward explaining some previously puzzling phenomena. On the other hand, the experience one has in viewing an ambiguous figure, such as Leeper's figure or Jastrow's duck-rabbit, suggests that the memory traces interact with the representation of the ambiguous figure and, perhaps, with each other. This interaction among items in short-term storage is in need of much more attention than it has yet received.

It is not possible to reduce all events in memory into verbal form. When recalling a scene, a person does not recite to himself that one object appeared closer to him than some other object. The perception of the color yellow, for example, can be produced by the mixture of two other colors, and no special verbal intervention is needed to see it. Nor, for that matter, is it required for seeing one of Julesz' squares as raised above its background of random dots. Visual storage and short term visual memory are, however, still vital constituents of perception.

The previous remarks should not be taken as meaning that verbal behavior is irrelevant to perception. Glanzer and Clark (1963, 1964) performed experiments indicating that verbal processes may well be important in the perception of form. They presented a number of forms to observers and had them try to reproduce the forms after seeing them, and then had them describe the forms verbally. The experimenters simply counted the number of words needed for each description. The result was that the ability of an observer to reproduce a form was highly correlated with the number of words needed for him to describe it. If a form needed many words to describe it, it was less likely to be reproduced correctly than if few words were needed. Thus, the number of words needed to describe a form is both an index of its complexity and a negative correlate of its reproductibility. According to Glanzer and Clark (1964), an observer translates sensory information into words and uses them as the basis for his final response. This is known as the *verbal loop hypothesis.*

The verbal loop hypothesis makes a great deal of sense when it is related to many psychological functions. In immediate-recall tasks, for example, it is of considerable importance. Aaronson, Markowitz, and Shapiro (1971), for example, found that the immediate recall of sequences of auditorily presented digits may be enhanced if the period of time between digits is made longer. Thus, keeping the rate of digit presentation constant, Aaronson and her associates found that compressing the duration of the sound of a digit (and thereby prolonging the silent period between digits) makes it easier for the observer to remember the order of a sequence of digits. This implies that the observer is better able to process and store items of information when he is not required to process sensory events simultaneously. The observer must be translating sensory information into some symbolic form that is subsequently utilized in recall.

The problem with the verbal loop hypothesis is that not all perceivers have linguistic ability; and again, there are situations that cannot be put into words. However, the fact that symbolic representation of any sort is related to recall behavior suggests that other kinds of symbolic representation may be involved in other activities related to perception. A hint as to the nature of such symbolic processes was given by Sperling (1970*b*), who noted that when an observer recalls a letter he must, in effect, decide that he is going to make a particular response. This response may entail writing the letter or pronouncing it. In both cases an extensive repertoire of motor behavior must be called upon. As Sperling has put it, it is useful to distinguish between the decision as to which response one wants to execute and actually executing such a response. Thus, *recognition* of a letter may be functionally identical to deciding which program of overt behavior is to be executed in order to indicate that one has recognized it.

Recognition, interpreted as setting up a program of action, is not limited to the programming of verbal action. The co-ordination of programs governing many kinds of activity—verbal, postural, and overt motor behavior—may well be involved. This complex co-ordination is undoubtedly the stuff of which attention is made.

ATTENTION

It is natural to think of attention as a special faculty of the mind. If one pays attention to something, he will see it more clearly and remember it better. If one does not pay attention, he will not remember the events he is ignoring. Hence attention may be thought of as a filtering function that excludes some things from the center of awareness and includes other things.

This common-sense interpretation has its counterpart in the world of science. One view holds that attention is made possible by filtering processes that attenuate information coming from a sense organ (cf. Hernandez-Peón, *et al.*, 1956). This physiological interpretation implies that there are feedback circuits from the brain to the sense organs, and that this feedback reduces the sensitivity of the sense organs. The experiments designed to demonstrate this filtering action have been devastatingly criticized on the grounds that the effects noted can be attributed to peripheral factors (Horn, 1965). Thus, the click-evoked potential recorded from the cochlear nucleus in the brain of the cat becomes smaller when the cat gets a sniff of sardines or sees a mouse. This is probably due to the fact that the cat's ears change their positions as he orients his body toward the more interesting stimulus.

A more sophisticated theory would place the filter at a higher level than that of the sense organ. The sensory data get to the brain but are not processed in any great detail when something else is going on that is of greater interest to the organism. This was Broadbent's (1957) original proposal. Since then various experiments in dichotic listening, in which one ear of an observer listens to one speaker while the other ear listens to another speaker (Cherry, 1953; Treisman, 1960; 1964; Treisman and Geffen, 1967), require that the filter be located after a good deal of processing of the sensory input.

In one variant on this position, Treisman (1964), and Treisman and

Geffen (1967), suggested that the unattended speech is not analyzed to the same degree as is attended speech, and further, that features of the attended and unattended speech are analyzed and that selection taking place during the analysis results in the identification of the verbal content of one of the messages and not in that of the other. When there were distinct physical differences between the two voices in Treisman's experiments, observers had no difficulty in keeping the two messages apart. When instructed to follow the meaning of a female voice, for example, observers could ignore a male voice. The more alike the voices were in physical and in linguistic structure, however, the more difficult it was to keep the messages separated.

According to Treisman's theory, messages may be selected on the basis of their physical features and, when necessary, also on their linguistic characteristics. The grammatical features of speech can be detected and used to sensitize the observer to certain signals. These more or less predictable signals are then passed onto the higher stage of processing for further identification. The ultimate perception occurs after all this processing. The signals that are unselected are generally unperceived unless they are confused with the attended message and passed on to the higher centers. In this model, therefore, perception occurs after a great deal of processing and filtering of incoming sensory information. Selection is based upon filtering of the physical attributes of as well as the linguistic features of the speech.

There are alternatives to this model of attention. The interested reader is referred to Deutsch and Deutsch (1963). Norman (1969) has given us a thoughtful review of the various alternatives. For our purposes, however, the approach taken by Hochberg (1970) seem to be more pertinent.

Hochberg (1970) makes the point that listening is an active process involving a special sort of covert speech. If an observer hears a particular unit of speech sound, he may then select a program for the execution of a well-practiced larger unit of speech. If subsequent elementary speech units are consistent with the larger unit he selected, he goes on to program still larger articulations. He is trying to predict as many words ahead as he can. Following Miller, Galanter, and Pribram (1960), Hochberg proposed that the active listener is trying to formulate a speech plan. This plan is stored and checked against the ongoing speech. It is used to follow what another person is saying during listening and to follow oneself during active speech. In this theory, during dichotic listening, incoming messages are analyzed for their physical attributes as well as for elementary speech units (phonemes). Rather than having the unattended message excluded by means of a filter, the attended message is being matched against the anticipated events generated by the organism. The listener is aware of the attended speech because he is continually checking it against programs of articulatory sequences. What the listener stores or remembers is the confirmed representation of the speech. This is what enables him to reconstruct the heard words on request.

This brings us back to Sperling's point that recognition can be interpreted as initiating a program of action. Recognition as awareness entails the selection of a hierarchy of programs. Whatever is attended to is being responded to actively. We do not have a perceived image on an inner screen, and then respond to what we perceive. The things we perceive are perceived *because* they are responded to. This does not prove that unperceived sensory events have no effect on the organism. Clearly, features are extracted from speech and from visual patterns prior to awareness.

Hochberg (1970) made the point that we have a vocabulary of sequential visuomotor expectancies somewhat like the phonemes and morphemes of speech. Each fixation is checked against an inner plan or set of expectancies. The structure of visuomotor expectancies provides the basis for the selective perception of visual form much in the same way that linguistic expectancies provide the basis for the selective perception of speech. A schema of a scene represents the anticipated features that would be seen if particular eye movements were made. The confirmation of these expectancies is the basis for the selective perception of form. Thus, the phenomena of organization discussed in Chapter 12 may well be instances of a selective attention process based on these expectancies.

The visual scanning experiments of Neisser and his associates (Neisser, 1963; Neisser and Beller, 1965; Neisser and Lazar, 1964; Neisser and Stoper, 1965) are pertinent at this point. Figure 14–2 contains lists of various words. In a typical experiment observers had to scan one of the lists and identify the word containing some specified letter or letters, or the word from which a given letter was absent. The speed of accomplishing such a task was a function of the nature of the materials involved.

For our purposes there are two related points to be made on the basis of Neisser's results. For one thing, the ease with which a search task can be accomplished is related to the distinctiveness of the item being searched for. Thus, an angular letter in a background of round letters will be detected more quickly than would a round letter in a background of

a	b
ODUGQR	IVMXEW
QCDUGO	EWVMIX
CQOGRD	EXWMVI
QUGCDR	IXEMWV
URDGQO	VXWEMI
GRUQDO	MXVEWI
DUZGRO	XVWMEI
UCGROD	MWXVIE
DQRCGU	VIMEXW
QDOCGU	EXVWIM
CGUROQ	VWMIEX
OCDURQ	VMWIEX
OUCGQD	XVWMEI
RGQCOU	WXVEMI
GRUDQO	XMEWIV
GODUCQ	MXIVEW
DUCOQG	EMVXWI
CGRDQU	IVWMEX
UDRCOQ	IEVMWX
GQCORU	WVZMXE
GOQUCD	XEMIWV
GDQUOC	WXIMEV
URDCGO	EMWIVX
GODRQC	IVEMXW

Figure 14–2. Sample lists used in visual search experiments of Neisser (1963). The target Z is present in both lists. It is easier to detect the Z in list **a**.

round letters. This is reminiscent of Beck's (1972) findings. The observer is probably trying to detect specific features that make up a target letter.

The second point derives from the fact that Neisser's observers were able to seek and detect two target letters in a list as rapidly as they could one target letter. Moreover, with sufficient practice observers were able to detect ten different targets as rapidly as they could one target. This was interpreted by Neisser as indicating that observers were processing features of letters in parallel and not in a sequential manner.

E. J. Gibson (1969) wondered what it was that observers were learning to do when they scanned rapidly for ten letters in Neisser's lists. She suggested that observers may have been learning to get along with fewer features in detecting targets. Although these minimal features are not yet identifiable, her suggestion is supported by the fact that Neisser's observers made more errors with the increase in speed that resulted from practice. This would be expected if fewer features were used to identify a target letter.

The concepts developed by Gibson and Gibson (1955; see also E. J. Gibson, 1969, and J. J. Gibson, 1966) in their theory of perceptual learning are relevant at this point. Gibson and Gibson proposed that what is acquired in perceptual learning is a greater ability to differentiate features of the mass of stimulation impinging on the organism. An unfamiliar object can ultimately come to have recognizable attributes, as is illustrated in the at-first meaningless jumble of shades and colors on a microscope slide containing a section of nervous tissue. After sufficient training observers can identify features of the section, and this leads to an increased specificity of response—that is, the observer learns to differentiate features not detected previously. This in turn implies that the observer must learn also to ignore irrelevant features if he is to detect and respond to relevant features. It is clear from Neisser's experiments that observers do ignore irrelevant letters. Tests conducted after searching lists for target letters showed that observers had no memory whatsoever for the irrelevant background letters. (The reader may try this for himself, using the lists in Figure 14–2.) This is consistent with Hochberg's views about the selective perception of form. The observer's expectancies provide a schematic to guide his scanning of the distal stimulus. The stimuli impinge on his sense organs and are ultimately matched with the anticipated event. A distinctive figure is matched more easily because there is less confusion of irrelevant items with the anticipated item. Perception of the item occurs when a match is found. The program is ready for execution, and the observer responds accordingly.

It may well be that Hochberg places too much reliance on eye movements. Sperling, Budiansky, Spivak, and Johnson (1971) conducted visual search experiments in which successive matrices of letters were flashed onto the screen of a computer-controlled oscilloscope. A numeral was contained in one of the many rapidly presented arrays of letters. The observer's task was to identify the position of the randomly located numeral when it appeared. This means that he had to keep track of a number of positions in the display. At each position letters were rapidly changing from one to another. At one such position a letter changed for a few milliseconds into a numeral. This occurred far more rapidly than the eyes could move; indeed, some observers could perform this task when the changes were so rapid that they were processing 100 letters per second. This indicates that the limiting factor on visual processing is not the speed of eye movement. Of course the speed with which an observer could scan one of his lists was the limiting factor in Neisser's pioneering visual-search experiments.

None of this proves that the selection of programs of action is not involved in perceiving. Once the key numeral is presented, it is selected by the nervous system for further processing. The numeral must be stored for a short time in memory prior to the awareness of the subject. His selection of a response is what makes the observer aware of its presence. There is little doubt that after a run the observers in this experiment would be unaware of the names of the other background letters.

It would be tempting to build a theory of perception on the foundation of information processing; and yet, since most of the work in this area is based upon linguistic materials, it is not yet clear that this can be done. Moreover, this is one of the newer areas of investigation in perception, despite the fact that the literature is already extensive. Our purpose in this chapter was to outline some of the concepts emerging from the study of information processing. Particularly important in this connection is the concept of short-term memory and the ways in which attention is being studied. Much of what has been said about attention is highly speculative. This, together with the newness of these studies, make it impossible, at this time, to construct an information-processing-based theory of perception.

The work on information processing is like the peak of the growing pyramid of knowledge. If we try to turn the pyramid upside down to rest it on this new knowledge, it would not be very stable. Nevertheless, it is clear that we are now on the threshold of great progress.

bibliography

Aaronson, D., Markowitz, N., and Shapiro, H., Perception and immediate recall of normal and compressed auditory sequences. *Percept. & Psychophys.*, 1971, 9, 338–44.

Abney, W. de W., The sensitiveness of the retina to light and color. *Phil. Trans. Roy. Soc.*, 1897, 190A, 155–95.

Adler, F., *Physiology of the eye.* 4th ed.; St. Louis: C. V. Mosby Co., 1965.

Anstis, S. M., Size adaptation to visual texture and print: Evidence for spatial frequency analysis. Paper presented at annual meeting of *Assoc. for Res. in Vis. and Ophthalm.*, Sarasota, Fla., 1973.

——, and Atkinson, J., Distortions in moving figures viewed through a stationary slit. *Amer. J. Psychol.*, 1967, 80, 572–85.

——, and Moulden, B. P., After effect of seen movement: Evidence for peripheral and central components. *Q. J. Exp. Psychol.*, 1970, 22, 222–29.

Arduini, A., and Pinneo, L. R., The tonic activity or the lateral genicutate nucleus in dark and light adaptation. *Arch. Ital. de biol.*, 101, 1963, 493–507.

Atkinson, R. C., and Shiffrin, R. M., Human memory: A proposed system and its control processes. In Spence, K. W., and Spence, J. T., eds., *The psychology of learning and motivation. Advances in research and theory,* vol. 2. New York: Academic Press, 1968.

Attneave, F., Some informational aspects of visual perception. *Psychol. Rev.* 1954, 61, 183–93.

——, Symmetry, information and memory for patterns. *Amer. J. Psychol.*, 1955, 68, 209–22.

——, *Application of information theory to psychology.* New York: Holt, Rinehart and Winston, 1959.

Aubert, H., *Physiologic der Natzhaut.* Breslau: Morgenstern, 1865.

——, Die Bewegungsempfindung. *Arch. f. d. Ges. Physiol.*, 1886, 39, 347–70.

Averbach, E., and Coreill, A. S., Short-term memory in vision. *Bell Syst. Tech. J.*, 1961, 40, 309–28.

Bahnson, P., Eine Untersuchung uber Symmetrie und Asymmetrie bei visuellen Wahrnehmungen. *Zeit. f. Psychol.*, 1928, 108, 129–54.

Baird, J. C., Gulick, W. L., & Smith, W. M., The effects of angle of regard upon the size of after-images. *Psychol. Rec.*, 1962, 12, 263–71.

Baker, C. H., The dependence of binocular fusion on timing of peripheral stimuli and on cerebral process. I, Symmetrical flicker. *Canad. J. Psychol.*, 1952, 6, 1–10.

Barlow, H. B., Eye movements during fixation. *J. Physiol.*, 1952, 116, 290–306.

———, Retinal noise and absolute threshold. *J. Opt. Soc. Amer.*, 1956, 46, 634–39.

———, Temporal and spatial summation in human vision at different background intensities. *J. Physiol.*, 1958, 141, 337–50.

———, Blakemore, C., and Pettigrew, J. D., The neural mechanism of binocular depth discrimination. *J. Physiol.*, 1967, 193, 327–42.

———, and Hill, R. M., Selective sensitivity to direction movement in ganglion cells of the Rabbit retina. *Science*, 1963, 139, 412–14.

———, Hill, R. M., and Levick, W. R., Retinal ganglion cells responding selectively to direction and speed of image motion in the Rabbit. *J. Physiol.*, 1964, 173, 377–407.

———, Levick, W. R., and Yoon, M., Response to single quanta of light in retinal ganglion cells of the cat. *Vis. Res.*, 1971, 11, Suppl. 3, 87–101.

Bartlett, N. R., Thresholds as dependent on some energy relations and characteristics of the subject. In Graham, C. H., ed., *Vision and visual perception.* New York: Wiley, 1965, 154–84.

Bartley, S. H., *Principles of perception. 2nd ed.;* New York: Harper and Row, 1969.

Beck, J., Apparent spatial position and the perception of lightness. *J. Exp. Psychol.*, 1965, 69, 170–79.

———, Perceptual grouping produced by line figures. *Percept. & Psychophys.*, 1967, 2, 491–95.

———, Similarity groupings and peripheral discriminability under uncertainty. *Amer. J. Psychol.*, 1972, 85, 1–20.

Békésy, G. von, Neural inhibitory units of the eye and skin. Quantitative description of contrast phenomena. *J. Opt. Soc. Amer.*, 1960, 50, 1060–70.

Berenson, B., *Italian Painters of the Renaissance.* New York: Meridian, 1957 (first pub. 1952).

Bishop, P. O., Coombs, J. S., and Henry, G. H., Responses to visual contours: spatio-temporal aspects of excitation in the receptive fields of simple striate neurons. *J. Physiol.*, 1971, 219, 625–57.

Blakemore, C., and Campbell, F. W., On the existence of neurons in the human visual system selectively sensitive to the orientation and size of retinal images, *J. Physiol.*, 1969, 203, 237–60.

———, and Cooper, G. F., Development of the brain depends on visual environment. *Science*, 1970, 228, 477–78.

———, and Sutton, P., Size adaptation: A new aftereffect. *Science*, 1969, 166, 245–47.

Bonnet, C., La vitesse perçue et la relation V=E/T. *Année Psychol.*, 1964, 64, 47–60.

Boring, E. G., Apparatus notes: A new ambiguous figure. *Amer. J. Psychol.*, 1930, 42, 444.

———, *The physical dimensions of consciousness.* New York: Century, 1933.

———, *Sensation and perception in the history of experimental psychology.* New York: Appleton-Century-Crofts, 1942.

———, The moon illusion. *Amer. J. Physics.*, 1943, 11, 55–60.

Bower, T. G. R., Discrimination of depth in premotor infants. *Psychon. Sci.*, 1964, 1, 368.

———, Stimulus variables determining space perception in infants. *Science*, 1965, 149, 88–89.

Braine, L. G., A developmental analysis of the effect of stimulus orientation on recognition. *Amer. J. Psychol.*, 1972, 85, 157–87.

Brecher, G. A., Form und Ausdehnung der Panumschen Areale bei fovealim Sehen. *Arch. f. d. ges. Physiol.*, 1942, 246, 315–28.

Brewster, D., On the conversion of relief by inverted vision. *Edinb. Phil. Trans.* 1847, 15, 657.

Brindley, G. S., *Physiology of the retina and visual pathway.* London: Edward Arnold, 1960.

———, and Merton, P. A., The absence of position sense in the human eye. *J. Physiol.*, 1960, 153, 127–30.

Broadbent, D. F., A mechanical model for human attention and immediate memory. *Psychol. Rev.*, 1957, 64, 205–15.

———, *Perception and communication.* New York: Pergamon Press, 1958.

Brosgole, L., An analysis of induced motion. *Acta Psychol.* 1968, 28, 1–44.

Brown, J. L., Afterimages. In Graham, C. H., ed., *Vision and visual perception,* New York: Wiley, 1965, 479–503.

Brown, J. F., The visual perception of velocity. *Psychol. Forsch.*, 1931, 14, 199–232.

Campbell, F. W., The human eye as an optical filter. *Proc. IEEE*, 1968, 56, 1009–14.

———, Cooper, G. F., and Enroth-Cugell, C., The spatial selectivity of the visual cells of the cat. *J. Physiol.*, 1969, 203, 223–35.

———, and Robson, J. G., Application of Fourier analysis to the visibility of gratings. *J. Physiol.*, 1968, 197, 551–66.

———, and Rushton, W. A. H., Measurement of the scotopic pigment in the living human eye. *J. Physiol.*, 1955, 130, 141–47.

———, and Westheimer, G., Factors involving accommodation responses of the human eye. *J. Opt. Soc. Amer.*, 1959, 49, 568–71.

Carr, H., The autokinetic sensation. *Psychol Rev.*, 1910, 17, 42–75.

Charnwood, J. R. B., *Essay on binocular vision.* London: Halton Press, 1951.

Cherry, C., On the recognition of speech with one, and with two, ears. *J. Acoust. Soc. Amer.*, 1953, 25, 975.

———, On human communication. Cambridge, Mass.: M.I.T. Press/Wiley, 1957.

Clark, B., An eye-movement study of stereoscopic vision. *Amer. J. Psychol.*, 1935, 47, 82–97.

Cohen, J., and Gordon, D. A., The Prevost-Fechner-Benham subjective colors. *Psychol. Bull.*, 1949, 46, 97–136.

Conrad, R., Acoustic confusions in immediate memory. *Brit. J. Psychol.*, 1964, 55, 75-84.

Cook, F. H., and Mott-Smith, J. C., The influence of repetition rate on apparent movement. Air Force Cambridge Res. Lab. Report No. AFCRL–66–86, 1966.

Cooper, S., Daniel, P., and Whitteridge, D., Nerve impulses in the brainstem of the goat. *J. Physiol.*, 1953, 120, 471.

Coren, S., Brightness contrast as a function of figure-ground relations. *J. Exp. Psychol.*, 1969, 80, 517–24.

———, Subjective contours and apparent depth. *Psychol. Rev.*, 1972, 79, 359–67.

———, and Keith, B., Bezold-Brücke Effect: Pigment or neural locus? *J. Opt. Soc. Amer.*, 1970, 60, 559–62.

Cornsweet, T. N., Determination of stimuli for involuntary drifts and saccadic eye movements. *J. Opt. Soc. Amer.*, 1956, 46, 987–93.

———, *Visual perception.* New York: Academic Press, 1970.

Cornwell, H. G., Prior experience as a determinant of figure-ground organization. *J. Exp. Psychol.*, 1963, 65, 156–62.

Crovitz, H. F., and Lockhead, G. R., Possible monocular predictors of binocular rivalry of contours. *Percept. & Psychophys.*, 1967, 2, 83–85.

Daw, N., Colour-coded ganglion cells in the goldfish retina: Extension of their receptive fields by means of new stimuli. *J. Physiol.*, 1968, 197, 567–92.

Daniel, P., Spiral nerve endings in the extrinsic eye muscles of man. *J. Anat.*, 1946, 80, 189.

Dartnall, H. J. A., *The visual pigments.* New York: Wiley, 1957.

Davson, H., ed., *The eye.* Vol. 2, *The visual process.* New York: Academic Press, 1962.

Day, R. H., Inappropriate constancy explanations of spatial distortions. *Nature,* 1965, 207, 891–93.

Deutch, J. A., and Deutsch, D., Attention: Some theoretical considerations. *Psychol. Rev.*, 1963, 70, 80–90.

De Silva, H. R., An analysis of the visual perception of movement. *Brit. J. Psychol.*, 1929, 19, 268–305.

De Valois, K., Black and white: Equal but separate. Paper presented at annual meeting of *Assoc. for Res. in Vis. and Ophthalm.*, Sarasota, 1973.

De Valois, R. L., Color vision mechanisms in Monkey. *J. Gen. Physiol.*, 1960, 43, Suppl. 2, 115–28.

———, Abramov, I., & Jacobs, G. H., Analysis of response patterns of LGN cells. *J. Opt. Soc. Amer.*, 1966, 56, 966–77.

———, and Jacobs, G. H., Primate color vision. *Science,* 1968, 162, 533–40.

Dewey, J., *Experience and nature.* 2nd ed.; New York: Open Court, 1929.

Dichganz, J., and Bizzi, E., eds., *Cerebral control of eye movements and motion perception.* Basel: Karger, 1972.

———, and Brandt, T., Visual-vestibular interaction. In Dichganz, J., and Bizzi, E., eds., *Cerebral control of eye movements and motion perception.* Basel: Karger, 1972.

Dimmick, F. L., and Scahill, H. G., Visual perception of movement. *Amer. J. Psychol.*, 1925, 36, 412–17.

Dinnerstein, D., and Wertheimer, M., Some determinants of phenomenal overlapping. *Amer. J. Psychol.*, 1957, 70, 21–38.

Ditchburn, R. N., and Ginsborg, B. L., Vision with a stabilized retinal image. *Nature*, 1952, 170, 36–37.

Dodwell, P. C., *Visual pattern recognition.* New York: Holt, Rinehart and Winston, 1970.

———, and Engel, G. R., A theory of binocular fusion. *Nature*, 1963, 198, 39–40, 73–74.

Dove, H. W., Über Stereoskopie., *Ann. Phys.*, 1841, series 2, 110, 494–98. Cited in Julesz, B., *Foundations of Cyclopean perception.* Chicago: Univ. of Chicago Press, 1971.

Dowling, J., and Wald, G., The biological function of Vitamin A acid. *Proc. Nat. Acad. Sci.*, 1960, 46, 587–608.

Dudley, L. P., *Stereoptics: An introduction.* London: MacDonald, 1951.

Duncker, K., Über induzierte Bewegung (Ein Beitrag zur Theorie optisch wahrgenommener Bewegung. *Psychol. Forsch.*, 1929, 12, 180–259.

Elliot, H. C., *Textbook of neuroanatomy.* Philadelphia: J. B. Lippincott Co., 1963.

Epstein, W., The influences of assumed size on apparent distance. *Amer. J. Psychol.*, 1963, 76, 257–65.

———, and Baratz, S. S., Relative size in isolation as a stimulus for relative perceived distance. *J. Exp. Psychol.*, 1964, 67, 507–13.

Emmert, E., Grössenverhaltnisse der Nachbilder. *Klin. Monatsbl. d. Augenheilk.*, 1881, 19, 443–50.

Ewert., P. N., A study or the effect of inverted retinal stimulation upon spatially coordinated behavior. *Genet. Psychol. Monogr.*, 1930, 7, Nos. 3 and 4.

Exner, S., Über das Sehen von Bewegungen und die Theories des zusammengesetzen Auges. *S. B. Akad. Wiss.* (Wien), 1875, 72, 156–90.

Fain, G. L., and Dowling, J. E., Intracellular recordings from single rods and cones in the Mudpuppy retina. *Science*, 1973, 180, 1178–81.

Falmagne, J. C., Foundations of Fechnerian psychophysics. In Atkinson, R. C., Krantz, D. H., Luce, R. D., and Suppes, P., eds. *Contemporary developments in mathematical psychology.* New York: Academic Press, 1974.

Fantz, R. L., The origin of form perception. *Sci. Amer.*, 1961, 204, 66–72.

Festinger, V., Allyn, M. R., and White, C. W., The perception of color with achromatic stimulation. *Vis. Res.*, 1971, 11, 591–612.

———, Burnham, C. A., Ono, H., and Bamber, D., Efference and the conscious experience of perception. *J. Exp. Psychol.*, 1967, Monogr. Suppl. 74 (4, whole no. 637).

———, Coren, S., and Rivers, G., The effect of attention on brightness contrast and assimilation. *Amer. J. Psychol.*, 1970, 83, 189–207.

———, and Easton, A. M., Inferences about the efferent system based on a perceptual illusion produced by eye movements. *Psychol. Rev.*, 1974, in press.

Finchman, E. F., The accommodation reflex and its stimulus. *Brit. J. Ophthalm.*, 1951, 35, 381–93.

Fineman, M. B., Facilitation of stereoscopic depth perception by a relative-size cue in ambiguous disparity stereograms. *J. Exp. Psychol.*, 1971, 90, 215–21.

Foley, J. M., Disparity increase with convergence for constant perceptual criteria. *Percept. & Psychophys.*, 1967, 2, 605–8.

Fraisse, P., *Psychologie du temps*. Paris: Presses Universitaires de France, 1957.

Fry, G. A., A photo receptor mechanism for the modulation theory of color vision. *J. Opt. Soc. Amer.*, 1945, 35, 114–35.

———, and Bartley, S. H., The brilliance of an object seen binocularly. *Am. J. Ophthalm.*, 1933, 18, 687–93.

———, and Bartley, S. H., The effect of one border in the visual field upon the threshold of another. *Amer. J. Physiol.*, 1935, 112, 414–21.

Ganz, L., Mechanism of the figured aftereffects. *Psychol. Rev.*, 1966, 73, 128–50.

Garner, W., *Uncertainty and structure as psychological concepts*. New York: Wiley, 1962.

Gelb, A., Die 'Farbenkonstanz' der Sehdinge. *Handb. Norm. Path. Physiol.*, 1929, 12 (I), 594–678.

Gettys, C. F., and Harker, G. S., Some observations and measurements of the Panum phenomenon. *Percept. & Psychophys.*, 1967, 2, 387–395.

Gibson, E. J., *Principles of perceptual learning and development*. New York, Appleton-Century-Crofts, 1969.

———, Gibson, J. J., Smith, O. W., and Flock, H., Motion parallax as a determinant of perceived depth. *J. Exp. Psychol.*, 1959, 58, 40–51.

Gibson, J. J., Adaptation after-effect and contrast in perception of curved lines. *J. Exp. Psychol.*, 1933, 16, 1–31.

———, *Perception of the visual world*. Boston: Houghton Mifflin, 1950.

———, *The senses considered as perceptual systems*. Boston: Houghton Mifflin, 1966.

———, and Gibson, E. J., Perceptual learning: Differentation or enrichment? *Psychol. Rev.*, 1955, 62, 32–41.

Gilinsky, A. S., The effect of attitude upon the perception of size. *Amer. J. Psychol.*, 1955, 68, 173–92.

———, Orientation specific effects of patterns of adapting light on visual acuity. *J. Opt. Soc. Amer.*, 1968, 58, 13–18.

———, and Mayo, T. H., Inhibitory effects of orientational adaptation. *J. Opt. Soc. Amer.*, 1971, 61, 1710–14.

Gillispie, C. C., *The edge of objectivity: An essay on the history of scientific ideas*. Princeton, N.J.: Princeton Univ. Press, 1960.

Glanzer, M., and Clark, W. H., Accuracy of perceptual recall: An analysis of organization. *J. Verb. Learning and Verb. Beh.*, 1963, 1, 289–99.

———, and Clark, W. H., The verbal loop hypothesis: Conventional figures. *Amer. J. Psychol.*, 1964, 77, 621–26.

Gogel, W. C., The tendency to see objects as equidistant and its reverse relations to lateral separation. *Psychol. Monogr.*, 1956, 70 (whole no. 411).

————, Convergence as a cue to absolute distance. Fort Knox, Ky.: U.S. Army Med. Res. Lab., Report No. 467, 1961, 1–16.

————, Equidistance tendency and its consequences. *Psychol. Bull.*, 1965, 64, 153–63.

————, The adjacency principle and three-dimensional visual illusions. *Psychon. Monogr. Suppl.*, 1970, 3 (whole no. 45), 153–69.

————, Hartman, B. O., and Harker, G. S., The retinal size of a familiar object as a determiner of apparent distance. *Psychol. Monogr.*, 1957, 71, 1–16.

————, Wist, E. R., and Harker, G. S., A test of the invariance of the ratio of perceived size to perceived distance. *Amer. J. Psychol.*, 1963, 76, 537–53.

Gold, T., *A psychophysical study of the Gestalt proximity law of perceptual organization.* M.A. thesis, Hofstra University, 1960.

Gottschaldt, K., Über den Einfluss der Erfahrung auf die Wahrnemung von Figuren, *Psychol. Forsch.*, 1926, 8, 1–87.

Graham, C. H., Visual space perception. In Graham, C. H., ed., *Vision and visual perception.* New York: Wiley, 1965a, 504–47.

————, Perception of movement. In Graham, C. H., ed., *Vision and visual perception.* New York, Wiley, 1965b, 575–88.

————, Baker, K. F., Hecht, M., and Lloyd, V. V., Factors influencing thresholds for monocular movement parallax. *J. Exp. Psychol.*, 1948, 38, 205–23.

Graham, N., and Nachmias, J., Detection of grating patterns containing two spatial frequencies: A comparison of single-channel and multiple-channel models. *Vis. Res.*, 1971, 11, 251–59.

Graybiel, A., and Hupp, D. E., The oculogyral illusion. *J. Aviat. Med.*, 1946, 17, 3–27.

Green, D. M., and Swets, J. A., *Signal detection theory and psychophysics.* New York: Wiley, 1966.

Gregory, R. L., Distortion of visual space as inappropriate constancy scaling. *Nature,* 1963, 199, 678–80.

————, *Eye and brain.* New York: McGraw-Hill, 1966.

————, *The intelligent eye.* New York: McGraw-Hill, 1970.

————, Cognitive contours. *Nature,* 1972, 238, 51–52.

————, and Wallace, J. G., Recovery from early blindness. A case study. *Exp. Psych. Soc. Monogr.*, No. 2, Cambridge (England): 1963.

Gruber, H. E., The relation of perceived size to perceived distance. *Amer. J. Psychol.*, 1954, 67, 411–26.

Guilford, J P., and Dallenbach, K., A study of the autokinetic sensation. *Amer. J. Psychol.*, 1928, 40, 83–91.

Gulick, W. L., *Hearing: Physiology and psychophysics.* New York: Oxford Univ. Press, 1971.

Haber, R. N., A note on how to choose a mask. *Psychol. Bull.*, 1970, 74, 373–76.

————, ed., *Information processing approaches to perception.* New York: Holt, Rinehart and Winston, 1969.

————, and Nathanson, L., Post retinal storage? Some further observations on Park's camel as seen through the eye of a needle. *Percept. & Psychophys.*, 1968, 3, 349–55.

Hamilton, C. R., Intermanual transfer of adaptation to prisms. *Amer. J. Psychol.,* 1964, 77, 457–62.

Harker, G. S., Interrelation of monocular and binocular acuities in the making of equidistance judgment. *J. Opt. Soc. Amer.,* 1958, 48, 233–40.

Harmon, L. D., and Julesz, B., Masking in visual recognition: Effects of two-dimensional filtered noise. *Science,* 1973, 180, 1194–97.

Harris, C. S., Adaptation to displaced vision: Visual, motor, or proprioceptive change? *Science,* 1963, 3, 71–72.

———, Perceptual adaptation to inverted, reversed and displaced vision. *Psychol. Rev.,* 1965, 72, 419–44.

———, and Gibson, A. R., Is orientation-specific color adaptation in human vision due to edge detectors, afterimages or "dipoles"? *Science,* 1968, 162, 1056–7.

Hartline, H. K., The neural mechanisms of vision. In *The Harvey Lectures.* New York: The Harvey Society of New York, 1942, 37, 39–68.

Hartridge, H., *Recent advances in the physiology of vision.* Philadelphia: Blackiston, 1950.

Hay, J. C., and Pick, H. L., Jr., Visual and proprioceptive adaptation to optical displacement of the visual stimulus. *J. Exp. Psychol.,* 1966, 71, 150–58.

———, Pick, H. L., Jr., and Ikeda, K., Visual capture produced by prism spectacles. *Psychon. Sci.,* 1965, 2, 215–16.

Haynes, H., White, B. L., and Held, R., Visual accommodation in human infants. *Science,* 1965, 148, 528–30.

Hebb, D. O., *The organization of behavior.* New York: Wiley, 1949.

Hecht, S., Schlaer, S., and Pirenne, M. H., Energy, quanta, and vision. *J. Gen. Physiol.,* 1942, 25, 819–40.

Hecht, S., and Verrijp, C. D., Intermittent stimulation by light. III. The relation between intensity and critical fusion frequency for different retinal locations. *J. Gen. Physiol.,* 1933, 17, 251–65.

Hein, A., and Held, R., A neural model for labile sensorimotor coordination. In *Biological Prototypes and Synthetic Systems.* Bionics Symposium, 1961. New York: Plenum Press, 1962.

Heinemann, E. G., Simultaneous brightness induction as a function of inducing and test field luminance. *J. Exp. Psychol.,* 1955, 50, 89–96.

———, Tulving, E., and Nachmias, J., The effect of oculomotor adjustments on apparent size. *Amer. J. Psychol.,* 1959, 72, 32–45.

Held, R., Plasticity in sensory-motor systems. *Sci. Amer.,* 1965, 211, 84–94.

———, and Bossom, J., Neonatal deprivation and adult rearrangement: Complementary techniques for analyzing plastic sensory-motor coordinations. *J. Comp. Physiol. Psychol.,* 1961, 54, 33–37.

———, and Freedman, S. J., Plasticity in human sensorimotor control. *Science,* 1963, 142, 455–62.

———, and Gottlieb, N., A technique for studying adaptation to disarranged hand-eye coordination. *Percept. Mot. Skills.,* 1958, 8, 83–86.

———, and Hein, A., Adaptation of disarranged hand-eye coordination contingent upon re-afferent stimulation. *Percept. Mot. Skills,* 1958, 8, 87–90.

———, and Hein, A., Movement-produced stimulation in the development of visually-guided behavior. *J. Comp. Physiol. Psychol.,* 1963, 56, 872–76.

————, and Rekosh, J., Motor-sensory feedback and the geometry of visual space. *Science*, 1963, 141, 722–23.

Helmholtz, H. von, *Treatise on physiological optics*. vols. 1 and 2. Trans. from 3rd German ed., J. P. C. Southall, ed. Opt. Soc. Amer., 1924. Republished as one volume, New York: Dover, 1962.

————, *Treatise on physiological optics*, vol. 3 Trans. from 3rd German ed., J. P. C. Southall, ed. Opt. Soc. Amer., 1925. Republished New York: Dover, 1962.

Henle, M., An experimental investigation of past experience as a determinant of form perception. *J. Exp. Psychol.*, 1942, 30, 1–22.

Hepler, N., Color: A motion-contingent aftereffect. *Science*, 1968, 162, 376–77.

————, "Where have all the colors gone?" Paper presented at meeting of *Assoc. for Res. in Vis. and Ophthalm.*, Sarasota, 1973.

Hering, E., *Beitrage zur Physiologie*. Leipzig, W. Engelmann, 1861–64.

Karpinska, L. von, Experimentelle Beiträge aur Analyse der Tiefenwahrnehmung.

————, *Outline of a theory of the light sense*. Trans. L. M. Hurvich and D. J. Jameson. Cambridge, Mass.: Harvard Univ. Press, 1964.

Hermans, T. G., The relationship of convergence and elevation changes to judgements of size. *J. Exp. Psychol.*, 1954, 21, 204–8.

Hernandez-Peón, R., Scherrer, H., and Jouvet, M., Modification of electrical activity in the cochlear nucleus during attention in unanaesthetized cats. *Science*, 1956, 123, 331–32.

Herrick, R. M., Foveal luminance discrimination as a function of the duration of the decrement or increment in luminance. *J. Comp. Physiol. Psychol.*, 1956, 49, 437–43.

Hershenson, M., Visual discrimination in the human newborn. *J. Comp. Physiol. Psychol.*, 1964, 58, 270–76.

————, Munsinger, H., and Kessen, W., Preference for shapes of intermediate variability in the newborn human. *Science*, 1965, 147, 630–31.

Hess, C., and Pretori, H., Messende Untersuchungen über die Gesetzmässigkeit des simultanen Helligkeits-Contrastes. *Archiv. f. Ophthal.*, 1894, 40, 1–24.

Hirsch, H. V. B., and Spinelli, D. N., Visual experience modifies distribution of horizontally and vertically oriented receptive fields in cats. *Science*, 1970, 168, 869–71.

Hochberg, J. E., Nativism and empiricism in perception. In Postman, L., ed., *Psychology in the making*. New York: Knopf, 1962, 255–330.

————, Contralateral suppressive fields of binocular combination. *Psychon. Sci.*, 1964a, 1, 157–58.

————, A theory of the binocular cyclopean field: On the possibility of simulating stereopsis. *Percep. Mot. Skills*, 1964b, 19, 685.

————, In the mind's eye. In Haber, R. N., ed., *Contemporary theory and research in visual perception*. New York: Holt, Rinehart and Winston, 1968, 309–31.

————, Attention, organization and consciousness. In Mostofsky, D. I., ed., *Attention: Contemporary theory and analysis*. New York: Appleton-Century-Crofts, 1970, 99–124.

————, Perception. In Riggs, L. A., and Kling, J. W., eds., *Woodworth and Schlosberg's experimental psychology, third edition*. New York: Holt, Rinehart and Winston, 1971, 396–546.

————, and Brooks, V., The psychophysics of forms: Reversible perspective drawings of spatial objects. *Amer. J. Psychol.*, 1960, 73, 337–54.

————, and Hay, J., Figural after-effects, after-image, and physiological nystagmus. *Amer. J. Psychol.*, 1956, 69, 480–82.

————, and McAlister, E., A quantitative approach to figural "goodness." *J. Exp. Psychol.*, 1953, 46, 361–64.

————, and Silverstein, A., A quantitative index of stimulus similarity: Proximity vs. difference in brightness. *Amer. J. Psychol.*, 1956, 69, 456–59.

————, Triebel, W., and Seaman, G., Color adaptation under conditions of homogeneous visual stimulation (Ganzfeld). *J. Exp. Psychol.*, 1951, 41, 153–59.

Holst, E. von, Relations between the central nervous system and the peripheral organs. *Brit. J. Animal Beh.*, 1954, 2, 89–94.

————, and Mittelstaadt, H., Das Reafferenz-princip. *Die Naturwissenschaften*, 1950, 20, 464–67.

Holway, A. F., and Boring, E. G., The moon illusion and the angle of regard. *Amer. J. Psychol.*, 1940, 53, 509–16.

————, and Boring, E. G., Determinants of apparent visual size with distance variant. *Amer. J. Psychol.*, 1941, 54, 21–37.

Horn, G., Physiological and psychological aspects of selective attention. In D. F. Lehrman *et al.*, eds., *Advances in the study of behavior.* Vol. 1. New York: Academic Press, 1965, 115–217.

Hsia, Y., Whiteness constancy as a function of differences in illumination. *Arch. Psychol.* (N.Y.), 1943, 284.

Hubel, D. H., and Wiesel, T. N., Integrative action in the lateral geniculate body. *J. Physiol.*, 1961, 155, 385–98.

————, and Wiesel, T. N., Receptive fields, binocular interaction, and functional architecture in the cat's visual cortex. *J. Physiol.* 1962, 160, 106–54.

————, and Wiesel, T. N., Receptive fields and functional architecture in two non-striate visual areas (18 and 19) of the cat. *J. Neurophysiol.*, 1965, 28, 229–89.

————, and Wiesel, T. N., Receptive fields and functional architecture of monkey striate cortex. *J. Physiol.*, 1968, 195, 215–43.

————, and Wiesel, T. N., Stereoscopic vision in macaque monkey. *Nature*, 1970, 225, 41–42.

Hurvich, L. M., Color vision deficiencies. In *Color Vision.* Symposium Conducted at Spring Meeting, 1971. Washington, D.C.: National Academy of Sciences, 1973.

————, and Jameson, D., An opponent process theory of color vision. *Psychol. Rev.*, 1957, 64, 384–404.

————, and Jameson, D., Some quantitative aspects of an opponent colors theory. II. Brightness, saturation, and hue in normal and dichromatic vision. *J. Opt. Soc. Amer.*, 1955, 45, 602–16.

Husserl, E., *Ideas: General introduction to pure phenomenology.* Trans. W. R. Boyce Gibson. New York: Collier Books, 1962 (first pub. 1931).

Ishak, I. G. H., Radwan, M. H. S., and Ibraham, M. M., Convergence and steroscopic vision. *Opt. Acta*, 1965, 12, 213–21.

Ittelson, W. H., Size as a cue to distance: Static localization. *Amer. J. Psychol.*, 1951, 64, 54–67.

———, *Visual space perception.* New York: Springer, 1960.

Ives, H. E., Critical frequency relations in scotopic vision. *J. Opt. Soc. Amer.*, 1922, 6, 254–268.

Jameson, D., and Hurvich, L. M., Note on factors influencing the relation between stereoscopic acuity and observation distance. *J. Opt. Soc. Amer.*, 1959, 49, 639.

———, and Hurvich, L. M., Complexities of perceived brightness. *Science*, 1961, 133, 174–79.

Jampel, R. S., Representation of the near-response on the cerebral cortex of the Macaque. *Amer. J. Ophthal.* 1959, 45 (no. 5, pt. 2), 573–82.

Jastrow, J., The mind's eye. *Pop. Sci. Monthly*, 1899, 54, 299–312.

Judd, D. B., Appraisal of Lands' work on two primary-color projections. *J. Opt. Soc. Amer.*, 1960, 50, 254–68.

Julesz, B., Visual pattern discrimination. In *IRE Transactions on Information Theory*, 1962, It–8:8492.

———, Binocular depth perception without familiarity cues. *Science*, 1964, 45, 356–62.

———, Some recent studies in vision relevant to form perception. In Wathen-Dunn, W., ed., *Models for the perception of speech and form*, Cambridge, Mass.: M.I.T. Press/Wiley, 1967, 136–54.

———, *Foundations of Cyclopean perception.* Chicago: Univ. of Chicago Press, 1971.

———, and Stromeyer, C. F., III, Masking of spatial gratings by filtered one-dimensional visual noise. Paper presented at 10th annual meeting of *Psychon. Soc.*, San Antonio, Texas, 1970.

Kahneman, D., Method, findings and theory in studies of visual masking. *Psychol. Bull.*, 1968, 70, 404–25.

Kalil, R. E., and Freedman, S. J., Persistence of ocular rotation following compensation for displaced vision. *Percept. Mot. Skills*, 1966, 22, 135–39.

Kaneko, A., Physiological studies of single retinal cells and their morphological identification. *Vis. Res.*, 1971, 11, Suppl. 3, 17–26.

Kanizsa, G., Marzini quasi-percettivi in campi con stimolozione omogenea. *Rivista di Psicologia*, 1955, 49, 7–30.

Kaplan, M., Study of apparent movement. Research paper submitted to Department of Psychology, New York University, 1972.

Karpinska, I. von, Experimentelle Beiträge aur Analyse der Tiefenwahrnehmung. *Zeit. für Psychol.*, 1910, 57, 1–88.

Katz, D., *The world of color.* Trans. R. B. MacLeod and C. W. Fox. London: Kegan Paul, 1935.

Kaufman, L., On the spread of suppression and binocular rivalry. *Vis. Res.*, 1963, 3, 401–15.

———, Suppression and fusion in viewing complex stereograms. *Amer. J. Psychol.*, 1964a, 77, 193–205.

————, on the nature of binocular disparity. *Amer. J. Psychol.*, 1964*b*, 77, 398–401.

————, Some new steroscopic phenomena and their implications for theories of stereopsis. *Amer. J. Psychol.*, 1965, 78, 1–20.

————, Bacon, J., and Barroso, F., Stereopsis without image segregation. *Vis. Res.*, 1973, 13, 137–47.

————, Cyrulnick, I., Kaplowitz, J., Melnick, G., and Stof, D., The complementarity of apparent and real motion. *Psychol. Forsch.*, 1971, 34, 343–48.

————, and Locker, J., Sensory modulation of the EEG. *Proc. 78th Annual Conv. Amer. Psychol. Assoc.*, 1970, 179–80.

————, and Pitblado, C. B., Further observations on the nature of effective binocular disparites. *Amer. J. Psychol.*, 1965, 78, 379–91.

————, and Pitblado, C. B., Stereopsis with opposite contrast conditions. *Percept. & Psychophys.*, 1969, 6, 10–12.

————, and Richards, W., Spontaneous fixation tendencies for visual forms. *Percept. & Psychophys.*, 1969, 5, 85–88.

————, and Rock, I., The Moon illusion. I. *Science*, 1962, 136, 953–61.

Keesey, U. T., and Lindsley, D. B., Effects of eye movements and sharp edges in a flickering field. A paper presented at the annual meeting of *Western Psychol. Assoc.*, 1962.

Kelly, D. H., Effects of sharp edges in a flickering field. *J. Opt. Soc. Amer.*, 1959, 49, 730–32.

Kelly, D. H., Visual responses to time-dependent stimuli. I. Amplitude sensitivity measurements. *J. Opt. Soc. Amer.*, 1961, 51, 422–29.

————, Sine waves and flicker fusion. *Doc. Ophthalm.*, 1964, 18, 16–35.

Kessen, W., Salapatek, P., and Haith, M. M., The visual response of the newborn to linear contour. *J. Exp. Child Psychol.*, 1972, 13, 9–20.

Koestler, A., *The Watershed: A biography of Johannes Kepler.* New York: Doubleday, 1960.

Köhler, W., *Gestalt Psychology.* New York: Liveright, 1929.

————, *Dynamics in psychology.* New York: Liveright, 1940.

————, and Wallach, H. Figural after-effect, an investigation of visual processes. *Proc. Amer. Philos. Soc.*, 1944, 88, 269–357.

Koffka, K., *Principles of Gestalt psychology.* New York: Harcourt, Brace, 1935.

Kohler, I., *The formation and transformation of the perceptual world.* Trans. H. Fiss. New York: International Universities Press, 1964.

Kolers, P. A., Some differences between real and apparent movement., *Vis. Res.*, 1963, 3, 191–206.

————, and Rosner, B., On visual masking (metacontrast). Dichoptic observation. *Amer. J. Psychol.*, 1960, 73, 2–21.

Korte, A., Kinematoskopische Untersuchungen. *Z. Psychol.*, 1915, 72, 193–206.

Krauskopf, J., Light distribution in human retinal images. *J. Opt. Soc. Amer.*, 1962, 52, 1046–50.

————, Graf, V., and Gaarder, K., Lack of inhibition during involuntary saccades. *Amer. J. Psychol.*, 1966, 79, 73–81.

————, and Mollon, J. D., The independence of the temporal integration properties of individual chromatic mechanisms in the human eye. *J. Physiol.*, 1971, 219, 611–23.

————, and Sebro, R., Spectral sensitivity of color mechanisms: Deviation from fluctuations of color appearances near threshold. *Science*, 1965, 150, 1477-79.

Kuffler, S. W., Discharge patterns and functional organization on mammalian retina. *J. Neurophysiol.*, 1953, 16, 37–68.

Kuhn, T. S., *The structure of scientific revolutions*. 2nd ed., enl.; Chicago: Univ. of Chicago Press, 1970.

Kulpe, O., Versuche über Abstraktion. *Ber. ü. d. I Kongr. f. exper. Psychol.*, 1904, 56–68.

Kunnapas, T. M., Influence of frame size on apparent length of a line. *J. Exp. Psychol.*, 1955, 50, 168–70.

Land, E. H., Experiments in color vision. *Sci. Amer.*, 1959, 200, 84–99.

————, The retinex. *Amer. Scientist*, 1964, 52, 247–64.

Lange, H. de, Experiments on flicker and some calculations on an electrical analogue of the foveal systems. *Physica*, 1952, 18, 935–50.

————, Research into the dynamic nature of the human fovea-cortex systems with intermittent and modulated light. I. Attenuation characteristics with white and colored light. *J. Opt. Soc. Amer.*, 1958, 48, 777–84.

Latour, P. L., Visual threshold during eye movement. *Vis. Res.*, 1962, 2, 261.

Lawson, R. B., and Gulick, W. L., Stereopsis and anomalous contour. *Vis. Res.*, 1967, 7, 271–97.

Leeper, R. A., A study of a neglected portion of the field of learning: The development of sensory organization. *J. Genet. Psychol.*, 1935, 46, 42–75.

Leeuven, S. W. van, EEG during stimulation with flickering light. *Doc. Ophthal.*, 1964, 18, 151–58.

Le Grand, Y., Light, color and vision. Trans. R. W. G. Hunt, and F. R. W. Hunt, 2nd ed.; London, Chapman and Hall, 1968.

Leibowitz, H. W., The relation between the rate threshold for the perception of movement and luminance for various durations of exposure. *J. Exp. Psychol.*, 1955, 49, 209–14.

————, Graham, C., and Parrish, M., The effect of hypnotic age regression on size constancy. *Amer. J. Psych.*, 1972, 85, 271-76.

————, and Harvey, L. O., Jr., Size matching as a function of instructions in a naturalistic environment. *J. Exp. Psychol.*, 1967, 74, 378–82.

————, and Harvey, L. O., Jr., Comparison de l'approche expérimentale et non expérimentale de la perception de la taille. *Bul. de Psychol.*, 1969a, 276, XXII, 9–13.

————, and Harvey, L. O. Jr., The effect of instructions, environment, and type of test-object on matched size. *J. Exp. Psychol.*, 1969b, 81, 36–43.

————, Shiina, K., and Hennessy, R. T., Oculomotor adjustments and size constancy. *Percept. & Psychophys.*, 1972, 12, 497–500.

Lettvin, J. Y., Maturana, H. R., McCulloch, W. S., and Pitts, W. H., What the frog's eye tells the frog's brain. *Proc. Inst. Radio Engr.*, 1959, 47, 1940-51.

Levelt, W. J. M., On *binocular rivalry*. Soesterberg (The Netherlands): Institute for Perception, RVO–TNO, 1964.

Levinson, J. Z., Flicker fusion phenomena. *Science*, 1968, 160, 21–28.

Linksz, A., *Physiology of the Eye. Vol. 2, Vision.* New York: Grune and Stratton, 1952.

Linschoten, J., *Structuranalyse der binocularen Tiefenwahrnehmung.* New York: Gregory Lounz, 1956.

Lowenstein, O., and Lowenfeld, I. E., The Pupil. In Davson, H., ed., *The eye. Vol. 3. Muscular mechanisms.* New York: Academic Press, 1962.

Luce, R. D., and Galanter, E., Psychophysical scaling. In Luce, R. D., Bush, R. R., and Galanter, E., eds., *Handbook of mathematical psychology.* New York: Wiley, 1963.

McColgin, F. H., Movement thresholds in peripheral vision. *J. Opt. Soc. Amer.,* 1960, 50, 774–79.

McCollough, C., The conditioning of color perception. *Amer. J. Psychol.,* 1965a, 78, 362–68.

———, Color adaptation of edge–detectors in the human visual system. *Science,* 1965b, 149, 1115–16.

McDonald, R. P., Apparent interposition in binocular depth-perception. *Amer. J. Psychol.,* 1962, 75, 619–23.

McFarland, J. H., Sequential part presentation: A method of studying visual form perception. *Brit. J. Psychol.,* 1965, 56, 439–46.

McLaughlin, S. C., and Webster, R. G., Changes in straight-ahead eye position during adaptation to wedge prisms. *Percept. & Psychophys.,* 1967, 2, 37–44.

MacKay, D. M., Interactive processes in visual perception. In Rosenblith, W. A., ed., *Sensory communication.* Cambridge, Mass.: M.I.T. Press/Wiley, 1961.

———, Brain and conscious experience. In Eccles, J. C., ed., *Brain and conscious experience.* Berlin: Springer-Verlag, 1966.

MacNichol, E. F., Jr., Macpherson, L., and Svaetichin, G., Studies on spectral response curves from the fish retina. *Symposium on visual problems of colour,* Paper 39. Teddington, Middlesex (Eng.): Nat. Phys. Lab., 1957.

Mack, A., and Rock, I., A re-examination of the Stratton effect: Egocentric adaptation to a rotated visual image. *Percept. & Psychophys.,* 1968, 4, 57–62.

Marg, E., The accessory optic system. In Whipple, H. E., ed., *Photo-neuro-endocrine effects in circadian systems, with particular reference to the eye.* Annals N.Y. Acad. Sci. 1964, 117, 35–52.

Marks, W. B., Dobelle, W. H., and MacNichol, E. F., Visual pigments of single primate cones. *Science,* 1964, 143, 1181–83.

Marriott, F. H. C., Colour vision: Colour matches. In Davson, H., ed., *The eye. Vol. 2. The visual process.* New York: Academic Press, 1962.

Marshall, W. H., and Talbot, S. A., Recent evidence for neural mechanisms in vision leading to a general theory of sensory acuity. In Kluver, H., ed., *Visual mechanisms.* Biological Symposium, vol. 7. Lancaster, Pa.: Cattell Press, 1942, 117–64.

Matin, E., Clymer, A. B., and Matin, L., Metacontrast and saccadic suppression. *Science,* 1972, 178, 179–82.

Matin, L., and Kibler, G., Acuity of visual perception of direction in the dark for various positions of the eye in the orbit. *Percept. Mot. Skills,* 1966, 22, 407–20.

————, and MacKinnon, E. G., Autokinetic movement: Selective manipulation of directional components by image stabilization. *Science,* 1964, 143, 147–48.

————, Pearce, D., Matin, E., and Kibler, G., Visual perception of direction in the dark: Roles of local signs, eye movements and ocular proprioception. *Vis. Res.,* 1966, 6, 453–69.

Mayzner, M., Tresselt, M. E., and Helfer, M. S., A provisional model of visual information processing with sequential inputs. *Psychon. Monogr. Suppl.,* 1967, 2, no 7. (whole no. 23).

Medewar, P. B., *The art of the soluble.* London: Methuen, 1967.

Metzger, W., Optische Untersuchungen am Ganzfeld. II. Zur Phänomenologie des homogenen Ganzfelds. *Psychol. Forsch.,* 1930, 13, 6–29.

Mikaelian, H., Failure of bilateral transfer in modified eye-hand coordination. Paper read at annual meeting of Eastern Psychol. Assoc., New York, 1963.

Miller, A., *Investigation of the apparent shape of the sky.* B.A. thesis, Penn. State Coll., 1943.

Miller, G. A., Galanter, E., and Pribram, K. H., *Plans and the structure of behavior.* New York: Holt, Rinehart and Winston, 1960.

Minnaert, M., *Light and color.* New York: Dover, 1954.

Mitchell, D. E., Freeman, R. D., Millidot, M., and Haegerstrom, G., Meridional amblyopia: evidence for modification of the human visual system by early visual experience. *Vis. Res.,* 1973, 13, 535–58.

Mollon, J. D., and Krauskopf, J., Reaction time as a measure of the temporal response properties of individual color mechanisms. *Vis. Res.,* 1973, 13, 27–40.

Muir, D. W., and Mitchell, D. E., Visual resolution and experience: Acuity deficits in cats following early selective visual deprivation. *Science,* 1973, 180, 420–22.

Nachmias, J., Two-dimensional motion of the retinal image during monocular fixation. *J. Opt. Soc. Amer.,* 1959, 49, 901–8.

Neisser, U., Decision-time without reaction time. Experiments in visual scanning. *Amer. J. Psychol.,* 1963, 76, 376–85.

————, *Cognitive psychology.* New York, Appleton-Century-Crofts, 1967.

————, Visual Search. *Sci. Amer.,* 1964, 210, 94–102.

————, and Beller, H. K., Searching through word lists. *Brit. J. Psychol.,* 1965, 56, 349–58.

————, and Lazar, R., Searching for novel targets. *Percept. Mot. Skills,* 1964, 19, 427–32.

————, and Stoper, A., Redirecting the search process. *Brit. J. Psychol.,* 1965, 56, 354–68.

Norman, D. A., *Memory and attention.* New York: Wiley, 1969.

O'Brien, B., A theory of the Stiles-Crawford effect. *J. Opt. Soc. Amer.,* 1946, 36, 506–9.

Ogle, K. N., *Researches in binocular vision.* Philadelphia: W. B. Saunders Co., 1950.

————, Precision and validity of stereoscopic depth perception from double images. *J. Opt. Soc. Amer.,* 1953, 43, 906–13.

Ono, H., Distal and proximal size under reduced and non-reduced viewing conditions. *Amer. J. Psychol.,* 1966, 79, 234–41.

Osgood, C. E., and Heyer, A. W., A new interpretation of the figural after-effect. *Psychol. Rev.*, 1952, 59, 98–118.

Pantle, A., and Sekular, R. W., Contrast response of human visual mechanisms to orientation and detection of velocity. *Vis. Res.*, 1968, 9, 397–406.

Papert, S., Stereoscopic synthesis as a technique for localizing visual mechanisms. *M.I.T. Quart. Progr. Rep.*, 1964, 73, 239–43.

Parks, T. E., Post-retinal visual storage. *Amer. J. Psychol.*, 1965, 78, 145–47.

Pastore, N., *Selective history of theories of visual perception: 1650–1950.* New York: Oxford Univ. Press, 1971.

Penfield, W., and Jasper, H., *Epilepsy and the functional anatomy of the human brain.* Boston: Little, Brown, 1954.

Piaget, J., *The mechanisms of perception.* Trans., G. N. Seagrim, New York: Basic Books, 1969.

Pieron, H., Le mécanisme d'apparition des couleurs subjectives de Fechner Benham. *Ann. Psychol.*, 1923, 23, 1–49.

Pirenne, M. H., *Vision and the eye.* 2nd ed.; London: Associated Book Publishers, 1967.

Pitblado, C. B., *Displacement of half-image during binocular viewing.* Ph.D. diss., Boston Univ., 1966.

———, and Kaufman, L., On classifying the visual illusions. In Kaufman, L., ed., *Contour descriptor properties of visual shape.* Sperry Rand Research Center Report SRRC–CR 67–43, prepared for Air Force Cambridge Research Laboratories, Project no. 4645, 1967, 32–53.

Plateau, J. A. F., Quatrième note sur de nouvelles applications curieuses de la persistance des impressions de la rétine. *Bull. Acad. Sci. Belg.*, 1850, 16, 254–60.

Polyak, S., *The vertebrate visual system.* Chicago: Univ. of Chicago Press, 1957.

Posin, R. L., *Perceptual adaptation to contingent visual-field movement: An experimental investigation of position constancy.* Ph.D. diss., Yeshiva Univ., 1966.

Posner, M. I., and Mitchell, R. F., Chronometric analysis of classification. *Psychol. Rev.*, 1967, 74, 392–409.

Pritchard, R. M., Stabilized images on the retina. *Sci. Amer.*, 1961, 204, 72–78.

———, Heron, W., and Hebb, D. O., Visual perception approached by the method of stabilized images. *Canad. J. Psychol.*, 1960, 14, 67–77.

Rashbass, C., and Westheimer, G. H., Independence of conjugate and disjunctive eye movements. *J. Physiol.*, 1961, 159, 361–64.

Ratliff, F., *The Mach Bands: Quantitative studies on neural networks in the retina.* New York: Holden-Day, 1965.

———, and Hartline, H. K., The response of *Limulus* optic nerve fibers to patterns of illumination on the receptor mosaic. *J. Gen. Physiol.*, 1959, 42, 1241–55.

———, F., Hartline, H. K., and Miller, W. H., Spatial and temporal aspects of retinal inhibitory interaction. *J. Opt. Soc. Amer.*, 1963, 53, 110–220.

Reimann, E., Die scheinbare Vergrösserung der Sonne und des Monde am Horizont. *Zsch. f. Psychol.*, 1902, 30, 1–38, 161–95.

Restle, F., Moon illusion explained on the basis of relative size. *Science*, 1970, 167, 1092–96.

Richards, W., Size-distance transformations. In *Pattern recognition in biological and technical systems*. Berlin: Springer-Verlag, 1971*b*, 276–87.

———, Anomalous stereoscopic depth perception. *J. Opt. Soc. Amer.*, 1971*a*, 61, 410–14.

———, Stereopsis and stereoblindness. *Exp. Brain Res.*, 1970, 10, 380–88.

———, Disparity masking. *Vis. Res.*, 1972, 12, 1113–24.

———, and Kaufman, L., "Center of gravity" tendencies for fixations and flow patterns. *Percept. & Psychophys.*, 1969, 5, 81–84.

———, and Miller, J. F., Jr., Convergence as a cue to depth. *Percept. & Psychophys.*, 1969, 5, 317–20.

———, and Miller, J. F. Jr., The corridor illusion *Percept. & Psychophys.*, 1971, 9, 421–23.

———, and Steinbach, M. J., Impaired motion detection preceeding smooth eye movements. *Vis. Res.*, 1972, 12, 353–56.

Riesen, A. H., The development of visual perception in man and chimpanzee. *Science*, 1947, 106, 107–8.

Riggs, L. A., Ratliff, F., Cornsweet, J. C., and Cornsweet, T. N., The disappearance of steadily fixated visual test objects. *J. Opt. Soc. Amer.*, 1953, 43, 495–501.

Robinson, D. A., The oculomotor control system: A review. *Proc. IEEE*, 1968, 56, 1032–49.

Rock, I., The orientations of form on the retina and in the environment. *Amer. J. Psychol.*, 1956, 69, 513–28.

———, *The nature of perceptual adaptation*. New York: Basic Books, 1966.

———, MS Textbook on Visual Perception, 1973. New York: Macmillan, in press.

———, and Brosgole, L., Grouping based on phenomenal proximity. *J. Exp. Psychol.*, 1964, 67, 531–38.

———, and Ebenholtz, S., The relational determination of perceived size. *Psychol. Rev.*, 1959, 66, 387–401.

———, and Ebenholtz, S., Stroboscopic movement based on change of phenomenal location rather than retinal location. *Amer. J. Psychol.*, 1962, 75, 193–207.

———, and Halper, F., Form perception without a retinal image. *Amer. J. Psychol.*, 1969, 82, 425–40.

———, and Heimer, W., The effect of retinal and phenomenal orientation on the perception of form. *Amer. J. Psychol.*, 1957, 70, 493–511.

———, Hill, L. A., and Fineman, M., Speed constancy as a function of size constancy. *Percept. & Psychophys.*, 1958, 4, 37–40.

———, and Kaufman, L., The moon illusion. II. *Science*, 1962, 136, 1023–31.

———, and Kremen, I., A re-examination of Rubin's figural after-effect. *J. Exp. Psychol.*, 1957, 53, 23–30.

———, and McDermott, W., The perception of visual angle. *Acta Psychol.*, 1964, 22, 119–34.

———, and Victor, J., Vision and touch: an experimentally created conflict between the two senses. *Science*, 1964, 143, 594–96.

Roelofs, C. O., Optische Lokalisation. *Arch. Augenheilk.*, 1935, 109, 395–415.

Rubin, E., *Visuell wahrgenomenne Figuren.* Copenhagen, Gyldendalske, 1921.

Rushton, W. A. H., Kinetics of cone pigments measured objectively on the living human fovea. *Annals N.Y. Acad. Sci.*, 1958, 74, 291–304.

———, Visual pigments in man. *Sci. Amer.*, 1962, 205, 120–32.

———, and Campbell, F. W., Measurement of rhodopsin in the living human eye. *Nature*, 1954, 174, 1096–97.

———, Campbell, F. W., Hagins, W. A., and Brindley, G. S., The bleaching and regeneration of rhodopsin in the living eye of the albino rabbit and of man. *Optica Acta*, 1955, 1, 183–90.

Ryle, G., *The Concept of mind.* New York: Barnes & Noble, 1949.

Salapatek, P., and Kessen, W., Visual scanning of triangles by the human newborn. *J. Exp. Child Psychol.*, 1966, 3, 155–67.

Schouten, J. F., Subjective stroboscopy and a model of visual movement detectors. In Wathen-Dunn, W., ed. *Models for the perception of speech and visual form.* Cambridge, Mass.: M.I.T. Press/Wiley, 1967, 44–55.

Schlodtmann, W., Ein Beitrag zur Lehre von der optischen Lokalisation bei-Blindgeborenen. *Arch. f. Ophthalm.*, 1902, 54, 256–69.

Schriever, W., Experimentelle Studien über stereoskopisches Sehen. *Zeit. f. Psychol.*, 1925, 96, 113–70.

Schumann, F., Einige Beobachtungen über die Zusammenfassung von Gesichlseindrücken zu Einheiten. *Psychol. Stud.*, 1904, 1, 1–32.

Sekular, R. W., and Ganz, L., Aftereffect of seen motion with a stabilized retinal image. *Science*, 1963, 139, 419–20.

Schade, O. N., Modern image evaluation and television (the influence of electronic television on the method of image evaluation). *Appl. Opt.*, 1964, 3, 17–21.

Senden, M. von, *Space and sight: The perception of space and shape in the congenitally blind before and after operations.* Trans. P. Heath. London: Methuen, 1960.

Shaffer, O., and Wallach, H., Extent of motion thresholds under subject-relative and object-relative conditions. *Percept. & Psychophys.*, 1966, 1, 447–51.

Sherrington, C. S., *The integrative action of the nervous system.* New Haven: Yale Univ. Press, 1906.

———, Observation on the sensual role of the proprioceptive nerve supply of the extrinsic ocular muscles. *Brain*, 1918, 41, 332–43.

Shipley, T., Visual contours in homogeneous space. *Science*, 1965, 150, 348–50.

Shortress, G. K., and Krauskopf, J., Role of involuntary eye movements in stereoscopic acuity. *J. Opt. Soc. Amer.*, 1961, 51, 555–59.

Skavenski, A. A., Inflow as a source of extraretinal eye position information. *Vis. Res.*, 1972, 12, 221–29.

———, Haddad, G. and Steinman, R. M., The extraretinal signal for the visual perception of direction. *Percept. & Psychophys.*, 1972, 11, 287–90.

———, and Steinman, R. M., Control of eye position in the dark. *Vis. Res.*, 1970, 10, 193–203.

Smith, O. W., & Sherlock, L., A new explanation of the velocity-transposition phenomenon. *Amer. J. Psychol.*, 1957, 70, 102–5.

————, and Smith, P. C., Developmental studies of spatial judgments by children and adults. *Percept. Mot. Skills*, 1966, 22, 3–73.

Smith, R., *Cours complet d'optique*. Avignon (France): Gerard (vf) & F. Sequin, 1767.

Smith, W. M., and Gulick, W. L., Dynamic contour perception. *J. Exp. Psychol.*, 1957, 53, 145–52.

Snodgrass, G., *Theory and experimentation in signal detection. Parts 1, 2, and 3*. Baldwin, N.Y.: Life Sciences Associates, 1972.

Snyder, F. W., and Pronko, N. H., *Vision with spatial inversion*. Wichita, Kan.: Univ. of Wichita Press, 1952.

Sokolov, Ye, N., *Perception and the conditioned reflex*, Trans. S. W. Waydenfeld, New York, Macmillan, 1963.

Spekreijse, H., and Norton, A. L., The dynamic characteristics of color-coded S-potentials. *J. Gen. Physiol.*, 1970, 56, 1.

————, and Tweel, L. H. van der, System analysis of linear and nonlinear processes in electrophysiology of the visual system. *Proc. Konenkl. Nederl. Akademie Van Watenschappen*, Series C., 75, no. 2, 77–105. Amsterdam, 1972.

Sperling, G., The information available in brief visual presentations. *Psychol. Monogr.*, 1960, 74 (whole no. 498).

————, A model for visual memory tasks. *Hum Factors*, 1963, 5, 19–31.

————, Linear theory and the psychophysics of flicker. *Doc. Ophthalm.*, 1964, 18, 3–15.

————, Successive approximations to a model for short-term memory. *Acta Psychol.*, 1967, 27, 285–92.

————, Binocular vision: A physical and neural theory. *Amer. J. Psychol.*, 1970a, 83, 461–534.

————, Short-term memory, long-term memory, and scanning in the processing of visual information. In Young, F. A., and Lindsley, D. B., eds., *Early experience and visual information processing in perceptual and reading disorders*. Washington, D.C.: Nat Acad. Sci., 1970b, 198–218.

————, Budiansky, J., Spivak, J. G., and Johnson, M. C., Extremely rapid visual search: The maximum rate of scanning letters for the preserve of a numeral. *Science*, 1971, 174, 307–311.

————, and Sondhi, M. M., Model for visual luminance discrimination and flicker detection. *J. Opt. Soc. Amer.*, 1968, 58, 1133–45.

Sperry, R. W., and Miner, W., Pattern perception following insertion of mica plates into visual cortex. *J. Comp. Physiol. Psychol.*, 1955, 48, 463–69.

Stecher, S., Luminance–difference thresholds and simultaneous contrast. *Amer. J. Psychol.*, 1968, 81, 27–35.

Sternheim, C. E., and Cavonius, C. R., Sensitivity of the human ERG and VECP to sinusoidally modulated light. *Vis. Res.*, 1972, 12, 1685–95.

Stevens, S. S., On the psychophysical law. *Psychol. Rev.*, 1957, 64, 153–81.

Stiles, W. S., The directional sensitivity of the retina and the spectral sensitivity of the rods and cones. *Proc. Roy. Soc.*, 1939, 127B, 64–105.

————, Increment thresholds and the mechanisms of colour vision. *Doc. Ophthalm.* 1949, 3, 138–63.

————, and Crawford, B. H., The luminous efficiency of rays entering the eye pupil at different points. *Proc. Roy. Soc.*, 1933, 112B, 428–50.

Stratton, G., Some preliminary experiments on vision without inversion of the retinal image. *Psychol. Rev.*, 1896, 3, 611–17.

————, Vision without inversion of the retinal image. *Psychol. Rev.*, 1897, 4, 341–60; 463–81.

Stromeyer, C. F., III, and Mansfield, R. J. W., Colored after-effects produced with moving edges. *Percept. & Psychophys.*, 1970, 2, 108–14.

Sutherland, N. S., Stimulus analyzing mechanisms. In *The mechanisation of thought processes*. London. H.M.S.O., 1959.

Svaetichin, G., Spectral response curves from single cones. *Acta. Physiol. Scand.*, 1956, 39, V Suppl. 134, 17–46.

Tastevin, J., En partant de l'expérience d'Aristote. *L'Encephale*, 1937, 1, 57–84.

Taub, E., A learning approach to compensation for sensory rearrangement. In Freedman, S. J., ed., *The neurophysiology of spatially oriented behavior*. Homewood, Ill.: Dorsey Press, 1968.

Tauber, E. S., and Koffler, S., Optomotor response in human infants to apparent motion; evidence of innateness. *Science*, 1966, 152, 382–83.

Tausch, R., Optische Täuschungen als artifizielle Effekte den Gestaltungsprozesse von Gestaltungs Grössen und Formenkonstanz in der natürlichen Raumwahrnehmung. *Psychol. Forsch.*, 1954, 24, 299–348.

Taylor, J. G., *The behavioral basis of perception*. New Haven: Yale Univ. Press, 1962.

Templeton, W. B., and Green, F., Chance results in utrocular discrimination. *J. Exp. Psychol.*, 1968, 20, 200–3.

Ternus, J., The problem of phenomenal identity. In *A source book of Gestalt psychology*. Trans. W. D. Ellis. London: Routledge & Kegan Paul, 1938.

Teuber, H.-L., Perception. In Field, J., Magoun, H. W., and Hall, V. E., eds., *Handbook of Physiology. Sect. 1. Neurophysiology. Vol. 3*. Washington, D.C.: Amer. Physiol. Soc., 1960. 1595–1668.

Thomas, F. H., Dimmick, F. L., and Luria, S. M., A study of binocular color mixture. *Vis. Res.*, 1961, 1, 108–20.

Tolhurst, D. J., Adaptation to square-wave gratings: Inhibition between spatial frequency channels in the human visual system. *J. Physiol.*, 1972, 226, 231–48.

Tomita, T., Electrophysiological study of the mechanisms subserving color-coding in the fish retina. In *Symposia on Quantitative Biology. Vol. 30*. Cold Spring Harbor, N. Y.: 1965, 559–71.

————, Kaneko, A., Murakami , M., and Pautler, E. G., Spectral response curves of single cones in the carp. *Vis. Res.* 1967, 7, 519–31.

Treisman, A., Contextual cues in selective listening. *Quart. J. Exp. Psychol.*, 1960, 12, 242–48.

————, Binocular rivalry and stereoscopic depth perception. *Quart. J. Psychol.*, 1962, 14, 23–27.

————, The effect of irrelevant material on the efficiency of selective listening. *Amer. J. Psychol.*, 1964, 77, 533–46.

————, and Geffen, G., Selective attention—perception or response? *Quart. J. Exp. Psychol.*, 1967, 20, 139–50.

Troland, L. T., The enigma of color vision. *Am. J. Physiol. Opt.*, 1921, 2, 23–48.

Troxler, D., Über das Verschwinden gegebener Gegenstände innerhalb unseres Gesichtkreises. In Himly and Schmidt, eds., *Ophthalmologische Bibliothek*, 1804, II, pt. 2, 1–53.

Tschermak-Seysenegg, A. von, *Introduction to physiological optics.*, Trans. P. Boeder. Springfield, Ill.: C. C. Thomas, 1952.

Tweel, L. H. van der, and Verduyn-Lunel, H. F. E., Human visual responses to sinusoidally modulated light. *EEG and Clin. Neurophysiol.*, 1965, 18, 587–98.

Verhoeff, F. H., A new theory of binocular vision, *Arch. Ophthal.*, 1935, 13, 151–75.

Vernon, M. D., The perception of distance. *Brit. J. Psychol.*, 1937, 28, 1–149.

Vitz, P., and Todd, T. Z., A model of the perception of simple geometric figures. *Psychol. Rev.*, 1971, 78, 207–28.

Volkman, F. C., Vision during voluntary saccadic eye movements. *J. Opt. Soc. Amer.*, 1962, 52, 571–78.

Wagman, I. H., Kreiger, H. P., and Bendham, M. B., Eye movements elicited by surface and depth stimulation of the occipital lobe of Macaque mulatta. *J. Comp. Neurol.*, 1958, 109, 169–93.

Wagner, H. G., MacNichol, E. F., Jr., and Wolbarsht, M. L., The response properties of single ganglion cells in the Goldfish retina. *J. Gen. Physiol.* 1960, 43, 45–62.

————, MacNichol, E. F., Jr., and Wolbarsht, M. L., Functional basis for "on" center and "off"-center receptive fields of the retina. *J. Opt. Soc. Amer.*, 1963, 53, 66–70.

Wald, G., The receptors for human color vision. *Science*, 1964, 145, 1007–17.

————, and Brown, P. K., Human color vision and color blindness. In *Symposia on Quantitative Biology*. Vol. 30. Cold Spring Harbor, N.Y.: 1965, 345–49.

————, Brown, P. K., and Gibbons, I. R., The problem of visual excitation. *J. Opt. Soc. Amer.*, 1963, 53, 20–35.

Walk, R. D., The development of depth perception in animals and infants. *Child Dev. Monogr.*, 1966, 31, Serial 107, No. 5, 82–108.

————, and Gibson, E. J., A comparative and analytical study of visual depth perception. *Psychol. Monogr.*, 1961, 75, (whole no. 519).

————, Gibson, E. J., and Tighe, T. J., Behavior of light- and dark-reared rats on a visual cliff. *Science*, 1957, 126, 80–81.

Wallach, H., On constancy of visual speed. *Psychol. Rev.*, 1939, 46, 541–52.

————, The role of head movement and vestibular and visual cues in sound localization. *J. Exp. Psychol.*, 1940, 27, 339–68.

————, Brightness constancy and the nature of archromatic colors. *J. Exp. Psychol.*, 1948, 38, 310–24.

————, Some considerations concerning the relation between perception and cognition. *J. Person.*, 1949, 18, 6–13.

————, The perception of motion. *Sci. Amer.*, 1959, 56–60.

————, and Adams, P. A., Binocular rivalry of achromatic colors. *Amer. J. Psychol.,* 1954, 67, 513–16.

————, and Floor, L., The use of size matching to demonstrate the effectiveness of accommodation and convergence as cues for distance. *Percept. & Psychophys.,* 1971, 10, 423–28.

————, and Frey, K. J., Adaptation in distance perception based on oculomotor cues. *Percept. & Psychophys.,* 1972, 11, 77–83.

————, and Karsh, E. B., The modification of stereoscopic depth-perception and the kinetic depth effect. *Amer. J. Psychol.,* 1963, 76, 429–35.

————, and Kravitz, J. H., The measurement of the constancy of visual direction and of its adaptation. *Psychon. Science,* 1965a, 2, 217–18.

————, and Kravitz, J. H., Rapid adaptation in the constancy of visual direction with active and passive rotation. *Psychon. Science,* 1965b, 3, 165–66.

————, and Kravitz, J. H., Adaptation in the constancy of visual direction tested by measuring the constancy of auditory direction. *Percept. & Psychophys.,* 1968, 4, 299–303.

————, Kravitz, J. H., and Lindauer, J., A passive condition for rapid adaptation to displaced visual direction. *Amer. J. Psychol.,* 1963, 76, 568–78.

————, and McKenna, V. V., On size-perception in the absence of cues for distance. *Amer. J. Psychol.,* 1960, 73, 458–60.

————, and Norris, C. M., Accommodation as a distance cue. *Amer. J. Psychol.,* 1963, 76, 659–64.

————, and O'Connell, D. N., The kinetic depth effect. *J. Exp. Psychol.,* 1953, 45, 205–17.

————, O'Connell, D. N., and Neisser, U., The memory effect of visual perception of three-dimensional form. *J. Exp. Psychol.,* 1953, 45, 360–68.

————, and Smith, A., Visual and proprioceptive adaptation to altered oculomotor adjustments. *Percept. & Psychophys.,* 1972, 11, 413–16.

————, and Zuckerman, C., The constancy of stereoscopic depth. *Amer. J. Psychol.,* 1963, 76, 404–12.

Walls, G., The problem of visual direction. *J. Optom.,* 1951a, 28, 55–83, 115–46, 173–212.

————, A theory of ocular dominance. *A.M.A. Arch. Ophthalm.,* 1951b, 45, 387–412.

————, Land! Land! *Psychol. Bull.,* 1960, 57, 29–48.

————, *The vertebrate eye and its adaptive radiation.* New York: Hafner, 1963.

Washburn, M., Retinal rivalry as a neglected factor in stereoscopic vision. *Proc. Nat. Acad. Sci.,* 1933, 19, 773–77.

Weinstein, S., Sersen, E. A., Fisher, L., and Weisinger, M., Is re-afference necessary for visual adaptation? *Percept. Mot. Skills,* 1964, 18, 641–48.

Wiesel, T. N., and Hubel, D. H., Comparison of the effects of unilateral and bilateral eye closure on cortical unit responses in kittens. *J. Neurophysiol.,* 1965, 28, 1029–40.

Weisstein, N., Scoz, R., and Tangney, J., Masking of bars and gratings by radially symmetric and aperiodic patterns. Paper presented at annual meeting of *Assoc. for Res. in Vis. and Ophthalm.,* Sarasota, 1973.

Werner, H., Studies on contour. *Amer. J. Psychol.,* 1935, 47, 40–64.

————, Dynamics in binocular depth perception. *Psychol. Monogr.* 1937 (whole no. 218).

Wertheimer, M., Experimentelle Studien Über das Sehen von Bewegung. *Zeit. Psychol.*, 1912, *61*, 161–265.

————, Untersuchungen zur Lehre von der Gestalt, II, *Psychol. Forsch*, 1923, *4*, 301–50. Abriged version, entitled "Laws of organization in perceptual forms," appears in Ellis, W. D., trans., *A Source Book of Gestalt Psychology.* London, Routledge & Kegan Paul, 1938.

Wertheimer, Michael, Psychomotor coordination of auditory and visual space at birth. *Science*, 1961, *134*, 1692.

Westheimer, G. H., Mechanism of Saccadic eye movements. *A.M.A. Arch. Ophthalm.*, 1954, 52, 710–24.

————, and Campbell, F. W., Light distribution in the image formed by the living human eye. *J. Opt. Soc. Amer.*, 1962, *52*, 1040–45.

————, and Mitchell, A. M., Eye movement responses to convergence stimuli. *A.M.A. Arch. Ophthalm.*, 1956, 55, 848–56.

Wheatstone, C., On some remarkable, and hitherto unresolved, phenomena of binocular vision. Roy. Soc. London, *Philosoph. Trans.*, 1838, 371–94.

Willmer, E. N., *Retinal structure and colour vision.* London: Cambridge Univ. Press, 1946.

Wohlgemuth, A., On the after-effect of seen movement. *Brit. J. Psychol. Monogr.*, Suppl. 1, 1911.

Wohwill, J., Developmental studies of perception. *Psychol. Bull.*, 1960, 57, 249–88.

Wolf, E., and Zigler, M. J., Excitation of the peripheral retina with coincident and disparate test fields. *J. Opt. Soc. Amer.*, 1965, 55, 1517–19.

Woodworth, R. S., *Experimental psychology.* New York: Holt, 1938.

Wright, W. D., A re-determination of the trichromatic mixture data. *Med. Res. Counc. Spec. Rep.*, 1929, No. 139, 1–38.

Wundt, W., *Grundriss der Psychologie.* Leipzig: W. Engelmann, 1896.

Yarbus, D. L., *Eye movements and vision.* New York: Plenum Press, 1967.

Zeigler, N. P., and Leibowitz, H., Apparent visual size as a function of distance for children and adults. *Amer. J. Psychol.*, 1957, 70, 106–9.

Zuckerman, C. B., and Rock, I., A reappraisal of the roles of past experience and innate organizing processes in visual perception. *Psychol. Bull.*, 1957, 269–96.

Zusne, L., *Visual perception of form.* New York: Academic Press, 1970.

Zusne, L., & Michels, K. M., Nonrepresentational shapes and eye movements. *Percept. Mot. Skills*, 1964, 18, 11–20.

name index

subject index

Acuity, measurement: with bar grating, 501; with sinusoidal grating, 501; with Snellen chart, 501

Aberrations, 246; chromatic, 246–47, 249; spherical, 246–47, 249

Accommodation, 241; contraction of pupil and, 247; and cue assimilation, 448; parasympathetic innervation, 242; and power of eye, 40; sympathetic innervation, 242. *See also* Aberrations

Adaptation: as contrast attenuation, 514; dark, *see* Sensitivity to light; frequency, specific nature, 514; to high-contrast gratings, 513; and lateral inhibition, 515; to rearrangement, 428

Aftereffects, figural, 511–15; field theory, 511; Osgood-Heyer theory, 511; and stabilized images, 512. *See also* Single-channel model

Allelotropia, 282; or assimilation of visual directions, 282; or displacement, 282; energy involved, 282; as fusion, 282. *See also* Fusion theory

Alpha wave, 123

Ambiguous forms: "duck-rabbit," 496, 500; and meaning, 496; "wife or mother-in-law," 495

Amblyopia ex anopsia, 421

Ame's distorted room, 344, 345 *fig.*

Angular size, 323; and size of retinal image, 324. *See also* Visual angle

Apparent (stroboscopic) movement, 392–95; of opposite contrast stimuli, 395; in random dot stereograms, 395; and real movement, 392–93, 396, 397; upper threshold for, 398. *See also Beta* movement; *Phi* phenomenon

Astigmatism, 247–49; and asymmetry of blur, 249; and direction of distance-differences, 248; and shape of blur circles, 247. *See also* Frequency selective channels

Attention: and click-evoked potentials, 534; as covert speech, 535; in dichotic listening, 534–36; as a filter, 19, 534, 536; to linguistic characteristics, 535; and perception, 19; to physical features, 535; physiological interpretation of, 534

Attitude, effect of, on size and distance judgments, 336–39

Aubert-Fleischl paradox, 376

Autokinetic effect, 405; eye-movement theory, 406; outflow theory, 406; with stabilized image, 406; with turned gaze, 406

Average evoked potentials, 122–27; coherent noise and, 125; effect of randomly flickering light, 126–27; and sinusoidally modulated light, 125; and spatial frequencies, 516; and stimulus-related activity, 125

Awareness: as selection of programs, 536

Bandwidth, 484

Benham's disc, 207